COLLECTED LETTERS OF

Samuel Taylor Coleridge

COLLECTED LETTERS OF
Samuel Taylor Coleridge

EDITED BY

EARL LESLIE GRIGGS

VOLUME VI

1826–1834

OXFORD
AT THE CLARENDON PRESS
1971

Oxford University Press, Ely House, London W. 1

GLASGOW NEW YORK TORONTO MELBOURNE WELLINGTON
CAPE TOWN SALISBURY IBADAN NAIROBI DAR ES SALAAM LUSAKA ADDIS ABABA
BOMBAY CALCUTTA MADRAS KARACHI LAHORE DACCA
KUALA LUMPUR HONG KONG TOKYO

PRINTED IN GREAT BRITAIN
AT THE UNIVERSITY PRESS, OXFORD
BY VIVIAN RIDLER
PRINTER TO THE UNIVERSITY

CONTENTS

Abbreviations and Principal References

Letters, Conversations and Rec.	Allsop, Thomas, ed.: *Letters, Conversations and Recollections of S. T. Coleridge*, 1836, 1858, 1864 (cited)
Letters from the Lake Poets	[Coleridge, E. H., ed.] *Letters from the Lake Poets . . . to Daniel Stuart*, 1889
Letters Hitherto Uncollected	Prideaux, W. F., ed.: *Letters Hitherto Uncollected by Samuel Taylor Coleridge*, 1913
Letters of Hartley Coleridge	Griggs, G. E. and E. L., eds.: *Letters of Hartley Coleridge*, 1936
Life of Joseph Blanco White	Thom, J. H., ed.: *The Life of the Rev. Joseph Blanco White, written by himself; with portions of his Correspondence*, 3 vols., 1845
Literary Remains	Coleridge, H. N., ed.: *The Literary Remains of Samuel Taylor Coleridge*, 4 vols., 1836–9
Memoir of H. F. Cary	Cary, Henry: *Memoir of the Rev. Henry Francis Cary, . . .* 2 vols., 1847
Memorials of Coleorton	Knight, Wm., ed.: *Memorials of Coleorton, being Letters . . . to Sir George and Lady Beaumont, . . .* 2 vols., 1887
Middle Years	De Selincourt, E., ed.: *The Letters of William and Dorothy Wordsworth: the Middle Years*, 2 vols., 1937
Nineteenth-Century Studies (Cornell)	Davis, H., De Vane, W. C., and Bald, R. C., eds.: *Nineteenth-Century Studies*, 1940
Poems	Coleridge, E. H., ed.: *The Complete Poetical Works of Samuel Taylor Coleridge, . . .* 2 vols., 1912
Poetical Works	*The Poetical Works of S. T. Coleridge, including the Dramas of Wallenstein, Remorse, and Zapolya*, 3 vols., 1828, 1829 *The Poetical Works of S. T. Coleridge*, 3 vols., 1834
Rem.	Cottle, Joseph: *Reminiscences of Samuel Taylor Coleridge and Robert Southey*, 1847, 1848 (cited)
Robinson on Books and Their Writers	Morley, Edith J., ed.: *Henry Crabb Robinson on Books and Their Writers*, 3 vols., 1938
Southey Letters	Warter, J. W., ed.: *Selections from the Letters of Robert Southey*, 4 vols., 1856
Table Talk	[Coleridge, H. N., ed.] *Specimens of the Table Talk of the late Samuel Taylor Coleridge*, 2 vols., 1835, 1836
Theory of Life	Watson, Seth B., ed.: *Hints towards the Formation of a more comprehensive Theory of Life. By S. T. Coleridge*, 1848
Wise, Bibliography	Wise, T. J.: *A Bibliography of . . . Samuel Taylor Coleridge*, 1913

ABBREVIATIONS AND PRINCIPAL REFERENCES

Abbreviations

Aids to Reflection — Coleridge, S. T.: *Aids to Reflection in the Formation of a Manly Character on the several grounds of Prudence, Morality, and Religion: illustrated by select passages from our Elder Divines, especially from Archbishop Leighton*, 1825, 1831

Alaric Watts — Watts, Alaric A.: *Alaric Watts. A Narrative of His Life*, 2 vols., 1884

Biog. Lit. — Coleridge, S. T.: *Biographia Literaria*, . . . 2 vols., 1817; ed. H. N. Coleridge, 2 vols., 1847; ed. J. Shawcross, 2 vols., 1907. (Unless otherwise indicated references are to the Shawcross edition.)

Campbell, *Life* — Campbell, J. D.: *Samuel Taylor Coleridge, a Narrative of the Events of His Life*, 1894

Campbell, *Poetical Works* — Campbell, J. D., ed.: *The Poetical Works of Samuel Taylor Coleridge*, 1893

Chambers, *Life* — Chambers, E. K.: *Samuel Taylor Coleridge: A Biographical Study*, 1938

Church and State, The — Coleridge, S. T.: *On the Constitution of the Church and State, according to the Idea of Each; with aids toward a right judgment on the late Catholic Bill*, 1830, 2nd edn. 1830 (cited)

D.N.B. — Stephen, Leslie, and Lee, Sidney, eds.: *The Dictionary of National Biography*, 22 vols., reprinted 1937–8

E. L. G. — Griggs, E. L., ed.: *Unpublished Letters of Samuel Taylor Coleridge*, . . . 2 vols., 1932

Early Rec. — Cottle, Joseph: *Early Recollections; chiefly relating to the late Samuel Taylor Coleridge*, . . . 2 vols., 1837

Gillman, *Life* — Gillman, James: *The Life of Samuel Taylor Coleridge*, 1838

John Hookham Frere — Festing, Gabrielle: *John Hookham Frere and His Friends*, 1899

Lamb Letters — Lucas, E. V., ed.: *The Letters of Charles Lamb, to which are added those of his sister, Mary Lamb*, 3 vols., 1935

Later Years — De Selincourt, E., ed.: *The Letters of William and Dorothy Wordsworth: the Later Years*, 3 vols., 1939

Letters — Coleridge, E. H., ed.: *Letters of Samuel Taylor Coleridge*, 2 vols., 1895

LIST OF ILLUSTRATIONS

1504. To Unknown Correspondent

MS. Princeton University Lib. Hitherto unpublished.

[January 1826?][1]

My dear Sir

I have not destroyed your paper—God forbid! But I was, on the moment of your Bearer's arrival, employed in noting down a few of the points, for the purpose of leaving with you tomorrow (when I had purposed to restore the MSS to you) a more specific Answer— Perhaps, You anticipate some prevention of our having the pleasure of seeing you on Thursday Evening?—If so, I will answer for it's being safely delivered into your hands on Friday Morning—or (should you let me know by return of Post, whether it will make any difference) on Thursday Morning.

Our Conversation yesterday had but one object on my part— The truth of the Christ. Rel. in *Idea*—& the *living power* & reality of Ideas, as Law or Productive Forms.—On this Basis I have no *fear* of satisfying you most completely & to the utmost tranquillity of mind, with regard to the Living forms in which it has cloathed itself—Your's

very truly
S. T. Coleridge

P.S. If you do not come, please to send your address—for I have mislaid [it]—

1505. To Mrs. Charles Aders

Address: Mrs Aders | 11 Euston Square
MS. Mr. W. Hugh Peal. Hitherto unpublished.
Postmark: Highgate, 3 January 1826.

3 Jany 1826

My dear Mrs Aders

I mean to punish you for supposing it possible that any thing, that Nature and God's good grace have left in your or Mr Aders's *power* to do, could alienate my or my Friends' Regard and Affection. And by way of punishment I purpose to inflict on you an attentive perusal of three close-written pages of metaphysical disquisition on the minor morals arising out of the Duty of respecting the free-agency & individuality of your friend, or intimate. But unluckily

[1] The MS. is endorsed 1826.

I began on a defective sheet, and was forced to finish it on a different scrap, so I must make a fair copy.—But when shall I find the time?—And how can *my* impatient eagerness to avenge myself on you endure the delay?—I will even inclose the Scraps, as they are —*demanding a promise* of you, that you will bring them with you the first time, you come—when if you should wish it, I will make a fair copy for you—. N.B. By the words, 'the first time, you come', I precisely mean, desire, hope, and expect Thursday next, i.e. the day after tomorrow, 5 Jany. 182 *six* (alas!)—Mrs Gillman trusts, that you and Miss James will come *early*—a full hour *at least* before dinner (4 o'clock)—and that nothing foreseeable can absolve you, but wicked bad weather.—I wish myself very much to converse with you on a subject that I feel in closer neighborhood to my heart than what I had imagined that any new prospect, or image of a possible Event, could have made way to. For in this bleak World of Mutabilities, & where what is not changed, is chilled, and in this winter-time of my own Being, I resemble a Bottle of Brandy in Spitzbergen—a Dram of alcoholic Fire in the center of a Cake of Ice.—But on this very account, that I do feel unusual interest in the question, I find greater difficulty in making my own thoughts sufficiently distinct and clear to communicate them, connectedly and consecutively, in writing. They are mature enough to climb up & chirp on the edge of their Birth-nest; but not fledged enough to fly away, tho' it were but to perch on the next branch.— You observe most truly, that the distance is the *menacing* obstacle —whether insuperable? this is the point, I would fain sift with you, previously to my being able to decide whether I should digest my reflections on this point and submit them to Mr Aders. Till the *possibility* at least of the scheme is ascertained, on any condition— it would (according to my judgement) be premature to think of aught else. Should it appear *possible*—then many points might purposely need to be understood, in order that you & Mr Aders may form a judgement whether it would be *convenient* to you, or feasible in compatibility with your other views & objects.—

But I shall lose the Post if I do not hurry off this letter—Pray, pray, do not let a *trifle* disappoint us of you on Thursday—for I am with true regard

Your & Mr Aders's | affect. Friend
S. T. Coleridge

1506. *To Derwent Coleridge*

Address: Derwent Coleridge, Esqre | John Macauley, Esqre | Plymouth.
MS. Victoria University Lib. Pub. E. L. G. ii. 366.

Grove
Highgate
4 Jany. 1826

My dearest Derwent

Mr Edward Lowndes has just brought me your letter—and I am writing in the same room with him.—From what I had before heard of Mr M. Lowndes I was a little shocked but not at all surprized at his abrupt discharge. But had I considered this as a misfortune, it would have been swallowed up in the Comfort and gladness which your determination to prepare yourself in good earnest for Orders has given me. I never indeed could fear that a young man of your acuteness and habits of reflecting on what goes on around & within you should fail to see that in certain points there must be an act of the *Will*, a hoc *credam*, as well as an acknowlegement of insight. It is this presence of the Will, as an equally essential Co-factor with the intellective Faculty, that distinguishes an *Idea* from a Conception, and removing the poetic drapery constitutes the true import of this *Platonic* Term—for without an act of the Will it is not possible to contemplate the Particular in the Universal, the Finite in the Absolute—& vice versâ the U. in the P., the Abs. in the F.—which every Idea supposes.—But of this hereafter. I send the Aids of Reflection by Mr Edward Lowndes—The Father, and not the Author, earnestly intreats that you will give a fair and (as far as is in your own power) an unprejudiced attention to it's contents.—I am going to bring out three Essays, as a Supplement to the 'Aids'—on Faith, the Eucharist, and Prayer—With these the Aids will answer all, I intended, by the volume—and I hope, prove for some few a preparation for my larger works.—I have been too unwell to go into town; but purpose to do so tomorrow—in order to see John Coleridge, from whom I wonder, I have not heard. I have some thought likewise of going thro' a course of the VAPOR BATHS—tho' alas! they can but palliate.—

And now, my dear Derwent, for I cannot write longer or write at ease with a stranger in the Room—is there any thing I can do or get done? Write immediately with your present address—I shall consult Montagu tomorrow—Would you have me write to Mr Skinner of Jesus?—Supposing, you could not get Pupils at Cambridge—have you fortitude & perseverance enough to employ half your time in compiling a School-book or two from a plan in detail that I would give you—provided, that you could be secured such a sum, as you might live on, near London, during the time, you were preparing for the Church?—Let me hear from you at all events.—

Mr E. Lowndes does ample Justice to your conduct & character at Buckfastleigh—He supposes, that his Brother must have suddenly met with some Clergyman whom it was necessary to engage at once, or lose—.

All here desire their Love.

God bless you | &

S. T. Coleridge

1507. *To Edward Coleridge*

Address: Revd. Edward Coleridge | at his Father's | Ottery St Mary | Devon [Readdressed in another hand] Eton College, | Windsor | Bucks.
MS. Pierpont Morgan Lib. Hitherto unpublished.
Postmark: 10 January 1826. *Stamped*: Honiton.

½ past 3, Tuesday Afternoon [10 January 1826]

My dear Edward

It does not often happen, that an intervention which compels me to write or rather scribble a few hasty lines instead of the seemly postage-paying Authentic Letter which four hours ago I was seated, pen in hand, to execute, can be looked back on with pleasure. Such, however, is the case—for I was interrupted by a Visit from John Hookham Frere—and have been enjoying the luxury of hearing him read his—translation? nay! his *equation* of the Knights—and recite several sublime passages of a religious and philosophic Poem, which I flatter myself, he will permit *me* to publish in my supplementary small Volume—(= The three disquisitions, on 1. Faith: 2. the Eucharist: 3. the philosophy of Prayer—with an introductory Dialogue on *Utility*, and the contempt of Logic & Metaphysics—tried in the Court of *Common Sense*.)—But I must hasten to my purpose—the less reluctantly, because the day after to morrow I propose to commence with an exact scrutiny into little Henry Gillman's Esse & Posse—and of the result I shall immediately send you a faithful report—i.e. of the Judgement, I shall have formed.—This, however, by having three or four times attended to him while doing his lessons with his elder Brother, and by Henry's general conduct & deportment, I can confidently assert—that he has improved far beyond what (you know from my Mem. Book) I had ventured to hope—*I* con-list gives it—1. Θεός. 2. ὁ ὤν,[1] ὁ μονογενής. 3. ὁ πατήρ. Plato was a prophetic Anomaly—all the prior Theologians of Greece (unless Heraclitus was an exception) were φυσιολόγοι—Their first principle was—῎Εστι:—the first of the Christian Scheme Εἰμί.—The former deduced the Persons—the latter begins with and from the Personal, or rather the Personëity itself.—

What the Jew said who turned Christian after [he] had returned from Rome to which he had gone against the intreaty of his pious Friend:—viz. that Christianity must be divine—or it could not subsist under such monsters as those of the Romish Hierarchy, often suggests itself to me—when I read Paley, Watson, or indeed any one of the Evidence-mongers.—They are outrages [on] Logic, and insults on Common Sense.— . . .[2]

1509. *To John Hookham Frere*

Address: John Hookham Frere, Esqre | 20. Gloucester Place.
MS. formerly in the possession of the late Arthur Pforzheimer. Pub. John Hookham Frere, *228.*
Postmark: Highgate, 12 January 1826.

Grove, Highgate
Wednesday Night. [11 January 1826]

My dear Sir

It is a great delight to me to be any where with you. And more than so—for to you I can say this, secure of the right interpretation —it is a source of Strength, and a renewal of hope—and of the hope, I most need—viz. that I am still in a region where the sympathy of sane minds can follow me, and have not been toiling after shadows. I shall have much pleasure in availing myself of Lord Hastings'[3] condescension, and still more in the preludium— Dared I shape my expectations to my wishes, I would say, I expect you on Friday at an early hour[4]—and if I might wish *aloud,* you would hear me craving & hoping that you might have a portion of your MSS. with you—

    With sincere respect, I am, | my dear Sir! your obliged
             S. T. Coleridge

 [1] ὁ ὤν underlined once in MS.

 [2] Three-fourths of a page of MS. cut off, thus destroying the address sheet.

 [3] Francis Rawdon-Hastings, first Marquis of Hastings and second Earl of Moira (1754–1826), governor-general of Bengal and commander-in-chief of the forces in India, 1812–21, and governor and commander-in-chief of Malta, 1824–6.

 [4] A notebook entry indicates that Frere did arrive early: '13 Jany. 1826 Thursday [Friday] Mr J H Frere passed an hour or two with me in my Garret, & then took me with him in his Carriage to the Marquis of Hastings, at the Burlington Hotel.' [MS. notebook, Huntington Library.]

than 4, successively. I more than suspect an ulcer in the stomach, or the pylorus, from the constant pain in that region every morning, for years past, on awaking—& which continues till I get up & move about in an upright posture. This is known by experience to be perfectly compatible with a look of good health—the texture of the Skin & the excessive action of the Kidneys, & torpor of the lower Bowels being the only symptoms, from which it can be conjectured.—But no more of this! We must all die of somewhat and ought, as the Irish Franciscan in a discourse of Final Causes observed—Let us all thank God and adore his wisdom and goodness in putting Death at the end of Life & thereby giving us all time for repentance.

I do not want you to read the Aids to Reflection thro', till you can sit down to it with calmness & in leisure. But one thing I *do* wish—viz. that before I see you, you would run your eye over the pages, which I have marked down overleaf.[1]—Mr Frere was particularly struck & pleased with a remark, I made to him, the day before yesterday—That our Divines had adopted the foundations of their Faith (which they call Natural Religion) from Paganism— they begin with *The Being*—'Ο "Ων—the necessary legitimate consequence of which is Pantheism, with Polytheism (i.e. the hypothesis of higher *Natures*, οἱ θεοί) as it's *utter*ance or exoteric Half.— The Deity, τὸ θεῖον, was (for the Theogonists) to the Divinities (οἱ θεοί) as Space to the Diagrams for the Geometrician. The space exists absolutely in each—Circle, Ellipse, Triangle, Parallelogram &c &c—but only in these does it *ex*ist at all.—Now St John would have taught them a deeper philosophy, and the only one compatible with a *Moral* religion—Θεόν = τὸ θεῖον, the Absolute, or Causa sui—Θεὸν[2] οὐδεὶς ἑώρακε πώποτε—i.e. essentially unutterable, deeper than all Idea—ὁ μονογενὴς υἱός, ὁ ὢν[3] ἐν τῷ κόλπῳ τοῦ πατρός,[4] οὗτος ἐξηγήσατο.[5]—Θεός *becomes* ὁ πατήρ by the Act of realizing in the Son—. It sounds paradox, but it is most certain truth, that in order of Thought, under the intrusive form of *Time*, the Father is a reflex from the Son—and that it does not appear so in human relations arises from our Fathers having had Fathers— The man is called a Father by anticipation, grounded on a Past. But in the Idea of the Christian Deity the order is as the Evange-

---

[1] (1) The Preface. (2) P. 4. *note.* (3) p. 14–17. (4) 26. *note.* Defin. of *Prudence,* generally.—40, 41. Def. of Pleasure & Happiness. (5) 51–56. (6) 67–71. *Definition of Nature.* See p. 73. (7) 81–82.—(8) 111–112.—116–121. (9) 131–135. 154. (10) 159–162. 176, 177.—Lastly, 229–233.—[References added 'overleaf' by S. T. C.]

[2] Underlined once in MS.　　　　　　　　　[3] ὁ ὢν underlined twice in MS.

[4] τοῦ πατρός, underlined once in MS.

[5] John i. 18. (with ἐν τῷ κόλπῳ for εἰς τὸν κόλπον, and οὗτος for ἐκεῖνος).

myself—but they [are] so very **expensive**—4. 4. for a dozen Baths—exclusive of the **Stage!!**—

Mr Frere is, I know, very anxious to get something *for me*; but of this in my next—. If I could but get a 200£ a year—[1]

Thou kenst not, Percy! how the Rhyme should rage!—

But I shall be too late—My best Love to My Brothers, James & George—

God bless you &
S. T. Coleridge

Pray, mention the state of your own health.—

1508. *To Derwent Coleridge*

MS. Victoria University Lib. Pub. E. L. G. ii. 370.

[Wednesday, 11 January 1826]

My dear Derwent

I answer your's of this morning (Wednesday) merely to say, that I shall be rejoiced to see you; and that Mr & Mrs Gillman desire me to propose your coming here immediately and spending the two or three weeks at Highgate. It might be not without it's advantages, and I am sure, could not but be a gratification to you, that you would on this scheme be likely to see a good deal of Mr J. H. Frere—to whom, should you publish a Volume of Poems, or Your Poems in a Volume, you might with great propriety dedicate it—. This, however, your own Feelings must determine, pro or con.

If you thought, that the School-book would prevent your bringing out a Volume of Poems, I would not press it on you. But with regard to the Profits, you should not begin it till I had secured a price for the first Edition, to be paid you on the delivery of the MSS, sufficient for your present purposes. I have talked with several Masters, at Eton & in London on the subject—and from each have received the most encouraging Predictions of it's success —. And should it succeed, it would be a little annuity for you. If I dared sacrifice the labors and Object of my Life to the almost certain Foresight, that I shall never gain a shilling by them—I would myself even at this late time of life make Books of this sort my constant employ—and had I twenty years ago known what I now know, I might in this way have rendered myself independent, without any detriment to my chosen Labors. But, alas! the Night draws on—and the Days shorten. Do what I will, I cannot work to any purpose more than five hours in the 24—and not more

---

[1] See Letters 1510–11.

template him singly, or in relation only to his past Self—and after
an interval of time—I see that the Hand of the Clock *has moved*;
tho' from the tedious space of the Orbit, it must needs seem motion-
less for an eye constantly fixed on it—especially, when it is impos-
sible to resist the effect of his slowness *compared* with other Boys.
His Brother, a sensible, matter of fact Lad, and not gifted with
any disposition to see things in a favorable light, is certain of his
improvement—and he spent three or four days at Basil Montague's,
in order that I might have Basil's & still more Mrs Montague's
opinion on this point—But I need not say, that we must estimate
the dormant *feracity* of the Tree not by the scanty and abortive
fruits on the known sickly branches but by the comparative pro-
ducts of the strongest & healthiest—But these lie in his *moral*
Being—and out of this, and out of his bodily growth, must his
intellectual powers evolve themselves—And this brings me to the
purpose of this letter.—Mr Stanley, the Surgeon of St Bartholo-
mew's, and my friend, Mr Green—(the two rising men of the
Medical World) have examined Henry—& were both of Opinion,
that his *Skin* was in a morbid state *per se*, and that his digestive
Organs & general Health must be acted on thro' the Skin, and not
vice versâ.—On this ground, they strongly recommended a Course
of the Sulphur Vapor Baths—which he has commenced—& with
such evident good effect, that it is of the utmost importance to the
child's ultimate Welfare, that it should not be interrupted.—In
order to this, however, he must be detained for ten days or a fort-
night after the re-commencement of School at Eton—(To give you
a slight notion of the state of his Skin, poor fellow—he bore during
the two first days a heat of *160* degrees without any perspiration
following!)—Beyond all doubt, a great part of his Idleness &
Wanderings of Mind must be attributed to the state of his half-
conscious *Sensations*. Now will you be so good as to let us know
what the forms are—whether a Certificate from the Medical
Advisers should be sent to Dr Keates—
    With regard to his Schooling I pledge myself to you, that *on the
whole* he shall sustain no loss by passing this fortnight under my
eye—for I have so arranged my time, that I shall take him myself
in hand, after his Brother returns to Merchant-Taylors'—and at
all events, you shall find him thoroughly master of his Greek
Grammar—tho' it must depend on his health, whether he will
at every moment be master of himself *extempore*. This however,
will. . . .[1] I have prepared a little catechism of the Greek Grammar,
in which he will be *dodged* every day, before and on his return from
the Baths in Red Lion Square. I have some thoughts of trying them

---

[1] Word illegible in MS.

myself—but they [are] so very expensive—4. 4. for a dozen Baths—
exclusive of the **Stage!!**—

Mr Frere is, I know, very anxious to get something *for me*; but
of this in my next—. If I could but get a 200£ a year—[1]

Thou kenst not, Percy! how the Rhyme should rage!—

But I shall be too late—My best Love to My Brothers, James
& George—

God bless you &
S. T. Coleridge

Pray, mention the state of your own health.—

1508. *To Derwent Coleridge*

MS. Victoria University Lib. Pub. E. L. G. ii. 370.

[Wednesday, 11 January 1826]

My dear Derwent

I answer your's of this morning (Wednesday) merely to say,
that I shall be rejoiced to see you; and that Mr & Mrs Gillman
desire me to propose your coming here immediately and spending
the two or three weeks at Highgate. It might be not without it's
advantages, and I am sure, could not but be a gratification to you,
that you would on this scheme be likely to see a good deal of Mr
J. H. Frere—to whom, should you publish a Volume of Poems, or
Your Poems in a Volume, you might with great propriety dedicate
it—. This, however, your own Feelings must determine, pro or con.

If you thought, that the School-book would prevent your bring-
ing out a Volume of Poems, I would not press it on you. But with
regard to the Profits, you should not begin it till I had secured a
price for the first Edition, to be paid you on the delivery of the
MSS, sufficient for your present purposes. I have talked with
several Masters, at Eton & in London on the subject—and from
each have received the most encouraging Predictions of it's success
—. And should it succeed, it would be a little annuity for you. If
I dared sacrifice the labors and Object of my Life to the almost
certain Foresight, that I shall never gain a shilling by them—I
would myself even at this late time of life make Books of this sort
my constant employ—and had I twenty years ago known what
I now know, I might in this way have rendered myself indepen-
dent, without any detriment to my chosen Labors. But, alas! the
Night draws on—and the Days shorten. Do what I will, I cannot
work to any purpose more than five hours in the 24—and not more

---

[1] See Letters 1510–11.

template him singly, or in relation only to his past Self—and after
an interval of time—I see that the Hand of the Clock *has moved*;
tho' from the tedious space of the Orbit, it must needs seem motion-
less for an eye constantly fixed on it—especially, when it is impos-
sible to resist the effect of his slowness *compared* with other Boys.
His Brother, a sensible, matter of fact Lad, and not gifted with
any disposition to see things in a favorable light, is certain of his
improvement—and he spent three or four days at Basil Montague's,
in order that I might have Basil's & still more Mrs Montague's
opinion on this point—But I need not say, that we must estimate
the dormant *feracity* of the Tree not by the scanty and abortive
fruits on the known sickly branches but by the comparative pro-
ducts of the strongest & healthiest—But these lie in his *moral*
Being—and out of this, and out of his bodily growth, must his
intellectual powers evolve themselves—And this brings me to the
purpose of this letter.—Mr Stanley, the Surgeon of St Bartholo-
mew's, and my friend, Mr Green—(the two rising men of the
Medical World) have examined Henry—& were both of Opinion,
that his *Skin* was in a morbid state *per se*, and that his digestive
Organs & general Health must be acted on thro' the Skin, and not
vice versâ.—On this ground, they strongly recommended a Course
of the Sulphur Vapor Baths—which he has commenced—& with
such evident good effect, that it is of the utmost importance to the
child's ultimate Welfare, that it should not be interrupted.—In
order to this, however, he must be detained for ten days or a fort-
night after the re-commencement of School at Eton—(To give you
a slight notion of the state of his Skin, poor fellow—he bore during
the two first days a heat of *160* degrees without any perspiration
following!)—Beyond all doubt, a great part of his Idleness &
Wanderings of Mind must be attributed to the state of his half-
conscious *Sensations.* Now will you be so good as to let us know
what the forms are—whether a Certificate from the Medical
Advisers should be sent to Dr Keates—

With regard to his Schooling I pledge myself to you, that *on the
whole* he shall sustain no loss by passing this fortnight under my
eye—for I have so arranged my time, that I shall take him myself
in hand, after his Brother returns to Merchant-Taylors'—and at
all events, you shall find him thoroughly master of his Greek
Grammar—tho' it must depend on his health, whether he will
at every moment be master of himself *extempore.* This however,
will. . . .[1] I have prepared a little catechism of the Greek Grammar,
in which he will be *dodged* every day, before and on his return from
the Baths in Red Lion Square. I have some thoughts of trying them

[1] Word illegible in MS.

than 4, successively. I more than suspect an ulcer in the stomach, or the pylorus, from the constant pain in that region every morning, for years past, on awaking—& which continues till I get up & move about in an upright posture. This is known by experience to be perfectly compatible with a look of good health—the texture of the Skin & the excessive action of the Kidneys, & torpor of the lower Bowels being the only symptoms, from which it can be conjectured.—But no more of this! We must all die of somewhat and ought, as the Irish Franciscan in a discourse of Final Causes observed—Let us all thank God and adore his wisdom and goodness in putting Death at the end of Life & thereby giving us all time for repentance.

I do not want you to read the Aids to Reflection thro', till you can sit down to it with calmness & in leisure. But one thing I *do* wish—viz. that before I see you, you would run your eye over the pages, which I have marked down overleaf.[1]—Mr Frere was particularly struck & pleased with a remark, I made to him, the day before yesterday—That our Divines had adopted the foundations of their Faith (which they call Natural Religion) from Paganism— they begin with *The Being*—'Ο "Ων—the necessary legitimate consequence of which is Pantheism, with Polytheism (i.e. the hypothesis of higher *Natures*, οἱ θεοί) as it's *utter*ance or exoteric Half.— The Deity, τὸ θεῖον, was (for the Theogonists) to the Divinities (οἱ θεοί) as Space to the Diagrams for the Geometrician. The space exists absolutely in each—Circle, Ellipse, Triangle, Parallelogram &c &c—but only in these does it *ex*ist at all.—Now St John would have taught them a deeper philosophy, and the only one compatible with a *Moral* religion—Θεόν = τὸ θεῖον, the Absolute, or Causa sui—Θεὸν[2] οὐδεὶς ἑώρακε πώποτε—i.e. essentially unutterable, deeper than all Idea—ὁ μονογενὴς υἱός, ὁ ὢν[3] ἐν τῷ κόλπῳ τοῦ πατρός,[4] οὗτος ἐξηγήσατο.[5]—Θεός becomes ὁ πατήρ by the Act of realizing in the Son—. It sounds paradox, but it is most certain truth, that in order of Thought, under the intrusive form of *Time*, the Father is a reflex from the Son—and that it does not appear so in human relations arises from our Fathers having had Fathers— The man is called a Father by anticipation, grounded on a Past. But in the Idea of the Christian Deity the order is as the Evange-

---

[1] (1) The Preface. (2) P. 4. *note.* (3) p. 14–17. (4) 26. *note.* Defin. of *Prudence,* generally.—40, 41. Def. of Pleasure & Happiness. (5) 51–56. (6) 67–71. *Definition of Nature.* See p. 73. (7) 81–82.—(8) 111–112.—116–121. (9) 131–135. 154. (10) 159–162. 176, 177.—Lastly, 229–233.—[References added 'overleaf' by S. T. C.]

[2] Underlined once in MS.   [3] ὁ ὢν underlined twice in MS.

[4] τοῦ πατρός, underlined once in MS.

[5] John i. 18. (with ἐν τῷ κόλπῳ for εἰς τὸν κόλπον, and οὗτος for ἐκεῖνος).

list gives it—1. Θεός. 2. ὁ ὤν,[1] ὁ μονογενής. 3. ὁ πατήρ. Plato was a prophetic Anomaly—all the prior Theologians of Greece (unless Heraclitus was an exception) were φυσιολόγοι—Their first principle was—Ἔστι:—the first of the Christian Scheme Εἰμί.—The former deduced the Persons—the latter begins with and from the Personal, or rather the Personëity itself.—

What the Jew said who turned Christian after [he] had returned from Rome to which he had gone against the intreaty of his pious Friend:—viz. that Christianity must be divine—or it could not subsist under such monsters as those of the Romish Hierarchy, often suggests itself to me—when I read Paley, Watson, or indeed any one of the Evidence-mongers.—They are outrages [on] Logic, and insults on Common Sense.— . . .[2]

1509. *To John Hookham Frere*

Address: John Hookham Frere, Esqre | 20. Gloucester Place.
MS. formerly in the possession of the late Arthur Pforzheimer. Pub. John Hookham Frere, *228.*
Postmark: Highgate, 12 January 1826.

Grove, Highgate
Wednesday Night. [11 January 1826]

My dear Sir

It is a great delight to me to be any where with you. And more than so—for to you I can say this, secure of the right interpretation —it is a source of Strength, and a renewal of hope—and of the hope, I most need—viz. that I am still in a region where the sympathy of sane minds can follow me, and have not been toiling after shadows. I shall have much pleasure in availing myself of Lord Hastings'[3] condescension, and still more in the preludium— Dared I shape my expectations to my wishes, I would say, I expect you on Friday at an early hour[4]—and if I might wish *aloud*, you would hear me craving & hoping that you might have a portion of your MSS. with you—

With sincere respect, I am, | my dear Sir! your obliged
S. T. Coleridge

[1] ὁ ὤν underlined once in MS.

[2] Three-fourths of a page of MS. cut off, thus destroying the address sheet.

[3] Francis Rawdon-Hastings, first Marquis of Hastings and second Earl of Moira (1754–1826), governor-general of Bengal and commander-in-chief of the forces in India, 1812–21, and governor and commander-in-chief of Malta, 1824–6.

[4] A notebook entry indicates that Frere did arrive early: '13 Jany. 1826 Thursday [Friday] Mr J H Frere passed an hour or two with me in my Garret, & then took me with him in his Carriage to the Marquis of Hastings, at the Burlington Hotel.' [MS. notebook, Huntington Library.]

1510. *To John Hookham Frere*[1]

Transcript British Museum. Pub. with omis. Coleridge on Logic and Learning, *by Alice D. Snyder, 1929, p. 153.*

The text of this letter is drawn from an imperfect transcript attached to Egerton MS. 2826, the second of two volumes containing a copy of Coleridge's unfinished treatise on *Logic*. For a brief description of Egerton MSS. 2825, 2826 see note to Letter 1324.

[January 1826][2]

My dear Sir

With this you will receive the copy of the Aids to Reflection, which I had been mustering courage to send to Lord Liverpool.[3] It came like a Breeze in one of our hot soundless Summer-noons, which one *sees* rustling in a Tree, and in the next moment feels on one's forehead, when you were so good as to say that you would present it yourself to his Lordship. And I should avail myself of your kindness without scruple, if the value of an offering were to be measured by the sincerity and *thoughtfulness* of the Respect which dictated it. But had you not been convinced of my sentiments on this point, you would not have undertaken the charge. I have three works, the fruits of a laborious life, if hard thinking and hard reading are labor—one finished and transcribed for the press, another and far larger work, my Opus Maximum containing

---

[1] While no correspondent is mentioned, this is the rough draft of a letter intended for J. H. Frere, who was anxious to secure a sinecure for Coleridge. See Letter 1507.

[2] On 19 Jan. 1826 Coleridge said that for 'certain strong motives' he had been engaged 'in writing sundry letters, one to Lord Liverpool, and the rest similarly prudential'. The present letter, with which Coleridge sent a copy of *Aids to Reflection* for Liverpool, was written, therefore, not long before Letter 1511.

[3] In September Frere received the following letter from Liverpool:

Fife House
Sept. 13th, 1826.

Private.

My dear Frere,

I return the Copy of Mr Coleridge's 'Aids to Reflection'.

When I have the Means, I will certainly endeavor to do something for him —but I will be obliged to you not to commit me.

When however you leave England, I wish you would let me have his Address, and at the same time inform me in what manner I had better communicate with him—I am with great truth very sincerely your's

Liverpool.

[Transcript Coleridge family.]

Before he left for Malta in September 1826, Frere obtained from Liverpool a 'positive Promise' of a sinecure for Coleridge of £200 a year. Liverpool, however, suffered a paralytic stroke before the matter was settled, and 'the King gave away the Place to another'. See Letters 1578–81, 1586, 1598, 1600, 1607, and 1609.

the sum and system of my philosophy and Faith on reason &
revelation, the life of Nature and the history of Man, of which the
MSS *materials* are complete, and somewhat more than a third of
the Work reduced to form, and in a *publishable* state—and lastly
a complete volume in which the main *Results* of the preceding are
given in a dramatic and popular form, entitled Travels in Body and
Mind, or the Sceptic's Pilgrimage to the Temple of Truth.[1] Of this
last work I expect to have the concluding sheet ready for the
Printer before the end of October next, so as either to appear at
the same time with the first work, or immediately after the publi-
cation of the first which (permit me to say out boldly what I think
and believe), in addition to the vast importance of the subject [for]
one intended for Public Life, in any scheme of education that
deserves the name of Liberal, and to its specific utility for all who
are in training for the Bar, the Pulpit or the Senate, or whose
stations require or incline them to speak in public, furnishes the
key, and contains the preliminaries to all my other works. The
object of this work and its principal contents are given in the Title
page, viz.—[2] The constitution & limits of the Understanding, with
the Canons of legitimate form in all conclusion, the criteria of Truth
& Falsehood in the Premises, with a reduction of all the modes of
deceptive argument to a few distinct classes, with examples of
each, commencing with some Bull, or broad & palpable Absurdity,
and thence shading off through intermediate instances, close with
some paralogism that has deceived a Nation, & tyrannized over a
whole Age: and yet resting on the same equivocation, as the first,
with the causes of the different effect on the Reader's or Hearer's
mind. Something of this sort, having the influences of psychological
causes on forensic Logic, Aristotle had annexed to his Organon—
I conjecture from one of the latter chapters, which is manifestly
a fragment. And as I have carefully selected the intermediate
examples from writers of great authority, or from popular works
with frequent references to facts of history, as demonstrating the
power of words for evil & for good, I flatter myself that I should
not overrate the practical utility of this chapter [work ?] if I
entitled it Organon verè Organon—and if I were consulted by a
Student for the Bar, or by a young man whose birth and fortune
entitled him to look forward to a Seat in the Legislature, [I could

---

[1] According to Miss Snyder, 'Folios 37–42 of Egerton 2801 contain an
autograph fragment that may well be a portion of the proposed "Travels in
Mind and Body"'. *Coleridge on Logic and Learning*, 1929, p. 153 n.

[2] The following title is cancelled in the transcript: 'The Elements of Dis-
course containing the Canons of Legitimate Form and the Criteria of Truth
and Falsehood.'

propose no better way]¹ of giving firmness & agility to his jud[g]-
ment than by framing a common-place book on this scheme, and
multiplying the examples under each head as they occurred in the
course of his reading &c, for with the *knack* of instantly detecting
a Sophism in whatever disguise, he would learn likewise the means
of exposing the fal[l]acy, how to discern it and strip it of its
plausibility.

By the publication of these two works I shall have disburthened
my conscience and then (if [it] please God to prolong my life) shall
interpose a year or two, which I mean to employ in bringing the
substance of my Lectures on Shakespear, Milton, Dante, and
Cervantes into publishable shape, and in poetic composition—
being assured by my past experience that no month will pass with-
out some addition to my Opus Maximum on which I chiefly rely
for the proof that I have not lived or laboured in vain. FAME, my
dear Sir! is a Wise Man's Object and a good man's Duty—where
ever the means have been vouchsafed. But reputation as distin-
guished from Fame, the word defines itself—Quod Maevius putat,
grex Baviorum *reputat*,² what that fool thinks (i.e. fancies) t'other
fool thinks over again. Nil omnibus vel paucis. The first is only
for one in an Age for whom, [as] in the instance of Sir Walter Scott,
the whirlwind of popularity is the Herald of the still small voice
of Fame! I certainly should be glad to have the fifth part of Scott's
reputation—but if I know myself—even this not for its own sake,
but as the means of obtaining that frugal competence which would
emancipate me from the hard, hard necessity of employing my
time and Talents on things which fifty others could do better, and
which might without loss to any one be left undone, not to speak
of the hours wasted in Spirit quenching anxieties! and permit me
to devote the whole man to the reaping and housing of the harvest
which I had myself sown anew, while it is yet untouched by the
rains & frost of late Autumn, and for which I have ploughed,
harrowed, manured, & weeded while it is yet standing, before the
approaching hour comes when no man can work—For the last
twelve years, the period of the intensest *conversion* of my mind
and spirit to this work—[*sic*] There is a noble passage in Spencer's
Calendar³ in which the sage & learned Poet had, doubtless, ine-

¹ The transcript is incomplete here, but Coleridge had made the same point
23 years earlier. His *Organum verè Organum*, he wrote to Godwin on 4 June 1803,
would contain 'instructions, how to form a commonplace Book by the aid of
this Instrument, so as to read with practical advantage—& (supposing
average Talents) to *ensure* a facility & rapidity in proving & in confuting'.
Letter 504. ² Cf. Virgil, *Ec.* iii. 90.
³ Coleridge refers to *The Shepheardes Calender, October*, especially lines 109
fol. He quotes and comments on the lines in Letters 1136, 1159, and 1228.

briations of his Master, Plato, in his thoughts, the *'sober inebria-
tion'*[1] to wit, from the contemplation of the Good, the True, &
the Beautiful in the absence of worldly anxieties: and during the
last twelve years, the period of the intensest studies, I could
never recall them without the homely mental translation—O that
I had but three hundred a year.—[Transcript breaks off thus.]

1511. *To Edward Coleridge*

MS. John Rylands Lib. Hitherto unpublished.

Thursday.—19 Jany. 1826
Highgate—

My dear Edward

Indeed, indeed, so far from any *'forthwith'* in your letter, the
impression left on my Mind as well as Mr Gillman's was the con-
trary—and so true was this, that on Sunday last Mr Green was
about to write the certificate in my Athenaeum Garret, when Mr
J. H. Frere came in—and as he stayed a long time, Mr Green asked
me, had I not better step down & write the certificate—as my car-
riage is waiting—and the answer was—Why on second thought,
it will be better for you to give the certificate on Sunday next—
that Henry may take it with him on the Monday—& your certifi-
cate will attest for the whole time of his medical Course.—

You would have had a *very long* letter from me; but that certain
strong motives have engaged me in sending to the press *immediately*
the supplementary disquisitions requisite for the completion of
'the *Aids* of Reflection'—& in writing sundry letters, one to Lord
Liverpool, and the rest similarly prudential.—You have not
exactly the right notion of Mr J. H. Frere's Character & Manners
—The ὁ φιλόκαλος,[2] and this Love, Taste, and Tact of the Seemly
and the Exquisite, expressed and realized in his Being, Doing, and
Saying, will best convey him to your mind.—In his Wit, in his
Humour, there is always a Fineness—he shaves with a guard to
his Razor, and the Razor is of *Steel & Rhodium,* which (says Mr

---

[1] Cf. Plato, *Phaedrus*, 243 E ff., 253 A, and 265 B. See also Philo Judaeus, *On
the Creation*, ch. xxiii. 71: μέθῃ νηφαλίῳ κατασχεθείς. In the Argument to *October*
Spenser speaks of 'Poetrie' as 'a divine gift and heavenly instinct not to bee got-
ten by laboure and learning, but adorned with both: and poured into the witte
by a certaine ἐνθουσιασμὸς and celestiall inspiration'. In *The Friend*, 1818, iii.
107 n., Coleridge himself defines Enthousiasmos as 'the influence of the divinity
such as was supposed to take possession of the priest during the performance
of the services at the altar'.

[2] Underlined once in MS.

Stoddart, the scientific metallurgist, alias, Cutler) admits of the highest polish and the smoothest as well as finest edge.

Have you seen or heard of the Translation of Schleiermacher's Essay on St Luke's Gospel with the Introduction by the Translator?[1] It will make the Bamptonists, Hulseans, &c shake their ears—It was sent to me by my Publisher (Mr Taylor) in a very handsome letter announcing *his own conversion* by the Aids to Reflection—But with Mr & Mrs G's cordial thanks & regards I must conclude—for the Man is waiting to take the letter to Town—

God bless you, | &
S. T. Coleridge.

You will soon hear from me again—

P.S. Will *you* be so good as to present Mr Gillman's respectful Assurances to the Provost and to Dr Keates, that neither neglect or forgetfulness on his part had occasioned the delay in sending the Certificate—but the belief, that the Certificate was to be retrospective &c—

1512. *To Mrs. Charles Aders*

Address: Mrs C. Aders | Euston Square
MS. Mr. W. Hugh Peal. Hitherto unpublished.
Postmark: Highgate, 20 January 1826.

20 Jany. 1826.

My dear Mrs Aders

I do not write to remind you of remembering not to forget to remember to bring my 'Scraps' with you tomorrow. No! for on the faith of a Christian Scrapster I do not think them worth the 3 Pence, which this Letter will divert from your purse to the defraying of the National Expenditure.—But I want you to give my kind Love to Mr Aders, with the request that if he could procure me the sight of Schleiermacher's Sermons[2] for a few hours only—for instance, during the time, you & he were here, & so that he might take them back with him—he would be doing me a service. —As likewise whether he has heard of any Translation on foot or intended? I have the highest reverence of Schleiermacher, as a good great man.—I have long had it in my wish and imagination

---

[1] F. D. E. Schleiermacher, *A Critical Essay on the Gospel of St. Luke*. . . . *With an Introduction by the Translator* [Connop Thirlwall], *containing an account of the controversy respecting the origin of the three first Gospels, since Bishop Marsh's Dissertation*, 1825. A copy of this work containing annotations by Coleridge is in the British Museum.

[2] Schleiermacher's *Predigten* appeared in six volumes, 1801–31. The set in the British Museum is made up as follows: vol. i, 3rd edn., 1816; vol. ii, 2nd edn., 1820; vol. iii, 2nd edn., 1821; vol. iv, 1st edn., 1820; vol. v, 1st edn., 1826; vol. vi, 1st edn., 1831.

to attempt the founding of a Teutonic Club, that should be connected with the gradual formation of a permanent German Library in London, on the plan of the Library at Bristol—the Tickets of Proprietorship being transferable, but with a Veto placed in the managing Committee, and the price of new Tickets increasing with the increase of the Library—every new Member to be balloted for.—By the bye, I took in Mr Aders's Letter to you —& being really most uncomfortably unwell, & sickish all over, from the change of Weather or indigestion, I—my imagination, at least—took the alarm.—What can have happened? Is Mr Aders taken ill? What can have occurred? It is plain, that the letter must be to hasten Mrs Aders back to town—& this must be urgent too—& so as to render an hour or two's delay a matter of importance!—Haunted by these Broodings and in this hypochondriacal Mood, I was (I confess) quite out of sympathy with my friend, Mr Gillman, & (a very unusual thing with me) could not enter at all into his Jokes. Nay, when Mrs G. told me that she had written to you, a laughing letter, the main of which Mr G. had dictated, I was ill-natured enough & *doggish* enough, to tell her—That Nature never intended her for a *Humming* Bird; and that she should be content to remain, as she was, a Bird of Paradise—. This is to shew you, that I can be out of sorts—tho' I hope it is excusable, & I know, that our dear Friend would readily excuse even a burst of ill-humour when it arise[s] from anxiety respecting two persons, not less dear to her than,

my dear Mrs A. | to your & Mr Aders's | sincere & affectionate Friend

S. T. Coleridge

1513. *To Mrs. Charles Aders*

Address: Mrs C. Aders | Euston Square
Transcript in the possession of Professor Robert C. Whitford. Hitherto unpublished fragment. Although the name, Mrs C. Aders, in the address was written by Coleridge, the direction, Euston Square, and the text of this fragment are in an unknown handwriting.

[January 1826?]

... dear Mrs Gill[m]an!—*Her* jokes are, I have observed, dutifully *adopted*, not of her own birth; and her smiles smiles of simplicity and of sympathy with the mirth of the true parent of the Jest— For I have from all my experience convinced myself that it is part and parcel of a truly feminine character of which Mrs G. may serve as a Representative, to be even laughably *obtuse* to what is commonly called wit & fun—God bless you &

S. T. C.

1514. *To Mrs. Charles Aders*

MS. University of Kansas Lib. Hitherto unpublished fragment.

23 Jany. 1826.

... P. 35. And is not God likewise the TIMELESS, and the INCOM-PREHENSIBLE, and the ALL ALWAYS? If so, what becomes of Schleiermacher's Logic? the Logic of these immutable *Predeci-sions*, and *anterior* Decrees?—I confess, it is only in a very quali-fied sense that I dare recommend either of the two first Sermons;[1] and the second I regard as in unsafe neighbourhood to the Theory described in p. 81 of the 'Aids to Reflection'.[2] The first is extremely pleasing and plausible, and there are few, if any, *parts*, which are in themselves objectionable.—But when I *feel* the Effect of the Whole, there is a Spirit of Moral Quietism, that would, I conceive, find the warmest friends and patrons in the Framers of the Holy Alliance. It is the very Morality that suits a Despotism. But as to the second, do not, my dear Mrs Aders! be too easily beguiled by this persuasive Writer into a moral Fatalism. Whatever result we may, and by the necessity of our Nature *must*, attribute to our Actions, considered as the appointed means to *rightly* desired ends, we may with equal reason expect from Prayer.

At all events, have confidence enough in my judgement not to make up your mind on this momentous question, till you have read my Essay, entitled, the philosophy of Prayer, which I am now preparing for the Press.　　　　　　　　　S. T. Coleridge

[1] The two sermons to which Coleridge refers are in the first volume of Schleiermacher's *Predigten*, 1801. They are entitled, 'Die Aehnlichkeit der Zukunft mit der Vergangenheit. Am Neujahrstage' ('The Similarity between the Future and the Past. On New Year's Day') and 'Die Kraft des Gebetes, in so fern es auf äussere Begebenheiten gerichtet ist' ('The Power of Prayer, when directed to External Events').

[2] The passage in *Aids to Reflection* (1825) reads:

If you have resolved that all belief of a divine Comforter present to our inmost Being and aiding our infirmities, is fond and fanatical—if the Scrip-tures promising and asserting such communion are to be explained away into the action of circumstances, and the necessary movements of the vast machine, in one of the circulating chains of which the human Will is a petty Link —in what better light can Prayer appear to you, than the groans of a wounded Lion in his solitary Den, or the howl of a Dog with his eyes on the Moon? At the best, you can regard it only as a transient bewilderment of the Social Instinct, as a social Habit misapplied! Unless indeed you should adopt the theory which I remember to have read in the writings of the late Dr. Jebb, and for some supposed beneficial re-action of Praying on the Prayer's own Mind, should practise it as a species of *Animal-Magnetism* to be brought about by a wilful eclipse of the Reason, and a temporary *make-believe* on the part of the Self-magnetizer!

P.S. *You* will think it worth my noticing that in a little blank
Verse Poem addressed by me to Charles Lamb on his Sister's Illness
in my 23rd Year I had expressed the same sentiments as Schleier-
macher in the conclusion of his 2nd Sermon, and in my 24th year
had already publicly recanted and renounced them in a Note to the
Poem—in the first Edition of my Juvenile Poems.—[1]

A child (says Schl.) is permitted and encouraged to pour forth
his Wishes and entreaties to his earthly Father—& so may we,
as God's Children, to our heavenly Father.[2] But would, I ask, a
wise and good Father permit and encourage this, if he did not per-
mit & encourage the Child to hope, that it's Wishes & Entreaties
might influence him?

1515. *To Derwent Coleridge*

Address: D. Coleridge, Esqre
MS. Cornell University Lib. Pub. with omis. Charles Lamb and his Hertford-
shire, *by R. L. Hine, 1949, p. 70.* The manuscript has been tampered with:
the address is heavily inked out, and the words *Derwent* in the salutation and
Father in the conclusion are altered to *Friend*.

[January 1826][3]

My dearest Derwent! Experto credes?—That the most heart-
withering Sorrow that can betide a high, honorable, morally sensi-
tive and affectionate-natured Man, (a guilty conscience excepted)

[1] Coleridge's lines, *To a Friend* [*Charles Lamb*] *together with an unfinished
Poem,* were first published in 1796. (See *Poems,* i. 78–79.) They were included in
a letter to Southey in 1794. (See Letter 77.) The following recantation appeared
in 1797, in the second, not the first edition of the *Poems:*

I utterly recant the sentiment contained in the lines—

> 'Of whose omniscient and all-spreading Love
> Aught to *implore* were impotence of mind,'

it being written in Scripture, '*Ask*, and it shall be given you,' and my
human reason being moreover convinced of the propriety of offering *peti-
tions* as well as thanksgivings to Deity. [Note by S. T. C. in *Poems,* 1797
and 1803.]

[2] The relevant sentence from Schleiermacher's second sermon, 'The Power
of Prayer', reads as follows: 'It [prayer] is one of the privileges that attach to
our status as children of God. It would be a family of slaves if children were
not allowed to express their wishes in the presence of their father, wiser though
he be.' *Predigten,* i. 29 (3rd edn., 1816). Translation by Mr. B. A. Rowley, who
examined the *Predigten* in the British Museum. See Letter 1512 n.

[3] On 30 Jan. 1826 Mrs. Coleridge wrote to Derwent: 'I hope no child of
mine will marry without a good certainty of supporting a family. I have known
so many difficulties myself that I have reason to warn my children!' Three
days later Sara reported to him: 'Your hint about "marrying as soon as may
be" has plunged mama into one of those bogs of doubt & discomfort.' [MSS.

is: to have placed himself incautiously in such a relation to a Young Woman as neither to have it in his power to discontinue his attentions without dishonor & remorse, nor to continue them without inward repugnance, and a future *life* of Discomfort, of vain Heartyearnings and remediless Heart-wastings distinctly before his eyes —as the alternative!—Either Misery of Remorse, or Misery of Regret!—a Regret too, which Thoughts and Remembrances of suicidal Weakness & Foolishness will make the Half-brother at least of Remorse! Consciously and intentionally to excite a Hope is in the code of Honor, is in *Your* code, to give a *claim.*—For God's sake, think and think again before you give the least portion of your own free-agency out of your own power! You give away more than Life.—

This is a case in which with my principles I can only give the general Rule—the application of it to persons and particulars I must ever leave to yourself—

Your affectionate & in this | faithful Father
S. T. C.

1516. *To George Skinner*

Transcript Coleridge family. Hitherto unpublished.

Grove Highgate
Thursday Evening [26 January 1826]
My dear Sir

I can scarcely sit up & guide my pen so fearful a shaking have I had since the breaking up of the first frost. I have been literally *weather-blighted* and this is the first morning I have been able to leave the house, for two or three turns in the sunshine.

My son Derwent Coleridge having (as indeed I never doubted that he would) sloughed the last skin of his Caterpillarage has made the first use of his eyes and wings into which he has unfolded by returning to Cambridge in order to prepare himself in good earnest for taking Orders. He hopes to be able to maintain himself during the time, in part by pupils.—If it should be in your power to serve him in this respect, I intreat you to confer this additional obligation on me—and I trust that the wrigglings of the Larva will be forgotten by you in the present *Psyche*, which I believe to be the very *Imago* sui.

Mr. A. H. B. Coleridge.] The present letter was evidently prompted by a similar intimation made to Coleridge, possibly while Derwent was at Highgate for three or four days in late January 1826. (See Letter 1517.) Although Derwent was probably engaged to Mary Pridham at this time, the marriage did not take place until Dec. 1827.

Need I say, how welcome you will be to me and to us all whenever choice or chance shall bring you to Highgate?—For with sincere & affectionate Esteem

I am my dear Sir | Your obliged Friend
S. T. Coleridge

1517. *To Edward Coleridge*

Transcript Coleridge family. Hitherto unpublished.

30th Jan. 1826.

My dear Nephew

Sick & low as I am, yet while I can hold myself up & guide a pen, Henry Gillman must not return to Eton without bearing a note from me: tho' it's whole purport were but to tell you so. And in fact I have neither strength nor spirits to do much more. From the first breaking up of the first frost, during which I had enjoyed a more than usual quantum of genial sensations, I was struck with a sort of weather blight. There seems indeed to have been a malignancy in the Atmosphere—the effect of which was a general influenza in this neighbourhood, that wreaked it's wicked will on me with peculiar virulence & persistency, all over & all through me. The pains in my back & limbs were trifles compared with the fatiguing frequency of cough & expectoration, which made my head feel like a Bruise, preventing any sound or continued sleep, & all the conditions of perspiration. I am certainly much better, but without any of the feeling of convalescence. It seems as if having been *floored*, I had got up again, not *from* the Blow but *with* it, my chest remaining sore as a boil, & the dreary sickishness & fever-feel in my eyes from the quantity of phlegm secreted during the night is worse than those who have not been fellow-sufferers could easily imagine. Unluckily Derwent arrived & past 3 or 4 days here on his way to Cambridge shortly after my confinement: so that I had but little power of talking with him. He has, however, sloughed (he gives me reason to hope) his last caterpillar skin— seen his infidelity in the true light of 0×0, or as a fulfilment of the threat that from him who had nothing, should be taken away even that which he had—& is resolved to sit down heart & soul to prepare himself for taking orders.

It has been & is a subject of painful regret to me that this long illness, happening unluckily just at the time that James Gillman returned to Merchant Taylors' has deprived Henry of the advantages, such as they are, that I had fully purposed to give him. Yet I hope that you will find him improved—at all events in his

Greek Grammar. He often appears far worse & more ignorant than he is, from the habit of always saying something—instead of stopping. Consequently, he utters some nonsense which strikes his own ear & completely bewilders him, while if he had paused, he would be found to have the whole very correctly. But alas! the want of power over his powers is his characteristic calamity.

Mrs G. begs me to say, that she will write out the Wanderings of Cain for you by Easter. I have sent Davison, the two volumes of Skelton (I should be glad to read his volume against the Deists), & the Matthiae—lest you should want them. I hope you did not understand by my words respecting the Essay on the third Gospel that I approved it or imagined it as aught to frighten the Bamptonians—I meant no more than that it would rouse them & send them forward in a new direction.

I have never heard from John & did I not know him, should be afraid that the freedom with which I had delivered my sentiments on reviewing had given him offence.

But I must close up this letter. As soon as I can do it to any purpose, you shall hear from, my dear Nephew, . . . [No conclusion or signature in transcript.]

1518. *To Basil Montagu*

Address: Basil Montague, Esqre | at his Chambers | Lincoln's Inn Square
MS. British Museum. Pub. with omis. Samuel Taylor Coleridge and the English Romantic School, *by Alois Brandl, translated by Lady Eastlake, 1887, p. 373.*
Postmark: Highgate, 1 February 1826.

[1 February 1826]

My dearest Montague

Tho' no other reason is wanting but the obvious one of the weather, for your long intermission of a Month—still I am haunted (not having even heard *of* you) with the apprehension that Mrs M. has been ill.

As it has happened, you & Mr Irving have been absent during a time when I could not have enjoyed, & for a fortnight at least not even have partaken of, your Society. From the first breaking up of the first Frost I was struck with a Weather-*blight*—and have been very much worse than during any indisposition for the last 3 years, even my Jaundice fit not excepted.—And tho' the pains in my Side & Limbs are gone, still the fatiguing frequency of Cough and the irritating Expectoration remains & has reduced me to great weakness & depression, from forcing me to start up every 3 or 4 minutes in bed, to eliminate the phlegm—

My excellent and filial Friend, Mr Watson, is with us—a great delight to us all. I hope, you will come on Thursday.

I was truly grieved to hear from Harriet Hall that Mr Irving looked shockingly ill—and had preached *two hours*—He will surely shorten his life & will find too late that he has been unjustifiably prodigal of reversionary property. He robs Mankind of his future Self.

I confess, I do not at all understand our Friend's late excursions into the prophecies of a sealed Book, of which no satisfactory proof has yet been given whether they have already been or still remain to be fulfilled. Cocceius, the best & most spiritual of all our learned Commentators interprets [the] Chapter on the Millennium as of events already past. But as I do not understand, I do not judge—but am willing to believe, that as preached by Mr Irving, it will be to edification—tho' for myself, I am not ashamed to say, that a single Chapter of St Paul's Epistles or St John's Gospel is of more value to me, in light & in life, in love & in Comfort, than the Books of the Apocalypse, Daniel, & Zachariah, all together. In fact, I scarcely know what to make even of the second Coming of our Lord. Is he not 'my Lord and my God'? Is there aught good in the Soul, and he not a Dweller there?—I am aware of the necessity of a mid course between Quakerism & a MERELY *historical* Christianity—But I dare not conceal my conviction, that on certain points we may have clearer views of Christianity than some of the Apostles had—

God bless you &
S. T. Coleridge

1519. *To Derwent Coleridge*

Address: Derwent Coleridge, Esqre | St. John's, Cambridge
MS. Victoria University Lib. Pub. E. L. G. ii. 367.

Grove, Highgate.
Thursday Afternoon [2 February 1826][1]

My dear Derwent

Mr Whiteford took your *Essays* and (by an odd and felicitous coincidence) the *Sponge*, which however we detached & diverted from it's critical invasion before it had done much mischief. I was not aware that you had left your Poems likewise, they being in Mrs Gillman's Parlour, till after Mr W. had left the house. And as Mr Johnson is going to Jesus (College, I mean) tomorrow morning, it was worth while to interpose this brief delay.—

[1] This letter is endorsed 'received—Feby. 6th—1826—D. C.'

I was glad of your letter. Be assured, that it will be for our mutual happiness that you should write me, once a fortnight at least— even tho' I might not always be well enough to answer you, letter per letter. It is afflictive enough, that we have not one family House, as the natural center for all of you & your Home, as often as your Calls admitted. I have felt this want very poignantly and not without an after-relish of *mortification,* with regard to your Sister: tho' as it is the only instance, and stands in contrast with the Rest, I should be an *Unthank,* if I did not turn away my eye from it—the more so, as the Obstacles have not been mere Excuses. —As the matter is, my intended argument holds—we must make the best of it—& not by neglect or long intervals of silence aggravate the evil.

O if I could but promise myself five or six years of practical health, and Hartley could but promise himself to be a *Self* and to construct a circle by the circumvolving line—what a comfort and delight it would be to have him with me, as a Literary Partner!—[1]

Since you left us, I have been much worse—and altogether confined to my Bed Room. This morning, tho' I have perhaps suffered more pain than on any day, my worst Symptoms (viz. Cough, Expectoration, and Affections of the Scrotum connected with the Bladder & Kidneys) are abated—and tho' weak almost as an Infant, I have been able to take three or four turns in the Grove.—

---

[1] Coleridge may have learned of the failure of Suart's boarding-school, an establishment with which Hartley Coleridge had recently been associated. In Apr. 1825 Dorothy Wordsworth said she had 'no hope of the school succeeding at Ambleside, as a Boarding School', and on 18 Oct. she reported to Mrs. Clarkson: 'Hartley's school is done up. He writes for Magazines.' *Later Years,* i. 197 and 230.

In a letter addressed to Thomas Poole early in 1826, Mrs. Coleridge revealed her uneasiness over Hartley's situation: 'H. has been writing some Essays in a yearly publication called *Janus* published at Edinburgh— . . . He talks of publishing a small volume of Poems, and printing them at Liverpool, but he talks of so many literary projects, which *end* [in] talk, that I never depend on his intentions. All I know is that if he do not write he cannot eat, for writing now is his sole dependance . . .—for his School is given up for the present, and I do not flatter myself he will resume it even if pupils might be had. I assure you, I am not a little anxious on his account, for he ought to be in town to pursue a literary career, but London will not do for him!' *Minnow among Tritons,* ed. Stephen Potter, 1934, p. 93 (letter misdated).

As his mother had feared, Hartley was never able to support himself by his writings. It was, indeed, 1833 before he published a volume of poems. Except for one or two brief intervals, he stayed on in the Lake Country until his death in 1849, and over the years he managed to produce a considerable body of poetry and prose. He is remembered today as the author of a number of excellent sonnets and as a minor critic and essayist.

My dear & truly filial friend, Mr Watson, surprized us by his
Apparition on Monday last—stays with us till Sunday, & then
makes for Cumberland. He is the *very same* and yet greatly im-
proved—the very same in heart, and principles, and looks—but
with more ease & confidence. He is indeed a delightful young man:
and I dare hope very highly of him. Most unlucky that you first
and then he should have come—nay, that is not what I mean—
but that I should have been so unusually incapacitated when you
& he came—It has been the sorest Shaking, I have had, since I
have been at Highgate, after the first year.—

The two Copies of the Aids were dispatched on the day after
your departure—the one with Mr J. Macauley's Name & mine, the
other with mine as in acknowlegement of friendship to my Son,
D. Coleridge—I understood Mr Whiteford to say, that they *had
been* forwarded to Plymouth.—

I can write no more at present.—Do not fail to let me hear from
you, whether you have or have not any thing to say.—Were I you,
I would for the next 5 or 6 months put the formation of opinions
wholly out of view and consider myself as merely collecting facts,
and the knowlege of what other men thought & said, wisely or
unwisely, to be hereafter scanned—. I should think it worth your
while to run your eye thro' the *Latin* Translation of the Apostolic
Fathers, collected by Dr Rowth[1]—just to form some general
notion, taking notes of any thing that struck you (viz. of the page
& line) to read it at some future time in the Greek—. It would be
no great Labor to *run thro'* in this way the Christian Writers, Greek
and Latin, down to Tertullian & Irenaeus—. It does seem to me a
very mean & false view of Christianity to suppose that even the
Apostles themselves had the degree of clearness & enlargement
which a philosophic Believer of the present day may enjoy—
Think only of the vast inferiority of the other Apostles to John &
Paul—and the distinct marks in the writings of the Latter that he
was becoming more and more doubtful of the Jewish Literarity
[Literality?] in which he as well as the rest had understood the
Second Coming of our Lord.[2] What is Christianity at any one
period?—The Ideal of the Human Soul at that period.—

Write to Keswick & tell your Mother how ill I have been. She is
troubled with yearly anxieties about the Ensurance Money—

---

[1] Martin J. Routh (1755–1854), *Reliquiae Sacrae; sive auctorum fere jam
perditorum secundi tertiique saeculi fragmenta, quae supersunt,* 4 vols., 1814–18.

[2] Cf. *Literary Remains,* iv. 14–15. 'The whole passage in which our Lord
describes his coming is so . . . intentionally expressed in the diction and images
of the Prophets, that nothing but the carnal literality common to the Jews at
that time and most strongly marked in the disciples . . . could have prevented
the symbolic import . . . of the words from being seen.' See also Letter 1584.

which rather annoys the Gillmans.—*Seven* (nay, 8) *years ago* my friend, Mr Green, assured me that as long as I lived, the sum was set aside for me—& I have no doubt, that he has put it in his *Will*, in e[ven] so unlikely an event as my Surviving him. Mr Gillman has nothing farther to do with it, than that of receiving it & paying it at the same time that he pays his own to the same office.—I trust, that I shall shortly be able to add—that whatever may be the state of my personal engagements to the Gillmans at the time of my death (& to no one else am I indebted) the whole proceeds of this Assurance will be held sacred, to your Mother & Sister, & secured beyond all dependency on the will or feelings of any person—. Not that I have any the least reason not to rely on Mr Gillman in this instance.

I shall bear in mind your need of a Title—God bless you & your affectionate | Father . . . [Signature cut off.]

P.S. You might, as well, call on Mr Johnston of Jesus. He is a civil friendly young man—& his Father a wealthy Neighbor & Patient of Mr Gillman's.

1520. *To Mrs. Charles Aders*

MS. Harvard College Lib. Hitherto unpublished.

Grove, Highgate
Monday
6 Feby 1826.

My dear Mrs Aders

I am ignorant of our excellent Friend, Mr H. C. Robinson's Address. Will you be so good as to re-direct this Letter for me: or at least the 3rd. and 4th. sides and send it to him?[1] My dear & filial Friend, Mr Watson, has been with us for 4 or 5 days— *greatly* improved and yet the very very *same.* He left us for Cumberland yestermorning: but in about 4 months will return, and sojourn with us an indefinite while. He *loves* Germany & Germans —*dislikes* the Italians, and ABHORS the French—all as a good man ought to do—just as I would have had it!—This was indeed among my last injunctions to him, when he was leaving England—Bring me back your prejudices, with the loss only of the *first* syllable. He has done so: and of course I rank him now among the *judicious* Lovers & Haters.—

[1] These pages have not come to light, but on 16 Feb. 1826 Robinson wrote in his diary: 'Then inquiry at the Red Cross Library after Eichhorn's *Commentarius in Apocalypsem* [*sic*] *Johannis* for Coleridge. To its reproach not there.' *Robinson on Books and Their Writers*, i. 332.

What weather! the equinoctial gales before their time! I hope, you keep yourself at home—and even there, with as few excursions & loiterings on the stairs & in the passages as possible. Mrs Gillman is not so much better as I would wish, but yet better.—As to myself, since Friday last I have been manifestly and feelably *convalescing* —and am yielding with a good grace to the conviction, that I am *aging* apace, passing to the feebleness of second (& in some measure, I trust, to the innocence of the first) Childhood—& MUST NURSE MYSELF!

Transmit my affectionate remembrances to [Ellen][1]—and my love to that sweet-countenanced Niece of your's whose name I have forgotten or did not catch.—

My love to Mr Aders is included in the assurance that I am *your* most

affectionate Friend
S. T. Coleridge

P.S. Read my note to Robinson: for it contains a request to you, or rather supposes one.

1521. *To Edward Coleridge*

Address: Revd E. Coleridge | the College | Eton
MS. Pierpont Morgan Lib. Pub. except for the postscript, *E. L. G. ii. 393.* The last four pages of the MS. beginning with the postscript and including the address have become separated from this letter and are erroneously attached to the MS. of Letter 1537.

[8 February 1826][2]

My dear Edward

Many thanks for your kind and interesting letter. It was very welcome and has been, I assure you, a great refreshment to my Spirits. During the last week I have been progressively convalescent: & am now at the *par* of my health. I thank the All-merciful with a full heart, that I can attest by my own experience the truth of your remarks respecting the loving-kindness as well as the wisdom and Justice, of these Visitations & Chastisements in the Flesh. In three points I trust that thro' his grace I have been spiritually benefited by this recent shaking. First, my Prayers

---

[1] Name heavily inked out in MS.

[2] The copy of *Remorse* referred to in the postscript of this letter bears the following dated inscription in Coleridge's handwriting: 'To the Revd. Edward Coleridge this Duplicate of the Remorse with Mrs Gillman's best respects 8 Feby. 1826.' A cancelled inscription reads: 'Mrs Gillman from the Author.' The volume is now in the possession of Mr. Henry Hofheimer.

had been too little formal, too exclusively meditative, too much
of thought and feeling, and too little of Will and Striving after
furtherance in grace. There was an indolence leavening the resig-
nation which it counterfeited. There was indeed that imperfect
Love which made me dread above all fears the falling out of God
into the abysm, the dreadful productivity, of my own corrupted
Soul, but not the Love, that should urge me to press forward and
lay hold of the *Promises*. My state of mind was too often in too
close a neighbourhood to the relaxing Malaria of the Mystic Divinity,
which affects to languish after an extinction of individual Con-
sciousness—the sickly state which I had myself described in one
of the Poems in the Sibylline Leaves—'the Lover's Resolutions'
—who sick in soul

> Worships the Spirit of unconscious Life
> In tree and wild-flower. Gentle Lunatic,
> If so he might not wholly cease to *be*,
> He would far rather not be that, he is,
> But would be something that he knows not of, &c[1]—

But a few days after the commencement of this bilious fever, the
first Volume of Schleiermacher's far-famed Sermons was sent me,
in German—the same Divine, whose Essay on St Luke's Gospel
has been recently translated: and among these Sermons was one
(greatly admired in Germany) on Prayer, grounded on the Scene
in the Garden—the Preacher's object being to shew, first, that we
may, and ought to, *pray*: for our Lord did so—but 2. that on no
account for a single moment should we allow ourselves to believe,
that our prayers & petitions would have any effect but that which
the act of praying produced on our own minds and feelings: for the
Disciple dare not hope for more than his Master obtained.—(One
instance this among many of the danger of turning away from the
express directions of Scripture on this or that part of duty in order
to draw consequences from some other part of Scripture, recorded
for a different purpose.)—This Sermon, however, occasioned me to
give the whole force of my mind to the Subject—to seek Light in
Prayer and from the Scripture, from the Scripture and in Prayer—
and the result has been a clear & steadfast conviction, that whatever
efficacy we may, and by the constitution of our Being *must*, attri-
bute to our *Actions*, considered as appointed means to rightly
desired ends, the same with equal rationality we assign to our
petitionary prayers—and that provided only that our *spiritual*
interests be, generally, the predominant, and *always* the ultimate,

---

[1] *The Picture, or the Lover's Resolution*, lines 20–24, *Poems*, i. 369–**70**. See
also Letter 933.

Object, neither our bodily, nor our temporal, needs & concernments are excluded from the requests that may be offered in Faith and in the name of our Mediator and Redeemer. And I am encouraged to hope, that in the Essay on the philosophy of Prayer (a phrase, which I have chosen instead of ' the duty and reasonableness ' in the expectation of winning a certain class of Inquirers, tho' at a sacrifice of my own feelings) my own convictions may be made an instrument of divine mercy to others.

The second point, in which additional Light has been vouchsafed me, respects the state of my thoughts & feelings in connection with the three Gospels—I scarcely know how to explain it to you, but by a difference in the impressions made and left on my mind from the perusal of Matthew, Mark & Luke compared with the 4th Gospel, the Epistles of Paul & John, the Psalms, the Prophets, the Book of Job—a difference too great to have been left so long a time unexamined and obscure—as long as this dimness, perplexity, and ferment continued, the New Testament could not be contemplated as an harmonious Whole. If the cause was in myself, (and I thank God's supporting Spirit, I was not so lost in presumption as not to consider this as incomparably the more probable) whether it were from defect of knowlege or from an unhealthy state of feeling, it was high time that it should be discovered and brought to trial. And here too, tho' I have still great need for further light on the relations of the three Gospels, each to the others, and particularly as to [the] relation of Mark to Matthew, yet I have to be thankful for a large portion of Quiet from the view, I have obtained, respecting their common relation both to the 4th Gospel and to the Epistles, and that they form a distinct yet inseparable integral Part of the Christian Volume. With this in conjunction with the third point, which follows, my faith has, I trust, become more duly proportioned to the *objective* and historical part of Christianity—to the Church Militant and to the Kingdom of Christ on earth, instead of dwelling with too exclusive a preference on the subjective, timeless, and individually spiritual. Not that if my former opinions were stated to me now, I could find any thing objectionable in the *words*; but the cast and tone of feeling was not right. And yet should I by God's Grace become fit to receive a clearer light, a more compleat & satisfying insight, I shall still have reason to be grateful, that I had begun with St John and St Paul.—

The third Point and which occupied the larger portion of the time, my Strength allowed me, reading for the greater part with my head on the raised pillows, I was led to, greatly against my inclinations, by a sense of duty, viz. a duty of friendship—The fact was **Mr** Irving has been lately very much with Hatley Frere[1] (*my* Mr Frere's Brother) a pious and well-meaning but gloomy & enthusiastic Calvinist, and quite swallowed up in the quicksands of conjectural prophecy—translating Ezekiel, Zachariah, Daniel and the Apocalypse into Journals and Gazettes for the year of our Lord 1827—[or] 6 as the present year happens to be—in short, one of the Revd. G. S. Faber[2] School. Mr Irving (as Mrs Montagu most sensibly observed) affected by Hatley Frere's solemn and intense earnestness, mistook the vividness of the impression for the force of truth—and has been preaching immeasurable lengths of Sermons, to the serious detriment of his health, and the bewilderment of his Auditors, on the Millennium—& I know not what—Armath Geddon [Armageddon] & the Jews—. I have not seen him for the last six weeks; but the last time, he was here, I felt that he was going wrong—& intreated him to beware, how standing as an Ambassador of Christ he interpolated his instructions by mere conjectures of his own fancy. I told him, that with the great activity and inventiveness of intellect, which I possessed in common with him, I should have been wrecked, had it not pleased the Almighty that it should meet with a Counter-check in my rooted aversion to the *Arbitrary*, and my solicitude to bring back all my positions to their *Premises*—to understand distinctly what I set off from.—Now, Sir! (I continued) you assume the Apocalypse to contain a series of events in an historico-chronological Arrangement—not simply first, A, second, B, third, C, & fourth, D,—but A so many years, B so many—in short, not as the Prophets predicted but as the Annalist in the Books of Samuel, Kings, or Chronicles *narrated*—nay, with an exactness not attempted even by the latter, but to be parallelled only in modern Chronicles. If so, then I ask you, from what *date* do you commence? And on what authority do you fix it?—I did not however, press the point —conscious that I had never given that degree of attention to the Apocalypse which might have authorized [me] to deliver a settled opinion of it's Contents.—But I have now studied it verse by verse in the original with the commentary of Cocceius, from which, however, I derived little or no assistance, tho' to this learned &

---

[1] James Hatley Frere (1779–1866), writer on prophecy. In 1815 he published *A combined view of the prophecies of Daniel, Esdras, and S. John, shewing that all the prophetic writings are formed upon one plan ... Also a minute explanation of the prophecies of Daniel; together with critical remarks upon the interpretations of preceding commentators, and more particularly upon the systems of Mr. Faber and Mr. Cunninghame;* and in 1826 *On the general structure of the Apocalypse, being a brief introduction to its minute interpretation.*

[2] George Stanley Faber (1773-1854), controversialist and author of several works on prophecy.

generally judicious Commentator the credit is due of having first
expunged the Nicolaitan from the List of Heresies, and of thus
adding one proof to the many of the little reliance to be placed on
the assertions of Irenaeus, and the early Fathers.—But unhappily
during the whole Work the ignis fatuus of the Pope keeps whisk-
ing and dancing before the good man's eyes—nothing but this
can he see, and this he sees every where.—The result, however,
has been such as beyond, nay contrary to my anticipations,
I am most thankful for. Not that many particular words and
symbols do not remain sealed for me: and doubtless many,
very many beauties & proprieties I have yet to discover. But the
whole scope of the Work, and all the main stages of it's magnifi-
cent March are perfectly clear to me—and I have no doubt of
establishing for all competent Inquirers the Conclusion, which
I have drawn for myself—that the Apocalypse is truly the Supple-
ment to the three preceding main divisions of the New Testament,
and the requisite Complement of the Christian Faith—of high
interest, use, and edification for *all* Believers, and without which
the New Testament would not be what with it it *is*, the compleat
Quadrature and Antitype of the Old.—

On running my eye over this sheet, I see that I have been putting
your patience to the Trial—but prosing and egotistic as it would
appear, and indeed *be*, to other[s], yet as a chapter in my Bio-
graphia Interior it will have an interest for *You*—were it but as a
humble instance of an earnest desire on the part of an Individual
to know what he is, and to be what he knows, in an age where
beyond all former precedent (such at least is my belief) men seem
to regulate their conduct by the Worldling's maxim—viz. to sacri-
fice the World to himself in all worldly concerns, and himself to the
world in all spiritual ones.—

My illness has prevented me from *having* sent my supplementary
disquisitions to the Press—I having layed it down as a By-law for
myself, never for the future to send a first sheet to the Printer till
I have written Finis to the fair Copy of the last. I expect, however,
to commence Printing before the close of next week. Did I tell you,
that I had received a letter from my Publisher, announcing to me
his conversion by the Aids to Reflection—principally, by the com-
ments on Original Sin and Redemption?—

The *occasion* rather than *cause* of my remarks on Mr J. H. Frere
was given by the words, 'Wit and *Drollery*' in your letter—but it
was exclusively with respect to Mr Frere's *external* manners that
I imagined your image of him to require modification—. Sir
George Beaumont & Mr Frere are both in a remarkable degree
highly mannered Gentlemen; but compared with Sir George

Beaumont there is a graver and more sensitive dignity of deportment in Mr Frere, and more of the *Morale* and the Thoughtful in his Courtesy.—By the bye I conjectured (for inferred is too positive a word) from something that half escaped him & was half retracted, that he, like every other person who has had any thing to do with the Man of Albermarle St, has had cause for dissatisfaction with him.—I should have pressed Mr Frere much more warmly on the subject of publishing his Aristophanics,[1] had I not some reason to believe that one of Mr Frere's motives for publishing them would be to give *me* the Honorarium, whatever it might be.—I cannot indeed adequately describe to you, my dear Edward! how very good and affectionate he is to me. I am convinced, that the thought of me was a serious aggravation of his vexation at his large Losses from the failure of both Houses, at which he banked, in addition to the incapacitation of his Tenants from the same causes in the Country.—[2]

I read with affectionate pride the part of your letter respecting the honor shewn in the honor proffered to your Brother. No higher Honor (especially, after what Mr Canning said in the House of Commons on the subject) is it in the power of Englishmen to bestow or of an English Gentleman & Scholar to receive.—I have

[1] Frere's translation of *The Frogs* was published in 1839, but the 'greater part' of the play had been printed 'upwards of twenty years', presumably by Murray. (See Letters 1014–15 and 1244.) Frere's translations of three additional plays of Aristophanes were privately printed in Malta in 1839 and in the following year were published by Pickering as *Aristophanes. A Metrical Version of the Acharnians, the Knights, and the Birds*. In July 1839 Frere wrote to his brother Bartle concerning the latter work:

> Some must be sold, not for my profit, but for poor Mr. [Gillman]'s, who is entitled to all kindness from the lovers of learning, and particularly from me, in this instance; for poor Mr. Coleridge had requested in his last will, that some of the transcripts which I had lent to him might be allowed to remain with Mr. [Gillman]. I have done, therefore, what I suppose he would have wished, by giving Mr. [Gillman] half the impression (250 copies). *The Works of the Right Honourable John Hookham Frere, with a Memoir by Sir Bartle Frere*, ed. W. E. Frere, 3 vols., 1874 (2nd edn.), i. 296.

As late as 1843 Frere asked his brother to inquire of Pickering whether Mrs. Gillman had 'profited by the sale of the Aristophanes'. Ibid. i. 322–3.

The relevant passage in Coleridge's will reads as follows: 'To Mr Gillman, as the most expressive way in which I can mark my relation to him, and in remembrance of a great and good man, revered by us both, I leave the Manuscript volume lettered, Arist: Manuscript—Birds, Acharnians, Knights, presented to me by my dear Friend & Patron, the Honorable John Hookham Frere, who of all the Men that I have had the means of knowing during my Life, appears to me eminently to deserve to be characterized as ὁ καλοκἀγαθὸς ὁ φιλόκαλος.' [For Coleridge's will see Appendix A.]

[2] In 1825 there were 2,683 bankruptcies, and 'through bubble companies' 770 banks stopped payment during the winter of 1825–6. *Haydn's Dictionary of Dates*, ed. B. Vincent, 1889 (19th edn.), pp. 86 and 663.

just received Henry's Book;[1] and have read almost half—I have received both amusement & instruction from it—it cannot but have an extensive circulation—One fault there is, that I would fain have had removed—an imitation of Southey, especially in his Letters from Portugal & Spain in the frequent obtrusion of offensive images, Sweating &c; and again a little too much & too often of eating—. Like Southey, too, his Levities border now and then on the *Odd*, and Grotesque—and he has not Southey's excuse. For I can venture to say to *you*, sub rosâ, that all men of cold constitutions are naturally immodest, as far as their Notions of Morality will permit. So Southey—while he keeps clean of *one* outlet, he does not care what filth comes out of the other Orifices.—But I could almost be angry with Henry for that very indiscreet & ex omni parte objectionable Episode on *Maria*, not to say a word of the infantile Silliness of 'but you do not know Maria, nor me either'. —It is idle to suppose that the Author of so interesting a Book, the only one that supplies any real reliable information on the present state & manners of the West Indies should not be generally known, and that he was the Bishop's Cousin and Secretary—nor is it probable but that the Book will be read in Madeira—& I know too many melancholy instances of the trouble, nay, ruin brought on Individuals & whole Families in Naples, Sicily, and Minorca by the unthinking *Blab* of English Tourists & Travellers.— Read, my dear Edward! the last §§ ph.—about carrying off a Nun, as a good Joke &c—not to say, that the impertinence & coxcombry of a perfect Stranger making love & asking a young Lady—Are you happy?—would have surprized me less from my own Derwent —I may be too severe—the Snows may have drifted from my head downwards & inwards—but believe me, the source of it is in affectionate apprehension of the consequences. Mr Gillman who has read it already twice over, when he should have been in bed, pronounces it a *right* pleasant Book & with a deal of valuable information in it—but he too complains of the Southeianisms. I shall take my very first leisure evening, possibly tomorrow, to finish it, and shall then write to Henry.—

I will not conceal from you that I take the Bishop's Conduct

---

[1] Henry Nelson Coleridge's *Six Months in the West Indies in 1825* was published anonymously in Feb. 1826. On 26 Dec. 1825 Southey wrote to John Taylor Coleridge: 'Henry's sheets are very amusing, with a hopeful exuberance about them, a yeastiness which will work off and leave the liquor the better for its working.' (Lord Coleridge, *The Story of a Devonshire House*, 1905, p. 142.) On 2 Feb. 1826 Sara Coleridge also refers to the work: 'Henry's "Six Months in the Antilles" is to be out this week—a few of the proof sheets have been sent here—it is delightfully vivacious & amusing, & my Uncle augurs well of the sale.' [MS. Mr. A. H. B. Coleridge.]

towards me as unkind. That he should neither have called on me, nor even written a line, having formerly visited here & been so cordially & affectionately welcomed, is a source of mortification to me, not on my own account but from the impression, it has made on my friends & neighbors—& the reasons conjecturally assigned. If your Cousin had any reason for this slight, prudential or of higher origin, I should have honored him for plainly communicating it to me. But enough!—Only this—My words will have utterly misrepresented my feelings if they suggest any feeling of *resentment*— If I have any feeling that relates to myself, it is only that of sorrow at any event that tends to keep up the appearance of my estrangement from the interests and affection of my nearest relations.—

The weather must improve & the days lengthen before I can with any chance of repeating my visit wait on Mr Geddes; but you may depend on my calling the first time, I go to town, and endeavoring to arrange my sittings.[1]—By the bye, I forgot to say that I shall be glad to receive old Luther. He shall occupy the only picture place in my Book-study-bed-room—over the fireplace.[2] His Table-talk is next to the Scriptures my main book of meditation, deep, seminative, pauline, beyond all other works in my possession,[3] it *potenziates*[4] both my Thoughts and my Will. I would, I had all his works—. The scanty result of my reflections on the Book of Daniel I will communicate in my next—As to Jacob's Ladder, I can conceive no other interpretation than that which you have given—Nor can I imagine the need of any other— none more beautiful, more appropriate, or bearing in the grandeur & importance of the truth intended a more authenticating character of patriarchal & pastoral Sublimity. Especially striking to me, when I call to mind that the immediate Descendants of Jacob were destined to become Sojourners in EGYPT, a Country in which Pantheism was even then pregnant with it's proper offspring, idolatrous *Polytheism*—the Deity of Egypt was the World or Nature, the Elements, the Birds, Beasts, Reptiles were his Reve-

[1] No portrait of Coleridge by Andrew Geddes (1783–1844) has come to light.

[2] The drawing of Coleridge's room does not show a picture of Luther over the fire-place. See Letters 1566 and 1568.

[3] Coleridge refers to *Dris Martini Lutheri Colloquia Mensalia: or, Dr Martin Luther's Divine Discourses at his Table*, &c. Collected first together by Dr. Antonius Lauterbach, and afterward disposed into certain Common places by John Aurifaber. Translated by H. Bell, 1652. A copy of this work with annotations by Coleridge is in the British Museum. The annotations are printed in *Literary Remains*, iv. 1–65, and T. J. Wise, *Two Lake Poets . . .*, 1927, p. 119–22.

[4] See *Biog. Lit.* i. 189: 'I have even hazarded the new verb potenziate, with its derivatives, in order to express the combination or transfer of powers.'

lations, the ἱερὰ γράμματα. What could be more fitted to counteract this sensual Apostacy than the image presented to the Patriarch, of a direct and immediate connection with Heaven, with rational Creatures *superior* in form and glory to man, as the Internuncios? Remember that the Personality of God, the living I AM, was the distinctive of the Hebrew Faith: & *personal* Revelations, a connected series, their privilege. As to the systematic Commentators, as far as they inform me respecting the radicals of words, with their Cognates, or supply parallel or illustrative passages from sacred or profane Writers, I am thankful—. Even for the true sense and force of the Texts I owe them few obligations—and as to the inward and spiritual power of the Passages I have long ceased to expect any help from them. Cocceius indeed affords occasional exceptions. I prefer our Church (by which I mean the scheme of Faith and Doctrine contained in the Liturgy, Catechism & Articles) because it is *Lutheran* in it's spirit—and the Reformation in my belief fell back after Luther, instead of advancing. But I shall make myself more intelligible to you on this point when I have leisure to state my reflections on the nature of the Romish Apostacy—the retrograde movements of which began soon after if not rather in, the apostolic Age—as both Paul & John assert—tho' it could not openly and fully manifest itself till after the disruption of the Latin Empire—

My judgement is in perfect coincidence with your remarks on Sir Walter; and when I think of the wretched trash, that the Lust of Gain induced him to publish for the last three or four years, which must have been *manufactured* for the greater part, even my feelings assist in hardening me. I should indeed be sorry if any ultimate success had attended the attempt to unite the Poet and the Worldling.—Heaven knows! I have enough to feel for without wasting my Sympathy on a Scotchman suffering the penalty of his Scotchery.[1] In whatever remote corner of recluse life a man

---

[1] The ruin of Scott's fortunes occurred during the severe financial crisis of 1825-6 and was involved in the failure of three firms: Constable and Co., Edinburgh, Scott's publishers; Hurst, Robinson, and Co. (John Hurst and Joseph Ogle Robinson), Constable's London agents; and Ballantyne and Co., a printing business in which Scott and James Ballantyne were partners. The affairs and fate of the three firms were inextricably interlocked through a system of accommodation bills. Thus a stoppage of payments by Hurst, Robinson, and Co. on 14 Jan. 1826 'brought down Constable and Co.', with whom they had carried on 'an exchange system of bills and counter-bills'. Both firms were forced into bankruptcy. Furthermore, the collapse of Constable and Co. 'in turn occasioned the failure of James Ballantyne and Co., who had been engaged in bill transactions with them'. The Ballantyne firm, however, was not made 'technically bankrupt', Scott persuading the creditors to accept a trust deed, whereby he and James Ballantyne 'as partners and as

may hide himself, and however unworldly & 'unpartaking in the evil thing' he and all his pursuits may be, the calamity of the World's frenzies will hunt him out! I am at this moment heart-sick with fruitless anguish from the ruin of a Man who loved me as a Father, but whom I had in vain sought to defascinate![1]

God bless you &

S. T. C.

P.S. ὡς περὶ Δερϝεντου, the *Genus* is (as you say) Self-conceit; but the *species* is Coxcombry—which shooting across the ground-thread of the Simplicity of Nature which he inherits as a Coleridge, produces such a betraying *veracious* Falsetto, that my vexation at the mischief is sure to break up in a Laugh at the comicality & absurdity of it. I wish, you had the Drawing of him by a Signor Betsy which he has just sent me—full length to a little below the knees, standing in a College Gown, his arm resting on a sort of Balcony, with a dirty-faced Moon 5½ inches (by measurement)

individuals . . . conveyed all their assets to trustees for the creditors', and whereby he agreed to employ 'his time and talents in the production of literary works, the sums arising from which to be applied to the payment of the debts owing by him'. Since Scott had settled the estate of Abbotsford on his son Walter early in 1825, the property was not included among his assets. He had, however, reserved the right to borrow £10,000 on the estate and did so on 3 Jan. 1826. According to James Glen, who made a detailed study of Scott's financial affairs, the total indebtedness (apart from the mortgage of £10,000 secured against Abbotsford) amounted to £116,838. 11s. 3d.

Although much controversy arose over the apportionment of responsibility for the catastrophe, the disaster was in large measure due to Scott's extravagance and improvident borrowings. The expenditure on Abbotsford alone has been estimated at £76,000. To Scott, according to James Glen, must go 'the chief blame for running the accommodation bills, both an expensive and hazardous system of borrowing'. Furthermore, Constable and Co. 'had either to grant bills or to risk the loss of their most valuable connection'. Grierson points out that Constable regarded Scott as 'an asset to preserve which almost any risk must be taken'. The consequence was that Constable 'accepted bills, both "value" bills for work done or undertaken, and "accommodation" bills, loans, to an extent that went far beyond his means if, as at the end, there should come any pressure to realise'. See *D.N.B.* under Walter Scott and James Ballantyne; H. J. C. Grierson, *Sir Walter Scott, Bart.*, 1938, pp. 237 and 253–77; James Glen, 'Sir Walter Scott's Financial Transactions', included in *The Letters of Sir Walter Scott, 1787–1807*, ed. H. J. C. Grierson, 1932, pp. lxxx–xcv, and Grierson's Introduction to the *Letters*, pp. xxxi–xlix; and J. G. Lockhart, *Memoirs of Sir Walter Scott*, 5 vols., 1914, iv. 384 and 403–4. See also Letters 1538 and 1540.

[1] Chambers (*Life*, 317) suggests that Coleridge may refer to Thomas Allsop. If so, Coleridge had in mind his attempts in 1825 to dissuade Allsop from engaging in various speculative schemes with which he was wholly out of sympathy and in which he found it difficult 'to draw the line between honorable enterprize, and a feverish spirit of Gambling'. See Letters 1428–30, 1434, 1436, and 1443.

from his nose, in the sadness of a most humorous *Melancholy*.[1]
I took it at first for a Copy of some Portrait of Lord Byron's!
Do you remember the first of my three Nehemiah Higginbottom
Sonnets?—

> Wandering at Eve on the hard world I mus'd
> And my poor Heart was sad! So at the Moon
> I gaz'd: and sigh'd and sigh'd! For oh! how soon
> Eve saddens into Night!—&c—.[2]

Had Cruikshanks made a drawing purposely for the visible im-
personation of this Sonnet, he could not have hit off so felicitous
a Fac Simile.—But if you had seen him (I having objected that it
was no more like him, than a wig-block to a Jew's harp) put him-
self as Signr. Betsy took him—It was EXQUISITE! Why (quoth I)
dear Son of mine, Derwent by name—that Signor Betsy, or Eliza
Martin or any other of the My Eye Tribe[3] may have the gift of
portraying Faces of *your* Making, is very possible; but that this
same Something which I now see bears no resemblance to the Face,
that God made, I am as positive as Sight compared with Memory
but two Seconds old can make me.—To be sure that quantity of
black excrement under the Chin is, to my shame & sorrow, very
like indeed—but if you love me, do, pray, let it become an *Ideal*
Charm, confined to Signr. Betsy's Alter Tu, the very next time,
you take a razor in hand.—

[1] This much abused portrait of Derwent Coleridge was drawn by a some-
what distinguished second-rate Artist—Ball of Plymouth where a *good*
altar-piece of his is placed in St. Andrew's Chapel. The drawing in question
may be considered as a very fair likeness (a copy of it is much valued by a
member of D. C's wife's family); it is open to the charge of sentimentality—
the taste of the Artist giving it a romantic turn but there was hardly any-
thing sufficiently amiss to give rise to the charge of *absurdity* or of *conceit*.
The good Father was prone to see in it what he feared that he might find in
his youthful & very handsome son.

The '*Signor Betsy*' mistaken as the unlucky artist was an Italian Gentle-
man of high accomplishments. The mistake probably arose from the fact
of the picture having been done at his request. He was Signor Giovanni
Bezzi, a Piedmontese—afterwards Secretary for many years to the Arundel
Society—now resident both in England & Italy. [MS. note by Mrs. Derwent
Coleridge.]

[2] *Poems*, i. 209.

[3] Robinson in 1812 says: 'Coleridge . . . gave an explanation of "All my Eye
and Betty Martin". This is a corruption of a ridicule by the Protestants at the
time of the Reformation of the Catholic address on the feast of St. Martin.
*Mihi beate Martine. Se non vero è ben trovato.' Robinson on Books and Their
Writers*, i. 114. For Joe Miller's explanation of the phrase, see E. C. Brewer,
Dictionary of Phrase and Fable, 1901, p. 33. See also *Biog. Lit.*, i. 101:

> All my I! all my I!
> He's a heretic dog who but adds Betty Martin!

But to turn to serious matters, his present plans and intentions are a great relief to my mind: and if he will but persevere for the next 12 months in learning *what* other men know and believe before he takes in hand the business of deciding on the value of the knowlege and the rationality of the Belief—in collecting and connecting for himself the *Materials* for judgement—all, I trust, will end well and happily. He professes—and to the extent of his own consciousness most sincerely, I doubt not—to be convinced, that the first great Premise, in which all his legitimate conclusions will lie as an Oak in an Acorn, must be a *Postulate*—and the Concession a Choice, an Act of moral Election. Either 1. I determine that Nature is *all*—and I reject, as a phantom, whatever is presumed to be more or other than a Link of the Chain. Why? I *see* no exception—and I can *conceive* none—or—2. I determine, that I am a self-determining Agent to the extent, that my Conscience makes me a responsible one—Therefore, I am not altogether a Link determined wholly by the Chain, with which I cohere: and I instance the reality of my Will in and by the free act of determining to believe the contrary. Why?—Because it is a sufficient proof of it's truth for an honest man, that whatever is most abhorrent from human nature would be the legitimate consequence of it's falsehood. But that the Moral Interest has no voice or vote in the decision of this question, is but another assumption of the same stuff with that of an all-including headless and tail-less Nature, and to be payed in kind by a 'Mentiris in corde tuo, Bestia bipes!'—I see no reason to fear a *relapse*; but whether Derwent will press forward to the Goal, and have that *within* which will render him in tone and manners, as well as life and doctrine, an *exemplary* Clergyman, will, I suspect, depend (humanly speaking) on circumstances—perhaps, on afflictions. He has a very fertile but somewhat shallow Surface-soil—below, I hope & I believe, there is rock and springs of pure water; but between, and as the *immediate* Sub-soil, there is a stratum of blue Clay, abundant in wild waters, strongly impregnated with earthy irony vanities and self-regards, and an unfit menstruum for the preparation of *nutritious* substances.—Blessed for him will be the Affliction that shall bore through this barren *Leck* which diseases every root that shoots deeper than the upper Mould!—He has many good points in his character—ex. gr. he is kindly natured, open, unsuspecting, and you never hear from him—any more than from Hartley—an unkind word, or aught that borders on detraction—and if I could keep the Press, and Critical Essays out of his head, I trust, he will be a comfort to me on the whole.

S. T. C.—

The remark on *Favere linguae* is Leighton's, tho' not the inference
—I dare say, you are right; tho' for a *moral*, Leighton's may pass.
But the whole §§ph. might be omitted without loss—it is but a
witticism.[1]

Mrs Gillman has found a Copy of the Remorse which I had given
her: and as there are two in the House besides, she desires me to
beg your acceptance of it.[2] She likewise sends a Transcript of the
WANDERINGS OF CAIN: it was a mortification to her that it was not
in her own hand-writing—but her wrist was so weak and painful,
that she feared on the score of legibility—

With regard to Henry Gillman I must defer what I meant to
say to my next. His Father looks forward to milder & warmer
weather for an amendment, & is about as much perplexed what to
prescribe as all other medical men in the obscure diseases of Boys
before puberty—obscure in the causes, I mean. There is defect of
vital vigor; but whether constitutional, et in Ente toto, or from
disorder of any particular organ, who shall decide? There are no
external marks of mesenteric affection.—At present, palliatives only

[1] Coleridge refers to the concluding paragraph of Aphorism XXXIII of the
Moral and Religious Aphorisms, *Aids to Reflection*, 1825, p. 108:

It is characteristic of the Roman Dignity and Sobriety, that, in the Latin,
to favour the tongue (favere linguae) means, *to be silent*. We say, Hold your
tongue! as if it were an injunction, that could not be carried into effect but
by manual force, or the pincers of the Forefinger and Thumb! And verily—
I blush to say it—it is not Women and Frenchmen only that would rather
have their tongues bitten than bitted, and feel their souls in a strait-waistcoat,
when they are obliged to remain silent.

[2] Coleridge wrote the following note in the verso of the title-page of the
copy of *Remorse* sent to Edward Coleridge:

It is scarcely worth noticing; but as an instance of damning with faint
praise, one might refer to the criticism on this play in the Quarterly Review
[Apr. 1814]—the only work of mine which the Quarterly ever condescended
to notice. As a notable *improbability* gross even to absurdity the Reviewer
gives the surprize of Valdez's Castle by a party of Morescoes!—Within the
space of the 18 months preceding the publication of this criticism no less
than five perfectly parallel incidents had taken place in Ireland.—But
what should render it improbable, or why the Reviewer conceived it to be
such, I cannot even conjecture—.

The concluding Paragraph of this Review, far more injurious to me than
all the Malignities of the Edingburgh, affords an instance of insolent intrusion
into the sacredness of private Life, surpassed only by the detestable attack
on my dear friend, Charles Lamb, perpetrated by the same Aristarchus, Mr
J. Gifford.

                                                S. T. Coleridge.

N.B. The great and serious defect in this Play is the representation of a
solemn Shew of Magic with not a single Believer in it's reality among the
supposed Spectators. Each in a different way indeed but yet all alike know
or presume it to be a Trick, Alvar, Valdez, Ordonio and Teresa.

can be suggested—And his Father would have him take three of
the Pills, he has with him, regularly just before his Dinner, and if
still his Costiveness continue, then to take about the same time
and in addition to the Pills, two or three tea-spoonfuls of the
Compound Tincture of Aloes, known by the name of Baume de
vie, Miss Bramble's favorite Medicine in Humphry Clinker.—
The Tincture may be taken in a little water.

I believe, one Subject only remains unnoticed—and this is
Sidney Walker's Poems.[1] I have read them once; and with great
pleasure—I should speak highly of them. But I must read them
over again, and each more than once, in a somewhat quieter mood
than the necessity of writing at large to a distressed and agitated
Friend permits at present, before I can do what you wish. I have
therefore retained the poems, as I confidently calculate on writing
to you in less than 10 days, so that a little parcel by the Coach
will be less expensive than the Postage—and I will then together
with the Poems give you my full and frank opinion. A Poet is one
thing: the Poets of the Age, we live in, are or may be another
thing—on the one our judgement must be positive, on the other
relative & comparative—Now this much I can venture to say, after
one perusal—that in the *latter* point of view, my opinions are favor-
able.

Again and again, my dear Edward! may the divine Grace &
Protection be vouchsafed & continued to you, temporally and
spiritually, is the heart-felt wish and the expressed nightly Prayer
of your affectionate

Friend & Uncle

S. T. Coleridge

If you possess the 2nd Lay-sermon, favor me by reperusing the
passage from p. 95 to the end of p. 104—and p. xi of the INTRO-
DUCTION.

1522. *To Mrs. Charles Aders*

MS. Yale University Lib. Hitherto unpublished.

8 March 1826.

My dear Mrs Aders

To say, I think of you, is idle. I can do nothing else—sitting,
lying, walking, and often, every day often on my knees. I am not a
superstitious man; but yet I have no ambition to over-fly my
Nature. And if I believe in a God, to whom I can with the consent
of my reason say, Our FATHER! I do not see, how without grievous

---

[1] William Sidney Walker (1795–1846), poet and Shakespearean critic.

inconsistency I should hesitate to pour forth the anguish of my
Wishes before him, whenever they are such as my Conscience dare
sanction.—And O, assure dear Mr Aders from me, that Religion &
Philosophy are a Pair wedded in Heaven—and that their offspring
are Love, Comfort, Strength, and Tranquillity. O that the time may
soon arrive when you & he may steer your Vessel up some safe Bay,
and thence up a Majestic Stream far inland—and it would make
me wish to live, if I might live to know it.

[Mrs G. has *sent* a Bottle of Brandy—lest Mr Aders should be
out before you can order—][1]

I am *pretty* well—and not the worse for my walk to Grosvenor
Square—I had got very near the Turn down Road to your House
when it came on raining—so seeing a Two penny Post Office I went
into the Shop, & had just time to scrawl the line to you when the
Highgate Coach passed & I *mounted*—

Again & again, my dear Friends both! may God give you a happy
issue out of all Trials—

S. T. Coleridge

1523. *To Edward Coleridge*

Address: Revd E. Coleridge | College | Eton
MS. Pierpont Morgan Library. Hitherto unpublished.
Postmark: Highgate, 8 March 1826.

[8 March 1826]

My dear Edward

I now sit down to fulfil my two promises—first, to share with
you the scanty product of my study and lucubration respecting
the Book of Daniel: and secondly, to give you my best judgement
on the poems of Sidney Walker, which I herewith return to you,
both in themselves and as indications of the Writer's poetic Call.—
The first will, I think, more conveniently occupy a scrip of paper
by itself under the title of 'Tinder-stars', or Parson, Clark and
Congregation of the (not virgin tablet secundum Aristotelem, or
blank Sheet secundum Lockium; but) bescribbled folio of my Brain,
in the attempt to throw light on the ἀναμνημονεύματα καὶ ὀπτασίας
τοῦ Δανιῆλος—which will have this advantage, that at any moment
you choose, you may literalize my Metaphor, and amuse yourself
with their successive Exits. But to speak seriously. The time is
passed, when a Clergyman, who does or may occupy a distin-

[1] Sentence in brackets inked out in MS.
[2] Miss Brinkley, who prints three sentences from this letter, erroneously
gives the addressee as Edward Irving. See *Coleridge on the Seventeenth Century*,
1955, p. 554 and note.

guished station in society, may build up his own faith in ignorance
of other men's doubts—at all events, on a subject like this, viz.
where the Book is, on the one hand, the especial mark, the very
target, at which the more learned Sceptics shoot their arrows, and
on the other, the favorite Shield and Buckler, which a large and
zealous party of Believers hold before the most momentous truths
of Revealed Religion.—Both the opposite Parties likewise being
composed of very unlike Materials—the former of Infidels by
wholesale and (n.b. *these* only I meant when I used the word *learned*)
Sceptics respecting this one Book while they hold the authenticity
of all the other Scriptures as extra litem: the latter of learned, and
judicious Divines, and of dreaming ignorant Fortune-tellers, begot
by Nostradamus on Mother Goose, and who profanely use their
Bible in the pagan game of Sortes Virgilianae.—Yes!—it is almost
necessary to know the state of the question: and the strong points
on both sides—tho' thank God! it is by no means necessary for
you, or for me, to enter further into the dispute, than we find
profitable to ourselves. The arguments in favor of the *Authen-
ticity* of the Book may sufficiently preponderate to render that
acquiescence in the decision of the Church, which would be one's
duty, had the scales been but even, an act of one's own judgement,
and to raise assent into Consent. And yet our spirits may hold a
more intimate communion with other parts of the Sacred Volume.
Other proofs, evidences and displays of the truth and excellence
of our Religion may be better suited to, may be more readily
assimilated by, our minds; and we may justifiably leave this or that
department to those whose more vivid impressions or greater pre-
paration for the work, shall call or invite them thereto. Particular
Circumstances imposed on me the duty of investigating the grounds
of the received opinions concerning the interpretation as well as
authenticity of Daniel and the Apocalypse—but I can truly say,
that I am glad, the task is finished.—Somehow or other, I seemed
dried up; my thoughts & feelings were infected by the very doubts,
I was removing—or as if you should look at a Chain thro' a
Herschel's Magnifier, that made less than a single link fill the whole
field of vision—and turned every speck of rust or casual Air-blacks
into startling deformities. I could not help contrasting my state
of feeling with that which accompanied my Collation of St Paul's
Epistles with the Gospel of St John. I remember a strange fan-
tastic legend somewhere in Josephus (but in Mr Gillman's vil-
lainous English Josephus I cannot find it) of a certain Root of
wondrous efficacy in strengthening the Brain & purging the eye-
sight; but which no Man can pull up without imminent hazard,
alienation of mind & so forth—But that if it be fastened by a string

to a Dog, and the Dog be made to draw it up into light, then it may
with proper precaution, be used &c. At the time, I read it, I thought
of the root, Haemony, in Milton's Comus—which that it should
have been left to *me* to discover the meaning of, viz. that it is an
allegory of the Gospel Dispensation or Redemption by Christ as
represented in the Eucharist—αἷμα οἶνος[1]—surprizes me to this
hour[2]—& in like manner I conjectured, I remember, that this
root of Josephus's meant Philosophy, and the Dog, the Pagan
Greeks—or the σοφοὶ τῶν ἐθνῶν, the wise men of the Gentiles,
generally. Something like this I am inclined to say of inquiries
περὶ αὐθεντείας, ἢ περὶ ἀρχῶν τῶν γραφῶν τῶν κανονικῶν.—As
Painters have a green cloth or turn to a green field when their eyes
have been tried by dazzling colors or by obscure & minute objects—
so in the course of my studies in sacred Bibliology I found it, of
daily necessity, to stop and divert the whole attention of my
Spirit to the Everlasting Gospels, τῇ ἀληθείᾳ πανοψίᾳ, to the green
pastures whither the Flock follows the Shepherd and where the
Yearling Lambs can feed in safety—and if there be any one occa-
sion in the life of a learned Christian on which more than any other
he ought to follow the Apostolic Advice, '*Pray* always', this is it.

Sidney Walker has been here—. Rather unluckily, he came on
the day & hour when I had made an appointment with Mr Irving,
to go thro' the Apocalypse with him, chapter by chapter—if so I
might withdraw him from what I cannot regard as other than a
Delusion, of a very serious nature, were it only for it's consequences
on his character, and therewith on his Utility. The great source
of Error in all, or only not all, the Commentators & Expositors is,
that instead of seeking for the particular truth, for that portion of
the Christian Belief, which formed the IDEA of the Work, and to
which it was the writer's object to give a *prominence* not elsewhere
given, to make it fill a space in the mind of the Believer propor-
tional to it's importance, they took up the Apocalypse in the ex-
pectation of finding new *matter*—& a great deal more & other,
than was to be found in the preceding Books of the New Testament—
whereas the fact is, that there is much less. Hence & hence alone
the obscurity of the sublime Drama, combining in itself the
characters of the Greek Tragedy (the *Eschylian* for instance) and
of a magnificent *Poly*mime. The obscurity is wholly . . .[3] At all
events, there ought to be none for a man who has made himse[lf
master] of the preparatory notices. I can truly say, that there are

[1] These two Greek words underlined once in MS.

[2] For similar comments see Coleridge's letter to Sotheby of 10 Sept. 1802,
and *The Statesman's Manual*, 1816, Appendix C, p. xxvi.

[3] MS. torn.

not a[bove] 4 or 5 *words* in the 22 Chapters, the meaning and inten-
tion of which are dark or doubtful to me—and when I reflect,
how large a portion of the work was high treason, jeoparding
even the Possessors of the Book, the perspicuity is not the least
of the many excellences of this truly wonderful Composition.—
But I have digressed from Sidney Walker—I returned his Mss to
him—& told him, as with sincerity I could, that it depended on
himself and the judicious choice of a Subject, to place himself in
the first class of the Poets of his own Age & standing—& that
Wordsworth was my only reason for adding this last qualifying
clause—But I advised him to expend as much thought as possible
in the selection of his Subject, and the formation of the Plan—&
that there appeared to me three sources, which had not yet been
opened by a competent Man—& pressed him to call on me on his
return from Cambridge—.

I thank you again & again for your Letter. Your Letters have
indeed all been refreshments to me—& the happiness, it enabled
me to communicate to Mr & Mrs Gillman, was a cordial to my own
Spirits—When do you come?—Be so good as to write all particulars,
as to the day when Henry comes—& where he is to be met—and
what day, or days rather, we may hope to see you—in order that
I may set about securing Blanco White, Charles Lamb—& on one
of the days, I hope, I shall *try*,—J. H. Frere—Your Daniel &c
shall be ready for you. Mrs G. is so anxious to have these questions
answered that I must run off to the Post—. I have seen Henry
Coleridge—& *urged* him not to add ANY Advertisement to the 2nd
Ed. much less not what he intended.[1] It would be folly—

Again God bless you & all whom you love—
S. T. Coleridge

1524. *To Lady Beaumont*

MS. Pierpont Morgan Lib. Pub. with omis. Memorials of Coleorton, ii. 246.

Dear Madam   Saturday 18 April [March] 1826[2]
Tho' I am at present sadly below even *my* Par of Health or rather
Unhealth, and am the more depressed thereby from the conscious-
ness, that in this yearly resurrection of Nature from her winter
sleep, amid young leaves and blossoms and twittering nest-building

[1] A second edition of *Six Months in the West Indies in 1825* was published
anonymously in 1826. No Advertisement was included.

[2] Coleridge may inadvertently have written 'April' for 'March', since both
Saturday the 18th, which he mentions in the date, and Friday the 24th, to
which he refers in his letter, are correct for March rather than April 1826.

Birds, the sun so gladsome, the breezes so with healing on their
wings, all good and lovely things are beneath me, above me, and
every where around me—and all from God—while my incapability
of enjoying or at best languor in receiving them, is directly or
indirectly from myself, from past procrastination, and cowardly
impatience of pain—yet I am so far from *indisposed*, in relation to
your Ladyship's kind invital, that I can truly and with an inward
seriousness in the disguise of Levity assure you, that Prince
Hohenlohe's Advertisement of the Day & Hour on which he pro-
posed to commence his thaumaturgic Operations never evinced
a more rousing power or acted as a stronger 'soliciting Spell'[1] on
his ultra-catholic Patients, than the imagination of a long Evening
past in your society with *both* Sir George Beaumont & Mr J. H.
Frere exerts on *my* Will & Wish. For in the very heart of simple
Sincerity I can affirm, that when I think of Sir George, the only
person that (almost mechanically) becomes associated with his
Idea, is Mr J. H. Frere—and vice versâ, when my mind dwells on
Mr Frere (and o! how many many reasons I have to think of him
with Esteem, Admiration, and grateful Love!) I naturally recur
to Cole-orton & Grosvenor Square—In fact, it comes so natural to
me, and is so habitual, that whenever I have been talking of the
one, my House- & Hearth-mates regularly expect the name of the
other.—They are not my own words, or of my suggestion, but
Mrs Gillman's—that they (Sir G. & Mr F.) seem intended to shew
us, what and how much is comprized in the phrase—a perfect
Gentleman—but (let me add this necessary comment) as Edmund
Spenser sang and Sidney realized the Idea.—

Nothing short of moral or physical impracticability will prevent
me from availing myself of your Ladyship's invitation, for Friday
the 24th.

Actual feebleness has kept me still a Debtor to the Clergyman at
Cole orton; but I intend to answer him, and trust that I shall
answer him by Monday's Post. In Jeremy Taylor's Holy Living
I have met a passage completely co-inciding with & so far sanc-
tioning the view of Infant Baptism in the Aids to Reflection[2]—
viz. that the assertion of regeneration in the Baptismal Service is
symbolical & prospective, and instructs the Members of the Church
to *feel* and *act* toward the Babe by anticipation of a lively & assured
Hope AS IF it were already a Christian by individual Faith &
Election—

---

[1] *The Destiny of Nations*, line 11, *Poems*, i. 132.
[2] See *Aids to Reflection*, 1825, pp. 330–3 and 354–76. In the fifth edition of
the *Aids*, 2 vols., 1843, i. 301–3, H. N. Coleridge included a passage on baptism
from one of Coleridge's notebooks. See also *Literary Remains*, iii. 291 n.

My dear old Friend, Charles Lamb, and I differ widely (& in point of Taste & Moral Feeling this is a rare Occurrence) in our estimation & liking of George Herbert's Sacred Poems. He greatly prefers Quarles—nay, he *dis*likes Herbert—But if Herbert had only written the two following stanzas—& there are a hundred other that in one mood or other of my mind have impressed me—I should be grateful for the possession of his works—. The stanzas are especially affecting to me, because the folly of over-valuing myself in any reference to my future lot is *not* the sin or danger that besets me—but a tendency to self-contempt, a sense of the utter dis-proportionateness of all, I can call *me*, to the promises of the Gospel—*this* is *my* sorest temptation. The *promises*, I say: not to the *Threats*. For in order to the fulfilment of these, it needs only, that I should be left to myself—to sink into the chaos & lawless productivity of my own still-perishing yet imperishable Nature— Now in this temptation I have received great comfort from the following Dialogue between the Soul & it's Redeemer—(The Church—p. 107.)[1] . . .[2]

1525. *To Lady Beaumont*

Address: Lady Beaumont | South Audley Street | Grosvenor Square
MS. Pierpont Morgan Lib. Pub. Memorials of Coleorton, *ii. 194.*

Saturday, ½ after 11.—[18 March 1826][3]
Dear Madam
My Messinger, a descendant from the old Kings of Tipperary, and skilled in the craft of List-slipper-making and Shoe-mending— more over under my auspices during the last nine years has made such progress in Literature as to be able to pick out the letters of a Direction if the MSS be of large type & it had been read to him previously—this trusty Messinger (for such he had hitherto proved to *me*: tho' I had heard it whispered that he was one of those Mortals whom Nature had made of bibulous Sand instead of the *Red Clay* (for so does the Hebrew '*Adam*' signify) which is the more orthodox material)—this once trusty and often trusted Messinger on his return from Mr George Frere's at Hampstead, (to which place he had been dispatched yesternoon with a letter from

---

[1] Herbert's *Dialogue* appears on p. 107 of *The Temple*, 1633. For Coleridge's annotations in Herbert's *Temple* and Harvey's *Synagogue*, see *Notes and Lectures upon Shakespeare*, ed. Mrs. H. N. Coleridge, 2 vols., 1849, ii. 255–63. See also *Biog. Lit.*, ii. 73–76 ; *The Friend*, 1818, i. 67 n. ; and Letter 1159.

[2] Almost the whole of page 3 of MS. is cut off, removing address on verso.

[3] This letter was written after Letter 1524 was posted.

me inclosing your Ladyship's Card & a note of my own to Mr J. H. Frere) unfortunately meeting some royal 16th Cousin in the disguise of a Hay-maker had drank such copious draughts of Oblivion as to all present Humilities, and of Remembrance of Glories long past, that he presented himself to me in the form of a Penitent pushed on by his Wife, weeping and scolding, at 9 o'clock this morning—the first time of his appearance—. He *had* received a letter from Miss Frere—& he believed, that there was likewise a verbal message for Mrs Gillman—but of neither were either his Brain (Skull, I should say) nor his Pocket continent or cognizant.— But lo!—some ten or fifteen Minutes ago a Girl called to ask whether any one in this house would own a Letter, she had picked up in a ditch in Milfield Lane—which proved to me [be] the Card with the inclosed from Mrs George Frere.

I am now going to seek an Envoy with a less numerous regiment of itinerant Relatives, to dispatch with this note, & with a note & the Card to Mr Frere at Lady Orde's[1]—I shall direct him to go first to Gloucester Place, & thence to Grosvenor Square.—

With my best respects to Sir George, I | am, dear Madam, | Your obliged Friend

S. T. Coleridge.

1526. *To Daniel Stuart*

Address: D. Stuart, Esqre | Harley Street
MS. British Museum. Pub. Letters from the Lake Poets, *289.*

[18 April 1826][2]

My dear Stuart

I will not *say* a word of yourself or your accident:[3] for you know, that this time (and I was getting up when your letter reached me) is the worst of my daily Bad, in point of healthy feeling. I tremble at the very imagination of what has happened.

But now for the business. Mr & Mrs Gillman in passing thro' their minds thus on the sudden all the lodgings, they can at present think for [of ?], are not so satisfied as to be able to fix on one without an actual going round which he will do without delay—But a comfortable Bed-room, in which a Chair-bed for a Nurse or Servant to sleep in may be put, is ready *immediately* for Miss Stuart at our

---

[1] Lady Orde was J. H. Frere's sister.

[2] This letter, which is endorsed '1826 April', was written in response to Stuart's 'first note this morning', Tuesday, 18 Apr. 1826. See next letter.

[3] Stuart had been thrown from his carriage and run over by a passing vehicle. Though no bones were broken, he was confined to his bed for several weeks.

house[1]—& if Mr Gillman should not find something in the Neigh-borhood that he can pledge himself for, as likely to be comfortable, (and of this Mrs Gillman is very doubtful) I can venture to assure Mrs Stuart, that on such an occasion we shall *make* the accomodation for her *here*, which out of our house we cannot find.

My dear Stuart! You cannot know to the fullness and extent with which a ten years' day and night Domestication has enabled me to know, the *disinterested* anxiety of Mr and Mrs Gillman to exert themselves in all instances in which an old & kind friend of mine shall be concerned—or indeed the comparative Worth of these two *rare* Persons—. Mrs Stuart might attend her daughter with a more loving eye (for a mother's Love is above all) but not with a tenderer or more careful one than Mrs Gillman will—and all I *entreat* of you, my dear Stuart! is, that you interpret this, as it truly is—a mark of regard & respect—

I am so agitated by the thought of your accident that what with this and what with the time of the day I scarcely know what I have written—but the Substance is this—

A bed room with convenience for a Servant for Miss Stuart is at your service immediately—for a lodging such as you mention Mr Gillman will forthwith look out—but if it cannot be found, they do not doubt, that they shall be able to contrive so as to re-ceive Mrs Stuart likewise—and that we all hope, that they will come up *immediately* without waiting for the very uncertain result of Mr G's enquiries. Mrs Gillman is at this moment arranging the room for Miss Stuart—

God bless you | &

S. T. Coleridge.

1527. *To Daniel Stuart*

Address: D. Stuart, Esqre. | Harley St
MS. British Museum. Pub. Letters from the Lake Poets, *292.*

Tuesday 19 [18] April 1826

Dear Stuart

It is a great satisfaction to my mind, that you have so decided. All will be ready and in expectance for Mrs & Miss Stuart. We have so handy, gentle, and *feminine* a Creature in Dina, a former servant and still especial favorite of Mrs Gillman's, who will be with us during the day, while Miss Stuart remains, and such a staid attentive young woman in the present Needle-maid (for Mrs

---

[1] Miss Stuart, 'just recovering from a bilious fever, was sent up at this time to Highgate for change of air'. *Letters from the Lake Poets*, 291 n.

G. does not like to hear of Lady's Maid—tho' in fact she is the
especial attendant on her person) and without being at all *out* of her
proper rank she is really both in manners & morals a *superior* sort
of Girl *in* it—that I really think, and so does Mrs Gillman, that
Mrs Stuart will find herself more comfortable without bringing a
Servant. At all events, be so good as to assure her, that Mrs Gillman
will not in the least degree be inconvenienced by it—and that if
Mrs Stuart should not wish it on her own account or Miss Stuart's
from any *accustomedness* to her own Maid or other ground of pre-
ference, there will be no *other* occasion for one—. With regard to
all the rest, you may rely on it's complete correspondence to your
wishes, which I believe myself pretty well able to understand &
measure. Perfect neatness, comfort, and respectability are aimed
at, habitually in this family—& I venture to add, successfully—
in bed & board, house and home—and more than these you would
consider as rather detracting from Ease & Quiet, than as adding
to happiness or even to pleasure.—You will be received as *friends*—
and I *intreat you*, let the Balance of Obligation be struck between
you and me exclusively—if such a word or thought is to intervene
at all—& you know, I have a pretty long account in your favor.—

Tho' I believe myself from my own studies and pursuits better
qualified to appreciate the medical talents & reliability of any man,
of whom & of whose practice I have had any long experience, than
most unprofessional men—and tho' it is my maxim, that presuming
the average quantity of science & practice, the superiority of one
medical Man over another is determined by the union of general
good sense with a sort of medical *tact*, or good common sense shewn
in presence & readiness of mind at the individual bed side—yet I
should not in the present instance express my high opinion of my
friend, Gillman, as a general Practitioner, especially in the wise
treatment of young people, did I not know the high estimation, in
which he stands with the first and ablest men of his profession in
London—as Abernethy, Gooch, Green, Stanley, &c. And I say it
now, only because it may, perhaps, be some small comfort &
satisfaction to Mrs Stuart.—

Dear Stuart! if your first note this morning greatly affected me,
by your second I have been deeply impressed.—Within the last
two years and more particularly within the last, my mind without
sustaining any revolution in faith or principles has yet undergone
a *change*; I trust, a progression—and I am more practically per-
suaded, that toward the close of our Lives, if we have been at any
time sincere in cultivating the Good within us, events & circum-
stances are more & more working towards the maturing of that
Good, even when they are hardest to bear for the moment. I have

not the slightest cause for even apprehending any tendency in my feelings to a servile & selfish religion of fear—or for applying to myself Pope's remark

That Beads & Prayer-books are the Toys of Age.[1]

[On the] contrary, on all religious subjects I think & reason with a more cheerful sense of *freedom*—because I am secure of my faith in the main points—a personal God, a surviving principle of Life, & that I need & that I have a Redeemer—But in one point I have attained to a conviction which till of late I never had in any available form or degree—namely, the confidence in the efficacy of Prayer. I know by experience, that it is Light, Strength, and Comfort.—

May God bless you & your's! I shall trust, that you will be able to pay us a visit by the time you mention—And if in the meantime you should wish to see me, a single Line will bring me to your House—

For I am with no every day feeling your | obliged & affectionate Friend,

S. T. Coleridge

1528. *To Mrs. Daniel Stuart*

Address: Mrs Stuart
MS. British Museum. Pub. Letters from the Lake Poets, *296*.

4 May 1826—
Grove, Highgate—

My dear Madam

Two jars of Black Currant (alias, Corinth) Jelly, tho' charged by the censorious with a tendency to create intestine jars, and to produce a spurious fruit, differing from Grapes by the substitution of i for a, are nevertheless in my deliberate judgement and taste excellent Articles, and in and for themselves well worth thanks—yea, thanks of the inward Man. But indeed, and indeed, truth & sincerity compel me to avow, that they are but poor compensations for the loss of the Donor's Society—and a very imperfect atone-ment for the Absenteeism of innocent Mirth, frank and genial Manners, and cheerful Good Sense. But

To know, t' esteem, to like—and then to part
Is an old tale with every genial heart[2]—

and so I rest in hope, and 'I' here expresses the whole Household—especially Mrs Gillman and little Susan—that we shall meet again,

---

[1] *An Essay on Man*, ii. 280.
[2] *To Two Sisters*, lines 1–2, *Poems*, i. 410.

without our being obliged to such an affrightful accident as in this
instance.—

Remember me most kindly to Mr Stuart—& beg him from me to
remember that too little exertion is far safer than even a little
too much—& believe me, with best wishes for all that [are] dear
to you, and kind regards to Mary,

My dear Madam, | Your & his | obliged Friend
S. T. Coleridge

1529. *To Gioacchino de' Prati*

Address: Dr De Prati | 31 | Oxenden Street | Haymarket
MS. New York Public Lib. Pub. E. L. G. ii. 373.
Postmark: Highgate, 9 May 1826.

Grove, Highgate
Tuesday Morning, 8 [9] May 1826

My dear Sir

Neither my long and spirit-quenching Illness and Languor; nor
the despondence and procrastination induced by the accumula-
tion of engagements unperformed and of work called for by my
own needs yet called in vain; nor the yet sadder and more agitat-
ing trials of my strength by the deplorable state of the Times
brought home to me by the distresses of many and the ruin of
some of my dearest connections; can reconcile my conscience to
the long silence & neglect with which I have afflicted you. I had,
however, till yesterevening believed in some words of Mr Gillman's
which I had misunderstood, that he had written to you—to assure
you, that you had wrongly interpreted a letter of mine which was
never intended to express my unfitness for the enjoyment of my
friends' society on Thursday Evenings beyond the Thursday
Sennight, from the date of my letter—. I have often wondered at
not seeing you—& have 50 times intended to write to you—but
either illness or the bewilderment of having so many things to do,
that I left all undone, or interruption from visitors, have prevented
me. In some *small* part, likewise, my perplexity about your Essay
acted as a Drag on my Feelings—my vexation, namely, that you
should have chosen a subject which had been so recently and in
different forms, Magazines, Reviews, and one separate work either
published or announced for publication, forestalled with the
Public—and I had well nigh said, hackneyed. And this was the
more unfortunate, that a Life of Schiller had already appeared in
Blackwood's Magazine,[1] the only Publisher, that could answer

---

[1] Coleridge probably refers to the *London Magazine*, where 'Schiller's Life
and Writings' by Thomas Carlyle, appeared in 1823–4.

your purposes, over whom *I* possess the least influence. Besides, as I have before told you, it is not any single essay, which would weigh with the Editor so as to induce any terms of decent remuneration—unless it possessed some more than common attraction from Novelty or Popularity of Style or Subject; but a succession of Articles, that might form a regular dish at the Monthly Ordinary—And on this account it was, that I so strenuously recommended a series of critical & biographical Sketches of the most remarkable revolutionary minds, in the manner of Meiners's Work— and mentioned in particular Giordano Bruno, and Cornelius Agrippa, as advisable subjects to begin with.—But I hope, that if the weather permits, you will recommence your Thursday Visits on Thursday Sen'night. I mention Thursday Sennight; because the day after tomorrow a large party of Mr Gillman's Friends are expected, and the House will be in a bustle, and I shall not be able to have any conversation with you. But on the Thursday following I shall have much to say to you, particularly as to your *composition* in English. Half a dozen pages fresh from your hand (if you did feel yourself equal or disposed to a biography of Bruno; yet a spirited Sketch of Vico's Life and great Work, your copy of which I have, would be more attractive to the Learned Public, and easy and *readier* to yourself)—half a dozen pages fresh from your hand, I say, would enable me not only to form a better judgement respecting the probability of your success as an English Writer, but to point out to you mistakes and give you some general Mementos, that might prevent a week's work in the correction of your after writings.

But there is one circumstance, which must be considered in order not to condemn me as lacking in disposition to serve a literary friend, beyond my actual demerits—and this is my own almost utter friendlessness among the influencive and accredited Guides of the public taste, the Dispensers of Passports to writers' Books. I have not had interest enough to procure my 'Aids to Reflection' even a *mention* in any one of our numerous Reviews, Magazines, or Literary Gazettes—but on the other hand, numerous Detractors who have been successfully industrious in exciting a prejudice in the minds of the London Publishers against any work from my pen, as obscure, brain-wrenching and unsaleable. Still there is no way of serving you, that I can attempt with any tolerable probability of success, which would not be tried for by, my dear Sir,

Your sincere Friend & Sympathizer

S. T. Coleridge

1530. *To Richard Cattermole*

Transcript Coleridge family. Hitherto unpublished.

Thursday Morning
25 May 1826.

My dear Sir

About five minutes after you left me Mrs Gillman meeting me asked—'What! is Mr Cattermole gone?' *Yes.* 'You asked him to dine with us of course?' *No, I never thought of it, I am ashamed to say.* 'And it is Thursday too: and there will be two or three persons here that he would like to see.' *And I never thought of its being Thursday either, but perhaps I can overtake him.* And off I ran, or rather shuffled; but alas! my speed is defunct, and I have left its Ghost to skip with the Echoes and vault from rock to rock on our Cumbrian Mountains: and have Sinbad's Old Man pick-a-back across my shoulders instead, with the Drag, Obesity, at my hind wheels, and I returned not a little vexed and mortified at myself. In sober truth, I turned away with angry shame from the ugly vizard of Inhospitableness, that my Forgetfulness must have worn to you—not to say, Ingratitude—you having come all the way from town on my business,[1] and at near 4 o'clock to return to Brixton, and without having taken any refreshment even!

All this transmuted regret into mortification, that I am (and for the last fortnight have been) pre-engaged to dine at Mr Chance's, a very valuable friend of Mr and Mrs Gillman's (to whom under Heaven I owe my Life and more than words can express!) on Friday. Anxious, however, to answer your very kind, undeservedly kind, letter in the affirmative, as soon as I had read it, I called on Mr Chance, to try if he could let me off, for which I have an additional excuse in Mr Southey's arrival in town. He frankly told me, that it would depend on an answer he expected to an invitation to a Family who reside nine miles from Highgate who had repeatedly expressed a wish to meet me, and whom he had invited expressly for this purpose. They had accepted the invitation conditionally, viz. if some country visitors should have left them,

[1] The following receipt has been preserved in the archives of the Royal Society of Literature:

May the eighteenth, 1826. I received from the Rev. R. Cattermole on the part of the Royal Society of Literature, the sum of One Hundred Guineas, payed to me as Associate of the R. S. L.

S. T. Coleridge.
Highgate.

[From a transcript kindly made by Mrs. J. M. Patterson, Secretary of the Society.]

time enough to announce that they actually would come. It was not till last night that their answer came and this morning Mr Chance sent word that he could not excuse me.

Now, my dear Sir! I *know* of no other engagement till June 9th—unless I should receive one from Sir George and Lady Beaumont to meet my Brother-in-law, Southey—which if I do, I will let you know—and I shall be highly gratified in being introduced to Mrs Cattermole. Need I tell you how much, how very much I shall prefer spending a long day with *you* in the bosom of your family to a dinner *party*?

I must make haste or I shall miss the Post—but cannot conclude without entreating you not to consider my strange negligence when you last called, as a *specimen*—or, as symptomatic. I am desired and commissioned by Mrs Gillman (of whom the more you see, the more you will esteem and admire her) to assure you in her and Mr Gillman's name, how happy we shall be, when you have the leisure, to see you at all times in our plain family way—and to beg, that should you be inclined to join our weekly conversazione on any or every Thursday Evening, that you will take pot luck with us and come early. On Thursday we dine a little after 4—on all other days, an hour later.

With best respects to Mrs Cattermole, believe me,

My dear Sir, | With respect and every anticipation of | cordial regard, | Your obliged

S. T. Coleridge

1531. *To Mrs. Charles Aders*

Address: Mrs C. Aders | 11. Euston Square
MS. Cornell University Lib. Hitherto unpublished.

Grove, Highgate
3 June 1826.

My dear Friend

I wish, that word, friend, had not been so soiled in it's passage from hollow hearts thro' vulgar mouths to unbelieving ears, in the market of the World—and you are not old enough to be even my *youngest* Sister—Nevertheless, You, as well as Mrs Gillman, must put up with the Affront and allow me to begin again with

My dear Friend and Sister

I have during the last fortnight or more been so haunted by day-thoughts and night-fancies of and concerning *you*, that *if* I had been some 25 or 30 [years] younger; and *if* some months ago I had not been possessed and lorded over in the very same way &

with the same exclusiveness and monopoly of my Thoughts, Solicitudes and Imaginations by Mr Aders's Image; I should verily have been half afraid that I was in love—in which case I do not know what you could do, unless you could persuade Mrs Gillman to be either ill or absent, and thus get rid of the annoyance by shifting it to another Object. To be sure, it would not be acting a friendly part on your side; but really I cannot think of any other person, that would answer your purpose, or draw off the complaint from you!

A few days [ago] Mrs G. was expressing her wonder—I might have said her admiration—that with all the intense Suffering, you had undergone, you looked just the same, and neither pain or anxiety seemed to have any power over that beautiful face of your's. With this remark in my head as I layed it on my pillow I fell asleep, and out of the weeds that spring up in the garden of Morpheus, I wove next morning the accompanying wreath[1]—which I intended to have presented to you with my best Bow, this afternoon when I called with Mr John Hookham Frere—who was delighted, nay (as he himself said) 'absolutely overset' by the *Von Eyk*[2]—and astounded with your Copy.[3] I am sure, *I* was. Indeed, my dear Mrs Aders! I cannot find words to express adequately the feeling of Delight and Exultation, that took possession of me, as I stood gazing on it, and observed the same emotion in Mr Frere, the polished Gentleman, the Scholar, the Man of Genius! and yet the *good* man shining out in him above all!—I felt so proud of you!! You should not make your friends so abominably vain of you, Mrs Aders! It is very wrong in you—and remember, that I tell you so, who am verily verily and indeed indeed your & dear Mr Aders's most faithful and affectionate Friend

S. T. Coleridge

[1] The 'accompanying wreath' was *The Two Founts*, the MS. of which is no longer with the letter. Coleridge later copied the lines and part of the present letter into Mrs. Aders's album. See Letter 1572.

[2] Among the paintings in the Aders collection was 'a fine old copy of the famous *Adoration of the Lamb*, of Hubert and Jan van Eyck'. The original painting was formerly placed on an altar in the church of St. Bavon in Ghent. The various panels had long since been dispersed to the galleries of Brussels and Berlin, but the copy belonging to the Aders showed the altar-piece as a whole. Alexander Gilchrist, *Life of William Blake*, ed. R. Todd, 1945, p. 331; *Encyclopaedia Britannica*, 1910–11, x. 90; and *Robinson on Books and Their Writers*, i. 292.

[3] Mrs. Aders was 'much admired for her clever copies after the old masters', and in 1830 she exhibited at Berlin 'un tableau de la *Vierge*, d'après Van Eyck'. This may have been the 'copy' which delighted Frere. See Ellen C. Clayton, *English Female Artists*, 2 vols., 1876, i. 408, and E. Bénézit, *Dictionnaire . . . des Peintres, Sculpteurs, Dessinateurs et Graveurs*, 1948.

P.S. I hope to bring Mr Frere again, some Morning after Monday. I dare promise myself, that you are prepossessed in his favor, were it only on the score of his Love and Kindness toward me—and eke because he is such an *immense* Favorite with my other Mrs Aders, your Sister in Soul, dear Mrs G.—

1532. *To John Hookham Frere*

Address: The Honorble J. H. Frere | at G. Frere's, Esqre | Hampstead—
MS. New York Public Lib. Pub. with omis. John Hookham Frere, *227*.

Grove, Highgate.
6 June 1826.

My dear Sir

Shall I be presuming on your kindness if I tell you that on Friday my excellent Friend, Mr Green, and Mr Tulk, the late Member for Sudbury (a thoroughly good and amiable man, and in many ways worth knowing) dine with us; these two with Mr and Mrs Gillman and myself constituting the whole party: and if I venture to request the honor—to express the wish at least—of your joining us— should you chance not to be pre-engaged? Of Mr Green I need only say, that to him I look with confidence for the excitement of a philosophical Spirit, and the introduction of Philosophy in it's objective Type, among our Physiologists and Naturalists—the one side of the Isosceles Triangle, the Basis of which is the Dynamic Logic, and the Apex Religion. The Historic *Idea* is the same in Natural History (Physiogony) as in History, commonly so called— but polarized, or presented in opposite & correspondent forms. The purpose of the latter is to exhibit the moral Necessity of the Whole in the freedom of the component parts: the resulting Chain neces- sary, each particular link remaining free. (Our old chroniclers and Annalists satisfy the latter half of the requisition; Hume, Robertson, Gibbon the former half; in Herodotus, and the Hebrew Records, alone both are found united.) In the History of Nature the same elements exist in the reverse order.—The absolute Free- dom, WILL both in the form of Reason ($\Lambda\acute{o}\gamma o\varsigma$; $\upsilon\grave{\iota}\grave{o}\varsigma\ \mu o\nu o\gamma\epsilon\nu\acute{\eta}\varsigma$; $\acute{o}\ \H{\Omega}N$ $\grave{\epsilon}\nu\ \tau\hat{\wp}\ \kappa\acute{o}\lambda\pi\wp\ \tau o\hat{\upsilon}\ \pi\alpha\tau\rho\acute{o}\varsigma$) and in it's own right as the Ground of Reason ($\beta\upsilon\sigma\sigma\grave{o}\varsigma\ \H{\alpha}\beta\upsilon\sigma\sigma o\varsigma$) is the Principle of the Whole in the necessity of the component Parts. And in this spirit my Friend contemplates and is laboring to make others contemplate, the Law of Life both as a Surgeon and as a Professor of Comparative Ana- tomy and Physiology.

Mr Tulk would interest you, were it only that it is something to meet with a Scholar, and a Man of Taste and Talent, who is a

Partizan and Admirer of the Honorable Emanuel Swedenborg;
but of the genuine School, with the Revd J. Clewes,[1] Rector of
St John's, Manchester, who oppose strenuously all sectarian feeling
and remain sincere and affectionate Members of the Established
Church. But the substance of Mr Tulk's character is, that he is
a sensible, well-informed Man, of great sensibility and delicacy of
mind—and worthy of being introduced to you. We dine at ½ past 5
—the ostensible hour being 5.

With best respects to your Brother and Mrs G. Frere

I am, my dear Sir, | Your obliged and affectionately grateful |

Friend

S. T. Coleridge

1533. *To Edward Coleridge*

Transcript Coleridge family. Hitherto unpublished.

Grove, Highgate
13 June 1826

My dear Nephew

It is painful to me that I should from the little intercourse with
those of my blood be able to acquit myself of idly superfluous words
when I say, that of all your letters I felt the last not only as the
most direct but as the most affecting & gratifying proof of your
Friendship & Regard for me. But as I have already said two thirds
of what I have to say respecting the contents of that letter, in an
answer which you would have received more than a week ago, but
for interruptions of sundry kinds, black, white & particoloured, &
which you will I trust receive in a few days, I shall say no more on
it at present.—I write now indeed not in my own name—tho' that
again neither is or ought to be true on any point in which Mr &
Mrs Gillman's feelings or interests are concerned. At Mrs G's request,
however—who, having at Henry's request sent him a Virgil &
Horace & Case of Instruments & inclosing in the parcel a Copy of
my friend Hurwitz's Vindiciae Hebraicae for you with Mr Gillman's
best respects, wishes me to say that Mr Gillman is so far solicitous
about the state of Henry's Teething, this being the time which Mr
Parkinson had mentioned as the period at which it would be
necessary or highly expedient for the boy's future comfort (& if I
mistake not present health) that his teeth should be looked after

---

[1] John Clowes (1743–1831), rector of St. John's Church, Manchester, from
1769. In 1773 he was introduced to the writings of Swedenborg. He became an
ardent Swedenborgian but on the advice of Thomas Hartley retained his in-
cumbency of St. John's. Clowes published translations of several works of
Swedenborg.

& one of them filled up, that if there existed no objection, & if the measure met *your* approbation, he would prefer a request for permission to have Henry at home for two days & if possible from Saturday or Friday evening if possible till Tuesday. Will you be so good as to give me a single line by return of Post—first whether you deem it fit & not inexpedient—2. whether any formal application beyond that of his having (as *per me*) intreated you to communicate his request to Dr Keate—& lastly, supposing he should be allowed to come, where & at what hour we may send for him on his arrival in London?

Mr J. H. Frere has passed a considerable portion of his time with me lately—& the more I see of him, the more reason I find to love & admire him—the polished Gentleman, the exquisite Scholar, the man of Genius—but the Good Man, the CHRISTIAN, shining out among all & beyond all.

May the Almighty bless & make happy you & your's is the matin & evening song of your affectionate Uncle

S. T. Coleridge

1534. *To Edward Coleridge*

Transcript Coleridge family. Hitherto unpublished.

My dear Nephew Monday. [3 July 1826][1]

I cannot permit Derwent to leave me for Eton without taking with him some token, however brief, of my constant remembrance of you. I have been very unwell, & depressed spirits as much a constituent as a consequent of my illness. But likewise I was aware, that you were & could not but be nostril deep in business & strong tho' I trust painless solicitudes. Have you any of my Mem. books— or did you send all back? I do not know which is in the greater litter & confusion—my head or my Room—From one or the other cause I miss the Book I happen to want—hour after hour—to the sad waste of my time. But I trust this will be amended as soon as our Landlord will come to a settlement.

Be assured that I remember you and her, who will, I fervently hope, be your support & comfort, often & most affectionately in my prayers.

If by advice or interest you can help my poor boy in his present object of procuring a title or curacy,[2] I know you will do it for the sake of Your true friend & affectionate Uncle

S. T. Coleridge

[1] This letter was delivered by Derwent Coleridge on his way to Plymouth in July 1826. See next letter.
[2] See note to Letter 1568.

1535. *To Derwent Coleridge*

Address: Derwent Coleridge, Esqre | 5 | Gloucester Place | Plymouth
MS. Victoria University Lib. Pub. E. L. G. ii. 375.
Postmark: Highgate, 15 July 1826.

> Saturday 15 July 1826.—
> Grove Highgate—

My dear Boy

The weather and the recurrence in an aggravated form of a complaint, that in itself is in the last degree irritating and enfeebling, at once disquieting and dispiriting, and which arises from and alternates with a deranged state of the Kidneys, the Bladder, and the bowel ending in the rectum—these have so overcome me that for the last fortnight I have lost the power of even *reading*. But yet paradoxical as it will sound, there has been one other more efficient cause of my not writing to you—namely, the constant thinking about you, and the vexatious recollections connected with the subject of the Curacy.—Of course, I applied to Lady Beaumont—who, I must do her the justice to say, did her best. For the next time, she was in the Bishop of London's company with Mrs Beaumont (the Bishop's Daughter) she mentioned the circumstance, adding how great an interest she felt in procuring you a Title—But the Bishop persevered in silence—and after the Bishop retired, Mrs Beaumont told Lady Beaumont that her Father made a point of never interfering in the disposition of Titles; but that *she* (Mrs Beaumont) would speak to the Bishop's Chaplain when he returned and try to obtain his interest for you— but—(& this was the part, that was Gall & wormwood to me) she wondered, your *Cousins*, especially John, had not been applied to— for that his word would go a great way with the Clergy—& that, tho' every one must have a high opinion of my genius & many did justice to my motives, yet I was not supposed to be a *high* Church Man &c—I have little doubt, indeed none, that your episcopal Cousin has contrived to sigh & look sad or remain intelligibly silent whenever my name was mentioned—in short, has done every thing in his power to injure me—and I must ever contrast the manly indignation, with which Edward Coleridge expressed himself of William's conduct toward me, with that of your Cousin Henry— tho' in his last note he raised a smile on my lip by subscribing himself *dutifully* &c. You know my fixed principle on this subject. After my Children have reached the years of discretion, my advice is at their service if they ask it in earnest & when it can be of any use—but as a Father, I have only my Prayers & my Blessing.—

A second attempt I made for you—Thomas Murray had both

a Curacy to give & Pupils to transfer—and this somewhere near
Totness. As he had appeared much interested in my conversation,
and his family are intimate with the Gillmans, I applied both
thro' Mr Mence to Mr T. Murray himself & thro' Mrs Gillman to
his Father & Mother—and heard that he was conditionally en-
gaged—that a Clergyman was to return an answer & if he did not
take the Cure——in short, a sort of a kind of a promise of which I
could make nothing.—Besides this, I have spoke or got others to
speak to all, I could think of, with whom I had any acquaintance—
& tho' it is much against my feelings, I certainly will write to John,
or see him on the subject—as soon as I have strength & spirits
enough—& in a letter, which will go with this to the Post, I have
pressed it urgently on Edward to do what he can when he can—.
Further I mean in my next letter to Sir George (who is now at
Coleorton) to express my mind & feelings respecting my not being
friendly to the Church (for that was the true meaning of the Speech)
—Be assured, nothing shall be lost from any neglect on my part—
and on your's you have only (but what an *only* is that?) to be pru-
dent in speech. I read (and for the far greater part with great satis-
faction and delight) your lecture on Wordsworth;[1] but I would
have given a finger-joint to have prevented the composition &
not merely the publication of the whole passage on Wordsworth's
later poems—The quotation from the Edingburgh Review[2] was
Verum usque ad limen mendacii ultra verum—It was Truth con-
vulsed and swoln by the poison of Malignity—and even had it been
nothing but the truth, both the citation & your own comment, a te,
mi fili, neque bonum neque decens erat. Charles Lamb justly
observed that if these poems had been discovered among Words-
worth's Papers a century after his death, there are portions that
would have given a glory to the whole.—To have the appearance
of conspiring with the Ed. Review—whose whole literary existence
has been marked with the most assassin-like hate & slander of
every Man of Genius, whose names must be sacred to you by
private affection—this was want of *thought*—If you knew a Wretch
infamous for s[elling] books & prints of unnatural obscenity, you
would not recommend the Shop for good drawing-paper or any
other trifle, tho' it might be the fact.—
    As soon as I am a little better, I will write to you—for the
present, I am unable to do any thing—even to think—I can only
feel—. I had a letter from your Mother this morning, announcing
that Sara will be here about the 26th of this month—.[3] It is one

---

[1] Published in the *Metropolitan Quarterly Magazine*, 1826, 457–79.

[2] See *Edinburgh Review*, vol. xxxvii, Nov. 1822.

[3] Much to her father's disappointment Sara Coleridge was forced to postpone

aggravation of my unwellness that I cannot express what I fain would with regard to the Friends with whom you now are.—I wish, I could afford to have a duplicate taken of a very fine Likeness in Chalk of me by Catharine de Predl (a noble Bavarian Lady by birth, tho' by the ruin of her Father during the Revolution & her own strong inclinations, now an Artist)—and I would send it to Mrs Pridham.[1] Mam'selle de Predl is making or to make a Copy of this (but much enlarged) in Oil colors for Mr Aders: & another for Mr Green.[2] Her painting is more like the best specimens of Andrea del Sarto and Fra Bartholomeo, than I have ever seen— and as to Drawing, I question whether any of our English Artists, unless it be Lawrence, that could approach to the perfect science & firm yet delicate stroke of her pencil. She has taken Mr and Mrs Gillman, Mr & Mrs Mence, Mr and Mrs Holmes—all admirable Likenesses. Mine cost her more trouble than all the rest—& she was the least satisfied with it. But Mr Green, who carefully studied it, & occasioned several alterations, declared his conviction that it was the utmost that could be atchieved in chalk. At all events, it is the best—& greatly preferable to Phillips's in the character &

her visit. She arrived at Highgate on Sunday, 17 Sept. 1826. See Letter 1551.

Sara Hutchinson, on the other hand, used the news of the postponement of Sara Coleridge's journey to London as an excuse for an excess of malicious gossip and thereby reveals something of her personality:

Sara Coleridge set off for Town with Mr Gee about a month ago—but unluckily her mother accompanied her to Kendal & there persuaded her she was not fit for the journey, dosed her with Laudanum to make her sleep at a time when she could not have been expected to sleep if she had had the feeling of a stone—viz upon leaving her friends & home under affliction (for it was not more than a week after the poor Child's burial [Isabel Southey]) and brought her back—leaving poor Gee to go alone—after having waited 17 days for her convenience & procured a Carriage in which she could travel at ease—& have the advantage of staying on the road at Night. Now S[ara] is in despair—Her Father disappointed—Her Lover too (but why does he not fetch her?) and Mama is to accompany her to Derby—So if you want to succor a distressed Damsel you may go thither & escort her up by *slow stages* which is the only mode by which she can travel.—O how I do pity her! & hope that if she gets rid of her Mother that she may turn out something useful before she ceases to be ornamental. I am sorry to tell you (but it is a secret) that she is engaged to one of her Cousins—he who has written the conceited work about West India and who is very delicate in constitution —having had an affection of the spine—without fortune but what he can make by his wits & the Law—Now I am quite tired of gossip—I hope there is no scandal—tho' I know you will call me *cross* with regard to Sara—but I am vexed at her weakness—& I am more *illnatured to you* because you do not like my favorite Edith [Southey] so well. (Sara Hutchinson to Edward Quillinan, 23 Aug. 1826. *The Letters of Sara Hutchinson*, ed. Kathleen Coburn, 1954, pp. 322–3.)

[1] No such drawing has come to light.
[2] See Letter 1566.

expression, and at least equal in point of the Likeness.—God bless you! I share in head & will in all your pleasures—& if my frame contained a pleasurable sensation, that too would have been evoked in your service.

Your affectionate Father,
S. T. Coleridge.

P.S.—Mr & Mrs Gillman's kind Love.

1536. *To Edward Coleridge*

MS. Pierpont Morgan Lib. Pub. E. L. G. ii. 378.

Grove, Highgate
27 July 1826

My dear Edward

Since you last heard from the Grove, I have been ill enough not only to account for my silence but even in my own Conscience to justify it. The excessive Heat was, I doubt not, the principal *exciting* Cause: tho' anxiety and intestine Conflict have been accessories. My Daughter (God permitting) will arrive here on Saturday —and in mourning for her Cousin, Isabel. (When her death was announced to Southey, he paused a few moments and then mildly desired that the whole Household should be called in to his Study— and he then read to them the 15th of Corinth: I.—What more effective Comfort could an afflicted Father give or receive?) You will wonder at my simplicity; but I assure you, that even after I had read the 'Six Months in the W.I.', I had no suspicion of any *serious* attachment on the part of Henry to his Cousin, Sara—and first learnt it vaguely and generally from Mrs Gillman, in consequence of my complaining of his thoughtlessness in not foreseeing, that his in all respects very objectionable phrase—my Sister ere my Wife—might be applied by many persons to Sara[1] —and besides this, the mingling of Romance in a book of facts and of very important ones too, was not pleasant to my feelings. After this, I wrote to Mrs Coleridge, mentioning what I had heard, adding that if it was more than an idle rumour founded on the flights about Eugenia[2] I should, I suppose, learn the particulars

---

[1] See *Six Months in the West Indies in 1825*, p. 117: 'I love a cousin; she is such an exquisite relation, just standing between me and the stranger to my name, drawing upon so many sources of love and tieing them all up with every cord of human affection—almost my sister ere my wife!' Sara and her cousin Henry Nelson Coleridge had been secretly engaged since early in 1823.

[2] Several times in his *Six Months* Henry Nelson Coleridge speaks of Eugenia, ex. gr.: 'Eugenia, with every faculty do I love thee; thine am I, in union or separation, to my life's end. . . . In visions by night, in musings by day, in noise

from Sara herself, when we met—and concluded with the following words. I have no fortune to leave, no *trust* of this kind in the transfer of which I have any interest of duty: and therefore it has ever been my fixed principle in respect of marriage that after my children have reached the years of discretion—as a friend, I was ready to give them my best advice if it were asked while it could be of any service; but as a Father, I had only my Prayers and my Blessing to give.—The answers to this—for both the Mother and the Daughter wrote to me at large—left me nothing to be informed of. What I should have thought, had I been her Confidant at her first knowlege of Henry's intention, it would now be a great deal worse than idle to say[1]—I do not conceive it to be my duty—I

and in silence, in crowds and in the wilderness, I have thought I saw thee. . . .
O could I really see, could I really hear, really hold that white and soft and
faithful hand.' (p. 290.)

[1] Coleridge had misgivings concerning the marriage of first cousins. See,
for example, his inquiry to Stuart in Letter 1538 and his comment in *Table
Talk*, 10 June 1824:

  If the matter were quite open, I should incline to disapprove the marriage
  of first cousins; but the church has decided otherwise on the authority of
  Augustine, and that seems enough upon such a point.

Consider, too, the following autograph note:

  First: the motives ordinarily assigned for the prohibition under the highest
  penalty of marriages between Brothers and Sisters apply with diminished
  force indeed but which Circumstances of no unfrequent occurrence may render
  all but equal, against marriages between First Cousins. . . . All the domestic,
  political and moral advantages, all the honor, beauty and loveliness of
  dividing the relation of Brother and Sister from that of Husband and Wife
  by an impassable chasm; and consequently the evil and unseemliness of
  confounding these two so diverse relations, the universality of the contrary
  practice, and that the Law which enacts it, admits of no exception, no dis-
  pensation, being that which gives it's peculiar sanctity to the brotherly and
  sisterly Affection; all these, I say, plead with an inferior but still with a
  great and prevailing force for preserving the tie of the next nearest Con-
  sanguinity, the Love between Brothers' or Sisters' children single and
  sufficient of itself. How much truth there is in this plea, Henry himself has
  let out, unawares, in the words, 'my Sister ere my Wife'—words which have
  given offence, I find, to three or four persons of our acquaintance, and I own
  shocked *my* feelings even tho' in my simplicity I took the whole for a Romance.
  Surely, the best interests of Society render it expedient, that there should
  be some *Outworks* between the Citadel, that contains the very *Palladium*
  of the Human Race, and the Open Country: that we should not pass at once
  from the Horrible to the wholly Blameless: especially where both Nature &
  the Law of Custom have so evidently pointed out and provided an inter-
  mediate Bulwark by the existence of an intermediate Relationship. Nor
  will it be altogether without weight, what is recorded in ecclesiastical
  History, that when by the influence of St Augustin's Authority the Decision
  of St Ambrose had been annulled, and the cruel Law of Theodosius de in-
  cestuosis etam in secundo gradu'comburendis repealed—still no use was made
  of the permission in any part of the Empire, so fixed and universal was the

thank God, that I do not—for the man and the father are too strong
in my soul, for me not to shrink from the thought of my only
Daughter—& *such* a daughter—condemned to a miserable Heart-
wasting; or not to regard the Alternative as a *lesser evil*. I have
not the heart either to pass such a sentence, or in any way to be
aidant thereto. To no other person (with the one exception of Mrs
G. and that involuntary) have I said, or would I have said, as
much as I now have, *to you*: and I trust, that I am not requiring
any thing incompatible with the friendship between you and your
family, when I earnestly request you to bury it in silence—and
not to breathe even a hint of what I have written. On the other
hand, allow me to assure you, that the not opening out the whole
of my mind and of what would have been my mind arises from no
want of confidence, and no want of the longing wish to have you
to open out my heart to; but solely and altogether from the appre-
hension, that I might place you in a painful and perplexed state
of feeling relatively to those, who have far higher claims on you
and a far deeper Right of interest, than I either have or ought to
have.—And moreover, this is not the time for doleful tales—
Were it in my power, no bird of less happy omen than the Halcyon
or the Wood-dove should cross your path for the next fortnight!
If to think of you many times a day, aye, and in the night too,
if to pray, to hope, and to rejoice in the full belief of your hap-
piness, be proofs of paternal love, I can confidently assert that
You and Miss K. have a Son and Daughter's place in my heart.—

And now I must revert to the subject of your last letter, without
entering into any particulars of the ill-health that has delayed
my answer.

Before the receipt of this strongest proof of your regard, I had
been aware of the fact, that particular trains of thought had estab-
lished a sort of *eddy* in my mind—or I might easily have found
excuses for believing, that the impression on your and your
Brothers' minds had been the result of accidental circumstances.
Mrs Gillman was doubtful, but inclined to your point of view—But
Mr & Mrs Montagu, and Mr Gillman, to whom but without men-

prejudice against and the aversion to the marrying the Child of a Father's or
Mother's Brother or Sister. If the first be *detested*, the next to it ought,
methinks, to be disliked; and the next but one (the marriage of second
Cousins) *tolerated*, but (caeteris paribus) not commended. [British Museum,
Egerton MS. 2800 f. 151.]

On 19 Aug. 1826 Coleridge remarked: 'If first cousins may marry, then I
should confidently decide that a man may marry his Wife's Sister. But as I
do not approve of the former, neither dare I give a positive opinion for the
lawfulness of the latter.' (Marginal note in Luther's *Table Talk*. See T. J. Wise,
Two Lake Poets . . ., 1927, p. 121.)

tioning your name or that I had received any hint of the kind from any one—these counted up the different persons, that had at different times been with me during the last 3 or four months—Merchant, Manufacturer, Physician, Member of Parliament & keen politician, chemist, Clergymen, *poetic* Ladies, Painters, Musical Men, Barristers & Political Economists—to each of whom, in turn, I had talked in his own way, & that they had all expressed their admiration of the *clear* point of view, in which I placed things—Mr Frere & Mr Green in a conversation with Mrs Gillman coincided in one remark—viz. on the entire absence of *effort* and of any painful groping or staggering of mind—'his forehead is like a Child's'.—But all this weighed not with me—tho' it is to a certain extent true, that from several causes the tendency has appeared stronger to you, more habitual & despotic at least, than it actually is—and as to any influence on my *health*, would to Heaven! that it were so, or had been so! But I could soon convince you, that it is my *mind* that alone feeds & supports my crazy *body*—and that the best medicine is that which unconnected with *sensations* of any sort, has most power to make me forget it. The subjects, on which you wish me to correspond with you, would not answer the purpose, you have in view—for the whole system of my Thoughts on Subjects of Poetry &c is so digested in my mind, that it would be a mere business of the passive Memory, or of Transcription from my Notes. Yet for your sake I would gladly do it, but that it would stand in the way of the removal of the true cause & occasion of that eddying of my mind, on the particular subjects mentioned by you—Namely, the ever increasing conviction of their importance and the dread of leaving a task unperformed which I believe to have been made a duty, on the one hand; and the perpetual interruptions, from ill-health, and other people's business and the (truly called) *a*vocations to tasks imposed on me by the want of a competent income and the obligations & vexations consequent thereon, on the other; these have kept the thoughts constantly *on my mind*, and no other cure is possible even were it desirable but that of satisfying my sense of duty by reducing them to a publishable state.—All the *particulars*—& that less than a 12 month, should I be vouchsafed any tolerable health, will set me at freedom for the lighter and more popular muses, you will find in the Copy of a Letter written to my Publisher, Mr Taylor—himself a literary man, whom the Aids to Reflection had restored to Christianity and the doctrines of the Church. (O Edward! I have six or seven letters—the larger half from Clergymen of our church, which would shake your opinion of the *in nubibus* character of my speculations—if the Tree is to be judged of by it's fruits. I suspect, that you are not aware of the extent to which the *Shaking* of men's minds in the educated classes has gone!—and in both Universities.)—But respecting my views and plans, I must refer you to the Copy of the Letter, which you will be so good as to let me have again by Mr Henry Hall—should he be returning to Town.—The other Letter[1] (to you, & in my own hand) you may read at your leisure—two months hence, if it suits you.—Yet should we meet again, it may furnish you with matter for a few questions; & I will take care not to advance a yard without ascertaining whether you are alongside of me, and if you are not *up to me*, I will step back and rejoin you.— Long, long, my dear Edward! may you enjoy the strength of *the Prime*, & find sufficient support in the consciousness of being honorably & usefully active, and in your natural Gladness. But nevertheless the Time will come, when it will be remembered with delight that you had been called on to another well-head of Strength.

I had intended to transcribe some verses for you; but I shall be too late for Mr Henry Hall—and therefore must hurry to the (I trust) superfluous assurance that I am most truly,

my dear Edward | Your affectionate Friend & Uncle
S. T. Coleridge

P.S. Be so good as to give me *two* lines—one concerning the Inn, at which Henry Gillman will be set down on his arrival in town; and the *other*, what you would have him be employed in, during his vacation.—Mr & Mrs G.'s most affectionate thanks & remembrances.—

1537. *To Edward Coleridge*

MS. Pierpont Morgan Lib. Pub. with omis. The Church and State, *223.*

[Endorsed July 27 1826]

My dear Edward

In emptying a Drawer of under-stockings, Rose-leaf Bags, old (but too many of them!) unopened Letters, and Paper-scraps or Brain Fritters, I had my attention directed to a sere and ragged half-sheet by a gust of wind, which had separated it from it's companions and whisked it out of the window into the Garden. Not that I went after it. I have too much respect for the numerous tribe, to which it belonged, to lay any restraint on their movements, or to put the vagrant act in force against them. But it so chanced that some after-breeze had stuck it on a standard Rose-tree: and there I found it, as I was pacing my evening walk alongside the lower Ivy-wall, the bristled Runners from which threaten to entrap

---

[1] Coleridge refers to the next letter.

the top-branch of the Cherry Tree in our Neighbor's Kitchen-Garden. I had been meditating a letter to you—& as I ran my eye over this fly-away Tag-rag and Bob-tail, and bethought me that it was a By-blow of my own, I felt a sort of fatherly remorse & yearning towards it, and exclaimed—If I had a frank for Eaton, this should help to make up the Ounce!—It was far too decrepit to travel per se—besides that the Seal would have looked like a single Pin on a Beggar's Coat of Tatters—and yet one does not like to be stopt in a kind feeling, which my Conscience interpreted as a sort of promise to the said Scrap—& therefore (frank or no frank) I will transcribe it—

A dog's leaf at the top worn off, which contained the syllable, Ve, I conjecture, —rily, quoth Demosius, of Toutoskosmos, Gentleman, to Mystes the Allocosmite,[1] thou seemest to me like an out of doors' Patient of St Luke's, wandering about in the Rain without Cap, Hat, or Bonnet, poring on the Elevation of a Palace—not the House that Jack built, but the House that is to be built for Jack, in the suburbs of the City which his Cousin German, the lynx-eyed* Dr Gruithuisen,[2] has lately discovered in the Moon. But for a foolish kindness for that Phyz of thine, which whilome belonged to an old School-fellow of the same name with thee, I would get thee shipped off under the Alien Act, as a Non Ens, or Pre-existent of the other World to come!—To whom Mystes retorted—Verily, Friend Demos! thou art too fantastic for a genuine Toutos-cosmos man! and it needs only a fit of dyspepsy or a cross in love, to make an Heterocosmite of thee—this same Heteroscosmos being in fact the endless shadow which the Toutoscosmos casts at sunset! But not to alarm or affront thee as if I insinuated that thou wert in any danger of becoming an Allocosmite, I let the whole of thy courteous Address to me pass without comment or object[ion,] save only the two concluding Monosyllables—and the preposition (*Pre*) which anticipates them. The world, in which I exist, is *another* World indeed, but not *to come*.—It is as *present* as (if it be at all) the magnetic Planet, of which, according to the Astronomer HALLEY, the visible Globe that *we* inverminate, is the *Case* or travelling Trunk—a neat little world, where Light still exists *in statu perfuso* as on the third day of the Creation, before it was

---

[1] 'TOUTOS cosmos—*this* world . . . . ALLOCOSMITE—a Denizen of another world.' See *The Church and State*, Glossary, p. 211.

* The Dr tells us that he can see distinctly with his Frauenhofer [Fraunhofer] Telescope of the power 90 what the best living observers can barely see with one of 270. Entdeckung &c p. 33. [Note by S. T. C.]

[2] Franz von Paula Gruithuisen (1774–1852), German astronomer and author of *Entdeckung vieler deutlichen Spuren der Mondbewohner, besonders eines colossalen Kunstgebäudes derselben*, 1824.

polarized into outward and inward (i.e. while Light and Life were one and the same, NEITHER *formally* yet BOTH *eminenter*) and when Herb, Flower and Forest rose as a Vision in proprio Lucido, the ancestor and unseen Yesterday of the Sun & Moon. Now, whether there really is such an elysian *Mundus mundulus* incased in the Macrocosm, or Great World, below the adamantine Vault that supports the Mother waters that support the coating Crust and over-all, the Mundum immundum on which we, and others—less scantily furnished from Nature's *Legg*ery, crawl, delve and nestle (—or shall I say the Licēum, οὖ περιπατοῦμεν οἱ τούτου κόσμου ψιλόσοφοι?) —the said Dr Halley may perhaps by this time have ascertained: and to him and the philosophic Ghosts his compeers I leave it. But that an other World is inshrined in the *Microcosm*, I not only believe but at certain depths of my Being, during the solemner Sabbaths of the Spirit, I have held commune therewith, in the power of that Faith which is 'the substance of the things hoped for', the living Stem that will itself expand into the flower, which it now foreshews. How should it not be so, even on grounds of natural Reason and the Analogy of inferior Life? Is not Nature prophetic up the whole vast Pyramid of organic Being? And in which of her numberless predictions has Nature been convicted of a Lie? Is not every Organ announced by a previous instinct or act? The Larva of the Stag-beetle lies in it's Chrysalis like an infant in the Coffin of an Adult, having left an empty space half the length, it occupies—and this space is the exact length of the Horn that distinguishes the perfect animal, but which, when it con-structed it's temporary Sarcophagus, was not yet in existence. Do not the Eyes, Ears, Lungs of the unborn Babe give notice and furnish proof of a transuterine, visible, audible, atmospheric world? —We have eyes, ears, touch, taste, smell. And have we not an answerable World of Shapes, Colors, Sounds, and sapid and odorous bodies? But likewise—alas for the Man, for whom the one has not the same evidence of Fact as the other!—the Creator has given us spiritual Senses and Sense-organs—Ideas I mean! the Idea of the Good, the Idea of the Beautiful, Ideas of Eternity, Immortality, Freedom, and of that which contemplated relatively to WILL is Holiness, in relation to LIFE is Bliss: and must not these too infer the existence of a World correspondent to them? There is a Light, saith the Hebrew Sage, compared with which the glory of the Sun is but a cloudy Veil: and is it an ignis fatuus given to mock us and lead astray? And from a yet higher authority we know that it is a Light that lighteth every man that cometh into the world: and are there no Objects to reflect it? Or must we seek it's analogon in the Light of the Glow-worm, that simply serves to distinguish one reptile from all the rest, and lighting inch by inch it's mazy path through weeds and grass, leaves all else before, behind, and around it in darkness? No! Another and answerable World there is: and if any man discern it not, let him not, whether sincerely or in contemptuous irony, pretend a defect of faculty as the cause. The Sense, the Light, and the conformed Objects are all there, and for all men, and the difference between man and man in relation thereto results from no difference in their several gifts & powers of *intellect*, but in the WILL. As certainly as the Individual is a Man, so certainly should this other world be present to him: yea, it is his proper Home. But he is an absentee, & *chooses* to live abroad. His freedom and whatever else he possesses which the Dog and the Ape do not possess—yea, the whole revenue of his Humanity is derived from this—but as with the Irish Land-owner in the Theatres, Gaming-houses and Maitresseries of Paris, so with *him*. He is a voluntary ABSENTEE! I repeat it again and again—the Cause is altogether in the WILL, and the defect of intellectual power, and 'the having no turn or taste for Subjects of this sort', are effects and consequences of the alienation of the WILL—i.e. of the Man himself. There may be a defect, but there was not a deficiency, of the intellect. I appeal to facts for the proof. Take the science of Political Economy—No two Professors understand each other— and often have I been present, where the Subject has been discussed in a room full of Merchants & Manufacturers, sensible and well-informed men—and the conversation has ended in a confession, that the matter was beyond their comprehension—and yet the Science professes to give light on Rents, Taxes, Income, Capital, the Principles of Trade, Commerce, Agriculture—on *Wealth* and the ways of acquiring and increasing it—in short, on all that most passionately excites and interests the Toutoscosmos men. But it was avowed, that to arrive at any understanding of these matters requires a mind gigantic in it's comprehension and microscopic in it's accuracy of detail. Now compare with this the effect produced on promiscuous crowds by a Whit[e]field, or a Wesley—or rather compare with it the shaking of every leaf of the vast forest to the first blast of Luther's Trumpet. Was it only of the world *to come*, that Luther and his Compeers preached? Turn to Luther's Table-talk: and see if the larger part be not of that other world which now *is*, and without the Being and the working of which the world *to come* would be either as unintelligible as Abracadabra, or a mere refraction & elongation of the world of Sense—Jack Robinson be-tween two Looking glasses, with a series of Jack Robinsons in secula seculorum.

Well—but what *is* this *now* and yet *other* World?—

The Sneer on that Lip, and the arch Shine of Laughter in those eyes, Friend Demosius, would almost justify me tho' I should answer that question by retorting it in a parody—What—quoth the Owlet peeping out of his Ivy-tod at Noon, with his blue fringed eye-curtains dropt—what is this Light which is together with this Warmth, we feel, and yet is something else?—But I read likewise in that same face, as thou wert beginning to prepare that question, a sort of a misgiving from within, as if thou wert more *positive* than *sure*, that the reply, with which you meant to accomodate me (viz. the Brain of a man that is out of his Senses) is as wise as it is witty. Therefore, tho' I cannot answer your question, I will give you a hint, how you may answer it for yourself.—First, learn the art & acquire the habit of contemplating Things abstractly from their *relations*. I will explain myself by an instance. Suppose a body floating at a certain height in the air, and receiving the light so equally on all sides as not to occasion the eye to conjecture any solid contents & circumference—and now let six or seven persons see it at different distances & from different points of View. For A it will be a Square; for B a Triangle; for C two right-angled Triangles attached to each other; for D two unequal Triangles; for E it will be a Triangle with a Trapezium hung on to it; for F it will be a square with a Cross in it ⊠ ; for G it will be an oblong quadrangle with three Triangles in it ◹ ; and for H three unequal Triangles ◺ —&c &c—Now it is evident that neither of all these is the Figure itself (which in this instance is a four-sided Pyramid) but the contingent *Relations* of the Figure.—Now transfer this from Geometry to the subjects of the real (i.e. not merely formal or abstract) Sciences—to Substances and Bodies, the materia subjecta of the Chemist, Physiologist & Naturalist; and you will gradually (that is, if you choose & sincerely *will* it) acquire the power and the disposition of contemplating your own imaginations, wants, appetites, passions, opinions etc on the same principle—and distinguish that which alone is and abides from the accidental and impermanent Relations arising out of it's co-existence with other things or Beings.—

My second Rule or Maxim requires a prolegomena [*sic*]:

In the several Classes and orders that mark the scale of Organic Nature from the Plant to the highest order of Animals each higher implies a lower in order to it's actual *existence*—and the same position holds good equally of the vital and organic Powers. Thus: without the 1st Power, that of growth, or what Bichat[1] & others

---

[1] M. F. X. Bichat (1771–1802), French anatomist and physiologist, published *Recherches physiologiques sur la vie et sur la mort* in 1800. Coleridge

name the Vegetive Life, or Productivity, the 2nd. power, that of total and loco-Motion (commonly but most infelicitously called, Irritability) could not exist—i.e. *manifest* it's being. Productivity is the necessary Antecedent of Irritability: and in like manner, Irritability of Sensibility. But it is no less true, that in the *idea* of each power, the lower derives it's *intelligibility* from the higher: and the highest must be presumed to inhere latently or potentially in the lowest, or this latter will be wholly unintelligible, inconceivable. You can have no *conception* of it. Thus in Sensibility we see a power that in every instant *goes out* of itself & in the same instant retracts and falls back on itself: which the great Fountains of pure Mathesis, the Pythagorean and Platonic Geometricians illustrated in the production or self-evolution of the Point into the Circle. Imagine the going-forth and the retraction as two successive Acts, the Result would be an infinity of angles, a growth in zig-zag; in order to the imaginability of a circular line the extroitive and the retroitive must co-exist in one and the same act and moment, the curve line being the Product. Now what is *ideally* true in the generations or productive Acts of the intuitive Faculty (τῆς Αἰσθήσεως καθαρᾶς, or *pure* Sense) must be assumed as truth of fact in all living growth: or wherein would the Sport of a Plant differ from a chrystal? The latter is formed wholly by apposition ab extra: in the former the movement ab extra is consequent on (i.e. in order of thought) and yet coinstan[tan]eous with the movement ab intra.—Thus, the specific Character of Sensibility, the highest of the three powers, is found to be the general Character of Life; and supplies the only way of *conceiving*, supplies the only insight into the *possibility* of, the first and lowest power. And yet even thus, Growth taken as separate from and exclusive of Sensibility, would be unintelligible, nay, contradictory. For it would be an Act of the Life, or productive *Form* (vide Aids to Reflection, p. 68) of the Plant, having the Life itself as it's *source* (since it is a going-forth from the Life) and likewise having the Life itself as it's *object*—for in the same instant it is *retracted*—and yet the Product (i.e. the Plant) exists not for *itself*, by the hypothesis that has excluded sensibility—i.e. that self-*finding* (N.B.—the German word that answers to our 'Feeling' is *Empfindung*, an *Inward Finding*) which is absolutely necessary to integrate the conception.—*Therefore* Sensibility cannot be excluded: and as it does not exist *actually*, it must be involved *potentially*. Life does not yet

quotes Bichat's definition of life in *Hints towards the Formation of a more comprehensive Theory of Life*, 1848, p. 22: 'Life is the sum of all the functions by which death is resisted'—and adds, 'in which I have in vain endeavoured to discover any other meaning than that life consists in being able to live'.

manifest itself in it's highest *dignity*, as a *Self*-finding; but in an evident tendency thereto, or a Self-*seeking*—and this has two epochs, or dignities. Potential Sensibility (1) is Growth: Potential Sensibility (2) is Irritability. In both it must have pre-existed (or rather pre-inhered) tho' as *latent*: or how could the Irritability have been evolved out of Growth (ex. gr. in the Stamina of the Plant in the act of impregnating the germen) or the Sensibility out of the Irritability? (ex. gr. in the first appearances of nerves & nervous Bulbs in the lower Orders of the Insect Realm.) But indeed Evolution as contra-distinguished from apposition, or superinduction *ab aliunde*, is implied in the conception of *Life*:[1] and is that which essentially differences a living fibre from a Thread of Asbestos, the Floscule, or any other of the Fairy Shapes of animalcular Life, from the Frost-plumes on the window-pane.[2]

Again: what has been said of the lowest power of Life relatively to it's highest power—Growth to Sensibility, the Plant to the Animal, applies equally to *Life* itself relatively to *Mind*. Without the latter the former would be unintelligible: and the Idea would contradict itself. If there had been no self-*retaining* Power, a Self-finding would be a perpetual Self-*losing*. Divide a second into a thousand or if you please a million of parts—yet if there be an absolute chasm separating one moment of Self-finding from another, the chasm of $\dfrac{1}{100,000,000}$ would be equal to all time. A Being that existed for itself only in moments, each infinitely small & yet absolutely divided from the preceding and following, would not exist *for itself* at all. And if all Beings were either the same or yet lower, it could not be said to *exist* in any sense—any more than *Light* would exist as *Light* if there were no Eyes or Visual Power: and the whole conception would break up into contradictory positions —an intestine conflict more destructive than even that of the two Cats, where one Tail alone is said to have survived the battle. The conflicting Factors of our Conception would eat each other up, Tails and all.—Ergo: the Mind as a self-retaining power is no less indispensable to the intelligibility of Life as a self-finding Power, than a self-finding, i.e. Sensibility, to a self-seeking Power, i.e. growth.—

Again: a self-retaining Mind (i.e. Memory, which is the primary

[1] For a brief discussion of Coleridge's concept of evolution see J. H. Muirhead, *Coleridge as Philosopher*, 1930, pp. 130–6. See also note to Letter 1613.
[2] Cf. the following footnote in Coleridge's *Theory of Life*, p. 40: 'The arborescent forms on a frosty morning, to be seen on the window and pavement, must have *some* relation to the more perfect forms developed in the vegetable world.'

sense of Mind—& the common people in several of our provinces still use the word in this sense—ex. gr. Don't you *mind* him ? i.e. remember him ?—*Mind*, you call on Mr—— when you get to Ottery) —a self-*retaining* Power supposes a self-*containing* Power—a self-conscious Being. And this is the definition of *Mind* in it's proper and distinctive sense—a Subject that is it's own Object—or where A contem*plant* is one & the same subject with A contem*plated.*

Lastly (that I may complete the ascent of Powers for my own satisfaction and not as expecting or in the present habit of your thoughts even *wishing* you to follow me to a Height, dizzy for the strongest spirit, it being the apex of all human, perhaps of angelic knowlege to know, that *it must be*: since all absolute Ultimates can only be seen by a Light thrown backward from the Penultimate—John's Gosp. I. 18)—Lastly, I say, the Self-*containing* Power supposes a self-*causing* Power. *Causa sui, αἰτία ἡ ὑπερούσιος.* Here alone we find a Problem which in it's very statement contains it's own solution—the one self-solving Power, beyond which no question is *possible.* Yet short of this we dare not rest: for even the ὁ ὤν, the supreme Reality, if it were contemplated abstractly from the Absolute Will, whose essence it is to be causative of all *Reality*, would sink into a Spinozistic Deity. That this is not evident to us arises from the false notion of Reason (ὁ *Λόγος*) as a quality, property, or faculty of the Real, whereas Reason *is* the supreme Reality, the only true *Being* in all things visible and invisible! the Pleroma, in whom alone God loveth the World! Even in Man *Will* is deeper than *Mind*: for mind does not cease to be *mind*, by having an antecedent; but Will is either the First (τὸ ἀεὶ πρόπρωτον, τό nunquam *positum*, semper *sup*ponendum) or it is *not* Will at all.—

Now then for the second Rule: in all things accustom yourself to seek the solution of the lower in the higher.—

And the first Rule was—?

I will comprize both in one sentence. Accustom your mind to distinguish the Relations of Things from the Things themselves: think often of the latter independent of the former, in order that you may never think of the former apart from the latter—i.e. mistake mere relations for true and enduring Realities—and with regard to *these*, seek the solution of each in some higher Reality.—

The contrary process leads demonstrably to Atheism—and tho' you may not get quite so far, it is not well to be seen travelling on the road with your face toward it.—

I might add a third rule. Learn to distinguish permanent from accidental Relations: but I am willing that you should in the first instance take permanent *Relations* as real Things—confident that you will soon feel the necessity of reducing what you now call *Things* into relations which immediately arising out of a somewhat else may properly be contemplated as the *Products* of that somewhat *else*, and the means by which it's existence is made known to you—but as what? Not as a *Product*: for it is the Somewhat *else*, to which the Product stands in the same relation as the words, you are now hearing, to my living soul—. But if not as Products, then as productive *Powers*: and the result will be, that what you have hitherto called *Things* will be regarded as only more or less permanent *Relations* of Things, having their derivative reality greater or less in proportion as they are regular or accidental Relations; determined by the pre-established fitness of the true Thing to the Organ and Faculty of the Percipient, or resulting from some defect or anomaly in the latter.

With these convictions matured into a habit of mind the man no longer seeks, or believes himself to find, true reality except in the *Powers* of Nature, as made known to him, determined in respect of their *kind* and measured in respect of their Force, by their proper Products. In other words, he thinks of the Products in reference to the productive *Powers*: each of these presents a Problem, the solution of which he seeks in some higher power—and thus possessing the same world with the Toutoskosmites, save only that he does not *bark* at the Image in the Glass because he knows what it is, he has in present possession another World to which he can transport himself by a swifter vehicle than Fortunatus's Wishing-Cap, whenever he is tired of doing nothing, & passively *done up.*—[MS. breaks off thus.][1]

1538. *To Daniel Stuart*

Address: D. Stuart, Esqre | 9 Upper Harley Street
MS. British Museum. Pub. with omis. Letters from the Lake Poets, *297.*
Postmark: Highgate, 29 July 1826.

> Friday Night
> 28 July 1826.—

My dear Sir

We are all uneasy at your not coming nor your Son. Every thing was prepared. Surely my letter which I put myself into the Post, Monday Afternoon, could not have miscarried.—The substance being—how happy Mrs Gillman would be to have him here, and that I was glad to say that my health presented no obstacle to my

---

[1] See *The Church and State*, p. 241, for Coleridge's conclusion to this 'epistolary Essay'.

endeavors to give you a clear account of what he has learnt, and of his progress hitherto, and my best opinion of his talents.

I had not quite half finished a letter in reply to your remarks on Woodstock[1] & the causes of Sir Walter's unprecedented *Run*—with which I entirely co-incide—& to which I should add one or two others on the character of the Works themselves, and their bearings on the characteristic traits of the Age. I wished likewise (for in a letter to a friend one is not forced to be on one's guard against the charge of envy & such like amiable dispositions) to point out clearly and distinctly the essential difference in character of the Scotch Novels from those of Shakespear, 2. of Richardson, 3. of Smollett, 4. of Fielding & 5. of Sterne—and then to give the *Recipe* for the construction of these stories in Scott's Novels.—I say, Scott: tho' I hear that he has written to the French Translator or his Publisher, contradicting the belief & insisting that his name should be removed from the Title-pages.[2] But this does not shake me[3]—and I venture to assert, that tho' he were the Author, he would be entitled to do this, if he had reasons for it, without breach of moral Veracity. Otherwise every man's secrets would be at the mercy of every knave or fool whose curiosity was on a par with his impudence. It is idle to say—You might be silent. In how many occasions would silence give consent?—The common inference is— I asked him: and he could not *deny* it, tho' he would not own it. At least, for Sir Walter's sake I would much rather it were so— than that he should justify himself to his own conscience by some paltry reserve, that he was not the only Writer—or that he bonâ fide was in no sense entitled to the credit—and cash. Miss Baily is keen in the faith that they were written by Scott's Brother who has fled the country for debt![4]—Precious Morality, Master Walter!

[1] *Woodstock* was published in June 1826 by Longman, Rees, Orme, Brown, and Green. See H. J. C. Grierson, *Sir Walter Scott, Bart.*, 1938, pp. 264–5, and J. G. Lockhart, *Memoirs of Sir Walter Scott*, 5 vols., 1914, v. 1 and 529.

[2] In his General Preface to the *Waverley Novels* dated 1 Jan. 1829, Scott remarked that while the 'paternity of these Novels was from time to time warmly disputed in Britain, the foreign booksellers expressed no hesitation on the matter, but affixed my name to the whole of the Novels, and to some besides to which I had no claim'. The collected edition of the *Waverley Novels*, the 'author's favourite edition', for which Scott wrote new prefaces and notes, appeared in 48 vols., 1829–33.

[3] By Mar. 1820 Coleridge had read *Ivanhoe* (issued in Dec. 1819), and his discovery in that work of three lines from his then unpublished poem, *The Knight's Tomb*, convinced him that Scott was the author of the Waverley novels. He had previously recited the lines to J. H. Frere as an experiment in metre. The following day Frere dined in company with Scott and repeated the poem to him. Gillman, *Life*, 277, and Letters 1228 and 1413.

[4] From the time *Waverley* was published anonymously in 1814, Scott countenanced and gave publicity to the rumour that the Waverley novels were written

if this were true—and so you contrive to have the whole world
believe a falsehood in order to defraud your Brother's Creditors!—
And was the Brother in debt to the tune of 120,000£: for so
much Constable assured me on his honor, he had himself paid
into the hands of the Author of Waverly.—That a large part
may have been paid in Bills drawn on himself, does not alter the
argument.[1]—

But enough of this. I was about to say, that I was interrupted
by a run of Visitors, from 1 at noon to 10 at night—but as soon as

by his brother Thomas, who after failing in speculations and in debt was made
paymaster of the 70th regiment. Thomas Scott accompanied the regiment to
Canada in 1813 and died there ten years later. To Thomas, Scott wrote in 1814:
'You must know there is also a counter-report, that *you* have written the said
Waverley. . . . Keep this matter a dead secret, and look knowing when Waverley
is spoken of.' In Jan. 1817, in his own review of *Tales of my Landlord* (first series,
1816) in the *Quarterly Review*, Scott pointed directly to his brother as the author:

> We intended here to conclude this long article, when a strong report
> reached us of certain transatlantic confessions, which, if genuine, (though
> of this we know nothing,) assign a different author to these volumes, than the
> party suspected by our Scottish correspondents. Yet a critic may be excused
> seizing upon the nearest suspicious person, on the principle happily ex-
> pressed by Claverhouse, in a letter to the Earl of Linlithgow. He had been,
> it seems, in search of a gifted weaver, who used to hold forth at conventicles:
> 'I sent to seek the webster, (weaver) they brought in his *brother* for him:
> though he maybe cannot preach like his brother, I doubt not but he is as
> well principled as he, wherefore I thought it would be no great fault to give
> him the trouble to go jail with the rest.'

On the basis of this statement Murray, the London publisher of *Tales of my
Landlord*, was convinced of Thomas Scott's authorship and wrote to William
Blackwood in Jan. 1817: 'I can assure you, but *in the greatest confidence*, that
I have discovered the author of all these Novels to be Thomas Scott, Walter
Scott's brother. He is now in Canada.' See J. G. Lockhart, *Memoirs of Sir
Walter Scott*, 5 vols., 1914, ii. 479 and 483–4, and iii. 79–83; H. J. C. Grierson,
Sir Walter Scott, Bart., 1938, pp. 104, 110, and 210–11; Samuel Smiles, *A Pub-
lisher and His Friends. Memoir and Correspondence of John Murray*, 1911,
pp. 185–9; and *D.N.B.*, Walter Scott.

According to Scott, the failure of his publishers, Constable and Co., in 1826,
'and the exposure of their accompt-books, which was the necessary consequence,
rendered secrecy no longer possible'. At a public dinner in Feb. 1827 he admitted
that he was the sole author of the Waverley novels, and in the same year he
acknowledged his authorship in the Introduction to the *Chronicles of the
Canongate*. See Scott's General Preface to the *Waverley Novels*, 1829.

[1] Scott wrote in his journal on 18 Dec. 1825:

> My extremity is come. Cadell has received letters from London which all
> but positively announce the failure of Hurst and Robinson so that Constable
> & Co. must follow and I must go with poor James Ballantyne for company.
> I suppose it will involve my all. . . . I have been rash in anticipating funds to
> buy land, but then I made from £5000 to £10,000 a year, and land was my
> temptation. (*The Journal of Sir Walter Scott, 1825–26*, ed. J. G. Tait, 1939,
> p. 45.) See also Letter 1521 and n.

I can find a leisure hour, I will compleat my Outline & send it for your amusement in Oxfordshire—

I hope & trust that this letter will cross you on the road—for I shall be—indeed all three of us—increasingly uneasy till we see or hear from you—and I have another reason for wishing to see you & Mrs Stuart, that my Daughter is to be here some time to-morrow—& tho' I know, Mrs Stuart has seen her, yet it was if I mistake not some years ago.—Let me request to have your—and likewise Mrs Stuart's—opinion of marriage between First Cousins. Do you or do you not think them objectionable?

Mr & Mrs Gillman unite with me in kindest remembrances to Mrs Stuart, and Mary—and be assured that I am with sincere esteem & regard   your obliged Friend

S. T. Coleridge

P.S. The Sprinkles of Ink on this paper are a Warning not to *clap* at a Gnat with a pen in one of the hands—if there be ink in it, at least.

1539. *To Mr. Mundell*

MS. Huntington Lib. Hitherto unpublished.

13 Aug. 1826

My dear Sir

The Burmese Mss shall be returned in the same state and relative positions as received by the earliest time, you mention. I only wish, that I were able to remunerate you for the Loan by some account of the Contents; but alas! I am wholly unalphabeted in the Languages of the Farther East.—For the Image except my best thanks—It's most valued Function will be that of recalling to my mind the image of the Donor, who will never be other than kindly & respectfully

remembered by

S. T. Coleridge

Remember me cordially to Mrs Mundell.

1540. *To C. A. Tulk*

Address: Ch. Augustus Tulk, Esqre
MS. Cornell University Lib. Hitherto unpublished.

Grove, Highgate.
17 August 1826.

My dear Sir

Mr Gillman being *called out*—for better purposes than to take a life or to lose it—has appointed me his Amanuensis pro tempore—& has commissioned me to inform you, that

On the evening of the day, on which you left Highgate, He obtained from the Assignees a promise of the refusal of Mr Hurst's House.[1] Mr Chapman, of the Temple, who is their Surveyor, was from home at the time; but Mr Kinderley has been very urgent with him, and accordingly he viewed the Property last week, and *re*viewed it yesterday: and it is expected that he will make his Report (*canonical*, I (*viz. S.T.C.*) presume as I suppose the Assignees are not so infected by the first Syllable of their official Name as to employ a Blunderbuss) tomorrow or next day—and they will then without further delay decide on the Sum, they shall think themselves entitled or bound to ask for the Property. The moment that Mr Gillman receives their decision as to the Price, he will advertise you of the same; but thought that it would be not unacceptable to you that he should *report progress* in the mean time.—

I know you will be pleased to hear that for the last three days my health & state of Spirits have received a perceptible improvement. For nearly three months I have not known a single genial Sensation; but have felt, even in the intervals of Freedom from Pain and distressful Feelings, just as the imprisoned Spirit in the enchanted Wood of Tasso, or in Virgil's Tree—like a naked Intelligence, a Mind detached from Life.—Mrs Gillman desires her kind regards to You and Your's—. Give if you please my best love to all your dear Children and my assurances of cordial respect to Mr Hart—and be assured, my dear Sir, that the Hope and Prospect of your residing at Highgate are like a new life to your sincere & affectionate Friend

S. T. Coleridge

[1] When in 1825 Hurst, Robinson, and Co., booksellers, found themselves in a precarious situation as the result of reckless speculation, especially in hops, John Hurst, one of the partners, applied to his younger brother Thomas for assistance. Thomas Hurst, who was then a partner in the Longman firm, complied by drawing accommodation bills in the name of the firm. Some of these bills were paid, but they became so numerous and were for such large amounts that Longman and Co. demanded an explanation. As a result, the partnership was dissolved and Thomas Hurst made personally responsible for all further outstanding bills. Although he received more than £40,000 as his share in Longman's, the sum was insufficient to meet his liabilities and he became insolvent. Thus Winchester Hall, his home at Highgate, was put up for sale by the assignees of his bankruptcy. See *The Auto-Biography of John Britton*, 2 vols., 1850, i. 209 n., and Letters 1542 and 1544–9.

1541. *To the Editor of 'The Times'*

Pub. The Times, *31 August 1826.*

> Grove, Highgate, Tuesday Evening.
> [29 August 1826]

Sir,—I have just received a note from a city friend, respecting a poem in *The Times* of this morning ascribed to me. On consulting the paper, I see he must refer to '*A Vision*, by the author of *Christabel*'.[1] Now, though I should myself have interpreted these words as the author, I doubt not, intended them, viz., as a part of the fiction; yet, with the proof before me that others will understand them literally, I should feel obliged by your stating, that till this last half hour the poem and its publication were alike unknown to me; and I remain, Sir, respectfully yours,

> S. T. Coleridge.

1542. *To C. A. Tulk*

Address: Charles Augustus Tulk, Esqre.
MS. Historical Society of Pennsylvania. Hitherto unpublished.

> Grove, Highgate.
> Thursday Afternoon
> 31 Aug. 1826.

My dear Sir

I inclose the Assignees' terms—ut mons a *non* movendo, et lucus a *non* lucendo, so perhaps termini a non terminando. It is one of the blessings of a Mammon Land, a Mammondom, where the Market is the Mint of Language, that any word may mean any other word— and if a Professor of this busy School had said Terms and you or I had replied—tentative Proposals, ea quae *posuisti pro*—i.e. *before* or instead of the Sum, you really have made up your mind to take—the Professor would answer—Aye! aye! Terms, or Proposals—just as you like—all one!—

However, I talk of what I know nothing about—I mean, as far as the Price of the House is concerned. Provided, You and your's are within a 10 minutes' walk, I shall be well satisfied.

I am sorry to say that since I last wrote, my health has suffered a worse than relapse—and my friend, Mr Green, does not know what to make of it. He can discover no mark of organic injury—no symptom of inflammation in Liver or Kidney, or (tho' the functions

---

[1] Thomas Moore's poem by this title was printed in *The Times* on 29 Aug. 1826.

are greatly deranged) any structural ailment in the intestinal Canal—. But he is inclined to think the ganglionic System, pectoral & abdominal, to be the seat of the disorder—the more so, from the worst sufferings being in sleep, and my greatest weakness and languor during the two or three hours after my last Sleep.—These disturbances have almost forced my attention to the obscure subject of dreams—and the extraordinary tendency to a sort of allegoric personification of the processes & incidents of vital Action, that is so characteristic of Sleep when the lower Bowels are deranged. How many hundred times have I thought of Swedenborg's impure Spirits collected by the colluvies, as flies.—I have derived great comfort from praying the 71st. Psalm—and much support from Hooker's Sermon on the perpetuity of Faith,[1] appended to his Ecclesiastical Polity.

Mr and Mrs Gillman beg to be cordially remembered—and with my affectionate regards to all your household I remain,

My dear Sir, | With most sincere and | earnest esteem | your affectionate Friend

S. T. Coleridge

1543. *To T. J. Ouseley*[2]

Pub. Letters Hitherto Uncollected, *44.*

2nd September, 1826.

Oh it is sad, Sir, to know distress and to feel for it, and yet to have no power of remedy. Conscious that my circumstances have neither been the penalty of sloth, nor of extravagance, or vicious habits, but have resulted from the refusal, since earliest manhood, to sacrifice my conscience to my temporal interest, and from a practice of writing what my fellow citizens want, rather than what they like, I suffer no pang of shame, in avowing to you that I do not possess as many shillings as you mention pounds; and that if I were arrested for a debt of eight sovereigns, I have no other means of procuring the money but by the sale of my books,—that are to me the staff of life. The whole of my yearly income does not amount to the prime cost of my necessary maintenance,—clothes, shelter, food, and medicine; the rest I owe to the more than brotherly

---

[1] See *Literary Remains*, iii. 49–52 for Coleridge's marginal notes to this sermon.

[2] This letter is printed in part in the Nov. 1834 issue of the *Gentleman's Magazine.* No correspondent is mentioned, but the letter is described as having been 'lately published in the newspapers'. In Apr. 1839 the letter was published in full in the *Birmingham Iris and Midland Counties Monthly Magazine,* a short-lived periodical, started by T. J. Ouseley.

regard of my disinterested friend, Mr. Gillman, to whose medical skill I owe it, under God, that I am alive, and to whose, and his amiable wife's, unceasing kindness I am indebted for all that makes life endurable. Even when my health is at the best, I can only exert myself for a few hours in the twenty-four, and these I conscientiously devote to the completion of the great works, in the matter and composition of which I have employed the last twenty years of a laborious life—if hard thinking and hard reading constitute labor. But for the last six months such has been the languor and debility of my frame—languor alternating with severe pain, that I have not been able to maintain the scanty correspondence with the few friends I possess. By publications I, or rather two or three generous friends, have lost about 300£, for I cannot, at least will not, write in reviews; and what I can write the public will not read, so that I have no connection with any magazine, paper, or periodical publication of any kind; nor have I had interest enough to procure, in any review or journal, even the announcement of my last work—the *Aids to Reflection.* I neither live for the world nor in the world.

I read your poem,[1] not without pleasure, or what would have been pleasure, could I have detached the lines from the distress of their writer. My utter want of access to all the editors of magazines, and of influence with the London publishers, will explain my remitting them to you, together with your letter, which no eyes but mine have seen since its receipt; and with most sincere wishes that the occasion of this correspondence may be of short continuance, and that I may, without knowing it, hereafter meet you more than a conqueror over your present perplexity, I remain, Sir, with every kind wish, and distressed that I have only that to offer,

Yours respectfully,

S. T. Coleridge.

1544. *To C. A. Tulk*

Transcript Coleridge family. Hitherto unpublished.

Grove Highgate

5 Septr. 1826.

My dear Sir

Knowing that the Royal Dane, Hamlet (the Jeweller, I mean) is actually after Mr Hurst's House, we are all of us becoming

---

[1] In 1833 Ouseley published *A Vision of Death's Destruction . . . and Miscellaneous Poems.* The reviewer in *Fraser's Magazine* (Sept. 1833) advised him to 'cast off all intention of becoming a bookseller's drudge', and added: 'If you *must*, spite of all advice, stick to literature, turn your fist to prose; for you have no hand for poetry.'

anxious at not receiving any answer from you to my last, which was enclosed under cover to —— Hart Esqre, 28 Walbrook, & which I myself put into our Highgate Post Letter Box. And yet we are afraid it may have miscarried—the contents were that the terms, or to speak more accurately, the *proposal* agreed on by the Assignees is £6500 which however includes two tenements let for £40 a year.—I was in great hopes that we should see you, in order that Mr Gillman might communicate to you all he knows & thinks.

I informed you that I had had a very severe relapse; but I trust that my present convalescence will proceed tho' slowly yet steadily. —May the All Merciful Lord give to you and your's that next to Faith and inward Peace—the blessing of Health.

Mr & Mrs Gillman unite in all kind and cordial wishes and affections with your sincere Friend

S. T. Coleridge

1545. *To Marmaduke Hart*

Address: Hart, Esqre. | 28 Walbrook
MS. Massachusetts Historical Soc. Hitherto unpublished.
Postmark: Highgate, 6 September 1826.

Grove, Highgate
Wednesday Afternoon.—[6 September 1826]

Dear Sir

Anxious in consequence of not hearing from Mr Tulk in answer to my last Note inclosed under cover to you, 28. Walbrook—the contents of my note being that the Terms proposed by Mr T. Hurst's Assignees are 6500£—including two tenements now rented at 40£ yearly—Mr & Mrs G. have begged me to write again, lest my former should have miscarried.—It is thought here, that it will not go under 6000£.—Hamlet, the Jeweller, being it is said (Mr T. Hurst at least assured Mrs Gillman so) *keen* after it.—Mr Gillman, I believe, supposes the true market-price, at this present time, & putting all *fancy* influences out of the question, to be 5500£— tho' Mr Hurst, who had no motive for falsehood, declared on his word to Mrs Gillman, that it had cost him 12000£—original cost, repairs, improvements &c—. You will not wonder at my solicitude —as there is [no] earthly incident, I know of, that would add so much to my happiness as the having Mr Tulk & his Family near Neighbors.—

Accept, dear Sir! of the assuran[ce of my] unfeigned Respect and Regard

f[rom y]our obliged

S. T. Coleridge

P.S. Mrs Gillman has advised me to direct the note, I had inclosed, at once to Mr Tulk, at Brighton—and to send this to you as a duplicate.

1546. *To C. A. Tulk*

Address: Marmaduke Hart, Esqre | 28 Walbrook   For Mr Tulk with request
to be forwarded immediately.
MS. Indiana University Lib. Hitherto unpublished.
Postmark: 8 September 1826.

Friday Afternoon—
8th Septr 1826.—

My dear Sir

You well know our Friends', Mr and Mrs Gillman's, solicitude on the subject of your residence in our immediate neighborhood; and that independent of my own at least equal earnestness, I cannot but take an interest in their feelings, knowing, as I do, that this anxiety originates in their deep and more than disinterested affection towards myself, and their appreciation of the genial effects, your society would have on my spirits and active powers—a belief inspired by and grounded on their own esteem and (even before Length of acquaintance had sanctioned a higher word) 'warm *Liking*' of you.—I can not therefore withstand Mrs Gillman's wish that I should write to you—in consequence of what we have heard from the Assignees, and yet more from a recent conversation which Mrs Gillman has had with Mr Hurst, who had just left her when I returned from my Morning Stroll in Lord Southampton's Grounds.—

Mr T. Hurst has (he I doubt not truly says) no pecuniary interest in the Sale; but he has a sort of Father's Yearning toward the House, in which, at a time when his Hopes seemed to have consolidated into certainties, he had promised to himself the fruits of his past Labors by at once enjoying and employing his fortune and his leisure in the several relations of a hospitable Neighbour and an active Member of the Hamlet—& with these feelings the character and pursuits of his Successor cannot be indifferent to him—. He assured Mrs Gillman, that there was not even a Chance of the Property going at the Price, you have offered.—This, however, is not the principal motive or occasion either of my writing or of Mrs Gillman's uneasiness—but the necessity of removing an erroneous impression which my former letter was at least calculated to make—. When Mr Gillman stated 5500£ as his valuation of the Property at the now *market*-price, & supposing no accession from the influence of Fancy in the Purchaser, he had not included either the Furniture or the Tenements—and he does not hesitate to say, that (these included) the Property is a cheap bargain at £6000.—

I sadly dislike this writing on points, on which I am most profoundly unlearned—an unalphabeted Child. But I do wish, that your avocations would allow you to step into one of our Highgate Stages, and talk the matter over with Mr Gillman—. I shall be glad when the affair is settled—for there are two or three subjects, on which I would gladly obtain your opinion—as that of Inspiration, whether predicable of *all* the canonical Books, the Hebrew and the Greek—and if so, yet whether predicable in the same kind and equal degree. I confess to you, that I regard the Evangelium Infantiae *pre*fixed to Luke's Gospel & evidently intertruded between the Evangelist's Letter dedicatory and the Gospel itself—and concorporated with the Gospel *according* to St Matthew, which I conjectured to have been brought into it's present form from the Syro-chaldaic of the κηρύγματα, καθὼς ὁ Ματθαῖος ἐκήρυξε[1] (see Luke I. 2.) καὶ παρέδωσεν [*sic*]—I confess, that I regard both these, as symbolical throughout, and applications of various passages in the Psalms, evidently messianic, to our Lord's spiritual Manifestation. The omission in Mark, whose Gospel is demonstrably grounded on the same materials with those of our Matthew, and composed apparently with the view of uniting with the *prophetic* character of Matthew, (the continued reference I mean to the fulfilment of the Old Testament Predictions) the purely *historic* and chronologic character of Luke's—the absence of all allusion in John & Luke (with exception of one very *suspicious* word 'supposed')[2] and even in the remainder of Matthew—above all, the profound silence, if not direct negative, of St Paul & the Author of the Ep. to the Hebrews, who it might have been thought *must* have mentioned it in his series of Parallels between our Lord & the Saints under the Law in proof of the superiority of the former—all these & many other arguments, weigh heavily on my mind against the *historic* character of these Chapters—Likewise—of the connection between the Symbols & Correspondences of the Written Word, and those of the visible Creation—& whether a certain Philosophy of Symb[ols] might not unite all the Friends of a spiritual faith, so as that they might co-operate so far—all meeting in the Trunk, however they might diverge in the After Branches—. But the Clock has struck *four*—& I have yet to inform you, that Mr Chance on the part of a Friend—is about to make offers for Mrs Rodwell's House—.

[1] This Greek passage underlined once in MS.
[2] Luke iii. 23.

If you *can* come, it would be a great comfort to me, & to us all, to have some conversation with you on this business—May God bless you & your's—& most
unfeignedly your Friend
S. T. Coleridge

1547. *To Marmaduke Hart*

Transcript Coleridge family. Hitherto unpublished.

Grove
Highgate
Saturday Noon [9 September 1826]

My dear Sir

The accompanying Letter for Mr Tulk[1] will explain my motives for troubling you with another Letter. If on perusing my note to Mr Tulk you see no objection to it, we should be obliged to you if you would inform the Messenger (who is, I find since I wrote the word Messenger, Mr Gillman's eldest son) whether Mr Tulk is still in Town, or whether he have proceeded to Brighton, as he informed Mr Kinderley he meant to do—and if the latter that you would instruct my young Friend, James Gillman, as to the best Coach to send the little parcel by—And permit me to assure you, that I am with no everyday impression of respect & regard

Yours most truly
S. T. Coleridge

1548. *To C. A. Tulk*

Address: C. A. Tulk, Esqre.
MS. Harvard College Lib. Hitherto unpublished.

[9 September 1826]

My dear Sir

The conversation, which Mr Gillman had with Mr Kinderley yester-evening, left on *his* mind and made on mine and on Mrs Gillman's a strong impression, that you had not been put in possession of all the particulars concerning Mr T. Hurst's Property; not at least with the clearness, which [you] might have desired. Mr G. feels so much anxiety on this account, that he would even have run down to Brighton, or have met you in town, had it been feasible and there had been any certainty of not missing you. He has however persuaded Mr Kinderley *to try* to put off the Auction

[1] See next letter.

and Public Sale for a week, so as to allow time for due considera-
tion & for correspondence by letter. The particulars, stated as the
result of Mr Gillman's deliberate judgement after inquiries in every
direction, and after he had collated his own determination with
the opinions of those whose competence to give a sound opinion he
knew & from whom he felt confident of receiving an honest judge-
ment, are as follow:

1. The House & Grounds, taken *per se,* are worth £6000.
2. The Fixtures are valued at £400.
3. The two Tenements let at present for 35£ a year; but would
fetch 40£: the present Tenant having been Mr T. Hurst's Coach-
man.
4. The Furniture (i.e. Wine, Books, Pictures, &c, as per Catalogue,
which I have inclosed with this letter) is rated at £1300; but will
fetch a thousand Pound at the Hammer.—

Finally, it is Mr Gillman's Belief, that £6500 would be accepted
at once; that less than six thousand four hundred will not be
accepted: that the Property (House, Fixtures, Furniture, Wines,
Books, Pictures, &c) and the two Tenements are *cheap* at 6500£:
and that tho' you should succeed in purchasing it at 6200£, at the
public Auction, yet that three hundred Pound would not compen-
sate for the deterioration of the House by the confusion and
diffractions that a public Sale on the Property is sure to bring with
it—nor for the *Risk,* supposing the Place to suit you in all respects
and that you would like to have it.—

You will, I am sure, be pleased to hear, that my Health is con-
siderably improved—especially with regard to my Sleep, and the
tumults and afflictions of that mysterious state of the Soul in which
the Fancy and the Understanding work for themselves in the
eclipse of the Reason.—

Mr & Mrs Gillman desire their best regards—and with my love
to your dear family believe me with unfeigned respect and regard
Your affectionate Friend
S. T. Coleridge.

P.S. Mr Kinderley goes this morning to Mr Cadell, to ascertain
whether he can influence him to put off the Sale, but should he not
succeed, Mr Gillman will not fail to give you minute & immediate
information as to the result; and as to the deterioration of the
Property consequent on a public Auction, & the then value of the
Same.

1549. *To C. A. Tulk*

Address: Charles Augustus Tulk, Esqre | Brighton
MS. Bodleian Library. Hitherto unpublished.
Postmark: Highgate, 13 September 1826.

Wednesday
13 Septr 1826

My dear Sir

As I promised, I would write after the Sale, & Mr Gillman is desirous that I should, I will trouble you with the expence of one more letter—to inform you—that owing to the apparent indifference of the Assignees, none of whom would stay in town, the Sale could not be put off—that the Furniture, (Books, Wine and Pictures included) have sold at a price that has more than borne out the estimation of the Appraiser—the Results will exceed 1200£—The Wines sold remarkably well—the old Sherry fetched six guineas a dozen, and the other wines three and four—Of the Books the only one that sold cheap was the Unique Copy of the Encyclopaedia for 100 guineas, thought to be worth 200 at least. The Prices given for the Pictures made me *stare*—for with exception of a Teniers, I should not have pledged myself for their originality.—All together, you would certainly have had an excellent bargain, had you taken the whole for 6500£.—Now at present Mr Gillman has little doubt that you may have the House, Fixtures and two Tenements for 6000£—and he does not after further enquiries hesitate in assuring you that the Fixtures are worth 800£, and that for the two tene-ments, for which Mr Hurst gave 750£, *he* (Mr Gillman) could get you 500£ immediately.—So much more can be said & conveyed by an hour's conversation than by half a score Letters, that Mr Gillman was strongly inclined to have taken a run down to Brighton: & still if you think that he could be of any use to you in the way of minute information, he would come to you as soon as he had received your letter.—

I had a very interesting conversation with Mr Harrison[1] yester-morning—I like him very much—the whole frame of his mind.—

Do let me trouble you with the request to receive a line or two from you by return of Post—& believe me, my dear Sir,

with most sincere regard | and esteem | Your obliged
S. T. Coleridge—

P.S. I am glad to find, that the Oil Cloth which cost 90£, and would have fetched little, has been reserved—together with some other things, the value of which is greatly dependent on their re-

---

[1] Probably 'the Quaker Barrister' mentioned in Letter 1446.

maining in the House—If you mean to make any offer, let me advise you (if you will excuse my presumption) to do it thro' **Mr Gillman**—You may then be assured of it's being executed in a sensible man of business way—which I cannot promise (*inter nos*) from our very worthy but not very *clear-headed* Neighbor.—

1550. To Sara Coleridge

Transcript Coleridge family. Hitherto unpublished.

[September 1826?][1]

My dear Sara

As I think that the following delicate morsel of information from the other World is not at all likely to produce the same effect on your fancy, during the time when you are Fancy's rather than the Fancy your's—i.e. in sleep—that it has produced on me ever since I first read it, I will begin my letter by transcribing it in my informer's own words, from p. 119 of the 'De Coelo et Inferno et eorum Mirabilibus ex Visis et Auditis' of that very credible Traveller, the Honorable Baron Emanuel Swedenborg[2]—Datum etiam est scire, unde homini anxietas, dolor animi ac tristitia ea interior quae Melancholia vocatur. Sunt Spiritus, qui nondum in conjunc-

---

[1] This letter was probably written not long after Coleridge's daughter arrived at Highgate on 17 Sept. 1826. See next letter. E. H. Coleridge noted that the present letter is written on paper watermarked 1825.

[2] In a notebook entry dated 26 Apr. 1826 Coleridge refers to the passage from Swedenborg cited in the present letter:

> Since I first read Swedenborg's De Coelo et de Inferno ex Auditis et Visis, every horrid Dream that I have, my thoughts involuntarily turn to the passage in p. 119, §§ 299 (indeed to the whole Book I am indebted for imagining myself always in Hell, i.e. imagining all the wild Chambers, Ruins, Prisons, Bridewells, to be in Hell)—Sunt Spiritus, qui nondum in conjunctione cum Inferno sunt illi amant indigesta et maligna, qualia sunt sordescentium Ciborum in Ventriculo—Swedenborg had often talked with them, & driven them away, & immediately the poor Sleeper's frightful Dreams were removed, they being the spiritual Linquifacture of these Toad-Imps' whispers. Only that I modify this Miltonic Theory by supposing the Figures in my Dream to *be*, or to be assumed by, the Malignant Spirits themselves— for it is very curious, that they are more or less malicious.—One good effect, I trust, I may attribute to these half and quarter earnest Melancholies—the deep sense of the exclusion from God's Presence to me (for this has for many years been my Conception of REASON, & I think it sanctioned by the First Chapter of St John's Gospel)—But in serious whole Earnest, and however hypochondriacal the Spirit-theory may be, I dare avow, that no Explanation of Dreams or attempt to explain them, that I have seen or heard, has in the least degree satisfied my Judgement, or appeared to solve any part of the mysterious Problem. [MS. notebook, Huntington Library.]

tione cum Inferno sunt, quia adhuc in primo* suo statu sunt. Illi amant indigesta et maligna qualia sunt in Dyspepticorum Ventriculis: quapropter adsunt (sc. hi Spiritus) ubi talia apud hominem quia illa iis sunt jucunda; atque ibi inter se ex malâ suâ affectione loquuntur (*have a little scandal-conversazione, these spirits being the only proper Ventriloquists*). Affectio loquelae eorum influit inde apud hominem, who mistakes & is maliciously made to mistake their vile gossip in the language of Vision (thoughts in sleep being mostly translated into sights and sensible impressions) for his own thoughts. The Baron proceeds to relate, that he had often in the spiritual world driven away a coterie of these spirits from their haunts in the inside of some sleeper troubled with indigestion, as one would spring a covey of Blue-bottle Flies, & he ends the paragraph with the following remark: Inde patuit mihi, quod quidam qui non sciunt quid conscientia est ex eo quod non sit illis conscientia, adscribunt huic dolorem qui re verâ locum habet in ventriculo. Now a sorrowful lot of this ventricular conscience have I had to harrass me during the eclipse of Sense and Reason, and to make me ask for a Sleep for sleep itself to rest in during the last 6 weeks[1]—

Yours affectionately,

S. T. Coleridge.

1551. To C. A. Tulk

Address: Charles Augustus Tulk, Esqre. | Brighton
MS. Cornell University Lib. Hitherto unpublished.
Postmark: Highgate, 21 September 1826.

Grove, Highgate.
Thursday Afternoon
20 [21] Septr 1826.

My dear Sir

Tho' I always considered my friend, Gillman, as a Man of Business, I have never had so strong an impression of it as of late—first, in the way of planning and executing the Repairs of our own House; & next, in the skill with which he has steered the vessel and sounded his way in the shelvy and unbuoyed channel of Bankrupt Property, between Assignees, Solicitors, Appraisers, &c—. His information respecting the Property not only beyond what the Assignees chuse to communicate but beyond what they actually possess, gives him the Vantage-ground. However, it would

---

* According to Swedenborg there are three intermediate States between a man's Death and his final passing into Heaven or the other place. [Note by S. T. C.] For the three states after death see *De Coelo*, paragraphs 491–520.

[1] Coleridge's comments in this letter may be compared to those in Letters 1242, 1418, 1542, and 1548.

be far too difficult a task for me to attempt the detail of all the motives and reasons which have determined Mr Gillman's Judgement—that it would be *highly* ADVISABLE for you to come to town for a few days, as soon as you can make it convenient—and still better, if you could take up your sojourn at Highgate—and I am desired by Mrs Gillman to say, that she can procure you a bed at a next door but one Neighbor, and if you can sufficiently tolerate the *incondite* state of a House with Carpenters in the upper story to be our Guest for the time, you will afford us all a high gratification—and to me the greater, because I shall have the opportunity of introducing my Daughter to you, who arrived here on Sunday last—and is all, the most ambitious Father could desire—if his ambition was within the circle of *wise* wishes—with exception only of her bodily strength—tho' (the Author of all good be thanked & glorified!) she is in much better health, than I had ventured to anticipate.

On the subject of Inspiration, I will only say thus much—that if my scheme does not satisfy every moral, and every spiritual purpose, that has or can be pretended for the popular belief, which reducing the Sacred Writers to passive instruments, *pens* in the hand of an invisible Agent, might be called the *Automaton* Scheme; and if it do not increase, rather than diminish, the reverence and deep spiritual interest, in relation to the Canonical Books collectively;—I will be myself the first to renounce it.—I too contend for their *Inspiration*; but I contend, that πνεῦμα and λόγος are distinct operations, that may or may not be united in the same act, and that Inspiration is not in *all* cases accompanied by, much less the same with, *Miraculous dictation*.

'Whatsoever is spoken of God or of things appertaining to God, otherwise than as the Truth is, tho' it *seem* an honor, is an injury. And as incredible praises given unto men do often abate and impair the credit of their *deserved* commendation: so we must likewise take great heed, lest in attributing unto Scripture more than it can have, the incredibility of *that* do cause even those things which it hath most abundantly, to be less reverently esteemed.' Hooker's Eccles. Pol. B. III ad finem, p. 124.[1]—

Be pleased to remember me with cordial affection to all of your dear Household—& believe me
        most truly your's
                    S. T. Coleridge

[1] This quotation is taken from the last paragraph of Book II of Hooker's *Of the Laws of Ecclesiastical Polity*. Three of Coleridge's annotations in a copy of the 1682 edition of Hooker's *Works* now in the British Museum 'are dated "*12 August, 1826*", "*12 August, 1826*", and "*8 September, 1826*" respectively'. Wise, *Two Lake Poets . . .*, 1927, p. 132.

1552. *To Mrs. J. J. Morgan*

Address: Mrs Morgan | 11 Coburg Place | Kennington Lane
MS. Pierpont Morgan Lib. Hitherto unpublished.
Postmark: Highgate, 2 October 1826.

Grove, Highgate
2 Octr 1826.
Monday Afternoon

My dear Mary

Tho' I have kept up no acquaintance with the inmates of Christ's Hospital, and tho' with the exceptions of the Matron, and of Dr Trollope[1] (who, I understand, is no friend or admirer of his junior School-fellow, S.T.C.) I do not even know their names; yet I doubt not, that by some medium or other I could contrive to obtain whatever was obtainable—and I hope, I need not add that what I *could* do, I promptly and readily *would* do or set about doing. But I really must apply to you for a *commentary* on your letter—You say, 'a Youth *from* the Blue coats' School'. Do you mean one, who had been educated there & who has left it? Or a Youth still in the School? A Blue coat Boy? or one who *was* a Blue-coat Boy? If you mean the latter, the probability is, that he will be either at one of the Universities, supposing him to have been a Grecian; or if he was not selected for the Church, and left the School at 15 as a Deputy Grecian, that he will be apprentice, Articled Student, Clerk or the like to some Medical Practitioner, or Attorney, or Surveyor, or Architect, or in some Compting House. A youth competent in manners and attainments to instruct children in a respectable Preparatory School, a youth, in short, who has left Christ's Hospital, as a Deputy Grecian, will almost always (if it have not been grievously his own fault) be found in some respectable situation, in the mercantile or the professional Line of Life. Tenant, now the First Grecian,[2] happened to be with me at the time, your letter arrived. And he knew of no one, who was unemployed or so employed as to be able to undertake the office you want him for—If on the other hand, you mean a youth still in the School—it would not be possible for him, consistently with the rules of the School, to attend you more than once in a week—viz. Saturday Afternoons—and then only by special indulgence, or what is called a Ticket. And I am afraid, that the Treasurer & the Head-master would hesitate in making a Precedent of this kind. I induced Tenant during the

---

[1] A. W. Trollope (1768–1827) succeeded James Boyer in 1799 as headmaster of Christ's Hospital and resigned his post on 28 Nov. 1826.

[2] According to the records at Christ's Hospital, Robert John Tennant was the Senior Grecian in 1827.

Bartholomew Tide Holidays to come three afternoons in each week, to *grind* Henry Gillman during *his* Eton Vacation. But at the end of the Holidays, which were only half the length of Henry's, Tenant was obliged to give it up—tho' he is so greatly liked and esteemed by his Superiors, that nothing, that could be granted or allowed, would have been denied him—and tho' they were days of delight to *him*! You have not spoken of any terms—or of the particular times, whether daily, or every other day—. But while the practicability of the thing itself—that is, in relation to Christ's Hospital, and it's Nurslings—is so questionable, it would have been perhaps premature to enter into particulars—And I am so utter a Recluse, and so out of the way of hearing of any one likely to suit you, that I could only cause inquiries to be made at some of the Preparatory Schools in or near Highgate, if they knew & could recommend a person—And what would this be? I should know nothing of the Recommenders—or what reliance was to be placed on their word or judgement—and the result might be, that some dozen raw-boned Scotch Lads or Irish Honeys might tumble in, in quick succession, upon you. Mrs Gillman in her anxiety about Henry would against my humble opinion make an inquiry of this sort & thro' this channel—and Lord have mercy on our poor Knocker—and on *my* eyes & ears!—For a week afterwards I had a vision of *Rum Faces* haunting me.—

Mrs Gillman is very unwell and reduced almost to a Shadow—and I am worse than usual, from want of rest at night, the consequence of a very distressing local irritation connected with some affection of the lower Bowel, for which my medical friends expect no alleviation but by change of Scene & Salt-water Hot Bathing.—At length, by the kindness of two or three friends, this has been rendered practicable—& I shall leave Highgate for Ramsgate in a few days.—If you have occasion to write to me after Friday next, you must direct to be left at the Post office, Ramsgate.

Would that I had myself set about my scheme of the Domestic Tutor—instead of leaving it to poor dear Hartley who had promised to fill it up—You would not then have needed a Latin Tutor. Any sensible Mother, who could read, might without difficulty have prepared a Boy from his 6th or 7th to his ninth year for either of the Public Schools, so as that in his 9th year he might be put to his Sallust, Terence &c—or what is called the 5th Form at Eton.—

My Love to Charlotte—I shall miss the Post, if I do not hasten to
Your's sincerely & affectionately
S. T. Coleridge

1553. *To Marmaduke Hart*

Address: Marmaduke Hart, Esqre. | Walbrook—
Transcript Mrs. W. K. Denison. *Hitherto unpublished.*

Grove, Highgate.
Octr. 4, 1826

Dear Sir

If you are likely to see Mr Tulk, or to send a packet or parcel to him, I should be obliged by your giving him the enclosed or enclosing it. For there is no occasion of sending it by the Post—even were it more worth the charge than it is—since it may as well be read a month hence as now.

With respect to Mr Hurst's House, my humble opinion is that if a respectable Tenant could be secured before hand for Cromwell House, for a lease of years and at a rent that would pay good interest for the purchase money, Mr Tulk would act prudently in purchasing both houses if he purchased either. For I confess that the possibility of an unpleasant neighbor as an occupant of Cromwell House (and this becomes less improbable in proportion as the House should be sold below its value) weighs more with me, than any chance of the same kind in respect to the two small tenements—

But these matters are so much out of my line as to require an apology for the mention of them from,

my dear Sir, | Your's with cordial Respect
S. T. Coleridge

1554. *To C. A. Tulk*

Transcript Coleridge family. Hitherto unpublished.

4 Octr. 1826
Grove Highgate

My dear Sir

Your first condition viz. that the mind of the Reader of Holy Writ should be under an influence ejusdem essentiae tho' not ejusdem *formae* as that of the inspired Writer, and (so to speak) in the opposite Pole, a susceptibility correspondent to the Activity, and both the working of the same Spirit—this condition, so uniformly insisted on by all the Reformers, and by none more expressly than by the Compilers of our Church Homilies, is of so great importance as to render every other Opinion which a spiritual Believer can be supposed to entertain respecting inspired Writers a matter almost of Indifference. If it be otherwise to me, it is not on my own account but for the sake of those (and there are many such) who

are still in the Wilderness, tho' with their hearts and faces toward
the Land of Canaan, men perplexed in the extreme, not from any
presumptuous confidence in their understanding, but by objec-
tions suggested by natural piety and a dread of attributing aught
to the Supreme Being not commensurate or compatible with his
Love, Holiness and Majesty. In my communion with persons in
this state I should be content first to present the whole magnifi-
cent system of revelation with the evidences that it is true, real
and actual—true as Idea, real as History, and actual by the per-
petuity of its operation in the spiritual World, and thro' this in the
sensible or symbolic World—and secondly, that this system is
contained in the Canonical Writings, which therefore perform the
office of Witnesses that this Faith was from the Beginning—that
that portion, for instance, which it is part of our faith to receive as
having been revealed thro' Moses, was really in existence from the
age of Moses, that the Doctrines ascribed to Christ and promul-
gated as such by the Apostles, really existed in the Apostolic Age.
Likewise, that the said writings afford a strong presumption at
least, that Doctrines not contained, either expressly or by evident
implication, in the Scriptures were added at a later period and by
men not especially inspired for this purpose or of whose inspiration
we have not the same, nor in fact any satisfactory proof. But at all
events that no doctrine or institution contradictory to doctrines
preached by the Apostles, and proved to have been so by their
being repeated and propounded as such in writings of the Apostolic
Age, can be admitted as Articles of the Christian Faith. For tho'
a Vine may produce new tendrils & additional Grapes, a Vine can-
not bear thorns. I should be content, I say, to secure *these* points
in the first instance, leaving the question whether more than the
scheme of Catholic Faith (i.e. the doctrines &c necessary for and
binding on all Christians, and in all ages under all circumstances of
the Church) may not be contained in these Scriptures—or whether,
on the contrary, the Scriptures were the exact *Duplicate* of the
Religion, in all respects commensurate and co-incident, and now
therefore the Code & only criterion of Faith. The determination of
this I would leave to flow from the study of the Scriptures them-
selves, after the individual's mind and affections had been pre-
pared for a right understanding of the same by a previous knowledge
of the System of Faith common to all the Churches—i.e. to the
Greek and the Latin, & to the Romish and the Protestant Divisions
of the latter. *A.* Are the Scriptures in part, particularly those of the
Christian Canon, *occasional* Writings—most important indeed, but
yet occasional, and containing therefore more or fewer passages of
occasional and *temporary* obligation and expediency, and attesting

their authenticity by the occurrence of notions and traditions held
by the Writers, as men of that age & not exempt from the innocent
errors common to their contemporaries & compatriots—these pas-
sages not referred by them to any revelation as their source, not
delivered by authority or for the sake of the notions or traditions
themselves, as the primary purpose of the Writers, but occurring
as illustrations, argumenta ad hominem, or as ornaments of per-
suasive Rhetoric? *B.* Or was each and every Book, whether
history, epistle or poem, intended in each and every sentence for
all times, and as of equal certainty and obligation, consciously by
the Writer himself—or (if this should be found of too difficult recon-
ciliation with the time of the Writings, with the absence of any
claim of this kind, & with several seeming declarations or implica-
tions of the contrary, yet) by the divine Power, secretly inspiring
and without the Writer's being conscious of the operation, con-
trolling his thoughts & faculties to the production of words divinely
pre-determined?—State the problem thus. We will exclude every
contra-distinguishing doctrine, ceremony &c of *particular* churches:
and the remainder, held in common by all* who receive Christ as
the Son of the Living God who submitted to become Man in the
flesh in order to redeem mankind, we comprize in a Creed as
forming the Catholic *Universal* Faith. And if of any one or more
of these, which we know to be universal at this present time, we are
challenged to prove that they have been universal from the be-
ginning, we have no other proof than that the article in question
is contained in the Apostolic Scriptures. Well!—but an individual
or a sect arises, and asserts not only as a truth but as a truth to be
received of necessity by all Christians, some position which does not
enter into the Creed or Catalogue of Articles semper ubique et ab
omnibus Ecclesiis creditorum—Will the citation of a sentence from
any part of the Scriptures containing the same position (ex. gr. the
washing of Feet,[1] the saluting with a holy Kiss,[2] the Dispute be-
tween the Devil & Michael over the Corse of Moses,[3] or that the
law was given to Moses by Angels,[4] &c) bear out this demand, and
oblige us in conscience to insert this in our creed as a competent
part of—not the *universal*, but the universally *necessary*, Faith?[5]
If the answer be affirmative, one consequence is evident—that
necessary and universal are no longer equivalent terms: and that

* N.B. Assemblies of men who do not profess to have faith in Christ, as the
Lord & the Son of God that taketh away the sins of the World, are not
Christian Churches. [Note by S. T. C.]

[1] John xiii. 5–16.
[2] Romans xvi. 16.   [3] Jude 9.
[4] Acts vii. 53; Galatians iii. 19; Hebrews ii. 2.
[5] Cf. *Confessions of an Inquiring Spirit*, ed. H. N. Coleridge, 1840, Letter IV.

the old and venerable criterion, **Quod semper ubique et ab omnibus**, must be given up as precarious and unsafe, and we shall never know when our Creed is complete. By the increase of Antiquarian Learning and a more critical understanding of the Language, Customs and Opinions of the Apostolic Age new meanings may by ingenious and gifted men be discovered in the Canonical Books—The individual at all events may be fully persuaded, and succeed in persuading a more or less numerous party of men, that this is indeed the meaning of the passage—Now as God must be obeyed rather than man, *then* if the hypothesis B (i.e. the miraculous dictation or infusion of the whole of the Books collected into a Canon—when or by what authority we do not exactly know) be adopted both as truth and as an article of Christian Faith, it must be the Duty of such men or man to protest against, and separate from, the Church that perseveres in rejecting this truth, or forbidding it to be preached as an article of saving Faith. Now rather than meet this consequence, I would confine the public & universal obligation to the common & universal Creed—& all beyond these articles I would leave to the enlightening of the Spirit, vouchsafed to each sincere Searcher according to his individual needs & capacity, neither denying nor asserting the hypothesis B. [Transcript breaks off thus.]

1555. *To Daniel Stuart*

Address: D. Stuart, Esqre | 9. Upper Harley Street | Cavendish Square
MS. British Museum. Pub. Letters from the Lake Poets, *300.*
Postmark: 18 October 1826

My dear Sir   Saturday [14 October 1826]

I acknowlege with the feelings, which after so long an acquaintance I need not express, your kind inclosure ; which will put it in my power to effect to the extent necessary what I had more than self-concerning reasons to wish.—Nothing would give me more pleasure, than to pass a week or two with you at Banbury—so much so, that any time after my return from Ramsgate—the last week of November,[1] at latest, you and Mrs Stuart should find it convenient, at any time before you come for good to your House in Harley Street, you have only to write me that you wish, and I will be with you.

I have been writing to you on a subject, which is the only public matter that spite of myself takes hold of me—and that is, Ireland.—

---

[1] Coleridge left Highgate for Ramsgate on 11 Oct. 1826 and returned on 14 Dec. [Notebook, Huntington Library, and Letter 1567.]

Soon after your arrival at Banbury, if no unforeseen *knock-me-down* interferes, you will receive my notions—in the form in which I have thought of giving them to the Public, by some Newspaper—but this, I tell you beforehand, depends entirely on your judgement.—I will add no more to this Note—for you must most unjustly think me a hypocrite if you do not know, that I rely more on your knowlege & judgement of men and things, than on those of *any* other individual.

God bless you | &

S. T. Coleridge

1556. *To the Editor of a London Newspaper*

Pub. Book-Auction Records, *ed. Frank Karslake, 1913,* p. ix. In printing the letter Karslake prefaced it with this explanation: 'The following letter, signed "S.T.C." and undoubtedly written by Coleridge, appeared in some London newspaper in 1826, and a cutting of it has just come into my hands. It *may* have been reprinted, but is not likely to have been, so here it is,verbatim.'

[October 1826][1]

Mr. Editor,—Among the numerous forced sales which the cruel necessity of the present times has produced, the sales of books, either in small parcels or whole libraries, form a striking and very unpleasing feature; and I am, I confess, desirous to draw, through the medium of your valuable paper, the public attention to it, because I conceive that there are none (at least as now conducted) which unite so much severe pain to the former possessor, with so little pecuniary advantage to him, his creditors, or the public at large. You will have anticipated my invective against the slovenly, ill-judged Boeotian way in which *lots* of books are at present made up. Mr. Editor this is no small evil: it prevents country gentlemen and men of literary habits, but small incomes, from purchasing volumes which they *do* want, because lotted with a host of others which they do not; it causes the well-selected and valued stores of the former possessor to be sold for a very inadequate consideration, and it throws nearly the whole into the hands of booksellers exclusively. If a farmer on attending a sale of cattle were to find a bull and half a score fat sheep sold in the same lot, he would I suspect be apt to grumble, and 100 clamorous tongues would up-braid the folly of the auctioneer. Yet that farmer might keep the bull if he liked, and so long as good mutton is sold and consumed, he could be at no loss to find a *ready market* for the sheep which he

---

[1] The reference to 'a general sale of property' which Coleridge 'attended last week not 100 miles from London' suggests that this letter was written while he was at Ramsgate in the autumn of 1826. See headnote.

did not want. But in books the case is widely different, and in proportion as the consumers are fewer, their value less accurately appreciated, and the market duller—in that same proportion is this evil the greater. I attended last week not 100 miles from London a general sale of property under an act of bankruptcy, where, among other things, more than 150 lots of books came to the hammer. The auction-room presented as usual some mere loungers, a considerable number of country gentlemen and professional men who wished to buy, as literary men, some wealthy retired tradesmen, who bought in order to appear so, and booksellers! The lots were large, the country gentlemen hung their despairing heads, and the book-sellers bought, and bade, and bought and bade again. 'Lot 76. Citizen, 2 v.; Calvary, 2 v.; Carey's Poems, Death of Abel, Little's Poems.'[1] Mr. Editor, I fable not, Calvary, Death of Abel, and Little's Poems *were* in the same lot, and the catalogues are alive to testify it. I sat by a neighboring gentleman of literary taste, liberal mind, and good fortune, who would have been glad to buy a large number of volumes if sold separately, but neither could nor would be saddled with books which he already possessed. This gentleman, myself, and sundry others, *hujusmodi*, went off dolorous and malcontent, while the booksellers revelled in cheap purchases. Mr. Editor, it is high time that the powerful voice of the public press should be raised against this iniquitous system. I mean not to impute fraudu-lent design to the auctioneers, who are frequently (as in this case) men of good character and immensely rich; they overrate the value of their time, know as much of books as Moses in the School for Scandal, and acting on inherited maxims, think it saving of time to act as they do. Would they be persuaded to make their lots smaller, the biddings would be brisker, time would not be wasted in calcu-lating the division of a bidding between the sterling works and the heavy lumber tagged on, like weighing meat on a prime joint, time would eventually be saved, and the proceeds increased 50 per cent.

S. T. C.

1557. *To James Gillman, Jr.*

MS. New York Public Lib. Hitherto unpublished.

[October 1826?]

The Proneness of mankind to judge of Measures by the *event* forms a frequent topic of Complaint. That it is a false rule is

---

[1] Coleridge refers to Goldsmith's *Citizen of the World*, 2 vols., 1762; to Richard Cumberland's *Calvary*, 1792; to the poems of Henry Carey; to an English translation of Salomon Gessner's *Der Tod Abels*, 1758; and to *The Poetical Works of the Late Thomas Little, Esq.*, 1801, a work by Thomas Moore.

generally admitted. Scarce a season passes, in which some one or other of our Public Men do not deprecate it's application. And yet the influence of this tendency both on Nations and on Individuals is as strong and epidemic as ever. If indeed under the term we comprehended the whole range of Consequences, direct and indirect, Events, tho' still a very unfair criterion of the merits of the Agent, might be fitly employed in determining the character of the action. But in the ordinary sense of the word, and that here intended, namely, the immediate Event, and the success or failure of a measure or enterprize in respect to it's primary and ostensible Objects, the rule is alike inapplicable to Act and Agent. If from the crowd of Examples it were proposed to select some one instance especially striking, & which should at once illustrate [the] wide Spread of this tendency, and it's influence in misleading the Judgement, it would perhaps be difficult to adduce one better calculated for both purposes than the CRUSADES.

If the supporter of this Opinion were allowed to anticipate his proofs, so far as (for argument's sake) to assume the truth of the latter half of the preceding proposition, namely, that the reprobation of the Crusades is an error in judgement, the word itself would supply sufficient proof of the former half—that is, of the wide diffusion of the error. For it has passed out of it's particular & historical meaning: and is now a general, I might say, a proverbial term of contempt for any enterprise undertaken by blind Zealots for worthless or unattainable Objects—for any undertaking, described retrospectively or by anticipation, as unnecessary or from inadequate grounds; unjustifiable in it's commencement, and fruitless in it's results.

As the Undertaker's character is expressed by *Quixotism*, so is the Measure itself characterised by calling it a *Crusade*. In the definition above given of the latter word as now generalized, I exclude the two other grounds of reproach commonly included, viz. calamitous in the process, and failing in the direct object.—For so was the late heroic Enterprise of Kosciuski, and of the Prussian SCHELL[1]—and yet no man, no Briton at least, will call either a Crusade. But there is yet a stronger reason for excluding them.—For it is the including them in the charge against the Enterprise in question, that constitutes it's reprobation a case in point, an instance of the very error of which I complain, the disposition to judge of measures by their events.

Let us then try this stupendous Enterprize of the great republic

---

[1] T. A. B. Kosciuszko (1746–1817), Polish patriot. F. B. von Schill (1776–1809) attempted to liberate his country from French domination and was killed at Stralsund.

of Christendom by the existing import of the Word. Was this Measure commenced without necessity? Were there no adequate Motives, no justifying ends? Our Ancestors failed in their immediate Objects, we admit. But *were* those Objects worthless or extravagant? And lastly, *was* the Enterprize in all it's several & successive parts fruitless in the final Results? Now I undertake to maintain the direct Negative on all the points expressed in these Questions.

1. The Crusades not commenced idly but from urgent necessity.—The wide spread of the Saracen Power—Conquests in Spain —the danger of Germany thro' Hungary—

2. Not without justifying ends, but the very contrary—the dreadful Intolerance of the Mahometan Fanaticism—a Religion professing universal Conquest by the Sword, as it's great Principle. The instinctive Foresight, & prophetic Presentiment of our Ancestors respecting the soul-withering character of Mahometanism, ensuring Universal Slavery, Barbarism &c—

3. The objects not worthless—The preservation of the Greek Empire (were our Ancestors answerable for the melancholy fact, that the Greeks & their Emperors were too vicious & degenerate to be preserved?)—the finest district on Earth—But need we other proof of the contrary than the state of Minor Asia & Turkish Europe ever since? than the dreadful circumstances, from which the Greeks are at this hour heroically rescuing themselves?—

4. Not fruitless in their final results—Arts of Civilization, Splendor, Architecture, Poesy, Science—. Even the ruined Estates of the haughty Barons led the way to the gradual abolition of the Feudal System, and to the commencement of English Freedom in the Aera of Henry the 7th.—

These, my dear James! are the main facts—which by consulting Rapin, & (when you come home) Warton's History of Poetry, you will be able to embody in definite form.—I doubt not, that by beginning to exert yourself in good earnest from motives of *Duty*, you will soon *push onward* from the allurements of pleasure and intrinsic interest in your studies for their own sake.—

Your's with paternal regard

S. T. Coleridge—

1558. *To James Gillman, Jr.*

Address: James Gillman, Esqre. Junr | Grove | Highgate
MS. New York Public Lib. Pub. with omis. Coleridge at Highgate, *by Lucy
E. Watson, 1925, p. 127.*

[22 October 1826][1]

My dear James

There was a time—and indeed for the Many it still continues—
when all the different departments of Literature and Science were
regarded as so many different Plants, each springing up from a
separate root, and requiring it's own particular soil and aspect: and
Mathematics and Classics, Philology, Philosophy, and Experi-
mental Science, were treated as *indigenae* of different Minds—or
of minds differently predisposed by their original constitution.
Under this belief it was natural, that great stress was laid on the
Student's having a *Turn*, or *Taste*, for this or that sort of Know-
lege; and it was a valid excuse for reluctance in the study, and
want of progress in the attainment, of any particular Branch, that
the Individual had no *turn* that way.—But it is the Boast of
genuine Philosophy to present a very different and far more hope-
ful View of the Subject. Without denying the importance or even
the necessity of an original Tendency, or what is called a *Genius*,
for the attainment of *Excellence* in any one Art or Science, but
likewise without forgetting that even among the liberally educated
Classes the fewest can or need be eminent Poets, Painters, or
Naturalists—but that all ought to be well-informed and right-
principled *Men*—the Philosopher considers the several knowleges
and attainments, which it is the Object of a liberal Education to
communicate or prepare for, as springing from one Root, and
rising into one common Trunk, from the summit of which it
diverges into the different Branches, and ramifies without losing
it's original unity into the minutest Twigs and Sprays of practical
application: and so that in all alike it is but the same Principles
unfolding into different Rules, and assuming different names &
modifications, according to the different Objects, in which these
Principles are to be realized. Now as in the present stage of your
Studies, & indeed for the next two years of your life, you are en-
gaged in forming the *Trunk* of the Tree of Knowlege, which *Trunk*
belongs entire to each and every Branch of the Tree, singly as well
as collectively—(the Clergyman must have the *whole*, the Lawyer
the whole, the Physician the whole, yea, even the naval and the

---

[1] At the conclusion of the present letter Coleridge says he will 'defer' the
continuation of his comments 'to the next Post but one'. Since the next letter
is dated Tuesday 24 Oct. 1826, the present letter, therefore, was posted at
Ramsgate on the preceding Sunday.

Military *Officer* must possess the *whole,* if either of these is to be
more than a mere Tradesman and *Routinier,* a *hack* Parson, a *hack*
Lawyer, &c, in short, a sapless *Stick*—for that is the right name for
a Branch, in which the juices elaborated by the common trunk do
not circulate—and for all the uses, that a stick can be applied to,
such a man is good for—and good for nothing else!) it must be
evident to you, that to have no *Taste,* no *Turn,* no Liking for *this*
or for *that* is to confess an unfitness or dislike to a liberal Education
in toto—And what is a liberal Education? That which *draws* forth
and trains up the germ of free-agency in the Individual—Educa-
tio, quae *liberum* facit: and the man, who has mastered all the
conditions of *freedom,* is *Homo Liberalis*—the classical rendering
of the modern term, *Gentle*man—because under the feudal system
the *men of family* (Gentiles, generosi, quibus *gens* erat, et *gen*us)
alone possessed these conditions. I do not undervalue *Wealth,* but
even if by descent or by Lottery (& since Mr Bish mourns in large
Capitals, red, blue, and black, in every—corner over the Last, the
downright *Last,*[1] you have but small chance, I suspect, of a snug
£30,000 from this latter source, and your dear Father is too rational
& upright a Practitioner and Highgate too healthy a Place for you
to expect any one of the nine Cyphers as the Nominative of 000£
from the former)—but even if you had an independent fortune, it
would not of itself suffice to make you an independent man, a
free man, or a Gentleman. For believe me, my dear young Friend!
it is no musty old Saw but a Maxim of Life, a medicinal Herb from
the Garden of Experience that grows amid Sage, Thyme* and
Heart's Ease, that He alone is *free* & entitled to the name of a
Gentleman, who knows himself and walks in the light of his own
consciousness.—

But for this reason, nothing can be rightly taken in, as a part of
a liberal Education, that is not a Mean of acquainting the Learner
with the nature and laws of his own Mind—as far as it is the re-
presentative of the Human Mind generally—. By knowing what it
ought to be, it gradually becomes what it ought to be—and *this,*
the Man's *ideal* Mind, serves for a Chronometer by which he can
set his own pocket Watch and judge of his Neighbour's.—Most
willingly, however, do I admit, that the far greater part of the
process, which is called Education, and a classical, a liberal

[1] In 1826 lotteries were abolished in England, the last being held on 18 Oct.
* This word reminds me of an Ode to PUNNING which I wrote at School,
when I was of your age—& which began with 'SPELLING, avaunt'!—[Note by
S. T. C.] No such poem has come to light, but in 1803 Coleridge 'thought of
writing an Ode on Punning, of which the first words were to be, SPELLING
[avaunt]'. See Letter 522.

Education, corresponds most vilely to the character here given!—
But that all knowlege, not merely mechanical and like a Carpen-
ter's Ruler, having it's whole value in the immediate outward use
to which it is applied, without implying any portion of the science
in the user himself, and which instead of re-acting on the mind
tends to keep it in it's original ignorance—all knowlege, I say,
that enlightens and liberalizes, is a form and a means of Self-
knowlege, whether it be grammar, or geometry, logical or clas-
sical. For such knowlege must be founded on *Principles*: and those
Principles can be found only in the Laws of the Mind itself. Thus:
the whole of Euclid's Elements is but a History and graphic Ex-
position of the powers and processes of the Intuitive Faculty—or
a Code of the Laws, Acts and ideal Products of the pure Sense. We
learn to *construe* our own perceptive power, while we *educe* into
distinct consciousness it's inexhaustible *constructive* energies.
Every Diagram is a Construction of *Space*: and what is Space, but
the universal antecedent Form and ground of all Seeing? Now
that *Space* belongs to the mind itself, i.e. that it is but a *way* of
contemplating objects, you may easily convince yourself by trying
to imagine an outward space. You will immediately find that you
imagine a space for *that* Space to exist in—in other words, that you
turn this first space into a *thing* in space: or if you could succeed in
abstracting from all thought of Color and Substance, & then shut-
ting your eyes try to imagine it—it will be a mere Diagram, and no
longer a construction *in* space but a construction *of* Space.—Not
less certain and even more evident, is this position, in it's applica-
tion to *words* and language—to Grammar, Logic, Rhetoric, or the
Art of Composition. For (as I have long ago observed to you) it is
the fundamental Mistake of Grammarians and Writers on the
philosophy of Grammar and Language [to assume] that words and
their syntaxis are the immediate representatives of *Things*, or that
they correspond to *Things*. Words correspond to Thoughts; and
the legitimate Order & Connection of words to the *Laws* of Think-
ing and to the acts and affections of the Thinker's mind.

In addition to the universal grounds on which I might rest the
immense superiority of this method—i.e. Instruction by *insight*,
and by the reduction of all Rules to their sources in the mind itself—
over the ordinary plan (for *method that* cannot be called, in which
there is no μέθοδος, no intelligible guiding principle of Transition
and Progress) I recommend it to *you* as the most efficacious corro-
borant of the active Memory and the best Substitute for any de-
fect or deficiency of the passive Memory.—Let us indulge our fancy
for a moment and suppose that you or I or Sir Humphry Davy had
discovered an easy and ready way of decomposing, rapidly and on

a great scale, the Water of the Sea into it's component Elements of Oxygen and Hydrogen, with a portion of Carbonic gas: so as to procure by an extemporaneous process a Fuel to any desirable extent, capable of boiling the undecompounded Water—How poor a thing would the most capacious Hold that ever Steam-Frigate could boast of, and the most abundantly stocked with Wood or Coal, and with the largest reservoirs to boot established at different Points, which the Vessel might stop at in the course of the Voyage from London to Bombay or Van Dieman's Land—how poor an affair would it all be, compared with the facilities given us by this discovery! The only danger would be, that the Colliers, Pitmen and Coal Merchants might waylay the Discoverer, and cut his throat.—Now, my dear James! not much unlike this is the difference between the reproductive power consequent on the full, clear and distinct Comprehension of PRINCIPLES, and a familiar acquaintance with the Rules of Involution and Evolution of Particulars in Generals, and the memory that results spontaneously from the impressions left on the Brain & Senses, and may be destroyed by a fit of Sickness, or be suspended at the very moment, you want it, by a Flutter or a dyspeptic Qualm, in favor of the former. In this Memory, to which we trust whatever we learn by rote and all insulated knowleges, seen each for itself without it's relations and dependencies, the recollections stick together like the Dots in Frog-spawn by accidents of Place, Time, and Circumstance (Vide Essays on Method, FRIEND, Vol. III: Essay the First) or like the eggs in a Caterpillar's Web, by threads of capricious and arbitrary Associations. At the best, the several knowleges are in the Mind as in a Lumber-garret: while *Principles* with the Laws, by which they are unfolded into their consequences, when they are once thoroughly mastered, become the mind itself and are living and constituent parts of it. We know what we want: and what we want, we reproduce—just as a neat-fingered Girl reconstructs the various figures on a Cat cradle. That this is no mere fancy, you have a proof in my own instance. In the gifts of passive or spontaneous Memory I am singularly deficient. Even of my own Poems I should be at a loss to repeat fifty lines. But then I make a point of speaking only on subjects, I understand on *principle* and *with insight*: and on these I set my Logic-engine and spinning jennies a going, and my friends, I suspect, more often complain of a superabundant, than of a deficient, supply of the Article in requisition.

To exemplify this method of instruction by applying it to the principal points of an academic or classical Education—and in the first instance, to the analysis (= parsing), hermeneusis (= construing) and synthesis (= composition) of the Learned Languages—the Greek in comparison and collation with our Mother Tongue affords, I think, the greatest facilities.—The Latin, at all events, is least suited to the experiment—both as being only a very scanty Dialect of the oldest and rudest Greek, and the derivation of it's significant prefixes and affixes (or cases and tenses) requiring all the arts of the veteran Etymologist, τὰς γραμμάτων καὶ συλλαβῶν μεταμορφώσεις.—Accordingly, with the Greek I have already begun with you, tho' but in a fragmentary way hitherto, and rather for the purpose of breaking down the *chevaux de frize*, which the *newness* & strangeness of the Subject throws round it, than in the expectation of leaving any distinct impression of the particular truths. For there is a state of mind the direct opposite to that which takes place in making an Irish *Bull*. Miss Edgeworth has published a long Essay on *Bulls*—without understanding the precise meaning of the word which she makes synonimous with *Blunders*. But tho' all Bulls are Blunders, every Blunder is not a Bull. In a Bull there is always a *sensation* without a *sense* of connection between two incompatible thoughts.—The thoughts being incompatible, there cannot of course be any *sense* of—i.e. insight into—their connection or compatibility. But a *sensation*, a *feeling*, as if there was a connection, may exist, from various causes: as when for instance, the right order of the Thoughts would be thus— a b c d e f, of which *b* and *e* are incompatible ideas, tho' b is in just connection with c, c with d, and d with *e*—Now if from any heat & hurry of mind and temper such an extreme and undue vividness is given to b and e, as to bedim and practically extinguish the consciousness of (or distract the attention from) c and d, in this case b and e will appear next door neighbors, while the actual, tho' unconscious intervention of c and d, produces a *sensation* of the connection—just as in forgetting a name that was quite familiar to you—you have a *feeling* of remembering it, tho' the recollection is suspended.—Read this over till you understand it.—Now the opposite of this [stat]e is when we have the sense of the connection between any given series of Thoughts, but from their entire strangeness to the mind not the wonted, & therefore craved for, sensation. You understand them, & yet have the feeling of not understanding. The philosophy of the dead Languages I propose therefore to recommence systematically with you, beginning with the Greek Alphabet—then to the significant sounds or elementary *positions*, the Helms & Rudders of words, rather than *words*—and then to the different sorts of words. But for my present purpose, viz. of helping you to write Latin, I shall suppose all this done—& begin by pointing out the characteristic difference between Latin

Sentences & English—& from this deduce the Rules & the Helps—
This I defer to the next Post but one.—God bless you &
S. T. Coleridge.

P.S. Your Mama has not got over the *shock* of this Morning's
Letters[1]—for Mr Stanley wrote a very kind & considerate Letter
to me. What *might* have been the result keeps your mama's imagi-
nation & feelings at work. She thanks you for your letter—& sends
her kind love, & will write tomorrow or next day.—Till this shock,
your Mama's Health & Looks had improved far beyond what I had
dared anticipate—Susan Steele seems Hygeia herself—& I am
pretty well, all but——

1559. *To James Gillman, Jr.*

[Addressed by Mrs. Gillman] Mr J. Gillman, Junr | Mr Ingram's | Coleman
Street | Cheapside
MS. New York Public Lib. Hitherto unpublished.

Tuesday
24 Octr 1826.—

My dear James

In all languages there are some ἡμιρήματα or semi-vocables that
exist only as attachments to words; and some ῥημάτια, that often
occur as attachments but likewise as entire words. The function of
both is the same—to express, namely, the postures and accidents of
Words, whether they represent Things and Persons, or Acts, in
time, place, dignity (i.e. Subject or Object), & other relations, if
other there be. I comprize them under the common term, Positions:
that may or may not be found (in the same language) as conjunc-
tions, prepositions, pronouns or numerals.—And I say, that the
characteristic Difference of Languages consists in the *comparative*
number of such attachable Positions; and in the comparatively
greater or smaller number of those that are not detachable.—This
then is our first Principle.—

PRINCIPLE. The characteristic difference of the Latin as com-
pared with the English Language consists in the greater number
and more frequent occurrence of Positions; and of these again, in
the greater number of such as exist only in attachment.

One consequence is obvious—a diminished necessity for the gram-
matical Sequence of the words in order to their intelligibility.—
N.B. The grammatical disposition is (the Scholastic Logicians

---

[1] An entry in one of Coleridge's notebooks shows that Gillman was thrown
from his gig on Friday, 13 Oct. 1826. See also postscript to Letter 1560.

would tell you) '*the universal*' order of words in their syntaxis: to which you might very naturally reply—What the grammatical position is, I know tolerably well; but *a universal* order—*that* is satis noti per ignotius Obscuratio, to my humble apprehension. And truly, the term, universal, is not the happiest that could be chosen—but with regard to the Latin and Greek, it means that order, in which the words of a sentence would follow, independent of any change produced by the order in the mind, as affected by the comparative emphasis and interest of this or that thought, by connection with other sentences, retrospectively or prospectively, preceding or following, &c &c—in short, it is the order which the words follow, when either the paramount obligation of perspicuity does not permit, or the Interests of Logic or of Rhetoric do not require or suggest, any other. Perhaps, the best name would be the *indifferent* order of the words—tho' it may not be amiss to add, that 'universal' in it's technical use means that which is common to all sentences alike if you abstract from all the modifications which particular motives and purposes may give rise to in any & every particular sentence.

And here let me digress for a few lines, by way of meeting or anticipating a thought or feeling which both my Conversation generally and these letters in particular are calculated to excite in your mind.—Southey once observed to me—I (said he) hunt by the eye, like a Grey-hound. I see what my Object is: and dash in a strait line towards it. But you hunt with your nose to the earth: track the Prey thro' every bend & zigzag, in and out thro' the whole maze of Puss' or Renyard's Feet—and at the end what do you catch?—Why, the *Scent*, perhaps, of the Hare or Vermin which I had killed an hour before, after a five minutes' Run.—The Man, I replied, that plays at Tennis, *gets* nothing [at] all but the Tennis Ball, he brought with him—& that, perhaps, has flown over the wall—but he is well content if he acquires health, long breath, quick eye, and elastic muscles. It is a mistake to suppose, that the *end* is in all cases higher than the *means*: or that the *means* always derive their whole, or even their chief, value from the *end*. Strict integrity with courteous manners and charity in act and speech are the surest *means* to the regard and good opinion of our Acquaintances; but of ditch clay inspirited by the Soul of a Scotch Pawnbroker must *He* have been made, who values the former merely on account of the latter, or who can even put the *end* in this case on a level with the *means*.—

And so it is, my dear James! in the present instance. It is my object to put you in the way of writing good Latin, and for this purpose to make you understand the characteristic elements of the Language. But I want you so to understand these as at the same time to understand your own Understanding—to cultivate in you the power and the habit of forming not only clear but *distinct* conceptions on whatever subject, you may be required to study. In short, I would fain mechanize your mind into a Kaleidoscope, which shall secure a *symmetry* to all sorts of objects placed within the field of vision, in an endless variety of forms.—Shift the things to be looked at, as choice or chance may dictate, the result is sure to be symmetrical: for this excellence belongs to the kaleidoscope itself, and is communicated to the subject-matters, not received *from* them. And be assured that the time will come, when the particular knowleges themselves taken separately from the forms, in which the mind arranges them, the mere cognoscenda seorsim a principiis cognoscendi, will appear to you of not much greater comparative Value, than the fragments of glass, snips of silk, beads, spangles &c when removed from the drawer (or whatever it is called) of the kaleidoscope compared with the consummate beauty of the Patterns that are created out of them by applying the magic Instrument. Had I been the inventor, I would have named the kaleidoscope (a sound to conjure imps by!) the Talisman of Beauty—and it is the business of Education to render the human mind the Talisman of Truth and intellectual Symmetry and thus make it cognizant of it's own immortality—teaching it to call forth from the pipe of sycamore or viler hemlock-stem, the ram's horn, or the sea-drifted Tortoise-shell (*Testudo*) sounds that betray the Exile God, the Apollo tending the Herds of Admetus.—But to descend from the poetic to the sober element of prose, like the Sky-larks, from the purple Clouds to the Corn field—I have especially in view—one object indispensable to free and comprehensive Thinking—the accustoming you to *generalize* your knowleges, by reducing them to more and more comprehensive expressions, or (what the Mathematicians call) higher and higher *formulae*. But in order to this, or as the first round in this Logic-ladder, you must acquire a readiness in defining the terms, you employ—this being the only way, quo scias, te scire—the only way, by which you can know *what* it is that you know.—Definitions differ according to the Subjects and Purposes. They may be either *constitutive*, as all legitimate mathematical Definitions ought to be: and inasmuch as they supply the ground and condition of the reasoning (on which account they are likewise called *hypothetical*, or fundamental—*sub-positae*) they are of necessity antecedent. Ex.—A Circle is the Figure formed by the circumvolution of a strait line fixed at one end.—Thus is a circle constituted.—

Or they are simply *diagnostic*. Ex. A circle is a figure, having all the lines from the center to the circumference equal.—This enables you to *distinguish* a circle from all other figures; but it is only *one* of the numberless properties of the Circle, and therefore, tho' adopted by Euclid, it is not a legitimate *geometrical* Definition. Again. Definitions are either synthetic or analytic: Synthetic, when they *increase the quantity* of your knowlege: analytic, when they only *improve it's quality*. Examp. of the *analytic*: The Atmosphere is the Substance that surrounds the earth and is the sphere in and by which animals breathe. Here nothing is said which you did not know before; but yet it may bring that knowlege more distinctly into *consciousness*—et te, quod sciebas, tibi *conscire* facit. *Ex. of Synthetic Def.* The atmospheric Air is a mixture, or (as some believe) a lax combination, of an inhalable Gas capable of supporting flame, and named Oxygen, with a Gas in which Bodies can neither breathe nor burn, and entitled Nitrogen: the latter being to the former in the proportion of 4 in 5.—Dissolved, interfused, or floating in these is a variable quantity of aqueous vapor, in different states of rarefaction and condensation according to the variation of the temperature, from height, electricity, &c.— The total aqueo gaseous Mass, extending to about 40 miles from the surface of the Planet, is called the Earth's Atmosphere.— *Here* you have the quantity of your knowlege increased by learning the component parts of that, which you previously knew only as a whole or in the *Result*. The Definition is σὺν θετικόν,[1] com-*positive*.—

Thirdly—Definitions are either presum[p]tive or deductive. This, however, (with exception of mere verbal explanations) belongs rather to Rhetoric than to Logic: since in strict truth, mathematical or constitutive definitions alone are by right *antecedent*: and tho', to smooth the way for our being understood, we may begin by defining our terms, yet such definition is either anticipative, asserting beforehand what it is the purpose of the Essay to prove: or it has been deduced from former reasoning and assumed as already proved. In geometry the Definition *makes* the thing; it's existence is contained in the definition. The Circle in the diagram is only a picture or *remembrancer* of the Circle, on which the mathematician is reasoning. In all other studies, the Definition only *tells* and *compacts* or *compresses*, what had been already *shewn* or *found* by the Definer.—Lastly,—definitions are either general or specific —i.e. declares either the essential characters common to several species, or gives the specific character of some one in particular. For instance.—Things out of their right place, is a general definition, comprizing the three sorts or species—*Litter, Dirt*, and *Filth*.

---

[1] Greek words underlined once in MS.

Litter is whatever is out of it's proper place, which can be removed without danger of leaving any portion of it behind, or on the instrument with which it is removed.—Instead of '*can be*' read 'can *not* be': and you have the definition of *Dirt*—and if to this you add 'offensive to the Senses', you have the specific definition of Filth.—Filth is any thing out of it's right place & offensive to the Senses, which cannot be removed &c—. *Assa* Fetida is very offensive to the Senses: and a bit of it might be on the parlour mantle-piece instead of it's Drawer in the Surgery—and you might complain of it—but you would not call it *Filth*—Nor would any but a Cockney or a fine Lady or fine Lady's still finer maid call the Dung strewed on the field or pitted in the Farm-yard *Filth*.— Now I will readily agree with you, my dear James! that by these definitions (by the bye, *Litter* supposes a *plurality*, and is always a nomen *collectivum*, which ought to have been expressed in my definition) I have added little or nothing to your practical knowlege of Litter, Dirt and Filth; but you, I think, will likewise agree with me, that they must contribute somewhat to a greater decision and steadiness in the application of the words, and give a confidence and sense of security in the preference of one or the other. And if in a stage-coach or steam-packet there had been a dispute on the precise meaning of the three words, and the two disputants having appealed to [a] third person (likewise a Stranger to you) he had without any pomp or Johnsonian mouthing quietly given the preceding definitions—as the way in which he had been accustomed to desynonimize the words in question—you would have been impressed with his being a man *above the common*, and would be disposed to pay attention to any thing, he might say afterwards. And believe me, this is no trifling advantage to a man, in any one of the professions or the higher departments of Trade & Commerce.— And that I may knit on this long digression to our original subject, tho' you knew what the thing meant by 'grammatical order' was, that is not all that it [will] be well to know. Such or such words mean such a thing—Right! but what does *the Thing* mean? Of late years, our Newspaper-writers in recording a thunder-storm or a high wind, scorn to employ any less scientific words than 'the electrical fluid—the elastic Fluid'.—Pray, Papa! (might little Miss say) what is the electrical Fluid?—Lightning, my dear!—Aye, Father! (might her Brother rejoin) and what is Lightning?—And the sensible Lad would not find his question answered to his mind, tho' his Sister should exclaim—Why, that which we saw the night before last, to be sure! What a silly question, William! Who does not know what Lightning is? *Who* does not? Why, *you*—Miss Pert!—I know that the *word*, Lightning, means that which we saw the night before last; but I want my Father to tell me in other words, what *that* is.—

And now to return—for good & all. Our first Principle was—that the characteristic differences of the Latin from the English consist and rise out of, the greater number of it's syllabic attachments, generally; and of such as are found only in attachment, especially.

The first and obvious consequence is, that the necessity of arranging the words of a sentence in the grammatical sequence or order of syntax far less frequently stands in the way of the writer's arranging his words in the order of the corresponding thoughts and feelings, and likewise of placing them so as to express the connection of the sentence either with the preceding or the following, in respect of the dependency or of the similarity of the thoughts. Consequently, it enables the Writer to render his language more impassioned, more expressive of continuity, dependency, retrospection and anticipation by a closer approach to the logical, psychological, and sentimental order of the thoughts and feelings, which by means of words he wishes to transfer or (as it were) *copy off*, from his own mind to the minds of his Readers. It enables him, in short, to give a greater liveliness and Symmetry in the composition of his periods and paragraphs; and to communicate to eloquence some of the finest properties of Music, as described by me in the FRIEND, in the introduction to the Essay on the characters of Voltaire and Erasmus, Luther and Rousseau.—[1]

Secondly: as these semi-vocables or POSITIONS (See p. 1. l[ine] 8. of this Letter) have the force of, and where they do not exist in a Language must be supplied by, Conjunctions and Prepositions—the far greater number, at least—it follows almost of necessity, that what in the one Language (the Latin, for instance) may be expressed in a single and simple Sentence, must in the other (ex. gr. the English) be broken up into several sentences, parenthetically interwove—which will be the case, when the Latin *Position* has the force of a *Conjunction*. And even when it has the force of a preposition, or of a Pronoun, or of an auxiliary Verb, still the substitution of these for the Position cannot fail to give the latter Language, in comparison with the former, a more *friable* and fragmentary character, & to cumber it, as in English, with monosyllabic and unemphatic words. Add to this too, that the Latin, which requires fewer parenthetic sentences than the English, can nevertheless introduce them with far less risk of interrupting the sense or of rendering it obscure or doubtful: as at whatever distance the agreeing words may be, the Positions or semi-vocables of Case,

[1] See *The Friend*, 1818, i. 215.

Tense, Number, Gender &c, will shew the agreement and the grammatical syntaxis.—(In deriving the contra-distinguishing points of the Latin from this Principle as from their main source, I do not mean to deny, that several other causes, the surly, soldierly, lordly, patrician, magistratual and legislatorial character of the Romans, co-operate with the original poverty of the Latin Language itself in giving a sort of *memorandum* character to their prose— whence the Latin is eminently suited to Satires, moral sentences, Points, aphorisms & the like. Hence, Juvenal, Persius, Martial, Lucan, Sallust, Seneca, and Tacitus, are characteristically *Latin* Writers & Thinkers—but for that reason all more or less *Mannerists*. But in it's kind it was the *Manner* of Rome.)—

On the other hand, the Latin Language in proportion to the quantum of it's difference from the English, as produced by the original structure of the words, has one disadvantage—or what is occasionally such—It is this: that in most instances you must have heard the whole sentence before you can ascertain the sense of any part—the last word or words being necessary to determine the meaning of all the foregoing. Among the modern Languages the German is the nearest to the Latin in this respect: and hence neither the German nor the Latin suit well for Comedy or works of light wit and colloquial rapidity and interchange of thought.—

And now for the application of this Principle with it's *general* Consequences. Read a page of Cicero thoughtfully, sentence by sentence, rendering it word by word in English, in the exact order in which they stand in the Latin. Then observe whether it makes English; such as Hooker, Milton, Jer. Taylor write—tho' not such as the style, introduced since the Revolution in 1688, might require—or such as even now would be admitted. But wherever the Latin order of the words would make *no* intelligible sense, or would be at best obscure & uncouth—take a *note* of this, and add the *cause* of it, as resulting from the different genius of the two Languages. I am persuaded, that twenty such Notes would exhaust all the points of difference: and that by keeping the Sheet of Paper containing these notes, reduced to some convenient order, as a sort of Map, before you, you would soon become familiar with all the changes, which it would be necessary or *classical* to make, in turning English into Latin: & vice versâ, but with still more ease, in translating Latin into English.—The only Work of Cicero's, I can procure at Ramsgate, is the De officiis—and while I am here, I will devote half an hour daily to the reading of a page or two, and extracting some one or other instance, illustrating or exemplifying the general rule in detail—under the two main heads—I. the sequence of the words: and II. the conversion of one Latin Sentence

into two or more sentences in English.—But I would have you try
your own hand, in the mean time—and especially to note in Mel-
moth's Translation the places in which two or three sentences are
required to *English* one in Latin: and to refer this to the causes in
the significant terminations & more interlinking property of the
Latin Words.—

And now God bless you, my dear Jam[es.] I am anxious to hear,
how your Father goes on—esp[ecially] whether the bruise on the
Elbow has produced any distressing sensations or symptoms in
his arm—& whether he suffers from the Paint.—The weather is
close & gloomy & muzzy; but your Mama keeps well, tho' her
progress is certainly somewhat dragged by the suspension of her
Donkey Rides and Drives, and breezy Pier & Cliff Ambulations.—
I am tolerable all day; but have bad nights, owing to the local irri-
tation, I have so long labored under—

Susan desires to be kindly remembered to you—and I remain,
with little less than paternal love & solicitude,

my dear James, | your affectionate Friend
S. T. Coleridge

1560. *To Edward Coleridge*

Address: Revd. E. Coleridge | College | Eton | Bucks
MS. Pierpont Morgan Lib. Pub. E. L. G. ii. 386.
Postmark: 27 October 1826. *Stamped*: Ramsgate.

8 Waterloo Plains.
Ramsgate: Thursday Afternoon, 25 [26] Octr 1826.

My very dear Edward

With no other or longer delay than till the receipt of an answer
to a letter to Highgate, which will be put into the Letter Box to-
gether with this, Henry Gillman will be taken away according to
your advice—or rather, for the propriety of the measure does not
admit of a doubt, in resignation to the plain necessity of the case.
There is nothing more to be said except what a knowlege of Mr &
Mrs Gillman's minds & principles would render superfluous—the
assurance of their deep sense that every thing has been done by you
that *could* be done, and more than with every disposition to rely on
your kindness they had ventured to anticipate—that their grati-
tude is proportionate; and they will withdraw their Boy with
indelible impressions of affectionate esteem and respect for his
(alas! fruitlessly) anxious Tutor.—My advice to my 'more than
friend' Gillman is that his Brother James, a Youth of excellent
principles and now the Head Boy at Merchant Taylors', should go

off to Eton on Saturday, if possible, or on Monday—take Henry
with him to the House, in which he himself boards, and put him on
board the Ramsgate Steam Boat—and that here he should be
immediately placed under the care of a School-master with whom,
& with whose plans, regime, &c I am more than usually well-pleased
—as likewise with his Wife.—

Alas! Mrs Gillman! If ever Mother deserved a different result,
she has deserved it!—What has not been done or attempted for
this Boy!—I do not recollect in the whole retrospect of my ex-
perience a child who has enjoyed such a conflux of favorable
Circumstances, moral and intellectual—systematic undeviating
good example, & indefatigable Watchfulness!—

In the New Testament I have observed that wherever *the Father*
is spoken of, not as inclusive of the Word and the Spirit, or as
synonimous with the Godhead but *distinctively*, the WILL, as the
source of Being, and therefore in the order of thought antecedent to
Being itself (Causa Sui) is meant—And not a week passes, in which
some incident or other does not recall to my mind our Saviour's
words—No man cometh to me unless *the* FATHER leadeth him. In
vain the informing Reason, in vain the inspiring Life, the fecun-
dating Love, if there be not that germ in the *will*, which *is* the
Individual in his essential individuality, which is deeper than all
understanding—& till it have been stirred and actualized by that
ineffable *Will*, which is the mysterious Ground of all things visible
and invisible.—O what affecting lessons does not a School-master's
experience afford, for the right appreciation of all that can be
given from without, of all that man can do for Man!—

But I shall write to you again, before long—and shall run the
risk of losing the Post if I do not subscribe myself, with affectionate
respects to Mrs E. Coleridge   your's most sincerely,

S. T. Coleridge.—

P.S. We have all our little superstitions. Mrs Gillman's Mind was
so impressed with the fancy, strong in spite of her excellent under-
standing, that (to use her own words) the ill-luck of the year is sure
to come when she is away, that, reduced as she was, and necessary
as the change of air had become for her, Mr Gillman was obliged
almost to scold her away, before she [cou]ld make up her mind to
leave home.—And true enough (as the old folks say) on the day
but one after we left Highgate, Mr Gillman was thrown with vio-
lence out of his Gig, as he was driving down Highgate Hill—the
Horse having stumbled & the Shafts of the Gig breaking. God be
praised! the damage has not been serious—a bruised Elbow &c—but
what it might have been!—and now this woful account of Henry!—

1561. *To Edward Coleridge*

Address: The Revd. Edward Coleridge | College | Eton
MS. Pierpont Morgan Lib. Pub. E. L. G. ii. 388.
Postmark: 30 October 1826. *Stamped*: Ramsgate.

8. Waterloo Plains, Ramsgate.—
Saturday Morning
28 Octr 1826

My dear Edward

I inclosed your kind tho' afflicting letter to my Friend, to whom & to whose Wife you do but justice when you describe them as little Gillman's '*excellent* Parents'. If strict integrity, disinterested friendship, native generosity of mind, an instinctive antipathy to the mean and circuitous, and lastly, a keen sensibility to excellence in others, establish a right to the title of excellent, an experience of ten years, such and under such circumstances as render ten years more than equivalent to a Life of ordinary Acquaintance-ship, justifies me in claiming that name for Mr Gillman. I have this moment received his answer, in a few lines which the contusion in his arm by his late accident from that projectile engine yclept, a Gig, evidently made it a painful effort to shape in a legible fashion—without taking in the agitation of his spirits, and *the stunning* proposition, which he was called on to decide. For his time and attention, all at least of both that he could spare from his professional duties, had for the last four or five months been so engrossed, first by the languid and lifeless state of *my* health; then by the gross misconduct and sullen ungracious demeanor of his 'articled Student' as Surgeons' Apprentices are now by law new-christened; then by the alarming decline of Mrs Gillman's strength, whose loss, I am persuaded, he would not long survive; and lastly, by a House (the repairs of which from the way-wardness of that old Bashaw, General Fit[z]roy, in withholding the terms of the new leases of the Houses in the Grove to the last hour almost, had become perilously necessary) filled with a succession of Masons, Carpenters, and Painters under Mr Gillman's own superintendence— by which means, however, he has done it for less than half the expence, it would have cost another man—in consequence, I say, of this Confluence of anxieties & occupations, his thoughts had beyond his Wont been so much drawn off from Henry, (No news having, from these causes, the effect of good news) that your letter took him as by surprize—and to transcribe his own words—'the *Stun* of the Tidings' incapacitated him for the exertion of mind and will, which they so imperiously demanded. 'I have (he continues) such a sinking within me, and—owing in part, no doubt, to the well-known effects of Bruises on the nervous system—such a feeling of weakness & despondency, that I dare not rely on my own judgement—and therefore intreat you, my dear Coleridge, to judge and act for me. It is a heavy Blow! But if only he can be made fit to gain his bread as an honest man, I ought to be content—& with your friendly support I hope that I shall be able to say with sincerity, God's will be done!'

I am aware, my dear Edward! that I am writing a gloomy letter —But you in all human probability will be a Father yourself: and independent of all anticipated feelings, you are too good [a] man even to wish to be exempted from a portion of the pain, which this extinction of a Father's and Mother's hopes cannot but inflict. As far as circumstances went, as far as the scheme can be abstracted from the character and capacity of the Subject of it, I cannot wonder that the Hope was fondly cherished. Their joint attachment to *me* personally, and only too high estimation of my powers and principles, and of my heart even more than of my intellect, were the basis—and with such sentiments and persuasions it was natural, that they should feel an interest, and have a sort of affectionate pride in having a child, who had grown up under *my* eye & had been taught to look up to me as to [a] second Father, pass under the patronage and protection of so near a relation of mine, and of the same name—. In addition to this, came their unfeigned and lively admiration of you, and the impression—and on the part of the Mother naturally a more vivid tho' not perhaps stronger impression, which your address, person, and cordial frankness made on them—endeared and as it were sealed by their knowlege of your affectionate Attentions to me. Then the special advantages, that the Boy (had he proved receptive of them) would have enjoyed during his vacations, by the efforts, I should have made, to sustain his school acquirements, and to *inseminate* his intellect during the latter period of his residence at Eton & while he was at the university. Lastly, you are too well aware, how much our family (with the single exception of myself occasioned by my Father's sudden Death) owe to your Grandmother's maternal ambition, to condemn the same aspirations, the same forward-looking schemes and wishes in Mrs Gillman. In whatever relationship these may stand to Self-love, it is impossible not to regard as more than venial an unconscious Selfishness which seeks it's gratification by every species of Self-denial, and by the enduring systematic sacrifice of all immediate Self. Therefore I say again, you cannot wonder that such hopes are not resigned without a bitter pang—or that for the time this pang is rather exasperated than alleviated by her insight into the necessity of the measure, by her full and cloudless conviction, that *you* have done all, that the Boy's kindest & most anxious Friend could do; and by the fact, that Mrs Gillman is too good a woman, and tho' a plain *un-high-flying* Church of England Christian, too pious, *practically* to hesitate between *any* outward & circumstantial advantage, literary attainment or future rank, and the risk of her child's moral and spiritual Well-being.—

I am myself in certain moments under the temptation of fancying, that Misfortune and the Sojourn at Ramsgate are inter-linked. Scarcely at any former time of our last four or five *maritimations* had Mrs Gillman's Health so urgently required the Sea Air, Bathing, and Far niente: and never had the benefit been more manifest, and the improvement in her Looks, Strength &c so steadily progressive. If ever, on the one hand, I feel a stronger anger, a nearer approach to *dislike*, than either the age or the extenuating circumstances of the Boy would justify; or on the other hand, give way to the intruding wish, that one more Trial should be allowed him—it is when I cast my eye on the woeful change, which three days and nights have worked on the afflicted Mother's appearance. But God's will be done! Fortunately, her Sisters—both exemplary and Miss Lucy Harding a most amiable woman, & made for a Comforter, are here—& Miss Steele is as a Daughter.—

I have a half-finished Letter for you, on subjects of more general interest, which I shall fill up as soon as my mind is a little more at ease. May God bless you & your's! your affectionate Uncle & | Friend

S. T. Coleridge

P.S. James Gillman will wait on you, on his arrival at Eton: and any instructions, you may give him, he will gratefully receive.—

1562. *To Edward Coleridge*

Address: The Revd. Edward Coleridge, | the College | Eton | Bucks.
MS. Pierpont Morgan Lib. Hitherto unpublished.
Postmark: 20 November 1826. *Stamped*: Ramsgate.

[19 November 1826]

My dear Nephew

After so long and for this place so unusually long a Spell of raw dull gloomy weather it is quite a relief to hear the Wind as now growling, roaring and working itself up into a passion. We are in the onset of a hard Gale, by landsmen yclept a Storm.—What with this shock of Henry Gillman's Removal, and what with the effect of a most melancholy Letter from Mrs S. Coleridge from Keswick respecting my poor First-born[1]—Lacrymae gemitusque precum mearum, and the sick anguish of my silence—I could repeat with more than the first feeling the beginning of my Ode on Dejection—

> Those Sounds which oft have rais'd me while they aw'd,
> > And sent my Soul abroad—
> May now perchance their wonted influence give,
> May startle this dull pain and make it move and live![2]—

And I am grieved to add, that the following Stanza is but too exact a delineation of Mrs Gillman's State of mind and spirits during the last three weeks. Alas! and she had been so rapidly and evidently improving in her Looks and Sensations, in strength and general health—but God's will be done!

I had no anticipation, that Henry would have been so deeply shaken by the event. For the first three nights he had scarcely any sleep—and in his broken sleep he was heard talking, & woke with a scream—At length the agitation of his mind brought on a fever, from which by help of febrifuge medicines, blisters and starving he is now recovering.—After all had been settled between Mrs G. & Mr & Mrs Whitehead, Mrs G. received a letter from Mr Whitehead, who had been confined for two or three days by indisposition, intreating her to release him from his engagement. The impression had become so strong on his mind of the moral corruption that was likely to be imparted by any boy fresh from Eton, that tho' he gave full credit to my assurances as to my own convictions of the uncorrupted state of the Boy's Morals, yet he was responsible to the Parents of nearly a hundred children—& any risk was too great a risk—This seemed to give a new shock to the Boy—& for the first time, I have seemed to observe something like serious reflection mingled with his emotions. It occasioned, however, a relapse of the Fever.—

I have, of course, been a good deal with him, since his removal hither, and have neither observed nor been able to detect, any sign or symptom of positive Taint in his Principles or Imagination— nor yet any the least disposition to shuffle—Idle, wilful, egregiously

---

[1] Coleridge's wretchedness of mind was occasioned by Hartley's irresponsible conduct after the failure of the boarding-school at Ambleside in the autumn of 1825. (See note to Letter 1519.) Released from the restraint imposed on him during his three years as a schoolmaster, Hartley was now cast adrift. Prone to alcoholic indulgence, he soon reverted to his old habits of procrastination and irregularity. From time to time he made fitful efforts to gain a livelihood by his pen, but he was too unsteady to earn a regular income, and upon Mrs. Coleridge had already fallen the burden of seeing that his bills were paid. [2] *Dejection: an Ode*, lines 17–20, *Poems*, i. 363.

unreflecting and irretentive of impression—these are *small-capital'd* in Block Letter on the very forehead of his Character. But whether his Unthinkingness have it's origin in defect of Sensibility, or his apparent Want of Heart result from Want of Sense, I cannot decide. One thing I have observed thro' the whole course of my experience, that the faculty of Sense (i.e. the due Equilibrium of the Objective and Subjective, and the almost instinctive power of referring each Object, that engages the Attention, to a correspondent Conception or generalization in the Subject, & vice versâ) is more than any other faculty of the mind connected with the developement of the Body. Now tho' the baptismal Register records Henry Gillman as 13, Nature makes him only ten. Yet he reads *uncommonly* well—and gets thro' any book that entertains him quicker than most boys. He read the four small Volumes of Lewellin Penrose's Journal (an excellent Book for Boys & Girls) in one day—and when I reproved him for skimming and skipping, he assured me, he had read every word, and surprized me by the clear and correct detail, he gave, of the contents. Yet scarce a day passes in which he does not exhibit some proof & instance of his utter want of SENSE. His refractory and ungracious behaviour to you puzzled me—especially when I found that he was fond of Eton & that his removal cut him to the very soul. (He is much in the habit, when any thing has agitated him, of talking loudly in his sleep: and one night (he sleeps next room to mine & with his door open) I heard him cry out piteously—And will nobody ask for me to stay? And a few minutes after in a low muttering voice—And there was nobody to beg for me!) But a few days after his arrival Miss Susan Steel repeated a conversation, she had with him that seems to throw some light on it—. Susan had asked him, how he could behave so 'to his good Tutor'—Henry muttered a sort of dissent from this Epithet—[to] which she replied, as surprized— Why, you used to say, you *loved* your Tutor. And so I do, he answered—I love him very much and he was very good, but he was not a good tutor to me—all the *fellows* said so—You may ask —— (I won't repeat names) if they did not think, that he was unfairly severe to me.—His Mother, I need not say, on hearing of this, pointed out to him the extreme folly of such a notion, and how grossly it was in contradiction to what he had himself told her of what both you and Mrs Edward Coleridge would have done for him if he had behaved well—as taking him out with you, &c &c—and asked him, how he could be such a fool as to expect that his Tutor was to begin first, that is, to reward him for being idle and impudent.—Doubtless, his Idleness and Wilfulness were Principals in the Baseness and gave double efficacy to this Ear-poison as well as ready admission—but all acting together, with his utter want of Sense, and Mr Bloxam too being absent, he had got into one of his moody fits—& found out his blunder too late.—The worst of all is that affair of the Drawing—As far as I could receive any thing like pleasure in the moment that I had received a Shock far beyond what your account of it had led me to anticipate, I *was* pleased with the straight forward way in which after some requests not to be asked, he told the whole truth, without attempting to palliate or disguise it.—How deep the poison may have penetrated—and how much of senseless daring there may have been in this worst of his misdemeanours, I know not, tho' most anxious to know. But I will say no more on this head—at least, till we meet.—The Handing it up to you was, he says, an ill-natured & treacherous act. I thank God, that it was handed up to you.—The seemingly insolent Reply he solemnly assures me was a mistake. He had muttered—that his Father would not *remove* him (i.e. to another School) but would bind him apprentice to some poor trade—and on your demanding to know what he had said, he was ashamed to say this aloud 'before all the fellows'.—

Mr Gillman informs me, that by advice of Mr Mence whose excellent friend, the Revd. Mr Bather[1] is a Trustee, he has resolved on sending him to the Free Grammar School at Shrewsbury under Dr Butler—and to the House of the Under-Master, Mr Iliff, late of Trinity, Cambridge, & a Christ's Hospital Man.—What a curious coincidence—Myself, Dr Keate, and Sam. Butler, the 3 Candidates for the Univ. Scholarship[2]—and then myself, Tenant, Leighton, & now Iliff, as the Boy's Assistant Tutors—. However, there must be a Letter or Testimonial, I find, from Dr Keate to Dr Butler, that the Boy had not been expelled; but had been removed by his Father on your opinion of his unfitness for Eton.—And now farewell to this subject. Will you be so good as to write a few lines to Mr Gillman on this subject—

I am sorry to say, that neither my body nor my state of spirits are at all in a desirable state. Mrs Gillman bids me express her earnest hopes that we may see you, should you and Mrs Edward be in town, during your Christmas Holidays—& assures you of her cordial & grateful Regards. We remain here to the end of the month.

God bless you & your's & S. T. C.

[1] Edward Bather (1779–1847), at this time vicar of Meole Brace, became archdeacon of Salop in 1828.

[2] In 1793 John Keate, Samuel Butler, Christopher Bethell, and Coleridge were 'declared equal' in the competition for the University Craven Scholarship. According to the terms of the bequest, therefore, the youngest, Samuel Butler, was awarded the scholarship. See Letters 23 and 24.

1563. *To James Gillman*

Address: James Gillman, Esqre | Grove | Highgate
MS. Harvard College Lib. Hitherto unpublished.

Monday—[20 November 1826]

My dear Friend

Henry suffered a Relapse on Thursday last, with smart attack of fever, oppression on the chest and dyspnoea. Mr Snowden blistered him (by the bye, he lets the Blister remain only from 20 minutes to half an hour) and he has now no other apparent Ailing but Weakness.—He walked out with his Mother, Susan and myself this morning, to the Sea Sands; but [we] were soon driven in by the menace and *spit*fulness of the South-West, which is at this moment grumbling and growling and working itself up to a Passion. There is good promise of a Hard Gale. But in fact, the Weather has been for the last ten days so raw, dull and cheerless, and has been such an Accomplice *post factum*, as the Lawyers say, with the Events that had struck gloom and dejection into us, that a noisy bustling Storm would be a Relief.

> Those sounds, which oft have rous'd me while they awed,
>   And sent my soul abroad
> Might now perchance their wonted influence give,
> Might startle this dull pain, and make it move & live!
>   Ode to Dejection—

The Lines, that follow these, are, I grieve to say, only too exact a delineation of Mrs Gillmans state of Mind and Spirits: and it is but a melancholy and equivocal comfort, that I have to offer in the comparison of her & your vexation from Henry's Idleness with my calamity & hopeless Heart-gnawing from the evil spirit that has taken possession of my eldest born.—

I have tried to sift Henry to the bottom; but I cannot detect any mark or symptom of moral deterioration. His School-fellows had persuaded him, that his Tutor was unfairly severe to him—and his Idleness, no doubt, aiding the operation of this ear-poison, he got into one of his wilful moods—and as Ill-luck would have it, his good Friend Mr Bloxam was absent. In the affair of the Drawing (done, as I had supposed, in bravado) he was behaved treacherously to—a most ill-starred Drawing for *him*—since but for this and one other sentence in my Nephew's Letter, to which this incident supplied the comment in my mind, I should have gone to Eton myself.—But I am willing to believe that all will prove for the best.—It has made a vehement impression on the Boy's mind:

and is calculated to make a lasting one. Mr Whitehead's refusal to take the charge of him affected him deeply—it has been his first lesson as to what a Loss of Character is.—Every thing, I can learn respecting Mr Whitehead's School, makes me regret Whitehead's determina[tion,] tho' I cannot blame him.—My only fear would have been, of it's being too much for the Boy—to rise 20 m. after 5, to be three hours before breakfast, and with but two or three hours for Play & Dinner, to be at work or attending at least, till 8 at night—But the Boys are healthy and apparently happy & in high spirits.—I intend calling on Whitehead this evening—not from any expectation of changing his purpose, as of learning his plan of [preventi]ng Idleness—

Henry puzzles me. It seems to me impossible that a Boy who can read so unusually well, can read thro' a Romance or Travel of two Volumes in a day & retain so much of it, should be deficient in intellect. He does not want Talent, certainly, and he is, I am persuaded, *negatively* innocent at least.—

I have nothing more to say—& indeed write now lest you should be surprized by my silence—We want to know, how your arm goes on—&c &c—

God bless you & your faithful Friend
S. T. Coleridge

1564. *To Edward Coleridge*

Transcript Coleridge family. Hitherto unpublished.

[Sunday, 26 November 1826]

My dear Nephew

I did not *expect* a letter from you on the account of my two last *Dull*-and-*dolefuls*; for I know, how little time you have at your free disposal, and there was nothing in either that seemed to require an answer. But yet wishing the comfort a few lines from Eton would have administered, I had that quantum of Hope, which finds a ventage in conjectural comments on the Postman's professional knock, ex. gr. 'I should not wonder if there were a letter from Edward'. But on Saturday (i.e. yester) morning, the day on which there is no Post *from* Ramsgate, Mrs Gillman received a letter from her Husband, evidently written in vexation of spirit—& announcing, first, that he had been & continued seriously distempered with the smell of paint—that James Gillman, who slept at Highgate only two nights, had been made ill & caught a white lead cough as well as his Father; & that we must stay here a week or ten days beyond the appointed time, before he can recommend our return;

(For myself I dared not venture: for the smell of paint is poison to me.) but secondly, & what was most on his mind, he had not received from Eton either Dr Keate's certificate or a line from you. You probably are better acquainted than I am with the usual form on such occasions; but what I understood from Mr Gillman's brief account of Mr Iliff's letter is that before Henry's name can be inscribed for admission to the Shrewsbury Free School, Dr Butler must have a certificate that he was not expelled from Eton, or chargeable with any crime, but removed by his Parents. If you have not written to Mr Gillman or sent the requisite assurance, let me entreat you as a favour to myself to do it by the first post.

I have sifted the Boy in every way that my Brain could suggest, & if there is anything *positively* bad or corrupt in him, it has completely eluded my search. His pursuits & modes of amusing himself, his passion for shells & minerals, his questions when he is reading, are all symptomatic of childishness & a child's indistinction of all things beyond a Boy of 11 years old. And poor Boy! it would be a black day indeed for him, when he was sent under such seemingly happy auspices to Eton, if a year's residence there should have branded a mark on his character that would punish him for Life & almost preclude all the means of making him as well as placing him out as a respectable man. But I can not imagine that any hesitation can be the occasion of your not having written to Mr Gillman. On the contrary, this would have produced the very contrary result. But I have really suffered so much of late by wretchedness of mind respecting Hartley & by sympathy with poor Mrs Gillman, that I have not strength to repel any gloomy thought, however improbable, that attempts an entrance into my ;ancy. I do not ask you to write to *me*—but hope that in a short time I may tempt you by a letter that may contain something worth commenting on. [Transcript breaks off thus.]

1565. *To Mr. Hunt*

Address: Mr Hunt
MS. Mr. Geoffrey Keynes. Pub. E. L. G. ii. 391.

[December 1826][1]

Dear Sir
    The Courier sent & now returned contains only the same debate, as I had before in the New Times—If there be a Thursday's

[1] Coleridge wrote 'Mr Hunt' in the address page of the MS. To this the following endorsement has been added: 'Bookseller of Ramsgate—1827'. A notebook entry of 9 Dec. 1826 indicates, however, that Coleridge was reading Bruce's *Travels* at Ramsgate in 1826. Since both the letter and the notebook

Morning Paper at liberty, you would oblige me by letting me have it
—and likewise, the 3 & 4th Vol. of Bruce[1]—a great and for a long time
most ungratefully calumniated Man—His remarks on Polygamy,
Vol. II. p. 178–185, are curious;[2] but if the facts are accurate,
still I would rather deem them the *effect* of Polygamy than believe
God by a law imposed on Nature the Author and Sanctioner of a
Practice, evidently & notoriously incompatible with the develope-
ment of our Moral Being—the source of such frightful depravity
and degeneracy.[3] 'It was not so from the beginning'—i.e. It does
not result from any necessity of God's making, but from hardness
of heart—ex. gr. predatory Wars, Murder of male Captives, sale
of the females—then (avarice prevailing over Blood-thirstiness)
sale of male & female—and that accursed Slave Trade which Bruce
likewise vindicates!! These, however, are but Specks in a Diamond.
—By the bye, the fact that Christianity in any genuine or ennob-
ling form exists only in the northern, or rather in the temperate
climates, and degenerates in proportion to the increase of Heat—
say from the 40 Deg. of N. L. to the Equator—is one of deep interest
for a reflecting mind— . . .[4]

1566. *To Mrs. Charles Aders*

MS. Cornell University Lib. Hitherto unpublished.

[Ramsgate, December 1826]

My dear Friend, and (by the privilege of silvery Locks and a
heart pure as burnished Silver, in defiance of Beauty and Genius
I dare add) beloved Sister!

As you have been the innocent occasion of getting me into a
Scrape, you must assist me, as far as words will go, in getting out

entry refer to the same pages in volume ii of Bruce's work, it seems likely that
they were written about the same time.

[1] James Bruce, *Travels to discover the Source of the Nile* . . ., 5 vols., 1790.
Coleridge had long been familiar with Bruce's work. See *Poems*, i. 119 n., and
J. L. Lowes, *The Road to Xanadu*, 1930, pp. 133–4, 162–3, 183, 187, 370–9, and
397–8.

[2] Coleridge refers to a later edition of Bruce's *Travels*. The passage on poly-
gamy will be found in i. 280–8 of the first edition of 1790.

[3] Coleridge's notebook entry of 9 Dec. 1826 may be cited here: 'The maze
& exquisite subtlety, and yet the probable dependance on moral *individual*
causes, of the disparity of male and female Births in different families. Suppose
Bruce's Statements, Vol II. p. 178–185, to be relied on, yet it is more likely
that they are the results of Polygamy, and not (as B. would have us believe)
it's natural occasion & justifying cause.' [MS. notebook, Huntington Library.]

[4] One-half of page three of MS. cut off.

of it.—For Sufferings, I have undergone since the first fortnight after we had left Highgate, what from sympathy with Mrs Gillman's anguish about Henry's sudden removal from Eton, at the somewhat more than request of his Tutor, my Nephew, and it's blighting effect on her health (which up to that time had been improving beyond my most sanguine hopes) and what from a withering Letter from Mrs Coleridge respecting my own First-born, have so depressed my spirits, and with the supererogatory aids of an erysipelatous inflammation of my left leg, a previous but latterly aggravated local irritation elsewhere, and a series of disturbed nights and convulsive dreams of terror, have so confused and bewildered my faculties, that I really have not the power of expressing myself intelligibly in any language but my own—and scarcely in *that*.— I must, however, try to put you in possession of the facts—as I understand them, and at first understood them.

When Madame von Predl was making the Chalk Portrait of my Face, and before it was quite finished, we were all anxious both to serve her, and to give her spirits—and in this feeling various possibilities and probabilities were talked of—especially, if my Portrait should be (as we then sanguinely hoped, it would be) generally admired, I did not doubt, that my Nephew & Mr Green would have *copies*. I was then informed that Mr Aders was so much pleased with the Likeness, as it then stood, that he had determine[d] to have one (for which, however, I was to give one or two sittings) on a larger scale and in oil—and the great superiority of Madame's Portraits in oil was strongly urged.—Hearing this, and to encourage Madame, I having first consulted Mr Gillman, told her that if the Portrait in Oil for Mr Aders was, what I did not doubt it would be, I felt confident that there would be two if not three Copies ordered —and then asked her on what terms she could make them—always supposing Mr Aders' to be done first, his order having already been given, before I had thought of the thing, and wholly without anticipation of or in reference to, these Copies thus conditionally talked of.—Her answer was, that if she had two or three, so that she could be working on one while the other was drying, she could do them for 15£ or Guineas (I forget which) apiece.—So Mr Gillman understood the matter: and so did Mrs Gillman. In proof of this, I distinctly remember the words that Mr Gillman used, when I asked his opinion—If the Portrait in Oil for Mr Aders should answer to what we expect, I would not mind giving 20 guineas, were it only for a Present for your Nephew. But we shall see how your Nephews like it—. So strongly was the *conditionality* of all this impressed on my mind, that tho' it grieved me, I was not surprized when Mrs Green speaking of Madame's great anxiety to succeed in the Oil

Portrait for Mr Aders and her dissatisfaction & difficulty in satis-
fying herself, told me, she had begun it over again three times—
and when I asked her what she thought of the Oil Portrait, she
answered doubtingly, that Madame had been still less successful
in the Mouth & Lips than in the Chalk.—Such was my impression
when I called with my Daughter—having been once there before
to have my Coat drawn—& I cannot describe to you the effect,
that the sight of the Pictures produced on me.[1] Tho' unwilling to
give pain & in fact unable to say all I thought, I however confessed
to Madame that I would not give the Chalk Drawing with all it's
imperfections for a dozen of the oil portraits. To prevent all pre-
possession & prejudice, I did not say a word to my Daughter of my
disappointment—and never shall I forget the tone & look, with
which on Madame's quitting the room the moment after she had
received us, with which my Daughter exclaimed—Dear Father!
pray, do not ask me before Madame how I like these Portraits!—
I was glad to find that she admired Mr Green's—(whom, you know,
I to serve Madame had solicited to sit, and for the first time in my
life humbled myself to say to him—Dear Friend! I wish to put
something in this Lady's pocket, and I should like to have a
Portrait of you over my fire-place.[2] Make me this *present*. For you
know, I have not the money myself.)—& still more her Rafaelesque
Pictures—& I went home scheming, what I should do, when my
Nephew came to town—whether to ask Madame to let me sit
again in some other view—still possessed with the notion, that a
really fine Portrait of myself might be the means and introduction
to Madame's future success. For she must have known, and in fact
Mrs Gillman repeatedly told her, that this was the only way in
which I *could* serve her—for that in all but my friends I was more
penniless than herself. I remember that two or three things were
said when I was there with my Daughter, which I did not under-
stand—but Madame's Deafness & mode of pronouncing German
and my own difficulty in understanding German except when

---

[1] See Letter 1535. Neither of these portraits has come to light.

[2] In his edition of Crabb Robinson's *Diary*, Thomas Sadler quotes the fol-
lowing comment signed 'G. S.', i.e. Sir George Scharf (1820–95), director of the
National Portrait Gallery: 'His [Green's] portrait hung over the chimney-piece
in Coleridge's bedroom at Highgate, and I remember seeing it there when I
went with my father to see the room after Coleridge's death. My father made an
elaborate drawing of the room, which was afterwards lithographed.' *Diary,
Reminiscences, and Correspondence of Henry Crabb Robinson*, ed. Thomas
Sadler, 2 vols., 1872 (3rd edn.), i. 294 n. This water-colour drawing by the elder
George Scharf (1788–1860), draughtsman and lithographer, was in the pos-
session of the late Walter H. P. Coleridge. For a reproduction of the lithograph
see Letter 1568, p. 659.

slowly and distinctly spoken; & with this, my own vexing thoughts
prevented me from attending to them;—especially as I thought that
by the time, my Nephew came to town at Christmas, I should
have hit on something or other. What was my surprize when the
day before yesterday Mrs Gillman received a letter from Madame,
of which I will only quote the literal translation of two sentences—
'Tell him to send for his two Portraits—and to send me the 30£
and (mark you) *immediately.*'

Now the very short answer to this mandate is, that I have not
30 Shillings in the world; & therefore can not send 30 Pound. But
yet as soon as I come to town, I will *endeavor* to make some com-
pensation to Madame for her expenditure on the Portraits—& will do
(as I have always done) my very utmost to serve her—and more
I can not say.—From the causes above stated there has been a
misapprehension on my part & Madame's from the beginning; and
I am willing, as far as I can, to pay for my half of the Mistake—
But that I should, before I had the opportunity of shewing my
friends a specimen of Madame's Portraiture, on my own risk and
at a moment's warning, purchase & pay for them, she must have
known was out of my power.—Now this is what, my dear Mrs
Aders! I must trouble you to make her understand. I expect to be
in town before the 14th of Decr. unless my Leg should confine me.
God bless you & your

most sincere Friend

S. T. Coleridge.

P.S. Mrs Gillman desires her kindest love—She is better & her
spirits calmer. I am sorry to make you pay double post, yet am
afraid of affronting you by franking it.—

1567. *To Sidney Walker*

Address: Sidney Walker, Esqre.
MS. Victoria University Lib. Hitherto unpublished.

Grove, Highgate
Friday 15 Decr 1826.

My dear Sir

If you should be in our vicinity, will you be kind enough to let
me see you, at your first leisure?—for I cannot make the attempt of
finding you out, or of going to you even if I were sure, you were at
your Mother's. For during the last 3 weeks of my Sojourn at Rams-
gate I have been confined at full length to Sopha and Mattrass
with an erysipelatous affection of my left Leg (pity that none of

our Fire-insurance Officers will provide one with an exorcism for St Anthony!) which a too free use of my Nails during sleep in the commencement of this Arson has *nucleus'd* with an orifice that shews no disposition to heal. We left Ramsgate Yester Morning and did not reach home till 9 o'clock: which, you may guess, did the wound no good—and I am sentenced to another spell of the Sopha, and all walking or even sitting forbidden. So, you see, if I had nothing else, I have a claim on your Christian charity for a visit. But the fact is as follows. Our friend, **Mr Gillman**, has, *I am happy to say*, removed Henry Gillman from Eton, and decided on sending him to Shrewsbury; and his name is already entered on the list. Mr Gillman received a letter, some ten days ago, from Mr Iliff, in which he speaks of your Brother in a way that could not [but] delight you and his Mother—the more so, that the whole style of Mr Iliff's Letters prove[s] him to merit the character, he bears, of a very sensible and amiable man—*as in truth we Christ's Hospital Boys generally are*. But without joking, I was highly pleased with both the matter and manner of his correspondence— and gratified on your account no less than on our own with the encomia, he bestows on your Brother.—Now what is at my heart is, that you would be our Mediator with your Mother to confirm by her assent Mr Iliff's recommendation, that our Henry, who is a generous boy free from all vice & has always been much liked by his school-fellows, should accompany your Brother on his return to School: and further that on his arrival at Hampstead Mrs Walker would have the goodness to permit him to pass a day with us at Highgate, that *he* may learn & see what sort of a companion de voyage is proposed for him, and that we may learn from him, in what studies & books it would be desirable to occupy Henry's time during the Vacation. To you, who know my excellent Friend, Mr Gillman, and his every way good and amiable Wife, any assurances would be worse than superfluous; and knowing likewise, that their more than friendship, their disinterested services and unwearied constancy of affection to me, are more than I can express, you will not wonder at the interest felt in every thing that concerns them, by

my dear **Sir** | Your's very sincerely

S. T. Coleridge

P.S. If your Mother should assent to your request (for you see, I rely on your appropriating it) the earlier the day, the more obliged we shall be—and without any flattery Mr Iliff's character of your Brother would have made us wish to be acquainted with him, even without our additional motive.—

1568. *To William Worship*

Transcript made by Professor R. C. Bald from a copy in the handwriting of Mrs. Gillman. Hitherto unpublished.

29 Decr. 1826

Dear Friend

The Turkey κατ᾽ ἐξοχήν, the very Constantinople of Turkey-land with its suburban sausages arrived safely as the holy Chapel did at Loretto after a somewhat longer voyage a few hundred years ago. It was *an Exquisite*; and aided by genial recollections of the Sender forms now, I doubt not, some of the best-conditioned Flesh on our Bones. Mr Gillman was not in the mood or state of spirits for company; so to my great satisfaction we sate down to our Christmas Dinner: *a family* (with the exception of one Guest, Miss Bradley), to wit Mr and Mrs G, James, Henry, and the Bard. My dear Adorabit, I *can* sympathize with you thoroughly and believe me I *do* sympathize with you most sincerely in the depression of your spirits by the loss of a beloved and love worthy Friend, the solitary Fountain in your sandy Desert, whose waters nourished the roots of your social Being and were as the dews of Heaven on your Branches in a place where no dew fell; and not less so in your annoyance from those unclean Grunters the Saints, who are ready at all times to rip up a Clergyman's Character with their Tusks of Calumny and who beholding, i.e. fancying, impurity & evil in the most innocent things, may be truly said to have a *Sty* in their eye. Verily, these *Bêtes Priantes* fall right naturally under the latter of the two sorts, in which I class the folks in my immediate vicinity—Neighbours, and Nigh *Bores*! What a contrast between these Pseudo-evangelicals, and the great Father and Founder of the Evangelical Church, that dear large hearted Man of God, the heroic Luther—he whose Faith removed Mountains, whose wide, deep, and rapid Stream of Genius and Gospel truth rolled and roared thro' the Augean Stable of the Babylonian Harlot and swept away the accumulated dung and filth of ten centuries—His Table talk has long been my *Bosom* book: and I am now reading his Postille, i.e. short sermons on the Gospels and Epistles of the Day for every Sunday in the year.[1] Judge of the spirit of his doctrines by the following specimens, taken at hap hazard.

1st. *On the Marriage feast at Cana.* 'I am pressed by sundry Brethren to prohibit dancing. I cannot do it. Whether the young Jews and Jewesses danced at the marriage feast at Cana I know not; but this I know that it is the custom of this country, and when

---

[1] Coleridge was probably reading Luther's *Hauspostille* in the Erlangen edition. See *Sämmtliche Werke*, vols. i–vi, ed. J. G. Plochmann, 1826.

I see the merry lads & lasses frisking their heels, and ask myself why God gave them youth, health, tingling blood and dancing spirits if he did not mean them to enjoy these Flowers of their season, so it be with innocence & in moderation and on suitable occasions, I cannot, no! I cannot find it in my heart to condemn it —If people dance unchastely and immodestly, it is not the dancing but the *unchaste* immodest dancing—not the dancing but the inward impurity that infects and corrupts a gracious art—that is damnable—Rather than that the Guests should want Wine Christ wrought his first miracle—shall I call wine a bestial Drink, because some men make beasts of themselves with it? A sober cheerfulness is the Water of Young people, their ordinary and work day Drink, but on Wedding Days and birth days, we may do as our Lord did, turn the Water to Wine, the Pipe, the Rebec, the Song, and the Dance, and no offence—Besides to tell you a bit of my mind—a Christian Faith and Love that can be *danced away, sung away,* or *played away,* is in my opinion not worth the keeping.'

2. 'When you are employed in acts of love & kindness, your whole soul should be directed towards your fellow-men, the objects of your benevolence, and not be thinking of God and your reward in Heaven—So only do you imitate God and Christ, who gave us all good gifts from pure love and tender mercy—and if you had indeed the mind and heart that were in the dear loving Saviour, your souls would be so filled with love and Compassion for your afflicted Brethren as to leave no room for other thoughts—Selfishness does not change its nature according to its object—Selfishness remains Selfishness, nay is worse rather than better in that you expect to make God the instrument to gratify it—*Then* is the *love of God* in you when you are thinking what you can do for your poor fellow-creatures, not when you are thinking what God will do for *you.* For to love God is to keep his commandments & this is his command, yea, all his commandments in *one,* that ye love one another.'

This, my dear Adorabit! is the divinity you & I will teach; and now you will expect a little news, but these tho' not wanting, are not of the kind to answer my wish—viz. to cheer & amuse you— During the whole summer I was affected by the extraordinary weather to a degree never before experienced—one black cloud of Dejection & Languor varied only by severe and now painful now irritating sleep-disturbing ailments—&c—Mrs Gillman was little better—In September I recovered a portion of my spirits & my daughter was with us till Octr. 8 when we (i.e. Mrs Gillman, Miss Steele and myself) went to Ramsgate, which had now become threateningly necessary for Mrs Gillman and for the first 10 days her convalescence was great & rapid beyond all former examples. I never saw such a change in looks & spirits—But soon came the old Nemesis that the ill-luck of the year should be accumulated during our absence from home's fireside. Mr Gillman was thrown out of his Gig & sustained, not a fracture, but a serious bruise & strain of his right arm & wrist of which he has even now but an imperfect use. This however was in its true extent not imparted to Mrs G. But then came a letter from my nephew at Eton, Henry's Tutor, requesting, I might say demanding, the Boy's sudden removal. Had the Simoon or Poison blast of the Desert passed over Mrs G. the effect could scarcely have been greater or more sudden. James went down—brought Henry to us and 5 weeks of such continued heart-ache may I never know again. For Mrs G. it blasted all the purposes of our sea-sojourn & by little & little the truth dawned into full daylight of conviction, that the child had been idle, treated with most injudicious severity by his Tutor whom he loved very much!

> And to be wroth with one we love
> Doth work like madness in the brain[1]—

thought himself ill used (no wonder, for his school fellows all told him so), & so got into a restive mood—In short, for I am sick at heart of the subject, the whole charge against the child was *smoke*, & my nephew has betrayed throughout a deplorable want of Temper, Sense and Delicacy. Henry is now admitted at the free school Shrewsbury, under Dr Butler and Mr Iliff (a fellow Blue coat & Grecian). Hen Pen is a thoughtless Chap, but a better hearted, better principled Boy does not exist—For 5 weeks at Ramsgate I was confined to Sofa & Mattrass with Erysipelas & a wound in my left leg. Since my return Gillman has brought Madam Leg to her senses again by strait waistcoating her, i.e. forced the wound to heal by bandaging the leg. We are all now pretty well. I have barely room to say in the name of us all—

God bless you, my dear Worship—
S. T. Coleridge

Our house repaired from top to bottom and so altered for the better. G. has done wonders—

P.S. Derwent has taken orders—is going to settle at Helston in Cornwall with a perpetual curacy and a school.[2] I hear from all

---

[1] *Christabel*, lines 412–13.

[2] Derwent Coleridge was ordained deacon by the Bishop of Exeter on 29 Oct. 1826 and for a short time served as a curate in Cornwall under his cousin, the Rev. James Duke Coleridge. He was master of the grammar school at Helston, Cornwall, from 1827 to 1841.

Samuel Taylor Coleridge's Bed- and Book-room, No. 3 The Grove, Highgate. Not long after Coleridge's death, George Scharf, the elder, made a water-colour drawing of the room which he afterwards lithographed. The copy of the lithograph reproduced here bears Scharf's name and is in the possession of the Revd. Nicholas F. D. Coleridge

quarters of his great success as a Preacher. Altogether he is going on as I could wish, & is engaged to a Miss Pridham—

Poor dear dear Hartley! alas! alas! [the] object of every one's love & admiration, the subject of every one's sorrow and compassion.[1]—Why cannot you relieve your health & spirits by coming up to Highgate?

Love from all, especially from your paternal friend & Lover—

S. T. Coleridge

I am specially delighted with my room.[2] James has got his election to St John's by the death of old Matthews.[3] Have you a copy of my 'Aids to reflection'? if not, I would send one.

1569. *To Alaric A. Watts*

Address: Alaric Watts, Esqre. | 9 North Bank | Regent's Park
MS. Victoria University Lib. Pub. with omis. Alaric Watts, *i. 290.*
Postmark: 1 January 1827.

1 Jany 1827.—

My dear Sir

Under no imaginable circumstances, that I can think of in connection with your name, should I have suspected you of discourtesy, much less ingratitude—even if the latter were less inapplicable to the relation, in which I stand and have long stood to you, as the obliged party. I was not positive as to my own recollection of your words; but assuming their accuracy I explained the non-arrival of the Volume on your knowlege of my Absence from Highgate and your ignorance of my return. I am truly sorry, that the cause was of so much more serious a nature. What will be your pecuniary Loss eventually?[4]

[1] Mrs. Coleridge came to realize that Coleridge had been right in insisting on Hartley's return to the North: 'Almost ever since poor H's great misfortune', she wrote to Poole, 'he has resided in the Vale of Grasmere, a place the most desirable for him, in his very peculiar circumstances; for he is known, from infancy, by all the Vale—&, I may add, spite of his errors, much beloved & cared for by his many friends there.' Wordsworth also came to the same conclusion. *Minnow among Tritons*, ed. Stephen Potter, 1934, p. 166, and *Gentleman's Magazine*, June 1851, p. 584.

[2] According to Mrs. Watson, the Gillmans 'rebuilt for their honoured guest his attic room, transforming its original sloping ceiling (traces of which are still visible), into rectangular dignity'. Lucy E. Watson, *Coleridge at Highgate*, 1925, p. 51. See also Letters 1359–60, 1376, and 1566.

[3] Probably James Matthews, fellow and scholar at St. John's College, Oxford, who died on 10 Dec. 1826. James Gillman, Jr., matriculated at St. John's on 25 June 1827.

[4] After publishing the issues of the annual, *The Literary Souvenir*, for 1825 and 1826, the firm of Hurst, Robinson, and Co. failed early in the latter year,

You have decided wisely as well as prudently in omitting the Lampoon on Butler.[1] And I thank you on my own account. Not that I should so much have disliked it's publication, as the publication of the Lines without my name, and this too at my own request. The fact was: that I had hastily repeated—rather than deliberately adopted—a friend's advice—a 'Were I you, I would not put my name to it.'—Now a Lampoon (tho' I must still think, most richly deserved in the present case) is but of equivocal morality, perhaps, at the best; but unequivocally bad, when anonymous. He who thinks it his duty to give pain to another, and to excite his resentment, is bound at least to give this proof, that he is indeed actuated by a sense of duty, that he does it openly, and faces the consequences.

Of the 3 Volumes I have merely looked thro' the plates of the last[2]—and they deserve more than all, you have said. But I shall devote one day this week to the regular perusal of the 3rd Vol—& before the close of next week I shall have read the other two—& then, should any thing occur to me that I imagine might be useful—I will not conceal it. For the present, you must be content to accept my best thanks for the SPLENDID COPY of the two last, 1826[3]—1827[4]—and my Daughter's by anticipation—for she is at present at her Cousin's, John Coleridge (the Barrister) in Torrington Square—The Vol. will be inclosed in a parcel which is going off to her, tomorrow morning—& I doubt not, she will acknowlege your kindness in her own hand.—Mrs Gillman in returning her thanks begs me to add, how much she & Mr Gillman will be gratified by seeing you & Mrs Watts—should the weather & your leisure allow of an excursion to our House—

Accept, my dear Sir! for yourself and Mrs Watts my very sincere Wish—A happy New Year & a succession of healthy & happy Years to you.—I will endeavor to send you one or two small poems

and Alaric A. Watts, the editor, became the proprietor. 'Monstrous charges' and 'omissions of credits' in the accounts involved Watts in the affairs of the firm. See *Alaric Watts*, i. 234.

[1] Coleridge refers to his *Sancti Dominici Pallium. A Dialogue between Poet and Friend*, a poem written in 1826 and given to Watts for publication in *The Literary Souvenir* for 1827. See Letter 1607 for Watts's reasons for not including the poem.

[2] Watts had sent Coleridge copies of *The Literary Souvenir* for 1825, 1826, and 1827, the first three volumes of that annual. Each number was published and 'presented to the trade' during the latter part of the year preceding that given in the title-page.

[3] Coleridge's *The Exchange* appeared in *The Literary Souvenir* for 1826.

[4] *The Literary Souvenir* for 1827 contained Coleridge's *Lines suggested by the last Words of Berengarius*, along with *Epitaphium Testamentarium*, which was printed as a footnote to the title of the *Lines*.

for 1828,[1] of a more imaginative character & better suited to your Work—for believe me, that with a lively interest both in your success *circumstantial,* and in the genial evolution of your own strong intellectual powers I remain, my dear Sir,

Your obliged & sincere Friend
S. T. Coleridge—

1570. *To Basil Montagu*

Address: Mr Montagu
MS. Private possession. Hitherto unpublished.

3 Jany. 1827.

My dear Basil

I am always happy to see you: & Mr Irving will ever be a welcome Guest—& I have a double reason for wishing to see Mrs Montague for from Charles I am led to apprehend, she is not so well as from my heart's heart I would have her be—But in addition to the above I am in hopes that you will meet our good old Friend, T. Poole—

God bless you | & your obliged & faithfully | affectionate Friend

S. T. Coleridge

Mr & Mrs G's kind remembrances—happy New Years & the &c of kind thoughts.

1571. *To Thomas Poole*

Address: Thomas Poole, Esqre | Old Hummums | Covent Garden
MS. British Museum. Hitherto unpublished.
Postmark: Highgate, 3 January 1827.

Grove, Highgate
3 Jany 1827.

My dear Poole

I write now, *not* to say how glad I shall be to see you tomorrow: for that would be wasting ink & paper & postage, not to add pen, time, and daylight, in mere superfluities—but to transmit to you Mr and Mrs Gillman's best respect, and that *we* all take it for a settled thing & of course that you will dine & spend the day with us—that there is a right comfortable Bed Room & thoroughly well-aired Bed at your service—and that *we*, and they, and more

---

[1] See Letter 1596, in which Coleridge promised to send a copy of *Youth and Age.*

especially Mr Gillman (whose professional duties make him an absentee or may do so, before dinner) will be grievously disappointed, if you do not.—We will dine at ½ past 4, or 5 or ½ past 5, or at any hour, you may prefer. I saw the Fay this morning with her Cousin, Edward Coleridge—who expressed her delight in having seen you—. Atherstone is in town; and absolutely in spite of all my evasions forced from you [me ?] John Coleridge's address in order to wait on my Daughter, with whom he is very far from being a favorite. Your address I would not attempt to recollect—so told him, I did not know—& doubted whether you were in town. Pity that a man of really considerable vigor of intellect should be deficient in moral or at least mannerly tact—. Nature wove him well but with coarse threads. His Epic Poem in 24 Books on the Siege of Nineveh, the whole of which with exception of one or two Proper Names is to be of his own invention, is the most ridiculous thing, I ever heard of—and I wasted some wisdom upon him to no purpose.[1]—Martin, the Painter,[2] had rendered all I could say *Betty* Martin—

Mr Irving & Basil Montague will meet you, after dinner—.

God bless you, my dear Friend | and your obliged & ever faithful & | affectionate

S. T. Coleridge

1572. *To Mrs. Charles Aders*

MS. Harvard College Lib. Hitherto unpublished. This letter is written in the opening pages of an album formerly belonging to Mrs. Aders.

[January 1827 ?][3]

My dear Mrs Aders!

It is your wish that I should myself transcribe the poem addressed to you, entitled To Eliza in pain, in your Album. Even if a Wish from you to have a thing done had not been, as at all times it *is*, sure to awake it's echo in my heart in a Wish to do it; yet that a memorial of my esteem and affection should be privileged

[1] In 1828 Edwin Atherstone (1788–1872) published the first six books of *The Fall of Nineveh.*

[2] John Martin (1789–1854) painted *The Fall of Nineveh.* He was a friend of Atherstone, and the two men worked in friendly rivalry.

[3] Mrs. Aders called at Highgate early in 1827, and it may have been during this visit that Coleridge complied with her request to copy into the opening pages of her album his lines, *The Two Founts.* (See Letters 1578–9 and 1586.) Later in the album there are a number of Charles Lamb manuscripts, including a letter to Aders postmarked Apr. 1827.

to head this splendid Volume, is too gratifying a proof of a correspondent sentiment and feeling on your part, to permit me a moment's hesitation in complying with your request.

But that I may restore the Thought, on which the Poem is grounded, to the original Concipient, as it's right Owner, and at the same time give you an additional pleasure by connecting with your name that of our dear and admired (how deservedly dear, how justly admired) Mrs Gillman, I shall introduce the Lines by transcribing the explanatory part of the Letter, in which they were inclosed, from

your and Mr Aders' ever faithful and affectionate Friend
S. T. Coleridge.

Transcript from a Letter dated 3 June, 1826

My dear Friend

I wish, that word, Friend, had not been so unhandsomely soiled in it's passage from hollow hearts through vulgar mouths to unbelieving ears, in the market of the World!—And You are scarcely old enough to be even my *youngest* Sister—Nevertheless, you must, as Mrs Gillman has before you, put up with the affront, and allow me to begin again with

My dear Friend and Sister

A few days ago Mrs Gillman was expressing her wonder—I might have said her admiration that with all the intense Suffering, you had undergone, you *looked* just the same; and that neither Pain nor Anxiety seemed to have any power over that beautiful Face of Your's. With this remark in my Head, as I layed it on my pillow, I fell asleep: and out of the gay weeds that spring up in the garden of Morpheus, I wove next morning the accompanying wreath— which I intended to have presented to you with my best Bow, the afternoon I called with Mr John Hookham Frere: who was delighted, nay, as he himself expressed it, 'absolutely overset' with the Von Eyk, and astounded with your Copy. I am sure, *I* was. Indeed, my dear Mrs Aders! I cannot find words to express adequately the Delight and Exultation, that took possession of me, as I stood gazing on it and observed the same emotion in Mr Frere, the polished Gentleman, the Scholar, the Man of Genius! and yet the *Good* Man shining out in him through and above all! I felt so proud of You!—You should not make your friends so abominably vain of you, Mrs Aders! It is very wrong in you!—and remember, that *I* tell you so, who am verily verily and indeed indeed your and dear Mr Aders's most faithful and affectionate Friend

Grove, Highgate.   S. T. Coleridge

To Eliza in pain.[1]

'Twas my last waking thought—How can it be,
That Thou, sweet Friend! such anguish should'st endure?
When strait from Dream-land came a Dwarf: and He
Could tell the cause, forsooth, and knew the Cure.

Methought, he fronted me with peering Look
Fix'd on my Heart; and read aloud in game
The Loves and Griefs therein, as from a Book
And mutter'd praise like one, who meant to blame.

In every Heart, quoth he, since Adam's Sin
Two FOUNTS there are, of Suffering and of Cheer—
That to let forth, and *this* to keep within;
But She, whose aspect I find imaged here,

Of Pleasure only will to all dispense,
Will ope *that* Fount alone by no Distress
Choked or turn'd inward; but still issue thence
Unconquer'd Cheer, persistent Loveliness!

As on the driving Cloud the shiny Bow,
That gracious Thing made up of Tears and Light
Mid the wild Rack and Rain that slants below
Stands smiling forth unmov'd and freshly bright

As though the Spirits of all lovely Flowers,
Inweaving each it's Wreath and dewy Crown,
Or ere they sank to earth in sparkling Showers
Had built a Bridge to tempt the Angels down!

Even so, Eliza! on that Face of thine,
On that benignant Face whose Look alone
(The Soul's translucence through her crystal Shrine!)
Has power to soothe all anguish but thy own,

A Beauty hovers still and ne'er takes wing;
But with a silent charm compels the stern
And tort'ring Genius of the Bitter Spring
To shrink aback and cower upon his Urn!

[1] First published in *The Bijou*, 1828, with the title, *The Two Founts.
Stanzas addressed to a Lady on her recovery, with unblemished looks, from a
severe attack of pain.* See *Poems*, i. 454.

Who needs then wonder if (no Outlet found
In Passion, Spleen or Strife) the FOUNT of PAIN
O'erflowing beats against it's lovely Mound,
And in wild Flashes shoots from Heart to Brain?

Sleep, and the Dwarf with that unsteady Gleam
On his rais'd Lip which aped a critic Smile,
Had pass'd: yet I, my sad thoughts to beguile,
Lay weaving on the tissue of my Dream:

Till audibly at length I cried, as though
Thou had'st indeed been present to my eyes—
O sweet sweet Sufferer! if the case be so,
I pray thee, be *less* good, *less* sweet, *less* wise!

In every Look a venom'd arrow send!
On those soft Lips let Scorn and Anger live!
Do any thing, rather than thus, sweet Friend!
Hoard for thyself the pain, thou wilt not give!

S. T. Coleridge

To Mrs Aders. 3 June, 1826

1573. *To Mrs. John Walker*

Address: Mrs Walker | Squire's Mount
MS. British Museum. Hitherto unpublished.

26 Jany 1827.—

Dear Madam

Mrs Gillman has desired me to take my pen in her behalf in order
to express, first, her & Mr Gillman's sense of your kindness, and
how much regret they will feel, should any circumstance prevent
Curzon's staying with us a day or two before his return to Shrews-
bury; but in still stronger terms to convey the importance which
they attach to the formation of a friendship between him and our
Henry—but that since we had the pleasure of passing an hour with
you, Mr Gillman, who has long looked forward with anxiety to
Henry's *night* journey, and more uneasily since this sharp weather
has set in—for as you saw, Henry has but a delicate frame, has
received an offer from the Revd Mr Bather, to take Henry down
with him on Wednesday, and to send him to Mr Iliff on Friday
from *his* House, which is a mile from Shrewsbury—& so that he will
not have to pass a night in the Coach. Other motives conjoined—
& Mr Gillman accordingly has resolved to avail himself of this

excellent Man's friendly proposals.—Lest therefore any delay should occur in taking the place for Curzon, Mrs G. will send off our Servant with this note—

Be pleased to remember me kindly to Sidney, whom I am always glad to see—& be assured that I am

With respect & | every friendly feeling | dear Madam, | Your's truly

S. T. Coleridge

1574. *To Unknown Correspondent*

MS. Professor Thomas O. Mabbott. Pub. Notes and Queries, *2 May 1931, p. 317.*

Dear Lucius   [January 1827][1]

Would that you had come on Sunday by which time I promised you to have revised your Verses—For in part from the p[ossession], which Mr Bather & his adm[irable] Discourse, took of my mind—and in part, from 3 or 4 letters which Mrs Gillman was anxious that I should *get off*—Mr Porter's Question came like a *flash* on me—Not that I had not read your verses—for that I did, within an hour after they were sent to me, and spoke of them to Mrs Gillman, as I now speak of them to *yourself*—that the composition is *very* creditable to you—and were I your Tutor, I should be much gratified.—In the first line, *frantic* is too harsh a word for your side of the Question—Better put—

He comes, fit Herald of that frenzied Storm—

All the other lines are very well, in relation to the Thought—I do not know when you return. But if you return to Highgate two or three days before your Holidays are over, I will with pleasure devote a [day] to you—and even a few hours, when we were alone in my Room, and you with your pen in your hand, would enable me to suggest alterations & improvements & to aid you in making such, more effectually than days, in your absence.—

I would have Peter's Speech somewhat *compressed*—and then pass off into some reflection of this kind—So spake the Enthusiast —in the spirit of his times—But a prophetic Spirit, and truths unknown to himself, were working beneath the agitated surface of his Zeal—and so pass to the real justification of the Crusade, and end with the beneficial consequences. While you are gone, I will not let it out of my mind.   S. T. C.—

[1] The reference in this and the preceding letter to Edward Bather, vicar of Meole Brace, suggests that the two letters were written about the same time. See Letters 1562 and 1573.

1575. *To Thomas Allsop*

Address: T. Allsop, Esqre
MS. Cornell University Lib. Pub. Nineteenth-Century Studies (*Cornell*), *58.*

Grove, Highgate
1 Feby 1827.

My ever dear Allsop

You do not know me if you think that even a week, in a peck of troubles as I have myself been, has passed without earnest most anxious thoughts about *you*—In answer to your's what can I say but that if I knew how to answer, you would have heard long long ago—. For Heaven's sake come up to us—disburthen your whole mind & feelings to us—believe me, my dear friend, and never dearer than now, sad and perplexing as your affairs are, they are not so great an evil, as that incapability of plucking your hopes and fears & difficulties out from your own heart and mind and giving them that distance without which we can see nothing with our eyes and nothing as it really is with our mind's eyes.—This has been the occasion of all your sorrows—and if you could once conquer this thoroughly, I should see no reason why you should not yet be a prosperous, at least a happy man—Now as to myself, what can I say ? Be assured, no self-love will weigh with me an atom in any feasible plan of serving you. I will do any thing but what in your own judgement (if you will but give that judgement even tolerable play, by relieving your oppressed spirit & opening yourself out to us) would be seriously, very seriously injuring myself and the friends who have not only on me but on themselves other peremptory claims in addition to those of friendship, without even a *chance* of benefiting you.[1]—Come to us—and you shall yourself be the judge —& I doubt not, that with manly fortitude looking the worst in the face the Result will not be more than with the help & comfort of those, who love you, a man ought to bear. Pray, do not even for a single week longer keep away from us—I had written, from yourself, by mistake—& yet it truly *is* keeping away from your true self.—If you knew what poor Mrs Gillman has been suffering on poor little Henry's account (tho' that is now over, thank God!) you would appreciate the strength of the feeling which in the midst of all her anxieties has kept you prominent in her daily thoughts—Come— & believe me, my dear Allsop, | most earnestly your affectionate |
Friend
S. T. Coleridge

[1] On 1 Feb. 1827 Crabb Robinson called on Lamb and 'found him in trouble about his friend, Allsop, who is a ruined man'. *Robinson on Books and Their Writers*, i. 344.

1576. To Henry Brougham

MS. University College Library, London. Hitherto unpublished.

Grove, Highgate.
9 Feby. 1827

Dear Sir

I hope, you will acquit me of presumption in this intrusion on your time, when I assure you that in refusing to write I must have evaded what I believe to be a Duty. The Council of the London University having announced their intention of appointing a Hebrew Professor, my friend, Hyman Hurwitz, Author of the Vindiciae Biblicae, the Hebrew Tales, and some philological Works, has declared himself a Candidate and earnestly intreated me to mention his name to you. The Convictions expressed as to the rare attainments and high moral Worth of this excellent Man in my 'Aids to Reflection' and which have, I find, been extracted in the last number of the Quarterly in the Review of Mr Hurwitz's Hebrew Tales, place me beyond the suspicion of exaggerating his claims for any present purpose. Assuredly, I feel a strong personal attachment to Mr Hurwitz; but if I know myself, this would only tend to make me jealous of every word of praise uttered on such an occasion—had I not a moral certainty, that the noble Ends and Aims of the New University will have in Mr Hurwitz a most able and most sincere Supporter.[1]

Some years ago I made the History and Constitution of Universities the subject of particular study; and when the London University was first proposed and under your auspices, I had intended to have troubled you with the result of my reflections; but I was deterred by the belief that I might be suspected of a wish to intrude my Hook in a Vin[e]yard pre-occupied by abler Labourers —but I have my particular reasons for intreating your permission to add, that there does not exist a warmer admirer or more zealous advocate, of all the great exertions in behoof of that Liberty, which the Knowlege of Truth must ultimately confer, by which your public Life has been distinguished—or a more impassioned Echo of all the sentiments, by which you retrieved the character of our Country, in the defence of an injured Lady,[2] than he is, who now has the honor of subscribing himself, with unfeigned respect,

dear Sir, | Your obed. humble Servant
S. T. Coleridge

[1] In 1828 Hyman Hurwitz was elected professor of the Hebrew language and literature in the University of London.
[2] Queen Caroline (1768–1821).

1577. To J. H. B. Williams

Address: J. B. Williams, Esqre. | Surgeon | &c &c | Aldersgate Street
MS. Harvard College Lib. Pub. Underbrush, *by J. T. Fields, 1877, p. 48.*
Postmark: 13 February 1827.

Grove,
Highgate
Tuesday Afternoon
13 Feby 1827.

My dear Williams

I shall, God permitting, be in town and in your neighborhood tomorrow—& shall at least make the attempt of doing, what I have some half score of times proposed to Mr G. that we should do conjointly—that is, shake hands with you in your own ΑΣΚΛΗΠΕΙΟΝ, Latinè Esculapium.[1] Your time, I am well aware, is not at your own command; and unluckily I am not acquainted with the Horology of your daily Routine, or the relations of the *Whens* to the *Wheres* in your scheme of successive Self-distribution. But I will call between One and Two; and if I find that you will be in at any mentionable time between that and half past Two, I will return at the said time, and billet (I *should* have said, *label*) myself on you for a Mutton chop and a Potatoe— or what I should like better, a few sausages and a Potatoe—. Were my duodenal Digestion brisk enough for me to work after dinner, I should always dine from $\frac{1}{2}$ past I to $\frac{1}{2}$ past 2—for that is the only time of the 24 Hours, in which I have any appetite for animal food.—

Gillman has been very poorly, & complained much of his head; but he is now much better—& Mrs Gillman is at *par*—something between *so so,* and *pretty tolerable, I thank you.*

With my kind respects to Mrs W. and Love to the young Galenicals, believe me, my dear Williams,

with affectionate Esteem & Regard | Your sincere Friend
S. T. Coleridge

1578. To Daniel Stuart

Address: D. Stuart, Esqre | U. Harley Street
MS. British Museum. Pub. Letters from the Lake Poets, *301.*
Postmark: Highgate, 20 February 1827.

Tuesday 20 Feby 1827
Grove, Highgate—

My dear Sir

Before Mr Frere left England, he had a conversation with Lord Liverpool respecting me, in which Lord Liverpool promised that he

---

[1] More properly ΑΣΚΛΗΠΙΕΙΟΝ and Æsculapium.

would do something for me—and mentioned the sum—desiring
that he might be reminded of it.[1]—Some month ago Mrs Aders'
Brother in law exerted his interest to procure a sine cure place,
the salary of which is exactly the same as that mentioned by Lord
L. to Mr Frere, but was answered—The place (viz. Paymaster of
the Gentlemen Pensioners, held by the late Mr Gifford,[2] the
Quarterly Review Man) was reserved for Mr Coleridge.—Not
hearing any further, I wrote (as by Mr Frere I had been advised
to do—only (*as usual* in all matters relating to my own pecuniary
interests) not half as early as I ought to have done) to Lord Dudley
& Ward[3]—I received about 10 days ago a very kind answer, dated
from Brighton, assuring me that he would speak to Lord Liverpool
immediately on his arrival in town which would be in ten days—
that he would *rather* talk with him about it, than write; but that
if it needed hurry, I was to say so, and he would instantly write.
What has since happened[4] will probably recall these words with
a sad feeling to Lord Dudley's mind—and *you* will not suspect me
of hypocrisy when I say, that had not my Daughter's Face & the
Faces of those to whom I have been so deeply obliged, forced my
duties on me, I should not, or more properly I *could* not, have
mingled any anxiety or regret respecting my own pecuniary Loss
or Gain with the grief and alarm, I feel as an Englishman—

Now, my dear Friend! of all men in the world You are the man,
on whose good sense & knowlege of the World I rely the most, &
whose advice has always been as an oracle to me.—Advise me what
to do—. I will write to Lord Dudley, of course—but in the mean
time if I knew any person likely to be distinctly & officially ac-
quainted with the situation in Question, & the real existing state
of the matter (tho' I have not the slightest reason to doubt the
Authority above mentioned)—Do you know any one of the
Treasury? Lord Lowther?[5] or A. McNaughten?[6] I am so ignorant
as not to know what the Gentlemen Pensioners are.—If Mr Can-

---

[1] See Letter 1510 and notes.

[2] William Gifford, who as paymaster of the gentlemen-pensioners received
£1,000 a year, died on 31 Dec. 1826.

[3] John William Ward, fourth Viscount Dudley and Ward (1781–1833).
He became foreign secretary in Apr. 1827 and was created Earl of Dudley in
Sept.

[4] On 17 Feb. 1827 Liverpool suffered a stroke of paralysis combined with
apoplexy. 'Rarely conscious' during the remainder of his life, he died on 4 Dec.
1828.

[5] Lord Lowther (1787–1872), later the second Earl of Lonsdale, was on the
treasury board from 1813 to 1826.

[6] Edmund Alexander Macnaghten (1762–1832), a lord of the treasury
1819–30.

ning had been in town & well, I should have written to him[1]—
Pray, give me your advice—& if you see any thing that can be
done by you, do it for, my dear Sir,

Your obliged & affectionately | attached Friend
S. T. Coleridge

Our kindest regards to Mrs Stewart—

1579. *To Mrs. Charles Aders*

[Addressed by Mrs. Gillman] Mrs Aders | Euston Square
MS. Francis Edwards Ltd. Hitherto unpublished.
Postmark: Highgate, 20 February 1827.

Tuesday, 20 Feby 1827
Grove, Highgate—

My dear Mrs Aders

I had written to Lord Dudley & Ward, and received from him
(*from Brighton*) a very kind answer one sentence of which, I doubt
not, he will often think of—'I shall be in town in ten days, and
should greatly prefer *speaking* to Lord Liverpool to *writing*; but
if the thing require *hurry*, let me know & I will write immediately.'
—Alas! how little could he then have been aware of the melan-
choly Event—so melancholy that I declare to God, that if the
Faces before me (N.B. My Daughter is with us) did not remind me
too forcibly of an urgent *Duty*, I should not, nay, *could* not, have
mingled the grief, I feel as a man & an Englishman, with any
regret respecting my own Loss or Gain—Now what am I to do?—
The first thing, it seems to me, is to ascertain the *existing* state of
the Affair.

But to whom can I apply for this information? Can you learn
from Sir George P.[2] the name of the Gentleman, from whom he
received his information?—

If you *can*, or can from him procure me any advice, I am quite
sure, that you will not follow the bad example of S.T.C. in the
procrastination of his duty to himself in your exertions for the
service of the same S.T.C.—or—sad Culprit, but your very affec-
tionate Friend!—

S. T. Coleridge.—

[1] Canning, who became prime minister on 10 Apr. 1827, was informed of
the matter, though not by Coleridge himself, and intended to do something.
His death on 8 Aug. 1827 gave 'the settling Blow' to Coleridge's hopes. See
Letters 1586, 1598, and 1600.
[2] Mrs. Aders's brother-in-law. See Letters 1578 and 1609.

1580. *To Daniel Stuart*

Address: D. Stuart Esqre. | U. Harley Street
MS. British Museum. Pub. Letters from the Lake Poets, *304.*
Postmark: 26 February 1827.

Sunday Night [25 February 1827]

My dear Sir
    I wrote immediately to Lord Dudley on the receipt of your's—
and a letter which, I think, will please him. At least, the Gillmans
and my Daughter admired it very much. I ended by soliciting his
advice—whether I should write to Mr Canning—or whether I might
presume so far on his Lordship's kindness as to request him to
state the case to Mr Canning himself. Now I had no certain informa-
tion whether Lord Dudley was still at Brighton or had returned to
Park Lane—so—Mr Allsop happening to be here—& it being ½ 4,
our latest Post from Highgate, I entrusted my Letter directed
Brighton to him, who undertook to proceed instantly to Park
Lane, to learn whether Lord D. was or was not returned—if the
former, to leave the Letter; if the latter, to hasten with it to the
General Post—And this I doubt not, he did: tho' I have not seen
Allsop or heard from him since.—But I trust, I shall hear from
Lord D. tomorrow morning—& regulate my measures accordingly.
But if I should be disappointed of an Answer from Lord Dudley,
I shall go to town & try to see Mr Rogers—& to get him to go with
me to some one or other.—I have some ground for believing, that
the intimation of the Place held by Gifford was reserved for me
came from a Mr Hancock, Army Agent.—
    However, I write to you now, my dear friend! for a less impor-
tant purpose.—Mr Gillman with Mr Jameson (the Chancery
Barrister) have undertaken to superintend an Edition of all my
Poems to be brought out by Pickering[1]—that is to say, I have
given up the Poems as far as this Edition is concerned to Mr
Gillman—and he is desirous to procure a Copy of the Devil's
Thoughts as it originally appeared in the M. P.[2] (It is very curious
that both at Peele's & the Chapter Coffee House, carefully as they
both profess to guard against mutilation of their Series, almost
every poem of mine has been cut out.)—If therefore you happen
to have a Copy with you in town, you will oblige Mr G. by either

----

[1] *The Poetical Works of S. T. Coleridge, Including the Dramas of Wallen-
stein, Remorse, and Zapolya,* 3 vols., published by William Pickering in 1828.
[2] For the text of *The Devil's Thoughts* as it appeared in the *Morning Post*
on 6 Sept. 1799, see Campbell, *Poetical Works,* 621. In publishing the poem in
his *Poetical Works* of 1828 Coleridge reduced the stanzas from 14 to 10 and made
numerous changes in the text. See also Letter 1686.

entrusting it to him for a day or two, or favoring him with a Transcript.

While the Wind & Dust continue to act the part, they are now doing, I do not even wish to see you, for I am sure, the less you expose yourself, the more likely you will be to receive the full effect of the mild Weather when it comes.

Be so good as to remember me respectfully & affectionately to Mrs Stuart—or rather for *me* read *us*. For I need not tell you, she is a universal Favorite with the Circle of this Fire-side.—God bless you & your's—and your obliged

and sincerely attached Friend

S. T. Coleridge

P.S. Excuse the Paper—I did not observe that I had taken a sheet on which Mr Green had [drawn the] digestive organ of an Oyster.—

1581. *To Thomas Allsop*

Address: T. Allsop, Esqre | [in Mrs. Gillman's handwriting] Princes St.
MS. formerly in the possession of the late C. K. Ogden. Hitherto unpublished.

Tuesday Night [27 February 1827][1]
Grove, Highgate

My dear Allsop

It is not from any the most distant approach to a Suspicion, that any thing *doable* was left undone by You, of and concerning my letter to Lord Dudley, that I now write to you. But the non-receipt of an Answer from him has set my Fancy *a ferreting* into all the holes, and corners of Possibility—if peradventure it might chance to unearth the cause or occasion. And among other improbable possibles, driven or dragged out of it's Snug Burrow in the Warren of my Brain, it occurred to me that in my hurry and confusion I might not have conveyed to you the object & exigence of my troubling you with the charge of my Letter—instead of making a duplicate & directing one to Brighton, the other to Park Lane—and this way, to ascertain as speedily as possible where Lord Dudley *then* was, & if not in town, on what day expected. In my hurry, however, I forgot to ask you to drop a line in the 2d Post that evening, to acquaint me with the result—viz. whether the Letter was left in Park Lane or went by the General

[1] The erroneous date of '15 May 1827' appearing in the MS. is in Allsop's handwriting. The letter was written on the Tuesday after that to Stuart of Sunday, 25 Feb. 1827.

Post—so that I might have received [word] next morning by the
first delivery.—Meantime I have hourly expected to see you—tho'
with no better reason than that I have been wishing it.—Do drop
me a line on the receipt of this—& how is it to get to you? For Mrs
Gillman has both forgot & mislaid both your address & Mr Jame-
son's! She is *sure*, it is something about Princes, Dukes, Earls, and
that it is neither King's, nor Bishop's nor Dean's Street—but
Lord bless me! this won't do for the direction of a Letter![1]

So you see I am in a wood—the time passing, and I not knowing
what to do—for I cannot help thinking that my Letter can not
have reached Lord Dudley—and yet not sure of this, I am averse
from writing to Mr Canning, having solicited Lord Dudley's
advice whether I should—and almost equally averse from *boring*
Lord Dudley with a second Letter—tho' this last is what I be-
lieve I must do if I do not hear from him by Tomorrow's Post.—

Give my kind love to Mrs Allsop, | And hold me, my dear Allsop,
| ever your faithful & affectionate | Friend

                                                S. T. Coleridge

1582. *To Basil Montagu*

MS. University Library, Cambridge. Hitherto unpublished.

                                             [1 May 1827][2]

My dear Montagu

I presume, the passage which hovers before your recollection, is
Biogr. Literaria Vol. I. p. 58, 59, 60. The passage begins, p. 58,
last line but 5. 'In times of old Books were little less than RELIGIOUS
ORACLES. They then became VENERABLE PRECEPTORS. With the
still further diffusion of Literature, they next descended to the
rank of INSTRUCTIVE FRIENDS. The numbers still increasing, they
sank still lower to that of ENTERTAINING COMPANIONS. And at
present they seem degraded into CULPRITS, to hold up their
hands at the Bar of every self-elected yet not the less peremptory
Judge who chuses to carry on the trade of anonymous Criticism
from humour or interest, from enmity or arrogance; and to abide
the decision *"of him that reads in malice or him that reads after
dinner"*. (*Jer. Taylor.*)

---

[1] This letter was sent by messenger. Mrs. Gillman wrote the following note
on the address sheet: 'You will be so good as to deliver the Book to Mr Picker-
ing himself there are directions on a paper within side.'

[2] This and the two following letters were written on the same day, 1 May
1827, the date of the third letter.

'The same retrograde movement may be traced in the relation which the Authors themselves have assumed towards their readers. From the lofty address and prophetic self-reverence of BACON— "These are the Meditations of FRANCIS OF VERULAM, which that Posterity should possess, he deemed *their* interest":[1]—from Dedication to Monarch or Pontiff, in which the honor bestowed was asserted in equipoise to the patronage acknowleged: from PINDAR'S

$$———ἐπ' ἄλλοι-$$
-σι δ' ἄλλοι μεγάλοι. τὸ δ' ἔσχατον κορυ-
-φοῦται βασιλεῦσι. μηκέτι
πάπταινε πόρσιον.

Εἴη σέ τε τοῦτον
'Υψοῦ χρόνον πατεῖν, ἐμέ
Τε τοσσάδε νικαφόροις
'Ομιλεῖν, πρόφαντον σοφίαν καθ' "Ελ-
-λανας ἐόντα παντᾷ.

OLYMP. OD. I.

there was a gradual sinking in the etiquette or allowed style of pretension.[2]

'Poets and Philosophers, rendered diffident by their very number, addressed themselves to "*Learned* Readers": then aimed to conciliate the graces of "the *Candid* Reader": till, the critic still rising as the Author sank, the Amateurs of Literature collectively were erected into a municipality of Judges and addressed as THE TOWN! And now finally, all men being supposed able to read, and all readers able to judge, the Multitudinous PUBLIC, shaped and condensed into personal unity by the magic of abstraction, sits nominal Despot on the throne of Criticism. But alas! as in other despotisms, it but echoes the decisions of it's invisible Ministers, whose intellectual claims to the guardianship of the Muses seem, for the greater part, analogous to the physical qualifications which adapt their oriental Brethren for the superintendence of the Harem.'

P.S.[3]—As William thinks, that you have not a Copy of the Biog. Liter. I have transcribed the passage from Mr Gillman's Copy corrected by the Author.—S.T.C.

---

[1] See *Novum Organum.*
[2] This concluding clause ('there was a gradual sinking' etc.), which is necessary to complete the sentence beginning 'From the lofty address', does not appear in the first edition of the *Biographia Literaria.* It was, however, added in the second edition of 1847.
[3] This postscript appears at the top of page one of the MS.

1583. *To Basil Montagu*

MS. University Library, Cambridge. Pub. with omis. The Philosophical Lectures of Samuel Taylor Coleridge, *ed. Kathleen Coburn, 1949, p. 454.*

My dear friend   [1 May 1827]
The only other passage in my published Works respecting Lord Bacon is that in *Friend*, Vol. III. p. 204. Essay VIII.[1]—

In one of Goethe's least known Works and in a *Note* too, there is (I distinctly recollect) an elaborate Character of Lord Bacon[2]— and in some one of my Manifold Many-Scraps on Many Scrips in my own Manuscript, alias Manuscrawl, there are sundry additamenta, judicia emendata, and overruling of the Goethian Dicta— & a comparison of Plato and Bacon.—Altogether, if I could afford the time, there might be framed out of it a highly polished Character of Lord Bacon, as Man, Statesman, and Philosopher—

Now positively the time and concentration of Mind more than equal to a Poem of the same length, which must be given to it if it should be what I should wish to render it, the Gem of all my Compositions, to which I should refer as the Proof and Specimen of my powers in Style and Substance, would—if the Money were to come from forth of the Bookseller's Till—sanction me as an honest man having a tender conscience for his own interests, in asking the *Sir Walter Scott* Price of 50£ for it—

The Over leaf Matter is for Mrs Montague—God bless you | &
                                                    S. T. Coleridge.

1584. *To Mrs. Basil Montagu*

MS. University Library, Cambridge. Hitherto unpublished.

My dear Mrs Montagu   May 1, 1827—
Can you let me know by a twopenny post note whether Mr Irving is likely to accompany you & Basil on Thursday—or whether (as William tells me, he will be engaged on Thursday next Week) whether I could rely on seeing him the Thursday After?—Some friends of mine (Mr & Mrs Stutfield, of Hackney—You may spell

---

[1] Essay IX in subsequent editions of *The Friend*. In the list of Errata in vol. i of *The Friend*, 1818, Coleridge points out that in vol. iii, p. 168 [163], line 6, 'a new Essay (VI.) should have begun. . . . The Essays following to be counted accordingly, viz. VII. VIII. &c.'

[2] *Geschichte der Farbenlehre*, Dritte Abtheilung: Sechszehntes Jahrhundert. Bacon of Verulam, Goethe's *Werke*: Vollständige Ausgabe letzter Hand. Vol. 53, Cotta (Stuttgart, 1833) pp. 149–64.

the word, *frens*, if you like—as there ought to be distinctions) have
been for the last 3 months asking & asking me to invite them when
Mr Irving will be with us—and I have as regularly forgot it.—

And now I will give you, my dear Friend, what appears to me to
comprize in few words the strongest objection to Mr Irving's View,
and the strength of the Anti-millenarian Plea.—

'And then shall they see the Son of Man coming in a cloud with
power and great glory.'[1] What is the true import of this momen-
tous phrase '*coming in a cloud*'? Has not God himself expounded
it for us? To the Son of Man (so the Great Apostle assures us) all
power was given in Heaven & on Earth.[2] He became PROVIDENCE
—i.e. that Divine Power which behind the cloud & veil of Worldly
Events and seeming Human Agency controls, disposes, and directs
both events and actions to the Gradual unfolding and final Con-
summation of the vast Scheme of Redemption, in and by which
the evil and alien Nature shall be cast forth, & the Union effec-
tuated of the Creature with the Creator, of Man with God, in and
thro' the *Son* OF Man, even Him, the Son of God Manifested! Now
it cannot surely be denied or even doubted by any intelligent and
unprejudiced reader of Matthew, Ch. XXIVth, that the Son of
Man did come in the utter destruction and devastation of the Jewish
Temple and State during the period from Vespasian to Hadrian
(both included).—And is it a *sufficient* reason for rejecting the
Teaching of Christ himself, of Christ glorified and in full possession
of his kingly Rights, that the Apostles, who themselves disclaim
all pretension to any certain knowlege on this subject, had under-
stood our Lord's Words in a sense more commensurate with the
notions and imaginations common to them with their Age and
Countrymen? They communicated their conjectures, but only *as*
conjectures, and these too (happily for the cause of Christianity)
guarded by the avowal that they had received no special revela-
tion, no revealed commentary on their Master's Words, 'the great
Apocalypse of Jesus Christ while yet in the Flesh'—for by this
title was the prophecy (Luke 17th) known and distinguished among
the Christians of the Apostolic Age.[3] GOD *has* taught *us* the true

---

[1] Luke xxi. 27.   [2] Matthew xxviii. 18.

[3] This paragraph corresponds closely to one of Coleridge's marginal notes
in *The Coming of Messiah in Glory and Majesty*, 2 vols., 1827, a work translated
by Edward Irving from the Spanish of Manuel Lacunza, a converted Jew who
wrote under the pseudonym of Juan Josafat Ben-Ezra. (See *Literary Remains*,
iv. 412–13.) A copy of Irving's two-volume translation with annotations by
Coleridge is in the British Museum. For these annotations see *Literary Remains*,
iv. 399–415. For a further criticism of Irving's views on 'the Millennium, and
the return of Jesus in his corporeal individuality' see *Literary Remains*, iv.
14–15. See also Letter 1519.

meaning of the phrase, *in a cloud*—and is any other interpretation less than *childish*?—God bless you &

S. T. Coleridge.

1585. *To Mrs. Gillman*

Address: Mrs Gillman
MS. Cornell University Lib. Pub. Letters, *ii. 745.*

3 May 1827.

My dear Friend

I received and acknowlege your this morning's Present, both as Plant and Symbol, each with appropriate thanks and correspondent feeling. The Rose is the Pride of Summer, the Delight and the Beauty of our Gardens; the Eglantine, the Honey-suckle and the Jasmin if not so bright or so ambrosial, are less transient, creep nearer to us, clothe our walls, twine over our porch, and haply peep in at our Chamber window, with the nested Wren or Linnet within the tufts warbling good morning to us.—Lastly, the Geranium passes the door, and in it's hundred varieties imitating now this now that Leaf, Odor, Blossom of the Garden still steadily retains it's own *staid* character, it's own sober and refreshing Hue and Fragrance. It deserves to be the Inmate of the House, and with due attention and tenderness will live thro' the winter, grave yet chearful, as an old family Friend, that makes up for the departure of gayer Visitors, in the leafless Season. But none of these are the MYRTLE! In none of these, nor in all collectively, will the MYRTLE find a Substitute.—All together, and joining with them all the aroma, the spices and the balsams of the Hot-house, yet would they be a sad exchange for the MYRTLE! O precious in it's sweetness is the *rich* innocence of it's snow-white Blossoms! And dear are they in the remembrance—but these may pass with the Season, and while the Myrtle Plant, our own myrtle-plant[1] remains unchanged, it's Blossoms are remembered the more to endear the faithful Bearer; yea, they survive invisibly in every *more than* fragrant Leaf. As the flashing Strains of the Nightingale to the yearning Murmur of the Dove, so the Myrtle to the Rose—He who has once possessed and prized a genuine Myrtle, will rather *remember* it under the Cypress Tree, than seek to *forget* it among the Rose-bushes of a Paradise.

---

[1] For various anecdotes concerning this myrtle plant and slips taken from it, see Lucy E. Watson, *Coleridge at Highgate*, 1925, pp. 132–5, and *Letters*, ii. 745 n.

God bless you, my dearest Friend! and be assured that if Death do not suspend Memory and Consciousness, Death itself will not deprive you of a faithful Participator in all your hopes and fears, affections and solicitudes, in your unalterable

S. T. Coleridge

1586. *To Henry Nelson Coleridge*

Address: H. N. Coleridge, Esqre | 1. New Square | Lincoln's Inn—
MS. Victoria University Lib. Hitherto unpublished.
Postmark: Highgate, 9 May 1827.

Tuesday, 8 May 1827.
Grove, Highgate.

My dear Henry

As to Lord Dudley & Ward, I fear, that nothing good would come from *my* application to him. But you shall judge. Before dear Mr Frere left England, he informed me that he had at length procured a positive Promise from Lord Liverpool to do something for me to the amount of 200£ a year, without withdrawing me from my studies—that Lord Liverpool had himself suggested that before Christmas he should be reminded of it, if he had not by that time done it—& as Mr F. could not be himself here, he counselled me to write to Lord Dudley & Ward, who had made *me* (to tell the whole truth, as I am myself persuaded—for and *only* for Mr Frere's sake and because it would gratify *him*, and in consequence of an old offer of Lord Dudley's when Mr Ward) a pecuniary present.— The particulars I will tell you when we meet—in the same confidence with which I write this letter—(which is betwixt you & me. Of course, I do not mean to exclude Sara—unless and only as far as any thing, I may say, would in your judgement distress her feelings without any compensating good—). Well! You know enough of me, to supersede the necessity of my telling you that I have too few pleasant thoughts associated with my circumstances, or with the *I* in any other sense than as it is a synonime of the Italian *si*, the German *Man*, and the Anglo-gallic *one*, &c to think of it wilfully or oftener than I can help—So in this case I delayed & delayed writing to Lord Dudley, till Mrs Aders came up to Highgate to congratulate me, as she had taken for granted—her own Brotherin-law having, backed too with powerful influence, made interest for the late Gifford's place of Paymaster of the King's Gentlemen Pensioners—and received from the Treasury the immediate answer— The Place has been reserved by Lord Liverpool for Mr Coleridge—. A fortnight or so passed & no official confirmation reaching me,

Mrs Gillman's entreaties at length overcame my antipathy to the task and I did write to Lord Dudley & Ward—My letter followed him to Brighton—& from Brighton I received a civil answer, stating his disposition to comply with my request; but that he had much rather *see* Lord Liverpool on the Subject than write to him—that he should be in town within a fortnight, and as soon as he arrived in town, would make an opportunity &c. Ten days of this fortnight had elapsed and on the 11th Lord Liverpool lost all but that, of which Death itself will not bereave him! I again wrote what Sara thought a *mighty pretty* Letter to Lord Dudley, humbly intreating his advice—& whether he thought, I might without impropriety state the circumstance to Mr Canning—& whether I was presuming too much in asking his Lordship, should an opportunity occur, to mention it to Mr Canning—After about a week or more interval, I received a remarkable *cold* letter (even compared with the former which Heaven knows! was far enough from *Fever-heat*) in which he does not even notice the latter suggestion; but merely replies that from a gentleman of my reputation there could be no impropriety in my writing to Mr Canning; but that he feared, I was not likely to receive either a speedy or a satisfactory Answer.—In the mean time, the King himself filled up the Place—& since then I have not heard from Lord Dudley—But I have great reason to believe that the same Spirit of Calumny from the North and from the South had long ago been working on *his* mind, which had influenced Sir George Beaumont (who had taken leave of me with an unusual fervor of affection, affectionate as his manners had for the two last years been to a marked degree) to make one of the last acts of his Life an implicit but trumpet-tongued Brand on my Honor & character.[1] Poor Mrs C.—her hundred pound is but a poor compensation for the injurious influences on her children & herself, to which she has so long unthinkingly lent her aid in her rash and God knows! most unjust speeches & the impressions made & permitted to be made even on my own

---

[1] Sir George Beaumont died 7 Feb. 1827. By his will he left £100 to Mrs. Coleridge but nothing to Coleridge. According to Leslie, Lamb was 'indignant' at this action, said it 'seemed to mark Coleridge with a stigma', and added, 'If . . . Coleridge was a scamp, Sir George should not have continued, as he did, to invite him to dinner.' (*Autobiographical Recollections. By the late Charles Robert Leslie*, ed. Tom Taylor, 2 vols., 1860, i. 54.) Mrs. Coleridge reported to Poole that Beaumont left £100 each to Wordsworth and Southey. Noting that Wordsworth also received 'an Annuity for life of one hundred pounds', she went on to say: 'I find W. does not wish to have his Legacy spoken of—so—entre nous—Ly B. told Sara, that Sir G. meant to have made some additions to his will, if time had been allowed him.' *Minnow among Tritons*, ed. Stephen Potter, 1934, p. 137.

children!—How little did I anticipate the whole extent of the
injury when the fraudulent Bankruptcy of the Pater-noster Row
Fellow deprived me of the 1100£, which I had destined for Mrs
Coleridge to settle her obligations to the Southeys with—tho' there
is not (the Gillmans excepted) the Man, who has not derived from
me directly or indirectly more even in *pecuniary* RESULTS than
after deduction of Sara's Services[1] would remain to be accounted
for.—But I have long referred this and the whole web of positive
& negative Slander to a Tribunal that cannot misjudge—'O Lord
my God! if I have done any such thing knowingly or willingly; if
there be any such wickedness in my hands; if I have rewarded evil
unto him that dealt friendly with me—(yea, I have delivered him
that without any cause is my Enemy!) then let mine Enemy perse-
cute my Soul and take me—yea, let him tread my Life down upon
the Earth, and lay mine Honor in the Dust!'[2] God forbid! that I
should continue the appropriation to the verse that follows (Psalm
7.) & deprive myself of the greatest & best of my few remaining
Comforts, the undiminished power of saying nightly—Forgive me
my trespasses even as I from my heart & Soul forgive all them that
trespass against me!—

Now I scarcely need point out to you, in what a ludicrous light
an application from me for another to Lord Dudley might have—
But I have heard that Lord Lindhurst has spoken kindly of me—
& tho' I have no distinct personal recollections of him, yet his
private Secretary (Mr Charles Murray) thinks well of me, & if you
thought it was likely to be of service, I would write to Lord Lind-
hurst himself,[3] or to the Marquis of Lansdown or (tho' I do not
know on what terms he & Lord L. are) to Mr Brougham—or to
Sir James Mackintosh. I am sorry, as it happens that you are not in
town. I will, however, in the interval between this & the receipt of
your answer prepare a letter to Lord Lindhurst & a second that
may do for either of the other names.—Remember me affectionately
to Edward & with kind respect to Mrs E.—God bless you, and

S. T. Coleridge.

P.S. Lady L. (if she had in her Bosom what she ought to have &

---

[1] Sara Coleridge had for several years been a tutor to the younger Southey
children. More recently she had instructed Cuthbert Southey 'in Latin, French,
& anything that she could do for him'. [Unpublished letter, Mrs. Coleridge to
Derwent.] She was also helpful in other ways. 'Sara is secretary for triangular
affairs', Southey wrote in Mar. 1824, in reference to *The Doctor. Southey
Letters*, iii. 414. See also *Minnow among Tritons*, ed. Stephen Potter, 1934, p. 88,
and *Letters of Hartley Coleridge*, 108–9.

[2] Coleridge is here quoting *The Book of Common Prayer*, Psalm vii. 3–5.

[3] John Singleton Copley, Lord Lyndhurst (1772–1863), whom Coleridge had
met at Cambridge, became lord chancellor in Apr. 1827.

has not) is under obligations to Mr & Mrs Gillman, which she would thank no one for reminding her of—But she is what Helen was, beauty out of the question—& as I once pithily observed

A bitch and a Mare set Old Troy Bells a knelling:
The Mare was of Wood and the Bitch was call'd Helen!

P.S. I shall be in town tomorrow—& any time between 5 o'clock and 10 you would find me at Mr Tulk's, 19 Duke St, Westminster. If I sleep in town, it will be at Mr Hart's in Mecklenburg Square—& after breakfast I will call at your rooms. I had not read the latter part of your letter.

1587. *To Mrs. S. T. Coleridge*

MS. Victoria University Lib. Pub. E. L. G. ii. 405. This fragment consists of only a half page, recto and verso. It is the last letter which has come to light of those from Coleridge to his wife.

[*Circa* 8 May 1827][1]

My dear Sara

I have just heard that Mrs Gillman is sending off a Cap-casket (if Lester has rightly informed me of the contents) to Keswick—quite time enough to allow me no time to do more than scrawl a sentence or two with my name at the tail, the Carpenter fiddling impatiently with the . . .

. . . afflict me more than the Loss of the Place—which vexes me chiefly on Hartley's account—who is seldom, an hour together, out of my head, and still less often *off* my heart.—Something would have been done for me long before, but for the activity of calumny, direct and indirect, mute, and vocal—but enough of this! I have long since referred the cause to a Tribunal that cannot judge amiss —(Psalm VII. v. 3, 4, 5.)— . . .

---

[1] The mention of 'the Loss of the Place' and 'the activity of calumny' and the reference to Psalm vii in this and the preceding letter suggest that the two letters were written about the same time.

1588. *To H. F. Cary*

MS. Cornell University Lib. Pub. Memoir of H. F. Cary, *ii. 176.*

Friday Night—or Saturday Morning—
Grove, Highgate—[25 or 26] May 1827.[1]—

My dear Friend

I have been just looking, rectius staring, at the Theologian Croly's Revelations of the Revelations of John, the Theologian[2]—both Poets, both Seers—the one saw visions and the other dreams dreams; but John was no Tory, and Croly is no Conjurer. Therefore, tho' his Views extend to the Last Conflagration, he is not in my humble judgement likely to bear a part in it by setting the Thames on fire.—The Divine, Croley, sets John the Divine's Trumpets and Vials side by side. Methinks, Trumpets and Vi*ols* would make the better accompaniment—the more so, as there is a particular kind of Fiddle, tho' not strung with *Cat*-gut, for which Mr Croly's Book would make an appropriate Bow.

Verily, verily, my dear Friend! I feel it impossible to think of this shallow fiddle-faddle Trumpery, and how it is [and] has been trumpeted and patronized by our Bishops and Dignitaries, and not enact either Heraclitus or Democritus. I laugh that I may not weep. You know me too well to suppose me capable of treating even an error of faith with levity. But these are not errors of faith; but blunders from the utter want of Faith, a Vertigo from spiritual inanition, from the lack of all internal strength; even as a man giddy-drunk throws his arms about, and clasps hold of a Barber's Block for support—and mistakes seeing double for 'additional evidences'. I believe Luke, I believe Paul, I believe John, the Beloved of his Lord—I believe Moses, I believe the Prophets, and I mourn and rejoice and pray and complain and hope and trust and give thanks to the Lord with David. But I should study Daniel with more satisfaction, if it stood (*complete,* as in the Septuagint Version) between Maccabees & the Title-page of the Apocrypha; and I should read the Apocalypse with unqualified delight and admiration, if it took the Lead of the 'Shepherd', St Barnabas, and St Clement,[3] and (for I will confess to the whole extent of my Offending) the 3 Pastoral Epistles[4]—at all events the *first* Ep. to Timothy

---

[1] In Letter 1590, which was concluded on Monday night, 4 June 1827, Coleridge acknowledges Cary's reply to the present letter.

[2] George Croly, *The Apocalypse of St. John, . . . a new Interpretation,* 1827.

[3] Hermas, author of *The Shepherd,* Barnabas, and Clement, three of the Apostolic Fathers.

[4] St. Paul's two Epistles to Timothy and his Epistle to Titus.

—in a Volume by itself under the modest name of *Antilegomena*.—
It is true, that I hold the Pseudo-athanasian Creed to be pretty
equally divided into four parts, under the corresponding Heads of
—1. Presumption, and that brimstone-colored—2. Tautology or
Verbiage. 3. Nonsense. 4. Heresy—but I can conscientiously repeat
every syllable of the Nicene Creed, and likewise of that which I am
modest enough to think no bad Supplement for individual Catechu-
mens, the Confessio Fidei in p. 189–191 of 'the Aids to Reflection'
—and as a Man who has lost a Leg or Arm is still an integral *Man*,
so I trust that I notwithstanding the above-mentioned Decrements
may still pass for a Christian.

Now the object of this letter was to intreat you, with Francis's
assistance, to glance your eye over the theological part of the
Catalogue[1]—to see whether you have any number of Commen-
tators on the Apocalypse. I do not know, whether it would be
worth the time & trouble, it would cost; but a fancy has struck me,
that if one could select some one Interpreter & Prognosticator
from each *Century* from the tenth to the 16th Century—from
A.D. 1000 to 1600—and one for every half century from 1600 to
1827—and give the various *fulfilments* asserted or expected of any
two or three famous Passages in the Apocalypse, Trumpets or
Vials, in a sort of tabular form or synoptic map—it would be *one*
way of opening men's eyes. Another way would be to give a very
abridged interpretation of the Poem, chapter by chapter, according
to the true meaning of the Symbols; and then to abridge some one
of the most learned and rational of the Interpreters on the prog-
nosticating plan, Mede perhaps or Fleming[2]—and to print the two
in parallel Columns—so as to place the coherence and sequency
of the one with the backward, and forward, in and out, Jack a
lanthorn, *right-about-to-the-left-and-advance-backward* March of the
other in full contrast.

Finally, my dear Friend! the word, prophesy, may be taken in
three senses.—Organization is either simultaneous as in an indi-
vidual animal, or successive—as in one of Handel's or Mozart's
Overtures. Now in every scheme of Organization Successive (and
the great Scheme of Revelation is eminently such) every integral
part is of necessity both prophecy & history, save the last or
consummating Fact, which will be only History, and the initial
which can only be prophecy: but of all the intervening Components

---

[1] H. F. Cary was appointed assistant-keeper of printed books at the British
Museum in 1826.

[2] Joseph Mead (or Mede), *Clavis Apocalyptica ex innatis et insitis Visionum
characteribus eruta et demonstrata*, 1627; and Robert Fleming, the younger,
Apocalyptical Key, 1701.

of the Scheme every part is both at once—i.e. Prophecy in rela-
tion to what follows and History in relation to that which had
preceded.—Now in this sense of the word I believe the whole
Bible to be prophetic.—Secondly, in every perfect scheme there is
an Idea of the whole, and in every *real* (i.e. not merely *formal* or
abstract) Science there are Laws—& this is equally true in moral
as in physical Science. But where ever Laws are, Prophecy may be—
the difference between moral & physical Laws in this respect being
only this, that in the physical the *Prophecy* is absolute, in the moral
is it more or less conditional—according to the character of the
moral Subject in whom it is to be fulfilled. In certain cases it will
be *virtually* absolute—(Ex. gr. *If* that inveterate Sot and Dram-
drinker does not conquer his habit, and it is *next* to certainty he
never will—he will die of a rotten Liver.—Now would any man
hesitate to abbreviate this into—'That man will die of a rotten
Liver' ?—Yet it *is possible*, that the man might reform.) and there
are several instances of *verbally* unconditional Prophecies in scrip-
ture, both of Promise and of Threat, that were not fulfilled: and
yet 'tbe Scripture not broken'. Why ? because the condition, which
in all moral prophecies is *understood*, did not take place.—Now of
Prophecies in this sense of the word there are many and glorious
ones—and such as bear witness to the divinity of the inspiring
Spirit, the Santa Sophia, proceeding ἐκ τοῦ Ἀγαθοῦ, καὶ ἐκ τοῦ
Ἀληθοῦς. III. Prophecy is used for *prognostication*, with the precise
time, individual person, and name—and this two or 3 hundred
years before either the person was in existence or the name known.
—Now of Prophecies in *this* third sense I utterly deny that there is
any one instance delivered by any one of the illustrious Diadoche
whom the Jewish Church comprized in the name *Prophets*—and I
shall regard *Cyrus* as an exception when I believe the 137th Psalm
to have been composed by David only because the collection in
which it stands has, Psalms of David, for it's general Title.—Nay,
I will go further—and assert, that the contrary belief, or the hypo-
thesis of Prognostication, is in direct and irreconcileable oppug-
nancy to our Lord's repeated declaration, that the *times* hath the
Father reserved to himself—a declaration drawn from the very
depth of the profoundest Theology and Philosophy, aye and
Morality to boot! And now I must say, God bless you, and your's
—Good night—. I will remember you in my prayers & pray that
if I am in error, you or some other good man will be commissioned
to enlighten and recall me—

S. T. Coleridge.

1589. *To J. H. Green*

Address: J. H. Green Esqre | &c | Lincoln's Inn Fields
MS. Pierpont Morgan Lib. Hitherto unpublished.
Postmark: Highate, 30 May 1827.

Wednesday Morning, seven o/clock. [30 May 1827]
My dear Friend
   I have just received your letter—and am sorry that I cannot
name an earlier day than *Friday*: or Thursday night—for I must
have an hour or two to look thro' the pages, they have been so
thrown about—and to do [so] I am obliged to do what will employ
more than all the time, I have strength for—. How could you sup-
pose there could be any Objection? If I could transfer to you the
sheets of my Brain in a duplicate, you should have them without
omissions or hiatus.—
   A portly Dame, whose Good man has done well for himself in the
Carcase-Butcher Line, would fain have something, in the Otti-
graph way, from *me* in the splendid Book which by a somewhat
italianized mode of pronunciation she calls her *Ol*bum or *Awl*bum
—Would this do?

> Parry[1] seeks the Pólar Ridge:
> But rhymes seeks S. T. Cólĕridge
> Fit for Mrs Smudger's *Ol*bum
> Or to wipe her Baby's small bum.[2]

Another

Lines for a Lady's Album.

> A Dame of Fashion ask'd Sir Toby Jewett,
> What *Album* meant. Hem! quoth the Learned Knight:
> 'Clean Sheets—or your Chemise—or what's next to it—
> 'In fine, my Lady! *any thing that's white*'.

Sequel to the Above.

wants polishing

> Yes, yes! I see it now! rejoin'd the Dame—
> Last night when we were talking of the Name

---

  [1] William Edward Parry (1790–1855), brother of Charles and Frederick
Parry, Coleridge's companions in Göttingen, was at this time engaged in an
attempt to reach the north pole from Spitsbergen. Though unsuccessful, he
reached a point of 82° 45′ N. lat., the highest latitude attained for the next
49 years.

  [2] In publishing these lines in 1834, Coleridge substituted the couplet quoted
in Letter 1718 for the last two lines. See *Poems*, ii. 972.

Of the Turk's Bible, and you said to me,
You said, as I remember[1]—that *Al* meant *the*.
Me, I confess, it ne'er before did strike,
English and Latin were so near alike.—

S. T. C.—

God bless you &

S. T. Coleridge—

1590. *To H. F. Cary*

MS. State University of Iowa. Pub. Memoir of H. F. Cary, *ii. 181.*

Grove, Highgate—
Saturday Night—
[2] June, 1827.

My dear Friend

Haunted all day with that nervous necessity of repeating every two or three minutes the precious couplet

And there I saw beside of yonder Thicket

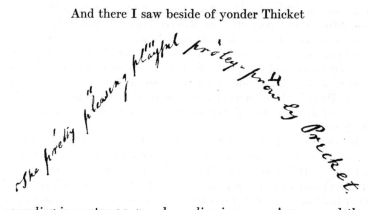

ascending in acutes ´ ″ ‴ —*descending* in graves ` ″ ‴ —and then in the pe- and antepe-nultimate words, there is a definite Indefiniteness, an accommodating ad libitum receptivity, such a promising wooing Meaningness *in general,* that you can't find in your Heart to supersede it's own natural *proley-prowliness* by attaching to it any Meaning in particular!—and further in aid of this nervous stammering of the mind there happens to be a family of Prickets in Highgate—the one a fine, tall, slim, swimmy, glidy Lass whose

---

[1] Coleridge first wrote, 'Aye—I remember now—' and then amended the words to read as above.

smiles curtsy to you as she bends and floats by—another a sullen, black, surly, burly, bum-bayly Lawyer, that is in league with the Spirit of *Irony* to recall the same Distich—and one or the other I am sure to meet in my walk—while a third is a Patient of Mr Gillman's, whose impatient Messages—Mrs Pricket would be very glad, Sir! if you would call as soon as possible—She is so very low & all over pain—are sure to start & make out-leap again

The pretty, pleasing playful, proley prowley Pricket—

It is a perfect Plague, a Jack o' lanthorn persecution—and I write this to you to try if I can get it *out* of my head, just as they send the Vaccine Virus in a twopenny post letter! I forward it, to wit, with the charitable hope of getting rid of the morbid matter by transferring it to another, according to a not yet wholly obsolete fancy & more than once acted on by the Devil's Vulgar, when inoculated with a worse Venom than Cow ever gave name or birth to.—

Monday Night.

I had thrown this sorry excretion, wherewith I had essayed to exonerate my nerves, aside, on a matter of doubt whether obtruding nonsense on a friend and making him pay 0£. 0s. 3d. for the same, was either quite respectful or strictly honest.—But this evening came your kind Letter—& as I can only write a few lines, in reply, the Above may serve to give my letter a letter-like primam faciem, without additional cost. (By the bye, it would be but civil in the Government to let all communications to the Librarians of the Imperial British Museum come free as presumably concerning the artistical, *bell-Let*tristical (not *belly**) or bibliographical interests of the Nation.)—

My dear friend! I made myself misunderstood about the 137th Psalm—I meant to say, that as no one thought that a Psalm of the imagery of Babylon was written by David, because the Compilers of the Canon had entitled the whole, 'Psalms of David', as little did I hold myself obliged to attribute the Oracle respecting Cyrus to Isaiah, because it stood in a collection or Florilegium of Isaianic Oracles. The main Obstacle, however, is not the word, Cyrus: tho' Eichhorn, a great Oriental Linguist whatever else he may be, asserts that neither the Language nor History affords the least sanction for the Conjecture.—It is the *unique* fact of the Camel and Ass Cavalry, and this originating in accident, and the thought of the moment—it is this, & one or two similar minutiae so wholly alien from the purpose & character of the Hebrew Prophecies re-

* ? belly-tristic no bad epithet for an author's banyan-day??—[Note by S. T. C.]

specting distant events, which gravel me.—It is no new notion—
Aben Ezra, the Coryphaeus of the uninspired Sages of Israel, and
undoubtedly a man of vast Intellect & almost portentous Variety
& Depth of Learning, states it as an opinion common among the
Learned of his Countrymen, and which he commends as removing
many 'troublesome difficulties', that the Oracles from the 40th
Chapter are by later Prophets who delivered their Oracles accord-
ing to the Isaianic Type.[1] Mr Hurwitz assures me, that the struc-
ture of the sentences & even the grammatical inflections are
strikingly distinguished.—But I attach no importance to this
point. Sufficient that I agree with you, in respect of the prophetic
character of the Bible in the two first senses of the word, Prophecy
—and I believe with you, that the whole chain of Predictions from
Adam to St Paul, given to Man in the five forms, necessary to the
full manifestation of the Manhood, 1. The Individual—2. the
Kind or Universal—3. The Races—4. Family. 5. Nation†—to be
such as could only proceed from a *special extraordinary* influence
of the Holy Spirit—and that you agree with me in the remaining
sense. It is scarcely possible that any one should estimate either
the prophetic Spirit or the particular prophecies of the Bible, at
a higher value than I do, as feeding, strengthening, deepening and
enlarging the faith of a Believer. The mistake is in the using them,
as the foundation-stones of the Edifice, instead of it's Pillars—in
beginning from them with Infidels, a[s] PROOFS of an Argument,
the very Data of which suppose the Belief that is to be produced
by it. The right use of the Prophecies is to regard them, as a
magnificent Scheme of *History* a priori, containing the Class, the
Orders of the class, and the Genera of the Orders, with the corre-
sponding classic, Ordinal, and Generic Characters—and then to
collate with these the series of actual Events, as so many Individua,
which with a wonderful Accordance arrange themselves into species,
that occur in the very sequency of the distinguishing Characters

---

[1] The father of the controversy concerning the authorship of these chapters
was Abraham ben Meir Ibn Ezra (Abenezra), who died in 1167.

† Christ promised—1. and 2. to Adam, at once the Individual & the kind,
the Man and *Man*—promised in his highest character, as first, the Destroyer
of Spiritual Evil—the crusher of the Serpent's Head, & 2. as the Healer of the
corrupted Humanity, the invenomed wound in the Heel—1st and 3rd—to Noah,
+ Shem, Ham, Japhet[h]—the Individual & the three Races—See the Epistle of
Peter—The Preaching of the Μετάνοια—the type of Baptism—the Rain-bow.
N. B. Baptism = φῶς δι' ὕδατος.—4. to the Patriarchs, the Family—Christ
promised as Shiloh, the Blesser of the Families of the whole Earth—and the
remover of the wall of Separation between them & the chosen Family—5. thro'
Moses and the Prophets, as the restorer of the Kingdom, in which the Elect
from the 4 Corners of the Earth shall be indenizened as children of Abraham.
[Note by S. T. C.]

which are found realized in them. Imagine for instance that the
first Chapter of Genesis had been revealed to the Angels, the future
minist[e]ring Spirits of our Earth, ere yet the Indistinction (Chaos)
was polarized by the Omnific Word into the Dyad of Light and the
Power of the Mass—Now with the same convictions, and with the
same feelings of Delight, with which one of these Angels would
peruse this Chapter on the 4th or 5th Day of the Week of the
Epochs of the Heaven & the Earth, do I in this 4th or 5th Day of
the yet diviner Week of the New Creation read the Prophecies.
I see all past History provided for in the Scheme: and I do not, say
rather I cannot doubt, that the Future will be found equally cor-
respondent as soon as the number of particular Events shall be
sufficient to form & fill up the next Epoch: for no Prophecy is of
private, i.e. individual Interpretation. And for this very reason is
every Prophecy instructive of the true meaning, the essential
character and import of the Events, in which they are fulfilled.
The Prophetic Word is the Light of the Present—and for the pre-
pared Organ the Source of *In*sight, without which Sight is but the
hollow Imago of a colored Shadow, of a Surface—i.e. a facies
super rem ipsam jacens vel fluitans.—My dear Friend! we are so
near each other in our convictions on this point, that with a little
modification on both sides we should soon accomplish a total Co-
incidence—

My Daughter is with me: and I am very anxious to pay you a
Visit with her, and Mrs Gillman—who is no less desirous of it than
myself. But I am afraid that I cannot make it Saturday. I will,
however, try to make some arrangement with Mrs G.—who
sends her kindest Love to you & Mrs Carey—& will let you know.—
God bless you & your's—in which last include

S. T. Coleridge.

1591. *To Unknown Correspondent*[1]

MS. formerly in the possession of the late Charlton Yarnall (transcribed by the late J. L. Haney). Hitherto unpublished.

9th June, 1827

My dear Sir

I fear you will find great difficulties in decyphering the handwrit-
ing, and more perhaps in correcting the errata of com- or o-mission
of my Pupil & Amanuensis, some 20 years ago. The thinner of the
two stiff covered Books is the first, and the flexible the third. I
shall not want them till we meet—which I should have wished to

---

[1] This letter may have been intended for J. H. Green. See Letter 1589.

have been at an earlier period . . .[1] as waste of Time and Thought
for which . . .[1] are but an inadequate consolation. But God's will
be done. I complain only as far as it suspends and retards my work
on the philosophy and history of Christianity, in contrast with the
Grotian and Paleyan defences of the same.

Believe me with | great respect | Your's sincerely
S. T. Coleridge

1592. *To William Sotheby*

MS. Mr. W. Hugh Peal. Pub. E. L. G. ii. 392.

Grove, Highgate
[June 1827][2]

My dear Sir

In what form of Thanks shall I acknowlege the receipt of the
Polyglot Georgics, that shall bear even a tolerable proportion to
the Magnificence of the Present? I will avail myself of some one
of those focal states of my Being, in which Head and Heart con-
verge, and record on the blank leaves all, I know, think, and feel
of the work, and of it's Author: and it shall be, as far as the full and
earnest expression of my Will can make it such, a[n] Heirloom in my
Family; which I shall, D V, deliver to my Daughter on her Wedding
Day—as the most splendid way, that I can command, of marking
my sense of the Talent and Industry, that have made her Mistress
of the Six Languages comprized in the Volume,[3] and of the fine
Taste and genial sentiment which will ensure her selecting the
English and the German Versions, as (in the only two legitimate
kinds of poetic translation) carrying the transfusion of the Spirit
and Individuality of a Poet, each in it's kind, to the highest point
of Perfection[4]—. And I shall make this Bequest the more willingly,
that in all present probability my dear Sara, whose worst fault is
that of tempting her Parents to be proud of her, will change her

---

[1] Erasure in MS. [Note by J. L. Haney.]

[2] In 1827 Sotheby issued a folio volume, *Georgica Publii Virgilii Maronis
Hexaglotta*, and sent presentation copies to many of the sovereigns of Europe
and to a number of friends. R. Gouch, librarian to King George IV, acknow-
ledged the volume on 9 June 1827. Coleridge's letter of acknowledgement, which
is endorsed 1827, was probably written about the same time.

[3] Sotheby's volume presented Virgil's *Georgics* in Latin, English (by W.
Sotheby), Spanish (by J. de Guzman), German (by J. H. Voss), Italian (by
F. Soave), and French (by J. Delille). Sotheby first published his English
translation in 1800.

[4] In 1828 Coleridge said he had made 'a very minute and critical Perusal
of the Georgics' and of the translations of Sotheby and Voss. See Letter 1645.

maiden state (whenever that may be) without changing her maiden name.[1]

I will not attempt any remark on *Your* Georgics. I have never had any other opinion, than that in a Poem of all others the most difficult to translate into English Metre it is the best Translation of *any* Work that exists in our Language and the nearest to the ideal *Alter et Idem*. The Diction and Versification are more highly polished, more exquisite than those of your Oberon: and both the Georgics and the Oberon are free from the one (and only notice-worthy) Defect of your later Compositions—the occasional excess of *fullness*—a strength and *co-acervation* that tend at times to retard the movement, and counteract the propulsive impetus of the total Spirit of the Poem. Were I asked, of any detached two or three hundred Lines in your Poems—ex. gr. Rome, Canto III.[2]—

---

[1] Coleridge specifically mentioned the polyglot *Georgics* in his will:

To my Daughter, Sara Coleridge, exemplary in all the relations of life in which she hath been placed, a blessing to both her Parents and to her Mother the rich reward, which the anxious fulfilment of her maternal Duties had, humanly speaking, merited, I bequeath the Presentation copy of the Georgica Heptaglotta [*sic*], given me by my highly respected Friend, William Sotheby Esqre—And it is my Wish, that Sara should never part with this volume: but that if she marry & should have a daughter, it may descend to her, . . . as a memento, that her Mother's accomplishments & her unusual attainments in ancient & modern Languages were not so much nor so justly the object of admiration, as their co-existence with Piety, Simplicity, and a characteristic meekness, in short with mind, manners, and character so perfectly feminine. And for this purpose I have recorded this my Wish in the same or equivalent words, on the first Title Page of this splendid Work— [For Coleridge's will, which is dated 17 Sept. 1829, see Appendix A.]

On his daughter's wedding day Coleridge wrote the following inscription in the fly-leaf of the Sotheby volume:

After my decease this splendid volume presented to me by William Sotheby, Esqr (and not the only mark of Regard and Kindness that I have received from this accomplished Scholar and truly worthy Man) is to belong, and I hereby give and appropriate it to my beloved and loveworthy child, Sara Coleridge. And I hope and trust that she will never willingly part with this volume or alienate the same. For if she should marry and should have a Daughter, it is my wish that this volume should descend to *her*, or (if Sara have daughters) to her eldest Daughter, who is to regard it as a Memento provided by her maternal Grandfather, that her dear Mother's accomplishments and her unusual attainments in ancient and modern Languages, were not so much nor so justly the objects of admiration as their co-existence in the same Person with so much piety, simplicity and unaffected meekness—in short, with a mind, character and demeanour so perfectly feminine.

S. T. Coleridge | 3 Sept. 1829 | Grove, Highgate.

[This volume is now in the Victoria University Library. I am indebted to Miss Margaret V. Ray, the librarian, for a copy of Coleridge's inscription.]

[2] *Farewell to Italy, and Occasional Poems*, 1818; reissued with additions as *Poems*, 1825.

what was wanted to make them *more* beautiful, I know not, how I could convey my mind more truly than if I should reply—To make 30 or 40 of them *less* so. You, I dare promise myself, will not be offended by my *heart-in-mouth* Openness.—

I will make an attempt to find you at home tomorrow—if I sleep in Grosvenor Square.—With respectful remembrance to Mrs Sotheby & Miss Sotheby, once more accept the thanks & admiration of

Your obliged Friend & Servt
S. T. Coleridge

1593. *To John Watson*

MS. Mr. W. Hugh Peal. Pub. Carlisle Patriot, *6 September 1834.*

This MS. letter is written on both sides of a single sheet, on the verso of which Coleridge had previously scribbled examples of metrical feet. It would seem, however, that he made a second copy of his letter. Not only does the text in the *Carlisle Patriot* differ considerably from the present manuscript, but the editor describes the 'original letter' as 'a letter written to a dear young friend upon the blank leaf of his "Aids to Reflection", with which the author had presented him on his leaving London in a hopeless state of consumption'.

[Grove, Highgate, 24th June, 1827.
Sunday evening.][1]

My dear Watson

Having month after month and season after season expected You with a Father's Longing, and at length received you with a Father's Joy, I should have found it grievous to part with you on any occasion. But to part from you in your present state of health, when the suspension even for a few days of the tenderest offices of Friendship cannot but fill my mind with anxiety, is very grievous! —On the restorative virtues of a Sea-Voyage, and the tried influence of your native air, I ground the right of looking forward to your return.—But in the thoughts and convictions, which produced the following work, I find my strongest support: for they teach me, that our meeting again is certain—and that the longer or shorter interval will be determined by the Friend who alone knows what is best for us, & who loves us more than we can love ourselves. To that all-wise, almighty Friend I consign you![2] His Love and the

---

[1] MS. undated. The place and date are taken from the text in the *Carlisle Patriot.*

[2] John Watson died on 9 July 1827, aged 28. In one of his notebooks Coleridge comments as follows:

Thurs. 2 Aug. 1827.—It is often said, that the Grief, we feel for the Death of the Innocent, of one who has departed in the Lord, is selfish for our own loss

Spirit, the Comforter, abide with you and with your paternally affectionate

S. T. Coleridge

1594. *To Mrs. Alaric A. Watts*

MS. Folger Shakespeare Lib. Pub. with omis. Alaric Watts, *i. 243.*

Monday Afternoon [2 July 1827.][1]
Grove, Highgate.

My dear Madam

You do me but Justice in believing that the part of your note respecting Mr Watts's Health would give me pain: tho' having had some little experience of a Newspaper Office in my own person, and the opportunity of an intimate knowlege of the toils of Editorship in a friend, I was almost as much surprized with what you told me on Saturday, as I am grieved with the information of this morning. O! dear Madam! the World is a stern and sour Goddess, that will not be conciliated without costly Sacrifices—and Life, and the Duties of Life, yea, even the very Affections, that give it zest and value, are pressed into the service, as her Whippers-on and Whippers-in. Were it in Mr Watts's power to set up a Paper, of which he would be the Master-WILL, as well as the Master MIND, and a Co-proprietor as well as the Controlling Editor[2]—tho' even so I should think it a costly Sacrifice—I could more easily reconcile myself to the thought—an early Competence is so great a Blessing—for a Man, I mean, of his powers and his activity of Mind. In this case it would be a benefit to Society, no less than to himself. And never was there a time, when a Paper of this kind, which

—tho' venial because natural. But this is a Saying extracted from *Words*—a Remark that is invented by the mind while thinking of words only, and deducing *words* of consequence from antecedent words according to the Rules of Logic.—It is not selfish—I am conscious in my own case & equally confident with regard to Mrs Gillman, when we heard of our dear young friend's Death—& so when we wept together over his mother's letter, that neither of us thought about ourselves, one way or the other—. The mistake is, in supposing that the passion of Grief always supposes the sense of Regret.—Grief is the appropriate feeling to the incident—Grief is sadness & the dissolving into tears—[MS. notebook, Huntington Library.]

[1] The 'old epigram' mentioned in the last paragraph of this letter appeared in the *Standard* on Friday, 29 June 1827.

[2] Watts was one of the sub-editors of the *Standard*, an evening newspaper established in 1827, the first number appearing on 21 May. He was also associated with the *St. James Chronicle*. See Letter 1598 and *Alaric Watts*, i. 260–3.

should bring the aims, acts, avowals and professions of both Parties, measure by measure and day after day, to the test of a pre-established Code of Principles deduced from a thorough insight into the Constitution of this Realm, and it's great constituent Elements and Interests, [was] more needed than at the present moment, or more certain of Success—supposing that means existed for securing it a fair tryal.—But these (the Knowers of the World will say) are *pia somnia*—Visions which Seers must shut their eyes to have—and alas! by *holding* them for pious dreams we *make* them so.—

On Thursdays I make a point of remaining at home: as on my account & to prevent my mornings from being at the mercy of Visitors, Mr and Mrs Gillman have given a general invitation to my London & Suburban Acquaintances for Thursday Evenings, a humble sort of Conversazione.—I will, however, soon take my chance of finding Mr Watts at home, and take my Tea with you.—

One subject I wished to talk over with him—namely, an Edition of Shakespear's Works, with notes that should bonâ fide explain what for the general Reader needs explanation, as briefly as possible, and with the expulsion of all antiquarian Rubbish.—After all the labors of the numerous Editors much remains to be done even for the Text of Shakespear—and this not consisting of trifles. The prominent Feature, however, would be the properly critical notes, prefaces, and analyses, comprizing the results of five and twenty Years' Study—the object being to distinguish and ascertain what Shakespear possessed in common with other great Men of his Age, or differing only in degree; and what was & is peculiar to himself.—I should prefer undertaking the work in concert with some other person—could there be found a man of letters, who had confidence in me and in whom I could have confidence.—Should Mr Watts think the scheme both desirable and feasible, and an opportunity should present itself, he would perhaps sound Colburn on the subject, or any other Publisher, that he thought proper.—

I saw an old epigram of mine in the Standard[1]—(Saturday's did not come—) If it would be of any service beyond the mere filling a gap, I will send him a Sheet-full, the far greater number of which have, I know, never been in print—but he will take what he likes— only I would not have my name subscribed to things that if they afford amusement for the moment of their perusal have answered all, they were intended for. Hoping that I shall hear better tidings

---

[1] This epigram was included in the *Standard* of 29 June 1827, the first line reading, 'George, grave or merry at no lie would stick'. The epigram was first published in the *Morning Post* on 23 Sept. 1802. See *Poems*, ii. 964.

of my friend's Health, I remain, dear Madam, with affectionate respect

your & his | sincere Friend

S. T. Coleridge.[1]

1595. *To Charles Aders*

MS. Lord Charnwood. Hitherto unpublished.

Grove, Highgate.
Wednesday
25 July 1827

My dear Sir

I—but why do I unjustly no less than selfishly say, *I*?—*we* were all pleased to see your hand-writing, and still more so with the contents of your Note.—God be praised! that your dear Wife is well in health—*that* secured, and you likewise well, all else Heaven has given you in yourselves—and believe me, my dear Sir! with exception of one or two Eels in this World's Snake-bag, it is in ourselves that we can alone expect to find peace and comfort. Mr Green (one of my prime *Eels*) well observed yesterday—The older I am, the more charitable I grow; and the worse I think of men in general—an apparent Paradox; but a Truth which every man who both *thinks* and feels, will sooner or later find the truth of.—I declare solemnly, that when in subscribing my name in a letter to you or *the other few*, I am beginning to write the words 'your sincere friend' I start back at the thought, how many scores of gossiping malignant Slanderers are probably at the same moment subscribing the same words in a letter or note of compliment to some one, whose hospitality and kindness they are prepared in the first conversazione or public dinner to repay by some *half-fact* which they must be sure will convey a *whole* LIE, and of the most fiendish character.—Did my Health & Spirits allow me the leisure, I could write a most edifying Article on the effect and influence of Newspapers, Magazines, Reviews, on the intellect and moral character of the English—especially, of Artists, and Authors—with advice

---

[1] In some notes printed by her son, Mrs. Watts reveals the warm regard she and her husband felt towards Coleridge: 'We named after him a son, Francis Coleridge Watts, born to us in 1827.' She also mentions an evening spent with Wordsworth when she 'happened to quote' some lines from *Christabel*. 'He did not dissent from my expressions of admiration,' she continues, 'but rather discomposed me by observing that it was an indelicate poem . . . . I could not forbear the impression that his sympathies were rather with his predecessors than his contemporaries. . . . I observed that he rarely left a commendation of the latter wholly unqualified.' *Alaric Watts*, i. 239 and 243.

to honest men respecting the expedience of setting Artist-guns and Author-traps in their Grounds.—But I am scribbling away in my spleen, & forgetting my main business—namely, to return Mr & Mrs Gillman's kindest thanks for the Ham, and the pleasure, with which they look forward to your passing Sunday next with them— and I am to beg you to come as early as you can—Sunday is now an unengaged day with me: as my dear Friend, Mr Green, is more generally with me on Tuesdays.—When you write, assure Mrs Aders, that she and yourself have an unforgetting, affectionate, and *sincere* Friend in

S. T. COLERIDGE—

and truly can I add, S. T. C.'s Mr & Mrs Gillman.—

1596. *To Alaric A. Watts*

Transcript Coleridge family. Pub. with omis. Alaric Watts, *i. 288.*

[August 1827][1]

My dear Sir

Well may you think that something strange has happened. It would be wasting my strength to enter into a detail of the afflicting incidents and accidents which have thrown in their several successive weights to aggravate the languor of volition, which is but too effectually palliated by an inwardly felt, though in my face scarcely perceptible, decay of life and almost constant pain. 'Sleep, the wide blessing, is to me distemper's worst calamity'.[2] The truth is, I have for the last three or four months been under a depression of spirits, which I cannot easily characterize. If there be an insanity of the muscular life and voluntary powers, compossible with an orderly and even unweakened state of the intellectual faculties, I have been *non compos voluntatis saltem.* I go on studying the Scriptures, writing notes, and even chapters of my philosophical works, and I can converse at times with a literary friend with unabated vigour; but all must be *continuous.* Meantime, never detected schoolboy was more fluttered, or played prettier tricks of cowardice, at the sight of a letter, if from anyone to whom I am attached, or for whom I entertain a high respect. I literally am afraid to open it; and though I am at this time somewhat roused, yet I will communicate a little secret *to you,* which one or two of my friends have found out, viz., that if you would be sure of my reading and answering a letter in my worst of times, you should

---

[1] The approximate date of this letter is established by Coleridge's reference to his conversations with Atherstone 'some 12 months ago', i.e., in July 1826.
[2] *The Pains of Sleep,* lines 35–36, *Poems,* i. 390.

enclose it under cover to Mrs Gillman (Mr Gillman is so much out
he is not so certain), who is an outward conscience to me, just
saying that you are anxious to have an answer. I really am at this
moment suffering a pang of shame, that I have to confess such a
tale; but anything is better than that you should suppose the
contrary to the truth—want of internal respect or regard for you.
If I had a sort of spiritual *Camera obscura* that could reflect the
constructions in my brain and fix them, you would have in your
possession a full volume of letters addressed to you. But let the
past be past—and let me try to make the compensation by im-
mediate exertion. In order to obtain a small sum for an old acquain-
tance, and at his earnest request added to my egregious cowardice
in the use of the monosyllable No! I suffered him to have a poem
(some 12 months ago) for some yearly publication for which I was
to have, as I understood, for that and a few things in verse and
prose 20£.¹ Poor as I am I would borrow 20£ to get the poem back

¹ Coleridge refers to his negotiations with Edwin Atherstone on behalf of
S. C. Hall, who founded *The Amulet* in 1826. On 15 July of that year Atherstone
had written to Hall: 'I called again on Mr Coleridge yesterday for the purpose
of hearing his intention respecting your Amulet. I would recommend you to
send him a few lines explanatory of your wishes, & of the *terms* that you might
think proper to offer. . . . He talked of furnishing about 200 lines.' [MS. Pro-
fessor R. C. Bald.] The 'verse and prose' transmitted to Hall as a result of
Atherstone's mediation consisted of (1) *The Improvisatore*; (2) three Letters
of 1799 describing Coleridge's Brocken tour (Letters 280–2); and (3) three
minor poems, *Love's Burial-place*, *The Butterfly*, and *A Thought suggested by a
View of Saddleback in Cumberland*. A holograph containing *Love's Burial-
place* and a portion of *The Improvisatore* is extant; it is part of the MS. sent
to Hall. Since nothing of Coleridge's appeared in *The Amulet* for 1827, pre-
sumably the MSS. arrived too late for inclusion.

As the present letter shows, the relations between Coleridge and Hall had
broken down. Of the MSS. received for publication in *The Amulet*, Hall selected
only *The Improvisatore* for the year 1828, and he reduced the remuneration
agreed upon from £20 to £10. He also rejected the letters describing the Brocken
tour and in 1827 returned them to Coleridge, not, however, 'without having
taken a copy'. In 1829 he printed in *The Amulet* large extracts from the first
two letters as 'Over the Brocken', though without Coleridge's 'consent'.
Coleridge considered this conduct 'not very reputable to the Editor, if Honesty
be a necessary ingredient of Repute', and rightly complained of the 'embarrass-
ment' which Hall had caused him. Coleridge alluded to an agreement made in
1828 with F. M. Reynolds, whereby he was to confine his contributions exclu-
sively to *The Keepsake* for 1829, except for those in *The Literary Souvenir*.
Later Hall told Reynolds that he himself had paid Coleridge 'but 10£' for *The
Improvisatore*. This tittle-tattle gave Reynolds an additional excuse to quibble
over payment for Coleridge's contributions to *The Keepsake*. Finally, in *The
Amulet* for 1833 Hall printed under the heading, 'Three Scraps. By S. T.
Coleridge', the three minor poems listed above which he had received in 1826,
but he neither asked Coleridge's permission nor made any remuneration. See
Letters 1602, 1612, 1634, 1639, 1650, 1667, and 1781.

—for in sentiment and music of verse it was equal to anything I ever wrote—Had it been asked of me a month afterward, I should have refused, but it had *that Day* as it were been written, and I had (as is always the case with me) made no comparative appreciation of it. Well! from the title of one of the minor copies of verses being to 'an ambitious mistress' the Editor too mistaking it for a *kept* Woman!!!¹ and the others being on lighter subjects, I am informed that they had *rather have*—what? Why the 'Wanderings of Cain', the Poem on 'Youth and Age', and one or two others of which they had heard my acquaintance speak in rapture! in other words, all the flowers of my whole poetic life—informing me that my first poem was only ten pages.² Of course I returned no answer, but desired to have the proportion—but no! not a penny have I received or ever expect to do.

This vexes me on many accounts—chiefly, that the poem ought to have belonged to you, and I shall never forgive myself for my indolence of mind and facility in letting it out of my hands. What you now ask of me I will willingly do—if in your judgement you think that the Critique will not be deemed an attack on Sir Walter Scott, tho' I have little reason to hold myself obliged to him—and yet I should be most unwilling to give a pretext for the rumour that I want to detract from his merits.

I have so many things to speak of that I must try to see you—Were I sure of finding you at home this evening, I would set off for Torrington Square. Another vexatious thing is about the Edition of my poems by Pickering—against my will and judgement from the beginning. Tho' it was expressly bargained to be only the Poems already published, yet under various pretences—but I must reserve this for your private ear—all I had to publish, and

---

¹ A reference to *Love's Burial-place*, the first of the 'Three Scraps' published in *The Amulet* for 1833. The poem was first published in Coleridge's *Poetical Works* of 1828 under the title, *The Alienated Mistress: A Madrigal (From an unfinished Melodrama)*.

² This was *The Improvisatore*, which fills ten and one-half pages in the 1828 *Amulet*. In the MS. transmitted to Hall, the full title reads:

New Thoughts on old Subjects—
or Conversational Dialogues on Interests & Events of common Life.
No. I. The Improvisatore—or John Anderson, my Jo, John.

Along with the MS. of *The Improvisatore* Coleridge sent Hall a note explanatory of his 'general' title, *New Thoughts*, etc. Hall printed this note with slight changes as an introduction to Coleridge's poem. It has not been reprinted, but the MS. is extant. *The Improvisatore* was included in Coleridge's *Poetical Works* of 1829 and 1834; but since no further dialogues were forthcoming, Coleridge dropped 'No. I.' from his title. The general title, *New Thoughts on Old Subjects*, appears, however, in both the table of contents and in the headlines of the pages containing the text of *The Improvisatore*.

much that had far better in their present state have remained un-
published, has been forced from me—and what is worst—I am as
clear as a prophet can be, that my dear friend, Gillman, to whom
I had given over the poems, will never receive a pickled herring
from this Pickering. Of the new poems I will select the best, especi-
ally the 'Youth and Age',[1] and you are heartily welcome to them
—for there is no doubt of your volume appearing before this
Edition. In short, I will take a lonely walk, and discover what
I can do, and you shall hear from me before the third day is over—
God bless you &

S. T. Coleridge.

1597. *To James Gillman, Jr.*

MS. Harvard College Lib. Hitherto unpublished.

[September 1827][2]

My dear James

Your success, as the result of your College Studies, and your
Happiness while you are there, will mainly depend on your follow-
ing a *system*.

I do not wish you to lay down any plan, beyond your own esti-
mation of the strength of your Will. Make it as light as you will:
only let it be systematic.

Systematic it cannot be, at all events, will not—if you do not
apportion a determinate number of hours at a fixed time or times
of the Day. If you should find it best to divide the hours dedicated
to your Studies into two portions, let *one* of them at least be sacred.
A week will suffice to make your acquaintance whether of the
same College or of other Colleges, understand, that you will not be
broken in upon during that time. But if you do not *begin* at once
(i.e. the very day after you are thoroughly settled in your Rooms)
you will never begin.

Two-thirds of your *reading* time should be employed on the one
thing, in which you propose to be examined. The rest may be
miscellaneous.

In your Greek never be satisfied with the Latin-pretended
Equivalent, or Equivalents, of Lexicon or Translation. With the
few exceptions of words imitating sound, every word has a primary

---

[1] Of these 'new poems' only *Youth and Age* (lines 1–38) appeared in *The
Literary Souvenir* for 1828. See Letters 1605 and 1639.

[2] This letter was obviously written just before James Gillman, Jr., left
Highgate to begin his first residence at St. John's College, Oxford, in the
Michaelmas term of 1827.

visual image, as it's proper, at least, it's original sense—and a man cannot be said to understand the WORD, tho' he may the whole sentence in which it occurs, unless he sees how that image was capable of such and such applications. In poetry, especially in the Greek Drama, it is incalculable the advantage which this tracking of words back to their Birth & Parentage will secure to you. You could not render a hundred Lines without making your superiority over an ordinary Lexicon Construer felt.

Respecting your moral being I will trouble you with but one hint.—Whenever you feel yourself inclined to assert your *Rights*, particularly if a *sensation* of Resentment or a swell of Pride should be the inclining cause, first ask yourself—if it be your *Duty* to assert the particular Right under the given circumstances. There are few things so hostile to *dignity* of character, and to manly Self-respect, as captiousness in the assertion of supposed Rights on trifling occasions.—

God bless you

S. T. C.

1598. *To Daniel Stuart*

Address: D. Stuart, Esqre | Wickham Park | near Banbury | Oxfordshire
MS. British Museum. Pub. with omis. Letters from the Lake Poets, *307*.
Postmark: Highgate, 8 October 1827.

Monday, 8 Octr 1827.
Grove, Highgate

My dear Sir

If Sunshine and Shadows are lying as beautifully on the woods and fields round your Mansion, as they at this moment are on Kane Wood and the landscape before my Window, while your health and power of enjoying them are, as I hope and trust, they are, the reverse of mine, now and for some time back, it is a selfish Wish which I seem inwardly to retract before I have expressed it—videlicet, that you were in town and that I could speak to you instead of writing.[1] The death of Mr Canning has, of course, given the settling Blow to all the hopes, I had built up on the foundation of poor Lord Liverpool's promise to Mr J. H. Frere: and by an odd Compound of Vanity and Low-spirits I could in certain moods bring myself to think, that my guardian Spirit had fore-seen that I should not have received the emolument long enough for it to compensate for ending my days, as a Pensioner and Sine-curist.

---

[1] At this point in the MS. Coleridge inserted the following sentence: '*Be so good, as to turn from here over leaf to the third side.*' He refers to the last paragraph of his letter, beginning 'I see that I have been giving way'.

Before Mr Canning's Death I had made a sketch of a Memorial, or rather of two or three Memorials, on the several distinct yet closely connected Subjects, the Catholic Question, the Population of Ireland, the Questions respecting Emigration and Colonization, and the Increase of Crime in the Country at large. On the two last subjects I especially want to know your sentiments—ex. gr. whether on the supposition that Parliament could or would devote a large sum to the alleviation of the Evil, there is any ground for the assertion, that the money would be more profitably expended in bringing the waste lands & bogs into a state of Cultivation than in shipping men off to Canada or Van Dieman's Land—Whether the said Waste and Bogland are susceptible of being raised into ordinary farm-land, I am perfectly ignorant—but one thing I seem to see clearly, that if the new Tenants were to be collected from the Irish Peasantry, in the present state of that priest-bedeviled Country, it would increase the evil, the troublesome symptoms of which it might for a short period suspend. In fact, any scheme of removing a portion of the Inhabitants of a Country which should leave those that remain in statu quo, would be but quackery. If you could improve the *quality* of the remainder so as to supersede the repetition of the costly Palliative—there would be some sense in it. It is unfortunate for the Country, in my belief, that the present Ministry do not possess the confidence or even the good will of the Clergy or the Land-owners: and I suspect, that even in our Cities and manufacturing Counties the attachment to the Cabinet collectively is of that lukewarm character which expresses itself in—But who is there *else*?—If the Ministry hold out, it will be, I fear, from the want of *accredited* talent in their opponents.—I have thought repeatedly of correcting the one Memorial on the only plan, on which the (so called) Emancipation of the Catholics could be either desirable for Ireland, or palatable to the Country at large—and of sending it to the Marquis of Lansdown.[1] But in all the great fundamental questions of Political Economy, of Religion as a public Concern, of Morality and of Education I differ so utterly from the leading Whigs, and am so well aware of their inaccessibility to any argument which does not take for granted the truth of *their* First Principles, that I shrink from any measure that would be interpreted as a sort of advance towards connecting myself with the Party—and had it not been for the rank & malignant personalities against Mr Canning, unmitigated even by his Death, by which that Paper has infamized it's name, I should have been disposed to accept of Alaric Watts's Overtures who would have purchased

---

[1] Henry Petty-Fitzmaurice, third Marquis of Lansdowne (1780–1863), was a strong advocate of Catholic emancipation. At this time he was home secretary.

these Sketches for the Standard, of which with two other Papers [persons?] he is a Triumvir—i.e. there are three Editors, the principal & *political* man being a Dr Gifford,[1] the third I don't know the name of—A. Watts takes the belles lettres department.—

I see that I have been giving way to my usual mental cowardice, and that infirmness of will which makes it little less than hateful to me to speak (almost, indeed, to *think*) of aught disagreeable that concerns myself exclusively—and that I am making myself appear what it is not in my nature to be, while I am shrinking from, and (to borrow a metaphor from my Malta experience) giving the *Quarantine Curve* to, the original purpose of the Letter. To the point then at once! and I must leave it at your own choice, whether you will consider your former kindnesses as excusing or aggravating the present application. If I might interpret the extreme reluctance, with which I make it, as a presentiment, I should have no difficulty in foretelling, which—nor could I, I believe, have brought myself to [it], but for my Daughter's increasing anxiety about my health, and the Gillmans' frequ[ent] expressions of regret, that from the late heavy expences in the repairs &c of the House, Henry's School-Bills, and in setting off and settling James at Oxford, they literally have it not in their power to give me a month or six weeks' Sojourn at Ramsgate this autumn. Now I frankly confess, my dear Sir! tho' with a *bitter* smile, that it does seem somewhat ridiculous in my own eyes, that because you have for the last three years given me 30£ for this purpose, I should expect the same this year, and in lieu of the Public Purse fasten myself, as a Pensioner on your's! But—if it be inconvenient to you, FOR GOD'S SAKE, do not think the worse, or feel the less kindly, of me for this letter: and from the very bottom of my heart I promise you, that your refusal will not detract a jot either from my sense of your past kindness, or from the sincere regard and attachment, which independent of all pecuniary obligations I habitually feel for You and your's.—

S. T. Coleridge

My Daughter sends her kind respects to you and Mrs Stuart— and Mrs Gillman I keep out of the way of, *quoad hoc*: as I hold it probable that her—'Tell Mrs S.—and ask—& Mary—&c &c'— would make a very pretty-sized letter of themselves. I need not assure Mrs Stuart, how truly and warmly attached to her and all the Household that bear her & your name, my good friend & her good Man are!—S. T. C.

[1] Stanley Lees Giffard (1788–1858), editor of the *St. James Chronicle*, was appointed editor of the newly founded *Standard* in 1827.

1599. *To Daniel Stuart*

Address: D. Stuart, Esqre | Wickham Park | near Banbury | Oxfordshire—
MS. British Museum. Pub. Letters from the Lake Poets, *312.*
Postmark: Highgate, 12 October 1827.

Friday 12 Octr 1827.

My dear Sir

Returning from a long walk taken for the purpose of a long con-
versation on family matters with my daughter I find & have barely
time by return of Post to acknowlege (I need not say, thank you
for) your kind letter and the order for 30£ inclosed. What you tell
me, I had so far anticipated, that the thought was one of the
Weights in the scale of my reluctance, in applying to you: for such
has been the confluence of events and either crude or unfortunate
measures, that I know and I hear of no one, however *well-off*, as
the phrase is, and however good a manager, within the bounds of
Good sense and that attention to appearances, which Society and
our best feelings for those most identified with ourselves render
a duty, who does not find himself straitened beyond what those
who know of him only as a man of good Property are disposed to
believe, and who does not find himself at times compelled to keep
his hand closed when a strong gush from the heart makes it a pain-
ful effort.—Such is the state of things, that with the exception of
the Jews on the Stock-exchange & their compeers, the lower
classes are demoralized by low wages & the nature of the supple-
ment, yet the higher and middle classes find it yearly more diffi-
cult to keep their places in society, and make both ends meet with-
out encroachment on what ought to be sacred to the Future—in
short, without doing what the Apes (Simia longi-cauda) are said
to do, when hungry,—i.e. eat a joint or two of the extremity of
their tail.—Allow me to assure you, my dear friend! that thrice
30£ would not have given me such lasting satisfaction, as the kind-
ness & frankness of your communication.

The other parts of your letter I must refer to another time—
I will only add, that *of late* the Standard has met with my thorough
approbation—

May God bless you, and your's—& your obliged & sincerely
affectionate Friend

S. T. Coleridge

1600. *To Derwent Coleridge*

MS. Victoria University Lib. Hitherto unpublished fragment.

[October 1827 ?][1]

My dearest and right reverend Boy[2]

The Εὐαγγέλιον κατὰ Δερούεντον blew on me as from the spice-islands of Youth and Hope, the two realities of this Phantom World—it being, you know, a first principle of the Ess-tee-ceean Philosophy (τῆς μὲν περὶ ἐποχῶν καὶ μεθόδων) that Reality is a thing of Degrees—from the Iliad to a Dream: καὶ γάρ τ' ὄναρ ἐκ Διός ἐστιν[3]—as far at least as Reality is predicable at all of aught below Heaven. Es enim *in caelis*, Pater Noster, qui tu veré *es*!—I did not add Love: for this is only Youth and Hope embracing and so seen as *one*.[4]—The most striking proof of the power your letter exercised over my mind is that it set me wishing, grieving, regretting, day-dreaming—every *ing* but *pray*ing—for a few thousand pounds, for the consolation of your and your Mary's schemes. —But alas!—remorseless Fate says, No! Lord Liverpool had promised Mr Frere to give me a sinecure of 200£ a year—He had even ordered the *place* to be reserved for me—Apoplexy interfered & King George the IVth gave the place to another. The hardship of the case was stated (not by myself, nor at my request) to Mr Canning, who meant to have done some thing for me instead—and Enteritis cried, Veto—& God knows, I grieved so much more for their *Deaths*[5] than for my own Loss, that but on poor Hartley's account I should not have heaved the 9th part of a sigh for the latter—& now you & Mary; and Sara and—for her sake & *since so it is*—Henry—but you & my Unseen Daughter Elect[6] more closely—are at my heart—& tempt me to the unworthiness of half-wishing, that instead of a voluminous System of Philosophy and Divinity, on God, Nature, and Man—&c &c—. . .

---

[1] In the present letter Coleridge refers to Mary Pridham as his 'Unseen Daughter Elect', and in his lines addressed to her and dated 15 Oct. 1827 (16 Oct. in a second MS.), he twice speaks of her as 'Dear tho' unseen'. It seems likely, therefore, that the poem and the letter were written about the same time. See *Poems*, i. 468.

[2] Derwent Coleridge was ordained to the priesthood by the Bishop of Exeter on 15 July 1827.

[3] *Iliad*, i. 63.

[4] The preceding lines appear almost word for word in *Table Talk*, 10 July 1834.

[5] Canning died on 8 Aug. 1827; Liverpool lingered on until 4 Dec. 1828.

[6] Derwent Coleridge and Mary Pridham were married on 6 Dec. 1827.

1601. *To James Gillman*

Address: James Gillman, Esqre | Grove | Highgate Favored by Mr J. Murray.
MS. Mr. Jonathan Wordsworth. Pub. with omis. Coleridge at Highgate, *by
Lucy E. Watson, 1925, p. 135.*

[Sunday, 28 October 1827][1]

My dear Gillman

There is one sort of Good Tidings (good, if there be truth in
proverbs) which, I have observed, always meet a sullen and thank-
less reception—the absence of all Tidings, to wit. Therefore tho'
there be nothing to communicate of sufficient urgence to levy on
you the tax of ten pence for an unprivileged letter, or to levy on
myself the heavier tax of applying to that knowing *Kid* of the
Commons' House, Mr Divett, for a frank wherewith to protect your
pence, I willingly avail myself of Mr John Murray's Return by the
Steamer tomorrow, rather than leave you to interpret no good
news into good No-news. I was so eager to learn the particulars
of your Voyage that I intercepted Captain Martin on the Plank
before he placed foot on the stone steps, and sympathized with
the triumph with which he announced your arrival at the Custom-
House Stairs Thirty five minutes after Two, and that he himself,
Captn Martin aforesaid, was transacting business in Lombard
Street Five Minutes before Three.—I never saw a Steam-boat look
beautiful—tho' always interesting—till yester evening $\frac{1}{4}$ past 4,
when it pencilled it's way toward the Pier and then described a horse-
shoe wake of grey lustre within the Harbour as it curved round in
the largest possible Circuit to the old Station at the Landing-steps,
all in a glory of the richest golden Light reflected from it's sides and
Uprights, & transmuting it's long pennant of Smoke into a huge
Cylinder or what shall I call it? of Topaz.—It had been a lovely
day, and continued lovely to the moment, I bade the sky Good
Night, about 11 o'clock—and all this day, from dawn to the
present hour, Sunday Evening, six o'clock, we have had & have
a steady deliberate soft thick soaking Rain, which yet does not
sufficiently disburthen the Atmosphere of it's ever contracting and
dilating, ascending and descending Aqueous vapor, as to quiet the
gusty winds or to smooth the white breakers.—

Mrs Gillman is anxious to hear from you, first and principally,
how your own health is—& what effect the change of Air has had
on your Boils, and on your Sensations—2ndly, whether & what
you have heard from James, the Oxonian—and 3rdly, any High-

---

[1] The consecration of St. George's Church, Ramsgate, to which Coleridge
alludes, took place on Tuesday, 23 Oct. 1827. The present letter was written
on the following Sunday.

gate News, Town, Grove, own House, that you may find time & patience to communicate.

I have bathed twice: and am on the whole less unwell than at your departure—as well as a man of my age with diabetes and intestinal torpor with pruritus senilis Scroti can be or I in particular have any right to expect—or the least pretence to murmur at. My chastisements compared with their causes, viz. mental cowardice, and staving off of apprehended terrors & the necessity of withdrawing my attention from the Objective in Thought to the Subjective in sensation—are Mercies: & I strive to make them Blessings.—But this is in a graver Note, than I intended.—Henry goes on quietly—and Miss Chance seems to me more *roused,* and under a mild continuous and inobservable influence she would, I think, be gradually awakened to a greater confidence in herself. She shews marks of attachment to Mrs Gillman, and seems more pleased when she has succeeded in doing any thing, Mrs G. has taught her to do, than distressed by being required to do it.—Miss Hunt, I believe, is improving in health—but Mrs Gillman most evidently. She feels herself much improved: and the improvement in her Looks, and complexion, in the clearness and brightness of her eyes, and the almost entire removal of all wrinkle & discoloration under the eyes, strikes every one—Harriet says, that she never saw her Mistress look so young.—I see more of her out of doors on my Walks, than within—as it is more convenient for Miss Hunt & better for Henry & Miss Chance to dine at an earlier hour than my arrangements & appetite can fall in with. I only regret, that as it is, a House with one bedroom more had not been taken: for the having to pass tho' but a few stones throw from a warm room every night, and often of course f[acing ra]in & wind, is a superfluous inconvenience for M[iss H]unt & no advantage to any one else—. For myself, this mode of living *solo* is a variety—tho' it would be insincere to say, that I look forward to a repetition of the experiment with any desire—even if to look forward at all to October 18*28* were not idle & presumptuous—.

I dined on Tuesday last at Sir Thomas Gray's & met Sir William Curtis—who gravely assured me, that an American, long before *my* Marquis of Worcester, & upwards of 20 years before Watt, had *found out* the Steam Engine[1]—. Sir Thomas told Sir Billy

---

[1] The American was probably Oliver Evans, who introduced the high-pressure steam-engine in the United States about 1800. For the part played in the early development of the steam-engine by Edward Somerset, second Marquis of Worcester (1601–67), James Watt (1736–1819), who received his first patent in 1769, and Evans (1755–1819), see *Encyclopaedia Britannica*, 1910–11, xxv. 818–22.

that my M. of W. lived in the reign of Charles the first—*Who*! quoth
Sir William—and what has Charles the first to do with Steam
Engines & them sort of things—*Who*!!—I acquiesced—& said—
Ah, Sir William! you have me there.— Aye, aye! quoth he—
with a friendly Jog with his arm—You Poets must not think of
coming over us in that way!!! I liked the old fellow for one observa-
tion—Ah! quoth he—I have always gone on the rule to live & let
live—I always wished for a *snug place* & I have got it—I have
lived a happy life, enough—& the worst is, that I must leave it—I
daresay, that is all very right; but I don't like it. I won't pretend
to say, but that I don't like it.—I forgot to say, that I attended the
Archbishop's consecration of the New church—& I liked the service
& the Anthem (admirably sung) and the Sermon; but Sir William's
Confession had more *unction* & edified me more, than they.—

Give my love to Eliza Nixon—& if she have returned, to the
little Truant, Susan Steele, God bless her!—& God bless you, my
dear Friend! & your sincerely affectionate

S. T. Coleridge—

1602. *To S. C. Hall*

MS. *Harvard College Lib. Hitherto unpublished.*

28 Wellington Crescent
Ramsgate.
Wednesday 14 Novr 1827.—

Dear Sir

I acknowlege the receipt of, and return you my thanks for,
Five Pound received by this morning's Post: if it should not be
inconvenient to you, it would certainly be an accomodation to me, to
receive the other half.[1]—As soon as I get the Amulet, I will go thro'
it—and if any thing strikes me, as likely to give your next Number
a *start*, I shall have pleasure in suggesting it to your judgement.

I cannot but think, that short biographies, from one page [to]
three or four, of men who played a great part in the revolutions of
the world, political, philosophical and religious, yet of whom little is
to be found in common reading, would be very well suited to a work,
like your's.—Occasionally, *maxims* of great depth and originality,
and exquisite single passages are to be found in works wholly out
of the routine of Literature—Believe me, dear Sir,

with every kind wish for | your success | your's truly
S. T. Coleridge

[1] Hall paid £10 for *The Improvisatore*, a contribution published in *The
Amulet* for 1828. Coleridge is here acknowledging receipt of the first instalment.
He did not receive the remaining £5 until 1828. See Letters 1596, 1612, and
1667.

1603. *To Hyman Hurwitz*

Address: Hyman Hurwitz, Esqre | Grenada Cottage | Old Kent Road
MS. University of Pennsylvania Lib. Hitherto unpublished.

Mr Neumagen's—
[23 November 1827]

My dear Friend

Last night, about 8 o'clock, I reached Highgate from Ramsgate —& just as I was undressing, found a letter of two lines from you, from which all I could infer was that some letter or letters must have been written by you—which from some cause or other I had not received.—This Evening (23rd) Mr Neumagen has sent me a letter from you, which lets me into the business, just time enough to make it possible for me to apprize you of the only scheme now in my power—namely, that I will be in town tomorrow morning, at *Mr Ingram's, Hatter,* in *Coleman Street,* by ten o'clock, and there wait for you, and go with you wherever it may be requisite or desirable—or write what or to whom you wish[1]—

Mr Neumagen has been so good as to say that he will send off this letter to you by a special messenger—God bless you &

S. T. Coleridge

1604. *To Leonard Horner*[2]

Address: L. Horner, Esqre | 12 Upper Gower Street
MS. University of Pennsylvania Lib. Hitherto unpublished.

Grove, Highgate
24 Novr 1827.

Dear Sir

For I hope, that my knowlege of your Brother and (I need not say) the reverence in which I hold him will be my apology for thus addressing you, tho' personally a stranger—I now write at the request of a very particular friend of mine, who will not be persuaded that my testimony respecting his character and talents will be as ineffectual, or as superfluous, as my estimation of my own influence, and my friend's well-earned Reputation in the literary republic, would lead me to apprehend.—I have known Mr Hyman Hurwitz most intimately for many years: I know, that the most learned of his own People rank him among their profoundest and

---

[1] See next letter.

[2] Leonard Horner (1785–1864), younger brother of Francis Horner, became warden of the University of London at its opening in Oct. 1828, a post he held until 1831.

most exact Hebraists—but of his strong and sound judgement in the use and application of his attainments, of his pure and exemplary moral Being, the liberality of his principles—in short, of Mr Hurwitz, as a man, a man of great natural abilities, and a philosopher, I can attest on the ground of my own knowlege: and have already given public testimony in my 'Aids to Reflection'.—Mr Hurwitz is a candidate for the Professorship of the Hebrew Language in the London University—About this time last year I wrote to Lord Dudley, the Marquis of Lansdown, Mr Brougham and Sir James Mackintosh[1]—and from the three former received such an answer, as from such men I had anticipated—an assurance, that *dabitur meliori*—and a kind acceptance of my testimony, as one among the Data on which their final Judgement would be formed.— In this view I intreat you to consider this letter—not as a request or solicitation—but as a simple testimony which as an honest man & a hearty well-wisher to the plan of *a* University in London I believe it my duty to offer—the more so, that my conscience bears me witness that if I knew another man in my belief more worthy of, or better suited to, the professorship, I would strike out my friend's, and substitute *his* Name.—With unfeigned respect, I intreat your favorable interpretation of this intrusion on your attention from

Your obedt humble Servant,

S. T. Coleridge

1605. *To Alaric A. Watts*

Address: Alaric Watts, Esqre
MS. McGill University Library. Hitherto unpublished.

24th Novr 1827.—

My dear Sir

I returned from Ramsgate on Thursday Night—& lay my head on my pillow like a man stunned with what I had to hear from Mr Gillman—I am not likely to find you at home, at this time—but yet I can [not] suffer an hour to pass without assuring you, that the Khan of Casimir or the Man in the Moon would be as fit subject for your resentment as myself—who till Thursday Night, 10 o'clock, had never even heard the Name of the Bijoux[2]—. The infamy on

---

[1] Of these letters of recommendation only that to Henry Brougham has come to light. It is dated 9 Feb. 1827. Hurwitz was elected to the post in 1828.

[2] The first issue of *The Bijou*, a literary annual launched in 1828 by William Pickering, contained five compositions by Coleridge: a prose work, *The Wanderings of Cain. A Fragment* (later published as Canto II), and four poems, *Work without Hope*, *Youth and Age* (lines 1–38), *A Day-Dream*, and *The Two*

the part of some one in obtaining from Mr Gillman under false pretence a MSS Poem, the publication of which was against my judgement & my express wish renders me a greater Sufferer than yourself[1]—. But I am really too much agitated to think it wise to *write* what I feel—I must see you—& make you acquainted with the business ab initio—I had not got over the vexation and mortification of having been induced by my nervous cowardice of that pain, which arises from the *disruption* of my thoughts by being solicited by any one, when I am unwell, to the giving the poem, I before apprized you of[2]—when this thunder-clap exploded at my ear—.

Besides this, before I left Highgate I had left the inclosed in an envelope for you, with orders to the Servant to send it to the Post —and on looking into my Drawer behold—there it stared me in the face.—I thought it possible, that some of them might be of

Founts. Coleridge had reluctantly released these unpublished pieces to Gillman for inclusion in his forthcoming *Poetical Works*, of which Pickering was the publisher. W. Fraser, the editor of *The Bijou*, however, not only printed them in that annual without Coleridge's knowledge but inserted the following 'impudent Paragraph' in the preface:

> In expressing the Editor's thanks in a separate paragraph to S. T. Coleridge, Esq., it must not be supposed that his obligations are the less important to those whose names have been just mentioned; but where a favor has been conferred in a peculiar manner, it at least demands that it should be peculiarly acknowledged. Mr. Coleridge, in the most liberal manner, permitted the Editor to select what he pleased from all his unpublished MSS., and it will be seen from the 'Wanderings of Cain,' though unfinished, and the other pieces bearing that Gentleman's name, that whenever he may favour the world with a perfect collection of his writings he will adduce new and powerful claims upon its respect.

Nor was this the end of Fraser's high-handed conduct. Coleridge was soon to discover that Blanco White's sonnet, *Night and Death*, had also been published in *The Bijou*. (See Letter 1608.) Coleridge later complained that he had never received any 'pecuniary acknowlegement' from the proprietor of *The Bijou*. See Letter 1639.

[1] Watts was justifiably indignant to find that *Youth and Age*, which he had received from Coleridge for inclusion in *The Literary Souvenir* for 1828 and which was printed as the first contribution in that annual, was also to appear in the 1828 issue of *The Bijou*. He inserted, therefore, the following footnote to the preface of the 1828 *Literary Souvenir*:

> I have just learned (too late, however, to notice the circumstance in the small paper impression of this volume), that 'Youth and Age,' by Mr. Coleridge, is about to be published in another annual work. I can only say, that I received it from the author, as a contribution to the Literary Souvenir.

Watts also printed *Youth and Age* in both the *Standard* (20 Oct. 1827) and the *St. James Chronicle* (18–20 Oct. 1827).

[2] A reference to *The Improvisatore*, which appeared in *The Amulet* for 1828. In Letter 1596 Coleridge gives the circumstances which led him to release the poem to S. C. Hall.

some use, in filling up a Gap—and that I could send you some ten or twelve more of such as you find in the first and second page of the inclosed—if they would be of any service to you in *the Paper*— only not with my name.[1]—

God bless you, till I see you—& do not suffer any *appearance* to injure me in your opinion, till you have it's confirmation from my mouth or hand. For so I will do by you.—

S. T. Coleridge—

1606. *To Richard Cattermole*

Transcript Coleridge family. Hitherto unpublished.

Wednesday 28th Novr. 1827
Grove, Highgate

Dear Sir

Instead of wasting my time and yours by entering into a detail of the Sorrows, Sicknesses, and Perplexities, which after all would not justify tho' they occasioned and might palliate my neglect, I will simply say, that I shall set to work immediately and that before this day week you shall receive a Paper from me—more *literary* at least and more likely to be easily understood than my first attempt.[2] So far however from entertaining any scruples respecting the truth or the importance of my views respecting the mid station of the genuine Greek Tragedy between the Mysteries and the Sacerdotal Θρησκεία, or the validity of the Clavis Aeschylo-Promethiana, the first data of which I have in that Essay set forth, my first leisure will be employed on an interpretation of the Prometheus, Scene by Scene, on this theory of the several Dramatis Personae. The whole difficulty consists in mastering the sense of IDEA and LAW in the Spirit of the eldest Philosophy: *this* once atchieved, it will be as little possible for a reflecting man to doubt the mythic (i.e. mixt-allegoric) meaning of the Prometheus, as of the Pilgrim's Progress.—Need I say, how happy you will always make me by a visit?—I have been at Ramsgate for 5 weeks: and have received great benefit from—the *Return* to Highgate.

With unfeigned respect, dear Sir | Your obliged
S. T. Coleridge

[1] Coleridge refers to the 'Sheet-full' of epigrams which he had promised to send for the *Standard*. See Letter 1594.

[2] Coleridge considered his lecture, *On the Prometheus of Æschylus*, which he delivered before the Royal Society of Literature on 18 May 1825, as 'preparatory to a series of disquisitions'. In the present letter he proposes to give an interpretation of *Prometheus*, but he did not carry out his intention. Indeed, in 1828 he confesses that he had failed to open 'Remembrancers' from the Society. See Letters 1442, 1463, 1614, and 1616.

1607. To J. Blanco White

Pub. Life of Joseph Blanco White, *i. 439.*

Grove, Highgate, 28th Nov. 1827.

My dear Sir,

It would be a waste of your time and feelings to enter into any detail of the sorrows, sicknesses and perplexities, in my own person, and from the misfortunes τῶν ἀμφ' ἐμέ, which after all would but palliate my unthankful silence and apparent neglect. I have now before me two fragments of Letters *begun*, the one in acknowledgment of the finest and most grandly conceived Sonnet in our Language,[1]—(at least, it is only in Milton's and in Wordsworth's Sonnets that I recollect any rival,—and this is not my judgment alone, but that of the man κατ' ἐξοχὴν φιλοκάλου, John Hookham Frere,) the second on the receipt of your 'Letter to Charles Butler,'[2] with the verses written on the blank page of Butler's Book of the Church,[3] with the motto, *Indignatio fecit*, as composed in the first Heat of my Feelings on reading the latter part of your Letter, from page 80.[4] They were to have been published in the Souvenir, with a long note declarative of my sense of your character, and of the nature and amount of your services to the Church of England, to Protestantism, and above all to the Faith in Christ. But Alaric Watts, the Editor, was afterwards advised, that it would probably expose his book to a persecution by the Catholics and Liberals— mislayed the copy, and afterwards applied for another copy, entreating permission to have the Lines inserted in the first Number of a Paper, undertaken on Protestant Principles. This was, as I afterwards found, the STANDARD,[5] to my no small annoyance—

[1] Blanco White's *Night and Death*, a sonnet composed in 1825 and dedicated to Coleridge. On 21 Dec. 1825 Coleridge sent a copy of this sonnet to Derwent.

[2] Blanco White's *Letter to Charles Butler, Esq. on his Notice of the 'Practical and Internal Evidence against Catholicism'* was published in June 1826. White sent Coleridge a copy of this work along with a letter dated 21 June 1826. The volume is now in the British Museum.

[3] Charles Butler's *Vindication of 'The Book of the Roman Catholic Church'*, which appeared in February 1826, contains the animadversions to which White replied in his *Letter to Charles Butler*.

[4] An extant holograph of Coleridge's poem is headed:

Poet and Friend:

a Dialogue occasioned by the Report of Mr Eneas M'Donnell's Speech at the British Catholic Association, Charles Butler, Esqre being present.— See the Revd. Blanco White's Letter to C. B. Esqre, *p. 80 usque ad finem.*

Facit INDIGNATIO Versus.

[5] Coleridge's poem appeared under the title, *A Dialogue written on a Blank Page of Butler's Book of the Roman Catholic Church*, in the *Standard* (21 May 1827) and in the *St. James Chronicle* (19–22 May 1827). In both newspapers the

first and least, because it was misprinted, and by the confusion of
the *Persons* of the Dialogue, rendered unintelligible; but secondly
and chiefly, from the *vampire* attacks and malignant Personalities
on Mr. Canning, with which the Paper infamized itself. The Poem
appeared likewise in the St. James's Chronicle. If you have not
seen it, I will transmit a correct copy to you. It may serve to assure
you, that I have *felt* as became one who loved and honoured you,
though I have failed in my duty, as an obliged Correspondent. You
have probably not heard, that by Lord Liverpool's (or rather the
Nation's) calamity I was deprived of a provision, to which he had
declared his intention of appointing me, as he had indeed engaged
his word to Mr. J. H. Frere—and which would have enabled me to
devote the scanty remainder of my breathing-time to the completion
and bringing out of the two Works, on which I have laboured for
thirty years past, and which it will be hard for me to effect under
my present necessity of scribbling what the Public *like*, instead of
giving what the mind of the country *wants*. God's will be done! One
of the books is now transcribing for the Press; of the other, the
materials are all collected, and the first part, and half of the second,
composed, and fit for the Press—and when I say, that this amounts
to three large volumes, and that the whole work, which, however,
is capable of being published as three several Works, will consist
of six, containing my system of Philosophy and Faith, as the result
of all my researches and reflections concerning God, Nature and
Man, you will not wonder that I name it my OPUS MAXIMUM, the
Harvesting of my Life's Labours. Yet as I awoke last night, or
rather with the poor relic of Volition breaking the Enchanter's
Talisman, succeeded at length in awakening myself out of a terrific
fantastic Dream, which would have required tenfold the imagina-
tion of a Dante* to have constructed in the waking state, I could
not but thank God on my knees for the lesson of Humility I had

poem is signed *ΕΣΤΗΣΕ*. In his *Poetical Works*, 1834, Coleridge altered his title
to *Sancti Dominici Pallium; a Dialogue between Poet and Friend, found written
on the blank leaf at the beginning of Butler's Book of the Church*. By adding the
date '(1825)' to the title, E. H. Coleridge (*Poems*, i. 448) pointed erroneously
to Charles Butler's first work, *The Book of the Roman Catholic Church: in a
series of letters addressed to R. Southey, Esq., on his 'Book of the Church'*, 1825,
to which Blanco White replied in May 1825 with his *Practical and Internal
Evidence against Catholicism, with Occasional Strictures on Mr. Butler's 'Book
of the Roman Catholic Church'*. In referring to Butler's *Book of the Church*, not
only in the various titles of his poem, but also in the present letter, Coleridge
certainly had in mind Butler's second work, the *Vindication of 'The Book of
the Roman Catholic Church'*, 1826, in which the author took 'Notice' of White's
strictures. See Letters 1476, 1569, and 1807.

* A large part of the imagery of the Divina Comedia was in fact supplied by
the Trances of a Monk, and it is certain that the monkish ἄσκησις may produce
the magnetic sleep. (Vid. Tertull. *de Animâ*. c. 9.) [Note by S. T. C.]

received, exclaiming, O vanity! I have but a few hours back an-
nounced myself to my friend, as the author of a SYSTEM of Philo-
sophy on Nature, History, Reason, Revelation; on the Eternal,
and on the Generations of the Heaven and the Earth, and I am
unable to solve the problem of my own Dreams! After many years'
watchful notice of the phaenomena of the somnial state, and an
elaborate classification of its *characteristic* distinctions, I remain
incapable of explaining any one Figure of all the numberless
Personages of this shadowy world—and have only attained to an
insight into the utter shallowness and impertinency of all the pre-
tended Theories hitherto advanced—and to look even on the *Visa
et Audita* of Swedenborg,[1] with his *spiritus* κοπροφίλοι, with more
respect than on the Lucubrations of Locke and Hartley! Well for
me if these vexations of the Night increase the dread of being
suffered to fall back upon the wild activities and restless chaos of
my own corrupt Nature! Well, if they increase the fervency with
which I pray, *Thy* kingdom come! in the world within me!

I have scarcely confidence to entreat you to re-commence your
correspondence with me, but if you will favour me with a letter, or
let me know how you are 'in mind, body and estate,' and what you
are doing, I dare give you my word that I will try to merit your
forgiveness. For I have much and of much interest to say to you,
arising in great part out of your own writings. You shall not again
have reason to complain of me.

This Letter will be delivered to you by James Gillman, a Fresh-
man and Probationary Fellow of St. John's, from Merchant
Tailors' School, which he left as Head Boy. He is the eldest of the
two children of my excellent friends and dear house-mates, Mr. and
Mrs. Gillman, a youth of thoroughly honest feelings and principles,
of fair abilities and respectable scholarship. He has in all his letters
from Oxford renewed his entreaties to be introduced to you by me,
as one who from his childhood has been accustomed to regard me
as a second father. I am assured that he will not discredit any
notice with which you should be so good as to honour him. I feel
an interest on this point, because I know enough of my young friend
to be convinced that the desire of winning and retaining *your*
esteem and approbation, will operate as a strong motive with him
to persevere in his studies, and closely linked with this, and of
still more importance, in his Temperance and Purity of Life. May
the Almighty bless you, my dear Sir! I am, with most sincere res-
pect and with affectionate regard,

Your obliged friend,

S. T. Coleridge.

[1] See Letter 1550.

1608. *To J. Blanco White*

Pub. Life of Joseph Blanco White, *i. 442.*

[Early December 1827]

My dear Sir,

James must not return to Oxford without bearing from me the
expression of my thanks, and of my thankfulness for your very
kind and to me most comfortable letter. But first of your Sonnet.[1]
On reading the sentences in your letter respecting it, I stood
staring vacantly on the paper in a state of feeling not unlike that
which I have too often experienced in a dream, when I have found
myself in chains, or in rags, shunned or passed by, with looks of
horror blended with sadness, by friends and acquaintance, and
convinced that in some alienation of mind I must have perpetrated
some crime, which I strove in vain to recollect. I then ran down to
Mrs. Gillman, to learn whether she or Mr. Gillman could throw any
light on the subject (though on reading your letter her heart was
so full of joy and thankfulness to you for your kind words about
her son, that it was some time before I could bring her back to the
point on which I came to question her). Neither Mr. nor Mrs. G.
could account for it. I have *repeated* the sonnet often; but to the
best of my recollection never either gave a copy to any one, or
permitted any one to transcribe it,—and as to publishing it with-
out your consent, you must allow me to say the truth,—I had felt
myself so much flattered by your having addressed it to me, that
I should have been half suspicious that it really might be, and half
afraid that it would appear to be, asking to have my own vanity
tickled, if I had thought of applying to you for permission to pub-
lish it. Where and when did it appear? If you will be so good as to
inform me, I may perhaps trace it out: for it annoys me to imagine
myself capable of such a breach at once of confidence and of deli-
cacy.—

My dear Sir, I pray you, do not consider this as any answer to
your letter. You will hear from me before James returns to us, i.e.
in about ten days. I mean this merely as a *skimming* of my mind,
that I may have nothing of this petty, personal gossip in my
thoughts, to interfere with matter of far deeper interest.

[1] Coleridge's letter of 28 Nov. 1827 elicited a prompt reply from Blanco
White, who mildly complained of the publication of his *Night and Death. A
Sonnet. Dedicated to S. T. Coleridge, Esq. by his sincere friend, Joseph Blanco
White.* The sonnet appeared in the 1828 issue of *The Bijou,* 'the Editor and
Proprietors' going so far as to offer their 'warmest acknowledgments' to Blanco
White for his contribution. Coleridge later learned that Gillman had 'let out
of his hands' a copy of White's sonnet, which Fraser published in 'spite of his
Honor thrice deliberately pledged to the contrary'. See Letter 1639.

You will hear from me in a few days, and then I shall dare hope
a continuance of your correspondence; for believe me, few indeed
are they to whom, with the same depth and entireness of regard
and respect, I can subscribe myself the obliged and affectionate
Friend,

S. T. Coleridge.

1609. *To Henry Taylor*

MS. Bodleian Library. Pub. E. L. G. ii. 403.

Grove,
Highgate.
[December 1827]

My dear Sir

Tho' the Constantia (I cannot decypher the word before it) is a
most exquisite Cordial—for Mrs Gillman being rather weakly and
dining by herself at an early hour, I insisted on opening a Bottle
for her, in the belief that as she scarcely ever tastes wine, a small
glass daily for four or five days would speed her convalescence,—
and tasted it myself, so as to be able to confirm her judgement,
that beyond any wine, I had ever tried, it deserved the description
of *pure*, and delicate—rich—and tho' I am learned enough in the
Heraldry[1] of Wine to be aware, that it was a Present for a Lord or
an Ambassador—yet you must do me and yourself the Justice to
believe me, that the proof, it implied, of your remembering me,
and my friends, and the Thursday Evenings at Highgate, and
thinking of us with kindness, was that which came first, and
remains uppermost in my mind. I assure you, that I felt quite
affected by it—for I have never ceased to follow you with inward
inquiries & wishes to know how you were going on, in this eddy of
Change and Chance.—Mrs Gillman was much gratified by your
friendly mention of her & Mr G.—and desires me to tell you so.

I am going on as usual—and hope, that soon after Christmas you
will see by a series of Works, that I have not been an idler, and
tho' infirm & hard pressed circumstantially, have yet kept 'the
Citadel unconquered'.[2]

Before Mr J. H. Frere left England, he received a positive pro-
mise from Lord Liverpool that he would do something for me, and
[Liverpool] requested that if I did not hear from [him] before
Christmas, he should be reminded of it. Mr Frere advised me to
write to Lord Dudley, & to tell him, that *he* (Mr F.) had advised

---

[1] 'Heraldly' in MS. The letter is carelessly written.
[2] *A Tombless Epitaph*, line 19, *Poems*, i. 413.

me, begging him to recall the circumstance to Lord Liverpool—. I did not however take this step, till a Lady informed me, that her Brother in law Sir G. Poetoch[1] had made great interest for the place held by the late Mr Gifford; but had received the direct Answer, 'Lord Liverpool has reserved it for Mr Coleridge'.—On this I wrote to Lord Dudley—then at Brighton—he replied, that in ten days he should be in town—that he would much rather speak to Lord Liverpool, which he would do immediately on his arrival in town, than write to him—unless I particularly wished it. On the seventh day after the receival[2] of his Lordship's Letter, the Earl of Liverpool was stricken: & in less than a month, I believe, the King gave away the Place to another.—So ended my first & only Dream of Patronage. God's Will be done! He knows, that poor as I am & hard put to it, thro' anxiety not to suspend works, from which I cannot derive any pecuniary emolument, to employ myself in more marketable commodities, I yet felt more for the Nation's Calamity than for my own!—

Need I say, how glad I should be to see you, whenever Chance or Choice should bring you in our neighborhood?

For I am with sincere | regard & esteem, my dear Sir, | Your
obliged
S. T. Coleridge

1610. *To Basil Montagu*

Address: Basil Montagu, Esqr | 25 | Bedford Square | or Mrs M.
MS. Huntington Lib. Pub. E. L. G. ii. 405.
Postmark: 21 December 1827.

20 Decr 1827—

My very dear Montague

Mrs Gillman has just set my heart in a beat and my bowells in a quiver by informing [me], that Mr Gillman, his thoughts bewildered by the pain and fever of these sad poison-boils, the sickness & irregular fever produced by them, and the necessity of driving out when it perplexes him how to sit, even on a pillowed chair, had forgotten that he had on my applying to him for directions concerning the *Fullers*[3] undertaken to write himself to you. On the

---

[1] This name in the MS. may be Poetoch or Pocock. Coleridge refers to Mrs. Aders's brother-in-law. See Letters 1578–80 and 1586. Sir George Pocock (1765–1840) was created a baronet at the coronation of George IV in 1821.

[2] 'received' in MS.

[3] For Coleridge's annotations in Thomas Fuller's various works, see *Literary Remains*, ii. 381–90; *Notes, Theological, Political, and Miscellaneous. By Samuel Taylor Coleridge*, ed. Derwent Coleridge, 1853, pp. 97–101; and *Notes and Queries* (Seventh Series), vi. 501–2 and vii. 35. Two volumes of Fuller's

same afternoon that I received your note & Mrs Montague's,
Henry Coleridge came up to inform me, that my Brother George,
the only one of my Brothers who from my 12th to my 22nd year
did act a brother's part by me & whom for many a year after that
I loved tho' with a filial rather than a fraternal affection, was
sinking rapidly under the oppression of Dropsy in the Chest—&
I could not help contrasting the calm sadness with which I received
this information with the agitation & I may truly say the misery
& the fright, into which your note threw me—and the possession,
it has taken of my mind, now blending now alternating with the
only grief that could have stood any competition with the imagi-
nation of your danger—a letter of gall and wormwood respecting
my poor dear bewildered Eldest born—Day after day, Mrs G. and
I have been talking about you—and really in my state of feeling I
could not write to Mr Irving—for I felt that it would have been hypo-
crisy to use the language of sympathy with his feelings for the loss
of an infant—so stunned had my ordinarily quick feelings been by
the thought of your illness, more alarming to me thro' recollection
of Sir Alex. Ball's case by the very circumstance of your extreme
temperance.—Pray, let Emily write me a line by return of Post,
how you are—I will however write to Mr I.—were it only, that Mrs
M. suggested it—& it is my duty.

   May God bless and preserve you for all of us—for me—for I most
truly love you, and the sight of you—

S. T. Coleridge

1611. *To George May Coleridge*

Address: Revd George May Coleridge | Warden House | Ottery St Mary |
   Devon
MS. Victoria University Lib. Pub. Letters, *ii. 746.*
Postmark: Highgate, 14 January 1828.

Grove, Highgate—
Monday 14 Jany 1828—

My dear Nephew
   An interview with your Cousin Henry on Saturday and a Note
received from him last night had enabled me in some measure to
prepare my mind for the aweful and *humanly* afflicting contents
of your Letter—& I rose to the receiving of it from earnest suppli-
cation to 'the Father of Mercies and God of all Comfort' that he

works with annotations by Coleridge are in the British Museum: *The Church-
History of Britain,* 1655, with which is bound *The Appeal of Injured Innocence,*
1659; and *The Holy State. The Profane State,* 1663 (4th edn.). See T. J. Wise,
Two Lake Poets . . ., 1927, pp. 122–3.

would be strong in the weakness of his faithful Servant, and his effectual Helper in the last conflict.—My first impulse on reading your letter was to set off immediately—but on a re-perusal I doubt whether I shall not better comply with your suggestion by waiting for your next.—Assuredly if God permit, I will not forego the claim, which my heart & conscience justify me in making, to be one among the mourners who ever truly loved and honored your Father. Allow me, my dear Nephew! in the swelling grief of my heart to say, that if ever man morning & evening and in the watches of the night had earnestly intreated thro' his Lord & Mediator, that God would shew him his sins and their sinfulness, I for the last ten years at least of my life have done so. But in vain have I tried to recall any one moment since my quitting the University, or any one occasion, in which I have either thought, felt, spoken, or intentionally acted of or in relation to my Brother, otherwise than as one who loved in him Father and Brother in one—and who independently of the fraternal relation and the remembrance of his manifold goodness and kindness to me from boyhood to early manhood should have chosen him above all, I had known, as the Friend of my inmost Soul—. Never have man's feelings & character been more cruelly misrepresented, than mine. Before God have I sinned—and I have not hidden my offences before him—but he too knows, that the belief of my Brother's alienation and the grief that I was a stranger in the house of my second father has been the secret wound that to this hour never closed or healed up.—Yes, my dear Nephew! I do grieve and at this moment I have to struggle hard in order to keep my spirit in tranquillity as one who has long since referred his cause to God, thro' the grief at my little communication with my family—Had it been otherwise, I might have been able to shew my self, my *whole* self, for evil and for good to my Brother—and often have said to myself—How fearful an attribute to sinful man is Omniscience! and yet have I earnestly wished, O how many times—that my Brother could have seen my inmost heart—with every thought and every frailty—But his Reward is nigh—in the Light and Love of his Lord & Saviour he will soon be all Light and Love, & I too shall have his prayers before the Throne.—May the Almighty, and the Spirit the Comforter, dwell in your & in Your Mother's Spirit.—

I must conclude—Only if I come, and it should please God that your dear Father shall be still awaiting his Redeemer's final Call,[1] I shall be perfectly satisfied in all things to be directed by you & his [your?] Mother—who will judge best whether the knowlege of

---

[1] George Coleridge died on 12 Jan. 1828.

my arrival tho' without seeing me would or would not be a satisfaction, would or would not be a disturbance to him—.

Your affectionate Uncle

S. T. Coleridge

1612. *To S. C. Hall*

Address: S. C. Hall, Esqre | 2 East Place | Lambeth
MS. Cornell University Lib. Hitherto unpublished.
Postmark: 15 January 1828.

Grove, Highgate

Tuesday 15 Jany 1828.

Dear Sir

The afflicting (humanly speaking, and to all who survive, & who honored & loved him)—the afflicting intelligence of the Death of my dearest Brother, the Revd George Coleridge, was the occasion of my not having received your letter with it's half-bank Note[1]—and I can now only acknowlege it, and beg you to send the other half, as before. When my mind is a little tranquillized, I will write to you more fully—At present believe me

with kind regard | Your's truly |

S. T. Coleridge

1613. *To J. H. Green*

Address: J. H. Green, Esqre | Lincoln's Inn Fields
MS. Pierpont Morgan Lib. Hitherto unpublished.
Postmark: Highgate, 25 January 1828.

[25 January 1828]

My dear Friend

Mrs Gillman bids me shift the blame of this Superfluity per Post from my own to her shoulders—& say, that she bothered (anglice, importuned) me not to wait for the chance of seeing you on Sunday but to ensure your coming against light obstacles.— Nay, quoth I, but a Surgeon hath no *light* obstacles. A pebble of an ounce weight might, it should seem, be easily kicked out of the way— but ask the Patient—and he will tell you (N.b.—I did not say this *out*) that one of a few grains is enough to gravel him—. But Women will have their way—& the purpose of this letter is to inform you, that my peccant Toe is not only very much sorer and more intolerant of the least pressure, but likewise not constantly but with

---

[1] Hall had sent Coleridge half of a bank-note for £5, the amount still due for *The Improvisatore*. See Letter 1602.

intermissions, perhaps three or four times during the 24 hours painful—I can scarcely call it throbbing—it is a kind of heavy deep-seated pain—In the mean time, there has appeared an erysypelatous inflammation beginning at the top of the knee on the outside, extending permanently 3 or four inches, but at night the blush has shot downward in a narrow slip to within an inch or two of the instep—the worst part & that on which there are unfortunately two or three scratches or abrasions is just where the Calf thickens but on the anterior ridge of the Leg. I am lame—& have tried to keep down the inflammation, and to stop and as much as I can to prevent the Itching & Heat by the Liquor Carbonat: Ammoniae, & (which I find more efficacious) by sponging the Stocking with cold water. This Morning I found that the Stocking which I had kept on during the night, & wetted every time I awoke, had stuck to one of the Abrasions which had been oozing blood.

Tuesday Night I was feverish, with little sleep & that little disturbed by flying whirling confused Dreams with a number of crimson colored & luminous objects. My Spirits are depressed; but my mind calm and active—& all above knee not worse than usual— The pain across my body just below the Thorax, or between that and the navel, as soon as I awake & as long as I remain in bed after waking, is not greater than it has been every morning for the last 6 or 7 years, is almost removed by rising and standing upright, and entirely removed the moment the faeces are eliminated. I have no pain & no soreness on either side; but make a great deal of light-colored clear Urine—and was thinking of boiling some over the candle in a Table-spoon to see whether it would co-agulate & thus (according to a Dropsy, Liver, and Kidney tall thin Quarto with a number of morbid-Anatomy Plates which I gave offence by calling *Cat's-meat*—not *quite* fresh) determine a schirrus, or abscess or tuburcle [tubercle?] in my Kidney—but I was afraid, it would co-agulate—& turned coward at the thought.—I know that nothing can be done, but by keeping myself still, & taking no stimulus that I can possibly do without—but yet it will be a great Comfort to me to see you next Sunday. And it is only on the possibility that something may have interfered or may interfere with *that*, that I could consent to avail myself of a leisure two hours on any other day, even tho' you should have them at your disposal.—If I know myself—& it is ten to one, I do not—but *if* I dare trust my own persuasions—I have no wish to have my life prolonged but what is involved in the wish to complete the views, I have taken, of Life as beginning in separation from Nature and ending in Union with God, and to reduce to an *intelligible* if not artistical form the results of my religious, biblical and ecclesiastical Lucubrations[1]—& as I ground my hope of redemption from the after-death on the capability of a righteousness not my own, I have no other fear of Dying than that of being seized with the stolen goods on me—the talents which had been entrusted to me & which I had retained from the Persons, for whose benefit they should have been traded with—.

May God bless you | & your very affectionate, obliged & |
grateful Friend
S. T. Coleridge

P.S. There is something very aweful in that necessary inference from the Phaenomenon of the Races—assuming the rejection of the Ouran outang Hypothesis[2] & that of Five Pairs of Adams & Eves—that Individual Depravity in a nation of depraved individuals may sink so deep & diffuse itself thro' all the acts, affections, faculties, passions and habits of the Man as at length to master the formative principle itself & involve the generative power in it's sphere of influence—. What a dreadful inversion! a *guilty* Nature, and a necessitated Individual—an Individual sunk below guilt!—

1614. *To George Skinner*

Transcript Coleridge family. Hitherto unpublished.

Grove Highgate
Saturday 16 Feby. 1828.

My dear Sir

I will not waste your time or hurt my own feelings by framing apologies for the following Request or for the Trouble, you will have in complying with it. For some months a medley of causes, events and incidents moral and physical has exercised a malign influence on my health and spirits, and at the moment I am pressing on the flying rear of the retreating enemy headed by *St Anthony*, tho' his Fire has become languid, and is yielding to the brisk and uninterrupted Shower of pump water, acetic acid and

---

[1] In May 1828 Coleridge wrote out in one of his notebooks a 'detailed synopsis' of his *opus maximum*. This account is printed by Alice D. Snyder in *Coleridge on Logic and Learning*, 1929, pp. 3–8. A briefer statement concerning his *opus* appears in a letter of 1833. See Letter 1795.

[2] In a letter to Wordsworth of 30 May 1815 Coleridge refers to the 'absurd notion . . . of Man's having progressed from an Ouran Outang state'. Likewise, in an autograph fragment quoted by J. H. Muirhead, Coleridge says he attaches 'neither belief nor respect to the Theory, which . . . contemplates Man as the last metamorphosis, the gay *Image*, of some lucky species of Ape or Baboon'. *Coleridge as Philosopher*, 1930, p. 132. See Letter 1537, p. 599.

muriate of Ammonia. In doleful earnest a series of very miserable
making Symptoms, of which involuntary fits of Stupor counter-
feiting sleep, and convulsive dreams night after night in ordinary
sleep ended in a serious attack of Erysipelas in both legs with
oedema of the right leg—and completely have I been for some
time past swallowed up in the one anxiety of arranging and in-
creasing my huge pile of Manuscripts, so that the *substance* at
least of the results of my logical, physiological, philosophical,
theological, biblical, and I hope I am entitled to add *religious* and
Christian studies and meditations for the last 20 years of my life
might be found in a state capable of being published by my dear
Friend Mr Green, who has for ten years devoted the only vacant
day of every week to the participation of my labors.[1] I thank God
that this is now so far effected that should He call me to morrow,
I shall leave the world in the humble trust that my daily morn-
ing and evening supplications offered in the very words of the
Psalmist (Psalm 71st.) had been heard, and that tho' the talent
intrusted to me had not been improved to an extent at all com-
mensurate with the unusual opportunities that had been afforded
me, it had not however been hidden in a napkin—and that the
power & life of Christ our Redeemer will so *precipitate* the remain-
ing evil of my corrupt nature as that cleansed by his spiritual
blood my spirit may rise a pure capacity of *him*, blind to be ir-
radiated with *his* light, empty to be filled from his fullness, and
naked to be clothed with *his* Righteousness—in him & thro' him
to be united with the Eternal *One*, the Author of my Being and its
ultimate *End*.—Before I pass to worldly concerns, let me say that

[1] In his will (see Appendix A) Coleridge described J. H. Green 'as the Man
most intimate with . . . [his] intellectual labors, purposes, and aspirations'.
To Green, therefore, he left 'upon Trust', for the benefit of Mrs. Coleridge and
after her his children, all his 'Books [and] manuscripts', with the rights of
publication. For his many annotated books, however, he made a special pro-
vision: 'My Friend, Mr Joseph Henry Green, shall in lieu of selling my Books
have the option of purchasing the same . . ., in as much as their chief value
will be dependent on his possession of them.'

After Coleridge's death, Green, as literary executor, devoted almost thirty
years 'to an attempt to realise his master's dream'. Despite his efforts, however,
he was unable to co-ordinate the mass of manuscript fragments into a coherent
and unified whole. His *Spiritual Philosophy; founded on the Teaching of the late
Samuel Taylor Coleridge*, 2 vols., was published posthumously in 1865. For a
sympathetic discussion of this work see J. H. Muirhead, *Coleridge as Philoso-
pher*, 1930, pp. 256–7 and 273–6. Campbell (*Life*, 280) says that 'in his Hunterian
Orations of 1840 and 1847 [*Vital Dynamics* and *Mental Dynamics*], Green prob-
ably accomplished more in the setting forth of Coleridge's philosophical views
than in the *Spiritual Philosophy*'. Miss Snyder comments that 'a reading of the
three works is bound to issue in an *a priori* agreement'. *Coleridge on Logic and
Learning*, 1929, p. 44.

of all the supplemental means of comfort and of growth that it has been given me to employ, the most fruitful has been the habit of making some one chapter of the Psalms or the Prophets, or St John's Gospel, or of St Paul's Epistles a regular part of my morning and my last prayers. This interposition of meditation, together with the act of self-examination in determining the appropriability of the several verses that either might form or suggest prayer or thanksgiving and previous to the appropriation, I have found most favorable to a devotional state—and among other advantages prevents those transient wanderings of the mind and transfers of the conscious attention from the Great Being addressed to the words and thoughts themselves & which the sound of one's own voice will at times occasion.—

And now, my dear Sir, I must proceed to my request. Owing to false, at least strangely mistaken information I had long abandoned in despair the proceeds of my dear Son Derwent Coleridge's Exhibitions from the Mercers' and the Goldsmiths' Company[1]— the latter remains hopeless. In fact my old friend Mr Sutton Senr. happened at the time to be abroad and Mr R. Sutton Junr., tho' as fashionable and of as imperative a Dash as any rich man's son & partner on the Stock Exchange, proved a very inefficient substitute for his Father in my son's case—Such is the first half of the Story. The second lies on my own shoulders—I am ashamed to confess that for the last three or four months mistaking the letters from the Clerk of the Mercers' Company for Remembrancers from the Royal Society of Literature, of which I have been (to my shame) but a sleeping partner, I *never* opened them till a friend came in a bustle to inform me, that an order was put up if not passed for transferring the proceeds to some other purpose. I applied to my old friend, told him the honest truth (I ought to say the truth honestly)—he bestirred himself and by his influence procured the order to be revoked,[2] and all I have to do is to get another certificate signed instead of the former, which has been lost—or if in

[1] For details concerning the exhibitions granted to Derwent Coleridge by the Mercers' and Goldsmiths' Companies, see Letters 1331 and 1395 and notes.

[2] On 7 Feb. 1828 the Court of the Mercers' Company ordered that notice be given to Derwent Coleridge of its intention to declare a vacancy in the exhibition at the next meeting. On 14 Feb., however, 'A letter from S. T. Coleridge Esq. dated Highgate February 1828, stating that it was entirely owing to a mistake as to the regulations of the Company with respect to exhibitions, that had prevented his son from claiming his Exhibition at an earlier period, and requesting that he might not be deprived of it, was read:—

'Whereupon the Notice given at the last Court for declaring the said Exhibition vacant was withdrawn.' (From information kindly supplied by Mr. G. E. Logsdon, the Clerk of the Mercers' Company.)

existence, I might as well take a trip to Ariosto's Limbo to look
after it as to any other place within my knowledge.—All that is
meant or wanted is simply that Derwent has not absented himself
from College *against the command of his Superiors*—that he stands
in a similar case as other young men after their first Degree. I have
enclosed the certificate—and if you know the Tutor and any kind
fellows of St John's, or have any resident friend that does, whose
services in this respect you can conciliate, you will very greatly
oblige me and serve my son, who since he has taken Orders, or
rather since he quitted the free-thinking Set, has been as great a
comfort & credit to me in *all* respects, as he was previously in all
but his silly opinions taken up at second hand on the credit of
Messrs Tom Macaulay and Austin.—Need I say how truly welcome
your visits will at all times be to, my dear Sir, your sincere Friend

S. T. Coleridge

P.S. Permit me to add, that it is of great importance that there
should be no delay.

1615. *To R. Sutton*

MS. Mr. W. Hugh Peal. Hitherto unpublished.

Grove, Highgate
16 Feby. 1828.

My dear Sir

I have sent the Certificate to Cambridge, and *till* I receive the
answer, I will content myself by so far anticipating the expression
of my feelings as to assure you, that it would not be easy for a man
the *most* impressed with the sense of another's persevering and
constant kindness to feel more affectionately grateful, than for
your fortitude and persistency in friendly services does

Your obliged

S. T. Coleridge

1616. *To Derwent Coleridge*

Address: The | Revd. Derwent Coleridge | Helston | Cornwall
MS. Pierpont Morgan Lib. Hitherto unpublished.
Postmark: 19 February 1828.

Grove, Highgate—
Tuesday 19th Feby. 1828

My very dear Children—for you are both as ONE in my Heart, a
joy, a thanksgiving, and a fervent prayer, morning, and night and
O! often & often in the watches of the Night—it will give you more
pleasure that it will come unexpected—But tho' it is not absolutely

certain, in consequence of an act of supererogation in Mr Tateham's Certificate—yet is next to certain, that I shall within a few days receive a hundred pound or more for you from the Mercers' Company, and for the future to the end of the time the 25 or 30£ yearly—Partly by my neglect—not *intentional*; but I had unluckily mistaken the Clerk of the Mercers' Company's Official Letters for Remembrancers of the Royal Society of Literature, of which I have been a Sleeping Partner, and *never opened them*—but principally from misinformation, and mistake on the part of R. Sutton Junr, who had given it up in despair & led me to do so—& his Father was abroad. Had he been at home, I almost believe that I should have got the Goldsmiths' Company's Withholding of the Exhibition over-ruled—In short, I wrote a long Letter to the Mercers' Company,[1] in which I modestly contrived to impress them with the importance of my *absorbing* Studies & (which is true enough) of the precarious state of my Health, and in a private Letter to Mr Sutton (which he read to the Wardens &c &c of the Company) gave a most *fascinating* account of *your* merits, my dear Dervy—it lies upon your conscience to make me *stand clear* on this score, & I am so full of faith that you will, that the affair lies very light on my own—The result was, that the Order for transferring the Proceeds was revoked, & it was agreed that nothing more should be required but that you had resided as much as the Heads of the College had required of you—. After I have got the money, You must write to R. Sutton, Esqre—who has really been most zealous in our behalf—& I could have done nothing without him—

In the meantime in order to prevent any unnecessary Delay You must send me your Authority for receiving the Proceeds from the Exhibition.

This I suppose will do: written one side of your letter to me—the front of course—

Sir

I have requested and I hereby authorize my Father, Mr S. T. Coleridge, to receive the Proceeds from the Exhibition, to which the worshipful the Mercers' Company nominated me, or any sums now due or hereafter to become due to me on this account: and with every sentiment of respect and gratitude to the Gentlemen of the Company for their indulgent kindness, I intreat you, Sir! to accept the respectful acknowlegements of

Your obliged humble Servant,
Derwent Coleridge

---

[1] Coleridge's letter has not come to light, but an account of it is given in the note to Letter 1614, p. 725.

To James Barnes, Esqre
    Clerk of the Mercers' Company.—

I have been long confined with erysypelas now in one Leg, now in another; but most seriously, and accompanied with considerable oedema in my right Leg—This is the first day, I have ventured out—. The sufferings from the intolerable Itching, the disturbance, and for ten days, all but the prevention of Sleep, and from the symptomatic prostration of Spirits have been great; but God has been gracious & I am convalescent— . . .[1]

The Gillmans' *earnest* Love[2]—

1617. *To Henry Nelson Coleridge*

MS. Victoria University Lib. Hitherto unpublished.

Wednesday Night
20 Feby 1828
Grove, Highgate

My dear Henry

I thank you for your Note—but thank God! every thing has been settled, and I wait only for Derwent's Answer to a Letter, which I dispatched by Yesterday's Post, desiring him to send me an authority for receiving the Proceeds on his account, and instruction in what way he would have the cash forwarded to him, to enable him to put a 100£ on his Wife's Lap—with nearly 60£ to come hereafter.[3]—

I am persuaded, that had Mr Sutton, Senr. been at home at the time, that the Archons of the Goldsmiths' Company would not receive the Certificate of Residence, & had taken it up instead

---

[1] A third of page 3 of the MS. cut off.

[2] This sentence is written at the top of page one of the MS.

[3] On 7 Nov. 1822 the Mercers' Company elected Derwent Coleridge to a Lady North Exhibition, which he was to 'enjoy' from Lady Day 1822 and 'during the pleasure of the Court'. On 16 Apr. 1829 the Court of the Company elected another candidate to the exhibition 'lately enjoyed by Derwent Coleridge'. Thus Derwent held his exhibition for 7 years. At £20 per annum the total amount would have been £140. If Coleridge is correct in saying in this and in the preceding letter that Derwent was to receive £100 at this time, then the payments were five years in arrears; and if, as seems likely, Derwent followed the instructions contained in his father's letter of 23 Apr. 1823 and applied for the £20 due at Lady Day 1823, the £100 was for the period from Lady Day 1823 to Lady Day 1828. Furthermore, since Derwent did not vacate his exhibition until Lady Day 1829, an additional £20 must have been paid to him at that time.

of his Son, I should have got that likewise—In fact, I should have gone myself to work, and canvassed the Wardens &c individually, but that Derwent had written to me after I had by Mr Sutton's powerful Interest secured his Election, that it would be of no use to him, as it would be out of his power to procure the requisite Certificate—. *A* certificate I did procure—& where the Inspectors are favorably inclined, they do not of necessity look to see how all the words are spelt.—But this is useless regret—tho' it would *smilify* my platter face to have had 200£ to send him instead of *one*.

I dined at Mr Green's yesterday—& have not laughed so loud and long for many a month, as I did on reading Leigh Hunt's character of me[1]—Green had had his Laugh before, and so sate with a face of secure, *fruitive*, anticipation enjoying my θαλάσσιον γέλασμα[2]—I do not, however, agree with him entirely in his description of the Portrait, as 'in *all* points (saving his compliment on my command of words) so whimsically contrary to the Truth'— Leigh Hunt's physiognomic Decision respecting my Sensuality is an Alethöid,[3] that *conveys* an untruth, because it *tells* but half the Truth—and does not *specify*.—It is just as true as Dryden's—

Great Wit to Madness sure is near allied[4]—

true so far, that Genius of the highest kind implies an unusual intensity of the modifying Power, which detached from the Discriminative and Reproductive Power might turn a Plat of Straw into a Royal Diadem—But it would be at least as true—that great Genius is most alien to Madness, divided from it by an impassable Mountain—viz—the activity of thought and vivacity of the accumulative Memory which are no less essential Constituents of 'Great Wit'[5]—Thus, I dare affirm, that the Antagonists of Sensuality are at least as noticeable parts of my Nature—of which I will only mention Constancy; the Love, almost the Passion, for the Permanent: and the tranquil Complacency in Beauty, as distinguished from the Interesting, the Agreeable, the Delicious—and of the Quality attributed to me two thirds might be more properly termed *Sensuosity*, and the remaining Third is of a feminine character, *continuous*, diffused, passive—nearer to the Elegiac Πόθος[6] than the Lyrical Ὄρεξις.—In short, in every thing *Continuity* is the characteristic both Quality and Property of my Being.—The

---

[1] See the article, 'Mr. Coleridge', in Leigh Hunt's *Lord Byron and some of His Contemporaries*, 1828.   [2] Cf. *Prometheus Bound*, 90.
[3] ἀληθοειδές τι [Marginal note by S. T. C.]
[4] *Absalom and Achitophel*, Pt. I, line 163.
[5] Cf. *Table Talk*, 1 May 1833. See also *Biog. Lit.* i. 30 n.
[6] Underlined once in MS.

peccatum originale with me might be, with friendly tenderness, expressed by Excess of *Power* with Deficiency of *Strength*— Facility, Infirmity, mental Cowardice of whatever might force my attention to myself, &c &c—. I hope, I do not scribble such notes of Egoism often enough to tempt you to add Vanity & Self-worship to the vices of your

affectionate Friend

S. T. C.—

1618. *To Joseph Hardman*[1]

Address: J. Hardman, Esqre | Hornsea Lane
MS. Mr. W. Hugh Peal. Hitherto unpublished.

Friday Night
7 March 1828

My dear Sir

The Night has set in with such seeming Obduracy of chilling Rain, that Mr and Mrs Gillman have put a Veto on my intended Walk to Hornesey Lane—I must, therefore (for I cannot with a good conscience expose Mrs Gillman to the Risk of having an additional Patient on her hands) defer the pleasure, I had calculated on, in passing the interval between Tea & Bed-time in your Fumatorium. My Thoughts will not *keep at home*. They dispose me to hope favorably of our Quarterly *Excursive* Magazine[2] (for excursions into foreign Literature, Incidents, &c, will form the permanent character of the Work, I presume, tho' not exclusively). As soon as I can find or make a leisure Day, I will devote it to the drawing up of a *Scheme* of the contents, and of the proportional spaces they should occupy, of a Publication intended to be popular.

Mrs Gillman begs me to give you, and Mrs H. her kind Regards— and believe me, my dear Sir,

with unfeigned Esteem & Regard | your obliged
S. T. Coleridge.

[1] Joseph Hardman, a frequent contributor to *Blackwood's Magazine*, was the father of Frederick Hardman (1814–74), novelist and journalist.
[2] Coleridge may refer to the *Foreign Review and Continental Miscellany*, 1828–30.

1619. *To Unknown Correspondent*

MS. Private possession. Hitherto unpublished.

17 March 1828

My dear Sir

I had intended to have delivered in person my acknowlege-
ments and deo permittente acceptance of your kind invitation for
Tuesday next—but I found myself a little exhausted, having
talked a good extent beyond my morning Wont at Lady B's[1]— &
likely to miss the stage—. With unfeigned respect,
            dear Sir, | Your obliged
                        S. T. Coleridge

[1] On her return to Coleorton after her visit to London, Lady Beaumont sent
Coleridge a letter postmarked 16 May 1828. The letter reads in part:

Let me remind you of our last conversation wherein you said that meta-
physics so far from deadening the spirit of imagination had added new wings
from the power of contrast, and the last specimen you read is a proof of
your not having deceived yourself. Do not let the last rays sink for want of
exertion, and give Fancy its full play. In this exhortation I shall be seconded
by Mrs Gilman. For *one* of the present—one that will profit by your labours,
hundreds will feel their purest thoughts kindle into life by the powers of
that precious gift you have received. Do not throw it away.

In the margins of Lady Beaumont's letter Coleridge scribbled the following
comment. The MS. is torn and partly illegible.

Lady B. in this letter urges me to resume Poetry.—Alas! how can I?—Is
the power extinct? No! No! As in a still Summer Noon, when the lulled
Air at irregular intervals wakes up with a startled *Hush*-st, that seems to
re-demand the silence which it breaks, or heaves a long profound Sigh in
it's Sleep, and an Æolian Harp has been left in the chink of the not quite
shut Casement—even so—how often!—scarce a week of my Life shuffles by,
that does not at some moment feel the spur of the old genial impulse—even
so do there fall on my inward Ear swells, and broken snatches of sweet
Melody, reminding me that I still have that within me which is both Harp and
Breeze. But in the same moment awakes the Sense of C[*hange*] *without*—
Life *unendeared*. The tenderest Strings no longer thrill'd.

In order to poetic composition I need the *varied* feeling—Thought charmed
to sleep;* and the too great *continuity* of mind broken up, to begin anew, with
new-power seeking & finding *new* themes.

* Thought's brief and genial Sleeps, that nourish Thought.
                        [MS. Mr. A. H. B. Coleridge.]

1620. *To Thomas Pringle*[1]

Address: Thomas Pringle, Esqre | 5 Bunhill Row | Finsbury Square
*MS. National Library of Scotland. Pub. with omis. 'Samuel Taylor Coleridge
and Thomas Pringle', by E. L. Griggs*, Quarterly Bulletin of the South African
Library, *1951, p. 3.*

Grove, Highgate
Thursday—
[Endorsed March 20, 1828]

Dear Sir

It is some four or five months ago since G. Thompson's Travels
&c in South[er]n Africa[2] passing it's book-club course thro' our
house, my eye by accident lighting on some verses, I much against
my Wont was tempted to go on—and so I first became acquainted
with your *Afar in the Desert*—.[3] Tho' at that time so busy that I
had not looked at any of the new Books, I was taken so com-
pleatly possession of, that for some days I did little else but read
and recite your poem, now to this group and now to that—&
since that time have either written or caused to be written, at least
half a dozen copies—and procured my friend, Mr Gillman, who, &
not I, is a Member of the Book-club to purchase the two Volumes
for me. The day before yesterday I sent a copy in my own hand
to my Son, the Revd D. Coleridge, or rather to his Bride, at Helston,
Cornwall—& then discovered that it had been re-printed in the
Athenaeum.—With the omission of about four or at the utmost
six lines I do not hesitate to declare it, among the two or three most
perfect lyric Poems in our Language—. Praecipitandus est *liber*
Spiritus, says Petronius: and you have thoroughly fulfilled the
prescript. I need not say that I shall dedicate my first leisure &
tranquil hours to the perusal of the other poems—& regret that
for the next two or three weeks I shall not have it in my power
consistently with urgent duties—in the mean time I shall be happy
to see you any time after One o'clock in the morning (for I am an
invalid)—and should it be convenient to you, on Thursday Even-
ings we commonly see a few intelligent friends from Town—from
6 to 10 or 11—& there will be a tolerable chance of getting you a
seat in Basil Montague's Carriage, for your homeward Journey—.

[1] Thomas Pringle (1789–1834), Scottish poet, spent the years 1820–6 in
South Africa. He was appointed secretary of the Anti-Slavery Society in 1827.
Two years later he became the editor of *Friendship's Offering*.

[2] George Thompson, *Travels and Adventures in Southern Africa*, 2 vols.,
1827. Pringle supplied materials for this work.

[3] Pringle's *Afar in the Desert*, his most popular poem, was also published in
his *Ephemerides; or, Occasional Poems, written in Scotland and South Africa*,
1828.

As to the rest, I will freely tell you how I stand when I see you—
indeed, I have scarcely read your Note thro', being anxious not
to detain your messenger—

believe me, that I am | with sincere interest and every kind |
anticipation | your obliged

S. T. Coleridge

1621. *To the Editor of the 'Quarterly Review'*

MS. *British Museum. Pub. E. L. G. ii. 407.*

[April 1828 ?]¹

Dear Sir

Soon after by occasion of a Scheme or Fancy bubble, to the
bursting of which the World owes the Thalaba, Curse of Kehama,
Don Roderic,—in short, Robert Southey, I had quitted Cambridge,
and from Opinions which less than two years sufficed for me to out-
grow, I had given up all my then very flattering Prospects in the
Church, and—MARRIED!—I was engaged, and if I recollect aright,
thro' the mediation of Sir James, then Mr, McIntosh to write for
the Critical Review:² and I wrote an Article on Lewis's Monk, and
another on Bishop Horsley's Tract on the Greek Metres, which
were perfected into Print.³ But I likewise had written some half
a score or more of what, I thought clever & epigrammatic &
devilishly severe Reviews, from a single sentence to the quantum of
half a page on sundry Fungi of the Press that had been sent to me,
to abide the operation which united Trial, Verdict, and Execu-
tion—but a Remark made by Miss Wordsworth, to whom I had in
full expectation of gaining a laugh of applause read one of my
Judgements occasioned my committing the whole Batch to the
Fire⁴—Since then, the Edingburgh & Quarterly effected a total

---

¹ The first volume of W. F. P. Napier's *History of the War in the Peninsula
and in the South of France* appeared in 1828 and is listed among 'New Publica-
tions' in the March issue of the *Quarterly Review*. The present letter, in which
Coleridge mentions this volume, was probably written, therefore, early in 1828.

² Coleridge first heard from Mackintosh in Nov. 1797, subsequent to his
connexion with the *Critical Review*. See note to Letter 214.

³ Both these reviews appeared in the *Critical Review* of Feb. 1797. (See Letters
159 and 183.) For a modern reprinting of Coleridge's review of Lewis's *The
Monk* see *Coleridge's Miscellaneous Criticism*, ed. T. M. Raysor, 1936, pp.
370–8; and of Horsley's tract see George Whalley, 'Coleridge on Classical
Prosody: an Unidentified Review of 1797', *Review of English Studies*, July
1951, pp. 238–47. For a further discussion of the review of Horsley's work see
C. I. Patterson, 'An Unidentified Criticism by Coleridge related to *Christabel*',
Publications of the Modern Language Association, Dec. 1952, pp. 973–88.

⁴ John Anster gives another version of this anecdote in a letter of 1835.
His account concludes: 'Coleridge described himself as so affected [by Dorothy
Wordsworth's reaction] that he never afterwards wrote a review, and he ap-
peared to me to have even a morbid feeling on the subject.' *Alaric Watts*, i. 247.

David V. Erdman attributes a number of reviews in the *Critical Review* to

Revolution, or only not total, in the object & character of Reviews—
and so far took away the grounds on which I had been led to con-
sider reviewing as an immoral Act. Nevertheless, from that time to
this it has so happened, that I have written but one Article in a
Review, & this wholly and solely to prevent Thomas Clarkson's
feelings from being turmoiled by any unhandsome treatment of
his History of the Abolition of the Slave Trade—But in this Mr
Jeffray outraged my sense of Right and Wrong by substituting for
an encomium on Mr Wilberforce and a Vindication of Mr Pitt two
or three infamously i.e. slanderously abusive Paragraphs on both—
the more offensive to me because I had been forced by the evi-
dence of Facts related to me & documented by Thomas Clarkson
to write what I wrote of two men, with one of whom (Mr W.) I
could never feel any sympathy, while the other (his measures &
notions, I mean) was and still is the object of my almost un-
qualified aversion—.[1] Permit me to say, that I have every reason
to believe that this & perhaps the ministerial Character of Lord
Castlereagh are the only political Points on which we should find
the least difference—. I mention the circumstance, however, as
having been the *cause* of my having kept aloof from Reviews after
all my former *Reasons* had ceased to exist—nay, tho' I have for a
series of years ranked the leading Reviews, on their present plan,
among the most powerful Moral Steam-engines, that the age has
produced.

    You begin—& not without reason—to wonder, for what purpose
I have been trespassing on your time and attention.—It is this.
I have re-perused with earnestness Napier's History of the Penin-
sular War—& have looked over some half-dozen or more of recent
Publications, having the same or similar character & tone of
principle & feeling—the principle I believe to be erroneous, and
the feeling, the evident predilection, in the highest degree *unhealthy*.
Possibly, the gross Mis[s]tatements and misrepresentations respect-
ing that admirable Man, John Hookham Frere, to whom of all men,

Coleridge. See 'Immoral Acts of a Library Cormorant: the Extent of Coleridge's
Contributions to the *Critical Review*', *Bulletin of the New York Public Library*,
Sept.–Nov. 1959, pp. 433–54, 515–30, and 575–87. See also C. I. Patterson, 'The
Authenticity of Coleridge's Reviews of Gothic Romances', *Journal of English
and Germanic Philology*, Oct. 1951, pp. 517–21.

    [1] Coleridge's memory played him false concerning the paragraph on Wilber-
force. In 1808 he insisted that Jeffrey had added 'a nauseous & most false
ascription of the Supremacy of Merit to Mr Wilberforce', and had substituted 'an
attack on Mr Pitt's Sincerity . . . for a Paragraph, in which I had both defended
it & him ; & proved that of all the parliamentary Friends of the Africans he was
the most efficient'. See Letters 717, 732, and 799, *Letters, Conversations and
Rec.*, 184–5, and *Edinburgh Review*, July 1808.

I have ever known, I should with least hesitation apply the epithets, φιλόκαλος, and καλοκἀγαθός, may have somewhat impassioned the decision of my Judgement.—But I have reason to hope, that I shall be assisted in forming a sane judgement by a military Man, of deservedly high character both as a Soldier, and as a scientific Man, who was in Spain from the commencement of the Insurgency to the return of the Army from Corunna—.[1] And the object of this letter is to enquire, whether you have already a Review of Napier's first Volume—and without any necessary connection with this particular Book whether an Article on the apparent revolution in the FASHION of estimating the character, and aims of Napoleon, and an attempt to reduce the recent magnificent claims of an almost exclusive efficiency on the part of military Institutions & Spirit within the bounds assigned by History and Sober Sense, without the least disposition to detract from their actual importance or to question their indispensableness in the existing state of the World,[2] would have a sufficient chance of finding admission into the Quarterly, to encourage me in writing it.[3] [MS. breaks off thus.]

1622. *To the Editor of the 'Berkshire Chronicle'*

MS. Fitzwilliam Museum, Cambridge. Hitherto unpublished.

Highgate London Apr. 20 1828.

Sir

I have just seen in the Berkshire chronicle of the 19th instant an Epigram professing to be written for your columns by a person signing himself *W. R.*[4] These lines I beg leave to inform you were published by me some time back in a periodical in London. I should not notice the imposition but that the quarter in which it occurs is of such high respectability. I have long read with pleasure the Poets' corner of the Berkshire Chronicle, and in particular the verses of Miss Mary Anne Brown,[5] your patronage of whom is at once an honor to your taste and liberality.

I am Sir | Yr obedient Serv.

S. T. Coleridge

To the Editor of the Berkshire Chronicle

---

[1] C. W. Pasley. See Letters 775 and 782.

[2] Cf. *Table Talk*, 26 June 1831.

[3] Coleridge did not contribute such an article to the *Quarterly*.

[4] Coleridge's epigram ('Charles, grave or merry, at no lie would stick') appeared over the initials W. R. in the *Berkshire Chronicle* of 19 Apr. 1828. The epigram was printed in the *Standard* on 29 June 1827. See Letter 1594.

[5] Mary Ann Browne contributed poems to the *Berkshire Chronicle* from June 1827 to early 1830. (From information kindly furnished by Mr. S. H. Horrocks, Borough Librarian, Reading.)

1623. *To William Sotheby*

MS. Cornell University Lib. Pub. E. L. G. ii. 411.

Grove, Highgate
Monday afternoon [28 April 1828][1]

My dear Sir

I have to beg your pardon for the delay in answering your note.
Have you not sometimes in revising a letter or other MSS found
that you had left out the very word, which you had had fullest and
liveliest in your intention? I was so fully prepared to write to you,
that having been prevented by a visit from my Brother, Colonel
Coleridge, from Devonshire, after he left me, I forgot that I had *not*
written—and there has been enough of Affliction in this house—
(*inter nos*, et sub rosâ Harpocratis loquor) what had *slipt* out of
mind to *keep* out. But I shall be most happy to see you and the
American Sir Walter.—P.S. I protest vehemently against your
remembering my reply to the worthy Pastor at Ratzeburgh when
he told me that Klopstock was the German Milton—'Yes! a very
German Milton indeed.'[2]—To speak seriously, it would be no less
unjust than injurious to Mr Cooper to institute a comparison be-
tween him and Sir W. S. (and Comparisons generally are in bad
taste, weeds of Criticism indigenous to shallow & coarse Soils). If I
mistake not, Mr Cooper's Genius would fit him better to fiction of
a more avowedly imaginative kind: the farther he is from Society,
the more he seems at home. His prominent fault is his forgetfulness
of the wise Hesiodic Line—

Νήπιοι, οὐκ ἴσασιν ὅσῳ πλέον ἥμισυ παντός[3]

With respectful remembrance to Mrs Sotheby and your Daughters
believe me, my dear Sir,

with unfeigned Esteem and | Regard your obliged
S. T. Coleridge

[1] On 25 Apr. 1828 Sotheby wrote to James Fenimore Cooper suggesting
that they call on Joanna Baillie at Hampstead and on Coleridge at Highgate.
The next day Cooper replied that he would take 'great pleasure' in paying his
respects to Miss Baillie and to Coleridge, 'since it is a compliment due to the
talents and sex of the one, and to the talents and years of the other', and pro-
posed 'any day, between this morning [26 Apr.] and Wednesday [30 Apr.]'. (*The
Letters and Journals of James Fenimore Cooper*, ed. J. F. Beard, 2 vols., 1960,
i. 261.) On receiving Cooper's letter Sotheby wrote to Coleridge. The present
letter was Coleridge's answer. For Cooper's account of this visit, as well as of
an earlier meeting with Coleridge and Scott at Sotheby's on 22 Apr. 1828, see
J. F. Cooper, *Gleanings in Europe: England*, ed. R. E. Spiller, 1930, pp. 157–63
and 332–4, and Lockhart, *Memoirs of . . . Scott*, 5 vols,, 1914, v. 193.

[2] See Letter 261 and *Biog. Lit.* ii. 180.

[3] Hesiod, *Works and Days*, 40.

1624. *To J. H. Green*

Address: J. H. Green, Esqre | &c. &c | Lincoln's Inn Fields
MS. Pierpont Morgan Lib. Hitherto unpublished.
Postmark: Highgate, 2 May 1828.

[2 May 1828]

My dear Friend

In the Medical Gazette,[1] 26 April, No. 21, the 2nd. Column of the first page I thought, I found a striking illustration (of course, a 1000 such might be found) of the observation, 'how small a part of what we mean by the Body and the bodily functions are really the immediate object of the outward Sense, or can be termed *material*, as the contrary of immaterial or spiritual'. In the Scarabaeus Nasicornis in it's first state 'we find the nerves arranged according to numerous small muscles attached to the *foot*—we see &c—muscles; but when this insect takes wing, there is a new developement of muscles for moving the wing; while those of the foot disappear, and (along) with them the Nerves'.—Now I humbly take for granted, that no one will pretend that the visible tangible molecules and fibres that compose the wing, were at the same time present and at work in manufacturing the new muscles and giving the nerves a new and correspondent arrangement; and likewise in the same moment in a third place removing and causing to disappear the muscles of the foot. But if not the component matter of the wing, then either the molecules of the wing muscles and those of the foot, the one moved *in* and the other moved by a fortuitous coincidence of opposite *freaks* without collusion which, I imagine, would protrude like the branching Antlers from the jaws of even a Boa Constrictor of Materialism who had contrived to swallow the whole Stag besides—*or* there must be a bodily Power or Power in the Body, working in evident reference to the wing.—And no less certain is it, that this is neither visible, audible, smellable, gustable, tangible, ponderable, nor any other ble but *intelligible*. Now I should like to hear first, what other definition of a spiritual Agent can be given but a presence that is intelligible but not sensible; and secondly, on what grounds the epithet, spiritual, can be denied to the bodily power aforesaid, seeing that the latter falls under the same definition. So true is the assertion of a Greek Neo-Platonist— τὸ καὶ Σῶμα πνευματικόν, ὅππο[σά]κις ζᾷ—i.e. Even the Body is

---

[1] The *London Medical Gazette*, a weekly journal, 1827–45. Robert Ferguson, whom Coleridge mentions in Letter 1486, was active in the founding of this journal 'as an organ of conservative opinion in medical politics and of academical views in medical science'. For a further reference to the *London Medical Gazette* see next letter.

spiritual as far as it *lives*.—Should you come up on Sunday (but do not put yourself to the slightest inconvenience—for I have no particular motive for wishing it) be so good as to bring with you the Letters on the true and false veneration of the Canonical Scriptures.[1]—

May God bless you &

S. T. Coleridge

1625. *To J. H. Green*

Address: J. H. Green, Esqre | &c &c | Lincoln's Inn Fields.
MS. Pierpont Morgan Lib. Hitherto unpublished.
Postmark: Highgate, 6 May 1828.

5 May 1828

My dear Friend

Were not the Steel, as I have faith that it *is*, 'of celestial temper',[2] your Razor must have been terribly notched and ser-rated by this time: for right tough, I ween, are the stumps of the lignum-vitae specimens, which you have had to cut into semblances of Humanity, and to elicit therefrom, if possible, some expression of sense and sensibility. And alas! in my own little way, few and unimportant as my experiences have been compared with your's, they have sufficed to convince me that the utmost, that can be carved out of a Block is—a Blockhead. Pygmalion indeed—but there are some doubts as to the truth of that Story. It is inter artes deperditas, at least. To be sure, on second thought, there is some ground for the belief, that your friend, Chantrey, has re-discovered it or by some means or other got possession of the Arcanum. But then Chantrey operates on Marbles: and 'out of these stones' children *may* be raised to Abraham.[3] But

> Sir Ass. and Sir Ant. and Sir Double you be[4]—
> Old Nic may turn Chiss'ler and chip 'em *for me*,

[1] In his synopsis of his *opus maximum*, dated at the end 27 May 1828, Coleridge refers specifically to the *Confessions of an Inquiring Spirit*. 'THE FIFTH PART', he writes, 'Takes up the inquiry (already instituted by me in my Eight [*sic*] Letters on the right and the superstitious Estimation of the Scrip-tures) whether the infallibility &c of the Jewish & Christian Canons is or ought to be an additional & distinct Article of Faith.' Alice D. Snyder, *Coleridge on Logic and Learning*, 1929, p. 7.

[2] *Paradise Lost*, iv. 812.   [3] Matthew iii. 9, and Luke iii. 8.

[4] Sir *As*tley Cooper, Sir *Ant*hony Carlisle, and Sir *Wil*liam *Bl*izard. [Note by E. H. Coleridge.] In 1780 William Blizard (1743–1835) was appointed surgeon to the London Hospital, where Coleridge's brother Luke began his medical studies in Oct. 1784 and remained for twelve months. It was during this period that Coleridge 'trudged' to the London Hospital every Saturday he 'could make or obtain leave' from Christ's Hospital. Gillman, *Life*, 22–23, and Letters 1 and 2.

While Orpheus's Dancing-kit plays Gramachree
To the crawl of a Louse and the skip of a Flea!

I cannot call this a digression, my dear friend! for I have not yet
put my foot on the way. Let us then shift the metaphor from the
turn-pike road of art to the great tho' somewhat narrow Turn-pike
Road of Nature on her travels to this World, and with Dr Gooch's*
leave, call it a *Breach Presentation*—the Head will be forthcoming
in due time and with a little management. Only wait a little—and
keep Dr Blundell[1] off! He looks as if he had a bloody mind to con-
sign it to the LANCET. It is a Privatissimum, Doctor! and Security
has been given to the Parish, that it shall not be burthensome.

Apropós—tho' . . .[2] for my life I cannot see, why *To the purpose*
might not have satisfied the first importer without running across
the channel for his contraband *Poes*.—There is no *Po* in the
English Language, as the Cockney Governess well remarked,
except Po Shay.[3]—But if we must have an exotic, let it be the
glorification of our Scholarship—THEREFORE

Ad propositum—I guess, that the last number of the Medical
Gazette with the poor weak petty every way impolitic reference to
the reception of Lawrence's Name[4] at a Students' Tavern Dinner in
the preceding Number has not tended to loosen your faith in the
soundness of your decision, to decline all concern procreative,
obstetric or sponsorial in this Babe of Grace. Already, Letters pro
and con from Hospital Students—already Informants by no lack

---

* Who, however, did not think it necessary to ask mine in his obstetric
delivery of my marginalia. [Note by S. T. C.] Robert Gooch (1784–1830) was
elected lecturer on midwifery at St. Bartholomew's Hospital in 1812. In Jan.
1826 he suffered a severe illness, and in view of the probable necessity of his
retirement from his practice in midwifery, one of his friends obtained his
appointment as librarian to the king.

[1] James Blundell (1790–1877), physician and lecturer on midwifery at
Guy's Hospital.

[2] Several words heavily inked out in MS.

[3] Colloquial for post-chaise.

[4] William Lawrence 'headed a public agitation against the management of
the College of Surgeons in 1826, and printed a "Report of the Speeches delivered
by Mr. Lawrence as Chairman at two Meetings of Members, held at the Free-
masons' Tavern." The college wisely elected him into its council in 1828,
Hunterian orator in 1834 and 1846, examiner for twenty-seven years in 1840,
president in 1846 and 1855, and he steadily maintained its privileges against
all agitators.' (*D.N.B.*) Lawrence published many essays and observations in
both the *Lancet* and the *London Medical Gazette*. Coleridge mentions the latter
journal in the preceding letter.

In 1827 or 1828 Lawrence withdrew from publication his early lectures at
the Royal College of Surgeons, *An Introduction to Comparative Anatomy and
Physiology*, 1816 (attacked by Coleridge in the *Theory of Life*), and a second
series, *On the Physiology . . . of Man*, 1819. See note to Letter 1235.

of Lying and mischief-making distinguishable from Informers, *alias* Blacking-brushes—and the reference above-mentioned—is it not an implied acknowlegement of the Right of Jurisdiction in the last instance inherent in Hospital Pupils by virtue of their Pupillage—in that respectable Court of Appeal formed of Striplings just let loose from their Indentures, and of course the most important personages & the best disposed to make a row—to vote by acclamation I mean—that ever bawled Hip Hip Hip to a Bumper? If their studies in *defunct* Anatomy are carried on with the same keen interest with which they attend to the viva sectio of any one of their Superiors & Instructors, what a House of Vesaliuses and Morgagnis will not England have to boast of!—The Medical Gazette may, I doubt not, do good—but even tho' it atchieve twice as much as I believe it likely to do, tho' it should deserve to be new-christened, Alexipharmacos Hebdomadalis Wakleicida,[1] comprizing in it's single bosom the spirits of Jack the Giant-killer, Tom Hickathrift and Ditto Thumb—still I am right glad that you have nothing to do with it.—

This, however, is not the Child, I asked you to wait for; but contrary to all good midwifery the mere Secundine—an after-birth —and now I must bring out the true Birth head & shoulders, indeed —to wit—I have been thinking a great deal since you left me of the subject of your intended Letter to the President & Council[2]—and it strikes me, that one argument might be grounded on the disgrace, that the Royal College of Surgeons will incur if they surrender to a knot of private Individuals uncountenanced by the Public Authorities & under strong suspicion of party purposes, the honor

---

[1] Thomas Wakley (1795–1862), medical and social reformer. In 1823 Wakley founded the *Lancet*, a weekly medical journal, and began an exposure of nepotism and of cases of malpractice in the hospitals. In opposition to the hospital doctors he insisted on publishing reports of their lectures. He also carried on a campaign against the whole constitution of the Royal College of Surgeons and aroused public support. On 18 Feb. 1826 he called a meeting of all members of the College at the Freemasons' Tavern and persuaded those in attendance to petition Parliament instead of offering a remonstrance to the council, a 'constitutionally rotten concern'. In response to a petition presented to Parliament on 20 June 1827 the House of Commons ordered the return of public money loaned or granted to the College. The influence of the council of the College was so strong, however, that it was 1843 before a partial reform was effected. Meanwhile, Wakley was elected to Parliament in 1835 and held a seat there until 1852. During his parliamentary career and subsequently he continued to wage war on medical restrictions and abuses as well as injustice elsewhere.

[2] Coleridge apparently refers to Green's *Distinction without Separation. A Letter to the President of the College of Surgeons on the present state of the profession*, published in 1831. The Coleridgean title suggests that Coleridge gave Green more than superficial assistance.

of instituting a School of scientific Anatomy & comparative Physiology, such as the present condition of the Sciences and of the Country require.—[1]

What I wish to learn from you, if you can find time to give me half a score lines by the Post, is—in what way, supposing you accepted the situation,[2] you are to be remunerated for resigning your private practice which must of necessity increase and (it is not improbable) rapidly, and (if I understood you aright) your Lectures &c at the Hospital. If you were to have *a Class* on similar terms, as at the Hospitals and as the Plan is at the London University, I can easily admit the probability—not of a result at all equivalent to what you would give up—but still in no outrageous disproportion. But if it is to be a SALARY & the Courses to be attended by right of Privilege, I cannot help doubting whether it would be either in the will or the means of the College to render it even consistent with your *duty* to turn your back on such prospects, as you now have.—I wish, I could hear you talk the matter over, before you sent in the Letter—tho' the Letter, indeed, would not bind you to any thing. Is the entire abandonment of your *private* Practice an indispensable Proviso?—I have written you a strange epistle—but I know that you will *make* what you do not find worth the reading, that comes from your affectionate Friend

                           S. T. Coleridge

1626. *To J. H. Green*

MS. Pierpont Morgan Lib. Hitherto unpublished.

                                [*Circa* 8 May 1828][3]

My dear Friend

Perhaps I ought to apologize for mooting a point bordering more closely on matters of private circumstances, than it is my Wont to start; and that in urging my opinion I had used a stronger phrase and of more serious import, than the opinion required or the arguments in support of it will be found to warrant. Such as they are, however, you shall have them; tho' more for the purpose of

---

[1] King's College, London, was founded in 1829 by Royal Charter as the rival of the University of London, later known as University College. (See Letter 1452.) Coleridge was right in suspecting 'party purposes'. The foundation of King's College 'under the leadership of the Duke of Wellington [by] a body of defenders of the established order' may 'in one sense be regarded as an answer to the challenge thrown out by the Whigs in establishing University College'. *University of London Calendar, 1963–4*, pp. 70 and 410.

[2] For details concerning Green's appointment at King's College, London, see next letter.

[3] The present letter was obviously written shortly after Letter 1625.

explaining the impressions under which I wrote than for any great
force that I myself in revisal attribute to them.

First—it was on my mind how much the Success of a new public
Institution depends on it's Eclat. I could not help thinking, that
in the first instance at least the Quot et Quales, the Conflux and
character of the auditors will be in no inconsiderable degree affected
by the Estimate, which the Public shall have been led to form of
the Situation; and that this Estimate again will be greatly in-
fluenced by the Value and importance, which the Royal College,
i.e. it's Magnates, shall appear to attach to it, and no less how the
Person who has accepted the appointment, himself appears to have
appreciated both the importance of the Trust and his own services.
Better not be done at all, than to be *so* done by the Council, as to
give the impression that it is *only an additional Course of Lectures
in Anatomy.* The *Truth* permits, and the interests of Science make
it most *desirable*, that the Government should be induced to con-
sider it as a *National* Concern; and as one most efficient & especially
needed Means, by which the Metropolis of the British Empire is to
be rescued from the *Impolicy* as well as the *Disgrace* of ranking
only fourth or fifth in scientific Attraction, inferior not only to
Paris, but to Vienna, to Munich—perhaps, to Berlin or Petersburgh.
Comparisons are weeds indigenous to coarse, sour and shallow
Soils—but yet I cannot hide from myself, that Comparisons *would*
be made between the Professorship of Zoonomy, Zoology and
Comparative Anatomy at the Royal College, and the similar Pro-
fessorship at the Democratical University:[1] and if what I have
heard lately of the Endowment and the contingent Emoluments
held forth by the latter be near the truth, and if the Provision in
the former be of a far humbler character, the Vulgar, that is (as
Machiavel somewhere observes) four fifths of Mankind (nay, of that
portion of it comprized in our 'Nobility, Gentry and People of
Dress') will be *after comparing*, & in their minds the Comparison
will work injuriously to the Dignity and by consequence to the
Utility of the Appointment.—Your Successor too, and the probabi-

---

[1] The position which Green was considering and to which Coleridge refers
in this and the preceding letter was the chair of surgery in King's College,
London. The College was granted a Royal Charter in Aug. 1829, and opened in
Oct. 1831. On the establishment of King's College, Green accepted the appoint
ment, and in 1832 he gave the opening address of the winter session. Published
under the title, *An Address delivered in King's College, London, at the commence-
ment of the medical session, Octr. 1832*, this lecture dealt with 'the functions or
duties of the professions of divinity, law, and medicine according to Coleridge'.
Miss Snyder says it 'was admittedly based on Coleridge's "Constitution of
Church and State"'. (*Coleridge on Logic and Learning*, 1929, pp. 43–44.) Green
resigned the chair at King's College in 1837.

lity of finding an Individual whose professional Character, Talents
and Attainments qualify him for so high and arduous an office,
filled as—it would be affectation in hesitating to say it—it will have
been by you, and whose private circumstances allowed him to ac-
cept it—even this is not wholly unworthy of consideration.—And
lastly, you must permit your *friends* to feel a little jealous and
touchy of the false judgement which notwithstanding it's false-
hood People in general may entertain of the rank and importance
of the advantages and prospects, the present and the reversionary
emoluments, you sacrifice, measuring the same according to their
own hearts and principles of action by the amount of the Com-
pensation.—

Thus did my thoughts run in this direction—then taking another
road, the great and daily moral, intellectual and professional Good
which you do & every year will do in a still greater degree, at St
Thomas's; and the reputation, authority, and influence accruing
to John Hunter, the Philosopher, from the private practice of
J. Hunter, the Surgeon, *would be heard at the Bar*, spite of Judge &
Cryer—& weighed with me—assuredly, not to change or affect
my ardent desire to see you in the situation best calculated to realize
that scheme of Life and Usefulness which you have so ably and
adequately delineated in the smallest possible space in your last
letter—but yet—to increase or rather to sharpen & render more
lively the reluctance and objection to such advantages being put on
an insecure venture—and under circumstances that do not give
me the assurance, I want, that the appointment will be favorable
to the execution of your designs and the realization of the high and
precious Objects, which you well and wisely no less than honorably
have proposed to yourself. When we have succeeded by persever-
ant effort not without harassing in clearing away the filth and
obstacles of 'the Way of Life', when we have surmounted the
steeper and more rugged portion of the Ascent, and are on the
ridge of the Hill, and (as it were) at the very Porch and Portal of
the Temple or Chapelry, which crowns it—it *does* seem to me, my
dear friend! something very near to a Duty, that a man should
not turn his Back on it and strike off in a new direction without
some *ostensible* motive that would explain his resolve to the World
(the sphere, I mean, over which his mind, character, influence, in
short, his powers extend) as well as to himself—We may not even
give up the means or probable prospect of benefiting and serving
our individual friends altogether without blame, unless where the
interests of our own tranquillity and therewith the developement and
growth of our Humanity (which are the interests of the Community)
would be seriously injured by not doing so.—To all these remarks

the *running Comment*, without which they have no force and no application in my thoughts & intentions, is the *supposition, and in case* that the appointment had not the circumstantial Rank, Dignity and Importance which might make it intelligible even to those, who really knew *what* you were about to sacrifice, and who had formed a fair estimate of your present worldly advantages and prospects, that a man of moderate desires, and not necessarily dependent on professional sources for the means of meeting them, might yet justifiably and to his honor give them up for such an Object and with such Views.

One other explanatory remark—. The observations both in this and in the former letter that furnished the occasion for this, represented & were only intended to represent a *mood* of my mind, a one side only of the subject taken exclusively for the purpose of letting the arguments appear in *more* than their due strength in order to be sure of seeing them in *all* their strength—and these were both conceived and looked at thro' a peculiar medium—the experience hitherto of the Objects, Plans and Proceedings of the President and Council. It was under apprehensions flowing from this source that I asked whether the Surrender of *both* your existing Resources, the Hospital Lectures, *and* your Private Practice were indispensable Conditions?—Would it not (I asked—not myself; but—in myself and on reflection I might have answered it myself in the *negative*) be always in my friend's power to limit his Practice to the more important departments of the Profession, in Consultations and in Operations [which] required more than ordinary Science, tact and experience? Were he in the situation for which he is especially and of all his *British* Contemporaries exclusively fitted, what with Correspondences, preparations of Specimens, of MSS, and (I trust) hereafter for the Press, the appointment ought to enable him, without incroachment on his private fortune, to have an intelligent Assistant and Secretary—And it was some confirmation of a part of my thoughts, that you had yourself included in your *idea*—'*professionally*, it's practical use and employment'.— But we shall have opportunities enough, I hope, to talk this matter over—& you will find no difficulty in putting me in another *mood* of mind. God bless you &

S. T. C.

1627. *To Frances Maria Kelly*

Address: Miss F. Kelly with Mr S. T. Coleridge's respectful Compliments.
MS. University of California Lib., Santa Barbara. Hitherto unpublished.

Grove, Highgate
31 May, 1828.

My dear Madam

Will the name, dear to us both, of Charles Lamb, and the chance of your recollecting having passed a fragment of an Afternoon with me under his Roof, warrant me in the favor, I am about to ask? If not—and my own Judgement whispers a vote against myself— I must shift my apology to my hope and faith in your Charity— which, should it not extend to the granting of my request, will I trust, induce you to forgive the liberty, I have taken in preferring it.—The Author of the accompanying Entertainment is a gentleman, for whom I entertain a more than ordinary regard, and who has indeed a right to the esteem and respect of all who know and are competent to know him. I am not about to solicit you to exert your interest in his behalf; but simply and solely to look thro' the piece and to honor me with your unbiassed judgement whether it contains the *groundwork*, the *materiel* of an After-piece, calculated to succeed at the Haymarket, or the Winter Theatres—supposing the Dialogue to be enlivened and rendered more stimulant and theatrical, in such scenes in which such improvement might be deemed desirable—in short, whether you think, it would *do* if what was alterable and addible were well altered and happily added.—

My dear Madam! I know from my own experience too well, how unpleasant a task one's friends sometimes impose on us in an *only* or *merely* if you will be so good &c, not to feel that I really am asking a favor of you, and that my own Conscience would justify you if you should complain of me as having intruded unwarrantably on your attention. I can only say that if on any occasion you will retaliate on me, I can think of nothing in my power to do, and which I should gratify you by attempting, that it would not give me pleasure to attempt.

Will you be so good as to favor me with a single line by the Two-penny Post, informing me whether your time and health will allow you to give the Piece a Perusal—and should I be so fortunate as to learn from you the affirmative, after what interval I or my friend might call for the MSS and your opinion respecting it's theatrical Capabilities?

Be assured, that with unfeigned esteem no less than admiration I am,

my dear Madam, | Your obliged
S. T. Coleridge

1628. *To George Dyer*

Address: George Dyer, Esqre | Clifford's Inn
MS. Cornell University Lib. Pub. with omis. Letters, *ii. 748.*
Postmark: Highgate, ⟨6⟩ June 18 ⟨28⟩.

Friday Afternoon
6 June, 1828
Grove, Highgate.

My dear long-known and long-loved Friend!

Be assured that neither Mr Irving nor any other person, high or low, gentle or simple, stands higher in my Esteem or bears a name endeared to me by more interesting recollections and associations than Yourself: and if Gentleman or Gentler Woman taking too literally the partial portraiture of Friends has a fancy to see the old Lion in his sealed Cavern, no more potent, 'Open, Sesame, open' will be found than an introduction from George Dyer, my elder Brother under many titles, Brother Blue, Brother Grecian, Brother Cantab., Brother Poet, and last best Form of Fraternity, a Man who has never in his long life by tongue or pen uttered what he did *not* believe to be the truth from *any* Motive, or concealed what he *did* believe to be such from other motives than those of tenderness for the Feelings of others, and a conscientious fear lest what was truly said might be falsely interpreted. In all these points I dare claim brotherhood with my old Friend—(not omitting *Grey* hairs which are venerable!) But in one point—the long toilsome Life of inexhaustible unsleeping Benevolence, and Beneficence that slept only when there was no Form or semblance of sentient Life to awake it, GEORGE DYER must stand alone. He may have a few Second Cousins; but no full Brother.

Now with regard to your Friends. I shall be happy to see them on any day, they may find to suit their & your convenience, from 12 (I am not ordinarily visible before—or if the outward man were forced to make his appearance, yet from sundry bodily infirmities my Soul would present herself with unwashed face) till 4—i.e. after Monday next. We having at present a Servant ill in bed, you must perforce be content with a Sandwich Lunch & a Glass of Wine—ἡδὺν οἶνον, ἡδυτέρας τε μοίσας.—But if you could make it suit you to take your Tea (an early Tea at or before six o'clock) and spend the evening, a long evening with us, on Thursday next, Mr and Mrs Gillman will be most happy to see you and Mrs Dyer with your Friends—and you will probably meet some old friends of your's. (On Thursday Evenings indeed, at any time between ½ past 5 and 11 you may be sure of finding us at home—& with a very fair chance of Basil Montague's taking you and Mrs Dyer back in their Coach.)

I have long owed you a Letter; and should long since have honestly paid the debt—but we have had a House of Sickness and of Mourning—my own Health has been very crazy and out of repair—and I have had so much work accumulated on me, that I have been like an overtired man roused from insufficient sleep, who sitting [sits?] on his bed post [*sic*] with one stocking *on* and the other in his hand, doing nothing and thinking what a deal he has to do.

But I am ever, sick or well, weary or lively, | my dear Sir, | your sincere and | affectionate Friend

S. T. Coleridge

1629. *To Dora Wordsworth*

Address: Miss Wordsworth | — Quillinan's, Esqre | 11 or 13 Bryanston St | Bryanston Square
MS. Dove Cottage. Hitherto unpublished.

[Circa 8 August 1828][1]

Thank you, my very dear Rotha! for your complementum of my mementos. You have saved me in a most satisfying manner, answering to the both general & particular Purpose, overflowing my full

---

[1] This letter was written soon after Coleridge, Wordsworth, and his daughter Dora returned from a tour of Belgium, the Rhineland, and Holland. They left London on 21 June 1828 and returned on 6 Aug. Writing to Charles Aders at Euston Square on 7 Aug. Wordsworth announced that the party 'arrived in good health yesterday' and offered 'a thousand thanks' for 'many kind attentions'. [MS. Central Library, Auckland, New Zealand.]

The plan to visit Germany was probably suggested by Aders, whose wife was spending the summer at their château at Godesberg. In an unpublished letter of 17 June 1828 Wordsworth writes to Coleridge that Dora 'is overjoyed at the thought of our proposed Tour' and goes on to say: 'Tell me how soon you can be ready . . . . Mr Aders will provide us all with passports & Letters of credit.' [MS. New York Public Library.] Dora Wordsworth's unpublished journal of the tour shows that on two occasions they stayed with Mrs. Aders for several days. Mrs. Aders was 'delighted' with Wordsworth, but as her husband reported to Crabb Robinson, she still claimed 'our old affectionate friend Coleridge as "her" Poet'. The presence of two famous English poets at Godesberg attracted various German 'illuminati' to Mrs. Aders's house, among them A. W. von Schlegel. According to J. C. Young, who was also staying with Mrs. Aders, Coleridge praised Schlegel for his translation of Shakespeare, and Schlegel 'returned the compliment' by declaring that 'Coleridge's translation of Schiller's *Wallenstein* was unrivalled for its fidelity to its original and the beauty of its diction'. Dora's journal records two further meetings with Schlegel. See *The Correspondence of Henry Crabb Robinson with the Wordsworth Circle*, ed. Edith J. Morley, 2 vols., 1927, i. 190, and J. C. Young, *A Memoir of Charles Mayne Young, with Extracts from his Son's Journal*, 1871, pp. 111–12.

expectation—My best Love to our 'Direction', for whom I inclose
the Dutch Latin Epitaph, funereal dry-flower of the chronologic
Muse—& the Dutch English for you.

If I understand the account, I am surprized at the smallness of
our expenditure—I say if I understand it, & that in addition to the
20£ I am only indebted to the 'Direction' 11£-15s.-4d.—Mr
Aders has a credit account of 10£ for me, from Mr Green—i.e. in
addition to the 20£. I desired Mr G. to settle with Mr Aders for
10£ which I might want—not knowing that my name was included
in his credit letters.—All—for I have this moment an opportunity
of sending off the Parcel which I shall lose if I delay two minutes in
this—Question two—Are 11, 15, 4 the total sum, I am indebted
to William on this account?—If so, can I settle it in the Settlement
with Mr Aders—or must I settle it, and pay the money in to any
where—or does William want the money immediately—?—Just,
dearest Rotha! give me one line—before you go—& give my kindest
love & thanks cordial to your dear Father from his most sincere &
affectionate

Friend and your loving Godfather
S. T. Coleridge

1630. *To Frederic M. Reynolds*[1]

MS. Mr. W. Hugh Peal. Hitherto unpublished.

8 August, 1828—Friday (I believe.)

Dear Sir

You must pack the whole blame on the sufficing shoulders of our
Friend, Mr Wordsworth—who had held forth to me, believing
Semi-bard! a three weeks' Tour, as the extreme Limit in Time—
and lo! the Poet, mihi magnus Apollo! and his fair Daughter have
by pure force of attraction carried me on, o'er Ditch and Dell,
River and Plain, not to speak of German Mountains and Dutch
Steeples and Rhenish Towers, like the Prodigal Son in Scripture
wasting my substance (i.e. my Obesity, especially during the hot
weather) in a foreign Land, on and on, & round about, even to the
commencement of the 7th Week—However, I am come back—
and trust that the Result will ultimately be to the advantage of the

---

[1] Frederic Mansel Reynolds, son of Frederic Reynolds, the dramatist, was
editor of *The Keepsake* from 1829 to 1835 and again in 1839.

Keep-sake[1] no less than it has been to the Health and Spirits of your obliged &c

S. T. Coleridge

P.S.—By Tuesday Morning I shall be prepared with the needful, in most calligraphic fitness for the Press—Will you come to me, and take a Sandwich and a Glass of Wine between 12 & 1, on Tuesday—or must I come to you?—Give me a line, (Grove, Highgate) by the twopenny Post.—

1631. *To Basil Montagu*

Transcript Coleridge family. Hitherto unpublished.

Friday afternoon. 8 Aug. 1828.

My dear dear M.

I have come to shew my face, with its appendages & dependencies to you, having just returned from Ostend,—Bruges,— Ghent, — Brussels, — Spa, — Aix-la-Chapelle,— Liege, — Namur, — Dinant, — Cologne, — Bonn, — Coblenz, — Bingen, — Sail down the Rhine — Nijmegen, — Utrecht, — Amsterdam, — Leyden, — Rotterdam, — Antwerp, — Ghent, — Bruges, — Ostend.

And thank you & dear Mrs M. over & over again for your friendship & kindness in your heartfelt attentions to Mr & Mrs Gillman &c during my absence.

S. T. C.

1632. *To Henry Nelson Coleridge*

Address: H. N. Coleridge, Esqre
MS. Victoria University Lib. Pub. E. L. G. ii. 418.

Tuesday [12 August 1828?]

My dear Henry

As I am afraid, I shall scarcely be able to reach Parliament Street, and have in fact nothing very particular to say that you do not

---

[1] Before Coleridge left for the Continent in June, Reynolds called at Highgate, offered £50 for contributions to *The Keepsake* for 1829, and selected the unfinished ballad, *Alice du Clos; or, The Forked Tongue, The Garden of Boccaccio*, and 'a few Epigrams'. It was further agreed that Coleridge would contribute to no other annual for 1829, with the exception of *The Literary Souvenir*, a previous arrangement having been made with Alaric Watts. Coleridge understood, too, that he would receive £50 for contributions to the 1830 *Keepsake*. Ultimately, his experience with Reynolds was to prove as disillusioning as those with S. C. Hall of *The Amulet* and with W. Fraser of *The Bijou*. See Letters 1634, 1637-8, 1639, 1651, 1667, and 1669.

know—videlicet, that my Health has been 'pretty considerably', and as far as I can at present judge, not transiently improved by my Tour—& that I am now employed in making out for the Press the first in the series of my Works, that on the Power and Use of Words— I have only to request you to see Mr Wordsworth, if he shall have been returned, as soon as you conveniently can—& to tell him, that at any place or person, he may inform me of, the 13 or 14£ odd, that are due to him on our Tour-account, it shall be deposited immediately on the receipt of the same—. Mr Green must have called, I apprehend, at your rooms, when they were shut up, in order to avail himself in my name of your going Northward—and as he is now either at St Thomas's, or on the round of his Patients as I find the Carriage is with him, I cannot learn the particulars—. So only give my best Love to Mr & Mrs Wordsworth, and Miss Wordsworth & Miss S. Hutchinson, and last not least, my dear God-daughter, and heretical Anti-Germanite, and that I do not consent to her being otherwise than in high health for the next six months—.

To them at Keswick what can I say more or other than that their happiness & comforts are an indispensable condition & part of the well-being and ease of mind of, my dear Henry,

Your affectionate Friend

S. T. Coleridge

1633. *To Richard Cattermole*[1]

Pub. Letters, ii. 750.

Grove, Highgate, Thursday, August 14, 1828.

My dear Sir,—I have but this moment received yours of the 13th, and though there are but ten minutes in my power, if I am to avail myself of this day's post, I will rather send you a very brief than not an immediate answer. I shall be much gratified by standing beside the baptismal font as one of the sponsors of the little pilgrim at his inauguration into the rights and duties of Immortality, and he shall not want my prayers, nor aught else that shall be within my power, to assist him in *becoming* that of which the Great Sponsor who brought light and immortality into the world has declared him an emblem.

---

[1] Despite E. H. Coleridge's note (*Letters*, ii. 750), this letter cannot have been intended for George Cattermole, who was not married until 1839. Possibly the letter was addressed to Richard Cattermole. In 1826 Coleridge was looking forward to being introduced to Mrs. Cattermole. See Letter 1530.

There are one or two points of character belonging to me, so, at least, I believe and trust, which I would gladly communicate with the name,—earnest love of Truth for its own sake, and steadfast convictions grounded on faith, not fear, that the religion into which I was baptised is the Truth, without which all other knowledge ceases to merit the appellation. As to other things, which yet I most sincerely wish for him, a more promising augury might be derived from other individuals of the Coleridge race.

Any day, that you and your dear wife (to whom present my kindest remembrances and congratulations) shall find convenient, will suit me, if only you will be so good as to give me two or three days' knowledge of it.

Believe me, my dear sir, with sincere respect and regard,

Your obliged

S. T. Coleridge.

P.S. I returned from my seven weeks' Continental tour with Mr Wordsworth and his daughter this day last week. We saw the Rhine as high up as Bingen, Holland, and the Netherlands.

1634. *To Charles Aders*

Address: C. Aders, Esqre | Euston Square   14 August—Thursday, your's is dated *Monday*.
MS. Mr. Thomas F. Madigan. Pub. E. L. G. ii. 409.

Grove, Highgate
14 August
1828.

My dear Friend

For indeed and in the verity of the Word I feel and have long felt that more than regard, that affectionate Predilection for yourself and your dear Wife, that in every outward and visible sign of Affection shewn to the one I find myself thinking of the other, and when on meeting I give a kiss to Mrs Aders it seems to me as if I were shaking hands with *you*—and perhaps, with the exception of *Henricus Krabius* Robinson, you will allow me to fancy myself of many of my Countrymen who esteem and regard you the only one capable of *justly* estimating your varied *Powers*, which from what I had observed & were confirmed to me by parts of your letters which Mrs Aders read to me, on Pasta and Sontag[1] &c, seemed to me like so many *Senses* corresponding to the different Forms in

---

[1] Madame Giuditta Negri Pasta (1798–1865) and Henriette Sontag (1805–54), famous opera singers.

which the Beautiful is revealed—in Form, in Color, in the mysteries
of Sound, and in the ministry of Language (even in one not your
Birth-tongue) to express the laws and life of all and to combine
with all the *thought* and *inborn* Humanity which give them their
proper and yet common Soul. And in addition to all this, you are
a Merchant—the combining & calculating and commercing Intel-
lect of a busy and bustling Compting-House!—

Now, my dear Mr Aders! all the above has been bubbling, and
steaming within me for some time—and you must receive this
letter, as the Escape-Valve.—So much Detraction is going on in
the World—that I feel it as a duty, where I can assure myself I
am out of the reach of all suspicion of insincerity or flattery, to let
an honest man know what an honest man and no fool thinks and
feels concerning him!

Now for Mr Ackerman.[1] I told the Gentleman, who is his
Editor, that I would tenfold rather *give* Mr Ackerman a Poem
under the recommendation of Mr and Mrs Aders, and as their
friend, than receive 20£ for it from another. But that previously
to the request I had engaged to furnish Mr Renyolds a parte Heath,[2]
for the Keep-sake, two Poems of no great length,[3] for 50£, (more
than all, *I* ever made by all my Publications, my week's Salary
of 5£ as Writer of the Leading Articles in the Morning Post during
the Peace of Amiens excepted) on the condition, that I was *not*
to give or sell any contribution to any other of these Annualists.—
Now I *had* previously given to Alaric Watts permission to print
(if he chose it) some fragmentary verses of mine—& so informed
Mr Renyolds—Another man without my consent has, I find, been
printing for the Amulet a prose-letter which he had last year re-
jected & sent back to me; but as it appears, not without having
taken a copy.[4]—What then can I say? Anything 'sent by a Lady'

---

[1] Rudolph Ackermann (1764–1834), fine-art publisher and bookseller, in-
troduced from Germany the fashion of the illustrated annual. He was the
publisher of the *Forget Me Not*, an annual edited by F. Shoberl. It contains no
contributions by Coleridge.

[2] Charles Heath (1785–1848), engraver and proprietor of *The Keepsake.*

[3] A reference to *The Garden of Boccaccio* and *Alice du Clos*. See Letter 1638.

[4] Coleridge refers to his three letters written from Germany in 1799 (Letters
280–2). They were delivered to S. C. Hall in 1826 but were 'rejected' and re-
turned in 1827, probably at the time of Hall's unsuccessful attempt to extract
from Coleridge for *The Amulet* such unpublished poems as *Youth and Age*. (See
Letter 1596.) Coleridge had only now learned that without his permission Hall
was, nevertheless, printing these letters. Large extracts from the first two were
published in the 1829 *Amulet* with the title, 'Over the Brocken'. Hall's unethical
conduct made it appear that Coleridge had violated his agreement with Rey-
nolds.

After Coleridge's death Hall published Letters 280–2 in the *New Monthly
Magazine* for Oct. 1835. They are introduced with this misleading statement:

I can have no objection to[1]—and if I can on Saturday next, when I am to have an interview with Mr Renyolds, procure his consent, I will (as I told Mrs Aders) give Mr Ackerman *the poem,* or if he thinks it worth any thing, sell him the poem, I am now finishing on the Rhine.[2] But I am not my own Master, in this instance— but the Slave of the Contract.

Mrs G. seems to me better—and in better Spirits, since I have given her a loving & christian Scolding for being so much otherwise—

I have scarcely left space to thank you for your kind present— but let the Thanks be included in the assurance, that I am, my dear Sir,

Most truly & with heart-felt respect | Your affectionate Friend | S. T. Coleridge

P.S.[3] I fear, you will scarcely be able to read this letter. But, your messenger had been long waiting before I came in; & the *first* preparatory Dinner Bell, but still more my unwillingly [*sic*] to delay him, has made me more than usually *scrawl*atory & illegible.

1635. *To Frederic M. Reynolds*

Address: Frederic Renyolds, Esqre. | at Mr MacPherson's Nursery | Ground | Archway Road.[4]
MS. Harvard College Lib. Pub. with omis. Athenaeum, *17 January 1835, p. 56.*

Monday Noon—[25 August 1828][5]

My dear Sir

I cannot bring myself to resign the pleasure, I have promised

The following letters of one of the most amiable and highly-gifted men of our age and country were presented, in 1828 [1826], by Mr. Coleridge to the gentleman who permits their insertion in the *New Monthly Magazine*, with the clear understanding that he was at liberty to publish them either altogether or in parts. He printed a few detached extracts from them, but the MS. having been mislaid, he was apprehensive that some accident had led to its destruction. The announcement that another distinguished poet was about to give an account of his travels suggested a further search: fortunately it was successful. The letters of Mr. Coleridge in 1799, from a country then almost as little known to Englishmen as Algiers in 1835, will not be found unworthy of association with those of Mr. Campbell.

[1] Coleridge refers to *The Two Founts.* As he points out in Letter 1639, the poem had already twice appeared in print.
[2] No such poem has come to light, although Coleridge again refers to it in Letters 1638 and 1641.
[3] This postscript appears at the top of page one of the MS.
[4] The address is written on a separate cover.
[5] In the present letter Coleridge says he saw 'yesterday', i.e. Sunday, two letters from young Mathews to his mother. The more recent letter, which is

myself, in being once more *hook*'d[1] on to the whirl-about Car of the
Portly God, Bacchus, with Wit, Laughter, Jest and Song on the
wooden-horses, like the children at Bartholemew Fair—Gladly
would I make on[e] in the Train, tho' in the character of Old
Silenus sitting on his Ass, as indeed, if one might judge by the *ear*
only, most other people do—. But if I am not with you before Six,
the cause will be, that I am either on my Bed, or *closeted* with my
Self, soliloquizing on a lesson of Ventriloquy.—Last night I sate
up late, writing—and probably, overwrought my nerves & thro'
them predisposed my Stomach to disordered functions—and then
taking my usual two table spoonfuls of white Mustard-seed, only
some three hours or more after my usual time, I went to bed—.
The Mustard-seed, which (I am persuaded) in all cases acts only
mechanically by blending with the digested food, like Carraway
Seeds in a plum-cake, and thus amassing it to the weight requisite
for the due Descent, lay, I doubt not, as a dead load on the torpid
organ in the first instance, and in the following Sleep produced
a true Hell of Dreams, so that literally I awoke the House with my
Shouts & Screams—and some night or other I shall probably die
as my Father did, and realize the Epitaph which, dreaming that
I had died I actually composed in my sleep, the first and only night
that I ever passed in Edingborough—& where I first had heard the
preceding evening the word pronounced *Embro'*—I well remember,
that I awoke from the pure delight of Vanity in the admiration of
my own imagined Calmness & Fortitude—The lines I immediately
put down.—

> Here lies poor Col at length, and without Screaming
> Who died as he had always liv'd, *a dreaming—*
> Shot with a pistol by the Gout within,
> Alone and all unknown, at Embro', in an Inn.[2]

dated Peroi, 13 July 1828, arrived from Istria while Coleridge was calling on
Mrs. Mathews, who read it to him before sending it on to her husband. Mathews
acknowledged its receipt in a note addressed to his wife from Ross on Sunday,
31 Aug. 1828. Coleridge's call on Mrs. Mathews took place, therefore, on the
preceding Sunday, 24 Aug. Next day Coleridge wrote to Reynolds. See *The
Life and Correspondence of Charles Mathews, the Elder, Comedian. By Mrs.
Mathews*, ed. Edmund Yates, 1860, p. 337.
   [1] On Monday night, 18 Aug., Coleridge had previously been '*hook*'d' at a
bacchanalian party at Reynolds's lodgings, Theodore Hook, Lockhart, and
William Jerdan being among the guests. For accounts of this jollification, and
particularly Hook's hilarious verse-making, see William Jerdan, *Autobiography*,
4 vols., 1852–3, iv. 230–6, and *Men I Have Known*, 1866, 121–2 and 128–30;
J. G. Lockhart, *Quarterly Review*, May 1843, pp. 65–66; and Lucyle Werk-
meister, '"High Jinks" at Highgate', *Philological Quarterly*, Jan. 1961, pp.
104–11.
   [2] See Letter 520 and *Poems*, ii. 970.

This morning my Head felt so loaded and my pulse was so full and
hard, that it would have been tampering with Suicide not to take
a few Calomel Pills, and since then a Black-dose—& of this I must
wait the Result—which in such cases is generally brief and once
for all—after which I am as well as ever I am.—

By the bye, I saw yesterday & read two really beautiful Letters
from Charles Matthews to his Mother from Peroi in Istria in a
Greek Village, where this little Colony speak Greek. They would
have been a Gem in the Keep-sake—& have left a lively impres-
sion of young Matthews's both Heart and Genius.—

Your truly obliged

S. T. Coleridge

1636. *To Mrs. Charles Mathews*

Pub. The Life and Correspondence of Charles Mathews, the Elder, Comedian.
By Mrs. Mathews, *ed. Edmund Yates, 1860, p. 337.*

[September 1828]

Dear Mrs. Mathews,—It would be a profanation even to alter
the position of a word in your dear son's sweet letter[s][1] in the
same language, much more to hazard such substitutes as rhyme
and verse might require. But even the genius of a Byron could not
be better employed than in translating them into a Greek poem.
They are poetry of the best kind—imagination—the power of
picturesque arrangement and playful will in the service of a pure,
most affectionate heart. From my own very heart I congratulate
you on such a son.

S. T. Coleridge.

---

[1] Coleridge refers again to the letters which young Mathews wrote to his
mother from Istria. (See Letter 1635.) Mrs. Mathews, who prints in full her
son's letter from Peroi of 13 July 1828, introduces Coleridge's letter to her as
follows: 'Mr. Coleridge happening to be with me when this letter arrived, I
read it to him, and he was so pleased that he begged me to lend it to him shortly
after, with other letters previously seen on the same subject, as he fancied he
could write a poem from them, and should like to try. In a few days he returned
the letters, with a note from himself, of which a mother may be pardoned for
being proud.'

1637. *To Frederic M. Reynolds*

Address: Frederic Renyolds Esqre | Macpherson's Nursery Ground | Arch
Way Road
MS. British Museum. Hitherto unpublished.

[September 1828]
My dear Sir
From not having the MSS Copy, or from my own oversights &
Slips of the Pen therein, I found so much to do when I came to
read it over that I could not get it off till it was too late for me to
find a messenger.—I have struck lines thro' all the parts of the
Note that are not absolutely necessary to the intelligibility of the
Poem, and have left only four Italian Lines, which are to be trans-
posed so as to conclude the Note.[1] I shall call on you on Thursday
evening, with the Ballad.[2]

S. T. C.

1638. *To Charles Aders*

Address: Charles Aders, Esqre | Euston Square
MS. Cornell University Lib. Hitherto unpublished.

[September 1828]
My dear Sir
It may be an accident of more genial Health and a freer ex-
pansion of the Chest in Breathing, or some still more accidental
coincidence—exempli gratiâ, the arrival of an affectionate letter
from the Person, of whom & of whose you happened at that very
time to be musing affectionately, that strikes the kindling Spark,
and gives utterance (i.e. outwardness, *Äusserung*) to the accumu-
lated Feeling. But at the age of 55, and with more thoughtfulness

---

[1] Coleridge refers to the proof-sheets of *The Garden of Boccaccio* and par-
ticularly to the footnote appended to line 100 of the poem. In *The Keepsake*
for 1829, where the poem was first published, the note concludes with a four-
line quotation from Boccaccio's *Filocopo*. A manuscript copy of the poem, in-
cluding a much longer version of the note, is extant. The present letter indicates
that the whole of the MS. note had been put into proof and that Coleridge was
shortening it, undoubtedly at the request of Reynolds. In the following year
Coleridge became involved in a dispute over the amount of his contributions
to *The Keepsake* and reminded Reynolds of this reduction: 'The smaller number
of pages was for your own convenience—even to the striking out of a part that
was sent.' (See Letter 1669.) The full MS. note has never been published.

[2] A reference to *Alice du Clos; or, The Forked Tongue. A Ballad.* Part of
the MS. undoubtedly was put into Reynolds's hands at this time, but as a
result of 'the Editor's being almost over-layed by the surplus Quantity of the
Contributions', the poem was not included in *The Keepsake* for 1829. Coleridge
did not complete the poem until 1829. See Letters 1651 and 1667.

acting on more experience and insight into character, than the un-
thinking part of my Acquaintance are aware of or are disposed to
give me credit for, I dare affirm to you, that every grain of the ex-
ploding material had been the contribution and *contingent* of a
sober reflection on an observed or ascertained Somewhat. Nor is it
a small support or consolation of my inmost and permanent Being,
that in my most languid mood my Reason & Conscience confirm
the almost involuntary self-revealings of my Heart in it's moments
of strong excitement. I love and highly esteem you, my dear Mr
Aders! and I deem it no inadequate compensation for a Life, dur-
ing which I have never seriously, or with the thought of being
understood as serious, written or spoken aught that from my whole
conscious Heart I did not myself believe to be true, that I can
without any mental stammering, secret misgiving, or fear of being
suspected of flattery, frankly tell you so.—

From Mr Renyolds I have heard—that my two Poems, the first
for an engraving, and entitled 'Boccaccio's Garden',[1] and the other,
a wild and somewhat long Ballad, are all, they can print this year,[2]
owing to the disproprotionate Length of Sir W. Scott's Prose (that
was to have been a Cannongate Tale, had not Mr Heath *outbid*);
but with expressions of the most courteous kind, that half the
number of Pages of such quality would have left them my Debtor.
—But as to my permission to give any thing to a rival publication,
directly & under my name by my own act, posterior to my contract
with Heath, I have had no opportunity to speak.—The Poem on
the Rhine which is extending to a length equal to Schiller's BELL
I must publish in some other way—For with the accompanying
Notes it would be too long for Mr Ackerman's purpose, and I my-
self should not think it right after having been handsomely treated
by Mr Heath & his Editor, to contribute it to a rival Publication.—
I have, however, a small poem which for Mrs Aders' Sake I should
be glad to give Mr A. if I *can*—& I will know this before the week
is over—tho' I am up to my chin in business for myself and
others.—

To the best of Mr Jones' Recollection he [has] sent you the
aperient Pills, which Gillman sent before—but Mr Gillman not
having noted this, as extra-practical, & little dreaming, God
bless him, of having such a Holiday,[3] *positively* certain he cannot

---

[1] Accompanying this poem in *The Keepsake* was a full-page illustration
drawn by T. Stothard and engraved by F. Engleheart. The 'Friend' men-
tioned in line 11 of the poem was Mrs. Gillman, who brought the engraving
to Coleridge's attention.

[2] *Alice du Clos* was later excluded from the 1829 *Keepsake*. See Letter 1651.

[3] In July 1828 Gillman accompanied the Duke and Duchess of St. Albans

be—but quite at ease, that no ill effect can follow, from 2 or 3 being taken when there is occasion. It vexes me, that I cannot obtain more decisive recollections.

I shall try hard (but I have something on hand that I must first do) to send a letter by you to E[llen][1]—Be so good as to remember the *Calderon*.—May God bless & protect you safe & in health to the Heart and Bosom of your beloved Wife[2]—

S. T. Coleridge

P.S. Thanks & cordial Love from Mrs Gillman—who has heard from Mr G.

1639. To Alaric A. Watts

Address: Alaric Watts, Esqre | 56 Torrington Square
MS. Harvard College Lib. Pub. with omis. E. L. G. ii. 412.

Grove, Highgate
Sunday Midnight—14 Septr, 1828—

My dear Sir

Your Wish shall at all events be complied with—whether my suspicion be well or ill-grounded, that you have not received (what yet to the best of my recollection I left at your own door) two letter-sheets of Verses—The first a pretended Fragment of Lee, the Tragic Poet, containing a description of Limbo,[3] & according to my own fancy containing some of the most forcible Lines & with the most original imagery that my niggard Muse ever made me a present of—for to compare one's own with one's honor [own?], is I trust no offence against Humility and may stand free of the Adage, that Comparisons are odious.—I likewise explained to you, in what manner by false and lying pretences, that the Edition of my Poems so many years [months?] pretendedly in hand was only stopped thro' a miscalculation in the quantity, so that it could not

as their medical adviser on a tour of the Continent. (See A. W. Gillman, *The Gillmans of Highgate*, 1895, p. 21.) The Duchess of St. Albans, widow of Thomas Coutts, had married the Duke in 1827.

[1] Heavily inked out in MS.

[2] Mrs. Aders had returned to London by 11 Nov. 1828. See *Robinson on Books and Their Writers*, i. 361.

[3] In his *Poetical Works* of 1834, where *Limbo* was first published, Coleridge gave no hint that the poem was 'a pretended Fragment of Lee'. See also Letter 1651, in which he mentions 'the conjectural Note of it's having been written by Lee while in Bedlam'. Nathaniel Lee (1653?–92), dramatist, was confined in Bethlehem Hospital in Nov. 1684 and remained there five years.

come for want of two Sheets more. (Observe, when against my own judgement I assented to Mr Gillman's wish, that I place the poems at his disposal, it was expressly stated that there should be no unprinted Poems—(had I possessed any of any importance in a finished state, there would have been still many and serious Objections to their making their first appearance in a Collection of Poems written in youth & earliest Manhood) and that all, that was or should be required of me, was to give a List of my printed Poems, marking those which, I thought, ought to be omitted.) Well—by pretences which I am entitled to call false—for at this very time the first Volume was not put to the Press, certainly not all printed— Mr G's mind was so worked on as repeatedly to intreat me to give what I had. I persevered in returning a denial, accompanied with my clear & (as has been proved) correct anticipations of the reprehension, it would bring on me, for three weeks—and this to a man, who had never heard the word, No! from my mouth during the eleven years, I had lived as a Brother in his family—At length, I could only say—Mrs G. has the Copies—do what you will—and being asked, whether they would not want correcting, I replied— Of these I *must* have *proofs*—and by that time I shall be in a fitter mood to supply the defects.—Could it have been believed, that the true cause of this application was to steal (it was no better) these original Poems for a Work, I had never even *heard of*—and to aggravate this by an impudent Paragraph, of thanks to Mr Coleridge for his great liberality!!—And the Copies—the greater part of which had been hastily transcribed from old and not very legible Scraps in my own hand, were (as how should they be otherwise, no Proof having been sent?) infamously incorrect! Not only no pecuniary acknowlegement was afterwards proffered, but to this hour I have never received a Copy of the Book which indeed I should have sent back—tho' 50£ was offered to me for less than the third part of them.—Nay! this was not the worst—By dint of the most solemn assurances made by a Mr Frazer, which had they been verified would not much have mended the matter, my friend (you will consider this letter as strictly *confidential*) at that time in weak health & his mind heavily oppressed and disturbed by the unhappy state of his younger Son, & other causes, let out of his hands a Sonnet addressed to me by the Revd Mr Blanco White in a friendly letter which containing a passage respecting his elder Son in his first term at Oxford I had given to Mrs Gillman—and this spite of his Honor thrice deliberately pledged to the contrary Mr Bijou published. What must have been, what were, *my* feelings, to whom all this was utterly unknown, when I received a letter from Mr White mildly complaining of my having published his Sonnet!—

And at the same time I first heard of *your* letter!—It turns me
deathy sick, even to recall those moments![1]—

But to make an end of this shameful Business; after the publica-
tion of this Bijou, a pretended half sheet Proof of some of the
additional poems were [*sic*] sent up, all in scraps, doubtless struck
off for the purpose—& so infamously incorrect, that it was impos-
sible to correct them in the ordinary way—accordingly, after
various attempts I sent the scraps back, and in dry words desired
Mr Pickering to send up a more decent Proof, immediately—.
None came—and I took the trouble to write out the Poems neatly,
& expressly ordered the omission of several, especially that which
is half prose,[2] & that the Contribution under my name in the
Amulet (*that*, which is perhaps the most polished of my composi-
tions, both the dialogue & the poem, was *my own* weakness &
facility!—)[3] has *occasioned* me another embarrassment, as you will
find below[4]—No attention whatever was paid to my request, no
notice taken, no further proof sent—& to this hour I have had not
a single Copy of my Poems, except an imperfect one that had been
brought up to our house by Mr B. Montagu, to prove to Mr G.
that the Volumes were really on the eve of being finished—Lastly,
Mr Pickering has sent word to Mr Gillman, that he has printed
only 300 copies (for which we have *his* Word) and therefore there
can be no *profit*, as it will bearly [*sic*] pay the expence of Paper &
Printing. I have as good grounds as an Author well can have, for
believing, that an Edition of a Thousand, properly advertised, and
befriended as it might have been, would have been sold within a
twelvemonth. Had it been, as it should have been, in two Volumes,
there is scarce a doubt of it.—As it is, neither I or Mr G. will ever
receive a penny, I dare prophecy.—So much for Mr Pickering and
Company!—[5]

[1] Coleridge is looking back to late 1827, when on his return from Ramsgate
he received an indignant letter from Watts and one of mild reproof from Blanco
White, and first learned that five of his own compositions (including *Youth
and Age*, which he had given to Watts for *The Literary Souvenir*) and the son-
net which White had dedicated to him had already been printed in *The Bijou*
for 1828. See Letters 1605 and 1608.

[2] *The Improvisatore* did not appear in Coleridge's *Poetical Works* of 1828.

[3] See Letter 1596 concerning *The Improvisatore*, first publ. *The Amulet*,
1828.   [4] See p. 762 and note 2.

[5] *The Poetical Works*, 3 vols., 1828, which Coleridge mentioned in a letter to
Stuart of 25 Feb. 1827, appeared in Aug. 1828 and had been 'sold off' by Oct.
(See Letter 1642.) The edition was fairly comprehensive. It included a selec-
tion from the juvenile poems, *The Ancient Mariner*, *Christabel*, *Kubla Khan*,
The Pains of Sleep, *Sibylline Leaves* (with omissions), a few poems previously
unpublished or reprinted from periodicals, and the dramas, *Remorse*, *Zapolya*,
and *Wallenstein*. For a list of the poems in this edition see *Poems*, ii. 1155–8.

And now, my dear Sir! I say as before that if you have not the Poems, I sent, or you deem them inapplicable (yet it puzzled me, that I had never heard from you, & if I had not myself delivered them, I should have imagined that they had miscarried) I will send you a short poem, the best I have of the two or three unpublished tho' far from what I could wish—and I am glad that it is in my power to do so without breach of engagement.[1] Some weeks before my late Tour up and down the Rhine and thro' Holland & the Netherlands, Mr Fred. Renyolds called on me with a letter of introduction from Wordsworth, in which Wordsworth informed me, that he had been induced, as likewise Southey and Sir Walter Scott, to furnish some poems to a Work undertaken by Mr Heath with Mr R. as his Editor—that the unusually handsome terms would scarcely have overcome his reluctance, had he not entertained the hope that I might be persuaded to give my name—and that besides Sir Walter, Southey, *he*, (Wordsworth) myself, Lord Normanby,[2] & (so Mr Renyolds then believed) Mr T. Moore, were to be the only or all but the only Contributors. In short, he hoped that I would write.—

I had not heard from you in answer to my letter, and was really uncertain whether you meant to continue the Souvenir. Mr Renyolds offered me 50£—more by the bye than all my literary Labors, if I except my Salary during the time, I wrote for the Morning Post, and the Courier, had procured me, as a set off against a *dead* loss of about 300£, by the weak Memories of the Subscribers to my 'Friend' when first published, and the necessity of buying up the half-copyrights & remaining Copies at Curtis & Fenner's fraudulent Bankruptcy—*not including* the 1100£ which according to their own Books were coming to me from the sale of the Lay-sermons, Zapolya &c—and this 50£ for a very small number of Lines. But the condition was annexed, that I was to contribute to no other Annual.—I caught at the opportunity— for spite of the Fifty Pound & it's convenience, the disinclination to reject W's request & advice, arising in part from feelings of friendship to Wordsworth & in part from the fear of my refusal to add my name to his & Southey's being misinterpreted at Keswick, was beyond all comparison the more efficient Motive.—I ought, however, to have told you that before this Condition was men-

---

[1] Only the lines, *What is Life?* appeared in *The Literary Souvenir* for 1829. In the preface, which is dated 10 Oct. 1828, Watts pointed out that contributions from Coleridge and others 'reached him too late for publication this year'. It would seem, therefore, that he received the 'two letter-sheets of Verses' mentioned in the present letter and in Letter 1651.

[2] Constantine Henry Phipps, Lord Normanby, later first Marquis of Normanby (1797–1863), contributed 'Clorinda' to *The Keepsake* for 1829.

tioned, [as] I was shewing Mr Renyolds the two or three things, that happened to be in the two or three little Common-place Memorandum Books on my table, and gave it as my opinion that they would not answer his purpose, he fixed on the rough, & imperfect Poem, which with numerous corrections and additions I had sent to you—and offered to close the bargain for this poem, & a shorter one—and before I could reply, he annexed the CONDITION above mentioned—. My answer was immediate—'The matter is settled then at once: for I have already, many months ago, given that very Poem with some other verses to Mr Alaric Watts, for the Souvenir if he thought them worthy, & should continue the Publication, or in any other way, he might think them usable by him—and at all events, till I have ascertained that Mr Watts does not mean to make any use of them, nay, till I know that he does not mean to publish a Souvenir, or does not intend to apply to me for a contribution, one or the other of which I hold probable from my not having heard from him, it is not in my power to accede to this condition.'—Well! (replied Renyolds) what is done is done! and the Condition therefore shall be understood *with exception of any contribution to the Souvenir.*—And so the Contract was concluded. —You will therefore let me hear from you—tho' tomorrow Evening or Tuesday Morning I am engaged to pay my long delayed first Visit to my dear friends, Charles and Mary Lamb, at Enfield, & shall probably not return before Wednesday Night, or Thursday Morning—or I would come to town.—If therefore you write by tomorrow's Post, directing, 'Charles Lamb, Esqre: Enfield Chace, next house to the Phoenix Fire-Office, for S.T.C.' I shall receive it there—or I should be happy to see you here, any time after Thursday Noon.

As to my Name being in other Annuals, it is not by any consent I have given—But I understand that Ackerman has taken a few lines from a Lady's Album, which he was quite at liberty to do, they having been printed twice before to my own knowlege[1]— and that in the other Annual I have just heard of, & that it is—not very reputable to the Editor, if Honesty be a necessary ingredient of Repute.[2] But I am weary of writing about these Reptilities—& must defer the rest to the time, I shall be able to talk with you.—

As some slight proof, that you have been in my thoughts, I inclose two sheets of the Observations & Criticunculae suggested

---

[1] A reference to *The Two Founts*, a poem which Coleridge copied into Mrs. Aders's album in 1827. (See Letter 1572.) The poem had been published in *The Bijou* for 1828 and in Coleridge's *Poetical Works*, 1828.

[2] Coleridge refers again to the unauthorized publication of his letters from Germany in the 1829 *Amulet*. See Letter 1634.

by your Volume of Poems[1]—& which a complexity of troubles & Anxieties prevented me from sending to you with an accompanying letter, months ago. Remember me respectfully and affectionately to Mrs Watts. She will be pleased to hear, that my Ramble on the continent has benefited my health, which in fact was such both in body and in mind as to require some such *Break-up* of the thoughts &c—

With Blessings on the little ones, believe me very truly your's,

S. T. Coleridge

1640. *To Thomas H. Dunn*

Pub. Advertiser, *Adelaide, South Australia, 28 July 1934.*

[September 1828]

Dear Sir—It has vexed me that I should have delayed settling our account so long beyond the time I had appointed. But indeed it had not been my fault, but a disappointment on the part of the Editor of an annual splendid volume,[2] who had promised me a given sum on the receipt of the contribution which I had engaged to furnish him with. After two applications, I have just received a letter of excuse from him that he could not get the money from the proprietary Bookseller till that portion of the work containing my articles was put in type, which he now assures me will be done in the course of this week, and that he will engage for my receiving the honorarium before the close of next week.—Yours truly and with sincere respect,

S. T. Coleridge.[3]

[1] The 'two sheets of the Observations & Criticunculae' suggested by Watts's *Poetical Sketches* (4th edn., 1828) are now in the Harvard College Library. A few of Coleridge's comments have been published. See *Alaric Watts*, i. 152–4.

[2] *The Keepsake*, the most sumptuous of the literary annuals. The 1829 volume was bound in red watered silk, and according to the preface, 'the enormous sum of *eleven thousand guineas*' was expended upon the work.

[3] Seymour Teulon Porter, Dunn's apprentice, has this to say of Mrs. Gillman's discovery that Coleridge was surreptitiously obtaining opium:

It must have been in the year 1828 that one day Mrs. Gillman entered our front-shop, and seeing Mr. Dunn there, desired to speak with him alone, though declining to enter the private house for the purpose. . . . Mrs. Gillman said that they had heard just previously for the first time that Mr. Coleridge obtained laudanum from us; that he lived with them in order that he might be restrained from the use of the drug; that they had supposed him cured of all desire for it; that they did not know how he procured money for it; but that, notwithstanding all their care, he seemed more thoroughly enslaved to it than ever. She insisted, moreover, that Dunn should promise to supply him no longer, & wished to extract a similar promise from each of his assistants. Dunn had long ago expected such an appeal some day, & had prepared

1641. *To Charles Aders*

Address: Charles Aders, Esqre | 25 | Laurence Pountney Lane
MS. Professor Earl Daniels. Hitherto unpublished.
Postmark: Highgate, 10 October 1828.

Friday afternoon [10 October 1828]

My dear Sir

I had so disturbed and distressful a night, with a worse the night preceding, which has explained itself by the re-appearance of an erysipelatous affection on my Leg, that the Servant did not chuse to awake me—& I overslept the Morning's Post—not having commenced the nap till 5—and now I am so depressed that I will not trust myself to write more than—Charles Lamb, Esqre. Enfield Chace, next door to the Phoenix Fire-Office—and that Mrs G. with her affectionate thanks will send the Errand Man tomorrow—that I shall devote, if I am well enough to go to Ramsgate, the time to the execution of the Poem, with the plan & component stuff of which I am more than commonly satisfied—and lastly—that I am most affectionately & with the truest esteem

your obliged Friend

S. T. Coleridge.

1642. *To Daniel Stuart*

Address: D. Stuart, Esqre. | Wyckham Park | near Banbury | Oxfordshire
MS. British Museum. Pub. Letters from the Lake Poets, *314.*
Postmark: Highgate, 14 October 1828.

14 Octr 1828.

My dear Sir

Tho' two or three times indisposed during my Tour on the Continent, and once for a few hours very alarmingly, I returned noticeably improved in health and it's agreeable Companions, good spirits and mental activity. And this state continued so long that I began to flatter myself, that I had taken a new lease of effective life—but a day or two before your very kind letter arrived, I had

himself for it. Nor did he now fail to act as he had proposed. He asserted his belief that the Gillmans had always known the truth of the case; . . . he positively & indignantly refused to enter into any engagement to withhold the laudanum; he complained that Mr. Gillman himself had not called; & he boldly declared his persuasion that without laudanum Coleridge would soon languish, fail, & die.

(E. L. Griggs, 'Samuel Taylor Coleridge and Opium', *Huntington Library Quarterly*, Aug. 1954, pp. 376–7.)

left the Grove in order to pay my long promised and often deferred visit to Charles Lamb & his Sister at Enfield Chace—and during my stay with them I lived temperately, and took a great deal of exercise. The last day but one I took a Walk beyond Cheshunt, the circle of which exceeded twelve miles; but unfortunately I had on a pair of tight-heeled Shoes, and the next morning I walked tho' in much pain about $3\frac{1}{4}$ miles across the fields to fall in with the Edmonton Stage—and on getting out of the Stage on Snow-Hill it was with great difficulty I could walk at all, from the almost torture that every step gave me, & not knowing what better to do, I went into the Druggist's Shop midway Skinner Street & Holborn, & breast-plated both heels with Diacolon Plaister—and not doubting that rest and the mere guarding against friction would bring all right, I kept on the plaister for the next 24 hours & more— when an inflammation of the left leg warned me to have my heels looked to—and in a miserable plight they were—and it was some days before by poultices & keeping my Limbs in a horizontal position I could bring them to heal—soon after which I was surprized by an indescribable depression of Spirits, a nervous dread of doing, hearing or reading any thing more or less remotely a matter of feeling, and a succession of disturbed nights

> When dreaded Sleep, each night repell'd in vain
> Each night was scatter'd by it's own loud screams[1]—

and worse still, I could not sit for ten minutes together, whether writing or reading, without an involuntary closing of my eyes followed by an inward *start* or subsultus. I do not remember having been in so thoroughly miserable [a] state, tho' the few days before I had the Jaundice some years ago, were the most like it—and never in the same time did I make one tenth of the appeals to my looking-glass, as I did in expectation of discovering the Yellow tinge. At length, however, the problem was solved by a smart attack of erysipelas in both legs, alternately, but most severe in the left, which unluckily I had scratched during my sleep before I was aware of the affection. But I trust, that by opening medicines and ammoniacal lotions I am on the eve of parting with this sorry Visitant—the heat is entirely gone, and the color become faint— parting till this time next year, at least: for I strongly suspect, that in my constitution it is a substitute for the Gout, to which my Father was subject. The Relief indeed is much less perfect, than is, I understand, ordinarily received from the first Fits of the Gout, in proportion perhaps as the Sufferings, or rather the pains, are less acute. Still, it *has* relieved me, and tho' I remain weak, with

---

[1] *The Visionary Hope*, lines 13–14, *Poems*, i. 416.

little or no appetite for animal food, and feel *low*, the weight has
been taken off from my spirits—or I should not have been able to
write even this doleful story, by way of reply to a Letter which
deserved and at any other time would have received a very
different as well as much earlier answer.—But as one instance of
the dream-like despondency into which I had sunk, I had to struggle
against the impression, counterfeiting a presentiment, that I
should never more see Ramsgate—and that if I did not die, I
should sink into a state which would render such a trip useless.
And tho' in my inward mind I estimated this bodement at it's true
value, yet it produced a hypochondriacal dread of applying to you
as long as I felt uncertain whether or no a sojourn by the Seaside
was likely to be of any use—&—FOR SICKLY CONSCIENCES ARE
ALWAYS SELFISH—I thought too little of dear Mrs Gillman, who
wants it indisputably and who would not go if I stayed behind. In
fact, Gillman has a nervous aversion, formed during the first
year of my inmateship in his family, to my remaining here for any
length of time, without his Wife—. Of course, for many years past
it can be merely a nervous caprice; but somehow or other he
attributes to Mrs G. a sort of talisman in respect to my health &
comforts—& is haunted with the thought, that some ill-luck would
happen.—If therefore by your kindness I am enabled to do it, I
propose to set off for Ramsgate on Monday next,[1] with Mrs Gillman,
whose Sister will join her there—and to spend the month of Novem-
ber by the Sea-side—and to do nothing but write verses, & finish
the correction of [the] last part of my Work on the power and use
of WORDS. The Edition of my Poems by Pickering is sold off—there
were only (so he says, and I can have no right to suppose the con-
trary) 300 printed. But I have much to write, both as suggested by
your letter, and of my own thoughts, which I will not blend with
this dolorous Scrawl—but begin anew without waiting for your
reply—Pray, remember me & likewise Mr & Mrs G. affectionately
to Mrs Stuart. What a lovely day!—

  May God bless you & your's | and your obliged & affectionate
         Friend
           S. T. Coleridge—

---

[1] A note of Stuart's shows that Coleridge received £20. [MS. British Museum.]

1643. *To Gioacchino de' Prati*

[Addressed in another hand] To Dr. De Prati | 3 Oxendon Street | Haymarket
MS. Private possession. Pub. Letters Hitherto Uncollected, *49.*

Grove, Highgate—
Tuesday 14 Octr 1828

My dear Sir

On hearing the contents of your Note I sought, and found the green book and delivered it to our friend, Mr Gillman: and more than ordinarily grieved am I, that the pressure or distraction of his professional Avocations precluded or prevented him from restoring it to you in person, and attending your lecture. I am myself barely emancipated from the RED ROVER, yclept Erysipelas—which at length had the grace to come forth with modest Blush, after having occasioned me a most miserable fortnight of torpid despondent Days, and affrightful nights, Dreams having been in fact the worst Realities of my Life.

Alas, my dear Sir! it is an additional Thorn to the Quickset Hedge of my Lot, that I am so generally talked of as being *well off* —so happily situated in the enjoyment of affectionate Friends, a beautiful Country, Philosophy, and all the Muses—in short, an enviable Man!—The sick, anxious, embarrassed Man, constantly forced off either by ill-health or the necessity of the To Day, from completing the Works, to which the studies and the Aspirations of more than half his Life had been devoted, and preserved from actual privations only by obligations to Friends, who themselves find it a hard and anxious task to make both ends of the Year meet —of THIS man they know nothing!—and the ignorance of these facts occasions many a request to me, which I have truly called superfluous Thorns—But these are trifles, the soft thorns on a budding Rose-stalk, compared with the sick dull pang at the very heart, inflicted by the sense of my inability to assist and be effectively serviceable to a man like yourself, with every claim that a Man and a Scholar can have! But what remains for one who has neither purse, interest, or time to offer? Alas! little more than empty tho' sincere prayers & good wishes—and the readiness to do any thing that is in my power, as soon as it is pointed out—And all these, my dear Sir, you may rely on from
Your sincere Friend

S. T. Coleridge—

Mrs Gillman sends her kind regards to you—

1644. *To James Gillman*

Address: James Gillman [, Esqre.] | Grove, [Highgate] | near L[ondon]
MS. Cornell University Lib. Pub. with omis. Coleridge at Highgate, *by Lucy E. Watson, 1925, p. 138.*
Postmark: 23 October 1828.

9, Waterloo Plains
Ramsgate
22 Octr 1828.

My dear Gillman

That the cargo real and personal was shipped on board the Dart Steamer without loss or breakage, Mr Jones will have announced to you: and I have only to add that it was landed in the same condition and snugly warehoused, about 7 o'clock P.M. of the same day. We did not set off before 10, the density of the fog preventing it—and having wind and tide for the greater part of the way against us we had rather a slow, tho' very fine Voyage—over leagues of Looking-glass—the Live-Stock not exceeding thirty head, and few of these Cattle of any Condition. My communion was confined to a short, fat, fashionably dressed and cloaked, little fellow, seemingly between 45 and 50, yet from the intermixture of grays in his very black hair possibly as old as myself, who for the first time on Monday last suffered my birth-day to pass undrunk (an omen, it is to be hoped, of the sobriety of the following year) and unblest. My Colloquist held his head brisk up, and somewhat thrown back, and had a very Jewish physiognomy—he had been travelling and sojourning with his family during the last three or four years in France, Netherlands, Holland, and the South of Germany—but was now settled at Wisbaden, and spoke of himself as an intimate Friend and Neighbor of the Sovran Duke of Nassau, whom, you will remember, I mentioned to you as so affectionately beloved by his Subjects—and whom this Gentleman described as amply meriting their attachment, and the esteem and admiration of good men every where.—From Wisbaden, of which and the society thereof, he spoke with raptures, he had recently come and thither was returning by the Ostend Pacquet from Margate. I found him quite at home on the Rhine, the Maese [Meuse], the Moselle, the Neckar &c—but unable to speak German, and with only a gentlemanly acquaintance with literature of any kind—The Duke, he says, speaks English like a native, and avowedly arranges his family on the English Plan, and both educates and dresses his children, as Boys and Girls are in England—and with the German Nobles who do not talk English, he speaks French—His name I could not fish out.—Mrs Gillman was not ill, but quite lifeless, during the voyage—She bathed this morning—but still complains of the strange *bony* feeling about the front of the head forming a sort of Oval, including the Eyes—and the look of these does in fact correspond to her statement. However, I trust that a few days of this most beautiful Weather and happy temperature of Air, with pony exercise, will bring her about again.—Miss Harding lives next door—and is chatty, as usual.—Poor Miss Bird has been forced to veil one of her visual Brilliants with a poultice— I tell her, it will be suspected that she looks forward to being married to a Mr Hog, as she has so manifestly a *sty* in her eye.—She is a good-natured, innocent and well-disposed Girl. The House is all, we want—and *enjoys* a fractional view of the Sea, which from the poke of the Neck necessary thereto is more, than I can pretend to do.—The rooms & beds are comfortable enough.—The Crescent has not a single empty house; yet the Natives speak of having had but a so so Season.—And this is all, I can squeeze out the interspace and interval between the Grove, Highgate, Tuesday ½ past 7, A.M. and 9, Waterloo Plains, Ramsgate, 3 o'clock P.M.— . . . [Conclusion and signature cut off.]

1645. *To William Sotheby*

Address: Wm. Sotheby, Esqre. | Fair Mead Lodge | High Beech | Essex
MS. Mr. W. Hugh Peal. Pub. E. L. G. ii. 423.
Postmark: Ramsgate, 11 November 1828.

> 9 Novr 1828
> 9. Waterloo Plains
> Ramsgate—

My dear Sir

It is a not unfrequent tragico-whimsical fancy with me to imagine myself as the survivor of

> This breathing House not built with hands,
> This Body that does me grievous Wrong[1]—

and an Assessor at it's dissection—infusing, as spirits may be supposed to have the power of doing, this and that thought into the Mind of the Anatomist. Ex. gr.—Be so good as to give a cut just *there*, right across the umbilicar region—there lurks the fellow that for so many years tormented me on my first waking!—Or— a Stab *there*, I beseech you—it was the seat & source of that dreaded Subsultus, which so often threw my Book out of my hand, or drove my pen in a blur over the paper on which I was writing! But above

---

[1] *Youth and Age*, lines 8–9, *Poems*, i. 439.

all and over all has risen and hovered the strong half-wish, half belief, that then would be found if not the justifying reason yet the more than the palliation and excuse—if not the necessitating *cause*, yet the originating Occasion, of my heaviest—& in truth, they are so bad that without vanity or self-delusion I might be allowed to call them my *only* offences against others, viz. Sins of Omission. O if in addition to the disturbing accidents & Taxes on my Time resulting from my almost constitutional pain and diffi- culty in uttering & in persisting to utter, No!—if in addition to the distractions of narrow and embarrassed Circumstances, and of a poor man constrained to be under obligation to generous and affectionate Friends only one degree richer than himself, the calls of the day forcing me away in my most genial hours from a work in which my very heart & soul were busied, to a five guinea task, which fifty persons might have done better, at least, more effec- tually for the purpose;—if in addition to these, and half a score other intrusive Draw-backs, it were possible to convey without inflicting the sensations, which (suspended by the stimulus of earnest conversation or of rapid motion) annoy and at times over- whelm me as soon as I sit down alone, with my pen in my hand, and my head bending and body compressed, over my table (I can- not say, desk)—I dare believe that in the mind of a competent Judge what I have performed will excite more surprize than what I have omitted to do, or failed in doing—Enough of this—which I have written because I sincerely respect you as a good *man* to whose merits as an accomplished Scholar and Man of Letters his Rank and Fortune give a moral worth, as rendering this dedication of his time and talents an Act of free choice, and *exemplary*—and by the beneficial influence of such an example in that class of society, in which the cultivation of the Liberal Arts and Sciences affords the best, almost I had said the only, security against Languor, and a refined but enfeebling Sensuality—the more enfeeb- ling, in proportion as it is diffused and inobtrusive. This is indeed the true meaning and etymon of the LIBERAL Studies—digna Libero viro—those, which beseem a Gentleman, as containing in themselves and in their reflex effects on the Student's own mind and character a sufficing motive and reward—and are followed for Love not Hire.—Because you possess my inward respect, I would not stand in a worse light, than the knowlege of the whole truth would place me, or forfeit more of your esteem than my Conscience assents to.—I need not tell you, that pecuniary motives either do not act at all—or are of that class of Stimulates [*sic*] which act only as Narcotics: and as to what *people* in *general* think about me, my mind and spirit are too awefully occupied with the concerns of another Tribunal, before which I stand momently, to be much affected by it one way or other.

So much for the Past. Now for the answer to your Lett[er], which I have but just received in a pacquet by the Coach, & which must have been detained at the Coach office for a day & a half, according to the date of a Letter to Mrs Gillman inclosed in it, who is here with her Sister.—I mean by this Post to write to Mr Blanco White, in answer to a Letter from him stating his scheme of a new Quarterly Review[1] & soliciting my immediate assistance—& I will offer to him without any particular mention of your name, an article on Didactic Poetry, the age & state of manners to which it belongs; the merits and defects of the Georgics; the comparative fitness of the principal European Languages & the comparative Success of the several Translators, whose Versions are collected in the splendid Polyglot—the former including the question of metres, and the two modes of translation, the identical, and the equivalent. I have not seen the Reviews, you mention; but do not entertain the least apprehension of having been anticipated. I shall have returned to Highgate (Deo volente) within ten days, and as I shall bring with me the first half of the Article, having luckily the notes, I took, during a very minute and critical Perusal of the Georgics, first by itself, and a second time with Voss's & your Version,[2] I hope & trust, that I shall be able to finish it before the close of as many days from the date of my return.[3]—I know of no other respectable Channel—certainly none, to which I have any access— unless indeed Blackwood's Magazine might be considered such.— Indeed, on reflection—the wide sale of this work, and it's undoubted influence on the Literary Public, make it a *question*—and I will defer the statement of any particular article to Blanco White, till I hear from you—which likewise will give me the time, I unfortunately must devote to an article for a Newspaper, necessary for my immediate affairs—O how my soul shrinks from *Politics*—in the present state of things at least!—With respectful remembrance to Mrs and the Miss Sothebies, believe that in thought, will, and wish, I have been & remain your faithful & sincere Friend & Servt

S. T. Coleridge

P.S. My motive for wishing to know your feeling respecting the new Review & the Edingburgh Magazine is—that a certain tone & coloring of style is requisite for each.

[1] This was the *London Review*, of which Blanco White was the editor. It was discontinued after two numbers appeared in 1829.

[2] Voss's German translation of the *Georgics* was included in Sotheby's polyglot edition. See Letter 1592.

[3] See Letter 1666, in which Coleridge again speaks of writing such a critique.

1646. *To Unknown Correspondent*

MS. Dr. Basil Cottle. Hitherto unpublished.

9, Waterloo Plains
Ramsgate—
[November 1828][1]

My dear Friend

I have received the Half of the 10£; tho' by a blunder jointly manufactured by our Servant & the Ramsgate Post Master, only in time to acknowlege it & to say that I will because [I] must defer all other sayings to the time when I shall have to acknowlege the other half only; this is not uninteresting to Naturalists as proving that Bank Notes are Polypuses. God bless you & your's &

included in the latter, I trust,
S. T. Coleridge

1647. *To Hyman Hurwitz*

Address: Hyman Hurwitz, Esqre | &c &c | Grenada Cottage | Old Kent Road | London.
MS. University of Pennsylvania Lib. Hitherto unpublished.
Postmark: Ramsgate, 21 November 1828.

[21 November 1828]

My dear Professor

Your Letter by this morning's Post made me eat my Round of Toast and sip my Cups of Tea in gladsomeness of heart. Need I say, that the contents gave me cordial delight: and Mrs Gillman, I can assure you, was scarcely less gratified, than myself, by this reception of your First Fruits; a reception equal to your Wishes, beyond your Anticipations and only inferior to your deserts.[2] Opposition from those whom he is most laboring to serve, is the *calthrop* on the road of Duty, for which every Benefactor of his Species or of any portion of it must prepare himself—even because they most need his Services. The Word in whom is Life and that Life the Light of Men fixed for every Recipient of that Light of Life in all ages the End and Aim of his Labors—that all may know the Truth and that the Truth may make them free. If there be shewn any milder and less startling vehicle of the Truth, than that in which your Convictions had first clothed themselves, willingly and

[1] During his many visits to Ramsgate Coleridge stayed at 9 Waterloo Plains only in 1828.
[2] Coleridge refers to *An Introductory Lecture delivered in the University of London, on Tuesday, November 11, 1828, by Hyman Hurwitz, Professor of the Hebrew Language and Literature*, 1828.

promptly adopt it—provided that the needful Truth is still con-
veyed, and not—as too often happens when Benevolence has taken
worldly Fear for her Privy Counsellor—softened away into False-
hood. Persevere! bearing in mind, that Some one must *begin*:
and that the very *Shock*, which you give the Patient, may help to
loosen the Obstructions & facilitate the operation of the medicines
that are to follow. What if the natives of the Sun should refuse to
avail themselves of the Light, which had called the Worlds around
them out of Death and Darkness—and chose to live in Pits and
Caverns & to see only by the taper shine of Candles—manufactured
for them by certain privileged Tallow-Chandlers, of no higher
birth than themselves?—If I say, that as the Solar Light to the
Candles, so the Bible to the Talmud—I do bare justice to the former,
and no injury to the latter. Yet I would not speak slightingly of
the Candles among the friends and admirers of the Tallow-
Chandlers; but neither would I refrain from extolling and setting
forth the manifold glories & virtues of the Solar Light.—Enough
of this.

We have taken our places for Tuesday next—and as I may prob-
ably need a day both to recruit myself from the Cramp of Mr
Cramp's Coach, the narrowest & scantiest, I believe, that runs on
British Roads, and to answer the cumulus of Notes, I will name
Thursday, if convenient to you, for your visit—any time after $\frac{1}{2}$
past 11.—Mean time, should you have the chance of meeting or
the means of finding, Mr Taylor the Publisher of the L.U.,[1] you
would oblige me by requesting of him a statement of the accounts
respecting the Aids to Reflection—of which I have heard dis-
crepant Reports, as that the work is—or is not—out of Print—i.e.
sold off. Now I want to know, how many Copies are at this present
time *on hand*—first, because it is my purpose immediately on my
return to put to the Press, if I can secure a fair Publisher on fair
terms, my long-announced Work on the power and use of *words*—
in short, an Organum verè organum, or Logic in it's living uses,
for the Senate, the Pulpit, the Bar—and secondly, I have been
strongly urged to re-publish the Aids to Reflection, considerably
improved—and I am anxious to understand Mr Taylor's wishes &
judgement on these heads—. [At a]ll events, press for this Account
between me [and] him. Something surely ought to be coming to me
—[for] two years ago only sixty Copies remained unsold.—And I
am reasonably anxious to understand Mr Taylor's inclination, as
to being the Publisher of the philosophical Works, I have either
finished, or shall shortly finish—The first part, amounting to 2
Volumes, of my Great Work, will be ready for the Press, God per-

[1] London University.

mitting, by the end of January—comprizing the ideal & scientific Truths of Religion—or Religion *true*, as *Philosophy*—whatever truths, in short, are in their nature, *pre*supposed in all history & Revelation, as historical fact—I live in hope, that you may have procured an interview with Mr Taylor by the time, we meet.[1]—

I made your relations, the Fancy Templars, who had made anxious enquiries, very happy this morning by assuring them that your *Talons* (= Talents) had gone off with *a Claw* = Eclat.—

God bless you & your sincere Friend
S. T. Coleridge

1648. *To Mrs. Joshua Bates*[2]

MS. Harvard College Lib. Pub. Coleridge the Talker, *by R. W. Armour and R. F. Howes, 1940, p. 408.*

Grove Highgate
Novr. 20 something—8? or 9?
1828.

Mr S. T. Coleridge returns La belle Assemblée[3] to Mrs Bates with his best respects & acknowlegements. Tom Hill, of convivial notoriety, said one day—If I am not witty myself, I am the cause of Wit in others. Even so, in reference to the *extract* of & respecting the Scribe S.T.C.—he may be allowed to say, that if he is not a fool himself, he is the cause of a great deal of folly in other Scribes!

There is one piece of information, which the said S. T. Coleridge learns from this Extract, and has had a hundred opportunities of learning—long and long ago—namely, that he is a most remorseless *Talker*—and that if his Ears were as long as his Tongue, his Consociates might well apprehend that their Patience would be *brayed*, tho' perhaps not *in a mortar*—and expect Rain in spite of Blue Skies and Sunshine. Instead of a *Neigh* Bore (for we do not find any thing either winning or *whynny*-ing in his tones; and yet He has been more than once addressed by the name of *Colt*ridge!) the Tenants of the Grove are recommended to call him a *Bray*-bore. The best that can be said of him, perhaps, is that he is thoroughly sincere when he subscribes himself Mr and Mrs Bates's obliged Friend & Servant

S. T. Coleridge

[1] See Letters 1649 and 1652.

[2] Mrs. Bates was the wife of Joshua Bates (1788–1864), American financier and subsequently senior partner in Baring Brothers and Co., London. In 1828–9 the Bates were neighbours of the Gillmans at Highgate.

[3] *La Belle Assemblée*, a monthly magazine, 1806–32. The file in the British Museum is incomplete.

1649. *To Hyman Hurwitz*

Address: Hyman Hurwitz, Esqre | Granada Cottage | Old Kent Road
MS. University of Pennsylvania Lib. Hitherto unpublished.
Postmark: Highgate, 3 December 1828.

[3 December 1828]

My dear Hurwitz

I have received but one Copy of the Lecture—which I am about
to send off with a few remarks, to one of our Literary Newspapers
—Curious that we neither of us noticed the '*characteristic distinc-
tion*' on p. 1—which might lead to a rather laughable mistake of
your meaning[1]—'the name & distinct history of my Race' would
have been far better.

I thank you for the Emplastrum Corroborans Mnemonicum,
you have applied to Mr Taylor.—If he does not come before Mon-
day next, I will inform you & request a repetition.—

God bless you | &

S. T. C.—

P.S. I have read the whole Lecture with great pleasure & unquali-
fied Satisfaction.—

1650. *To S. C. Hall*

Pub. Atlantic Monthly, *February 1865, p. 215.*

4th December, 1828.

Dear Sir

I received some five days ago a letter depicting the distress and
urgent want of a widow and a sister,[2] with whom, during the hus-
band's lifetime, I was for two or three years a housemate; and
yesterday the poor lady came up herself, almost clamorously
soliciting me, not, indeed, to assist her from my own purse,—for

---

[1] The sentence in Hurwitz's *Introductory Lecture delivered in the University
of London* reads: 'For can I forget—dare I suffer a false delicacy to prevent
me from expressing the reflection—that, novel as the situation is to *me*,
I myself, viewed in connection with the name and characteristic distinction
of my Race, am no less a novelty in this situation!'

On p. 23 of the *Lecture*, Hurwitz paid a graceful tribute to Coleridge:

Above all, it will be my most anxious wish to direct the students' atten-
tion to what the author of 'The Friend' and of the 'Aids to Reflection'—
a gentleman whom I am both happy and proud to call my friend—and
where is the man who knowing his vast learning, genuine piety, and goodness
of heart, that would not be proud of his friendship!—so justly calls the Science
of Words.

[2] Mrs. Morgan and Charlotte Brent.

she was previously assured that there was nothing therein,—but to exert myself to collect the sum of twenty pounds, which would save her from God knows what. On this hopeless task,—for perhaps never man whose name had been so often in print for praise or reprobation had so few intimates as myself,—when I recollected that before I left Highgate for the seaside you had been so kind as to intimate that you considered some trifle due to me,[1]—whatever it be, it will go some way to eke out the sum which I have with a sick heart been all this day trotting about to make up, guinea by guinea. You will do me a real service, (for my health perceptibly sinks under this unaccustomed flurry of my spirits) if you could make it convenient to inclose to me, however small the sum may be, if it amount to a bank-note of any denomination, directed 'Grove, Highgate,' where I am, and expect to be any time for the next eight months. In the mean time, believe me

Your obliged,

S. T. Coleridge.

1651. To Alaric A. Watts

MS. Cornell University Lib. Pub. with omis. E. L. G. ii. 419.

Grove, HIGHGATE
(not Hamstead)
[December 1828][2]

My dear Sir

The recollection, that a 40 or 50£ coming unexpectedly and not calculated on would perhaps go halfway to the removal of the only serious obstacle to my excellent and hard-working Friend and (as C. Lamb truly says) more than Friend, Gillman's sending his dear Wife off to Ramsgate for a month or six weeks' fresh Sea Air & Bathing—which exerts almost a re-creating influence on her

---

[1] This would have been the remuneration for 'Over the Brocken', which was published without Coleridge's consent in *The Amulet* for 1829. See Letter 1634.

[2] The present letter was obviously written in response to overtures from Watts, who was attempting to persuade Coleridge to confine his contributions exclusively to *The Literary Souvenir* for 1830. The approximate date is established by a letter to Reynolds of July 1829, in which Coleridge comments on the terms proposed by Watts, though without mentioning his name: 'At the close of the last year I was offered 50£ for any one poem, ... & this accompanied with a request, that I would state what further sum I would accept, on the condition of writing exclusively for the work.' Believing that he was 'under a tie of honor' to continue his contributions to *The Keepsake* for 1830, Coleridge referred the matter to Reynolds and was encouraged to decline the offer. This brought to a close his association with Watts. See Letters 1667 and 1669.

frame—while the weekly or even fortnightly Holiday from Saturday to Monday including the voyage *per Steamer* is scarcely less useful to himself—this recollection or other of the same genus may give to a Bank Note a charm not it's own—but if you knew me with all the sins and infirmities in, on, and around me, you would not need the assurance, 'the blast of the Self-trumpeter', that in my acts of intercourse with those whom I regard, or from all, I had known of them, feel disposed to regard, with esteem and affectionate interest, Money may have sometimes been tolerated as a *pretext* for others but has never been a motive for myself. It would be perhaps well, if it stopped here—and if from the sickly depressive sensation, given by the thought of connecting any thing with the exertions of my Intellect except the affections of my Moral Being, the plump Goddess, Pecunia, did not in a greater degree, than sound Judgement would sanction, exercise a repulsive force & awaken an impulse *ad contra*, that disenables her emissary Motive, or reverses it. I cannot help regretting, that a similar delicacy had prevented you from giving me the pleasure of seeing you, and from making me a Confidant in your views & wishes respecting the Souvenir. An hour or two's occasional Conversation would have left no doubt on your mind, that I should greatly have preferred confining myself professedly in all, that I was able to effect at all, to your Work, on just such terms, whatever they might be, as you with prudence & justice to Mrs Watts and your Little Ones could offer, than twice or three times the sum from Persons, of whom that which I call, *I*, knew nothing. And it was with the strictest truth, that I told you, that Wordsworth's urgent Letter, and the peculiar Relation, in which (N.b. by her own Choice) the Mother of my Children & my dearest Daughter have stood and stand in to Mr Southey, formed so very large a portion of my reason for assenting to the proposal, that Mr Heath's 50£ was at best but a make-weight—Even at this moment I do not feel perfectly comfortable in the thought of the transaction—and in confidence I will tell you, why.—I am well aware, how imperfect my information is respecting all Publishing Schemes, & therefore rely little on my own anticipations of Success or Failure. I know likewise that boastful Whispers & confidential Hints respecting the price of Copyright & the Capital hazarded, are among the Ways & Means of exciting curiosity &c &c—Still however, the sums expended in this work on the one hand, and the Proportions as well as Quality of the Contents on the other, are such, that a Sale adequate to the re-instatement of the former would overstep my conceptions of the Probable. To Sir Walter Scott a Sum (so I was assured) less than 600£ but more than 500 Guineas was given for certain

Tales, that occupy more than one third of the whole Volume.[1]
Southey had written a poem which would have occupied at least
one fourth of the Volume—& tho' this has been managed, & other
poems substituted[2]—yet on the whole, as far [as] I could judge from
a *very hasty* Over-look of the Volume, I could not help thinking,
that in the course of a Morning you and I could have sketched out
a Scheme incomparably better suited to a *Gaudy Book*, in every
respect.—Of Sir Walter's Powers I have as high admiration as you
can have—but assuredly, Polish of Style, and that sort of Prose
which is in fact only another kind of Poetry, nay, of metrical Com-
position, tho' metre *incognito*, such as Sterne's Le Fevre, Maria,
Monk &c—or the finest things in the Mirror—this is not Sir
Walter's Excellence. He needs Sea-room—space for developement
of character by Dialogue, &c &c—and even in his most successful
Works the *Tale* is always the worst part—clumsily evolved & made
up of incidents that are purely accidental.—Now in a fine Book,
with costly plates, &c &c each page should be or have the semblance
of being, something *per se*. A Cannon-gate tale on hot-pressed rich
paper &c &c—I do not know how—but it would [not ?] *read natural*
to my feelings.—However, it is done—and there is an end of it.
From a mistake, & from the Editor's being almost over-layed by
the surplus Quantity of the Contributions, he had received, the
only Articles of my writing are a few Epigrams which Mr Renyolds
selected from an old Memorandum Book of mine, and a Poem
written for one of the Engravings, 'Boccaccio's Garden'[3]—of

---

[1] Scott had insisted that he receive £500 for contributing one hundred pages
to the 1829 *Keepsake*, but since the material he submitted fell short of that
amount, he was notified that he was still in Heath's debt and contributed
The House of Aspen to the 1830 issue. He was, however, thoroughly aroused
when Heath offered to furnish engravings for the new edition of the Waverley
novels in lieu of a cash payment for further contributions to the 1830 *Keepsake*.
Thus ended Scott's relations with 'Heath and the conceited vulgar Cockney
his Editor'. *The Journal of Sir Walter Scott*, ed. J. G. Tait and W. M. Parker,
1950, pp. 478–9, 495, and 597–8.

[2] Southey was paid £50 for his poem, *All for Love*. It was afterwards excluded,
probably because of its length, and he was 'required' to substitute three addi-
tional poems, only two of which appeared in the 1829 *Keepsake*. Wordsworth,
too, was notified that his contributions, for which he received a hundred
guineas, were '*very short*' of the 'stipulated Mark', though four of his sonnets
had been rejected. He was also given to understand that he would be paid a
like sum for the next year, but neither he nor Southey was asked to con-
tribute to the 1830 issue of the annual. Indeed, he was later to declare that he
had been used 'most scurvily' by Heath and Reynolds and that Southey was
'much in the same predicament'. See *Southey Letters*, iv. 103, 113, 124, and
Later Years, i. 337–9, 344, 351–3, 378–9, and 385–7.

[3] Coleridge's eight epigrams and *The Garden of Boccaccio* amounted to
seven printed pages in the 1829 *Keepsake*, four short of the eleven pages

which if you should say, they are a vigorous *Copy of Verses*, you would confer all the commendation, I should be willing to receive from your Judgement.—

You in part misunderstood me with regard to the Poem—I said, or meant to say, that it was one, which Mr R. had desired to have, as *one*—not that he had offered 50£ for that alone.[1]—Surely, you must have received it—with the conjectural Note of it's having been written by Lee while in Bedlam—A rude Copy, I have—but in transcribing it for you I had made numerous alterations, and large additions, written more meo on sundry Scraps of Paper— which are either destroyed or in terra incognita—and as I cannot recollect & may not succeed in re-producing them—and moreover have had a certain influx of thoughts, that suggest an apt con- clusion, and would make the thing a compleat Poem—I should be obliged to you, if you would look over your papers, in case they should not have been destroyed. Of the little parcel, which I left, containing *two* (letter) sheets of Verses, at least, I have the most distinct recollection.—Perhaps, the Lines,

'Tis a strange place, this Limbo!—not a *Place*,
Yet name it such!—where TIME and weary SPACE
Fetter'd from Flight, with night-mair sense of Fleeing
Strive for their last crepuscular Half-being—
Lank SPACE and scytheless TIME with branny Hands
Barren and soundless as the measuring Sands,
Mark'd but by Flit of Shades!—unmeaning they,
As Moonlight on the Dial of the Day!

But that is LOVELY! looks like HUMAN TIME—
An old Man, with a steady Look sublime
That stops his earthly task to watch the Skies!
But He is blind: a Statue hath such Eyes.
Yet having moonward turn'd his face by chance
Gazes the orb with moon-like Countenance.
With scant white Hairs, with Fore-top bald and high
He gazes still, his eyeless Face all Eye.
As 'twere an organ full of actual[2] Sight*
His whole Face seemeth to rejoice in Light.

originally stipulated. Though the reduction was for the editor's convenience, Coleridge was later to find that he, like Scott, was expected to make up the deficiency by contributing without additional remuneration to the 1830 issue of that annual. See Letters 1667 and 1669.

[1] A reference to *Limbo*, 'the rough, & imperfect' copy of which Reynolds had seen when he called on Coleridge at Highgate. See Letter 1639.

[2] silent [Cancelled word in line above.]

* imperfectly recollected [Marginal note by S. T. C.]

Lip touching Lip, all moveless, Bust and Limb,
He seems to gaze on that which seems to gaze on him![1]

perhaps these lines, I say, may assist you in recollecting the circum-
stance.—At all events let me see you as soon as you can—or should
more needful Matters render this inconvenient, if you will state the
day & hour, in which I might be assured of finding you at home,
I will come to you—& then we can speak of Matters that in every
way it would probably be pleasanter to us both to *speak* than to
write—And if you have either space, or time, or wish for any poem
with my name in your Souvenir of this Year, I will shew you the
poor meagre *all*, I have, but which shall be at your service—for
believe me, my dear Sir, there are two or perhaps three Points in
which, with the deepest sense of my manifold infirmities, I yet
dare wish (& let me add, dare hope) that you in your 64th year
(for tho' the Earth has circled the Sun only 54 times since my eyes
opened to it, my poor Body is ten years at least older) may remain
as truly a child as your sincere Friend,

S. T. Coleridge.

1652. *To Thomas Hurst*

Address: Thomas Hurst, Esqre | Bank Side | Highgate
Transcript Coleridge family. Hitherto unpublished.

CONFIDENTIAL   Monday Night 19 January 1829
My dear Sir   Grove, Highgate

I am now giving you a perhaps troublesome proof of my esteem,
and of the confidence which I feel both in your Judgement, and in
your friendly disposition to exert it in my favor.

The 'Aids to Reflection' are out of Print, and the last Copies
have been disposed off [*sic*] many months ago—tho' to this hour
I have not received any account, nor till the last week, when Mr
J. Taylor permitted me to draw on him for 30£ on account, in
order to liberate me from the dread of a Bill* for that amount
which came due on the 15th of this month, have I ever received
any thing.

---

[1] *Limbo*, lines 11–30. See *Poems*, i. 430.

* N.B. The original Bill had been paid by me 12 years ago ; but I had trusted
the money for it's settlement with one who has been long in his grave & God
forbid! that I should for 30£ disturb his ashes—and alas! Need breaks thro'
stone walls, & the original words of the Lord's Prayer are—'Forgive us our
debts to thee, as we forgive our fellow men who are *Debtors* to us'—& [I] am not
quite sure that the interests of practical morality have been benefited by
generalizing the words into 'trespasses'. [Note by S. T. C.]

However, it is not my intention to introduce the subject by a complaint of Mr J. Taylor. The Past is past.—But I am about to send to the Press three works—the first, an almost entire *Rinfacciamento* [*sic*], or Re-construction of the Aids to Reflection, as a Second Edition, newly arranged & with large Editions [*sic*].[1]

Secondly—two Volumes, entitled, a System of the Faith and Philosophy of S. T. Coleridge.

Thirdly, (but which I ought perhaps to have put first) a Volume on the Power and Use of Words &c &c[2]—

Now I have inclosed the Terms, on which I wish these three Works to be published by Mr J. Taylor—and which appear to me equitable:[3] and my Request to you, My dear Sir! is to look over

---

[1] Although in Nov. 1828 Coleridge had planned to have John Taylor publish a second edition of *Aids to Reflection* 'considerably improved' and in the present letter mentions a rifacimento of the work, by 20 Feb. 1829 ill health had forced him to suspend the task. In Sept. 1829 he proposed, if he could 'contrive' to do so 'with honor', to transfer the second edition of the *Aids* to Hurst, Chance, and Company, and in August of the following year he reported that the first half was ready and that the second would be supplied as soon as required. The second edition appeared under the imprint of Hurst, Chance, and Company in 1831. See Letters 1647, 1657, 1676, 1696, 1700, and 1705.

[2] In 1823 Coleridge arranged to have Taylor and Hessey publish not only the *Aids*, but also the *Elements of Discourse* and the *Assertion of Religion*. See Letter 1345 and note.

[3] A manuscript containing these terms reads as follows:

That John Taylor takes on himself the risk of publishing the Edition of the Works hereafter named, namely, the cost of printing, advertising, and all other expences necessary or ordinarily incident to the publication of a Work.

That after deducting the sum repaying these expences, and actually paid by Mr John Taylor, (i.e. charged to the Author at the bonâ fide *Trade* and not at the nominal price) the Profits, if any, of the Edition shall be equally divided between Mr Taylor and the Author.

That the number printed

1. Of the Rinfacciamento of the Aids to Reflection shall be
2. Of the two Volumes, entitled 'ΕΣΤΗΣΙΣΜΟΣ, or the System of the Faith & Philosophy of S. T. C. shall be
3. Of the one large Volume of the Power and Use of Words, including a full exposition of the Constitution & Limits of the Human Understanding, &c with a compleat System of Logic in it's three functions, as Canon, or the Logic of *conclusion*; as Criterion, or Logic applied to the *Premises*; and as Organ, or Logic as an instrument of discovering the Truth of Things in themselves—shall be

That there shall be a yearly settlement of each of these three works, and that the division of the Profits, should there be any, shall not be deferred to the time, when the whole Edition shall have been sold off.

Lastly, that on the sale of these Editions the entire Copy Right shall revert to the Author, S. T. Coleridge—

P.S.—It is especially noted and agreed between J. T. and S. T. C., that no more shall be charged against the Works, or against any one of them,

(781)

them, and to give me the advantage (& I regard it as a very great advantage) of your Judgement & Experience, with regard especially to the following Questions—Are the Terms other or more than I am entitled to ask? Can you suggest any other precaution, or point which it would be advisable for me to have settled by [and?] agreed on between me & my Publisher?

Lastly (but this is a delicate Question, and I leave it at your own option to answer it or no) Can I do better[1]—in my two characters, as a poor man who wish[es] to obtain whatever [he sha]ll have honestly *earned*; and as a Christian who deeply convinced that he is offering truths of the highest importance, nay, indispensable utility, to the vital interests of his Fellow-men must be desirous to procure the largest sphere in his power?

My dear Sir! I am aware & I likewise feel that I am taking a liberty with you; but at the same time I promise myself, that you will find a *set-off*, or compensation, in the assurance that as the Request originated in the unfeigned Esteem & Regard, so your compliance with it will secure the gratitude of your sincere Friend & Servant

S. T. Coleridge

To Thomas Hurst, Esqre.

1653. *To William Pickering*

Address: Mr Pickering
MS. Mr. James M. Osborn. Hitherto unpublished.

[January 1829?][2]

Dear Sir

I have received your Note with the inclosed Draft[3]—& have left the first Volume corrected for the Press.—But I wish to know,

on the score of Advertisements than had been actually paid by J. T.— and that the mention of these Works in any general Sheet or Enumeration of Mr J. Taylor's Publications shall not be charged—it being at Mr Taylor's option, whether or no he thinks it to his own advantage to include these Works in his general List of Publications.—[MS. Mr. A. H. B. Coleridge.]

[1] Probably as a result of this inquiry, the firm of Hurst, Chance, and Company became the publishers of the two editions of *The Church and State*, 1830. Hurst and Chance dissolved their partnership in 1831. See Letter 1720.

[2] A note written in a presentation copy of Coleridge's *Poetical Works* of 1829, signed by him and dated 'May, 1829', suggests an approximate publication date. The present letter, in which Coleridge refers to the preparation of that edition, must have been written several months earlier, possibly in Jan. See *Poems*, ii. 1108, and Campbell, *Poetical Works*, 600.

[3] This draft was undoubtedly the £30 which Pickering advanced to Coleridge. Coleridge needed two-thirds of the sum for Mrs. Morgan. See Letters 1650, 1668, 1679, and 1748.

whether any new arrangement will be required, as it is my inten-
tion to add poems to the amount of five or six hundred lines at
least.—Will this render the second Volume of disproportionate
size?—I should be glad to receive a line from you on this point.—
One small poem under 20 lines, introductory to the Juvenile
Poems,[1] I shall send you on Monday—and the two other Volumes,
whenever you want them—as they are already corrected.[2]—

Your's truly,

S. T. Coleridge

1654. *To Henry Taylor*

Address: Henry Taylor, Esqre | Suffolk Street[3]
MS. Huntington Lib. Hitherto unpublished.
Postmark: Highgate, 3 February 1829.

Grove, Highgate.
3 Feby 1829.

My dear Sir

Mr and Mrs Gillman can only repeat their assurance, that You
are always welcome, both in your own person and your friends.
And I need not add, that I shall be happy to see Mr Romilly[4] and
Mr Charles Villiers[5] on next or any other Thursday Evening. I
mention Thursdays because on that day of the week there is the
least probability of your not finding us at home. I presume, Mr
Charles Villiers is a Brother of the Gentleman, who did me the
honor of accompanying you some time ago.—Do you know who
wrote the Article on the way of governing Ireland in the last
number but one of Blackwood? For a *red-hot unwise* Bravura it is
one of the cleverest I have seen on the Subject.—

Your's truly,

S. T. Coleridge

[1] No such 'small poem' was included in the *Poetical Works* of 1829.

[2] In revising his *Poetical Works* of 1828 for the new edition of 1829, Coleridge
made many corrections and alterations. He also added three compositions to
volume ii—*Allegoric Vision, The Improvisatore*, and *The Garden of Boccaccio*—
and omitted two short poems which had appeared in 1828—*Song* ('Though
veiled in spires of myrtle-wreath') and *The Alienated Mistress* ('If Love be
dead'). See *Poems*, ii. 1159.

[3] The following note appears on the address sheet of this letter: 'Opened by
Mr Henry Taylor, 2 Suffolk St Pall Mall and not for him. T. Rowe.'

[4] John Romilly, later Lord Romilly (1802–74), master of the rolls.

[5] Charles Pelham Villiers (1802–98), statesman and brother of Thomas
Hyde Villiers (1801–32).

1655. *To J. H. Green*

Address: J. H. Green, Esqre | Lincoln's Inn Fields
MS. Pierpont Morgan Lib. Hitherto unpublished.
Postmark: 7 February 1829.

[7 February 1829]
My dear Friend

The second Volume of my Eichhorn's Einleitung to the New
Testament has been long ago alibi in terra incognita—and now the
first part of Volume 3rd is missing—just at the very time, that I am
beginning my notes, chapter by Chapter, on the Epistles of Paul.
For to the reading of the N.T. and collating our version with the
Greek, I commonly appropriate the two last hours of my waking
day.—I should be much obliged to you therefore, should you come
up in the Carriage tomorrow, or should Mrs Green come up in the
carriage for you, to bring with you the two intermediate Volumes.—
If I do not deceive myself, I have brought it to a high degree of
probability that the Acts of the Apostles are two works of different
dates that (in the first instance possibly from their being transcribed
on the same Roll) have blended or as it were inosculated—The
first Chapter with the four first verses of the second common as
introduction to both works—from II. v. 4 to C. VIth the Acts or
Memorabilia of the Apostles in Jerusalem—certainly later than the
Apostolic Age—and from VI to the end, Acts or Memorabilia of
the Apostolate or Mission to the Gentiles, undoubtedly Luke's and
of the Apostolic aera.—This Hypothesis solves all the difficulties.

Thus I should divide the New Testament into two parts—
Apostolic and the earliest post-apostolic. Under the first, Luke's
Gospel, and Acts of the Mission to the Gentiles, John's Gospel and
three Epistles—Mark's Gospel, but with many interpolations
omitted—10 Epistles of Paul: the Ep. to the Hebrews: Ep. of
James & perhaps of Jude. Under the second—the Apocalypse,
Matthew, Acts of the Church of Jerusalem—and the Epistles to
Timothy & Titus.

God bless you &

S. T. Coleridge—

1656. *To Mrs. George Frere*

Transcript Coleridge family. Pub. Glimpses of the Past, *by Elizabeth Words-worth, 1912, p. 6.*

Grove, Highgate.
Monday afternoon [9 February 1829][1]

Dear Madam

A fatality seems to hang over every invitation, I have owed of late to your friendly remembrance of me.] When your note was put into my hands by the servant, I was engaged in a more than commonly interesting conversation with, or rather listening to, my nephew, Henry Nelson Coleridge, respecting his plans, which, you perhaps may have heard, include my daughter's change of *state* tho' not of name, & supposing Miss Frere at the gate, I hastily carried my eyes thro' your & Mr G. Frere's kind invitation & had read the word, Tuesday—& under this impression gave my answer to Miss Frere. This morning Mrs Gillman speaking of a gentleman who was to drink tea with us tomorrow, I said, giving her at the same time your note, I cannot meet him: I forgot to tell you that I am engaged to dine tomorrow at Mr Frere's. No longer ago than the minutes consumed in writing these lines, Mrs Gillman came to me with your note in her hand, & Bless me, why it is for *Thursday* that you have engaged yourself, & besides the usual Visitors, you have engaged to meet Mr Henry Taylor, who is to bring with him Sir S. Romilly's son & a Mr Mill;[2] & (quoth I with a deep respiration) Mr W. Hutt, a great traveller whose address I do not know, & Mr Irving with two Scotch Divines, & Mr Steinmetz from Hackney;[3] & then (continued Mrs G.) Mr Gillman has promised Dr Watson & the American Artist to introduce them to you—in short, the Room will be full & more than half perfect strangers to us. A moment's deliberation convinced me that I had but one way morally in my power—that of sending off a man immediately with this statement of the case, & of my vexation at my carelessness, not to mention, which yet with entire truth I might do, my regret on

---

[1] Since Coleridge's letter of 3 Feb. 1829 was first received by another Henry Taylor, the visit to Highgate mentioned in it cannot have taken place before Thursday, 12 Feb. The present letter, in which Coleridge refers to the forthcoming Thursday visit of Henry Taylor and two of his friends, was probably written, therefore, on Monday, 9 Feb.

[2] John Stuart Mill (1806–73). Mill's review of Coleridge's *Poetical Works* of 1829 and his celebrated essay 'Coleridge' may have owed something to this and later visits to Highgate. See *Westminster Review*, Jan. 1830 and Mar. 1840.

[3] Adam Steinmetz, Coleridge's friend and disciple, died in 1832. See Letters 1755–6.

my own account. For I am with most unfeigned Respect & regard, dear Madam,

Your & Mr G. Frere's obliged & attached Friend & Servant

S. T. Coleridge

1657. To F. A. Cox[1]

Address: Dr Cox | Library | University of London
MS. Lord Charnwood. Pub. Letters Hitherto Uncollected, *47.*
Postmark: Highgate, 20 February 1829.

Friday Noon. [20 February 1829]
Grove, Highgate—

Dear Sir

For some weeks past I have labored under an affection of the Chest and a functional derangement of the Bronchia, with cough and excessive expectoration for the two first hours after my getting up—tho' I am not wholly free from the latter during the rest of the day—and these distempers have been accompanied with a depression so completely incapacitating me from all literary effort that most anxious as I have been to put into Mr Taylor's hands the Copy for the new Edition or more correctly the rifacciamento of my Aids to Reflection, I have been compelled to suspend the task. A few days ago, however, an erysipelatous Affection made it's appearance in both my Legs, now in one, now in another—and in paroxysms, as it were, returning at night—so that a medical friend is inclined to think it a substitute for Gout which I have not strength enough to mature into a regular fit. My Spirits have been considerably relieved since the appearance of this whatever it be— but some (slight indeed but ominous) symptoms of the disorder on my *forehead*, the death-signal of my friend, Sir George Beaumont, and the continued oppression on my Chest, would stamp any promise of a literary kind from me whether positive or conditional with the character not only of rashness, but of a carelessness respecting my word, and a disrespect to you. Mr Colburn might be expecting a sheet for the Press, when the Author was being layed out for his winding sheet.—Believe me when I say that I have formed from what I have heard so high an opinion of you as a Man and a Christian, that I should, in a re-established state of body & mind, find an additional motive for acceding to Mr Colburn's proposals in the knowlege that I should be working under your

---

[1] Francis Augustus Cox (1783–1853), baptist minister, became librarian of the University of London in 1828.

auspices, and it will be a comfort to me that you should know me to be as I really am

with very sincere respect | and regard, dear Sir, | your obliged friend

S. T. Coleridge

1658. *To Henry Nelson Coleridge*

Address: H. N. Coleridge, Esqre | By H. Hall, Esqre
[Readdressed in another hand],— Patteson's Esqre | 9 Gower Street
MS. Victoria University Lib. Hitherto unpublished.

[Endorsed 23rd March 1829]

My dear Henry

It is with very great grief that I have this moment received from Mr H. Hall the information that you have been seriously ill. Of the particulars he has not spoken; tho' I need not tell you, that I am anxious about it's effects on your eyes. I have myself been without intermission, tho' with varying degrees of intensity, ill, since we met—have every night a paroxysm of Erysipelas on my Leg, and the distress of my general Sensations, my depression of Spirits and Incapability of combining an outward act of any kind with that of Thinking, to which I have to add some nephritic symptoms, seem to hold a sort of inverse ratio to the length and severity of these local Affections. Mr Green inclines to think the latter imperfect or abortive attempts at a Gout. But tho' I am now writing most about myself, believe me I have been all the while *thinking* only of you.

Who was the writer of the article in the Quarterly in which my Father's Crit. Gram.—& my [his ?] old Quare-quale—is introduced ?[1]—

I fear, I *fear* the want of *prominence* in our Friend, Blanco White's Review. I am glad to see you hunting down the villainous 'whose'. Did *you* write the Article on Scott's Novels ?[2]—

May God bless you!—But for my illness I should have by this time have had a few printed Sheets to send you on the ideas of the Constitution & the Church[3]—But tho' I have only half a dozen

---

[1] See *Quarterly Review*, Jan. 1829, pp. 111–12. The article, 'Elementary Teaching', was contributed by Southey. See also Letter 1484 for another reference to John Coleridge's *Critical Latin Grammar*.

[2] The first number of the *London Review* (Feb. 1829) contained an unsigned article on Scott's novels.

[3] Coleridge refers to his treatise, *On the Constitution of The Church and State, according to the Idea of Each: with Aids toward a Right Judgment on the late Catholic Bill*, 1830. The Catholic Emancipation Bill to which the title refers was passed

pages [to] compose in order to finish it, such has been the condition
of my mind & body that I have only wasted an extravagant quan-
tity of paper, writing and rewriting & nothing to my mind.—
Again God bless you, &

S. T. Coleridge—

1659. *To Thomas Allsop*

Address: Thomas Allsop, Esqre | Regent Street | corner | of Oxford Street
MS. Harvard College Lib. Hitherto unpublished.

[Early May 1829]¹

My dear Allsop

I am glad, your Letter did not come before last night—(it was
near Ten o'clock)—as very possibly it would not have been de-
livered to me—so ill have I been, that for the last month I have not
been in a state to admit even my most intimate friends to see [me],
with exception of Mr Green—Yesterday was the first day, I felt
any thing like convalescence—and letters, parcels, &c lay an
untouched heap.—Enough of this—

by the House of Commons on 30 Mar. 1829, by the House of Lords on 10 Apr.,
and received the royal assent on 13 Apr. As Coleridge remarked in *The Church
and State*, he was not unfriendly to Catholic Emancipation but had scruples
concerning 'the means proposed for its attainment'. He had been a 'strenuous
Opponent of the former attempts in Parliament', but he found the Bill 'lately
passed' to be 'much less objectionable than he had feared, and yet . . . much
less complete and satisfactory than he had wished'. Thus after a careful develop-
ment of his '*Ideas* of the Constitution in Church and State', he concluded his
work by offering 'Aids to a right appreciation of the Bill'.

   In 1825 Coleridge conceived of *The Church and State* as one of six disquisitions
supplementary to *Aids to Reflection*, and in the latter work he announced his
intention of publishing an 'Essay on the Church, as instituted by Christ, and
as an Establishment of the State' (p. 381). See also Letters 1447, 1450, 1458,
and 1480. In the Advertisement prefixed to *The Church and State* Coleridge
points out that the work was 'transcribed, for the greater part, from a paper
drawn up by me some years ago, at the request of a gentleman [J. H. Frere]
. . . and which paper, had it been finished before he left England [in Sept. 1826],
it was his intention to have laid before the late Lord Liverpool'. During his
stay in England, as Coleridge's letters of 1826 show, Frere actively exerted him-
self in Coleridge's behalf, and had *The Church and State* been completed, he
would certainly have brought it to Liverpool's attention. He not only forwarded
a copy of *Aids to Reflection* to Liverpool, but won from him a promise to
'endeavor to do something' for Coleridge. On 19 Jan. 1826 Coleridge himself
remarked that he had 'certain strong motives' for '*immediately*' sending his
supplementary disquisitions to the press. *The Church and State*, however, was
not published until Dec. 1829. See Letters 1510–11 and 1682.

   ¹ In his letter to Allsop of 5 May 1829 Coleridge says that the person to
whom he alluded in his last letter was Henry Taylor of the colonial office. The
present letter, therefore, was written a few days previously. The erroneous
date of '20 May 1829' appearing in the MS. is in Allsop's handwriting.

Need I say, that your Letter agitated me?—Tho' a stranger
even to the Name of Lady Louisa Murray,[1] it was sufficient that
you imagine a possibility of my being useful to you—I could not
hesitate a moment in doing what you requested and have accord-
ingly inclosed the Letter for her Ladyship, *undated*; and as I have
no particular seal, I have left it open for you to read & then seal—
only not with your own *T.A.*—But having done this, let me con-
jure you to reflect a little.—Is it not possible, that you may yet
go on? Would you not have done better if you had confined your
trade to ready money?—But if your present scheme be the result
of serious thought, what is it? What & where is this New Settle-
ment? Who are the persons likely to have influence? I have one
young friend in the colonial office—God knows, how helpless I am
—but I will write to any one of the few influencive persons, I have
been introduced to—if there was the least probability of the
influence being exerted in your favor.—But I am all in the dark—
even the inclosed letter I have written blindly.—Do arrange some
intelligible scheme of what you think possible & the means of achiev-
ing it.—

Nothing but this long and severe illness (a mixture of atonic
Gout and Erysipelas which last flew from my legs to my Neck and
Forehead & brought my inward head into a state, never before
experienced by me) has prevented me from calling on you—the
first day, I can get there, I will be with you—& settle this & *other*
matters—God bless you—! for the Post will not wait.

                                        S. T. Coleridge—

1660. *To Thomas Allsop*

Address: T. Allsop, Esqre | 251 | Regent Street | Oxford Street—
MS. New York Public Lib. Pub. with omis. Letters, Conversations and Rec. *242.*
Postmark: Highgate, 5 May 1829.

[5 May 1829]

My dear Allsop

The Person, to whom I alluded in my last as the only Acquain-
tance standing in any connection with your wishes, is a Mr Henry
Taylor, who within the last two or three Years has held a situation
in the Colonial Office: but *what*, I do not know. From his age and
comparatively recent initiation into the Office, it is probably not
a very influencive one; and on the other hand, from the rank and

---

[1] Lady Louisa Murray was the wife of Sir George Murray (1772–1846),
privy councillor and colonial secretary, 1828–30.

character of the friends, he has occasionally brought with him on our former Thursday Evening *Conver-* or to mint a more appropriate term, *One*versazioni, it must be a respectable one. Mr H. Taylor is *Southey's Friend*—and more than a literary Acquaintance to *me* only in consequence of my having had some friendly intercourse with his Uncle during my abode in the North. Of *him* personally I know little more than that he is a remarkably handsome, fashionable-looking, young man, a little too *deep- or hollow-mouthed* and important in his enunciation—but clever, and well-read—and tho' I hold a much lower place in his esteem & admiration than my Brother-in-law, the Poet Laureate, I have no reason to doubt that he would receive anyone whom I had introduced to him as a friend of mine in whose welfare I felt an anxious interest, with kindness and a disposition to forward his object, should it be in his power.—Of course, I should not hesitate a moment in writing to him—and indeed I will do so, at all events, by the *next* post. I say, the *next* post: because I do not recollect his Address, and Mrs Gillman who knows it or has his Card, is out & will not be at home till after our last post—i.e. ½ past 4:—and on receiving his answer will inform you when & where you may call on him.

But again, my dearest Allsop! you must allow me to express my regret, that I am acting in the dark—without any conviction on my mind, that your present scheme is not the result of wearied and still agitated spirits—an impetus of despondency—that fever which accompanies exhaustion. I can too well sympathize with you—and bitterly do I feel the unluckiness of my being in such a deplorable state of health just at the time when for your sake I should be most desirous to have the full possession of all my faculties.—May I ask—does Mrs Allsop think as you do—at least, as you feel?—Have you the judgement of any third person competent to form an opinion of your circumstances—and is there no possibility of your going on, in whatever unambitious a way?—I conjure you, my dear friend! do not interpret this as implying any slowness on my part to do any thing, that I can, & which you imagine likely to serve you—but I can not keep off the question, that has been put to me—Are you *sure* that you are not aiding Allsop to do what he will repent of?—Before tomorrow's Post I will know, what Mr Gillman thinks—& you had better let me know, something more precisely, how I should state your *object*, the precise Spot, you have been thinking of, in short, the character of your views in respect to your establishment as a Colonist.[1] By half an hour's Question

---

[1] Allsop says of this letter that it 'was written just after the utter, and as then it seemed, the hopeless ruin of my prospects'. *Letters, Conversations and Rec.* 243.

and Answer by word of mouth I should learn more than from 20 letters, written in your present agitation.—May God bless you, and your little-able but most | sincere Friend

S. T. Coleridge

1661. *To Hyman Hurwitz*

Address: Hyman Hurwitz, Esqre | Grenada Cottage | Old Kent Road.
MS. University of Pennsylvania Lib. Hitherto unpublished fragment.
Postmark: 11 May 1829.

[11 May 1829]

I agree with you, as to the repetition of 'it'. Perhaps, the whole §§ph would stand better thus:[1]

The Work is, in the strictest sense of the words, elemental and introductory, having been intended for Students, who duly estimating the advantages to be derived from a knowlege of the Hebrew Language are as yet unacquainted even with it's rudiments. To facilitate the acquisition of the language by a methodical unfolding of it's constituent parts, by a simplification of it's rules, and above all, by enabling the Student to distinguish the syllables or syllabic attachments that express the *modifications* of things, and to understand the distinct import of each—in these words I have explained at once the object, and the plan of the work. It stands at the first entrance of the route, and offers it's services to the Traveller in the double Capacity of Pioneer and Guide.

I am well aware, that Publications, which might seem to supersede the necessity of the present, are already numerous and that Hebrew Grammars, Guides, Introductions &c, both English and Latin, may be procured without difficulty. But whether—

P. ii. l[ine] 7. Qy?—Nay, the very display of Learning, which distinguishes many of these works, unfits them for this, the peculiar purpose of the present Work. A multitude of Particulars crowded on the mind by no previous discipline prepared to receive or assert them, is only too likely to bewilder and dishearten a Beginner: and at all events must tend to divert his attention from the main object.

I tear open the letter to say, that the de[lay is not] my fault but the forgetfulness of the Servant.[2]

[1] Coleridge refers to Hurwitz's Preface to *The Elements of the Hebrew Language*, 1829. The rewording suggested in the next three paragraphs was not, however, adopted. The Preface is dated 1 June 1829, and possibly the suggestions arrived too late to be of use. See the last sentence of the present letter.
[2] This sentence is written on the address sheet.

1662. *To Mrs. Joshua Bates*

MS. Bibliothèque Municipale, Nantes. Pub. Letters Hitherto Uncollected, *51.*

Grove, Highgate
23 June 1829

My dear Madam

I do not know whether *our* beloved, and (with good reason *my*) *revered* no less than beloved, Friend, Mrs Gillman, intended by the color of this paper, which she has placed on my writing-table, to hint that she perceived, I had the *blue* devils—but most true it is, that I do feel my spirits more than ordinarily depressed by the necessity of declining your kind invitation. *Declining*? That was a very ill-chosen word. For in the very act of writing it I was struggling with the rebellious *in*clination to accept it at all risks— But Conscience in the shape (i.e. to my mind's eye) of a Mouse gnawing at the bone of my knee, with an accompaniment at my stomach, came to my aid—and like those who interfere to protect Russian Ladies from the chastisement of their angry Husbands, got small thanks from me for her pains.—In grave earnest, my dear Madam! it vexes me more than the loss of any gratification ought to vex a grey-headed Philosopher, that I *must* not shew by the gladness of my countenance to yourself and Mr Bates what I am now about to write—to wit, that with

sincere respect and regard | I am, my dear Madam, | Your and his
obliged | Friend & Servt

S. T. Coleridge

1663. *To Mrs. Gillman*

Address: Mrs Gillman
MS. British Museum. Hitherto unpublished.

Apud
Ædes Nemorosas, super
Altam Portam, Apollini,
Æsculapio et Egeriae
Sacras.—

[July 1829]

My dearest Friend

When or before you take leave of Mr Anster, impose on him the task—or as the Oxford and Cambridge Youths say—set him an *imposition*—to compose, before he goes back to his Law Books, & during his passage, a poem—long or short as his Muse may be in the humor, entitled—'My Visit to the Grove, Highgate, in July, 1829'.—

ESTEESY.

1664. *To John Anster*[1]

MS. Cornell University Lib. Pub. Some Letters of the Wordsworth Family, *ed. L. N. Broughton, 1942, p. 110.*

[July 1829]

You desire me to exclude from the consideration what can*not* be excluded from the thoughts of a friend, so warmly attached to both parties and by an especial tie bound to the Younger—I mean, by her unlimited confidence in my affectionate watchfulness as to whatever might involve her happiness and her habit of implicit reliance on my Judgement. Whatever may hereafter fall to her lot on the decease of those of whose Life she is the main treasure and endearment, and with the loss of whom it is impossible for her to connect hope, wish, or ground of future advantage, at present [Susan][2] has no independence—nor is likely for some years to possess it. On the other hand she has not only been wholly fenced round and weatherfended from all anxieties & discomforts, but is by her nature & constitution unfit to struggle with them. Now tho' your prospects, I ought not to doubt, are improved, because I find your own opinion respecting them has undergone a change, and has become more chearful—still, my dear Mr A., you would not place the well-being of one, you loved, and with her's your own peace of mind on a mere—I hope & I do not see any reason why I should fear, &c. I am the very last person to be an advocate for taking security against Providence, or who would approve of the scheme of those Lawyers, who resolve that they will not marry till they can place their wives at the head of a complete establishment—a scheme, that in more than one or two instances has ended by their marrying their mistresses, with the appendage of a family, they are & ought to be ashamed of. But the means of comfort, but resources adequate to the expences of the five or six first years of a married life, the continuance of which may be so far calculated on even by a prudent man of the world, and with a judgement unwarped by any immediate wish, as to place you out of the reach of all rational causes of anxiety—these, I must think, are an indispensable condition, when as in the present instance, both parties have from infancy lived in the habitual enjoyment of the comforts, the appearances and the modest elegancies of genteel middle life.

Enough, however, on this point I have already [written.] I could

---

[1] This letter was probably addressed to John Anster, who visited Highgate in July 1829. See preceding letter.

[2] This name is partly erased in MS. Susan Steel was the daughter of an old schoolfellow of Coleridge's.

not wholly leave it out of Consideration, because it would necessarily have to be considered—But having once stated, I will now look at the question, wholly separated from this point—or what is tantamount, I will suppose that there exist no difficulties or objections on the score of pecuniary provision—.

But even on this supposition, I should be guilty of insincerity, I should be dishonest to my own convictions and—it is my belief—that I should be misleading and flattering you, if I pretended not to see, that very serious difficulties and Objections remain behind—difficulties, that render the accomplishment of your wish improbable, and objections, that scarcely allow me, from a heart-felt interest in the happiness & welfare of both parties, to wish it success.

First—[Susan's][1] constitution is very far from strong—and tho' with a good understanding, the steadiest principles and the deepest sense of Duty—she does not possess the *strength* either of mind, body, or health, to bear up under any accumulation of domestic Afflictions. A short continuance of Grief, anxiety, or the derangement either of her own health or of her Husband's, would make her *nervous*—and assuredly, it is a good general maxim, that two persons predisposed to weakness or unsteadiness of nerves are not fitted to come together, relatively to the purposes and probable contingencies of the marriage Union, however amiable they may be, and however in all other respects suited to each other, and in sympathy.

Second—the great difference in your ages.[2] [Susan just past her 18th year.][3] The difference may not strike you so much at present, but look at it as it will probably appear twelve years hence. Further—and in close connection with this inequality in the ages, tho' not with this exclusively, a

Third—namely, that I am persuaded and with the strongest grounds for my belief, that [Susan's] Parents, and particularly her Mother, whose only child she is, would never be reconciled to the Match.—

Fourthly—It was but a few months ago, that a young Oxonian,[4] a year or two elder than [Susan], and who had grown up in almost brotherly intimacy with her from Childhood, began to pay such marked attentions to her, and gave such evident signs of a transition in the nature of his attachment to her, as [Susan] must have

---

[1] This name is inked out here and elsewhere in MS.

[2] Anster was 36 years old in 1829.

[3] Sentence in brackets inked out in MS.

[4] The 'young Oxonian' was James Gillman, Jr., who would have been 21 on 8 Aug. 1829.

noticed, or could not long remain without noticing—and from her long & familiar regard might not have decided on repelling.—The parties were not unsuitable—& the Union, I have some reason to know, would at a proper time be looked forward to, not without predilection, by Mr and Mrs [S.][1] But neither party had seen enough of the World, or knew enough of themselves or their own characters, to be able to give any proof to themselves, that they knew their own minds, or might not hereafter, either the one or the other, or perhaps both, meet with some object, which would make them feel, that the former attachment had been but a creature of the fancy, like Romeo's for Rosalind [*sic*] before he saw Juliet.—[MS. breaks off thus.]

1665. *To James Gillman, Jr.*[2]

MS. *Cornell University Lib. Pub.* Saturday Review of Literature, *29 August 1942.*

[July 1829 ?][3]

It is too often the case, that a Young Man must more or less expressly declare—at least, signify—his intention of paying his serious addresses to a Young Lady, in order to have that degree of neighborly intimacy which is necessary or requisite for a true knowlege of her character. Or to convey the same truth more generally, it often happens, that two young persons must to a certain extent, (and so far at least, as to make a retreat difficult without wounding the delicacy of one or both parties) pre-engage themselves in order to possess the opportunities of studying each other's principles, habits, tempers, and of thus ascertaining their fitness for each other, in a point of such transcendent importance, as a union for life, a union of will, mind and body, in weal and woe, in sickness and health, thro' good report and evil report—in short, a combination of two individuals of different sexes into one moral and spiritual Person. Tho' to the corruptly sensitive ears of modern

---

[1] Inked out in MS.

[2] This fragment was intended for James Gillman, Jr. On 10 Jan. 1832 Coleridge wrote to him and Susan Steel concerning their betrothal.

In publishing this letter in the *Saturday Review of Literature*, Mr. George S. Hellman accompanied it with an introduction filled with false assumptions and entitled his article 'Coleridge on Trial Marriages'. Nothing could be more ridiculous than the suggestion that Coleridge advocated trial marriages, nor does the present letter contain even a hint of such a proposal.

[3] The 'Charles Y', aged 20 or 21, and 'Mary Z', aged 18 or 19, mentioned at the end of this letter were James Gillman and Susan Steel. Coleridge's comment on their ages here and in the preceding letter suggests that the two letters were written about the same time.

Manners the words may sound *coarse*, nevertheless most impressive and pregnant is the language, in which the Almighty first commanded and consecrated the Institution of Marriage—Therefore shall a Man leave his Father and his Mother, and cleave unto his wife: *and they shall be one Flesh.*[1] Contemplate a mother with her infant sleeping at her bosom and within her arms, & bending her eyes on it's countenance—sympathize with the feelings, which prompt that gentle pressure wherewith she brings the touching Babe yet closer to her heart—and you will be at no loss to interpret or understand the force & import of the concluding words. And remember too, that Marriage was instituted in Paradise, and previously to the FALL: in order to shew us that tho' it has been since mercifully made to serve as a remedy and consolation for our infirmities, yet the *origin* of Marriage, and it's primary most essential ends, purposes and benefits, must be sought for in the best, noblest and most god-like qualities and properties of our Humanity. It was the Image of GOD, which the first Lovers beheld and became enamoured of in each other. What but misery and discomfort can be expected, when a union so intimate has begun and been completed in passion, or caprice, or error from imperfect knowlege!—

Surely, therefore, when the circumstances are such as to supersede the only motive & plausible pretext for any premature engagements, whether express or implicit, that tend to foreclose or entangle the independence and freedom of choice in either party before they have the experience or the judgement requisite for forming a probable and well-grounded conclusion respecting their future and permanent mind—we ought to be thankful for them and give proof to ourselves, that we are so, by acting accordingly. Now this is the case, where the Parties have grown up in habits of intimacy—where the Parents on both sides have been & are connected by friendship & habitual intercommunion—& their children have grown up in or in all but, brother and sister familiarity. To bring the thing nearer, we will imagine an individual case—a Charles Y and a Mary Z, for instance, who have known each other, from early childhood—and whose families remain in the same habits and feelings of Attachment and Intimacy—Charles 20 or 1 and 20, & Mary 18 or 19. And we will suppose that Charles during his first or second Vacation at Oxford or Cambridge begins to think, that Mary would make a good Wife [MS. breaks off thus.]

---

[1] Genesis ii. 24.

1666. *To William Sotheby*

Address: W. Sotheby, Esqre. | 13. Lower Grosvenor Street
MS. Mr. W. Hugh Peal. Pub. E. L. G. ii. 427.
Postmark: Highgate, 13 July 1829.

[13 July 1829]

My dear Sir

I thank you for your kind Present: and not, you may be assured, with the less warmth for the delicacy with which you have wove a *Veil* for your kindness out of a Compliment, sufficiently gratifying in itself.

> Per bel velo l'amico Guardo
> Più bel e più cortese
> Discioglie il sorriso.

And I remit my Son's acknowlegements by anticipation. I doubt not that your friendly words will germinate in the soil, to which you trusted them. But have you not mistaken Derwent for his elder Brother, Hartley?—The only uneasiness, I ever suffered on Derwent's account, was from some falsely called free-thinking Opinions, which he had *caught* at Cambridge in the society of Austin, Macaulay, and some others whose talents & superior acquirements were but too well fitted to render their infidelity infectious. But tho' the circumstance provoked me for the time, it did not give me any serious disquietude—for I felt sure, that it was not the true IMAGO of the PSYCHE, but only one of the Larvae that he would soon *slough*. And the event, thank God! has verified my presentiment.—Derwent has very fine talents; and a particularly fine sense of metrical music. His lyric *Fantasie* are among the most musical schemes or movements of Verse, that I have ever met with —in our later poetry at least. But he is confessedly not equal to Hartley in original conception and either depth or opulence of Intellect.—Poor dear Hartley!—He was hardly—nay, cruelly— used by the Oriel men—and it fell with a more crushing weight on him, that with all his defects Love had followed him like his Shadow—& still does—. If you can conceive, in connection with an excellent heart, sound religious principles, a mind constitu[ti]onally religious, and lastly, an active and powerful Intellect—if you can conceive, I say, in connection with all these, not a *mania*, not a *derangement*, but an *ideocy* of Will or rather of Volition—you will have formed a tolerably correct conception of Hartley Coleridge. Wordsworth says—I lament it; but have ceased to condemn him. —All this I have written *in confidence.*—What Queen Mary said, on the loss of our last Stronghold in France—that if her Heart were opened, Calais would be found written at the Core—I might

say of my poor dear Hartley.[1] I can never read Wordsworth's delightful Lines 'To H. C. at six years old' without a feeling of awe, blended with tenderer emotions—so prophetic were they!—

And now for pleasanter themes. I trust, that before I see you again, I shall have brought together as a part of my Critique some remarks on translation on the principle of Compensation, proportional to the differences in the Genius of the two Languages that will be worth your attention. But I cannot help repeating my wish, that you could find leisure to amuse yourself with trying the Achilleis of Statius. The interest of the Tale, the Novelty, the interesting criticisms, you might prefix, on the genius & characteristic traits of Statius—conspire to recommend it—& then it is a finished *Whole* of only two Books.—

Present my cordial & respectful remembrances to Mrs Sotheby, to your Daughters and to all of your Household—and wishing you fine weather, and safe horses, I remain,

my dear Sir, | with unfeigned regard | your obliged
S. T. Coleridge

P.S. Hartley is at present, I believe, at Edingburgh with Mr Wilson. It is possible, that he may fall in your way.

Lines in a Lady's Album

in answer to her Question respecting the Accomplishments most desirable in the Mistress or Governess of a Preparatory School.[2]

> O'er wayward Childhood would'st thou hold firm rule
> Yet sun thee in the light of happy faces,
> LOVE, HOPE and PATIENCE—these must be *thy* Graces
> And in thy own heart let them first keep school!
>
> For as old Atlas on his broad neck places
> Heaven's starry globe and there sustains it: so
> Do these bear up the little World below
> Of Education—PATIENCE, LOVE and HOPE.
> Methinks, I see them group'd in seemly shew,[3]

---

[1] In his will, dated 17 Sept. 1829, and in a codicil added on 2 July 1830, Coleridge made special provision for Hartley. (For Coleridge's will see Appendix A.)

[2] This poem was first published in *The Keepsake* for 1830. (See note to Letter 1669.) In *Poetical Works*, 1834, it is entitled *Love, Hope, and Patience in Education*. The sheet containing Coleridge's poem is no longer with the MS. letter. Both the poem and the letter were formerly in the collection of the late Colonel H. G. Sotheby.

[3] Methinks, I see them now, the triune group, 'Qy? a living group'. [Cancelled version of line 9.]

The[1] straiten'd Arms uprais'd, the[2] Palms aslope,
And Robes that touching as adown they flow[3]
Distinctly blend, like snow emboss'd on snow.

O part them never! If Hope prostrate lie,
   Love too will sink and die.
But Love is subtle and will proof derive
From her own life that Hope is yet alive.
And bending o'er, with soul-transfusing eyes,
And the low murmurs of the Mother Dove,
Wooes[4] back the fleeting spirit, and half-supplies:
Thus Love repays to Hope what Hope first gave to Love!

Yet haply there will come a weary day
   When overtask'd at length
Both LOVE and HOPE beneath the load give way.
Then with a Statue's Smile, a Statue's strength*
Stands the mute Sister PATIENCE, nothing loth,
And both supporting does the work of both.

        S. T. Coleridge

[1] With [Cancelled word in line above.]
[2] and [Cancelled word in line above.]
[3] Robe touching Robe beneath, and blending as they flow! [Cancelled version of line 11.]
[4] Echoes [Cancelled word in line above.]
* In the first copy the Lines stood thus:
  'Then like a Statue, with a Statue's Strength,
  'And with a Smile, the Sister-Fay of those   = Fairy
   'Who at meek Evening's Close
   'To teach our Grief repose
  'Their freshly-gather'd Store of Moonbeams wreathe
  'On Marble Lips, a CHANTRY has made breathe,
  'Stands the mute' &c—
but they were struck out by the Author, not because he thought them bad lines in themselves (quamvis Della Cruscam fortasse paullulò nimis redolere videantur) but because they diverted and retarded the stream of the Thought and injured the Organic Unity of the Composition. PIÙ NEL UNO is Francesco de Salez' brief and happy definition of the Beautiful: and the shorter the poem, the more indispensable is it, that the Più should not overlay the Uno, that the unity should be *evident*. But to sacrifice the *gratification*, the sting of *pleasure*, from a fine *passage* to the *satisfaction*, the sense of *Complacency* arising from the contemplation of a symmetrical *Whole*, is among the last Conquests atchieved by men of genial powers. S. T. C.

1667. *To Frederic M. Reynolds*

MS. Harvard College Lib. Hitherto unpublished.

[Late July 1829][1]

Dear Sir

I inclose the Remainder.[2] It was my original intention to have annexed as a sort of Post-script Super-conclusion from six to eight stanzas in the legendary, supernatural, imaginative style of popular superstition. But in the first place, the Tale or Lyrical Ballad is already *lengthier*, as Brother Jonathan says, than you wish—and to say the truth, the report, my friend Mr G. made of his Conversation with you, gave me a sickening feeling incompatible with the genial mood—A misunderstanding so easily settled, as that of the pecuniary honorarium, most assuredly would not have annoyed me sufficiently to have tempted me to retort the annoyance by complaining of it to you.[3] It would be quite enough that the Experience on both sides had converged to the same conclusion   —had convinced *You*, that my name & the contributions of my   Muse were not worth the money and trouble, expended on   them —and me, that the money thrice told would not compensate for the anxiety, and vexation of mind and body, which from the circumstance of the depressing and incapacitating derangement of my health, and my frequent Relapses,[4] the effort of composition, and still more and more injuriously the haunting consciousness, that my word had been engaged, and that (tho' Heaven knows! most

¹ This letter was written a few days before the one to Reynolds of 6 Aug. 1829.

² Coleridge was sending Reynolds the conclusion to his ballad, *Alice du Clos; or, The Forked Tongue.* After hearing the first part of it in 1828, Reynolds had selected the poem as one of Coleridge's contributions to *The Keepsake.* Later finding himself with a surplus quantity of material he omitted it from the 1829 *Keepsake* and published only *The Garden of Boccaccio* and eight of Coleridge's epigrams in that issue. See Letter 1651.

³ Although they had originally agreed to pay Coleridge £50 for contributions to the 1830 *Keepsake*, Heath and Reynolds were no longer willing to do so. Furthermore, since Coleridge's contributions to the 1829 *Keepsake* had fallen four pages short of the stipulated eleven pages, they expected him to make up the deficiency by finishing *Alice du Clos* and contributing it to the 1830 issue with no additional remuneration. Coleridge himself had offered no complaint. Gillman, however, approached Reynolds without Coleridge's knowledge and protested vigorously against the injustice of thus obtaining 'contributions for two years at the price which had been promised for *one*'. See Letter 1669. See also Letters 1634 and 1639.

⁴ On 15 July 1829 Mrs. Coleridge sent Poole the account of Coleridge's health which she had just received from Mrs. Gillman: 'He has been a great sufferer of late, and has rallied at intervals of short duration only: he has been obliged to keep much in his room, even at Meals, & for the present, has given up his thursday-eveng. parties.' *Minnow among Tritons*, ed. Stephen Potter, 1934, p. 146.

involuntarily) I had been the occasion of several disappointments, have cost me—not to mention, what yet is not only severely the truth but *less* than the truth, that I have incurred the loss of as large a sum by deferring one work, which required no genial moods for it's completion, & by giving up another when more than half-completed. This indeed is no concern of your's, nor forms even the shadow of a claim on you or the Proprietor of the Keep-sake—and if you cast your eye back, you will see that my argument does not imply any such thing. The purport is simply this—It is a rule of conduct with me, that when I have understood one thing, and the other Party declares that he meant a different thing, and I have no means of proving the contrary, I act on the presumption that I had misunderstood him, and let the matter drop, consoling myself with the inward resolve (oftener made, I am sorry to say, than kept) of being more cautious the next time.— But certain observations dropt from you, which do not permit me to remain silent. First, that Mr Hall payed me but 10£. Can you suppose, that I am so utterly destitute, on the one hand, or so ignorant of the trading concerns of literature, on the other, as to have exerted myself in so highly polished and elaborate a Composition, every paragraph of which, (I speak of the prose-portion) cost me more time more effort, more correcting touches and remoulding of sentences, than double the number of lines in the most successful Poems, I have yet produced—for the sake of 10£?[1] Or that I am so poor in affectionate friends, as that they should have suffered me to work at a price, which taken as task-work per day, would not have afforded me the needful daily food during the time? In one fourth of the time I could have written an Article for a Review or a Sheet for Blackwood, for at least double the Sum—No, Sir!— I wrote at the earnest solicitation of a friend of Mr Hall's, having been led to think of him as a very deserving Man, anxious to maintain himself during his studies for his ultimate Object, the Bar[2]—& most desirous to serve him. It was not for myself, that I accepted the Sum at all.—Next point.—From the words, used by you, it might very naturally have been inferred, that if I did not make application for admission into the rank of Contributors to the Keep-sake, that at least it was the sum offered that determined me. But surely, you cannot have forgotten that I reluctantly

[1] Coleridge refers to *The Improvisatore*, which was published in *The Amulet* for 1828. While Hall paid only £10, in tattling to Reynolds he neglected to mention that Coleridge had originally been promised £20 for this composition and 'a few things in verse and prose'. See Letter 1596.

[2] Coleridge had met S. C. Hall through Edwin Atherstone. Although Hall began the study of law in 1824, he was not admitted to the bar until 1841 and did not follow a legal career.

acceded, & more than once expressly told you, that it was Mr Wordsworth's request, grounded on the circumstance that both he and Mr Southey had engaged to contribute, which (in addition to the morbid facility of my mind) alone decided me. Nor has the State of my Health been ever concealed from you—.

One other point you must permit me to notice. That you might have mentioned 11 pages, as the utmost you wished, or rather that your space would permit you to insert, I do not doubt. Tho' it had escaped from my mind when it was first mentioned to me, yet now I seem to recollect it. But most distinctly do I remember your after assurances, that it was not the number of pages, you wished me to think about—that 150 lines, or less, with two or three short poems, would best answer your purpose—on the supposition, that I gave you the best, that Nature had enabled me to give. I am not silly enough to expose my vanity to a Sneer by hazarding a comparison with other contemporary poets—but to compare my own with my own will scarc[ely] justify a charge of arrogance—and restricting my judgement to this point exclusively, I dare avow my belief, that I did produce, according to the Subject, the best within the productive power of my poetic Talent.—Had I been aware, that the eleven pages, that a given *quantity*, were to be exacted (which from your language it was scarcely possible that I should), I had verses enough by me, which I should not have been ashamed to let stand among the annual flowers of my Contemporaries, to have compleated the bargain without further trouble, or anxiety.—At the close of the last year I was offered 50£ for any one poem, tho' but a 'Sonnet', I might chuse to write—& this accompanied with a request, that I would state what further sum I would accept, on the condition of writing exclusively for the work[1]—I communicated the circumstance to you. Your reply was—that Mr Heath, you were convinced, would either forego his claim on the continuance of my assistance; or take care that I should be no loser by declining the above offer. You promised to have an interview with him on this subject—. Some time afterward I again spoke to you, but you had not found an opportunity—and I think but am not certain, that I a third time introduced the circumstance— Whether this would amount to any claim on the point of honor, I would rather any other should Judge than myself.—This, however, is not the main object, or the purpose of this Letter. I know, that I deserve your respect and that my maxims & motives of Conduct and action would secure the respect of every honorable Man, who really knew me—And conscious that from the hour, we

---

[1] This offer was made by Watts of *The Literary Souvenir*. (See Letter 1651.) Coleridge again mentions it in his letter to Reynolds of 6 Aug. 1829.

first saw each other, to the moment, in which I wrote the last verse of the inclosed MSS, the pecuniary Result never exerted even a momentary influence on my will, I cannot without remonstrance allow myself to be talked of as a trader in Verse, who had been slaving for 10£, & ought to thank Heaven & Mr Heath & the Keepsake for better wages.

S. T. C.

P.S.—I understood you to say, that you would bring up the Proof, & take the remainder. Of course, I shall be anxious to have one as soon as possible—especially as there are some stanzas to be inserted.

1668. *To William Pickering*

Address: Mr Pickering | Bookseller | Chancery Lane | Holborn
MS. Cornell University Lib. Hitherto unpublished.

Wednesday [5 August 1829][1]

Dear Sir

I beg you ten thousand pardons—but to tell you the simple fact will perhaps be more to the purpose. I had just opened your Note, but not read it, when Mr Montague came in—& taking him aside (for I had some reason for wishing the transaction to be confined to his & our knowlege) I began with—'I have this moment opened a Letter from Mr P.'—O! O! I know it—quoth M.—I was with him this morning—& all is settled—Oh!—replied I—I was really in a little flutter—for in consequence of my illness, & the number & severity of my Relapses I should have been in some difficulty—& with this I put your letter in my pocket, & till your last note reached me, had never looked at it—. Well! I had not thrown it into the Fire—Sir Walter Scott, tho' a Poet & a most successful One, manages these matters somewhat more prosaically—i.e. with more sense & discretion—

I thank God, that I am now so much recovered, my Convalescence too having been gradual & regularly tho' slowly progressive, that I can look forward with confidence to the removal of my difficulties before the expiration of this date[2]—Be so good, as

[1] This letter is dated conjecturally on the basis of the following notation which appears in the MS. in an unknown handwriting:

August
3 Mths ~~April~~   4—31 2—
due Nov 7

For Coleridge's reminiscent account of his financial dealings with Pickering and Montagu see Letter 1748.

[2] i.e. 7 Nov. Letter 1679 shows, however, that on 17 Nov. 1829 Coleridge renewed the loan and agreed to pay it on 10 Feb. 1830. Early in 1829 Coleridge had received £30 from Pickering. See Letter 1653.

to send by our Errand Man, who will call at your house tomorrow afternoon, a Copy of the last Edition of my Poems, & to put it to my Account—and by the arrival of these I shall know, without need of any written intimation, that the accepted Bill has been received by you. Believe me, dear Sir,

with esteem & regard | Your obliged
S. T. Coleridge

1669. *To Frederic M. Reynolds*

Address: F. Mansel Reynolds, Esqre | Warren Street | *48?* or *38?* Tottenham Court Road.
MS. Harvard College Lib. Hitherto unpublished. An incomplete first draft of this letter is in the British Museum.
Postmark: Highgate, 6 August 18(29).

Dear Sir   [6 August 1829]

If the Subject, the *Money* Part at least, was to have been brought forward at all—as a matter of feeling, and not because I find any impropriety in it's happening otherwise, I would rather that what was to be said had been said to you by myself. First, because I had never spoken of the Subject, as far as I remember; but certainly not with that detail of the particulars, which if Mr Gillman had been put in possession of, he possibly might have thought himself bound, as my friend, and on my account, to (forgive me if I say that the phrase smacks of the High Way) '*demand* more money'—. That he put a question to you, that he intimated his opinion that I should not have been treated liberally if no additional remuneration were made, I learnt from himself. But I am quite sure, that he made no *demand*; and, I take for granted, that you did not mean me to understand the words literally.—

Let this pass. Something was said. And I repeat, that I would rather, it had come from myself—as more consistent with the frank and confiding tone in which I have hitherto on all occasions talked matters over with you; and lest there should appear any ground for the suspicion, that I could stoop to do indirectly what I had given myself the credit of having shrunk from doing on the score of an affected delicacy. But having—in justice to myself and because it is the truth—made this acknowlegement, I am equally or rather far more bound, alike in truth, honor and justice, to protest altâ voce against the term '*officious*' as at all applicable to this interference on the part of Mr Gillman—whose tried and (in how many ways!) proved Affection, unintermitted during a period of fourteen Years, whose active and more than *dis*interested Friendship I justly regard as more honorable to me than all the Laurels on Parnassus could have been, tho' Apollo himself had woven and presented the Wreaths. No one, who has more than a surface acquaintance either with him or me, is ignorant that my Interests have at all times been as dear to him as his own, and in fact more anxiously looked after: and that no two Brothers living under the same Roof could have a more legitimate or more admitted Right to act as Proxy, either for the other.

If therefore Mr Gillman's Question, or Suggestion can be deemed officious, it must be on the supposition, that any such expectation or wish on my part, and as intimated by myself, would have been palpably unreasonable—and so devoid of all decent pretext, that even the partial Judgement of an old friend could scarcely demur to it's being cited as proof either of a grasping and greedy Disposition or of a most unconscionable Self-conceit. Now this I deny *in toto*—and now affirm that, whatever motives, or rather *moods*, might have prevented me from preferring the claim, *yet in honor and equity a Claim I had and have*. And in explaining to you why I think so, I will not at present say what yet a *friend* of mine might be excused for intimating—that *my* Name and the Poems in the last Year's Keep-sake were as well worth the money received as the same number of pages in any part of the Volume for which an equal Sum had been given. Nor will I now urge, tho' it is the fact, that I fully understood the agreement respecting the *eleven* pages, on which even at the first, and (as far as I can remember) the only time, it was mentioned, you layed no stress, to have been rescinded by your After-assurances.[1] As being the *fact* therefore, and not as *argument*, I say that without the shadow of a doubt on my mind I had taken for granted, that I was to receive the same Sum for the continuance of my efforts, as a Contributor, for the present year—only that I was under a tie of honor so to continue them, which I should not have been if I had furnished a few pages more—or rather (N.B.) if I had not given way to your preference of an unfinished Poem,[2] and had persisted in selecting for my contribution the Poems that I had offered, and read to you, and which in point of composition I judge equal to any thing, I have yet been able to produce. (I could add, that something more than this had been expressed by no ordinary judge of poetry, John Hookham Frere. But I speak now only, as my own conscience is concerned—and this must depend on what was my own Judgement.) In short, till the

[1] In 1828 Reynolds had assured Coleridge 'with expressions of the most courteous kind, that half the number of Pages of such quality would have left them my Debtor'. See Letter 1638.

[2] The rough draft of this letter in the British Museum contains the following sentence concerning *Alice du Clos*: 'But you preferred waiting for the contingency of the Legend being finished, of which you heard the first part.'

afflicting inroads on my Health, I neither felt nor affected to entertain the least doubt, that if in aught there was a minus in the first year, it would be so made up in the next, that I should not (*comparatively*, I mean) have been overpayed by 100£ for both.

You know yourself, dear Sir! and you edit the Work on the conviction, that it is the NAMES, singly & collectively, that you are to calculate on, not less than the Contributions even in their intrinsic comparative Worth—and much more than the quantity contributed by the Name-owner. And can it then be deemed *officiousness* in a friend of mine, that he expressed his discontent at your having obtained my Name & contributions for two years at the price which had been promised for *one*?

Now had there been no other grounds for my friend's View of the Case, even these would, in my opinion, have been entitled to the consideration of a man who professes to act with the liberality, which I had been led to suppose (and I have no disposition to think the contrary) that Mr Heath does. But these are *not* the grounds, on which I choose to rest a claim. For they imply an appeal to honor, and might seem like an appeal to liberality: and without the remotest intention of imputing to the present parties a deficiency in either, still it is a maxim with me, that where there is any necessity for *urging* a claim at all, it should be urged on grounds of common justice exclusively. And this I hold to be the case with the following.

Had I not acted in the full reliance that you had as little intention to make a trading bargain as myself, had I acted on any other feeling than an anxiety to do my best for the Keep-sake, & God knows! chiefly from my estimation of your manner of conducting it & your courtesy toward me, what was to have prevented me from returning 25£—not that it would have been altogether equitable that I should deduct so large a sum, as the smaller number of pages was for your own convenience—even to the striking out of a part that was sent—and tho' the deficiency in the number was the effect of your own choice—for Poems of at least as great merit (observe, I speak only, as comparing my own with my own) were at your command, & had been offered to you—and thirdly, it would have been but fair that my Name should have counted for something. I have not exposed myself to the risk of a Sneer by implying, that the value of the Name rests on any real poetic merits of it's owner. But I dare not even suspect you of the gross insincerity, with which you must have expressed yourself, if you were not impressed with the belief that my Name would be of some *use* to the Work.—What, I say, was to have prevented me from returning the 20 or 25£—when I have evidence to prove that I had only to transcribe a few pages or suffer them to be transcribed, to have received 50£ unconditionally—and if I would engage to confine my contributions to that Publication, a larger sum would have been at my acceptance.[1] What was to have prevented me? Rather let me ask you, could I have been such a *dolt* (had I learnt that the 50£ from Mr Heath was to have included two years, and that I had been under a delusion) as to have hesitated in paying back the proportion of the deficient quantity, in case Mr Heath had refused me any indemnification? On no other ground could he have been the Loser by this step, than on the one that would at the same time have established the equity of my claim—namely, his belief that my Name & the four or five Pieces contributed by me had been of use to the Keep-sake of 1828—and that the continuance of the like would be of service to that of 1829.[2]

And again I repeat, that the facts were related to you by me, and that I received and relied on your Assurance, that Mr Heath would either forego his claim on my Assistance or not suffer me to be a loser by continuing it. Accordingly, I have returned a negative to every solicitation that has been made me from other quarters. On these grounds I believe, and see nothing that should withhold me from declaring, that in all equity & justice I have a claim—tho' this conviction would not probably have extorted this setting forth of the *same*. But thinking as I do, if without vehement *recalcitration* I had permitted the term 'officious' (in any other than the primary sense of the word—i.e. zealous in the performance of the duties & services of a Friend or Relative) to be applied to a man whom Charles Lamb in one of his printed Essays has rightly characterized as my 'more than friend', I should be unworthy not only of Mr Gillman's Friendship but of any honorable Man's Acquaintance—unworthy to subscribe myself as notwithstanding this sudden *fog* I can with sincerity do, your's with every friendly wish

S. T. Coleridge.

P.S. I had well-nigh forgotten the business part of your letter.[3]

---

[1] Coleridge refers to the terms proposed in 1828 by Watts of the *Literary Souvenir*. (See Letter 1651.) In the MS. copy in the British Museum the sentence above reads: 'But supposing that you or Mr Heath had taken 20 or 5 & 20£ back from me, I have evidence to prove, that I had only to transcribe or suffer to be transcribed a few pages of my MSS to have received 50£ instead—if I would have added another poem, & bound myself to confine my contributions to that publication, a larger sum would have been at my acceptance—and of this I informed you—& you saw it at the time in the same light.'

[2] A reference to *The Keepsake* for 1829 and for 1830. The volumes, however, were printed and ready for distribution late in 1828 and 1829.

[3] The MS. draft in the British Museum breaks off with the words, 'And now for your proposal'.

I will tell you with open heart what I should *like*—that is, that you would accept for Mr Heath any portion of the 50£ not exceeding the half—& let me have back the MSS—. Other Poems I cannot say that I have not—for there are two or three; but one of them would require an introductory half page of prose—of another of about [a] hundred lines, an epigrammatic & (intended to be) comic narrative I have mislaid the concluding page—but let me write to you as I would talk.—I am not so foolish as to think the worse of any one for differing from me in matters of taste—nor when the difference is confined to Taste do I *feel* the less kindly or *like* the person the less. It often happens (& I rather think that it is the case between you & me) that tho' the person does not agree with *my* tastes, I can heartily sympathize with *his*. But where my highest aspirations or deepest feelings have been called forth in any production, I cannot but feel a sort of shrinking back from delivering them to a man of a different Taste & Judgement—better & saner possibly—but who would perhaps yawn or laugh at them—but this feeling becomes truly oppressive, when that person is in a *responsible* office, & I have any apprehension, that he might regard the contributions as a dead weight or (as the editorial phrase is) a *wet blanket* on the popularity of the Work, for the compilation of which he—& not I—must stand responsible. Besides, I had from the first planning of the Ballad conceived & intended what struck me as a highly lyrical & impressive conclusion—intimating the fate & punishment of Julian & the Traitor[1]—and tho' every thought & image is present to my mind, I have not, in the existing state of my feelings, the power of bringing them forth in the requisite force & fire of diction & metre. For Poetry (if any thing, I write, can deserve that name) is not a matter of will or choice with me. The *sickish* Feel, that is sure to accompany the attempt to compose verses mechanically, by dint of the head alone, acts like a poison on my health.—If therefore by returning half the money the dispute can be closed, let me have back the MSS—& the Money shall be given you on the re-delivery—and let me have a line from you by return of post, if you can—at the latest, by Friday Night.[2]— But whatever may be determined, for Heaven's sake, do not let it be the ground or occasion of any quarrel or unkindly thoughts or words between us. But that I dared not shrink from what I felt a duty to a friend, believe me—that poor as I am, it is not 20 or 50£ that would have influenced me to write this letter.

S. T. C.

---

[1] The conclusion to *Alice du Clos* described here and in Letter 1667 was not added to the poem.

[2] The controversy seems to have been settled without any money being returned. Coleridge received the MS. of *Alice du Clos* and substituted two

1670. *To James Gillman, Jr.*

MS. Cornell University Lib. Pub. Some Letters of the Wordsworth Family, *ed. L. N. Broughton, 1942, p. 102.*

August 10th[1] [1829]

My dear James

It will give you pleasure, I know, to receive a Letter on English Paper, and in a hand that will at once bring the Grove, Highgate, before your eyes—& to learn, that your Father, Mother & Aunt Lucy, with myself and other et ceteras of the Household are, each in his or her line, pretty well—mine, of course, being the better-most sort of the poorly line. We hope, that you have had something that more nearly resembles summer weather, than the Rain and Wind have allowed us to boast of—and I on this presumption take for granted that you have enjoyed that rich golden gleam which distinguishes the surface of the soil at evening twilight in the neighborhood of the Rhine & I suppose of the Neckar no less—the effect, probably, of the thinner & dryer Air, & in part of the absence or paucity of inclosures—and that you have been struck, as I was, with the somewhat scratchy, motley, & fantastic but amusing appearance of the terrass Vines and miscellaneous culti-vation of the Mountain Sides towards the River—with the endless Castles, too like mice-excavated Stilton Cheeses when one's near enough to see the materials, of which they are constructed. The condition of the lower Orders in the small towns, and hamlets, the inferior comforts & countenances of the peasantry who derive their livelihood from the vineyards principally; and how much of the appearance of poverty in the German Cottagers is grounded in actual poverty, and how much from their indifference to those comforts and that *entireness* of clothing, which if an Englishman does not possess & make shew of, it is because he absolutely can-not. The faces of the children, and the more or less uprightness in the persons of the Females from 14 to 20 or more are safer criteria. I was particularly pleased, I may say, exhilarated by the contrast, which the inhabitants of Coblenz presented to all, I had seen from Cologne included. Indeed, Coblenz delighted me altogether— . . .[2] so enchanting a view as that of Coblenz & it's . . .[2] [appr]oach it

poems, *Song, ex improviso, on hearing a Song in praise of a Lady's Beauty,* and *The Poet's Answer, To a Lady's Question respecting the accomplishments most desirable in an Instructress of Children,* both of which first appeared in *The Keepsake* for 1830. *Alice du Clos* was first published in Coleridge's *Poetical Works* of 1834, but it was offered to *Blackwood's Magazine* on 20 Oct. 1829. See Letter 1677.

[1] The date, 'August 10th', is in Mrs. Gillman's handwriting.

[2] MS. mutilated by removal of the conclusion and signature on the verso of the page.

from Horchheim—seldom a Landskip so marked with a character
of it's own, from the growth of the tall trees &c—And my dear
young friend will understand my hint, when I say, that a few re-
marks, like the above, in his Letters from Germany, will *gratify his
Father.*—It is not, I am quite sure, that you have not both the eye,
that sees, and the heart that feels, as well as the Head that reflects;
but it has not been your habit, and for that reason, you do not
possess the facility, of projecting your notices into set words. But
tho' this be among the lesser & dispensable accomplishments, and
tho' the neglect of it is incomparably better than a heartless affec-
tation of picturesque ecstasies or diplomatico-statistic Knowing-
ness, yet it is advisable not to stand under *par*—& besides, it
would gratify your Father, to know that you do keep yourself
present to the present, with your faculties on the alert.—

The main thing, however, next to your health is your acquiring
a sound solid *foundation* for a thorough Knowlege of the German
Language—in order to a command over the treasures of historical
& critical Learning, packed up therein—which may be worth
thousands to you, hereafter. As to your classical Studies, I can only
recommend that lexicographical accuracy, and that facility in the
collation of parallel or explanatory passages, in which the German
Scholars excel.—Make my kind remembrances to Mrs Tobin—
Your friend, Miss Kelly, is now Mrs Lee, or as her German Friends
would call her, die Frau Doctorin. I leave the News to your Mother.
The only novelty on my mind is that your Father to my great
annoyance has cleared the Garden of the Nasturtiums, which
especially at twilight eve were the very delight of my Eyes. God
bless you, my dear James!—I look back on my first sojourn in
Germany & at a German University, as on a spot of sunshine in
my past life—Do you so employ your time as that you may say the
same hereafter. . . . [Conclusion and signature cut off.]

In all my sorrows & adversities, I have found my dear James,
that next to the pleasures of religion those arising from a Taste for
Literature are the most delightful. S. T. C.[1]

---

[1] This paragraph appears in Mrs. Gillman's handwriting at the top of page
one of the MS. and was obviously written by Coleridge on a portion of the
letter now no longer extant.

1671. *To J. H. Green*

Transcript Coleridge family. Hitherto unpublished.

Wednesday 12 Aug. 1829

My dear Friend

Suppose an absent man to have been moving the tips of his fingers round & round a small space of sunshine on a table or the like, & wholly unawares slides his hand under the focus of a Lens: the close neighbourhood, in which his hand had been playing about & about it, will but add to the vivacity of the sting—For the four last words substitute 'novelty of the Idea' and I shall perhaps have conveyed to you one small ingredient of the total impression left on my mind by your theory of the Beautiful & which has occupied my thoughts from the hour you left us on Sunday last. It certainly did give a greater liveliness to the pleasure which every fresh inspection and turning round of the Idea afforded me, that tho' for years I had been experimenting on this or that fractional part of the Beautiful I could not recollect even an approximation to the Idea itself, to what the sense & state of Beauty *is*—and consequently with this the solution of the facts, that this or that quality is commonly found in objects which we call beautiful. The only thought indeed that I can recollect which possibly *might* have led me to the true Idea (for that it is such I have not the least doubt) but which most certainly failed of so doing, was an anticipation and half perception that in the distinctities of the Godhead the Beautiful or Essential Beauty belonged to the SPIRIT, or the Indifference (Mesothesis) of Will and Mind in the form of celestial *Life*, and in accordance with this and no less a consequence or corollary of your view, 1. the Good (= the Holy one, the abysmal Will) is the *Absolute* Subject—2. the Father, = I am, the Subjective: 3. the word or Reason (δ $\dot{\alpha}\lambda\eta\theta\dot{\eta}s$) the Objective: 4. the Spirit, or Life = Love, the Subjective Objective. But tho' this did not lead me to the central Idea, (of which to the utmost of my Book-lore you are the Fons et origo) your Idea necessarily leads to this, and both explains and confirms it. And this is not unimportant if (as I am disposed to think) in the enumeration of the Faculties or Attributes co-present in the *state* of the *sense* of Beauty, it shall be found requisite to place a higher Life ($\zeta\omega\dot{\eta}$ $\dot{\alpha}\pi\alpha\theta\dot{\eta}s$, cupido caelestis or $\H{E}\rho\omega s$ δ $o\dot{\nu}\rho\dot{\alpha}\nu\iota\sigma s$) at the vertex of the line as the representative of the Will above Mind, as well as a lower life, at the Base, as the Exponent of Sensation, which must be assumed as present, tho' not in that degree in which it is an object of distinct consciousness, i.e. not *as a* Sensation but only as far as it is a necessary element in the attribution

of independent Reality to objects of sense. But if the novelty &
originality of your view have been one source of pleasure, still
greater satisfaction have I received from the circumstance, that
it is evidently a beautiful continuation & completion of the Idea so
fully evolved in the introduction to the first of your two con-
cluding lectures—on the distinctive character of the Human
organisms—It is delightful to find that the same principle, which
applied to the bodily organs and the functions, faculties and modes
of Act and Being appertaining to or resulting from them distin-
guishes Man from the Beasts, constitutes in another form that
capability, that exclusively human Sense, which more than any
other distinguishes Man from Man, Nation from Nation—

I feel perfectly assured that you have only to reproduce the
idea and fix your mind on it for a while to be convinced that I do
not over rate it's value and importance, and that whatever zest
my personal affections may have given to the pleasure [of] the
discovery, they have nothing to do with the substance of my satis-
faction. As soon as I had full possession of your meaning, my mind
seemed to have a promise of a new Resting-place—and the oftener
I have reflected on it and the more relations and points of view
I have examined it in, the clearer has the central & centrific charac-
ter of the Idea presented itself. The happy illustration of the centri-
petal and centrifugal, the Beautiful representing the former and
the different modifications in the several Fine Arts corresponding
to the latter, renders it even easy (i.e. for those to whom it is not
impossible) to unfold the Idea into a complete Theory of the Fine
Arts. At the same time it settles (and for the first time *satisfactorily*)
the controversy respecting Taste—for it explains the difference of
Tastes relatively to different objects even in men of equal culti-
vation, while yet it establishes the permanence of the ground of the
sense of the Beautiful, and the independence of Beauty on acci-
dental associations—i.e. distinguishes the Beautiful *in genere* from
the agreeable. It will therefore be a comparatively light task to
shew in detail in what qualities positive and negative and what
forms the fitness to excite the state and sense of the Beautiful
consists, both as to the several material objects universally called
beautiful, and as to those which all highly cultivated Minds have
held such—But this is not all—I shall be wofully mistaken, if it
will not be found to cast a new and important light on Psychology
generally and to afford a clearer insight into the true essence of
our great constituent powers—to the dispersion of the cloudy
creations of Gall and Spurzheim.[1] For no living balance or union
of communion can exist as the Mesothesis except by virtue of an

---

[1] Coleridge was reading Gall and Spurzheim in 1815. See Letter 987.

Identity as the prothesis. Not only in the whole circle of the Fine Arts but in practical Morals, it will have a most salutary influence to have it an admitted principle—that the Beautiful is the centripetal Power, which dare never be *out of Act* even under the boldest and apparently wildest centrifugations. Another useful corollary is, that the Beautiful is an *Idea*—the *spirit* of this or that object— but not the object in toto—as Beauty adequately realized. As you truly observed, it is the subjective in the form of the objective—a fortiori, not the objective in contradistinction from the Subjective. We behold our own light reflected from the object as light bestowed *by* it. The Beauty of the object consists in its fitness to reflect it— But I am called down—a party to day—the Chances, Col. Aspenwall &c &c—and another tomorrow—and Mice or the Devil's Imps are gnawing and nibbling within my right knee—Liver? Stomach? Kidneys? [Transcript breaks off thus.]

1672. *To Thomas H. Dunn*

Address: Mr Dunn | Chemist and Druggist | Highgate
MS. Historical Society of Pennsylvania. Pub. E. L. G. ii. 330.

[August 1829]¹

My dear Sir

I am almost wild with pain affecting the sciatic nerve, as if four and twenty Rats 'all in a row' from the right Hip to the Ancle Bone were gnawing away at me. Thank Heaven! it is without any nervous disturbance, pure *pain* and not that worse than pain, miserable Sensations. Nevertheless, it is so severe, and so continuous (remitting only for four or five hours in the evening, say from 4 to 10 or 11) that it has deprived me of sleep for the last two nights—and if this continues, I shall be worn out. I must therefore have recourse to an Anodyne—till I can see my friend, Mr Green, that is, till Monday or Tuesday. You will therefore greatly oblige me by sending by the Bearer a Scruple of the Acetate of Morphium, in the accompanying little Bottle, which I shall try, a grain at a time, every six hours, till the Pain is sufficiently lulled to permit me to have some Sleep.—It sometimes goes off, after a pause has been once obtained— . . .²

I will do myself the pleasure of calling on you and winding up my little account, as soon as this damp-begotten Vagrant, Rheumatism by name (for want of a better) shall have taken to his Heels,

¹ This letter was probably written in Aug. 1829 when Coleridge was suffering severe pain, particularly in his right knee. See Letters 1671 and 1673.
² Three and a half lines heavily inked out in MS.

like the fugitive Turn-key in Sir W. Scott's Rob Roy, and left the
Prison Door open for,

my dear Sir, | your obliged Friend
S. T. Coleridge.

1673. *To Derwent Coleridge*

Address: Revd Derwent Coleridge | Helston
MS. Victoria University Lib. Pub. E. L. G. ii. 429.

Grove, Highgate.
Friday Afternoon [28 August 1829][1]

My very dear Derwent
    As I understand that Mrs Gillman has within the last three or
four days written to dearest Mary, I may take for granted that
you will have received all the Highgate News—of which there may
have been half a Letter-full, tho' I happen to be ignorant of the
same. On Wednesday Henry called and passed an hour or more
with me, as a leave-taking previous to his departure for Ottery,
from which he is to proceed via Bristol, Birmingham, Liverpool
&c to Keswick. Sara, he tells me, gave in a letter, he had just
received from her a more than usually satisfactory account of her
Health, tho' no doubt, her Nervous system finds an apter symbol
in a group of Aspens in breeze & Sunshine, than in the Weeping
Willow over the unwrink[l]ed Pool at breathless Twilight (vide
Vignettes, and Drawings in Young Ladies' Albums *passim*). The
Mel Lunaticum (Lunare is the purer Latin, I believe) Temporis
and gentle Privacy of recent Bliss is to have the Public House—
the little romantic Inn, I should say, at Patterdale for it's locality.
—When I add, that I am slowly but yet regularly convalescing,
that my animal spirits have in great measure got rid of their in-
trusive Visitors & ragged Relations, black Bile and blue Devils,
and that I have little else of bodily grievance to complain, but
certain Mice that seem to have nested within my right Knee,
nibbling & gnawing as if the sinews & muscles had been made of
Toasted Cheese—tho' mere Pain compared with miserable Sensa-
tions seems such an *out of door* disturbance, as to be almost amusing
—I have exhausted all my stock of tidings.—
    Poor Lady Beaumont has left me a Legacy of 50£[2]—which I

---

[1] Henry Nelson Coleridge left London on Wednesday, 26 Aug. 1829, paid
a brief visit to Ottery, and arrived at Keswick on Tuesday, 1 Sept., two days
before his marriage to Sara Coleridge. The present letter, therefore, was
written on 28 Aug.

[2] Lady Beaumont died on 14 July 1829.

shall send to your Mother, to lay out, as she thinks needful, for
dear Hartley. Would to God! it had been twice ten times the sum.
Had Lord Liverpool's promise & intention been realized, I should
have made over half to your Mother—as indeed it is & ever has
been my wish & purpose, should I obtain aught, be it more or less,
beyond my mere means of living.—Mr Gillman mentioned to me
what Montague had said to you. From any other man on earth it
would have annoyed me sorely—but from dear Basil it whistles
by my ears like the Wind—& I trust & take for granted, that it
has no other importance in your's.—

Before Mr Sotheby left town, in a very kind & affectionate
manner he begged me to send some little Friendship-offering in his
name to you or your 'lovely Wife'—& gave me 10£ for that
purpose. Now I am inclined to think, that the said Note had better
go in propriâ personâ to dear Mary's Purse or Cash-box, and there
await her own sentence respecting it's destination. I have not men-
tioned this to the Gillmans—therefore when you write, or rather
when Mary answers Mrs Gillman's Letter, just let her say—Derwent
has received his Father's Letter.—I am in a degree very unusual
for me fidgetty to see and kiss my little Derwent[1]—& it has not
been without doleful looks & much grumbling that I resign myself
to the thought of deferring my intended Journey to Helston—
but while this pain in my knee & the lameness that accompanies it
are too clear warning of my liability to a Relapse, and that either
Stomach or Liver or both are not yet brought back to their due
functions, I cannot oppose the decision of Mr Gillman & Mr Green,
who both think, it would be an unwarrantable imprudence on my
part to hazard it.

Tell my dearest Mary that she has left a genial life on the whole
state of my thought and feelings, has shed in upon my spirit a
new light of Love, and Hope & cheerful Purposes, which I could
not have anticipated and for which, I trust, that God will bless the
thanksgiving, which I offer to him in my morning and evening
Prayers—& often too in the watches of the Night.—

May the Almighty continue his Blessings on Her & you &
your's!—

Your affectionate Father

S. T. Coleridge

---

[1] Derwent Moultrie Coleridge was born on 17 Oct. 1828.

1674. *To H. F. Cary*

Address: Revd. F. Carey | &c &c | British Museum   By Dr Wiss.
MS. Pierpont Morgan Lib. Hitherto unpublished.

[Endorsed Sepr 1829]

My dear Friend

The Bearer of this is Dr Wiss, by birth an Englishman, and a Professor in the German University of Heidelberg—introduced to us with very warm com- and recom- mendations from Mrs Tobin (my old Friend, James Tobin's Widow) now resident at Heidelberg, and from James Gillman, Junr.—And Dr Wiss appears to us all to deserve the high character given of him.—His object in his present short sojourn in this country is connected with the literary treasures of the British Museum—and he has earnestly sought an introduction to you, who, I am sure, will receive him kindly—because you are you—& not the less kindly, because it will gratify Mr and Mrs Gillman and your sincere and very affectionate Friend

S. T. Coleridge

P.S. Remember us most cordially to dear Mrs Carey—I have had one severe Relapse but am now steadily convalescent—God be praised for both!—I heard this morning the very best sermon the best delivered, I ever heard, from Archdeacon Bather. I wished you had been with us—.

1675. *To Hyman Hurwitz*

Address: Hyman Hurwitz, Esqre | &c &c | Granada Cottage | Old Kent Road
MS. University of Pennsylvania Lib. Hitherto unpublished.
Postmark: Highgate, 16 September 1829.

[16 September 1829]

My dear Sir!

This was left by mistake—perhaps, it is scarce worth 3 pence—but perhaps likewise you may miss it—& therefore I send it—adding my *Logical Pentad*, or Heptad, of *forms*—.[1]

Prothesis

i.e. the identity or co-inherence of Act and Being of which there is and there can be but one perfect Instance—viz. The Eternal

---

[1] Coleridge refers to the two paragraphs which are here printed after the postscript. They precede the letter in the MS. where they are followed by Coleridge's '*Logical Pentad*, or Heptad, of *forms*', here printed last.

Coleridge was assisting Hurwitz with *The Etymology and Syntax, in continuation of The Elements of the Hebrew Language*, 1831. The Preface to that work contains a quotation from the Preface to *Aids to Reflection* on words as 'LIVING POWERS'.

I AM, who *is* by his own *act*—who affirms himself to *be* in that he is; and who *is*, in that he *affirms* himself to be. But the Image & Representative of himself is the personal Identity, the 'I am' of every self-conscious Spirit. In Grammar, this unique Thought or rather Idea is expressed by the appropriate name of Verb Substantive—that which is both Verb and Noun at once & in the *same* relation. The polarizing of this gives the Thesis, the Noun, and the Antithesis, the Verb—(or vice versâ, for this is conventional) the *Indifference* of the two, namely, that which is *either* Noun or Verb; or both Noun and Verb, but each in a different relation, is the Mesothesis, the Infinitive Mood—The Synthesis or combination of the Noun & Verb, is appropriately named the Participle.—These are the *essential* Parts of Speech—which *must* be in every language of civilized man—To these add the modification of the Noun by the Verb, and you have the Adnoun or Adjective: and vice versâ the modification of the Verb by the Noun, and you have the Adverb. And these are *all* the Parts of Speech that *can* be in any Language. For Conjunctions and Prepositions are but one or other of the foregoing seven—most often Participle or Verb in the Imperative Mood. When such an abbreviated verb governs a *whole* sentence, it is called a conjunction; when a part only, a Preposition. Cases are *Pre*positions affixed and agglutinated to the nouns or adnouns, they govern.—God bless you &

Your sincere Friend

S. T. Coleridge

P.S. Just as I was sending off this letter, your's arrived.—

p. 3.—But it proceeds on a mistake, which we have sought to preclude in our definition of Language—namely, that words primarily correspond to *Things*. Consequently, these writers have not perceived that tho' the Things must have existed and in most instances have been seen, prior to their modes of appearance by moving, acting, or being acted on; yet by means of the latter are they first brought into notice, so as to become the distinct objects of human Consciousness—that is, *Thoughts*—and the words *immediately* refer to our *Thoughts* of the Things, as Images or generalized Conceptions, and only by a second reflection—to the Things in themselves.[1]—

10. And this is indeed the process of the human mind, when it begins to *reflect*. An impressive single instance is taken or rather obtrudes itself on the recollection—it is then discovered, that the properties or attributes noticed in this instance are common charac-

---

[1] This paragraph is printed with slight changes in *The Etymology and Syntax*, pp. 8–9.

ters to a large number of instances—and thus the individual impression is raised into a general or generic Conception; and the Word, by which it was named, becomes a general term—And general terms applied to the purposes of classification, for the aid and ordonnance of the memory, are technical terms—without which no art nor science can be taught.[1]

Prothesis[2]
Verb Substantive

Thesis	Mesothesis	Antithesis
Noun	Infinitive Mood	Verb

Synthesis
Participle

Mod. of Noun by Verb		Mod. of Verb by Noun
Adnoun		Adverb

Prothesis
Red

Thesis	Mesothesis	Antithesis
Yellow	Indecomponible	Blue
	Green	

Synthesis
Decomponible
Green

Mesothesis of Prothesis & Thesis	Mesothesis of Prothesis & Antithesis
Orange	Indigo

1676. *To Thomas Hurst*

Address: T. Hurst, Esqre | Highgate
MS. Liverpool Public Libraries. (Hugh Frederick Hornby Art Lib.) Hitherto unpublished.

Highgate
Septr 1829

Dear Sir

I inclose the Proofs and remaining MSS.—Having made a reference to an epistolary Essay on 'Another World that now is', and this reference being printed (See Appendix A.) and struck off—I have sent it, tho' if this had not been the case, I should probably

---

[1] This paragraph appears almost verbatim in *The Etymology and Syntax*, p. 23.
[2] Cf. *Aids to Reflection*, 1831, pp. 169–70 n., and *Notes, Theological, Political, and Miscellaneous. By Samuel Taylor Coleridge*, ed. Derwent Coleridge, 1853, pp. 401–5.

have hesitated.[1]—I have before me & needing little more than transcription, a Chapter that would amount to half a sheet, or more—with the title—What is to be done now ?—addressed principally to the Clergy of the Establishment—and which would certainly prove an interesting addition to the Volume and give an air of completeness to it.[2] But whether the Volume will not be larger, than you & Mr E. Chance would have recommended, even without this Chapter, I am doubtful—If your judgement is in favor of it's being added, it shall be sent with the next proofs.

My late severe visitations, with the frequency and suddenness of the Relapses, and the entire incapacitation which accompanies them, have made me form a Resolution never to send a Work to the Press till it has received my last Finish, and till some Friend has undertaken to revise and correct the Proofs for me. If I can contrive with honor to transfer my Aids to Reflection &c, my Nephew & now Son-in-law, Henry Nelson Coleridge, whose Chambers are in Lincoln's Inn Square, No. I., has undertaken to do this for me.[3]—For the past, I will not offer an apology for what I could not help—or if there were any fault or neglect, I have suffered more than the proportionate penance in the aggravation of my distressful sensations by the consciousness of your disappointment —Be assured that I am with very sincere esteem & regard your |

obliged

S. T. Coleridge

[1] On p. 150 of *The Church and State* Coleridge points to the Appendix in which this 'epistolary Essay' is printed. It was originally addressed as a letter to Edward Coleridge on 27 July 1826 (Letter 1537).

[2] Concerning the omission of this chapter Coleridge writes in the Advertisement prefixed to *The Church and State*:

> I had written a third part under the title of 'What is to be done now?' consisting of illustrations from the History of the English and Scottish Churches, of the consequences of the ignorance or contravention of the principles, which I have attempted to establish in the first part: and of practical deductions from these principles, addressed chiefly to the English clergy. But I felt the embers glowing under the white ashes; and on reflection, I have considered it more expedient that the contents of this small volume should be altogether in strict conformity with the title; that they should be, and profess to be, no more and no other than *Ideas* of the Constitution in Church and State.

[3] Henry Nelson Coleridge did assist Coleridge in preparing the second edition of *Aids to Reflection*, which was published by Hurst, Chance, and Company in 1831. See Letters 1700 and 1705.

1677. *To William Blackwood*

Pub. Annals of a Publishing House. William Blackwood and His Sons, *by M. Oliphant, 2 vols., 1897, i. 414.*

20th October 1829.

Dear Sir,—This is my birthday. But for the last fifteen or sixteen years I have (like most other men of the same date, I suspect) so lost the inclination to count the same from any Birth but that of our Lord that I am not sure whether it is the 57th or the 58th. This, however, I know, that for many years back, once or twice or thrice at least in every Twelvemonth, it has been (as the religious of the olden times were wont to phrase it) 'borne in on my mind' that I ought to write to you and thank you for your long-continued and very kind attention in sending me your Magazine. In a small volume on the right *Idea* of the Constitution in Church and State, which you will receive I think within a fortnight, and which but for severe sickness you would have received many months ago, you will find how highly I estimate the favour. I never intentionally flattered, and I am now old enough to measure my words, and in sober earnest I can say, that the spirit with which it is supported excites not only my admiration but my wonder.[1] I see but one rock the Magazine is likely to strike on: the (only however of late) increasing proportion of space allotted to party politics, and especially to political economy. I persuade myself that you will pardon my frankness when I declare my opinion that the Essays on the subject last-named, though written with great spirit, like everything else in the Magazine, are not in point of reasoning or breadth and depth of information equal to the political articles. By my little volume you will see that I am as little an admirer or convert of Ricardo and M'Culloch[2] as your correspondent.[3] But

---

[1] See *The Church and State*, 147 n. In his letter to Blackwood of 15 May 1830 Coleridge refers again to this 'public avowal' of his 'admiration' for *Blackwood's Magazine*.

[2] J. R. McCulloch (1789–1864), statistician and political economist, held the chair of political economy in the newly founded University of London from 1828 to 1832. His *Principles of Political Economy* was first published in 1825.

[3] See the following passage from *The Church and State*, pp. 229–30:

Take the science of Political Economy—no two Professors understand each other—and often have I been present where the subject has been discussed in a room full of merchants and manufacturers, sensible and well-informed men: and the conversation has ended in a confession, that the matter was beyond their comprehension. And yet the science professes to give light on Rents, Taxes, Income, Capital, the Principles of Trade, Commerce, Agriculture, on Wealth, and the ways of acquiring and increasing it, in short on all that most passionately excites and interests the Toutoscosmos men. But it was avowed, that to arrive at any understanding of these matters requires a

my opinion of the quality of the literary or economical articles forms no part of my objection. It is only the quantity, the relative proportion, and this again only as a subject of apprehension for the future rather than of complaint for the past. For Blackwood and Sir Walter's novels have been my comforters in many a sleepless night when I should but for them have been comfortless. I assure you that were I a man in easy circumstances I should need no pecuniary motive to be a frequent contributor, and the liberal terms you offered me might well be thought to supply that motive, my circumstances being what, alas! they are. But the fact is that, from whatever cause, it is out of my power to write anything for the press, except with the full effort of my mind, or to send off anything that is not the *best* I can make it. The consequence is that I compose and write three pages for every one that goes to the Printer, so that I could very well afford to *give* the Publisher all that I send, if he would pay me for all that, though written with the same care and effort, I keep behind.

But before I proceed, let me ask you one question occasioned by the L'envoy of your last number respecting the plethora of 'Maga.' Are your existing stores so abundant as to supersede the wish for any contributions at present? Do not, I entreat you, my dear sir, imagine that I shall be wounded by your frankly telling me so, if so it be.

I speak now therefore only on the supposition that a certain number of articles with my name would be, if not serviceable, at least acceptable. I have at present—first: and this I dare avow that I should send in confident anticipation of its receiving the admirable Christopher's suffrage as original, amusing, and suited to the spirit of the Magazine—a critique expository and vindicatory of Francis Rabelais' great work. 2. Ditto on the Don Quixote. The first is divided into three chapters, each of which, so far as I can calculate, will supply about a third of one of your sheets. 3. An article entitled, A Sequel to the Catholic Bill and the Free Trade measure, or What is to be done now? 4. A Lyrical Tale, 250 lines. 5. Three or four other poems, altogether about the same number of lines. If I did not think them creditable to me, or if my Friends thought otherwise, I would not offer them to you.[1]

mind gigantic in its comprehension, and microscopic in its accuracy of detail.
This passage also appears in Letter 1537.

[1] None of these proposed contributions was published in *Blackwood's Magazine*. The 'Lyrical Tale' was *Alice du Clos*. Possibly in anticipation of receiving a contribution from Coleridge, Blackwood sent him an order for £10. On 15 May 1830 Coleridge reported to Blackwood that he had destroyed the order, 'it being against one of my rules to receive payment for work not delivered'.

1678. *To Unknown Correspondent*

Pub. The Gillmans of Highgate, *by A. W. Gillman, 1895, p. 20 A.*

October 20th, 1829.

Of our fellow men we are bound to judge comparatively—of ourselves only, by the *ideal*. Now verily, judging comparatively I never did know the Master and Mistress of a Household, and the Household in consequence so estimable and so amiable as the Gillmans'! The general Hospitality, without the least *self*-indulgence, or *self*-respecting expenses, compared with their income; the respectability and even elegance of all the appearances; the *centrality* to whatever is good and love-worthy in the whole neighbourhood, old and young; the attachment and cheerfulness of the servants, and the innocence and high tone of principle which reign throughout, would really be a very unusual combination, even though Mrs. Gillman herself had been a less finely natured and lady-like Being than she is. Would to God that I had Health and Opportunity to add 5 or 6 hundred a year to remove all anxious thoughts,—and that I could but render it possible and advisable for dear Mr. Gillman to have a two months' tour whither he liked every year! God bless them!

S. T. C.

1679. *To William Pickering*

MS. New York Public Lib. Pub. E. L. G. ii. 431.

17 Novr 1829—

Dear Sir

I am so unversed in Bill Matters, that I must wait, till Thursday Evening, & then If I have not done all that I am to day [do?] at present, I will send the remainder by Mr Montagu—. At all events the Money shall be ready by the 10th of Feby.—I had been (unintentionally) misled, or it should have been taken up before—.[1] But I am anxious to keep this business to ourselves—and Letters by the *Post* are not always the safest Means—so few secrets have I, and therefore not in the habit of objecting to the letters for me being opened when I chance not to be at home at their arrival—

Your's, dear Sir, sincerely

S. T. Coleridge

[1] See Letters 1653, 1668, and 1748.

1680. *To Derwent Coleridge*

MS. Victoria University Lib. Hitherto unpublished. This letter is written in the fly-leaf of a copy of Hyman Hurwitz's *The Elements of the Hebrew Language,* 1829. The volume is inscribed 'To S. T. Coleridge Esqr with the Author's Compts'.

20 something Novr
1829.

I have had no sleep, at least but an hour and a half, for two nights—thro' torture of symptomatic Rheumatism accompanied with oppression of Spirits worse than the pain, (tho' that is more than I have fortitude to bear). It seems to alternate with the appearance of the Erysipelas on the right Leg—. I am so weak, I really cannot write—which I will do when a little better. Lord Lyndhurst's letter was a kind one—I shall send him my Book on the Constitution with a letter[1]—Heart-felt Love to Mary & the dear Boy. Shall I yet be permitted to kiss him?

S. T. Coleridge—

1681. *To Thomas Hurst*

Address: Thomas Hurst, Esqre | Bank | Highgate
MS. Mr. Robert H. Taylor. Pub. with omis. Letters Hitherto Uncollected, *53.*

Friday Night
5th (?) [4] Decr 1829
Grove
Highgate—

Dear Sir

A proof Slip appertaining to some other Knight of the Press has been sent by mistake—which I have here re-inclosed.—

As to my own, there will be no need of the Printer's sending me any further proofs—if only you will be so good as to see that the additional sentence, with which the Advertisement is to conclude, is correctly printed.

I have been very grievously afflicted by a sort of rheumatic fever, affecting principally the right side and the whole half of the Back Lengthways—the more grievous, that the paroxysms have come on, about midnight, & rendered it impracticable to lie down or even to sit still for many minutes together, till 7 or 8 in the morning. —But for two or three hours before the fit, there comes on an indescribable depression of Spirits, which my Reason finds it difficult

---

[1] The copy of *The Church and State* sent to Lord Lyndhurst is now in the Huntington Library. It is inscribed, 'To Lord Lyndhurst &c &c this Work is respectfully submitted by the Author, S. T. Coleridge'.

to over-rule, and impossible to prevent or remove—& after the fit, my whole Back feels hot and sore, as a Bruise.—But the Weather is sadly against me: & I can only pray, for myself and for all— May God either proportion the Sufferings to the Strength, or grant strength in proportion to the Sufferings. His Will be done!—Amen.—

Accept assurances of sincere | respect and regard from your | obliged

S. T. Coleridge

1682. *To Thomas Hurst*

Address: Thomas Hurst, Esqre | Bank | Highgate
MS. Harvard College Lib. Hitherto unpublished.

6 December 1829
Grove
Highgate

Dear Sir

I have a particular reason for being desirous to have a copy of my work, respectably bound & bound with one or two blank leaves at the beginning, as soon as possible.—I want it for a presentation Copy to a GREAT Man.[1]—Two or three other Copies will suffice for any *private* wishes of mine—but I think, I could direct 4 or 5 to persons, who might be effectually influencive on the 'Reading Public'.—

I have endeavored, and I believe successfully, to make such arrangements that in case of your consenting to be my Publisher for my future works you and your Printer would be secured from any delays & interruptions occasioned by the precarious Nature of my Health—as well with regard to the Mss as to the correction of the Proofs. But on this subject I will solicit a personal interview with you (if God prolong my life) shortly.

From the knowlege of the interest, I have felt in your trials and efforts, and the good wishes with which I have followed & still follow your journey thro' this Vale of Probation, I do not hesitate to infer that you will be pleased to hear that my health has been amending, and that I have to thank the Giver of all Good gifts for a suspension of my severer bodily Sufferings and for an alleviation of those that still remain.

With kind respects to Mrs Hurst be assured, Dear Sir, that I am
Sincerely your obliged

S. T. Coleridge

[1] Although the first edition of *The Church and State* bears the date 1830 on the title-page, according to the *English Catalogue of Books* the work actually appeared in Dec. 1829. The 'GREAT Man' was probably Lord Lyndhurst. See Letter 1680.

1683. *To Henry Nelson Coleridge*

Address: H. N. Coleridge, Esqre | 12 Bernard Street | Russel Square
MS. Victoria University Lib. Hitherto unpublished.
Postmark: 6 January 1830.

1830.—Jany—[6]

My dear Henry

I thank you for your kind letter—and am quite content to receive your 'plusquam' as an indemnification for the minus quam in other quarters. But I am particularly pleased with my Neighbor, Kinderley's attention. It was barely five days before I last saw you, that I first spoke to *him* (for long ago I had talked in a half jesting way with *Mrs* Domville)[1]—'You know,' (I said) 'that I not only would not *ask*, but that I would not even *wish*, aught that is not consistent with strict propriety on your part—But under this proviso, should it lie in your way to serve a young Chancery Barrister of acknowleged superior talents, you will not be the less willing from the recollection that H.N.C. &c is my Daughter's Husband.'—He took me by the hand, and very kindly whispered— Say no more. Be assured, I will not forget it.—A few hours afterward, he asked Mr Gillman who happened to have called professionally in consequence of a Slip in the frozen Snow by Mrs K., your address—and made his Son take a Note of it.—But I have every reason to think, that both Mr K. and Mr D. would be pleased with any opportunity of evincing a friendly feeling towards me: and at least *equal* grounds for believing, that even without reference to myself Sara stands so very high in their good opinion, and is so great a favorite with both the Families, that any thing, in which her feelings and interests were concerned, would be furthered gladly—the means being presented. I should imagine that Mr George Frere might, if the inclination existed, serve you. I will, at least, *sound* him—unless you see cause ad contra. Without puff and connections few men *begin* a reputation—tho' by talents and industry only it can be sustained and ripened.—

I quite agree with you, that half a guinea is a *choking* price—of the *policy* of it I am not competent to judge; but of the sufficiency of the reason assigned for it by Messrs. Hurst and Chance to warrant it's *honesty* I am somewhat scrupulous—Videlicet, that I had made unusually many corrections &c that increased the expence, and that *they* had only thought fit to *print* a *very* small edition—I believe, not 300.—Now *this* does to my simple mind look very like levying an *impost* on the regard and good predisposi-

---

[1] Mrs. Domville was the daughter-in-law of Sir William Domville (1742–1833), lord mayor of London 1813–14.

tion of the Author's personal or *Author*ial Friends—It is one way, no doubt, of preventing loss, and in the present case of precluding even *risk*, on the part of the *Publishers*.

In the hope, a more sanguine temper might have made it expectation, of a second Edition, I have already prepared a Copy for the Press, in which I have reduced the Work into CHAPTERS, with a *Head* to each, stating the Contents—with a small number of insertions, and not a small number of emendations. And I shall carefully attend to your suggestions.—I have not yet been able to make up my mind whether, or no, in case of a second Edition, I should add a third Part, under the title—*What is to be done now?* The materials are before me—and in part brought into publishable form.[1] But then there ought to be a number of Copies printed separately, for the Purchasers of the first Edition—& whether the Publishers will like this, is a question—

Of James I will only say, that his Father and Mother appreciate your kindness. But I will talk with you on the subject. I would not at present wish to place any additional weights in either scale; and least in that of the Law—accord[ing to] my estimation of James's strength of Constitution—And yet, had I not had convincing experience that what he feels to be his Duty, he will make himself do, & thus gradually mould himself into, I should not be so much an Advocate as I on the whole am, for his entering under the mild yoke of the Clerical Profession. But of some particulars as to *contingencies* hereafter.—

My Stomach and Bowels, I am sorry to say, are in a very irritable state—& I have much to do to stave off that miserable Depression—

Give my fondest love to Sara—& may God bless you both.

                                                    S. T. Coleridge.

1684. *To J. H. Green*

Address: J. H. Green, Esqre. | 46 Lincoln's Inn Fields
MS. Pierpont Morgan Lib. Hitherto unpublished.
Postmark: 12 February 1830.

                                    Friday Morning. [12 February 1830]
My dear Friend

I am haunted by fatalities. Last week in order to get rid in a courteous manner of Mr Whitehead's Manuscript Poem[2] and of his

---

[1] The second edition of *The Church and State* was issued before May 1830. (See Letter 1691.) As Coleridge says, emendations and insertions were made in the text and the work was divided into chapters. The proposed third part, '*What is to be done now?*', which he had thought of adding to the first edition, was again not included. See Letter 1676 and note.

[2] Charles Whitehead (1804–62), poet, novelist, and dramatist, published *The Solitary* in 1831.

Brother who had repeated his call I explained to him the impracti-
cability of conveying to any useful purpose my grounds for approv-
ing *this* and disapproving *that*, and generally for dissuading his
Brother from publishing it in it's present state by letter, without
a sacrifice of time which it was not in my power morally or circum-
stantially to make—but that if on the return of more genial weather
he thought it worth his while to extend his walk to Highgate, &
could contrive to be here between 12 and one—save that it must
not be Sunday—I would give him the hour that I employed in
walking—if he would accompany me.—On Wednesday Evening
came a Letter from Mr Whitehead, informing me that Saturday
was the only day at his own disposal—that he was exceedingly
anxious &c &c—This Letter, however, Mrs Gillman had opened
and forced the contents on my reluctant ears together with another
from Mr Sotheby, about his Translation of the Iliad—.[1] Yesterday,
I sent Harriet to Mrs Gillman for Mr Whitehead's Letter, in order to
send him word that I could not see him till the Saturday after—
Bless me!—why, I lit the wax-taper with it, about an hour ago—
but I can tell him the contents.—But what was the address? How
am I to direct to him—for I expect Mr G. here?—Yes! Mrs
Gillman distinctly recollected that there was an address given; &
in the City somewhere—and it began with Bank Something; but
what, the number &c—she had utterly forgotten.—

Do, pray, compliment her, the next time, you see her, on the
remarkable and rapid recent growth of her Organ of *Locality*—
that you could lay hold of it with your fingers—a charming improve-
ment of her frontal sinus!—

Now I cannot work myself up to send this poor Poet off, after
such a walk under such expectations—because he is, I more than
suspect, a poor *Man* as well as a very poor Poet—or to comprize
both in one—Mr Whitehead is in every sense a *poor Clerk*—.

If you could stay and take a beef steak with me, in my own room
at ½ past 5 or 6 o'clock, & came at 2 (for by the original promise
I am to quit him before that hour) this would make no difference.—
Otherwise, you will decide whether you can stay long enough, from
after Two, to make it worth the while. To say that I should be
glad to see you, would be to say less than the truth—for I am
anxious to have it determined, which I think might be done in two
consecutive days' work, whether—previous to the commencement
of the individual Organization in the Vegetable Forms, a consistent,
flexible, and organic *Terminology* can be strictly evolved out of

---

[1] William Sotheby's *The First Book of the Iliad, a Specimen of a New Version
of Homer*, appeared in 1830, and his translation of the whole of the *Iliad* (in
heroics) in 1831.

spiritual Postulates and the Data furnished by them. If in the evolution of the Dynamic Powers, of the Elements, of the Minerals and the geological formations you have proved by the fact the acquisition of a *Language* of *Arrangement* more systematic & synoptical, and more luminously displaying the order and inter-dependence of the Facts & Phaenomena—this is all that at this stage of the Undertaking ought to be required.—Whether it be the actual *history* of the creation in these particulars?—The dis-position to adopt the affirmative must be looked for in the after stages—namely, in the applicability of the Scheme, as an organ of insight, and of solution, to the facts of organized Bodies, and the correspondence of [the] Results by ideal deduction to the Results supplied by Experience.—The mere existence of a perfect *Harmony* supplies no mean evidence of a real truth—for it is one of the characters & criteria of Reality—as for instance, if the same Law which has made the difference of fixed and fluid intelligible should by the law of the identity still remaining in the Thesis and Anti-thesis supply equally the insight into the primary distinctions of the *Fixed*—i.e. of the mineral World.—But I must leave off. Do not forget the Hoffman's Tales[1]—& I hear high accounts given of a Novel by Professor Steffens, a Norwegian Tale—'DIE FAMILIEN WALSETH UND LEITH'.[2]—Possibly, Mr Aders may have had it among the Books of the German Book-Club, of which he is a member. Did you ever see or look into Hahnemann's Organ der Heilung,[3] the Homoeopathy Doctor, or Similia similibus mini-missimum dose man, I mean?—How is the great impression made by him on the German medical Press to be explained? Two crowned Skulls have built Hospitals for the System—Emperor Nic at Tulczin in Russia & the King of Naples.—God bless you, my best Friend!—

S. T. Coleridge.

1685. *To J. H. Green*

MS. British Museum, Hitherto unpublished.

My dear and kind Friend   [March 1830?]

One explanatory notice ere I enter on the subject to which my last was the gentleman Usher, or rather, I hope, a Pioneer. There are three distinct sources, from one or other of which we must

---

[1] Ernst T. A. Hoffmann (1776–1822), German romance-writer.

[2] Heinrich Steffens, *Die Familien Walseth und Leith*, 3 vols., 1827.

[3] S. C. F. Hahnemann (1755–1843), founder of homoeopathy, published his chief work, *Organon der rationellen Heilkunde*, in 1810. The homoeopathic system was introduced into Russia in 1823, into Italy in 1821.

derive our arguments whatever the position may be that we wish
to support or overthrow: and in subjects of highest dignity and
widest interest the true Philosopher will avail himself of all, yet
not by intermixture or promiscuous juxta-position of Brick, Log
and Marble, but of each in it's proper time and appointed place,
like cross Arches; and so that each singly may appear capable of
supporting the superincumbent weight, because in each the power
of all is actually tho' latently co-present. (Thus in the most insen-
sate parts of a living body, as the Hair, Nails &c, the sensibility
and irritability are hidden in the predominance of the Reproduc-
tivity, but yet are contained therein or the latter could not exist:
& thus, e contra, in a healthy eye the sensibility is latent in the
higher power of visual perception, but with the absence of sensi-
bility or in proportion to it's decrease below or increase beyond
a given degree, the power of sight goes likewise.) These sources are,
1. transcendental or anterior to experience, as the *grounds* without
which experience itself could not have been. 2. Subjective, or the
experience acquirable by self-observation and composed of facts
of inward consciousness, which may be appealed to as assumed to
have [a] place in the minds of other[s] but cannot be demon-
strated. Each man's Experience is a single and insulated whole.
3. Common and simultaneous Experience, collectively forming
History in it's widest sense, civil, and natural. [MS. breaks off thus.]

1686. *To H. W. Montagu*

Address:——Montagu, Esqre | the Editor of 'The Devil's Thoughts'[1] illustrated
by Mr Cruikshanks— | to the care of
MS. Texas Christian University Lib. Hitherto unpublished.

Grove, Highgate
April
Monday 1830

Mr S. T. Coleridge would not have troubled Mr Montagu about
such a trifle as the Devil's Thoughts if the reputation, that this
doggrel is capable of conferring had been the point in question.[2]

---

[1] In the MS. 'Thoughts' is crossed out and 'Walk' written above in an un-
known hand.

[2] After its anonymous publication in the *Morning Post* on 6 Sept. 1799, *The
Devil's Thoughts*, the joint work of Coleridge and Southey, came to be attributed
to Richard Porson, and in Mar. 1830 H. W. Montagu published the poem under
the title *The Devil's Walk; A Poem. By Professor Porson.* The volume contained
a biographical memoir by the editor and engravings 'after the Designs of
R. Cruikshank'.

As a result of Coleridge's letter of protest, Montagu in 1830 reissued the
work with a new title, *The Devil's Walk; A Poem. By S. T. Coleridge, Esq. and*

But by referring to Mr Coleridge's Poems, even in the form of the long ago published Sibylline Leaves, Mr Montagu will find (in the Apologetic Preface to the Fire, Famine and Slaughter) that Mr Coleridge had informed the reader that the Devil's Thoughts were written by himself and Southey—that Southey wrote the three first stanzas and the Stanza on the Cold Bath Prison, (*worth all the rest twice over*) and Mr Coleridge the Remainder.[1] In the compleat collection of Mr Coleridge's poetical writings by Mr Pickering, Mr Montagu might have found a *correct* copy of the Devil's Thoughts—for the Poem, as given in the Illustrations, is in many parts not only such as Mr C. *could* not have written, had he been idle enough to have suffered the publication, when written—but almost a libel on the name of Porson, the *tersest* of Writers. Now surely, Mr Montagu could not even suspect that such a Man as Southey, or even that Mr Coleridge, could be guilty of claiming the work of another—& that too such a trifle at the price of so *monstrous* a Meanness!—Sir Walter Scott and half a Score other men of Rank and Literary Name knew that Mr Coleridge was the principal author from it's first appearance in the Morning Post—Mr Daniel Stuart received the MSS from Mr Coleridge—and besides the Copies in the Morning Paper struck off two or three hundred Copies, to disperse among his friends.[2]—By the bye, by a strange coincidence, the Fire, Famine and Slaughter,[3] and the wild Copy of Verses, entitled—The two Round Spaces—beginning with the Lines—

> The Devil believes that the Lord will come
> Stealing a March without beat of Drum
> About the same hour that he came last,
> On an old Christmas Day, in a snowy Blast—&c[4]

have been published in an Irish Miscellany and attributed to Mr Porson.—

S. T. Coleridge's Comps.

Robert Southey, Esq. LL.D. &c., and in a prefatory note dated Oct. 1830 he mentioned 'a communication from Mr. Coleridge' and inserted an apology for the 'error respecting the Authorship'. He also omitted the last page of the preface or biographical memoir, wherein he had asserted that Porson was the author of the poem.

[1] In *Sibylline Leaves* (p. 98) Coleridge says of *The Devil's Thoughts* that 'the four [later corrected to three] first stanzas . . ., which were worth all the rest of the poem, and the best stanza of the remainder, were written by a friend of deserved celebrity'; in his *Poetical Works* of 1829 (ii. 90) he is more specific: 'The three first stanzas, which are worth all the rest, and the ninth [on the Coldbath Fields Prison], were dictated by Mr. Southey.'

[2] 'Our "Devil's Thoughts"', Coleridge wrote to Southey on 19 Dec. 1799, 'have been admired far & wide—most *enthusiastically* admired!'

[3] See *Poems*, i. 237.   [4] Ibid. i. 353, and Letter 356.

1687. *To Mrs. Thomas Hurst*

MS. Editor. Hitherto unpublished.

16 April [1830 ?]
Highgate

Mr Coleridge acknowleges the favor of Mrs Hurst's polite Invitation and will feel much disappointment if contrary to his expectations either Ill-health or other unforeseen Accident should deprive him of the pleasure of availing himself of it—

1688. *To Thomas Hurst*

Address: Thomas Hurst, Esqre | Bank Side | Highgate
[Readdressed in another hand] 65 St Paul's Church Yard
MS. Harvard College Lib. Hitherto unpublished.

[May 1830 ?][1]

My dear Sir

No man can undertake to do more than his best; but it is very possible for his swift wishes so far to outrun his slow powers, that not to have undertaken at all would have been better than his best.—However, almost any thing has a fair chance of being better than that which having nothing in the way of wit, originality or poignant appropriateness in its favor, has a strong *prudential*, and a still stronger *moral* reason against it. And this, I am persuaded, is the case with the title 'Comic Annual', under the particular circumstances and relations, in which You & your Partner stand.—In competition with *this*, therefore, I should not hesitate to prefer either of the two following—tho' I should be right glad to have hit on some third better than either. I have written them on the third side of this sheet—& it would not be difficult to find an apposite Motto, or title-page Quotation, for either.—As to the Pre-advertisement or Prospectus, it would be necessary to have the *Stuff*, or specimen of the Materials graphic & scriptorial, and to know the Editor's *plan & notions* of what the work is to be, in order to make it *tell*.—Besides, in all probability Mr Head would be more offended with the interference than obliged by any assistance in a thing of this sort. Yet I have no doubt, that a well *pointed*, well *turned*, page or so of sound sense wrapped up in Cervantic or Rabelaisian Humor, would have some effect in exciting attention to the forth-comer.—

[1] This letter was probably written in 1830 when the firm of Hurst, Chance, and Company was planning *The New Comic Annual for 1831*. Only one issue was published.

Any thing in my power (alas! that the wretched & uncertain state of my Health should so narrow that power!) will be at your service—for I am, my dear Sir,

very sincerely your's

S. T. Coleridge

P.S. I thank you for your prompt kindness in procuring the Books for me—I have not yet opened the parcel—but I will carefully return them in a few days.

1. Falstaff's or Sir John Falstaff's Annual:[1] or Genial Laughs, graphic, metrical and confabulatory—with a short motto of a Line & a half, probably from Shakespear.

2. Pun, Picture, and Poetry: or HEAD's (still better, perhaps, HURST and CHANCE's) ANNUAL for the Summer-Bower, the Winter Fire-side, and the Travellers' Room on a Rainy Day.—
A Motto

If any thing else comes into my head, I will communicate it.[2]

1689. *To Mrs. Gillman*

Pub. Coleridge at Highgate, *by Lucy E. Watson, 1925, p. 143.*

8 May, 1830,
Saturday night, 10 o'clock.

Dear Mrs. Gillman,—Wife of the friend who has been more than a brother to me, and who have month after month, yea, hour after hour, for how many successive years, united in yourself the affections and offices of an anxious friend and tender sister to me-ward!

May the Father of Mercies, the God of health and of all salvation, be your reward for your great and constant love and loving kindness to me, abiding with you, and within you, as the spirit of guidance, support and consolation! and may His Grace and gracious Providence bless James and Henry for your sake, and make them a blessing to you and their father!

And though weighed down by a heavy presentiment respecting my own sojourn here, I not only hope but have a steadfast faith

---

[1] The Dedication and the Preface to *The New Comic Annual for 1831* both refer to the work as 'Falstaff's Annual'. One paragraph in the Preface reads:

Your petitioner humbly conceives that he does not trust to a fragile reed, or rest upon a false staff, in thus ushering into the world his first number by the merry title of FALSTAFF'S ANNUAL; the joyous harbinger of 'genial laughs' or glad contributor of social mirth; ripe for all seasons—the winter's hearth or summer's shade.

[2] The following note in an unknown handwriting appears on page 3 of the MS.: 'This Letter was written when *Your* Comic Anl. was wanting a Name.'

that God will be your reward: because your love to me from first
to last has begun in, and been caused by what appeared to you a
translucence of the love of the good, the true, and the beautiful
from within me—as a relic of glory gleaming through the turbid
shrine of my mortal imperfections and infirmities—as a light of
life seen within 'the Body of this Death!'[1] because in loving me
you loved our Heavenly Father reflected in the gifts and in-
fluences of his Holy Spirit!

S. T. Coleridge.

1690. *To Basil Montagu*

Address: Basil Montagu Esqr | at his Chambers | Lincoln's Inn Square
MS. Pierpont Morgan Lib. Hitherto unpublished.
Postmark: 11 May 1830.

10 May 1830. Grove, Highgate

My very dear Montagu

I need not tell you that at *no* time could I possibly have felt any
personal, or any other than a moral, interest in the politics of our
Hamlet—and that least of all, am I likely to suffer any *warp* of
this kind in my present state of health and under my present
presentiments.—But a strong moral and religious interest I *do*
feel—in the establishment of a place of Worship with a regular
Clergyman in this place—and an effective School for the poor—
and from my *intimate* knowlege of the *excessive* malignity and most
mischievous motives of the opposition to the measure, from the
first dawn of this opposition thro' all it's progress—a knowlege
obtained by conversation with the main opponents & a thorough
insight into their characters, in addition to the vindictive *private*
feelings *avowed* to myself, at least in my presence, by the originator
of the Feud—I can truly say, that in the whole course of my life
I never found my religious faith in the worth and dignity of Man so
necessary to rescue me from the temptation to misanthropy.[2]—

[1] Romans vii. 24.

[2] Although the suit in the Court of Chancery against the governors of the
Free Grammar School at Highgate was initiated under the leadership of the
Rev. H. B. Owen in 1822 and hearings were held in Dec. 1823 and Jan. 1824
(see note to Letter 1310), it was Apr. 1827 before a decree was issued by Lord
Eldon, the lord chancellor. That decree 'dismissed so much of those suits as
sought the removal of the Wardens and Governors from the trust: and de-
clared, that "the charity founded by Sir Roger Cholmeley was a charity for
the sustentation and maintenance of a Free Grammar School *for teaching the
learned languages*;" that the Wardens and Governors were not bound further
to enlarge the Chapel out of the revenues of the charity, or to enlarge the
burial-ground, or to do any other acts with respect to the Chapel, for the
benefit of the relators or other inhabitants of Highgate, and it was referred to

Now I understand, that in the Bill (which after passing the House
of Lords has been obliged to be recommenced in the Commons
under some accidental clause which the Speaker thought made it
a money Bill)[1] the opponent and the *only* inveterate opponent, is
Alderman Wood[2]—induced to it, I am well aware, by false,

the Master [in Chancery, Robert Henley Eden, later Lord Henley,] . . . to
approve a scheme for the purposes therein mentioned'. Lord Eldon's decree
led to the subsequent revival of the decayed grammar school.

By a further order dated 16 Apr. 1829 Lord Lyndhurst, then lord chancellor,
directed Eden to provide for the disposition of the school chapel and the ad-
jacent burial ground in a manner 'beneficial to, or not inconsistent with the
interests of the Free Grammar School'. Eden's report of 18 Dec. 1829 speci-
fied that Bishop Grindal's grant of the chapel and premises should be confirmed
by Parliament; that 'the Chapel should be taken down, and a new one erected
on some other site by the Commissioners [for Building Churches]'; that 'the
burial-ground should be transferred to those Commissioners'; that 'sittings
should be secured in the proposed new Chapel for the Wardens and Governors,
[and] Master and Scholars . . . [of the Free Grammar School] *rent free for ever*';
that 'the charity estates should be exonerated from liability to repairs'; that
'the patronage should be vested in the Bishop of London'; and that 'applica-
tion should be made to Parliament for the required authority'. This report was
confirmed by Lord Lyndhurst on 23 Dec. 1829, and the governors of the Free
Grammar School were ordered to apply to Parliament. Accordingly, a bill was
introduced in the House of Lords early in 1830, and after being passed by both
Houses, received the royal assent on 17 June. Among other provisions, it
authorized the governors to contribute £2,000 towards the erection of the
proposed new chapel in Highgate, the funds to be raised by mortgage of the
Highgate Charity; 'to take down the old Chapel . . ., and to convey the site of
their then present Chapel and burying-ground to the [Church] Commissioners,
to be used as a place of interment belonging to the new Chapel'; and to transfer
'the endowments belonging to the preacher of the present Chapel to the new
Church or Chapel'. John H. Lloyd, *The History . . . of Highgate*, 1888, pp. 146–7,
and *Journals of the House of Commons*, lxxxv.

The new chapel was erected across from the Grove, Highgate, some little
distance from the old school chapel, and on 8 Nov. 1832 it was consecrated as
St. Michael's Church. The Rev. Samuel Mence not only retained his position
as master of the Free Grammar School but was also appointed the first vicar
of St. Michael's Church. He remained at Highgate until 1838, when he became
rector of Ulcombe, Kent. The old school chapel was torn down in 1833 and the
area added to the adjoining burial ground. See Appendix A for an account of
Coleridge's burial in Aug. 1834 on the site formerly occupied by the old school
chapel, the transfer of his remains to the near-by family vault in 1843, and his
reinterment in the crypt of St. Michael's Church in 1961.

¹ The parliamentary bill was passed by the House of Lords on 5 Apr. 1830
and sent to the House of Commons. On the same day it was read for the first
time in the Commons, but on 28 Apr. the second reading was put off for six
months. Reintroduced and read for the first time on 3 May 1830 and for the
second time on the 10th, the bill was passed, with certain amendments on 24
May. It was referred to the House of Lords, where it was passed on 3 June.
The royal assent was given a fortnight later. See *Journals of the House of Lords*,
lxii, and *Journals of the House of Commons*, lxxxv.

² Matthew Wood (1768–1843), lord mayor of London, 1815–17, and M.P.,

utterly false representations, from a certain Party—. Now I cannot help persuading myself from Alderman Wood's noble Conduct in his Mayoralties, that he is acting on good impulses from false & calumnious impressions—and that if by means of an excellent young Friend,[1] who knows that *if a competent*, I am most assuredly in every sense a most *disinterested* Informant, I could convey to his worthy Father the real facts of the case, the expedience, nay, the moral necessity of the measure, the extensive good of which it will be the means, and the ruin, almost, to the Charity in addition to the frustration of all that good, which will be risked by it's failure, it could not but tend at least to qualify and mitigate, if not to suspend, his hostility.—How *strong* a moral interest I feel it my ' *duty* to my Neighbor', to take in this matter, I afford some little proof by the wish, I now express & thro' you hope to convey to our highly esteemed & estimated young friend, to see him (feeble as I am—for otherwise I am ALWAYS *delighted* to see his face & hear his voice) either on Thursday Night—or any other time that he can spare—should he be able to spare any—in the course of this week —*That is*—supposing that he can with propriety, & that he thinks, that *being himself convinced & informed* he could with a probable success, attempt to transfer his convictions to his Father.—

I remain tranquil—my mind in the fullest possession of all it's powers—but so weak as to occasion great anxiety to Mr & Mrs Gillman on any continued exertion of them, tho' highly pleasurable to myself at the time—& without dread—did the sense of my duty permit it, I fear, I should have to say, with a languid yearning after an extrication from 'the body of this death'—I yet, against my own will, say nightly my last prayer under a presentiment, that it will be *among* the last.—I do not recover my strength—& the intestinal secretions do not improve in their *appearance*, tho' they no longer produce the same distressful restlessness—but these are my only tangible grounds for my apprehensions—

Kindest love to Mrs M.

God bless you & your obliged & most affectionate Friend,

S. T. Coleridge

I do not know Mr W. Wood's address—or I would not trouble you—tho' his coming with *you* & Mrs M. would *spice my* satisfaction.—

city of London, 1817–43. He was one of the chief friends and counsellors of Queen Caroline. In 1837 Queen Victoria conferred a baronetcy on him.

[1] William Page Wood (1801–81), later Baron Hatherley, translated the *Novum Organum* for Montagu's edition of Bacon. (See Letter 1695.) Wood was appointed lord chancellor in 1868. For Wood's comments on Coleridge see R. W. Armour and R. F. Howes, *Coleridge the Talker*, 1940, pp. 238–41.

1691. *To William Blackwood*

Pub., Annals of a Publishing House. William Blackwood and His Sons, *by*
M. Oliphant, 2 vols., *1897, i. 416.*
Postmark: Highgate, 15 May 1830.

[15 May 1830]

Within a few days after the receipt of your letter enclosing an
order for £10 on Messrs Cadell—which I have destroyed, it being
against one of my rules to receive payment for work not delivered,
having learnt from experience that by making me feel uneasy and
bound it would be more likely to prevent than to expedite the
execution, not the less however thanking you for the kindness in-
tended,—within a few days from this, I say, the Illness com-
menced which, in a succession of relapses so close to each other
as to form one chain of distemper, has conducted me to the very
brink of the grave, through sufferings that removed all horror
from the anticipation; and seems (so my anxious friends hope and
wish to believe) to have reached its height and crisis in an attack
during sleep: the sum of which is, that a noise of some heavy body
falling having alarmed one of the servants then on the stairs, I was
found on the floor pulseless and senseless, and continued thus about
half an hour, when animation was restored, chiefly, I believe, by
means of mustard-plasters applied to the chest and abdomen. But
there was no appearance of convulsion, the expression of the
countenance tranquil, and all my faculties returned entire, and in
the first instance exactly as from ordinary sleep. Indeed, before
I had opened my eyes, I merely found that my medical friends and
Mrs Gilman were flustering over me: my first words were, 'What
a mystery we are! What a problem is presented in the strange
contrast between the imperishability of our thoughts and the
perishable fugacious nature of our consciousness', when I heard the
voice of my friend exclaiming, 'Thank God! however, there is
nothing of apoplexy in this seizure'.[1] From this time I have been
freed from pain, and my nervous system more tranquil than had
been the case for months and months before. Only, my strength
comes back very, very slowly; and though my mind is as active and
vigorous as in the best times, and I sufficiently disposed to exert it,
I cannot bear the consequences of exertion.

Now, my dear sir! you will scarcely guess my motive for boring
you with the dull sick-bed detail of and all about myself, so I must
tell you. I am aware that the man who volunteers his advice and,

---

[1] Cf. Lamb's comment of 10 May 1830: 'I saw Coleridge a day or two since.
He has had some severe attack, not paralytic; but, if I had not heard of it,
I should not have found it out. He looks, and especially speaks, strong.' *Lamb
Letters*, iii. 270.

unasked, obtrudes his opinion on another, runs the risk of being set down for a self-sufficient coxcomb, or of being suspected of some selfish view: and the risk is the greater when the advisee happens to be a remarkably prosperous and influencive man who, like the centurion in the Gospel, can say Go, and he goeth; Do this, and he doeth it.[1] And I would fain have you feel how bitter [little?] in the existing condition of my health—and with an insupportable presentiment haunting me every night as I lay my head on my pillow that I shall go off in my sleep, as my dear father did, whose very *facsimile* I am, both in body and mind,—I can be disposed to play the officious or impertinent part, or to profess friendly purposes as a pretext for gratifying a silly vanity or giving vent to the flatulence of self-opinion. And now for the point.

My respected friend, the author of the 'Colonna',[2] &c., has induced me to read with attention the letters that have passed between you and him respecting the untoward accident of the 'Headsman';[3] and I seem to feel it will be a more frank and friendly

---

[1] Matthew viii. 8–9.

[2] Joseph Hardman contributed 'Colonna the Painter. A Tale of Italy and the Arts' to the Sept. 1829 issue of *Blackwood's Magazine*. It is unsigned, but in writing to Messrs. Blackwood in 1840 Hardman specifically identifies himself as the author. (See M. Oliphant, *Annals of a Publishing House. William Blackwood and His Sons*, 2 vols., 1897, ii. 287–8.) The story is headed with two stanzas translated from Goethe by Coleridge:

> Know'st thou the Land where the pale Citrons blow,
> And Golden Fruits through dark green foliage glow?
> O soft the breeze that breathes from that blue sky!
> Still stand the Myrtles and the Laurels high.
> Know'st thou it well? O thither, Friend!
> Thither with thee, Beloved! would I wend.
>
> Know'st thou the House? On Columns rests its Height;
> Shines the Saloon; the Chambers glisten bright;
> And Marble Figures stand and look at *me*—
> Ah, thou poor Child! what have they done to thee!
> Know'st thou it well? O thither, Friend!
> Thither with thee, Protector! would I wend.
>
> S. T. COLERIDGE, *from* GOETHE.

The text of the first stanza differs markedly from that published in the *Poetical Works* of 1834. The second stanza has not been identified as Coleridge's since its publication in *Blackwood's Magazine*. Coleridge mentions his version of 'Know'st thou the Land' in Letter 1417.

[3] 'The Headsman. A Tale of Doom' appeared, without a signature, in *Blackwood's Magazine* for Feb. 1830. It was also written by Hardman, who speaks of his 'romantic and piquant tales' drawn chiefly from German and Danish sources, 'freely altered from the original, and adapted to British taste and feeling'. According to Mrs. Oliphant, Hardman 'seems to have been supposed to be guilty of putting forth as original the English translation of a German work already known'. Op. cit. i. 416 and ii. 288.

course to communicate the impression left on my mind and my mistaken, perhaps, but assuredly most sincere and conscientious judgment on the disputed point, directly to yourself. Bear with me, then, when, after the public avowal of my admiration for your 'Maga', page 147 of 'Coleridge on the Constitution according to the Idea'[1] (*I hope you have received the copy of the 2nd edition, which I ordered to be sent to you*), you will not suspect me of any want of zeal for you and yours if I say that:

First, I have looked carefully over the bond, as Shylock says, and can nowhere find that any approach to omniscience on the part of your correspondent had been promised or stipulated for: and, verily, something very like it he must be supposed to possess, before it can be naturally required of him that he should be cognizant of every tale and novelette, in whatever vehicle and under whatever name, published during the last twenty years, or even the last five, when we have had such a rank crop of them that have beggared geography to furnish them with distinct names, in one volume or two, or three, besides annuals, and monthlies, and weeklies, that even novelty itself seems flat, and curiosity turns yellow at the sight of a Hungarian or a Californian tale, as an alderman under the horrors of surfeit might be supposed to do at a Scotch haggis steaming up against him; all short of this impracticable Bibliography, all that your correspondent could be expected or had undertaken to do, he assuredly did. His orders to his foreign correspondent were to send works fresh from the press, or recently published. Kruse is a popular novelist, to whose previous publications my friend was no stranger, and from the title-page of the volume itself a man must be a conjuror to have conceived any suspicion that there had been an earlier edition, or that the contents had appeared in another form.

But as this letter *about myself* was intended for yourself alone, while the other paper which states in a somewhat less rambling and unbusiness-like style my sentiments on the point in question will probably be communicated to you through your correspondent, I will only add two points which seem to me worth considering. 1st. That your correspondent has, to my knowledge, spared neither trouble nor expense to procure the best information from foreigners of good taste, and the earliest arrival of the books well spoken of, and that from his former command, and his existing personal connections with the Continent, he possesses more than ordinary facilities. Further, that he is a man of talent and a neat stylist, you know, and that he is a man of the highest respectability and purest honour you may believe on my assurance. 2nd.

---

[1] This phrase is clearly an interpolation by Mrs. Oliphant.

Have you not overrated the inconvenience of [this piece of]
unluck? Why, bless me! ten well-written [lines describing] the
case would have converted it into an additional interest. In all that
forms the true comparative merit of a Tale of this kind the con-
tributions to your Magazine have so unmeasurably the advantage.
Oh that I could persuade you how much more likely to be ulti-
mately injurious is the recent change of the character of 'Maga'
by the increasing disproportion of the party politics articles, with
the feelings and passions of which there is *no* sympathy in England,
and with the subjects themselves only a languid exhausted interest.
I speak without any reference to their merits or demerits as com-
positions. Be assured you have few more zealous advocates and no
more sincere well-wisher than your aged friend,

S. T. Coleridge.

1692. *To J. H. Green*

Address: J. H. Green, Esqre | *46.* | Lincoln's Inn Fields
MS. Pierpont Morgan Lib. Pub. Letters, *ii. 751.*
Postmark: Highgate, 1 June 1830.

Grove, Highgate
30 May? or 1 June? at all events,
My dear Friend   Monday Night, 11 o'clock. [31 May 1830]

Do you happen among your acquaintances & connections to
know any one who knows any one who knows Sir Francis Freeling
of the Post office sufficiently to be authorized to speak a recom-
mendatory word to him?—Our Harriet, whose Love and Willing-
mindedness to *me*ward during my long chain of bodily miserable-
nesses render it my duty no less than my inclination, to shew to her
that I am not insensible of her humbly affectionate attentions, has
applied to me in behalf of her Brother, a young man who can have
an excellent Character from Lord Wynford & others for sobriety,
integrity and discretion—and who is exceedingly ambitious to
get the situation of a Post man or Deliverer of Letters to the
General Post office.—Perhaps, before I see you next, you will be
so good as to tumble over the names of your acquaintances, and if
any connection of Sir Francis's should turn up, to tell me—& if it
be right and proper, to mention my request and it's motive—
Dr Chalmers[1] with his Daughter & his very pleasing Wife

---

[1] Thomas Chalmers (1780–1847), theologian, preacher, and philanthropist,
was appointed in 1828 to the chair of theology in the University of Edinburgh.
For an account of his first visit to Highgate in 1827 see R. W. Armour and
R. F. Howes, *Coleridge the Talker*, 1940, p. 127.

honored me with a Call this morning and spent an hour with me—
which the good Doctor declared on parting to have been 'a *Re-
freshment*' such as he had not enjoyed for a long season.—N.B.
There were no Sandwiches—only Mrs Aders was present, who is
most certainly a Bon[ne] bouche for both Eye and Ear—and who
looks as bright and sunshine-showery, as if nothing had ever
ailed her. The main topic of our Discourse was Mr Irving[1] and his
unlucky phantasms and phantasms.[2] I was on the point of telling
Dr Chalmers, but fortunately recollected there were Ladies &
Scotch Ladies present—that while other Scotchmen were content
with Brimstone for the Itch, Irving had a rank itch for Brimstone
—*Mem.* sublimated by addition of Fire.—God bless you & your

> ever obliged & affectionate Friend
> S. T. Coleridge

P.S. Kind remembrances to Mrs Green.—I continue pretty well on
the whole, *considering*—save the soreness across the base of my
chest.

1693. *To Mrs. Thomas Hurst*

Address: Mrs Hurst
MS. Cornell University Lib. Hitherto unpublished.

> Grove, Highgate.
> Friday, 2 July 1830.

My dear Madam
    Mr Chance was so kind as to let me have each Yesterday's Paper
by Breakfast time—the Monday's Times, for instance, on Tuesday

---

[1] Edward Irving had served as assistant at St. John's, Glasgow, from 1820
to 1822, during Chalmers's ministry there.

[2] 'I have', Coleridge wrote of Irving in *The Church and State*, 'no faith in
his prophesyings; small sympathy with his fulminations; and in certain pecu-
liarities of his *theological* system, as distinct from his religious principles, I
cannot see my way.' (p. 182 n.) Elsewhere Coleridge remarked: 'Mr. Irving's
notion [of the Trinity] is tritheism,—nay, . . . tri-daemonism. His opinion
about the sinfulness of the humanity of our Lord is absurd.' In 1833 he de-
clared that the Church of Scotland might have 'visited' Irving 'for the mon-
strous indecencies of those exhibitions of the spirit; . . . but to excommunicate
him on account of his language about Christ's body was very foolish. Irving's
expressions upon this subject are ill-judged, inconvenient, in bad taste, and in
terms false: nevertheless, his apparent meaning, such as it is, is orthodox.'
Table Talk, 15 May 1830 and 17 Aug. 1833.
    In *The Church and State* (182 n.), however, Coleridge remarked that Irving
possessed 'more of the Head and Heart, the Life, the Unction, and the
genial power of MARTIN LUTHER, than any man now alive; yea, than any
man of this and the last century'. See also *Aids to Reflection*, 1825, p. 372 n.

Morning, & so on—and this Paper I made a point of re-delivering myself at Mr Chance's early in the Afternoon, except when confined by illness.—And since Mr Chance's absence, our Servant brought me a message from Mr Hurst, to the purport that I was to *send* for the Paper to your House & to let it be returned there, when done with. Whether the message might not have been cracked in the carrying from the door to my Attic, I cannot say. It is not improbable: for our little Cook, Sarah, took it in—and I have not quite as reverend an estimation of her *Head*, as I have of her *Heart*. Meantime, Miss Chance assures Henry Gillman, that she never sees or receives her Brother's Paper—that it was never sent to her.—May it not be, that the Paper used to be sent in the first instance from Mr Chance's to Mr Cook's, and from Mr Cook's used to come to me the next day?

Mr Hurst, I dare say, will be so good as to *unpuzzle* us—but I am really very sorry to have given you so much trouble about such a trifle. Be pleased to make my kindest respects to Mr Hurst, and believe me, my dear Madam,

with great regard & esteem | Your obliged

S. T. Coleridge

1694. *To Thomas Poole*

Address: Thomas Poole, Esqre | Nether Stowey | Somerset   Favored by C. Stutfield, Esqre.
MS. British Museum. Pub. E. L. G. ii. 431.

Grove

Highgate

Friday, [2] July 1830

My dear Poole

Since we last met, I have been brought to the brink of the Grave thro' a series of severe sufferings that would have removed all terror from the anticipation, even if I had ever associated any painful thought with the extrication of my Spirit from 'the Body of this Death'.—I had intended to have written a *Letter* to you by our distressed Friend, Mr Stutfield—and in thanking you for your little pamphlet to have proposed some of the doubts and questionings which occurred to me during the perusal. But this is one of my *badly* days—and I am not equal to any exertion—Yet am determined that you shall at least receive a mss proof that I am yet in

the Land of the Living—& what I trust you would take for granted
without my adding it—most faithfully

and affectionately your attached Friend

S. T. Coleridge

I have sent you a Copy of the 2nd Edition of my 'Church and
State' by Mr Stutfield. Chapt. V, and from p. 143 to p. 183, will, I
flatter myself, interest you.[1]

S. T. C.

1695. *To James Gillman, Jr.*

[Addressed by Mrs. Gillman] James Gillman Esqr | The Revnd — Wilson's |
Chadlington | Near Chipping norton | Oxon
MS. Cornell University Lib. Pub. Some Letters of the Wordsworth Family,
ed. L. N. Broughton, 1942, p. 104.
Postmark: Highgate, 11 August 1830.

[11 August 1830]

My dear James

I was both affected and gratified by your last Letter to your
Mother. I can conceive two Individuals, both equally rather
above than below par in respect both of Head and Heart, yet
differenced in this, that the one has been led and directed by his
Head to the cultivation of his Heart, while the other has been
impelled and sustained by his Heart in the *tilling* and *stocking* of
his Head. And of the two Characters I should have most hope of
the latter: for whatever may be his success as to intellectual attain-
ments and the extrinsic honors and advantages connected with
them, he is sure to have strengthened and elevated his moral being
in the attempt, and thus improving the *quality* of his will, combine
with a lesser amount of attainments a clear healthfulness of Judge-
ment, a steady Good Sense that will make them go farther toward
securing his success in after-life, than a much larger stock acquired
for their own sake, unconnected or but slightly and casually con-
nected with the sense of Duty. That in the *World* it will have this
effect, I have not the least doubt, whatever may be the case at the
University. And when I look at the point in relation to your hap-
piness and early establishment in life, and to your comparative
Usefulness, it is sometimes a question with me, whether with your
constitution and dispositions a failure in obtaining the more shewy
academic honors with that quantum of well-connected, thoroughly
mastered, fundamental knowlege acquired during an honest *try*
for them—in the efforts, I mean, to prepare yourself for a respec-

---

[1] Coleridge did not call attention to his characterization of Poole in the note
to p. 115 of *The Church and State*.

table competition—might not ultimately turn up a better Prize in
the Lottery of After-life, than your success might have proved—
if namely, it made you feel that you had to rely on yourself, if it
gave you earlier *manly* cares, manly prudence, and that honorable
worldly-wisdom which enables a man to form valuable connections
by presenting the correspondent *pole* to the different characters,
included within his sphere of Action.—You will not, I am sure, so
entirely misinterpret what I have here said, as to infer that I meant
it as an advice or intended it to act a motive, to your *flagging* in
your present studies—or as a consolation *in prospectu* for having
languidly and heartlessly pursued them. No! I am anxious to
make you see and feel the immense value of the knowlege, you will
acquire during the Endeavor, independent of the immediate
contingent Object, and for *Ultra-academic* purposes, not to mention
the still higher motive of it's dignifying and liberalizing influence
on your own mind, character and conduct. Ignorant of, or very
imperfectly acquainted with, the *particulars* of the Oxford Exami-
nations for the First and Second Class, I cannot form an opinion
respecting your probable chances—and can only *guess* at, but in
no way appreciate, Mr Wilson's unfavorable anticipation—if in-
deed it has not been *attributed* to him by your own misgivings in a
head-achy hour, rather than fairly deduced from any thing, he has
himself said. From what I have seen & observed respecting your
scholarship, I should suspect that your most important defect and
desideratum was an accurate, systematic, well-digested knowlege
of Ancient History—comprizing the chronological Dates, Laws,
Manners, Customs &c. This was one great advantage of our edu-
cation at Christ's Hospital under old Orbilius Plagosus[1] Boyer—
that we were so thoroughly drilled in Greek & Roman History, and
in Ancient Geography &c, that we had Potter (both his Historical
volumes & his Antiquities) Stanley, Hook, and Prideaux (= Con-
nection)[2] at our fingers' ends, before we went to the University.—
And in this belief, my dear James! it is, that I feel some hesitation
regarding your *metaphysical* Questions. We have borrowed & your
Mother will send the only English Translation of Bacon's Novum
Organum as yet in print—Had you been in town, Montagu would
have lent for your perusal Mr Wood's new Translation—but it is

[1] Cf. Horace, *Epistles*, II. i. 70–71.
[2] John Potter, *Archaeologia Graeca, or the Antiquities of Greece*, 2 vols.,
1697–9, and included in the *Thesaurus* of J. Gronovius; Thomas Stanley, *The
History of Philosophy*, 4 vols., 1655–62; Nathaniel Hooke, *The Roman History
from the Building of Rome to the Ruin of the Commonwealth*, 4 vols., 1738–71;
and Humphrey Prideaux, *The Old and New Testament connected, in the History
of the Jews . . .*, 2 vols., 1716–18; also, with title, *The Connection*, 6 vols., 1716–
18.

MSS.—But honestly I must tell you, that in my judgement it would be an *unseasonable* application of your time & thoughts—if not a waste of them. You are not sufficiently prepared for that Work by a previous intimacy with the antecedent Schools of Philosophy— especially the *genuine* & the corrupt, Platonic and Aristotelean Schools—And nothing can be more unfair & often untrue, than Lord Bacon's attacks on both the one and the other. Besides, the Aphoristic and fragmentary character of the Work, aggravated by Bacon's frequent inconsistencies, is not likely to engender that state of intellect especially desirable for you at this time & for the next year or two of your studies. The *lucid order*, the clear Sequence, the neat articulation—in short, whatever facilitates the bringing a series of knowleges *in synopsi*—these should be your Ideal. You do not want to have your Mind an American Store House, but a well-stocked, neatly and *handily* arranged, Shop, for immediate Retail. However, I will transcribe the passage, from my [Common-] Place-Book, to which I suppose, you refer—. I have in concert with Mr Green evolved the whole doctrine of Ideas, as distinguished from sensuous Intuitions, pure or mixed, from the mediate knowleges, i.e. the conceptions, notions, generalizations of the Understanding, and lastly from the merely *formal* truths of the Reason, more clearly & more at large within the two or three last years. But for the present, if you persevere in wishing to know more on the subject, (tho' I would much rather you should defer it) I can only refer you to the latter pages of the Appendix to my Second Lay-Sermon,[1] and to the Essays on Method in the Third Volume of the Friend.—I have had a severe return of my old Bowel Complaint— with it's concomitant Restlessness and Depression; but am now recovering, I trust.— . . . [Conclusion and signature cut off.]

P.S.[2] Of course, much must depend on your Health—but should this remain pretty steady, a great deal with so good a grammatical & classical Ground-work as you have may be done in eight months. I cannot persuade myself, that there is (Health not interfering) any reason why you should not have a fair chance, and sustaining Hopes & pushing Thoughts. If you could do it without much expence of time, I wish you could give me a brief general sketch or outline of the average nature of the Examinations—the usual subjects, &c.—But if it will cost you much trouble, do not do it. S. T. C.

[1] Obviously a reference to *The Statesman's Manual*, 1816, Appendix E.
[2] The postscript appears at the top of page one of the MS.

1696. *To Thomas Hurst*

Address: Thomas Hurst, Esqre | Bank Side | Highgate
MS. Mrs. Sadie Spence Clephan. Pub. with omis. Letters Hitherto Uncollected, *55.*

23 Aug. 1830—
My dear Sir

I am vexed *with*, tho' (the cause being involuntary, viz. a relapse into the only not all-absorbing Bowel-Complaint) I dare not say, I am vexed *at*, myself for the neglect of returning the 4 Journals. The Evening, I last saw you, they were packed up *to be sent*— my ailments burst in on me—and I forgot to give direction to the Servant to have the pacquet left at your House. If, however, any thing amiss has taken place, so that you cannot with comfort to your own feelings return them to the Lender, pray, put them down to me—and I will, as in duty bound, pay the fine of my own procrastination. Believe me, very sincerely Your's

S. T. Coleridge

P.S. You may if you like & continue to wish it have the first half of the Aids to Reflection, on the understood condition that you shall have the second as soon as it is actually required, whether I have or have not made the additions or rather substitutions which I meditate, and which consisting almost wholly of transcription from MSS, my health only has prevented—This is the best compromise that in the present uncertainty and restiveness of my *Beast*-body I can make between my desire to improve the Book and my anxiety not to worry or disappoint you or your Printer.[1]

S. T. C.

1697. *To Thomas Hurst*

Address: T. Hurst Esq.
MS. Private possession. Hitherto unpublished.

Tuesday Night
[Endorsed 24 Augt 1830]
My dear Sir

Of course, I must elect the lesser evil, and take it as the fine for my improvidence in not having understood or precisely determined the conditions under which the Numbers were submitted to my perusal.—But as my friend, Mr Green, has expressed an intention of taking in this work, I wish for a day's respite.—I shall see him tomorrow or Thursday to know whether he has received

[1] Hurst, Chance, and Company published the second edition of *Aids to Reflection* in 1831. See Letters 1700 and 1705.

his set—for if not, you will perhaps be able at least to have the 4
Numbers charged at the Trade-Price—I write quite in the dark,
& cannot see the marks of my pen, but light or dark,

> I am your sincere tho' somewhat uncircumspect
> S. T. Coleridge

1698. *To Henry Nelson Coleridge*

MS. British Museum. Hitherto unpublished. This note is written in the fly-leaves of a copy of C. J. Blomfield's charge *To the Clergy of the Diocese of London*, 1830.

11 Septr 1830.

I am almost afraid, my dear Henry! that this being an Author's
= presentation Copy, and this Author a Bishop, and this Bishop
a Bishop of LONDON,[1] I may be thought, at least *felt*, by you to have
indulged my propensity to marginal Annotations somewhat out of
place. But I cannot (n.b. the usual lying Synonime for, I *will* not)
resist the temptation of observing to you, with respect to the first
half of this Charge, how manifoldly the worthy Prelate's Reasoning
is weakened, how unsteady it is thro' defect of the *foundation*, in
consequence of his constantly addressing his Clergy in the character
of a *Christian* Bishop, and this *exclusively*. What is the legitimate
Conclusion? *Either*, that the 39 Articles & Canons semi-personified
as the Church of England, are the One & only saving Church of
Christ—which the papal Church with undeniable *consistency* at
least, whatever may be thought of it's Modesty and Charity,
asserts of itself—*or* that the Church of England is a *favored Sect*, by
the partiality of the two houses of Parliament allowed and autho-
rized to exact such and such Sums from the Land-owners, Farmers
&c, no consent asked on their part, independent of their atten-
dance on it's Ministry and without any recognizable proportion
to the claimant's services!—Well may the good Bishop augur that
such an Institution stands in jeopardy!—I seem to see with the
clearness of an intuition, that only on the distinct conception of
the 3 (only possible) Forms of a church can our church be *vindicated*
on *principle*. And as to Expedience—alas! 'tis quaking Bog-ground.

My dear Henry, it is very easy to laugh or sneer down a literary
Man who has in various forms advanced and enforced any *con-
nexus* of (what in his earnest conviction are) fundamental Prin-
ciples, or seminal Ideas, and who in treating of the appertinent
Subjects, which will be numerous in proportion to the importance
and comprehensiveness of the Ideas, ever refers to them, and tries

---

[1] C. J. Blomfield (1786–1857) became bishop of London in 1828.

every point by these as by the criterion—'Hem!—*Ideas*—antece-
dent grounds and conditions—Reason distinguished from Under-
standing'—out it comes, as inevitably as the great *Bacon* from
B.M.—nolens volens, or like the Patentee of the Anti-friction
Powder who, on the motion of the Planets being spoken of, ob-
served, that he felt quite proud in admitting that the Creator was
the first original Anti-frictionist!—But after all the *legitimacy* of
this easy Criticism or *proleptic Set-down*, depends on the answer to
a previous question—Are the Principles or Ideas true or false?—
i.e. *Are* they Ideas, or mere verbiage? Are they fundamental?—
If they are both true & fundamental how could the Man avoid
recurring to them, without sacrificing truth and the duty of com-
municating truth to a cowardly fear of being cried down, as a
Pedant & a Crambist?—If false & trifling, expose their falsehood &
nothingness—and laugh as long as such worthless laughing-stocks
can supply the stimulus.

S. T. Coleridge.

1699. *To H. F. Cary*

Address: Revd. F. Carey | &c &c | British Museum.
MS formerly in the possession of the late Arthur Pforzheimer. Pub. Memoir of
H. F. Cary, *ii. 192.*
Postmark: Highgate, 29 November 1830.

Monday Afternoon—[29 November 1830]

My dear & in the very center of my Being respected Friend! tho'
I am so unwell as not without plausible grounds to suspect that
your remarks may come too late for me to make any practical
use of them; yet—should it please God to grant me a respite, such
a sufficiency of bodily *negation* as (his grace assisting) would enable
me to redeem the residue of my time—it would be so great a help
to my chances of being useful to receive from a Man, like you,
some *data* on which I might commence a sincere attempt to ascer-
tain the causes of the Obscurity felt generally in my prose writings
—whether in the way of expressing my thoughts, or in the in-
judicious selection of the Thoughts themselves—that I must press
on you your kind promise to run your eye once more through my
Work on the Constitution—All I ask is, merely that you would
mention the pages in the 2nd Edition, which you did not fully com-
prehend—for I am quite certain, that on such a subject what you
found a difficulty in understand[ing], ought not, without an adequate
preparation, to have been in the Book at all.—One cause of this
defect I suppose to be the contrast between the continuous and

systematic character of my Principles, and the occasional & frag-
mentary way, in which they have hitherto been brought before the
Public.

Yet when I look at my *second* Lay-Sermon, of which Mr Green
was saying yesterday—that any reader who had not looked at the
date in the title-page, would have taken for granted that it had
been written within the last fortnight, and in which I cannot be-
lieve it possible that any educated man would complain of any
want of common sense thoughts in plain mother English—I can-
not sincerely & conscientiously attribute the *whole* of my failure to
attract the attention of my fellow-men to faults or defects of my
own—You will believe me when I say, that to win their attention
for their own most momentous interests is the Wish that so en-
tirely predominates over any literary Ambition, as to render the
existence of the latter *latent* in my own consciousness.—

My kindest Love & Regards to Mrs Carey—and with every
prayer of the Heart for you & your's I remain—

Your's truly

S. T. Coleridge

1700. *To Henry Nelson Coleridge*

Address: H. N. Coleridge, Esqre | at his Chambers | No. 1 | Lincoln's Inn
MS. *Victoria University Lib. Pub. E. L. G. ii. 432.*
Postmark: Highgate, ⟨1⟩ December 1830.

1 Decr 1830.

My dear Henry

The concluding §§phs of your note so overlayed the main purpose
of it, that it has required no little effort to bring it to life again.
But my dear Henry!—Well aware, as you are, of the probable—
vexatious enough were they but the possible—consequences of
getting cold, why do you run the risk of an outside place?—I shall
wish the Aids to Reflection, or with more justice my own indolence,
to t'other place, if your hurried journey up to me has been the
cause or occasion.

As to your questions, I am somewhat puzzled for an answer,
not having the Corrected Copy. The best that suggests itself to my
mind, is to substitute 'Leighton' for 'the Arch-bishop', in the few
instances of formal quotation—: and to leave all the rest to be
explained in the preface—For my object, God knows! being to
convey what appeared to me truths of infinite concernment, I
thought neither of Leighton nor of myself—but simply of *how* it
was most likely they should be rendered intelligible and impressive

—The consequence of this was, that in so many aphorisms, taken in the main, from Leighton, I had so modified them, that a *contra-*distinction of these from my own was deceptive.[1]—In the preface, I shall state plainly the Leightonian Origin & still remain[ing] *ingrediency*[2]—and I assure you, that I have quite confidence enough in your taste & judgement to give you a Chart Blanch for any amendments in the style—

My tenderest Love to all at home.—Of myself, I can say little. For some Years back, but more particularly for the last 18 months, My Life has been an Ague, counted by days of intermission & paroxysm—To day & the latter half of Yesterday I have been better—able to eat my meat breakfast, & the load on my spirits relieved.—

God bless you! Take care of yourself.

Your affectionate

S. T. Coleridge

1701. *To John E. Reade*[3]

Pub. Italy: a Poem, in Six Parts, *by J. E. Reade, 1838, p. 383.*

[December 1830][4]

I think as highly of Shelley's Genius—yea, and of his *Heart*—as you can do. Soon after he left Oxford, he went to the Lakes, poor fellow! and with some wish, I have understood, to see me; but I was absent, and Southey received him instead.[5] Now, the very

---

[1] In the first edition of *Aids to Reflection*, 1825, the aphorisms are headed 'LEIGHTON', 'EDITOR', 'L. & ED.', etc. to indicate their authorship. (See Letter 1356.) In the second edition, 1831, these designations are omitted, thus eliminating from the headings all indication of the authorship of the aphorisms. In the 1825 *Aids*, too, such phrases as 'The Editor and Annotator of the present Volume' and 'REFLECTIONS BY THE EDITOR' appear in the text. In 1831 they are altered to read 'The Author of the present Volume' and 'REFLECTIONS BY THE AUTHOR'.

[2] The Preface to *Aids to Reflection* is the same in 1825 and 1831. The Advertisement prefixed to the first edition explains the 'Leightonian Origin' of the work. (See notes to Letter 1376.) In the second edition, however, this Advertisement was replaced by an address 'TO THE READER' in which Leighton is not mentioned. Coleridge wrote out this address in the fly-leaves of a copy of the 1825 *Aids* presented to Stuart. The volume is now in the British Museum.

[3] John Edmund Reade (1800–70), poetaster and novelist.

[4] In introducing this excerpt Reade says that after the publication of his *Cain the Wanderer*, 1830, he received 'on the same day, gratifying letters from Goethe, and from Coleridge'. In Dec. 1830, too, Coleridge spoke of Shelley to John Frere in terms similar to those in the present letter. See R. W. Armour and R. F. Howes, *Coleridge the Talker*, 1940, p. 220.

[5] Shelley resided at Keswick in 1811–12.

reverse of what would have been the case in ninety-nine instances of a hundred, I *might* have been of use to him, and Southey could not; for I should have sympathised with his poetico-metaphysical Reveries, (and the very word metaphysics is an abomination to Southey,) and Shelley would have felt that I understood him. His Atheism would not have scared *me*—for *me*, it would have been a semi-transparent Larva, soon to be *sloughed*, and, through which, I should have seen the true *Image*; the final metamorphosis. Besides, I have ever thought *that* sort of Atheism the next best religion to Christianity—nor does the better faith, I have learnt from Paul and John, interfere with the cordial reverence I feel for Benedict Spinoza. As far as Robert Southey was concerned with him, I am quite certain that his harshness arose entirely from the frightful reports that had been made to him respecting Shelley's moral character and conduct—reports essentially false, but, for a man of Southey's strict regularity and habitual self-government, rendered plausible by Shelley's own wild words and horror of hypocrisy.[1]

1702. *To Mrs. William Lorance Rogers*

Address: Mrs Rogers | Upper Bedford Street | Bedford Square
MS. University of London King's College. Hitherto unpublished.
Postmark: Highgate, 23 December 1830.

Grove, Highgate
Wednesday Evening, 22 Decr 1830

My dear Madam

You did me but justice in supposing, that I should feel interested in your Brother's Success. As *your* Brother and from the interest I feel in your & Mr Rogers's feelings, & no *moral* reason forbidding, I should have held myself bound, and (I am sure) should have felt myself desirous, to exert any influence I possessed, in promotion of his views—at all events, to *try* whether I had any or no. And with equal truth and sincerity I can say, that had he been a stranger to you, and I had only known him by his writings and the few opportunities, I have enjoyed of personal intercourse with him,

---

[1] Allsop reports Coleridge as saying of Shelley:
    I was told by one who was with Shelley shortly before his death, that he had in those moments, when his spirit was left to prey inwards, expressed a wish, amounting to anxiety, to commune with me, as the one only being who could resolve or allay the doubts and anxieties that pressed upon his mind. (*Letters, Conversations and Rec.*, 139.)

and after deliberate comparison of his with those, whom I have heard mentioned as his Competitors, it would have been my *duty* to have expressed my conviction both of his fitness and of his *superior* fitness for this Professorship,[1] when and where ever there was a chance of it's producing any effect—however little—And little, I fear, would the influence of my name & opinion be, with the Potentiaries of the World.

I could not see Mr Green till this Afternoon. He will do his best, and will without delay talk with Mr Brodie.[2] He has likewise desired me to draw up in writing my reasons for my high opinion of Mr F. Daniel as a man, a philosopher and an Experimentalist—and he hopes—but this, you must be aware, is the judgement of a partial *friend*—that it may avail something in his hands. At all events, it shall be done forthwith.

Remember me most kindly to dear Mr Rogers—and accept of an old poet's Christmas Blessing on all of your fire-side.

Mr and Mrs Gillman are pretty well—& we have cheerful & satisfactory accounts of and from Henry who, you know, is at Paris under Mr Mathurin. We expect James Gillman tomorrow or next day.—In these doleful times I will not enter on so doleful a ditty, as my own health—but assure you, that sick or well I am, my dear Madam,

with affectionate Esteem | Your sincere Friend
S. T. Coleridge

P.S. Dr Ure's[3] Name was at one time mentioned: there is no need to mention why it has ceased to be so.—But I have heard—but I cannot, will not, believe such an act of folly and degradation could ever have been even deliberated on, that the Professorship was to be offered to Mr Turner,[4] to hold it together with that of the *London*!!—so call it—for the Affix, University, is too gross a misnomer.—Mr Turner, in addition to a compilation from Henry, Murray, and Thompson,[5] published under the title of TURNER'S System of Chemistry, is the Author of a puft letter regularly advertised by the Patentee of English French-Brandy, John Street,

---

[1] John Frederic Daniell was appointed professor of chemistry in King's College, London, on its opening in Oct. 1831.

[2] Sir Benjamin Collins Brodie (1783–1862), sergeant-surgeon to William IV and subsequently to Queen Victoria.

[3] Andrew Ure (1778–1857), chemist and scientific writer.

[4] Edward Turner (1798–1837) held the chair of chemistry in the University of London from 1828 until his death. His *Elements of Chemistry* appeared in 1827, but his most important scientific work was on the atomic weights of the elements.

[5] William Henry (1774–1836), John Murray (d. 1820), and Thomas Thomson (1773–1852), chemists.

West Smithfield—in which the Professor of Chemistry to the London!! assures the Public that the Smithfield Brandy does not differ from *Spirits of Wine* more than the *French* Brandy—

1703. *To Mrs. William Lorance Rogers*

Address: L. Rogers, Esqre | 40 Upper Bedford Place For Mrs Rogers
MS. Mr. Walter T. Spencer. Hitherto unpublished.
Postmark: Highgate, 23 December 1830.

Thursday Afternoon [23 December 1830]
Grove, Highgate

My dear Madam

I have just detected a blunder in my direction of a Letter which I wrote to you last night—after Mrs Gillman with whom I had left your Note, had gone to bed—& which letter our Harriet found on my table this morning & took to the Post before I was awake—I unfortunately directed it, Mrs Rogers, Upper Bedford *Street*, Bedford Square—& am led by Mrs G. to fear that it may not have found it's way to you—

The Contents, however, were—that I had no opportunity of communicating with Mr Green before yesterday afternoon—that he will use whatever influence he has or may have—that he will take care to shew in the proper quarters a paper, I am by his advice drawing up, stating my judgement respecting Mr F. Daniel's *superior* fitness for the Professorship & the reasons on which it is grounded—in short, he will do his best. You will not require me to add, that I shall—for you know that with unfeigned Esteem and affection

I am, my dear Madam, | Your & Mr Rogers's attached Friend
S. T. Coleridge

1704. *To Hyman Hurwitz*

Address: H. Hurwitz Esqre | Granada Cottage | Old Kent Road
MS. University of Pennsylvania Lib. Hitherto unpublished.
Postmark: 27 December 1830.

Monday afternoon [27 December 1830]
Grove, Highgate

My dear Friend

I am afraid this note will not find you in time to answer it's purpose—But if it should reach you in time, can you let me see you either Wednesday or Friday instead of tomorrow?

God bless you | &

S. T. Coleridge

1705. *To Henry Nelson Coleridge*

Address: H. N. Coleridge Esqre | at his Chambers | 1 Lincoln's Inn Square
MS. Victoria University Lib. Hitherto unpublished.
Postmark: 1831.

[January] 1831

Introductory Aphorisms
on the duty and advantage of cultivating the power
and habit of reflection   P. 1–14
    Prudence, Morality, and Religion inter-distinguished   P. 15[1]
    Prudential Aphorisms &c—

My dear Henry
    I find myself too ill, too low, and by the frequent *subsultus* of
muscle & seemingly of the whole trunk too painfully interrupted,
to be able to finish what I had planned & begun—
    Just let the omitted part be added at the end[2]—and substitute
or rather insert the above in the CONTENTS Page—
              God bless you | &
                        S. T. Coleridge

1706. *To J. H. Green*

Address: J. H. Green Esqre | 46 Lincoln's Inn Fields
MS. Pierpont Morgan Lib. Hitherto unpublished.
Postmark: Highgate, 19 January 1831.

Tuesday Night. [18 January 1831]
My dear Friend
    Should this note not meet you in time, & you should have left
Lincoln's Inn Fields for Highgate—it may be for the better—as I

---

  ¹ As Coleridge directed in the second paragraph of the present letter, this
and the preceding entry were inserted in the 'CONTENTS Page' of the second
edition of *Aids to Reflection*, 1831.
  ² The 'omitted part' was printed as an Appendix in the second edition of
the *Aids*, pp. 407–8, and bears the heading: 'A Synoptical Summary of the
Scheme of the Argument to prove the Diversity in Kind, of the Reason and the
Understanding. See p. 227.' The Scheme of the Argument itself appears in
the text of the 1831 *Aids* on pp. 206–27, in the 1825 edition on pp. 208–28. An
autograph of the 'Synoptical Summary' is written in the fly-leaves of a copy
of the first edition of *Aids to Reflection* presented to Stuart and subsequently
acquired by the British Museum. The MS. note is headed: 'Preparative Notice,
to facilitate the understanding of the Disquisition, beginning at p. 228: or
Scheme of the Argument.' The reference should have been to p. 208.
    As Letter 1652 shows, Coleridge intended to make the second edition of the
Aids a rifacimento of the first. He was not able to carry out his plan, but in the
1831 edition he made numerous revisions, omitted many passages which had
appeared in the first edition, and added new material. See Letters 1676,
1696, and 1700.

am not certain that Derwent will have returned from Harrow
before tomorrow evening¹—But I had forgotten, on Sunday, that
Derwent is to quit us on Thursday Morning—& that of course I
should wish to dedicate to him the few hours between his return
from Harrow & his departure for Cornwall. I know of no other
gentleman, for whom I would defer seeing you, or lose a *day of you*
—unless you should be disengaged on Friday or Saturday—

God bless you &

S. T. Coleridge

P.S. I have been more than usually interested with the article in
the last Quarterly on Lyell's 'Principles of Geology'.² Lyell's
motto seems to be—As it was in the beginning, is now, and ever
shall be, World without end. As far as I can judge from the Review,
he has a *half*-truth by the tail—tho' not half *the* truth. He sees
(dimly indeed) the Eternity in the Time; but not—which is of no
less necessity—the *Time* in the Eternity. Nathless, to *see* any *truth*
(✠ a *fact*) is a merit in a hodiern english Naturalist, which has
for me the attraction of novelty.

1707. *To Henry Nelson Coleridge*

Address: H. N. Coleridge, Esqre | 1. Lincoln's Inn Favored by Mr Kinderley
MS. Victoria University Lib. Hitherto unpublished.

In May 1831, almost a year after the death of George IV, the Royal Asso-
ciates of the Royal Society of Literature were notified that their annual grants
of one hundred guineas each were to be discontinued. Ten Royal Associates
had been elected by the Society in 1824 in recognition of their achievements,
and they had regularly received these grants from a fund which George IV
provided each year from the Privy Purse. William IV, however, was unwilling
to contribute a thousand guineas annually for this purpose, and the royal endow-
ment of the Society came to an unexpected end. For Coleridge the loss was
overwhelming. For seven years his pension had given him a measure of inde-
pendence, and he had assumed that it would be paid during his lifetime. He
first sought the advice of his friends, and on 19 May addressed a letter to Lord
Brougham, the chancellor, and another to Sotheby, who had offered to act as
intermediary. Neither letter has come to light, but it is likely that Coleridge
appealed to Brougham in the hope of receiving a civil list pension or sinecure
equal to the annuity which he had lost. Sotheby immediately called on

---

¹ I have heard my mother [Mrs. Derwent Coleridge] say that a scheme was
propounded of my father's taking a large private school at Harrow, but that
the speculation turned out to be too formidable for the capital at his disposal.
[MS. note by E. H. Coleridge.]

² See *Quarterly Review*, Oct. 1830. The first volume of Charles Lyell's *Prin-
ciples of Geology: being an attempt to explain the former Changes of the Earth's
Surface, by reference to causes now in operation*, appeared in 1830. Vols. ii and iii
followed in 1832 and 1833.

Brougham, who in turn consulted Lord Grey, the first lord of the Treasury. In this roundabout way Grey seems to have first learned of the suppression of the grants hitherto paid to the Royal Associates. Convinced that Coleridge was now reduced to desperate want, Grey acted at once and provided a temporary donation from the Treasury. Brougham thereupon informed Sotheby that £200 had been 'found' for Coleridge's use: 'Let him have ½ each year.' An enthusiastic letter of 26 May from Sotheby conveyed the news to Coleridge.

As his letters show, Coleridge did not share Sotheby's gratification, and from the first he was reluctant to accept this gift in lieu of the 'public honor and stipend' formerly conferred on him. Meanwhile, too, he learned that others had intervened on his behalf, Rogers calling on Lord Grey, Lamb appealing indirectly through Grey's brother-in-law. More than ever Coleridge felt certain that the sole consideration of the ministers had been the relief of his poverty, and on 3 June he wrote to Sotheby declining the proffered grant.

On the very day Coleridge communicated his decision to Sotheby he discovered that the plight of the Royal Associates, especially in reference to his own case, was being discussed in the press. 'I have this minute', he informed Sotheby in the postscript to his letter of 3 June, 'seen a paragraph from the Magazine, called the Englishman, in the Times of To Day—& another in yester-morning's Morn. Chronicle.' The article to which Coleridge alluded had appeared in the June 1831 issue of the *Englishman's Magazine* under the title, 'Extraordinary Case of the Royal Associates of the Royal Society of Literature'. The specific and reiterated references to Coleridge suggest that it was written by a friend, probably Joseph Hardman. The writer begins with a brief history of the Society, lists the names of the ten Royal Associates, notes that four of them 'are actually, or in a great measure, dependent for their subsistence on the paltry pittance' hitherto derived 'from the King's annual bounty', and goes on to say: 'Intimation has actually been given on the part of the Crown, to Mr. Coleridge and his brother Associates, that they must expect their allowances "very shortly" to cease. Such is the melancholy and . . . most disgraceful fact. And this too, at a time when . . . the Pension List has been sacredly preserved in all its entireness of political infamy, and while Lord Brougham is attempting to persuade the House of Lords to settle a retiring pension of two hundred per annum on seventy Commissioners of Bankrupt.' Reminding Brougham that he is 'the official keeper of the royal conscience', the writer calls upon him to 'prevent his patriotic master from being *unconsciously* guilty of committing an action so unworthy of the dignity of the beloved sovereign of Britain', who 'can personally know nothing whatever of the matter'. But 'there can be no excuse for the Chancellor if he do not immediately interfere, and hinder a miserable attempt at economy'. The writer also exhorts Lord Grey, who had 'once declaimed most indignantly' against the Scotch for their ungenerous treatment of Burns, to prevent the English from incurring a similar reproach.

On 2 June a writer in *The Times* quoted extensively from this article, but took issue with the author for 'assuring the world, as an official authority', that the pensions of one class only, those 'doled out' to such men of eminence as 'Coleridge, Mathias, . . . and a few others', were 'one and all to be discontinued'. This charge against the government, he insisted, must be false: 'The King's Ministers know nothing of it. Lord BROUGHAM assuredly does not.'

On 3 June the same writer in *The Times* exonerated the ministers of any responsibility for the 'harsh' discontinuance of the pensions of the Royal Associates:

We are now assured, and on the best information, that 'His MAJESTY's Ministers are entirely guiltless of the act.' It is further known that Lord

GREY, on finding that Mr. COLERIDGE had lost, through the exercise of an authority distinct from that of the King's *responsible* servants, the pittance on which he had hitherto existed, has agreed to grant him an annuity equal to that withdrawn from him, though issuing out of a fund which is only temporary. This conduct does honour to Lord GREY, and we trust that his Lordship will ... put the colleagues of Mr. Coleridge also on some less miserable footing.

The writer in *The Times* admitted that the suppression of the pensions had been 'a *blunder*' but laid the blame on William IV:

'The truth is, that the pensions were supplied by order of GEORGE IV. from the Privy Purse, over which . . . no person has authority but the King himself.' The press, the writer concluded, is 'a powerful protector of the destitute'.

Thoroughly aroused by the public attention his poverty had attracted in the press and noting the false statement in *The Times*, purporting to be official, that Lord Grey had awarded him an annuity, Coleridge decided that the truth of the matter should be made public. Thus it was that on 3 June, Gillman, probably at Coleridge's dictation, addressed and signed the following letter to *The Times*, where it appeared on 4 June:

In consequence of a paragraph which appeared in *The Times* of this day, I think it expedient to state the fact respecting Mr. Coleridge as it actually is. On the sudden suppression of the Royal Society of Literature, with the extinction of the honours and annual honoraria of the Royal Associateships, a representation in Mr. Coleridge's behalf was made to Lord Brougham, who promptly and kindly commended the case to Lord Grey's consideration. The result of the application was, that a sum of 200 l., the one moiety to be received forthwith, and the other the year following, by a private grant from the Treasury, was placed at Mr. Coleridge's acceptance; but he felt it his duty most respectfully to decline it, though with every grateful acknowledgment of the prompt and courteous attention which his case had received from both their Lordships.

The writer in *The Times* of 3 June was not the only person who was misinformed concerning the action of Lord Grey. Samuel Rogers, to whom Thomas Pringle applied, was told by Grey that Coleridge was 'still to receive his annuity', and Grey's brother-in-law informed Lamb that the grant was 'renewable three-yearly'. Brougham's note to Sotheby, nevertheless, was specific and clearly indicated that Grey had in mind a temporary grant from the Treasury.

Sotheby was obviously affected by Coleridge's letter of 3 June and immediately called at Highgate. He made Coleridge a gift of £50 and attempted to persuade him that he could accept the grant of £200 'without any sense of degradation'. Coleridge, however, remained unconvinced, and on 14 June he dispatched a letter of explanation to Brougham. The letter has not come to light. On the same day he wrote to Sotheby. There, as far as Coleridge was actively concerned, the matter ended. (See Letters 1708–13.)

The affair of the Royal Associates, however, continued to receive publicity in the press. In the July 1831 issue of the *Englishman's Magazine*, for example, the writer of the earlier article again took up the subject. 'The heads of the Royal Society of Literature', he informed his readers, 'have made a formal appeal to the Premier, and their representations were heard with an attention, ominous, we trust, of the only measure befitting an administration professing a proper deference to the popular voice.' The 'mode' in which the press has espoused the cause of the Royal Associates, he continued, 'proves that the case is considered discreditable to Government'. He also renewed his attack

on the ministers: 'It may be readily believed that a Grey and a Brougham are guiltless of projecting this miserable piece of thrift, but it will be difficult to exonerate them . . . if they fail to repair the injury it has inflicted. . . . Should ministers be resolute in enforcing an inflexible economy, it will be necessary for their reputation to account for the Lord Johns and Lady Georgianas who crowd the pension list, ere they grapple with the mite appropriated to veteran scholarship.' The writer of the article did not mention Coleridge by name, but he put forward an 'illustrative case' which pointed directly to him.

Nothing came of the appeal made by the Royal Society of Literature. Later the title 'Royal Associate' was dropped and 'Honorary Associate' substituted. Unfortunately the minutes of the Society for this period are missing, as are many of the early archives which were lost during the First World War. (From information kindly furnished by Mrs. J. M. Patterson, Secretary of the Society.)

Although Coleridge was unaware of the fact, his case finally came to the attention of the king himself. On 19 July 1831 Stuart wrote to the Earl of Munster, the natural son of William IV. He pointed out that Coleridge had 'no other means of Subsistence' than 'the annuity . . . lately derived from the Royal Society of Literature', and spoke of the poet's age and 'growing infirmity'. It would be a 'reproach' to the nation, Stuart declared, to 'cast into Beggary at the Close of Life, a Man who by his writings has shed a lustre on the age he lives in'. Stuart also reminded Munster of the unfavourable criticism which had arisen: 'It has been reported and is generally believed that the discontinuance of this annuity is not the act of the Ministry but of your Royal Father, who if he saw & knew the Man and his circumstances would certainly have made an exception in his favour.' In his reply of 21 July, Munster promised that he would not fail to lay Stuart's letter before the king, but he offered no encouragement: 'The late King, whose income *doubl'd* my Father's, had the means of giving out of his Privy Purse £1100 a Year, but it was found quite impossible it should be continued in the present reign from the very reduced Income of His present Majesty.' [MSS British Museum. Pub. *Letters from the Lake Poets*, 319–22.]

In publishing the letters of Stuart and Munster, E. H. Coleridge added an incorrect note: 'The annuity which had been conferred on Coleridge in 1825 [1824] was not renewed, but a sum of £300 was ultimately handed over to him by the Treasury.' Likewise, there is no supporting evidence for Scott's assertion that J. H. Frere 'made up to Mr. Coleridge the pension of £200 from the board of literature out of his own fortune'. Only a few months before his death Coleridge said that he had not had 'a shilling of my own in the world since King William the Fourth took my poor gold chain of a hundred links—one hundred pounds— with those of nine other literary veterans, to emblazon d'or the black bar across the Royal arms of the Fitzclarences'. See *Letters from the Lake Poets*, 319 n.; *The Journal of Sir Walter Scott*, ed. J. G. Tait and W. M. Parker, 1950, p. 777; and Letter 1809.

Ultimately the government acted more liberally towards two of the ten Associates, but not before death had reduced the number by half, Edward Davies and William Roscoe dying in 1831, Coleridge and T. R. Malthus in 1834, and T. J. Mathias in 1835. Sharon Turner received a civil list pension of £300 per annum from 1835 until his death in 1847. James Millingen, too, was granted a civil list pension of £100 a year 'as a person devoted to literary pursuits'.

19 May 1831.

My dear Henry

Mr Carey & Mr Gillman agree in thinking that as Mr Sotheby

had offered his kind Services to me, and as he is on good terms with Lord Brougham, it would be wrong for me not to make my first request to him—the sole present Object being to secure the letter being delivered into the Chancellor's own hands, so that I might know it—

If therefore you would be so good as to call yourself on Mr Sotheby, a letter to whom I inclose, as soon as you can, and receive his answer from me [him?], you will be serving me. Should he for any reason decline the office, then if you would call on Mr Rogers & send in your Name & card as desiring to speak to him from me, I have every reason to believe that you would meet with a very courteous & friendly reception—Do as your discretion dictates— . . . [MS. cut off.]

1708. *To Henry Nelson Coleridge*

MS. *Victoria University Lib. Hitherto unpublished.*

[Endorsed 23 May 1831]

My dear Henry

I had so fully expected, *'cause* I wished it, rather than *reason* for requiring it—to have received a line from you this morning, that not having done so, I begin to fear lest some cross accident should have prevented your receipt of my letter—with the letters inclosed, left by Mr Kinderley at your Chambers on Friday Morning. On thinking the subject over, too late if I think aright, I almost regret that I had not taken the chance of committing my letter for Lord Brougham to the Post—so as to disconnect it altogether from any intercession made by others, which, I have had intimated to me, *includes* my name.[1] Now I would fain stand or fall for myself—and God forbid! my poverty should be made the plea, unless on the principle that it is not indeed laeta, but honesta Paupertas—that it is not only innocent in respect to the occasion, but honorable in regard of the Cause. However, let it now take it's course—Only let me hear from you, whether you have been able to see Mr Sotheby, & when—& in short, what has become of the Letter.

I have carefully read over your second Edition[2]—and on reading

[1] A reference to the activities of Joseph Hardman and Thomas Pringle. See Letter 1712.

[2] Probably *Notes on the Reform Bill, by a Barrister*, 1831. Edith Coleridge, who had a copy of the third edition, attributed the authorship to her father, H. N. Coleridge. A copy of this work containing annotations by Coleridge is in the British Museum.

the excellent paragraph against the scoffers of virtual representa-
tion—who by the bye, triumph in Lord Chatham's Speech during
the American War against the doctrine of virtual representation,
I could not help feeling that tho' representation is far more
appropriate than delegation, yet that both terms are fallacious—
O for Reason in the shape of Common Sense!
God bless you &
S. T. Coleridge.

1709. *To Henry Nelson Coleridge*

Address: H. N. Coleridge, Esqre. | Downshire Hill | Hampstead
MS. Victoria University Lib. Hitherto unpublished.

Friday afternoon. [Endorsed May 27, 1831]
My dear Henry

I am by no means disposed to question the positive nutriment
contained in a bread and milk poultice newly removed from a sore
leg—and whether it's nutritive virtues are or are not enhanced
by the animalization, I am content to leave undecided. Still farther
from my thought and inclination is it to controvert the ancient
adage which asserts the harmony and correlation of hungry dogs
and dirty dumplins. It is a beautiful instance of the distinction
between correspondent Opposites and belligerent Contraries—
a finely proportioned adjustment of ab extra to ad intra, of
Stimulus to Stimulability. Yet nevertheless (Miltonice, nathless)
a letter, of this morning's receipt from Mr Sotheby—rather let me
say, a trumpet *note* of gratulation from the friendly Resurrection-
Angel of Maeonides, hath somewhat startled me—gave my poor
intellects a touch of the *Staggers*—Mr Gillman doubts my inter-
pretation of it—therefore, I here transcribe it, verbatim et litera-
tim: except that the emphatic ===== under the first two lines are
comments of my own addition.

Lower Grosvenor St
May 26 1831.
My dear Coleridge

I have SUCCEEDED BEYOND MY HOPES tho' not BEYOND YOUR
MERITS! YET MY HOPES WERE HIGH, when I applied in your behalf
to men of such cultivated minds as the Chancellor and Lord Grey.
I have expressed my thanks by letter to Both—I need not recom-
mend that to you. For your further gratification I copy Lord
Brougham's letter to me—
ever most truly | yr
Wm Sotheby.

'My dear Sir

Lord Grey has taken a very kind interest in our Friend Coleridge's Affair; and he has found 200£ which he can and will forthwith apply to his use. Let him have ½ each year.

yrs &c H.B.'—

Now all I can make out of this communication is that as a compensation for a life annuity of One Hundred Guineas in connection with a title of Honor, suddenly taken away from me the very week when the 105£ should have been delivered to me, Lord Grey makes me a present of two hundred pound; but this to be entrusted into my hands in two installments, with a year's interval—so that on the supposition that a hundred pound would suffice to prevent me from starving for 12 months, I have a *respite* of a full year, before my deposition in the Work-house—For (as in my letter to Lord Brougham I distinctly stated) the 105£, due to me on May 1. 1831, formed the means, on which I had been authorized to rely, of defraying my Board &c from May 1. 1830—.

Now I really want your advice—and if you can by any means manage it, take this way to town tomorrow—and your breakfast with Mr & Mrs Gillman at your own hour—A place may be taken for you in the ten o'clock Stage—or if you must be at your Chambers before 11, there is a nine o'clock Stage to Holborn—. I must write tomorrow—& yet without talking it over with my friends, I know not what or in what tone & spirit to express myself.—Do you perceive any possibility that I have misconceived Mr Sotheby's note?—My best Love to Sara and the bonny Suck. Cubus[1]—& to the *original Sara*—God bless you | and

S. T. Coleridge

Just let me [have] a few words from you—for I cannot trust John's Memory for the safe transmission of a verbal answer.

S. T. C.

1710. *To Henry Nelson Coleridge*

Address: H. N. Coleridge, Esqre | Downshire Hill | Hampstead.
MS. Victoria University Lib. Hitherto unpublished.

My dear Henry   Saturday Afternoon [28 May 1831][2]

After you left me, it began to dawn on my mind what from the Selflessness of my habits of thinking had not risen above the horizon

---

[1] Herbert Coleridge was born on 7 Oct. 1830. After a distinguished career at Oxford he was elected a member of the Philological Society in 1857. His *Glossarial Index to the Printed English Literature of the Thirteenth Century*, 1859, laid the basis for the *New English Dictionary*, of which he was the first general editor. He died on 23 Apr. 1861.

[2] This letter is endorsed 29 May 1831, the date it was received.

of my consciousness—that under existing circumstances, incidents and accidentalities on all sides, and I having hitherto stood on the footing of a slowly growing but still growing, confidential, *equal* friendship with Mr Green—tho' for some years I have known, that he looked forward wishfully to a time when Success in life might enable him to enable me to devote the residue of my intellectual strength to the great Object of my life undistracted by the calls of the *To Day*—under existing circumstances there would be an *indelicacy* on my part in calling him into council with you and Mr Gillman—First of all, he is not at present in clear light respecting his own arrangements—concerning which & the occasion of which, what passed between us, you will hold sacred to your own thoughts —& then it might have if not a semblance yet the effect, of a question—Can you do any thing?—Mrs Gillman coincides with me in this—i.e. that it would be much better at once to write to Sotheby, and modestly decline the offered boon, and then inform my friend what I had done as a thing already done and settled.— I therefore recall my request respecting your interview with him tomorrow.—

This business does not within my consciousness produce painful thoughts or anxieties in my mind—but probably runs under ground and emerges in my body—for I am even more than usually unwell, sick and sinking. There is *Peace* however within.—Love to all.—

S. T. Coleridge

1711. *To William Sotheby*

Address: W. Sotheby, Esqre. | Lower Grosvenor Street
MS. Mr. W. Hugh Peal. Pub. E. L. G. ii. 434.
Postmark: Highgate, 3 June 1831.

[3 June 1831]

My dear Sir

A *metastatic* fit, or *fall-in*, of my nervous Rheumatism, which occurred on the same day with the receipt of your Note, or rather the Sickness, faintness, and inquietude consequent on and symptomatic of these Caprices of the Nerves, must be my apology for having allowed so many days to pass without any record of my thanks to *you* for the undelaying promptness with which you placed my letter to the L. Chancellor in his Lordship's own hands. Could I, indeed, have expressed my sense of your friendly service without reference to the contents of your Note, ill as I was, I should have replied on the instant. But I was jealous of the possible influence, which the extreme depression of Spirits incident to my Complaint might exercise on my judgement: and even on the ground of

respect to *you*—not to mention others, who without my knowlege
have, I find, taken a similar friendly interest in this affair,[1] I was
most anxious that my determination should be such as might stand
the test of my Reason, and Sense of *Duty*—such as might be sanc-
tioned by the Conscience at that hour, when the *feelings* whether
of Pride or of Vanity, with all that had stirred them, will be as
Toys by the bed-side of a sick and moaning child.

This I believe myself now capable of doing: and therefore, hav-
ing once more returned thanks to yourself for your kind wishes,
friendly intentions, and prompt efforts in my cause, I beg leave
thro' you to convey, both to the L. Chancellor and Lord Grey, my
grateful acknowlegement of the prompt attention, which my case
has received from their Lordships, and my due appreciation of the
humane desire, evinced by them, to prevent or obviate the *imme-
diate* distress or embarrassment, in which the sudden Withdrawal
and unforeseen Extinction of the honor and honorarium of a Royal

[1] Coleridge apparently refers to the activities of Charles Lamb. When
Lamb learned that Coleridge had lost his annuity as a Royal Associate, he
took up the matter with his friend Badams. The only information concerning
this intervention, which was made without Coleridge's knowledge, comes from
a confused and telescoped account included in Lamb's letter to Edward Moxon
postmarked 14 June 1831. The passage reads as follows:

> About 8 days before you told me of R.'s interview with the Premier, I,
at the desire of Badams, wrote a letter to him (Badams) in the most moving
terms setting forth the age, infirmities &c. of Coleridge. This letter was con-
vey'd by B. to his friend Mr. Ellice of the Treasury, Brother in Law to Lord
Grey, who immediately press'd it on Lord Grey, who assured him of imme-
diate relief by a grant on the King's Bounty, which news E. communicated
to B. with a desire to confer with me on the subject, on which I went up to
The Treasury (yesterday fortnight) & was received by the Great Man, . . .
[who] promised me an answer thro' Badams in 2 or 3 days at furthest.
Meantime Gilman's extraordinary insolent letter comes out in the Times!
As to *my* acquiescing in this strange step, I told Mr. Ellice (who expressly
said that the thing was renewable three-yearly) that I consider'd such a grant
as almost equivalent to the lost pension, as from C's appearance & the re-
presentations of the Gilmans, I scarce could think C.'s life worth 2 years'
purchase. I did not know that the Chancellor had been previously applied to.
Well, after seeing Ellice I wrote in the most urgent manner to the Gilmans,
insisting on an immediate letter of acknowledgment from Coleridge, or them
in his name to Badams, who not knowing C. had come forward so disinter-
estedly, . . . & from that day not a letter has B. or even myself, received from
Highgate, unless *that publish'd one in the Times is meant as a general answer
to all the friends who have stirr'd to do C. service*! [MS. Huntington Library,
from a transcript kindly furnished by Mr. H. C. Schulz. Pub. *Lamb Letters*,
iii. 315–16, where the postmark is erroneously given as 14 July 1831.]

Grey could not have assured Ellice of a 'grant on the King's Bounty', since
only the king himself controlled expenditures from the privy purse. Likewise,
there is no evidence that Grey proposed a grant which was 'renewable three
yearly'.

Associate of the Royal Society of Literature might otherwise involve me, by a private Grant from the Treasury of *200£:— but that I beg leave most respectfully to decline it.

This, my dear Sir! is all, I presume, that it is necessary for me, or that it would be becoming in me, to say to their Lordships. But to *You* I seem to myself to owe a statement of the reasons that have actuated me to this decision: and at some future opportunity, God granting any such, I hope to do this *at full*. But for the present let it suffice to remind you, that at no period of my life have I ever attached myself, or in fact belonged to, any Party, religious or political—that I have never labored for any lower purpose, than the establishment of PRINCIPLES, the discovery or determination of LAWS—(*see the inclosed scrip*).[1] But tho' neither Whig nor Tory, I am enough of the latter, I trust, sincerely and habitually to fear God: and to honor the King, as ordained of God—i.e. as no Reflection or Derivative from the (pretended) Sovereignty of the *People*, but as the lawful Representative, the consecrated Symbol of the Unity and Majesty of the *Nation*: and therefore, with all the possible deference and respect that can be felt toward a Nobleman personally a stranger to me, I cannot but find a most essential difference between a private donation from Lord Grey, and a public honor and stipend conferred on me by my Sovereign in mark of approval of the objects and purposes to which I had devoted and was continuing to devote the powers and talents entrusted to me.

* a moiety of which was (if I understand Lord Brougham's note aright) to be entrusted to me immediately, in discharge of any obligations for the liquidation of which I had relied on the 105£, that should have been received on the first of last Month—i.e. 1 May, 1831: the other 100£ to be held in reserve by you, & bestowed on me the year following. *S.T.C.*

[1] Coleridge's '*inclosed scrip*' reads:

'The remedial and prospective advantages of habitually contemplating Particulars in their universal or general Laws: the tendency of this habit at once to fix and to liberalize the morality of private life, at once to produce and to enlighten the spirit of public Zeal; and let me add, its especial utility in recalling the origin and primary import of the term, GENEROSITY (*a genere*—i.e. the qualities supposed native to men of noble Race, or such as their Rank & *Kind* are calculated to elicit—) to the hearts and thoughts of a Populace long tampered with by the Sophists and incendiaries of the revolutionary Faction—these advantages I have felt it my duty and have made it my main object to enforce and illustrate during the whole period of my literary labors from earliest manhood to the present hour! Whatever may have been the specific theme of my communications, and whether they related to Politics, Religion, Poetry, or the Fine Arts, still PRINCIPLES, their subordination, their connection, and their application, in all the divisions of our tastes, duties, rules of conduct & schemes of belief, have constituted my chapter of Contents.' Lay-sermon addressed to the Higher and Middle Classes on the existing Distresses and Discontents: INTRODUCTION, p. viii.—1817.

From the latter to the former would be indeed a μετάβασις εἰς ἄλλο γένος! At my first presentation to the Royal Society of Literature[1] I publicly stated—that I received 'the appointment with glad and grateful feeling, as powerfully confirming me in the assurance, that I had not mistaken my vocation, retrospectively: and prospectively as a means of enabling me to give my whole time and entire powers to the completion of those more important works, for which I regarded all, I had hitherto attempted, whether vivâ voce or by the Press, but as a preparatory discipline': and I ended with the same remark on the two orders of men of Letters, the distributors & popularizers of knowlege already in the possession of [the] Learned, and the Advancers or Perfectors of the knowlege itself,[2] with which I concluded my last note to you, accompanying my letter to the Chancellor.—

[1] Coleridge was formally presented to the Royal Society of Literature on 6 May 1824. See Letters 1382 and 1395.

[2] While the following fragment is not a part of Coleridge's letter to Sotheby, it was certainly written at this time.

Substance of my Address to the Pres. &c of the Royal Society of Literature on my election and introduction, as a Royal Associate.

'Men of Letters may be distinguished into two classes—of which the first and far more numerous have it for their Object to distribute and popularize the stores of knowlege already existing, and devote their talents to the instruction and entertainment of the Many. And these men, if they have not wholly mistaken their vocation, may rationally look for their own remuneration to the Public in whose service they labor; and, in our times at least, can scarcely fail to receive it in a tolerably fair proportion to the fitness of the means, they adopt, to the end, they propose. But in every age and country there is, or ought to be, a smaller class, consisting of those who labor in the service of Science itself, for the enlargement of it's precincts or the deepening of it's foundations: and who must needs narrow the circle of their immediate influence and diminish the number of their readers in exact proportion to the success of their attempts. And to whom shall such men look for support and patronage, but to the lawful Representative of THE NATION, contra-distinguished from the People, as the Unity of the Generations of a people organized into a State—that is, to the King, or the Sovereign.'—

I then adverted to the Works, to which I had dedicated, during the last 15 years of my life, all my means and talents, and every hour, which ill-health and the necessity of staving-off the wants of the To-Day had left at my own disposal—'that in the consciousness of this, I accepted with thankfulness my unsolicited appointment, as Royal Associate, as tending powerfully to confirm me in the trust, that in devoting myself to the higher Literature I had not mistaken my Calling, and the annual stipend attached to it (mem. £105), because with strict economy, and with my few and simple wants it would enable me to employ my whole time in the completion of that System of Truths respecting Nature, Man, and Deity, evolved from one Principle, undiverted by tasks, which many, very many, of my younger Contemporaries could execute far better than myself.'

The result.—I, S. T. Coleridge, faithfully abided by my engagement—but

Further: in this letter to Lord Brougham I did not indeed hesi-
tate to avow my Poverty. But grievously have I been misunder-
stood, if I have been supposed to plead that Poverty, for itself and
independent of it's Causes, as the ground of my application. I
avowed it because I knew it to have been not only a blameless but
an honorable Poverty—no consequence or penance of Vice,
Extravagance, Improvidence or Idleness—but the effect and
result of an entire and faithful dedication of myself to Ends and
Objects, for the realization and attainment of which I was con-
strained to believe myself *especially* fitted & therefore *called,* in
open-eyed and voluntary dereliction of those more lucrative
employments, equally and at many periods of my life in my power,
but which hundreds of my Contemporaries could fill with equal or
perhaps greater probability of success.—N.b. This argument
weighs & ought to weigh the more with me, that tho' I have
(perhaps, with faulty indifference) abstained from noticing the
strange reports of myself, of my philosophic *Indolence,* &c, &c in
sundry Reviews & Pseudo-biographies (as beyond the wont of
calumnious Gossip in direct contrariancy to the truth), I cannot
be insensible to the fact of such reports having been widely circu-
lated.—Should it please God to remove me to morrow, the MSS
Works already prepared for the Press, would abundantly document
the words of an honored & intimate friend, the concluding sentence
of a letter—'All Success attend you: for if hard thinking, hard
reading, and perseverant labor are merits, you have deserved it.'—
Might I request a favor from you, my dear Sir! it would be that you
would cast your eye thro' a few pages of my 'Biographia Literaria'
—If I mistake not, this work is in your library—p. 190–221: Vol. I.
—and the seven last pages of the second Volume.—

One other remark, my dear Sir! and you shall be released. The
issues of our life are with God! I place no reliance on my fancies,
as well aware that they are the fancies of a Patient—but if I dared
trust my own presentiments, I should hold it not improbable, that
this 200£ would suffice to *bury* me as well as to sustain me while
alive. But even on the assumption, that some such sum *must* be
received by me from some quarter, that in the prideless resignation
of a Christian it would be *my duty* to receive it—yet there is in my
estimation a wide difference between receiving it from *half a dozen*
or even *half a score Friends,* who had long known & loved me, who
had witnessed & respected the innocence & simplicity of my life,

when old age and increasing bodily infirmities had conspired to disqualify
me for undertaking any of the lighter & only bread-winning kinds of writing,
the annuity was suddenly withdrawn, not only without any notice or prepara-
tion, . . . [MS. Pierpont Morgan Library.]

and professed to hold themselves morally or intellectually in-
debted to my writings and conversations—and accepting the same
sum, in the dark as it were, from a Stranger who neither knows or
thinks aught of me but my wants, and on the score of the want
exclusively, without reference to or recognition of any merit, has
been induced to concede it as an eleemosynary Grant.—The two
prayers of my heart—for our *thoughtful* Desires, our earnest
Aspirations as soon as they are united with the sense of the Divine
Presence become *Prayers*—my two remaining Prayers, the one
conditional, namely, if it should be for the advantage of my Fellow-
men—the other, unconditional, are—that He who has hitherto
sustained my life, may yet enable me to put the last hand to the
works, so near their completion! and 'not to forsake me in my old
age, now I am grey-headed—until I have shewn his truth unto this
generation, and the breadth, depth, and exceeding Goodness of
his Laws, Ways, and Dispensations to them that are yet for to come'.
Psalm 71. v. 16 [18].—The other is—to die in the faith in which I
have lived, laying hold of the promises of mercy in Christ, the
trust in *his* perfect righteousness prevailing over the sense of my
own unworthiness.—

Commending myself respectfully to Mrs Sotheby's kind remem-
brance, I remain, my dear Sir, your obliged & grateful Friend &
Servant,

S. T. Coleridge.—

Friday Afternoon, 3 June 1831.

P.S. I have this minute seen a paragraph from the Magazine,
called the Englishman, in the Times of To Day—& another in
yestermorning's Morn. Chronicle.—Without noticing the strange
misstatement of the Times[1]—I need not assure you, that the whole
was written & published without my consent—but I ought, per-
haps, to say that it has not been without *surprize* on my part.—
The Publishers—Hurst & Hardman[2]—having some month ago
intimated to Mr Gillman, that a Contributor to the Englishman
had proposed to write an Article on the Suppression of the R.S.L.—
especially, in reference to my case—& wished to know, whether
I had applied to the Ministers or any of them, & what answer I had
received—. Mr Gillman at my urgence instantly waited on Mr

---

[1] *The Times* of 2 June included an extensive quotation from the *English-
man's Magazine. The Times* of 3 June contained the 'strange misstatement'
that Lord Grey had granted Coleridge an 'annuity'. See headnote to Letter
1707.

[2] Hurst, Chance, and Company published the first four numbers of the
Englishman's Magazine, Apr.–July 1831. (H. G. Merriam, *Edward Moxon*,
1939, p. 31.)

Hardman, from me—stating that I had (as was then the fact) sent no Letter to the Minister or to Lord Brougham, consequently could have received no answer—that in my judgement, any such article *could* do no good, and *might* work injuriously—but at all events, as a *personal* favor I INTREATED, that *my* name should not be introduced, nor any allusion made to any intercession that had been & should be, made in my particular behalf.

S. T. Coleridge

1712. *To Thomas Pringle*

Pub. Fraser's Magazine, *January 1835, p. 56.*

On 23 May, shortly after he had himself written to Brougham concerning the loss of his annuity, Coleridge wrote to his nephew of an 'intercession made by others, which, I have had intimated to me, *includes* my name'. Undoubtedly this information came from Joseph Hardman, who had asked Thomas Pringle to intercede on Coleridge's behalf. Pringle took up the matter with Colonel Fox (probably C. R. Fox, appointed equerry to Queen Adelaide in 1830), James Mackintosh, and Samuel Rogers. Mackintosh, who was at Harrogate, wrote to Pringle on 26 May 1831: 'To get a pension or a sinecure from the present Ministers is something like trying to pull down the moon. I should almost think a subscription more promising.' Rogers called at the ministry on 26 May, found that Coleridge's case had already been settled, and on the 27th reported to Pringle: 'I saw Lord Grey yesterday, and am happy to say that the work is done for Coleridge. He is still to receive his annuity. To you it must give double pleasure, for it is in a great degree your work.' Pringle immediately conveyed the news to Hardman, who replied on 28 May: 'I shall always consider that Mr. Coleridge is indebted *to you* for this important benefit, for *by you* and *your friends* alone has the impulse been given. I shall have the pleasure of leaving your note with Mr. Coleridge this afternoon, and you will doubtless hear from him.' (*The Poetical Works of Thomas Pringle*, ed. with a sketch of Pringle's life by Leitch Ritchie, 1839, 2nd edn., pp. cviii–cx.) The following extract is all that has come to light of Coleridge's explanatory letter to Pringle. The comments closely parallel those made in the letter to Sotheby of 3 June, and the two letters were probably written about the same time. It was, of course, Coleridge's own letter to Brougham and Sotheby's intervention which led Grey to offer a temporary *grant* from the Treasury—not an *annuity*, as Rogers stated.

[Circa 3 June 1831]

At no period of my life have I ever belonged to any party, religious or political; never laboured for any lower purpose than the establishment or maintenance of principles; but though neither Whig nor Tory, I am enough of the latter, I trust, sincerely and habitually to fear God, and to honour the king as ordained of God; as no reflection or derivation from the sovereignty of the *people*, but as the lawful and consecrated symbol and representative of the unity and majesty of the *nation*.

At my first introduction to the R. S. L., I stated that I received the appointment with glad and grateful feeling, as tending powerfully to confirm me in the hope, that I had not mistaken my vocation,—retrospectively, and prospectively, as a means of enabling me to devote my whole time and strength to the completion of the more important works, for which I regarded all I had hitherto published, *vivâ voce*, or by the press, but as preparatory discipline.

Grievously have I been misunderstood, if I have been supposed to plead that poverty of itself, and independent of its causes, as the ground of my application. I avowed it because I know it not only to be a blameless but an *honourable* poverty; not the consequence and penance of vice, improvidence, or idleness, but the effect of an entire and faithful dedication of myself to ends and objects to the attainment of which I was bound to believe myself peculiarly fitted, and therefore *called*, in open-eyed and voluntary dereliction of those more lucrative employments equally and at many periods of my life in my power, but in which hundreds of my contemporaries could engage with equal or perhaps greater probability of success.

1713. *To William Sotheby*

Address: W. Sotheby, Esqre | 13 Lower Grosvenor Street
MS. Cornell University Lib. Hitherto unpublished.

14 June 1831.
Grove Highgate

My dear Sir

The Gentleman, who will leave this at your House, is at the same time the Bearer of my Letter to the Lord Chancellor. You had advised, & I had promised to write this letter—and the nature of *it's* contents, that is, what I finally deemed it my duty to determine on, I thought of as the most important or rather to *me* important and to your kindness not uninteresting portion of the Letter which I likewise, *by a suggestion of my own*, promised to write to you—With this view I could not write the latter till I had effected the former—for as two only of my friends, yourself and Mr Green (Mr Cline's Nephew) were of opinion, that 'the receiving of an eleemosynary grant in commutation for an honor' was an exaggerated interpretation of the fact, and that I might take it without any sense of degradation, I labored at the time, you were with me, under an uneasy presentiment—and on that account deferred what might so easily have been done, giving you an acknowlegement of the receipt of the 50£ at the moment. But in fact it was my purpose to

make the acceptance of the one dependant on my declining of the
other—or at least that it should give me an opportunity of record-
ing in a letter to you, that in declining the Grant of 200£ or 300£
from the Treasury I was actuated by no feeling of pride or vanity—.

The next day I received a communication from a friend, who
had just seen a letter from Col. Fox on the subject & which
placed it out of doubt, that the grant had been both applied for &
granted *exclusively* in consideration of my *Want*—of my *distressed*
situation—This again did not affect, or even diminish, my sense of
Lord Brougham's and Lord Grey's kindness—but the annoyance
of having day after day to be thinking about myself brought on,
or mainly assisted in bringing on, so severe a relapse of my Com-
plaints, that till yesterday I could never finish such a letter to Lord
Brougham, as I could even myself think worthy of his perusal.—
Now, my dear Sir! I do not send this, *as* my acknowlegement of
the 50£, tho' it is such: but merely to explain the delay—& I will
write to you tomorrow, at all events, as soon as I can copy out
the draft of my Letter to the Chancellor which I wish you to have
—For whatever come of it, I shall never cease to feel & remember
that

I am your obliged & I trust grateful | Friend & Servt.

S. T. Coleridge

1714. *To Charles Stutfield*

Address: Charles Stutfield, Esqre | Grove Place | Hackney
MS. Cornell University Lib. Pub. Letters Hitherto Uncollected, *56*.
Postmark: Highgate, 22 August 1831.

Grove, Highgate.
Sunday Night
21 Aug. 1831.

My dear Stutfield

I thank you for your very kind letter. As far as I have been the
Sower of good Seed, I am willing to take my credit of the Harvest,
without however forgetting how much is to be set off for the genial
Soil.

I shall have great pleasure in pressing a Spiritual father's kiss on
your dear little girl—in the full belief, that it is both your and
Mrs Stutfield's earnest desire that she should grow up a daughter
of Christ. For Christianity is the Humanization of the Man, but it
is the Apotheosis of the Woman, in every name of Duty, Daughter,
Wife, Mother and Friend.—

A sad relapse, last night, from which I obtained a reprieve only
this Evening, makes me afraid to promise myself the enjoyment

of dining with you. But at all events, I shall be ready for your Carriage—and hope, I shall induce Mrs Gillman to accompany me.

Your lively account of your S[torm]y Polemic grieved but did not surprize me—But we will talk on this subject. It is strange that so vigorous a Thinker should not have remembered, that the Elective Franchise is but a means to a Legislature, and a Legislature itself but a means to a right Government—the best definition of which would be—that which under the circumstances most effectually provides Security for the Possessors, Facility for the Acquirers and Hope for All.

Give my affectionate respects to Mrs Stutfield—And believe me ever your sincere Friend,

S. T. Coleridge

1715. *To J. H. Green*

Address: J. H. Green, Esqre | &c &c | 36 Lincoln's Inn Fields
MS. Pierpont Morgan Lib. Hitherto unpublished.
Postmark: Highgate, 13 September 1831.

Grove, Highgate
Tuesday Afternoon
13 September 1831.

My dear Friend

I have had no relapse, since we last parted: and am at this moment so much better, that with some confidence of hope I can look forward to the pleasure of seeing you, either tomorrow or Thursday, on a tolerably fair speculation that it will not be a mere waste of your time in sympathy with the doleful. As my intestinal Canal has subsided into a Calm, the Bronchia have set to work, all hands or glands rather, in the production and excretion of phlegm—. The quantity, that yesterday and to day, I have expectorated, from the moment of quitting my bed to near dinner time, might alarm me: but that I see grounds for the hope, that nature is in this way relieving herself.—

Query. Wherein does Dr Stevens's new Fever-scheme differ from the theory and practice of old Sylvius?[1] With him all diseases were referred to excess or deficiency of Acid—all malignant Fevers to the excess of Acid in the Blood with deficiency of the Saline ingredients—& the Antidotes were the Alkalies & alcaline Carbonates. —Dr Stevens too is avowedly a Humoral Pathologist.—How a new theory may mystify a clever man's Logic! Dr St. himself starts or repeats a seemingly awkward matter-of-fact Objection

---

[1] Sylvius, originally F. de la Boë (1614–72), the founder of the iatro-chemical school of medicine.

to his System—viz. that all the signs of superacid Blood co-exist in
their utmost prominence in the malignant Sea-Scurvy—and yet
this is cured by Citric Acid, Sour-crout, Scurvy-grass & the like as
by a Charm.—What does our Sylvius redivivus answer to this?—
O—an American Gentleman had so weakened his constitution by
using citric Acid in excess, under the notion that it was a preventive
of the Yellow-fever, that he became Scorbutic, and Dr St. cured him
by Valeric medicines—and then as to the efficacy of the citric acid
on Scurvy generally, the Doctor gives a *knowing* shake of the head
at it, as a *mallem non credere!*—Now the only satisfactory answers
would have been—*either* a proof of a diversity of *kind* in the black
blood of Scurvy and that of malignant fevers from aerial poisons;
or a downright—You *lie!*—'Tis all a damned LIE! to the numerous
attestations of Naval Surgeons, admirals, Voyagers &c &c.—

Did you notice the §§ ph in Monday's *Times*—with the Lines in
Small Capitals inviting the Army to mutiny and refuse to obey
command in case of the House of Lords rejecting or trifling with
the Reform Bill?[1]—If this hellish Licence is suffered to go on, a

[1] The Grey ministry, which was pledged to parliamentary reform, had in-
troduced the Reform Bill 'to amend the Representation of the People in
England and *Wales*' into the House of Commons on 1 Mar. 1831, but at the
second reading on 22 Mar. the Bill had passed by a majority of only one. On
19 Apr. a hostile amendment was carried in committee by eight votes. Grey
now proposed an appeal to the country, and William IV reluctantly consented
to a dissolution of Parliament on 22 Apr. The elections gave the ministry a
large majority. The Reform Bill was again introduced into the House of Com-
mons on 24 June and passed the second reading on 7 July, the third reading
on 22 Sept. Lord Grey introduced the Bill into the House of Lords, but at the
second reading on 8 Oct. it was rejected by a majority of 41. Widespread
disorders followed. Parliament was prorogued on 20 Oct., and the Grey
ministry averted a dangerous crisis by deciding not to resign, but instead to
reintroduce the Reform Bill when Parliament reassembled. It was presented,
with alterations, to the House of Commons for the third time on 12 Dec. 1831.
It passed the second reading on 17 Dec., the third reading on 23 Mar. 1832.
Towards the end of 1831 Grey's ministers had debated in cabinet whether the
king should be urged to create a sufficient number of peers to ensure passage
of the Bill in the House of Lords. Grey at first opposed such a strong measure,
but on 1 Jan. 1832 the ministry agreed to advocate this course of action if
necessary, and the king was so informed. See note to Letter 1744 for details
concerning the passage of the Reform Bill in the House of Lords in 1832.
   Coleridge bitterly opposed the Reform Bill but he did not reject the idea
of reform itself. Writing to Poole in 1835, H. N. Coleridge declared: 'It suits
the M. Chronicle in a paragraph I saw the other day, to say that S. T. C. vitu-
perated Parliamentary Reform: no such thing; he only abused this Reform Bill
—a very different thing, I conceive.' John Colmer, *Coleridge, Critic of Society*,
1959, p. 107. For Coleridge's comments on the Reform Bill, see Letters 1726, 1730,
1741, 1742, 1744, 1751, and 1757; and *Table Talk*, 20 Mar., 25 June, 20 Nov.,
and 17 Dec. 1831, and 22 Feb., 24 Feb., 3 Mar., 20 Mar., 5 Apr., and 21 May
1832. See also H. N. Coleridge's Preface to *Table Talk*.

civil War will be the result.—The first thing the House of Lords ought to do should be, to pass and present a solemn address to the King on the system of intimidation carried on by the Journalists & Pamphleteers under the presumed protection and partially *expressed* approval of his Majesty's Ministers—including the abuse of his royal name, as an incentive to, and in sanction of, rebellion. —The last *Noctes* ambrosianae in Blackwood's September is worth your reading—it is an interesting political Gossip.—

Remember me affectionately to Mrs Green.

Ever truly your's

S. T. Coleridge.

1716. *To J. H. Green*

Address: J. H. Green, Esqre | &c &c | 36 Lincoln's Inn Fields
MS. Pierpont Morgan Lib. Hitherto unpublished.
Postmark: Highgate, 21 September 1831.

Wednesday afternoon
21 Septr. 1831.

My dear Friend

A menace, in truth a fraction, of a Relapse yestermorning, and the exhaustion & languor in which the Coughing, the Sickness and Expectoration left me, took away from me the heart to write you. After 4 o'clock, P.M. however, I cleared up, had a tranquil night, and bating the exantlation of the mucus from the hold and bilge of my poor crazy Lugger, feel at present pretty comfortable.—Still, however, I am not certain, whether the main object at present in my wish will not be more probably furthered by deferring our meeting till Sunday, and putting my thoughts into trim in the interim—the rather, that Henry Taylor has written to Mrs Gillman & likewise to me, requesting earnestly, if my Health will permit me even to pass an hour with him, to be allowed to bring two of his friends, Members of Parliament, on Thursday Evening—who are anxious to have some conversation with me—and as he has been twice put off, we did not choose to return a negative the third time.

Warsaw!—But what would the TIMES have the British & French Governments do, *now*? Join in attacking Austria, Prussia and Holland in order to fight their way northward to the re-conquest of Poland?[1]—The Hordes of the Tsar would, I doubt not, be polite enough to give them the meeting halfway—Well! it is a bold plan. —Remember me affectionately to Mrs Green: and do not forget to

[1] In Nov. 1830 a military revolt against the Russians began in Warsaw. By Oct. 1831 the Poles had been conquered and the former Congress Kingdom of Poland was reduced to the position of a Russian province.

ask Dr Elliotson[1] about the inhalation of chlorine in my case. I am strongly inclined to think, that this excessive Expectoration depends mainly on matter or secretions irritating the middle intestines: and that both the Expectoration and the sciatic weakness are effects of the same cause. But alas! who shall extricate my feet out of the Net which I have unhappily woven for myself?—

God bless you and your | obliged & faithful Friend

S. T. Coleridge

1717. *To W. D. Cooper*[2]

Pub. Catalogue of Goodspeed's Book Shop.

November 4, 1831.

. . . I plead guilty to the stains and spots on the cover of this book, and penitently take them on my own covering, hoping, they will be considered by you as only *skin-deep*, relatively to the character of your obliged friend and servant. But really, the deep interest which absorbed me in reading the political article in this number, made me forget that I was at the same time eating my breakfast. Believe me respectfully and with respectful remembrances to Mrs. Cooper,

Yours truly,

S. T. Coleridge.

1718. *To R. Fieldier*

Address: R. Fieldier, Esqre | 1 Freeman's Court | Cornhill
MS. Yale University Lib. Hitherto unpublished.

Grove, Highgate.

10 Novr 1831

Dear Sir

My Works, unrecommended, indeed wholly unannounced by the Reviews and other Dispensers of Publicity, have obtained so very scanty a circulation, that once, being asked for an autograph, I subscribed myself as

Author of Works, whereof, tho' not in Dutch,
The Public little knows, the Publisher too much.[3]—

---

[1] John Elliotson (1791–1868), physician, was appointed professor of the practice of medicine in the University of London in 1831, a position he was forced to resign seven years later as a result of his advocacy and practice of mesmerism.

[2] A Highgate neighbour. See Letter 1251.

[3] *Written in an Album*, lines 3–4, *Poems*, ii. 972.

It is not therefore without some surprize, that I find or hear of any of my writings, as being in the possession of a stranger, or elsewhere than on the shelves of my personal acquaintances—but when in addition, the Stranger professes to have received important benefit from them, every lower feeling gives way to an emotion of thankfulness to that Providence who has commanded us to cast our bread on the waters: and we shall find it again, tho' after many days.—

For more than a year past, my Life has been a rapid succession of Sickness, imperfect Convalescence, and Relapse—the most favorable form of the Complaint, whatever it be, being either Erysipelatous Affection of one or both Legs, or Sciatic Rheumatism; the worst and most formidable, the retrocession of the morbid action to the intestinal Canal in a type resembling Cholera.[1] At present, I am under the milder influence—tho' a cripple and almost a Prisoner by the weakness and paralysed state of the Sciatic Nerve, specially of the left thigh. Nevertheless, it is not such as to deprive me of the pleasure of receiving a valued Visitor in my room—only that I cannot promise to be visible before One o'clock. But from that hour till four I should be happy to see you, on any day next week—Sunday excepted—

I am not certain that I have succeeded in decyphering your name —for Mr and Mrs Gillman, the dear and honored friends, of whose family I have for the last 17 years been a member, & Mr Gillman's medical Pupil, each read it differently. I shall do my best to imitate the characters: and the address will supply what is wanting.—

Believe me | with every kind & respectful | anticipation, your's truly

S. T. Coleridge

1719. *To James Gillman, Jr.*

Pub. Coleridge at Highgate, *by Lucy E. Watson, 1925, p. 149.*

[November 1831 ?][2]

My dear James,—Oh! this unrelenting vexatious sciatica! Sharp as the pang from the aspic's tooth may be, it is a trifle compared with the torpor of the voluntary muscles which it induces. The compulsory *egoism* of pain is for me the venom of its fang, and

[1] In a letter to Poole of 7 Oct. 1831, H. N. Coleridge says that Coleridge 'has had two very severe attacks of the prevailing cholera, & suffered dreadfully under them'. [MS. Miss Alice Gibson Smith.]

[2] This letter was probably written in Nov. 1831, after James Gillman, Jr., had taken his degree at St. John's College, Oxford, and while he was preparing for his ordination, which took place later in the same year. See Letter 1721.

amongst the several causes of regret, the earnest wish to pass a portion of my time with you, and the cherished thought of being aidant in your present task, the development and discipline of your mind and powers, is not the least afflictive!

1720. *To David Scott*[1]

Address: To David Scott, Esq.
Pub. Memoir of David Scott, *by William Bell Scott, 1850, p. 48.*

Grove, Highgate, 19th November 1831.

Dear Sir—For twelve years, or more, weak and interrupted health, and the nature and object of the studies to which the hours that ill health left in my power have been devoted—studies, the honour of which, if any, will be posthumous, and the advantage that of others—have rendered my visits to London rare, and at long intervals. But during the last eighteen months, my life has been but one chain of severe sicknesses, brief and imperfect convalescence, and capricious relapses. It is comparative health and comfort for me when the morbid action, whether gout or nervous rheumatism, passes down, and settles for a time in the great sciatic nerve of one or the other thigh—but then I am a cripple, and my boldest excursion a crawl up and down the Grove walk before our front door. At present I am confined to my bed-room. At no time of my life had I much intercourse with book-sellers or publishers—*the Trade*, as they call themselves—and my little experience has all been of the most unfortunate kind. Were I to sum up the whole cash receipts from my published works, I should find the sum total something like this—

£	S.	D.		£	S.	D.
0	0	0		300	0	0

[1] David Scott (1806–49), painter. Having drawn a series of designs for *The Ancient Mariner*, Scott wrote to Coleridge to ask whether there was a publisher interested in his works to whom the drawings might be sent. The present letter was Coleridge's discouraging reply. In 1837, however, Alexander Hill, Edinburgh, and Ackermann and Company, London, published *The Rime of the Ancient Mariner . . . Illustrated by twenty-five poetic and dramatic scenes, designed and etched by David Scott.*

In his review of Coleridge's *Poetical Works* of 1834, H. N. Coleridge comments on Scott's engravings as follows: 'It was a sad mistake in the able artist—Mr. Scott, we believe—who in his engravings has made the ancient mariner an old decrepit man. That is not the true image; no! he should have been a growthless, decayless being, impassive to time or season, a silent cloud—the wandering Jew. The curse of the dead men's eyes should not have passed away. But this was, perhaps, too much for any pencil, even if the artist had fully entered into the poet's idea.' *Quarterly Review*, Aug. 1834, p. 29.

The little I ought to have had was lost in a fraudulent bankruptcy; and the house by which my latest publications—the 'Aids to Reflection,' and the 'Essay on the Constitution in Church and State, according to *the Idea*'—were printed and published, have dissolved their partnership I understand. I have found no reason for withdrawing my confidence in the honour and integrity of the partners, Messrs. Hurst, Chance, and Company; but whether the business is, or *is not to be* continued, I am wholly uninformed.

With this exception, I know of no one individual in the trade with whom I have any acquaintance; nor do I believe that there is one, of London publishers at least, with whom my name and authority would act otherwise than as a counterweight; for the Quarterly Review never notices any work under my name—the Edinburgh has reviewed only such as seemed to furnish an occasion for vilifying the writer—and the minor Reviews sometimes, I hear, mention my name, but never in any reference to my works. I question whether there ever existed a man of letters so utterly friendless, or so unconnected as I am with the dispensers of contemporary reputation, or the publishers in whose service they labour.

Such is the answer I must return to your friendly letter, adding only the assurance, that I acknowledge, and duly appreciate the compliment paid to me, in having selected a poem of mine for ornamental illustration, and an alliance of the sister arts—Metrical and Graphic Poesy; and that I would most readily have complied with your request had it been in my power.—Believe me, Dear Sir, with every friendly wish, yours respectfully.

S. T. Coleridge.

1721. *To J. H. Green*

Address: J. H. Green, Esqre. | &c | 36 Lincoln's Inn Fields
MS. Pierpont Morgan Lib. Pub. with omis. Letters, ii. 754.
Postmark: Highgate, 15 December 1831.

Thursday Afternoon, 4 o'clock.—
15 Decembr 1831.

My dear Friend

It is at least a fair moiety of the gratification, I feel, that it will give *you* so much pleasure to hear from me, that I *tacked* about on Monday, continued on smooth water during the whole day, & with exceptions of about an Hour's *muttering*, as if a storm was coming, had a comfortable night—I was still better on Tuesday, & had no relapse yesterday. Last night, I was kept wakeful for about the three first hours (from ½ past 11 to 2) with a painless sensation of *cold* in the stomach and smaller bowels, which was removed by the sudden descent and elimination of wind, and I slept comfortably—and *this* day, both for Looks and inward feelings, has been my *best* day. I have so repeatedly given and suffered disappointment, that I cannot even communicate this gleam of Convalescence without a little fluttering distinctly felt at my heart, and a sort of Cloud-shadow of dejection flitting over me. God knows with what Aims, motives, and aspirations I pray for an interval of ease and competent strength!—One of my present wishes is to form a better nomenclature or terminology—I have long felt the exceeding inconvenience of the many different meanings of the term, *Objective*—sometimes equivalent to apparent, or sensible, sometimes in opposition to it—ex. gr. the Objectivity is the Rain-drops and the reflected Light, the Iris, is but an Appearance. Thus, sometimes, it means real, and sometimes unreal—and the worst is, that it forms an obstacle to the fixation of the great truth—that the perfect reality is predicable, only where Actual and Real are terms of identity—i.e. where there is no *potential* being—and that this alone is *absolute* reality—and further, of that most fundamental truth—that the *ground* of *all* reality, the Objective no less than of the Subjective, is the *absolute Subject.*—How to get out of the difficulty, I do not know—save that some other term must be used as the Antithet to phaenomenal —perhaps, *noumenal.*—

James Gillman has passed an unusually strict & long examination for ordination with great Credit, & was selected by the Bishop to read the Lessons in the Service—. The Parents are of course delighted—& now, my dear Friend, with affectionate remembrances to Mrs Green, may God bless you | &

S. T. Coleridge

1722. *To Thomas H. Dunn*

Facsimile Canadian Magazine, *June 1909, p. 105.*

6 Jany. 1832.

My dear Sir

You will oblige me by filling the accompanying bottle with Tinct. Op.—I am at present confined to the House by an attack of Rheumatism, but on my very first Excursion I will call on you & settle this with what other favors I have yet to account for.— Believe me, with 'many happy new Years' to you, with regard and esteem

Your obliged

S. T. Coleridge

1723. *To James Gillman, Jr., and Susan Steel*

MS. Pierpont Morgan Lib. Hitherto unpublished.

My dear young Friends   10 Jany. 1832.

If two young Persons, both having arrived at years of discretion,
have formed such and so exclusive an attachment to each other,
that they calmly and reflectingly prefer the inward satisfaction
and sense of security grounded on a mutual avowal of their affec-
tion, and the pledge and prospect of an ultimate union, at an indefi-
nite period, to the chance—or even the probability of an earlier
settlement in life under circumstances of equal or even greater
worldly ease and respectability—I see no moral or religious objec-
tion to such a betrothment. In thus executing and interchanging
a *bond of Judgement* on their whole future Will, in thus making a
single Volition the luminous point, of which the entire Will hence-
forward is to be but the diverging pencil, in thus by one single Act
of inward Election—an act which in it's reciprocal *utterance*
acquires the nature & obligation of a *Deed*—raising a Wish into a
Duty, they will both indeed have done an *aweful* thing; but they
have done only what they have a *right* to do.[1]

The wisdom, the *prudence*, of the determination must depend on
their healths, habits, tempers, dispositions; on the correspondence
in respect of these (which, however, need not be a correspondence
of LIKENESS—I have known very happy and harmonious Unions
of grave and gay, of Enthusiasm with a tendency to over-hasty
judgements, in the one, and of forethoughtfulness too nearly akin
to timidity, in the other &c)—It will depend, further, on their
prospects, and probable chances; but *above all*, on their own know-
lege of their own minds and characters, and the opportunities,
they have had, of COMPARATIVE experience, as the best security,
that they have not mistaken a mere Love-kindness for *the very*
Love, the wide difference of which might be detected only by the
entrance of the true SIMON PURE—(tho' if you have not read the
old Comedy, you will scarcely understand the allusion).[2] And
observe—in the requisite Self-knowlege I include the question and
answer—'Do I possess that moral fortitude, that cheerfulness of
Hope, which will not only *neutralize* "the Delay that maketh the

---

[1] Cf. Letter 1665, in which Coleridge argues against 'premature engagements'
of young persons who 'have grown up in habits of intimacy', as was the case
of James Gillman and Susan Steel. By 1832, however, they had 'arrived at
years of discretion' and he saw no moral or religious objection to their betroth-
ment. In Feb. 1837 James Gillman married Sophia Riley.

[2] Simon Pure, the Quaker in Susannah Centlivre's *A Bold Stroke for a Wife*,
1718, who is impersonated by another character, Colonel Feignwell, during part
of the play.

heart sick ",[1] but convert it into an incentive to perseverant exertion '—for without this, the best years of life might be wasted away in day-dreams of feeble love-yearning—in sad contrast with the patriarch of old. 'And Jacob served seven years for Rachel: and they seemed to him but a few days, for the love he had to her.' (Gen. 39 [29]. 20.)

But be this, as it may—still in this formal avowal of your affections you have done no more than you had the right to do— (at all events, since the assent expressed to the copy of the Letter, proposed to be sent to Mr S.)—But here, my dear young Friends! your moral Right stops—it does not extend to the Union itself, except under the rightful Conditions. You have *no* right to lead each other into temptation, and that too of the most afflictive and perilous kind, by a rash transition from a whole life's *habit* of all the comforts, & even elegancies of Home to privations, anxieties, and embarrassments. This no *Love* can excuse for this plain reason—that *Love* could not dictate, could not but forbid, it—and the true ground and occasion of so cruel an act would be sought for in a sickly impatience of the old home, on the one side, and an impatience of a still lower origin, tho' not of a more culpable character, on the other. No good or wise man will wish or expect you to demand security against providence itself, and to defer your marriage till you have an independent fortune sufficient to set all contingencies at defiance! But every wise, every good man, and all who truly love you, must and will expect you not to marry, till there exist the regular means of maintenance adequate to the present expences, according to the rank of life, in which you have both been bred up, and to the Appearances desirable in a Clergyman, and with a fair probability of income increasing with increased demands. And I do trust, that in determining this point you will agree to take your Parents on both sides, but especially your Mothers, as the Arbiters. I say the *Mothers*; because as the experienced House-wives, they are most competent to determine the *Minimum*, on which you may with economy and no burthensome self-denial hope to live respectably. A pledge of this nature, on your parts, would, I should hope, go far to remove every important objection to what has now passed—and I have so much confidence in the good sense and good principles of both of you, that I will not doubt but that God will sanctify this betrothment to the present moral discipline of your minds, and to your future happiness, here and hereafter. Such, be assured, is and will be the earnest prayer of, my dear James & Susan, your paternal Friend

S. T. Coleridge

[1] Proverbs xiii. 12.

1724. *To J. H. Green*

Address: J. H. Green, Esqre. | 36 | Lincoln's Inn Fields
MS. Pierpont Morgan Lib. Hitherto unpublished.
Postmark: Highgate, 12 January 1832.

My dear Friend   [11 January 1832]

Tho' not so *total* in my feelings as I could have wished, I had, however, no relapse since you left till last night, or rather this morning—immediately after my first sleep. A *fear* indeed came upon me, while I was undressing—but I soon fell asleep, & slept for about two hours—but then came the sensation of *wakefulness*—heat about the back with soreness of the chest—& soon I found sweat-drops running down my face, like rain, and all my trunk was in strong perspiration for an hour or more, my feet and legs remaining, or having the *sensation* of being, as cold as ice.—I had uneasiness, but no positive pain, that in which or in the nerves correspondent to which I conceived the head quarters of my Malady to be situated—that is, the hand's breadth between the Navel and the Pit of the Stomach.—The fit worked itself off.—I slept till near nine—& got up pretty tolerable—with the dull pain and weakness shifted to my right Hip, and extending down the groin to the part next the Scrotum—But this has now almost ceased—and for the last hour or two I have been so depressed, so sickish and so uneasy in my bowels, that I lost all heart to write to you, so as to reach you before Thursday.

You remember the little black Shaving-Pot, that used to stand on the Hob in my Room—? While I was riding on the Chamber-horse, Harriet brought in a new Concern from the Tinman's, & took away my faithful old Mungo, assigning the causes—which satisfied my reason but not my feelings—These I got rid of, on the spur of the moment, and to the rise and fall, the sea-like hexameter & pentameter Rhythm, of my Pegasus in the following Elegy or hypertrophied Sonnet—.

God bless you, and your afflicted | but ever faithful & affectionate Friend,

                                                    S. T. Coleridge

A Sesqui-Sonnet—or Elegiac Farewell to my black Tin Shaving-pot.[1]

My tiny Tin! my Omnium-usüum Scout!
My Blackie! fair tho' black!—the wanton Fire

---

[1] E. H. Coleridge did not include these lines in his edition of Coleridge's *Poems,* but they were published by Mrs. M. Oliphant, *Annals of a Publishing House. William Blackwood and His Sons,* 2 vols., 1897, i. 421. See Letter 1747.

Hath long bit off thy pert one-nostril'd snout;
Unhinged thy lid; and wrought luxation dire,

Where of thy arching Arm the handless wrist
Press'd on thy side. On treacherous Coal or Grate
Twice hast thou stumbled, and in rebel Mist,
With smoke and filmy soot confederate,

Flown in my face! Yet did I not upbraid
Thy crazy cranks, nay, held thee the more dear:
And morning after morning with thee play'd
At Rouge and Noire a game of hope and fear.

And must we part? Thy tears on the hot Hob
Say, iss! iss! iss!—hard by the top Bar reeks,
And to each tear makes answer with a sob.
The Cambrian's Broth is none the worse for *leeks*;

Rents are the landed Noble's pride and glee;
Holes, side or bottom, both to Man and Gun
Are apt and seemly. Would, 'twere thus with *Thee*!
But 'tis not so! And let Time's Will be done!
Blackie, adieu! But mind you, 'twas not *me*
That did turn you away, but you that *run*.

S. T. Coleridge

Tuesday, Jany 10. 1832[1]
Grove, Highgate.

1725. *To Robert Baldwin*

Address: Messrs. Baldwin & Co., | Publishers, | Paternoster Row.   For Mr Baldwin.
MS. Public Library of New South Wales, Sydney, Australia. Hitherto unpublished.

Grove, Highgate
Jany. 25, 1832.

Dear Sir

In a late conversation with a young man of undoubted talent, and if I mistake not, of Genius, urging him to adopt, or rather to abide by, a means of livelihood, which required only in himself what at all hours he might reasonably calculate on, and most earnestly, not only on prudential but on moral grounds dissuading him from the choice of Authorship, as a profession, (i.e. *as his*

[1] Another MS. of these lines is dated 1 Jan. 1832.

bread-winner) I shewed him the collective amount of all, I had gained by my publications—with exception only of the writings in the Morning Post just before and during the Peace of Amiens, for which I received a Salary—and thus it stood—*Loss*, after subtraction of all my receipts, 280£—for about half of which I am still in debt to the generous Friend, but for whose interference I should probably have lost my liberty and regained it only by figuring among the insolvent Debtors.—And yet from the year, I left Jesus College, to the present day I have lived a strictly moral life, my wants few, my habits simple—I have been a hard Thinker, an incessant Student, and to the utmost extent of my health laborious. The only remuneration, I ever received, was the honor of the Royal Associateship, and the annuity of 105£—which was suddenly and without warning withdrawn from me by his present Majesty, just at the time that it pleased God to smite me with a bodily affliction, so that I lost at once the maintenance provided for me by my Sovereign, and the health and strength that might have enabled me to maintain myself. But God's will be done!—

Under these circumstances you will not wonder, if I recur to any chance, however light, of a relief, however small—and in order to this, it is necessary that I should take courage & look my affairs in the face—from which I have year after year shrunk, not without some remembrance of the unlucky mistake of an old friend, which I have recorded in my 'Literary Life', between *Sell*- and *Cell*-erage.[1]—

If therefore, you will be so good as to let me have an account, as far as any works of mine have been under your patronage,[2] you will oblige one who is with great respect,

dear Sir, | your's sincerely
S. T. Coleridge

For Mr Baldwin.

1726. *To Charles Aders*

Address: Charles Aders, Esqre | Laurence Poultney Lane | Cornhill.
MS. Cornell University Lib. Hitherto unpublished.
Postmark: Highgate, 13 February 1832.

11 Feby 1832.

My very dear Friend

If my memory has not deceived me, or rather if my *fancy* have not counterfeited *memory*, either You or the other *You*, dear Mrs

---

[1] *Biog. Lit.* i. 113–14.

[2] Baldwin was one of the assignees of the bankrupt estate of Rest Fenner. Coleridge later received £102. See Letters 1202 and 1748–9.

A., have some acquaintance with Ackerman—who, my Nephew-Son-in-law tells me, is a great man in the publication of Caricature engravings. Now if so, I should like to suggest to some of his able Artists what seems to me no bad subject for a Caricature—viz. the REFORM BILL, allegorized as a Loco-motive Steam-Engine, with all it's smoke & fury—& a long train of Waggons, carts, &c dragged on by it, one or two huge Caravans containing the ministerial Majorities, &c—while on the road two or three poor Devils,—the Church, chancery, the Colonial Interests, &c—symbolically characterized, lie with broken limbs—Each of the Waggons should represent some one of the dead weights, and dead blunders of the present Ministry—Belgium, Holland, Portugal, Irish Tythes, Miss *Budget* with Lord Althorp[1] pouting, Deficient Revenues—&c &c—In short, it is endless what an inventive & imaginative Artist might not introduce—all dragged on, with a *broken* rail-road, or perhaps, with the title, the Steam-Engine *run mad*, over hedge & ditch, toward a precipice—between which and the loco-motive-Engine, with Brougham & Durham[2] atop of it, should be seen part of a herd of swine, the one fronting the Engine & the Train with a Devil across his Rump, & half a Devil, with tail & legs *below*, as half-entered into the Pig.—

Let these blundering Catalines [*sic*] commit what blunders they may—and however palpable to the Common sense of the H. of C. they may be rendered—No matter!—Swear black is white—or else you will endanger the Reform Bill!—

The three Patriots—Cockney Snip, Irish Blarney, and Me—

Cockney Snip.
  I'se a *Riff*erman!
Irish Blarney.
  A *Raff*orman I!
Me.
  And I write them both, aloud I cry,
  And for this Riff-raff-form will live and die!

---

[1] John Charles Spencer, Viscount Althorp and later third Earl Spencer (1782–1845). With the formation of Lord Grey's administration in Nov. 1830, Lord Althorp was made chancellor of the exchequer and to him was entrusted the leadership of the House of Commons. He was a key figure in the passing of the Reform Bill.

[2] John George Lambton, Baron Durham and later first Earl of Durham (1792–1840) entered the cabinet of his father-in-law, Lord Grey, as lord privy seal in 1830. Long a proponent of parliamentary reform, he in conjunction with three others was entrusted by Grey with the preparation of the Reform Bill. After the defeat of the Bill in the House of Lords in Oct. 1831, Durham was one of those in the ministry who advocated the creation of peers to ensure passage of the Reform Bill.

I pray, that your dear Eliza may not suffer from the fatigue &
bustle of moving—but I shall hear the particulars from James—

For the 3 or 4 last days, thank God!—the nervous Rheumatism,
or whatever more expressive name the possessing Evil Spirit may
have, not yet known to the exorcizing Doctors, has changed his
lodgings from the Viscera to my Limbs. I am a cripple, but yet have
abundant reason still to thank God!—For believe me, *pain, local*
pain, is like a something *outside* of one—& a very tolerable *Bore*
of a Companion, compared with *miserable sensation.*—

May God bless you, and your | affectionate Friend

S. T. Coleridge

1727. *To Henry Nelson Coleridge*

Address: H. N. Coleridge, Esqre | 1. New Court | Lincoln's Inn
MS. Victoria University Lib. Pub. with omis. Letters, *ii. 756.*
Postmark: Highgate, 24 February 1832.

Thursday Night—[23 February 1832]

My dear Nephew & by a higher tie Son—

I thank God, I have this day been favored with such a mitiga-
tion of the disease as amounts to a Reprieve—& have had ease
enough of sensation to be able to think of what you said to me from
Lockhart—And the result is, a wish that you should—i.e. if it
appears right to you, & you have no objection of feeling—write for
me to Professor Wilson, offering the Essays, and the Motives for
the Wish to have them republished, with the authority (if there be
no breach of confidence) of Mr Lockhart.—I cannot with propriety
offer them to *Frazer*,[1] having for a series of years received Black-
wood's Magazine as a free gift to me—*until* I had made the offer to
Blackwood.—Of course, my whole & only object is the desire to
see them put into the possibility of becoming useful. But o! this is
a faint desire, my dear Henry! compared with that of seeing a fair
abstract of the Principles, I have advanced, respecting the National
Church, and it's Revenue—and the National Clerisy, as a co-
ordinate of THE STATE, in the minor & antithetic sense of the term,
State!—

I almost despair of the Conservative Party—too truly, I fear, &
most ominously self-designated, TORIES—& of course, Half-
truthmen!—One main omission, both of Senators & Writers, has

[1] The first number of *Fraser's Magazine for Town and Country* appeared in
Feb. 1830. The periodical was published by James Fraser but took its name
from Hugh Fraser. The first three or four numbers were principally from the
pen of William Maginn (1793–1842).

been, ὡς ἔμοιγε δοκεῖ—that they have forgotten to level the ax of their argument at the *Root*, the true Root, yea, Trunk of the Delusion, by pointing out the true nature, operation, & modus operandi, of the Taxes in the first instance—& *then*, & not till *then*, the utter groundlessness, the absurdity of the presumption, that any H. of C. formed otherwise and consisting of other men of other ranks, other views, or with other interests, than the present has been for the last 20 years at least, would or could—from any imaginable cause—have a deeper interest or a stronger desire to diminish the Taxes—as far as the abolition of this or that Tax would increase the ability to pay the remainder. For what are Taxes, but one of the forms of Circulation?—Some a nation must have, or it is no nation. But he that takes ninepence from me instead of a shilling, but at the same time & by this very act prevents sixpence from coming into my pocket—am I to thank him?[1]—Yet such are the only Thanks, that Mr Hume,[2] & the Country Squires, his cowardly back-clapping Flatterers, can fairly claim.—In my opinion, Hume is an incomparably more mischievous Being, than O'Connel,[3] & the gang of Agitators. They are mere *symptom*[*atic* and] significative Effects & . . .[4] the waves, the foam, the roar of the inwardly agitated Mass of the popular Sea. But Hume is a *fermenting Virus*—But I must end my scribble—God bless my dear Sara— Give my Love to Mrs C.—& kiss the Baby for

S. T. Coleridge.

1728. *To Unknown Correspondent*

MS. Columbia University Lib. Hitherto unpublished.

Grove, Highgate
24 Feby. 1832.

Dear Sir

Some months ago I received a letter from Doncaster, from 'York Gate' if I recollect aright, paying me the compliment of a similar request. But as I immediately complied with it, and the General

---

[1] For Coleridge's ideas on taxation see *The Friend*, 1818, ii. 47–80, *Lay Sermon*, 1817, pp. 25–34, and *Table Talk*, 31 Mar., 10 Apr., and 16 Aug. 1833. See also W. F. Kennedy, *Humanist versus Economist. The Economic Thought of Samuel Taylor Coleridge*, 1958, pp. 23–29, and John Colmer, *Coleridge, Critic of Society*, 1959, pp. 112–13.

[2] Joseph Hume (1777–1855) was for thirty years a leader of the radical party and the self-elected guardian of the public purse.

[3] Daniel O'Connell (1775–1847), Irish politician and an advocate of the 'tranquil and peaceable' repeal of the union of Great Britain and Ireland.

[4] MS. torn; one or two words missing.

Post does not often miss, I infer that the name must have been different. I have for many months been confined to my Room by severe Illness, and am at this present time so ill, that it is almost equally probable that this Autograph may be the last Letter as that this Letter may be the last of the Autographs of

S. T. Coleridge

1729. *To J. H. Green*

Address: J. H. Green, Esqre | &c | 46 Lincoln's Inn Fields
MS. Pierpont Morgan Lib. Hitherto unpublished.
Postmark: Highgate, 25 February 1832.

Friday Afternoon, 24 Feby 1832—

My dear Friend

On Tuesday morning, after a tolerable night of tape-worm Sleep, i.e. made up of many joints, I found my breakfast appetite again, and eat the two chops with much gust—But about an hour afterwards and as soon as the digestion began in the upper bowels— *pray, if you think of it, bring me a 3s. 6d. packet of Perryisian Pens,*[1] *or any equivalent, when you next come*—the storm of agitation and nervous excitement rushed on me, head as well as Bowels, and from Noon till past six o'clock I never *once* sate down, but continued pacing to the tune of my own prayers & groans from the window of my own to that in the Room opposite!—At night I took the Bed-air-bath, for a full hour, indeed for 75 minutes—Mr Gillman has greatly improved it by lowering the arches, and thus lessening the former great difference of temperature between the air above the body and the stratum occupied by it—The effect was great—the perspiration far more copious, than even in the medicated Air-bath—Unintentionally I had left on my Under-waistcoat & Breast-plate—& not only these but my Night-cap might have been, indeed the latter was, *wrung* out. And Harriet said, that she had never seen a Blanket in such a state, as that which was between my body & the Mattrass—Unluckily, I had no fresh Under-waistcoat to put on, so slept without it—& I passed a comfortable Night, of only two sleeps; but on Wednesday Morning, on stepping out of bed, and to the clothes' Horse for my under-stockings, I sneezed violently, & perceived a disagreeable fever-smell in my Nostrils—I proceeded, however, after the operation of the Enema, to divide my daily dose of L. into *three* parts, instead of *two* as usual. Mr Gillman altogether discouraged my proposal to

---

[1] James Perry of Birmingham is believed to have been the first maker of steel slip pens.

DIMINISH it—and instead of the fatal chops took to or three thin slices of Bread & Butter with my two cups of Tea—then at 3 o'clock a small Basin of thin yet strong Beef & Veal Soup, and at half-past 5 a few spoonfuls of Bread Pudding—and I went to bed, without having taken the third division of the Laud. Dose. I rose much better, pursued the same plan, & passed the afternoon & evening below stairs, without any relapse—At night, I took a Mustard Leg-bath; kept my legs in the Pail with occasional additions of hot water for an hour, and for the first time found my feet and legs as high up as the water reached of a lively *pink*, & they retained the same color this morning—with a most sensible return of warmth & pleasurable sensation to the Feet and Ancles. God of his free goodness grant a continuance of this Mercy.—

In the Morning Chronicle of Wednesday, 22 Feby. there is a long paragraph, containing the opinions of a Doctor Kirk, on this Cholera.[1] It is the first sensible, and philosophic Article, I have yet seen on the subject—and why?—Plain as a Pike-staff. It is in substance the very same that you have heard from *me*, that is, from *myself*. Yes! that Doctor K. *must* be a very clever man.—I think, however, that I could give the theory with an important completing adjunct, and so fill up the whole line of transit and connection from an Essex Ague thro' a Pontine Marsh-fever to the present Malignant Cholera—and explain the super-induction of the *Epidemic* on the two latter—the reason, I mean, why they are likely to be modified by aerial influences in unlucky states of the atmosphere—tho' of the three Factors of the Disease, viz. the Predisposition of the Patient, the unknown Virus, and the predisposing Circumstances, in which word I include quaecunque stant circum circa, state of atmosphere, soil, air, temperature & condition of the Habitat, &c—it is on the *first* that the *third principally* acts, tho' I will not say, exclusively. While yet in Malta, I had anticipated & distinctly asserted the Chemist's, *Henry's*, view of the action of the *fomites* on the morbific Virus, or Venena.—Now what is my complemental Adjunct? This—first, I am inclined to doubt the necessity of supposing a specific *Virus* for the different diseases—tho' perhaps it may end in a question of words, and yet not an idle or unprofitable question. If the Virus can be decomposed, it may as probably be susceptible of combination with some other matter: and this matter may either counteract or intensate it's prior qualities—and again the counteraction may be either neutralization, or a new Virus as the product.—But nevertheless

---

[1] Cholera appeared in England in 1831, and during the following year the disease continued to prevail in most of the cities and large towns in Great Britain and Ireland.

we ought not to presume this, without a necessity—& I incline to
think, that two very simple Data will go far to preclude the neces-
sity—The first is, Grades of intensity, which in most cases may be
fairly presumed to be accompanied by increase of subtilization:
if indeed in morbific matter the grade of subtilty does not deter-
mine the grade of it's intensity, as a *power* or agent.

The second is, the ratio which the *specific* Virus holds to the
ordinary sedative agents, those, I mean, which become sedative
and injurious, not by the kind but by excess in the degree—Damp,
for instance, Cold, & the like. Now we may readily conceive, that
in an ordinary Ague the Virus in the explosive Water-b[last] from
a stagnant or emptying Pond may be, to the damp, the co[ld], the
fatigue, the accidental depression, but as 1 to 5—& yet sufficient to
give to the consequent indisposition the type of *ague*—But conceive
the Patient exposed to a continued Volley of these Water-blasts, as
in the Pontine Marshes, and during a suspension of Active Volition
by Sleep—the *death in life* of the overwhelmed cutaneous and the
veno-glandular System with the subservient Nerves may have
penetrated to the irritable System, or to it's positive Factor, the
arterial, before the latter can have been called up to counteract or
counterbalance the derangement—But what if the Virus should
stand to the ordinary Sedatives as 4 to 1!—and it's subtlety or
diffusibility be in the same ratio?—What is more probable, than
that it should find an aerial instead of an aqueous Medium? And
instead of acting principally on the Skin, should act principally in
the path of the respiratory organs? and thus even in the first
place, or rather co-ordinately, on the arterial Life—and that
Nature makes her last effort, the irritable System a House divided
in itself, and the muscular Life roused to imitate the fever-fit
against the Ague-fit in the arterial[1]—The short of it is, Mr Green!
that unless you bring me some Perryisian Pens, you must not
expect to receive a legible scrawl from

Your affectionate

S. T. Coleridge.

1730. *To Henry Nelson Coleridge*

MS. Pierpont Morgan Lib. Hitherto unpublished.

1 March 1832

My dear Henry

There is such a thing, as *canis-genere-feminino*-ing a measure:
i.e. of *bitching* as well as *botching* a business. And I sadly fear, that
that good man and true patriot, the M. of Chandos, has done or did

――――――――――

[1] Cf. *Table Talk*, 7 Apr. 1832.

both, in his motion on Tuesday Night. By not confining himself to
the negative proposition, the simple rejection of the clause grounded
on the enormous and unqualified mischief of converting the metro-
politan district into vast multitudinous pot-walloping Boroughs,
a worthless Gift, perilous to the Legislature, and a Deijanira's
Shirt to the infatuated Hercules, the Metropolis itself; and by
attempting to bribe the vacillating, and to conciliate the less
tightly pledged, Reformers by a scheme of compensation, the
admission of the expedience or necessity of which extracted the
very pith out of his own argument, or what ought to have been
such—he layed himself fairly open to Mr Macaulay's Reply—which,
tho' easily answered and even as to it's point, viz. the already
existing power of the Metropolitan Population, turned back on
himself, was yet one of his best & least flashy speeches.[1] [MS.
breaks off thus.]

1731. *To Eliza Nixon*

Transcript Coleridge family. Hitherto unpublished.

March 13. 1832

Dear Eliza

From the languor of Illness, I read very slowly and get through
a book as a Fly thro' a Milk splash—And yet it is a great relief
to me to have my attention withdrawn from my own miserable
sensations, & from the object the least worthy of my thoughts, &
on which I dwell with the most reluctance—myself—I have there-
fore relied on Mr & Mrs Nixon & you & your sister to put down to
my account & not to Mr Gillman's, that Beechey[2] has been de-
tained in my sick room & on my sick bed two days beyond our

---

[1] Richard P. T. N. B. C. Grenville, second Duke of Buckingham and
Chandos (1797–1861), was Marquis of Chandos from 1822 to 1839. On 28 Feb.
1832 the House of Commons took up the question whether the Tower Hamlets,
Middlesex, should stand part of Schedule C of the Reform Bill. This schedule
provided for the creation of new boroughs, each of which was to send two mem-
bers to Parliament. Chandos opposed 'the giving of these additional Members
to the metropolis' by 'the formation of separate boroughs in the heart of
London'. He was effectively answered by Macaulay, and by a majority of 80
the House of Commons voted to place the Tower Hamlets in Schedule C. On
2 Mar. Finsbury, Marylebone, and Lambeth were likewise ordered to stand
part of the same schedule.

[2] F. W. Beechey, *Narrative of a Voyage to the Pacific and Beering's Strait,
to co-operate with the Polar Expeditions, in the years 1825–28*, 2 vols., 1831.
According to a note in the transcript, Coleridge's letter accompanied the first
volume of Beechey's work.

allotted time. Give me those days as part of your time & mark the date accordingly—

God bless you my dear young friend.

Your afflicted but affectionate
S. T. Coleridge

1732. *To Miss S. Lawrence*[1]

Address: Miss S. Lawrence | The Grange | near | Liverpool
MS. Victoria University Lib. Pub. with omis. Letters, *ii. 758.*
Postmark: Highgate, 22 March 1832.

Grove, Highgate.
Sunday, [18] March
1832

My dear Miss Lawrence

You, and *dear*, DEAR, DEAR Mrs Crompton, are among the few Sunshiny Images that endear my past life to me—and I never think of you—& often, very often *do* I think of you—without heart-felt esteem, without affection and *a yearning* of my better being toward you.—I have for more than 18 months been on the brink of the grave, under sufferings which have rendered the Grave an object of my wishes, & only not of my prayers, because I commit myself, poor dark Creature, to an omniscient & all-merciful, in whom are the issues of Life and Death—content, yea, most thankful if only his Grace will preserve within me the blessed faith, that He *is*, and is a God, that heareth prayer, abundant in forgiveness, & THEREFORE to be feared—no *fate*, no God, as imagined by the Unitarians; a sort of I know not what *law-giving Law* of Gravitation, to whom Prayer would be as idle as to the Law of Gravity if an undermined Wall were falling upon me; but a God, that made the Eye, & therefore shall *he* not see? who made the Ear, and shall he not hear?[2] who made the heart of man to love him, and shall he not love that creature, whose ultimate end is to love him?—A God, who *seeketh* that which was lost, who calleth back that which had gone astray[3]—who calleth thro' his own Name, Word, Son, from everlasting the *Way*, and the TRUTH, and who became Man that for poor fallen Mankind he might *be* (not merely announce, but *be*) the RESURRECTION and THE LIFE[4]—Come unto *me*, all ye

---

[1] Miss Lawrence had earlier been a governess in the Crompton family at Eton House, near Liverpool. Later she and her two sisters kept a school for girls at the Grange, near Liverpool. See *Letters*, ii. 758 n., and R. P. Graves, *Life of Sir William Rowan Hamilton*, 3 vols., 1882–9, i. 191 and 535.

[2] Psalm xciv. 9.   [3] Ezekiel xxxiv. 16.

[4] John xi. 25.

that are weary and heavy-laden, and *I* will give you rest![1]—O my
dear Miss Lawrence! prize above all earthly blessings the faith—I
trust, that no Sophistry of shallow Infra-socinians has quenched it
within you—that God is a God that heareth Prayer.—If varied
Learning, if the assiduous cultivation of the reasoning Powers, if
an accurate & minute acquaintance with all the arguments of
controversial writers; if an intimacy with the doctrines of the
Unitarians which can only be obtained by one who for a year or
two in his early life had been a convert to them, yea, a zealous,
and by themselves deemed powerful, Supporter of their opinions;—
lastly, if the utter absence of any imaginable wordly interest that
could sway or warp the mind and affections;—if all these combined
can give any weight or authority to the opinion of a fellow-creature,
they will give weight to my adjuration, sent from my sick-bed to
you, in kind love—O trust, o trust, in your *Redeemer*! In the
Co-eternal *Word*, the only-begotten, the living NAME of the Eternal
I AM, Jehovah, Jesus!—

I shall endeavor to see Mr Hamilton[2]—I doubt not his scientific
attainments—I have had proofs of his taste & feeling as a Poet—
but believe me, my dear Miss Lawrence! that should the Cloud of
Distemper [pass] from over me, there needs no other passport to a
cordial Welcome from me than a Line from you, importing that—
he or she possesses your esteem & regard and that you wish, I
should shew attention to him—. I cannot make out your address,
which I read—'The Grange'; but where that is, I know not, &
fear that the Post office may be as ignorant as myself. I must there-
fore delay the direction of my Letter, till I see Mr Hamilton—but
in all places & independent of place, I am, my dear Miss Lawrence,
with most affectionate recollections, | Your friend,
S. T. Coleridge.

1733. *To J. H. Green*

MS. British Museum. Pub. Inquiring Spirit, *ed. K. Coburn, 1951, p. 62.*

[Spring 1832?]

My dear Green

One of the many mysteries of Human Nature, of which as
inferior to many yet as good as most I take my own to be a pretty

---

[1] Matthew xi. 28.

[2] William Rowan Hamilton (1805–65), mathematician. In 1827 he was
appointed Andrews professor of astronomy and superintendent of the observa-
tory at Trinity College, Dublin, and soon afterward astronomer royal for Ireland.
Hamilton called at Highgate on Sunday, 18 Mar., 1832, but found Coleridge
too ill to receive him. On 20 and 23 Mar., however, he had two interviews with
the poet. See R. P. Graves, op. cit. i. 536 and 538–42.

fair average, is: the increasing desire of Repose as we grow older,
and yet an involuntary Repining at the very events & changes of
feeling, which we need only resign ourselves to, to be in possession
of the very Repose and wishless Tranquillity, for which we had
been sighing. I would fain be independent of any Will that is not
one and the same with Reason. I would fain live the short remainder
of my Life for God and universal Interests: and yet I find myself
tenaciously clinging to the shadows of past [MS. breaks off thus.]

1734. *To J. H. Green*

Address: J. H. Green, Esqre | &c &c | 36 or 46. Lincoln's Inn Fields
MS. Pierpont Morgan Lib. Pub. E. L. G. ii. 440
Postmark: Highgate, 23 March 1832.

[23 March 1832]

My dear Friend
    By the mercy of God I remain quiet; and so far from any craving
for the poison that has been the curse of my existence, my shame
and my *negro-slave* inward humiliation and debasement, I feel an
aversion, a horror at the imagining: so that I doubt, whether I
could swallow a dose without a resiliency, amounting almost to a
convulsion. For this Quiet I am most grateful, whether I sink or
rise.—But on the other hand, I have & have had, no sensation of
convalescence, no *genial* feeling, no remission of the weakness in
the voluntary Muscles, symptomatic of a paralysis—and still in the
region between the pit of the Stomach & the Navel there is con-
stantly that which makes it difficult for me to believe that it is a
mere *functional* derangement. The grasp of Mortality seems too
tight, too constant.—Mr Gillman says, I look a great deal better;
but during and after shaving when I look at myself in the Glass, I
see almost the contrary—and Harriet, our House Maid, who has
most kindly & christianly tended me during this affliction, told me
to day—'Sir! your face has not the same expression of Pain,
Anxiety, and the being worn out by Pain; [but] it is yellower, or
brown and yellow, m[ore] than I have ever seen it.'
    I write, my dear Friend!—not to prevent your coming on Sun-
day which is perhaps the greatest comfort and Soothing, next to my
faith in the God, that heareth prayer; but to prevent your sacrificing
any thing important—for I fear, you will find me as incapable of
evolving my inward mind next Sunday as you did the last—Still,
to be quiet tho' very weak and as far as this Life is concerned, hope-
less—for remember, I am past threescore—is a great blessing, and

I trust, I lifted up my heart in unfeigned thankfulness to Him, in whose will are the Issues of Life & Death.

God bless you &

S. T. Coleridge

1735. *To William Rowan Hamilton*

Pub. Life of Sir William Rowan Hamilton, *by R. P. Graves, 3 vols., 1882–9, i. 542.*

April [March], 1832.[1]

I believe that the preceding pages contain the lines which you did me the honour to wish to have transcribed in my own hand.[2] I wrote to dear Miss Lawrence in reply to the letter, to which I owe the gratification of having seen you. I was affected, not surprised, not disappointed, by her answer, but yet through great affection could not wholly suppress the feeling of regret to find her and her family still on that noiseless sand-shoal and wrecking shallow of Infra-Socinianism, yclept most calumniously and insolently, Unitarianism: as if a Tri-unitarian were not as necessarily Unitarian as an apple-pie must be a pie. But you have done me the honour of looking through my *Aids to Reflection*; and you will therefore, perhaps, be aware that though I deem Unitarian*ism* the very *Nadir* of Christianity, and far, very far worse in relation either to the *Affections*, the *Imagination*, the Reason, the Conscience, nay even to the UNDERSTANDING, than several of the forms of *Atheism—ex. gr.* than the Atheism of Spinoza—whose pure spirit may it be my lot to meet, with St. John and St. Paul smiling on him and loving him—yet I make an impassable chasm between *an* and *ism,* and while I almost yield to the temptation of despising Priestleyianism as the only *sect* that feels and expresses contempt or slander of all that differ from them; the poison of hemlock for the old theological whiskey and its pugnacious effects; yet I am persuaded that *the Word* works *in* thousands, to whose ears the *words* never reached, and remained in the portal at the unopened door. But more especially I hold this of women. Man's heart must

[1] Hamilton had been asked by a member of the de Vere family to obtain a copy of Coleridge's *Epitaph on an Infant* in the poet's handwriting. Coleridge forwarded the lines in the present letter. On 27 Mar. 1832 Hamilton reported to Aubrey de Vere that he had procured Coleridge's autograph and had sent it to Lady de Vere. Coleridge's letter, therefore, was written shortly before that date. R. P. Graves, op. cit. i. 539–40.

[2] On one of Hamilton's two visits to Highgate of 20 and 23 Mar., Coleridge spoke 'slightingly' of his *Epitaph on an Infant* 'as crude and imperfect' and 'extemporised an altered set of lines, on the same subject'. For the amended version see R. P. Graves, op. cit. i. 540.

be in his *head*. Woman's head must be in her heart. But how it is possible that a man should entirely separate and exclude the mysteries—*i.e.* the philosophy of Christianity—from the Traditions, as contained in the three Gospels κατὰ σάρκα, and profess to believe the latter for their sake, and on that ground alone to receive this nondescript '*It*' = O, or if it pretend to anything not as clearly delivered in the Old Testament and in the Greek moralists, a vain boast—and yet affect to smile with contempt at the quack doctor's affidavits or [on?] oath before the Lord Mayor—this would make me *stare*, if aught could excite wonder in my mind at any folly manifested by *knowing* folks. Now your *male* Unitarians are all of this *class*—they are *knowing* fellows. Never once have I met, or heard of, a philosopher, or a really *learned* Priestleyian or Belshamite;—Lardner, a dull man, but as far as industry of itself can make a dull man a man of learning, certainly a learned man, at all events a man of systematic reading, seems to me to have oscillated between Sabellianism and Socinianism;—but *mem*—the *Socini* were Christians—though grievously inconsistent in their logic. But it is not in the ways of logic that we can be raised to heaven.[1]

1736. *To J. H. Green*

Address: J. H. Green, Esqre | &c &c | *36* Lincoln's Inn Fields
MS. Pierpont Morgan Lib. Pub. E. L. G. ii. 441.
Postmark: Highgate, 29 March 1832.

[29 March 1832]

My very dear Friend

On Monday I had a sad trial of intestinal pain and restlessness; but thro' God's Mercy, without any craving for the Poison, which for more than 30 years has been the guilt, debasement, and misery of my Existence.[2] I pray, that God may have mercy on me—tho' thro' unmanly impatiency of wretched sensations, that produced a disruption of my mental continuity of productive action I have for the better part of my life yearning [yearned?] towards God, yet having recourse to the evil Being—i.e. a continued act of thirty years' Self-poisoning thro' cowardice of pain, & without other motive—say rather without *motive* but solely thro' the goad *a tergo* of unmanly and unchristian fear—God knows! I in my inmost soul acknowlege all my sufferings as the necessary effects of his Wisdom, and all the alleviations as the unmerited graces of his

[1] Cf. *Table Talk*, 4 Apr. 1832.
[2] Coleridge began taking opium regularly in 1801. See Letter 400, the Introduction to vol. iii. of the present edition, and E. H. Coleridge's note in *Letters*, ii. 760–1.

Goodness. Since Monday I have been tranquil; but still, placing the palm of my hand with it's lower edge on the navel, I feel with no intermission a death-grasp, sometimes relaxed, sometimes tightened, but always present: and I am convinced, that if Medical Ethics permitted the production of a Euthanasia, & a Physician, convinced that at my time of Life there was no rational hope of revalescence to any useful purpose, should administer a score drops of the purest Hydro-cyanic Acid, & I were immediately after opened (as is my earnest wish) the state of the mesenteric region would solve the problem.

I trust, however, that I shall yet see you, as Job says, 'in this flesh'[1]—& I write now tho' under an earnest conviction of the decay of my intellectual powers proportionate to the decay of the Organs, thro' which they are made manifest, & which you must have perceived, of late, more forcibly than myself—I write, my dear friend! first to acknowlege God's Goodness in my connection with you—secondly, to express my utter indifference, under whose *name* any truths are propounded to Mankind—God knows! it would be no pain to me, to foresee that my name should utterly cease—I have no desire for reputation—nay, no wish for *fame*—but I am truly thankful to God, that thro' you my labors of thought may be rendered not wholly unseminative. But in what last Sunday you read to me, I had a sort of Jealousy, probably occasioned by the weakened state of my intellectual powers, that you had in some measure changed your pole. My principle has ever been, that Reason is *subjective* Revelation, Revelation *objective* Reason—and that *our* business is not to *derive* Authority from the *mythoi* of the Jews & the first Jew-Christians (i.e. the O. and N. Testament) but to *give* it to them—never to assume their stories as facts, any more than you would Quack Doctors' affidavits on oath before the Lord Mayor—and verily in point of old Bailey Evidence this is a flattering representation of the Paleyian Evidence—but by *science* to confirm the *Facit*, kindly afforded to beginners in Arithmetic. If I lose my faith in *Reason*, as the perpetual revelation, I lose my faith altogether. I must deduce the objective from the subjective Revelation, or it is no longer a revelation for me, but a beastly fear, and superstition.

I hope, I shall live to see you next Sunday. God bless you, my dear Friend! We have had a sad sick House—& in consequence, I have seen but little of Mr Gillman, who has been himself ill—and likewise Miss Lucy Harding. For me, it is a great blessing & mercy, Life or Death, that I have been & still remain quiet, without any

---

[1] Cf. Job xix. 26: 'And though after my skin worms destroy this body, yet in my flesh shall I see God.'

craving, but the contrary. Compared with this mercy, even the felt and doubtless by you perceived decay & languor of intellectual energy is a trifling counter-weight.—

Again, God bless you, my dear friend! | and
S. T. Coleridge—

1737. *To William Rowan Hamilton*

Pub. Life of Sir William Rowan Hamilton, *by R. P. Graves, 3 vols., 1882–9, i. 545.*

April 4, 1832.

Through bodily weakness and the multiplied professional avocations of my young friend, Mr. Gillman's medical pupil, I have not been able in the wilderness of my books, that for sixteen years have always been *intended* to be catalogued and put into some arrangement, I have not been able as yet to find the first volume of Kant's *Miscellaneous Essays*.[1] They are in five volumes, and for the most part consist of the publications anterior to the famous *Critik of the Pure Reason*.[2]

But—have you misunderstood me? I have no *translation*, and am aware of none—or are you a reader of the German? If so, I trust that I shall, before you quit London, still succeed in rummaging out the two lost volumes, one essay in Latin[3] being an excellent introduction to Kant's revival of the distinction between the Noumenon = Nomen, Intelligible, Numen—and the *Phaenomenon*—both *potential* Entities, that *are* only in and for the mind or the sensation. With great respect, my dear sir, I remain your afflicted but respectful, &c.

[1] Coleridge refers to Kant's *Vermischte Schriften*, ed. J. H. Tieftrunk, i–iii, 1799, iv. 1807. There is no fifth volume. The British Museum has two incomplete sets of this edition with MS. notes by Coleridge: ii–iv (C. 43. a. 9) and i–ii (C. 126. e. 7). In 1816 Coleridge returned Crabb Robinson's copy of vols. i–iii of still another set of the *Vermischte Schriften*. (See note to Letter 1019.) These three volumes, which contain annotations by Coleridge, are now in University College Library, London.

[2] Kant's *Kritik der reinen Vernunft*, 1781. Coleridge's annotated copy of the 1799 edition is in the British Museum.

[3] Kant's *De mundi sensibilis atque intelligibilis forma et principiis*, 1770, is in vol. ii of the *Vermischte Schriften* and is followed by a German translation. In a manuscript note in *De mundi* (C. 126. e. 7), Coleridge discusses the work as an important forerunner of the *Kritik der reinen Vernunft*. (From information kindly supplied by Mr. B. A. Rowley.) See also Letter 1126.

1738. *To William Rowan Hamilton*

Pub. Life of Sir William Rowan Hamilton, *by R. P. Graves, 3 vols., 1882–9, i. 545.*

[April 6, 1832.]

Dear and respected Sir,

I have little hope that this scrawl will reach you in time; but since the receipt of your kind letter, this morning, I cannot but feel self-accused, if from any neglect on my part you should leave England without having seen Mr. Green, 36 or 46, I forget which, in Lincoln's-Inn Fields; it is some five or six doors, Covent-garden-ward, beyond the Royal College of Surgeons. You will be pretty sure of finding him at home if it should be in your power to call before 11 or 12 o'clock.

I am much weaker than when you saw me: and have but feeble hope of the accomplishment of your kind wishes. God's will be done! He knows that my first prayer is not to fall from Him, and the faith that He is God, the I AM, the God that heareth prayer—the Finite in the form of the Infinite = the Absolute Will, the Good; the Self-affirmant, the Father, the I AM, the Personeity;—the Supreme Mind, Reason, Being, the *Pleroma*, the Infinite in the form of the Finite, the Unity in the form of the Distinctity; or lastly, in the synthesis of these, in the *Life*, the *Love*, the Community, the Perichoresis, or Inter[cir]culation—and that there is *one* only God! And I believe in an apostasis, absolutely necessary, as a *possible* event, from the absolute perfection of Love and Goodness, and because WILL is the only ground and antecedent of all Being. And I believe in the descension and condescension of the Divine Spirit, Word, Father, and Incomprehensible Ground of all—and that he is a God who *seeketh* that which was lost, and that the whole world of Phaenomena is a revelation of the Redemptive Process, of the Deus *Patiens*, or Deitas *Objectiva* beginning in the separation of Life from Hades, which under the control of the Law = Logos = Unity—becomes *Nature*, i.e., that which never *is* but *natura* est, is to be, from the brute Multeity, and Indistinction, and is to end with the union with God in the Pleroma. I dare not hope ever to see you again in the flesh—scarcely expect to survive to the hearing of you. But be assured I have been comforted by the fact you have given me, that there are men of profound science who yet feel that *Science*, even in its most flourishing state, needs a *Baptism*, a Regeneration in Philosophy—so call it, if you refer to the subjective feeling—but if to the Object, then, spite of all the contempt squandered on poor Jacob Boehmen and

Law[1]—Theosophy. If your time should permit, and your inclination impel you, to call on Mr. Green, you have only to tear off the postscript, and send it to him.

May God bless you, sir, and your afflicted but I trust resigned well-wisher nay, fervent *prayer*,

S. T. Coleridge.

[2nd.] P.S.—Should you have the opportunity, do not forget to remember me with love, and earnest good wishes to Mr. Anster in Dublin. I feel confident that he is not infected with the O'Connell palsying cholera morbus of his unhappy and unhappy-making country. . . .

1739. *To J. H. Green*

Address: J. H. Green, Esqre | &c &c | Lincoln's Inn Fields
MS. Pierpont Morgan Lib. Hitherto unpublished.
Postmark: Highgate, 7 April 1832.

[7 April 1832]

My dear friend

I will attempt to devote to you and your love & unfailing kindness toward me the relique of strength, that is left me—in order to let you know, if not the truth in itself as fact, yet my own convictions of the Fact, as concerns myself—that you may not have the pain, which I am sure my speedy Loss would give you, aggravated by disappointment. I do not wish—how is that possible? that *my feelings* should influence your judgement, more than those of any other sick man—But I would fain, putting all feelings & sensations out of the question, or rather stating them for what they are—dream indicative of Reality or mere Dream—place before you the Facts.—Partly from Mr Gillman's odd aversion to allow any sick person in his own house; partly, that he has been himself so unwell & wretched in his sensations, that his necessitated Duties leave him exhausted; & partly, that he has made up his mind, that a man with such a pulse & such a tongue, cannot be dangerously

---

[1] William Law (1686–1761), author of *A Serious Call to a Devout and Holy Life, adapted to the State and Condition of all Orders of Christians*, 1728, and an ardent admirer of Jakob Boehme. After Law's death, G. Ward and T. Langcake published *The Works of Jacob Behmen, The Teutonic Theosopher, . . . with Figures, illustrating his Principles, left by the Rev. William Law*, 4 vols., 1764–81. A copy of this edition with Coleridge's annotations is in the British Museum. Generally known as 'Law's edition', the work was, with a few alterations, reprinted from earlier English editions by J. Sparrow. For Coleridge's comments on Boehme and Law see *Biog. Lit.*, ch. ix ; *Aids to Reflection*, 1825, 377–85 ; Alice D. Snyder, 'Coleridge on Böhme', *Publications of the Modern Language Association*, 1930, pp. 616–18 ; Kathleen Coburn, *The Philosophical Lectures of Samuel Taylor Coleridge*, 1949, pp. 327–31 ; and Letters 800, 1067, and 1150.

ill;—I have not seen him, tho' I have passed my days in moaning & groaning, for the last 5 or 6 days. In fact, I should almost imagine that every one in the House thought it a *lost case*—but I will make no complaints—Mayhap, it would be folly so to do—

First—I have felt no craving for the Poison, but rather the contrary. Secondly, my Nights have been, sometimes for the mid part feverish, but yet tolerable, & without sufficient Sleep.—My Diet has been—first, a Dish of Tea, & a bit of buttered Toast—then at noon a basin of Gruel with half-a-glass of Brandy in it—& at 5 o'clock a single Mutton Chop, with a Pint of Wine.—But in addition to this I take in the course of the 24 hours two grains of Acetate of Morphium, with a small portion of the Tincture of Cardamom, & some of Battley's Liquor Cinchonae with Port Wine— so that in three days I probably take near two Bottles of Port Wine. Whether this is more or less than adequate to the abstraction of the Ounce of Laudanum I cannot say—I mean, the difference between the Pint of Wine taken while I took the Laudanum & Brandy, and the Pint & $\frac{1}{2}$ I take now without it—

But I have no sign or symptom of revalescence—on the contrary, am weaker—with the morning commences the bronchial *gleet*, the excessive expectoration of mucus—I feel, as if all the death & disease were at the Pit of my Stomach, & my Bowels—Sense of Heat, Weakness, and (when alone) almost constant *Moaning* & laborious Respiration. That Wind or Gas is most often the proximate cause of any *positive* pain, that I feel, I am strongly disposed to believe, but the increasing weakness, that generates this wind, the retrogression rather than any however slight progression, in me, & the evident weakness of my Bowels; incline me to think that at my age, & after more than 30 years' Self-poisoning, I cannot but be in danger of a dysentery or other epidemic complaint, carrying off the weak & previously *venenated*, spite of pulse, tongue, & complexion.—This at least is certain—It is now 5 weeks since I have taken Laudanum—but tho' thank God! much quieter, I am daily weaker & weaker.—Scarce able indeed [to] sit up for 3 or 4 hours in the 24.

Perhaps, without offending Mr Gillman, you might ask some Physician's opinion, in whose Judgement you have any confidence— God bless you | & S. T. Coleridge.—

P.S. I have opened this letter again, because I had forgotten to note one symptom of my case—namely, that while my complexion seems clearer, my eyes are weak, suffused, in short to use a hateful expression, have a sort of *sottish* wetness & weakness in them which shocks me while I am shaving. S. T. C.—

1740. *To H. B. Owen*[1]

Address: Revd Dr Owen | &c &c With Mr S. T. Coleridge's respectful thanks.—
MS. Huntington Lib. Hitherto unpublished.

April 11. 1832—

Dear Sir

I return the Book of Jasher with thankful sense of your kindness, in affording me the sight of it.—What? a Hebrew Work of the Age of Joshua done into *English* by Alcuin, who (we all know) lived some two Centuries before any such Language as the English was in Existence?[2] And who, good man! knew as much of Hebrew by recollection, as he could have done of English, except by a pre-creation!—The Bristolian Editor must surely be a most unthinking, credulous Mortal!—Why, my dear doctor! the very first page proves to any scholar, that it can be nothing more than one of the numerous slovenly Eutropius-like Abridgements of the Pentateuch & the Books of Joshua & Judges by some ignorant Monk—the Blunder of taking *Light*, not as a Power, but as the Phaenomenon, the positive, of which Darkness is the Negative—the presumptuous connection therewith of the creation of the Sun & Moon—the Word, *Nature*, for which there is no Hebrew Word, as *indeed* there is no *ens* or meaning corresponding to it—in short, the only doubt is, whether it is a vile Epitome formed from the Septuagint, or from the Vulgate Latin—I can scarcely doubt, that it was the work of some Christian Monk—for a Jew would not, I think, have so frequently, if at all, interpolated the sacred Text with passages from the Apocrypha—. Ex. gr. In the first Chapter, the Comment of the Author of the Wisdom of Solomon, a work written about a century before the birth of Christ by some Platonizing Alexandrian Jew—'to be the image of his own Eternity'[3] is impudently substituted for the Text.—But it is not worth writing about—being *utterly* worthless: & I, alas! am too weak to be able to do more than express my acknowlegement of your attention—

S. T. Coleridge

To the | Revd Doctor Owen | Highgate

---

[1] A leader in the feud over the chapel belonging to the Free Grammar School at Highgate. See notes to Letters 1284, 1310, and 1690.

[2] In 1751 Jacob Ilive (1705–63) printed anonymously a clumsy fabrication, purporting to be a translation of *The Book of Jasher. With Testimonies and Notes explanatory of the Text. To which is prefixed various readings. Translated into English from the Hebrew by Alcuin, of Britain, who went a Pilgrimage into the Holy Land.* The work was reissued with additions by the Rev. C. R. Bond, Bristol, 1829. Nothing is known of the Hebrew Book of Jashar mentioned in Joshua x. 13 and 2 Samuel i. 18.

[3] Wisdom ii. 23.

1741. *To H. F. Cary*

Address: Revd. H. F. Cary | &c &c | British Museum
MS. Professor W. A. Osborne. Pub. Letters, *ii. 760.*
Postmark: 23 April 1832.

22 April 1832.—Grove, Highgate

My dear friend

For I am sure by my love for you that you love me too well to have suffered my very rude and uncourteous vehemence of contradiction & reclamation respecting your advocacy of the Catalinarian Reform Bill, when we were last together, to have cooled, much less alienated, your kindness: even tho' the Interim had not been a weary weary time of groaning & life-loathing for me—But I hope, that this fearful night-storm is subsiding—as you will have heard from Mr Green or dear Charles Lamb. I write now to say, that if God who in his fatherly compassion, and thro' the Love wherewith he hath beheld and loved me in Christ, in whom alone he can love the World, hath worked almost a miracle of grace in & for me by a sudden emancipation from a 33 years' fearful Slavery—if God's goodness *should* continue & so far perfect my convalescence, as that I should be capable of resuming my literary labors—I have a thought, by way of a light *prelude*, a sort of unstiffening of my long dormant joints & muscles, to give a reprint, as nearly as possible except in quality of the *paper* a fac Simile of John Asgill's Tracts, with a Life & Copious Notes[1]—to which I would affix Postilla et Marginalia—i.e. my MSS Notes, blank leaf & marginal, on Southey's Life of Wesley,[2] and sundry other Works—Now can you direct me to any sources of Information respecting John Asgill, a prime Darling of mine—the most honest of all Whigs, whom at the close of Queen Anne's Reign the scoundrelly Jacobite Tories twice expelled from Parliament under the pretext of his incomparable, or only with Rabelais to be compared, Argument against the base & cowardly Custom of ever *dying* ?[3]— O that Tract is a very treasure—and never more usable as a

---

[1] Nothing came of this proposal, which is mentioned in the next two letters. A copy of *A Collection of Tracts written by John Asgill, Esq; from the Year 1700 to the Year 1715,* pub. 1715, with Coleridge's annotations is in the British Museum. The notes were first published in *Literary Remains,* ii. 390–7.

[2] Coleridge's notes written in a copy of Southey's *Life of Wesley; and the Rise and Progress of Methodism,* 2 vols., 1820, were first printed by C. C. Southey in the third edition of that work, 1846.

[3] *An Argument proving that according to the covenant of eternal life revealed in the Scriptures, man may be translated from hence into that eternal life, without passing through death, although the human nature of Christ himself could not be thus translated till he had passed through death,* 1700. Asgill was expelled by the Irish House of Commons in 1703 and by the English House of Commons in 1707.

medicine for our Clergy, at least all such as the B. of L., Arch B. of
Cant.—of Dublin &c,[1] the Paleyians and Mageeites[2]—any one or
all of whom I would defy to answer a single paragraph of Asgill's
tract, or unloose a single Link from his chain of Logic[3]—I have no
biographical Dictionary—& never saw one but in a little sort of
one Volume Thing.—If you can help me in this, do—& give my
kindest Love to dear Mrs Cary—

Your[s] with unalterable as ever unaltered love & regard & in
all (but as to the accursed Reform Bill, that mendacium ingens on
it's own Preamble—to which no human Being can be more friendly
than I am—that huge tape-worm *Lie* of some 3 score & ten joints)
entire sympathy of heart & soul your affectionate

S. T. Coleridge—

1742. *To Henry Nelson Coleridge*

Address: H. N. Coleridge, Esqre
MS. Victoria University Lib. Pub. E. L. G. ii. 443.

[7 May 1832][4]

My dear Henry

Tho' with the most willing faith in the validity of the grounds,
for your esteem and regard & friendly & affectionate *Liking* for the
Revd.——Millman, I cannot yet persuade myself that it was con-
sistent with either the modesty of a much younger man, or with
the delicacy of a gentleman & a Scholar to consent and undertake,
at the instance & under the auspices of an Anthropoïd, like Murray
of Albermarle St, to select, omit, correct, and by a few felicitous
interpolations improve and adapt my poetic Works in a very
abridged form, a sort of half brew between Rifaccimento & Por-
table Soup, to the correct taste of the Age.[5]—I say, I cannot with-
out hypocrisy pretend to acquiesce in the right feeling of this—
first, because as aforesaid, Mr Millman, tho' a Fellow of Braze-
Nose, was yet my junior—& secondly, because (God forgive me,
if I speak the Truth in a spirit of arrogance) at 5 & 20 I had not
forgotten, but thrown aside or precipitated, more than the Revd.
——Millman had or ever will have the chance of possessing—&

---

[1] C. J. Blomfield, bishop of London, 1828, William Howley, archbishop of
Canterbury, 1828, and Richard Whately, archbishop of Dublin, 1831.

[2] William Magee (1766–1831), bishop of Raphoe, 1819, and archbishop of
Dublin, 1822.

[3] For Coleridge's estimate of Asgill, see *Table Talk*, 30 July 1831, 30 Apr.
1832, and 15 May 1833.

[4] This letter, which was written on Monday, 7 May, and the one following
are both endorsed 9 May 1832, the day they were received.

[5] See Letters 1339, 1344, 1438, 1448, and 1456.

nathless, He may be not a whit the less respectable Being in *his* eyes, in whose alone [it is] of any importance. Do not, my dear Henry! so utterly misunderstand me, as to infer that I feel, much less cherish, any dislike or resentment toward Millman. On the contrary, since Good! Good! Mr Sotheby's grave & *sigh*ful narration to me of his Conversation with Scott's Oliver le Diable (*vide* Quentin Durward), the Archbish. of Cant. I mean—respecting Millman & his History of the Jews,[1] I have, even on a bed of pain, repeatedly laughed myself into a sort of a love & kind feeling toward him—

But as to this Asgill business, I have no objection *at all* to it's being submitted to Lockhart; & since his noble exertions against the Catalinarian Riff-Raff-form Bill, no other objection to *Mr Croker* but my knowlege from one of his pamphlets of the mutually exclusive Contrariety of his principles to mine, respecting the National Clerisy—whom he, in one of his pamphlets, has declared to be neither more or less than Government Cooks in office, to be kept, or dismissed, by the Ministers & Majority of the Houses for the time being, whereas, it will be one of my principal Objects to expose the hollowness & bull-froggery of our (I could almost say, blasphemously called) Legislature—if I were not doubtful as to the true interpretation of the two last Syllables—To make *Laws*!— Only think of the men, ex. gr. Hume, Althorp, Duncomb[e],[2] O'Connell &c &c &c—and then think of *Laws*, & *Make*. Why, in a Senate consisting of Moses, Heraclitus, Plato, Spinoza, Macchiavel, John, & Paul, it would be *presumption*—But if 'lature' only means, to announce & declare them, in application to circumstances, it may pass—saving only, that it cannot be right to extracrepidate[3]—as the Cobblers in our even unreformed H. of C. are in the constant habit of doing.

The remainder of this Letter, which written in bed is somewhat undecypherable, I will write on a different Sheet;[4] the *expedience* and *worldly-wisdom* of which I expect you duly to estimate and admire.—

Monday. [7 May] This hot ante-date of July I have crawle[d] from my Lair, like the *Slugs* (by the bye, the Parisian & American Editors ha[ve] chosen to dignify my 'Slugs quit their Lair'—into

[1] Henry H. Milman published *The History of the Jews*, 3 vols., in 1829; a second edition appeared in 1830. The work was unfavourably received, Bishop Mant among others violently attacking the author.

[2] Thomas S. Duncombe (1796–1861), radical politician, was at this time M.P. for Hertford.

[3] Elsewhere Coleridge wrote 'ultra-crepidated'. See Letter 342.

[4] Coleridge refers to the next letter. In the address sheet of the present letter he wrote 'No. 1.'

'*Stags*',[1] which is really so much grander that I grieve, it should
be senseless)—my ejection, however, having been effected by the
Chimney Sweepers.—Dialogue between S. T. C. and Mr Gillman—
S. T. C. on the penultimate Stair.—

G.—What's the matter now, Coleridge?

S. T. C.—I was only begging & intreating that some one of them
should keep watch in my room during the whole operation from
entrance to exit—& have her eyes about her.

G.—Why?

S. T. C.—Why?—Half a dozen of the Books—the MSS by pre-
ference as being the heavier paper—would be off in the Soot bags
to a certainty, and sold for waste paper—. Whole Volumes of
fervid *Mind* swopped for glasses of ardent *Spirit*, *Worlds*, I might
say, of solid Intellect for mere Shooting-stars of fluid Fire!—Rain-
water, and Flashes of Lightning, reconciled in Blue Ruin!—What
with Carpenters, Bell-hangers, Fire-lighters and Chimney-Sweeps,
I am unable to describe or enumerate the Losses, I have sustained,
since I have been in this house.—

G.—Now that last sentence at least is *a God's Truth*—I do
believe, that you *are* QUITE unable either to enumerate or describe
them—&c &c.

God bless you &
S. T. Coleridge.

1743. *To Henry Nelson Coleridge*

Address: H. N. Coleridge, Esqre. | 1 New Court | Lincoln's Inn
MS. Victoria University Lib. Pub. with omis. and inaccurately Coleridge on the
Seventeenth Century, *ed. Roberta Florence Brinkley, 1955, p. 493.*

Grove, Highgate
Monday Afternoon—May 5? or 6? [7] 1832.

My dear Nephew

My only objection, the only possible objection that I can have,
to the submitting of my 'Asgill's Tracts', and my intended Prae-
ills, Postills, and Marginalia, or rather the Scheme thereof, to either

[1] In Coleridge's *Poetical Works* of 1828 and 1829 the first line of *Work
without Hope* reads:

All Nature seems at work. Stags leave their lair.

In *Poetical Works*, 1834, 'Stags' is corrected to 'Slugs'. See the MS. version of
the poem in Letter 1433, where Coleridge first wrote 'Snails' and then altered
the word to 'Slugs'. In *The Bijou* (1828) 'Slugs' appears. In the Galignani
edition of *The Poetical Works of Coleridge, Shelley, and Keats*, Paris, 1829,
and in the American reprint of this edition, Philadelphia, 1831, the reading is
'Stags'.

Mr Lockhart or Mr Croker or both, is—the difficulty of conveying to any one, who had not conversed with me on the subject, either by the Tracts themselves, or by the few MSS Notes, which the paucity & scant dimension of the Blank Leaves, & the lankness of the Margins allowed me to incorporate or inatramentate with the papyr: cacatiss: of the Volume itself.—All I can say is that first, I should prefix a Life of Asgill, the facts of which I must take wholly from the Biogr. Brit. and Dr Kippis[1]—(Books, I have never read) but, I gather from Mr Carey's account of these Biographies, with a very, very different interpretation of the said facts, moral, spiritual, and political. 2.—A critical & philosophical Essay on Whiggism, from Dryden's Achitophel (Astley Cooper)[2] the first Whig to Lord Grey, who, I trust in God's Mercy, will be the last— considering the last years of Queen Anne's Reign, as the Zenith or palmy State of Whiggism, in its divinest Avatar of Common Sense, or of the Understanding vigorously exerted in the right direction on the right & proper objects of the Understanding[3]— (Mr Croker, not having seen, or if he has, not very likely having had either the leisure or the inclination to read, either my 'Aids to Ref.'—or my Essay on the Constitution in Ch. and State according to the *Idea*—i.e. Ultimate Aim—will not apprehend the antithesis here implied of the Underst. to the Reason)—3. Asgill's political Tracts, which (reversing the present Order) I place first—with numerous notes, of which those in the printed Vol. are but the specimen handful.—4. A brief History or philosophico-theologico-ethical Sketch of the History of the *Clergy* of the Church of England, from Cranmer[4] to Bishops Blomefield, Maltby[5] & Wheatly— In both Whiggism & the Church Clergy-system (Mem. *not* the *Church*, whether as National or as Christian)—wide as the differences are in other respects—I trace the rise, & occasion, progress, and necessary degeneration of the Spirit of *Compromise*— 'Councils begun in *fear* still end in folly.' 5. A summary, with the proofs from Divines of the Church, after the Restoration, of the points assumed by Asgill, which were & had been assumed by & were in fact admitted as orthodox & true, by his Enemies—

6. Then—Asgill's *famous* Tract—or 'Argument against the

---

[1] Andrew Kippis (1725–95) was chosen by the booksellers to prepare a second edition of the *Biographia Britannica*. Only five volumes were published, 1778–93. Joseph Towers assisted in the undertaking.

[2] Anthony Ashley Cooper (1621–83), first earl of Shaftesbury.

[3] Cf. *Table Talk*, 28 Jan. 1832.

[4] Thomas Cranmer (1489–1556) was appointed archbishop of Canterbury in 1533.

[5] Edward Maltby (1770–1859) was at this time bishop of Chichester. He was translated to Durham in 1836.

base & cowardly Custom of *Dying*'—than which a more incomparable Reductio ad absurdum of a Religion of the Understanding cannot, I hold, be conceived, whether considered as sound Logic or as original Humor—rendered exquisite by Asgill's evident uncertainty as to his aim being in jest or in earnest—7. His Defence in the House of Commons previous to his Expulsion under the pretext of this Tract[1]—with my Notes.—

8. & 9. My Marginalia & Post-illa on Baxter,[2] Southey's Life of Wesley—Supposing, the Anthropoïd, Mr Murray, should deem the extension to two Volumes instead of one too thick one advisable—

This is all the explanation, I can offer, either to Mr L. or Mr Croker—with the Tracts themselves—which, pray take care of, that whatever may be the Result or M's final decision, I may have the Book back—*Mem.*—If M. thinks it worth his while, let him assign me a price—for I won't work for *nothing*, or what is = nothing, a possibility of an *Author's Half* of the by the Publisher admitted net profits, after the sale of the very last *Copy*—which a wise Publisher will take good care shall never be sold—unless he sanguinely resolves on the success of a second Edition—

God bless you, my dear Henry! and Sara, and the Babes apparent & presumptive—

S. T. Coleridge—

1744. *To J. H. Green*

Address: J. H. Green, Esqre | &c &c | 46 Lincoln's Inn Fields
MS. Pierpont Morgan Lib. Hitherto unpublished.
Postmark: Highgate, 18 May 1832.

[17 May 1832]

My dear friend

It is my trust & prayer, that avocation and the absence of any Answer to the Cui bono, of your coming, have prevented you from turning your Horses' Heads Highgate-ward—& that neither illness

---

[1] *Mr. Asgill's Defence upon his Expulsion from the House of Commons of Great Britain in 1707*, published 1712. See *Literary Remains*, ii. 397, for Coleridge's annotation.

[2] A copy of Richard Baxter's *Catholick Theologie*, 1675, containing annotations by Coleridge is in the British Museum. A copy of *Reliquiae Baxterianae . . .*, 1696, with Coleridge's annotations is in the Harvard College Library. For the notes in the latter work see *Literary Remains*, i. 263–6 and iv. 76–156. (The notes included in vol. i. are reprinted in vol. iv. 76–78.) Derwent Coleridge republished these annotations and entitled them 'Second Series'. See *Notes on English Divines. By Samuel Taylor Coleridge*, ed. Derwent Coleridge, 2 vols., 1853, ii. 49–119. Derwent also printed a different set of notes drawn from another copy of *Reliquiae Baxterianae*, 1696. These notes he entitled 'First Series'. Ibid. ii. 5–48.

nor vexation ab extra have had a finger in the Pie.—I grieve to
say, for I know, it will grieve you, that I can offer no rational
motive for your coming here next Sunday.—Sunday last I drest
at 12 o'clock—crawled down into the drawing-room & received
the gratulations of successive visitors on my bright eyes & clear
complexion—A large number of incendiary ½d & penny flying-
sheets, recalling and repeating the guilt & frenzy of the Septem-
brizers in 93 [1792][1] were successively brought in—Mr Steele, an
old School-fellow, was eulogizing Lord Grey[2]—& I two thirds
laughing & one third in earnest was hyper-bolizing on the other
side—in short, in apparent high spirits—But I was not myself
deceived. The painful Yawning with the suffusion of the Eyes with
water gave too convincing proof of the want of balance & harmony
between the respiratory & the circulatory systems.—Yet as at
5 o'clock I retired to my room, my Nephew & Son in law exprest
his delight at my improved appearance.—Soon after I took half
a mutton chop. Had it been a Sponge impregnated with nux
vomica or any more narcotic poison, it could scarcely have acted
more suddenly. All my limbs became torpid, with aching & a sense
of weight—I lay, quite unable to undress myself, in a distressful
Torpor, a rapid succession of startful dozings, & the never remitting
sensation of Heat & Uneasiness in the old place—from the pit of
the Stomach to the Navel, till Monday Noon—when Mr Gillman
found time to look in on me—He ordered me some tincture of
Rhubarb, with tinct. of Cardamom, & the two grains of Acetate of
Morphium, divided into 4 doses, at 6 hour intervals—& 2½ grains
of Blue Pill to be taken with each dose. Therefore, from Monday

---

[1] During the French Revolution a dreadful massacre of the political prisoners
took place in Paris on 2-5 Sept. 1792. The agents of the slaughter were named
Septembrizers.

[2] Coleridge's letter was written during the struggle over the passage of the
Reform Bill in the House of Lords. The Bill was passed by the House of Com-
mons at the third reading on 23 Mar. 1832. (See note to Letter 1715.) Lord
Grey moved the first reading in the House of Lords on 26 Mar., and the Bill
passed the second reading on 14 Apr. by a majority of nine votes. The opposi-
tion, however, intended to mutilate the Bill in committee, and on 7 May the
ministry was defeated when the House of Lords passed by a majority of 35
a motion 'that the question of enfranchisement should precede that of dis-
franchisement'. A crisis followed, since Grey had determined that the whole
Bill must pass, 'unmutilated and unimpaired in all its main principles and
essential provisions'. He urged William IV to agree to the creation of sufficient
peers to ensure passage of the Bill in the House of Lords. The king, however,
rejected the proposal, and on 9 May Grey resigned. Wellington was unable
to form a ministry, and on 17 May Grey was recalled, the king giving the
ministers his written authority to create the necessary peers. This threat over-
came the opposition, and the Reform Bill passed the House of Lords at the
third reading on 4 June 1832. It received the royal assent three days later.

Noon to Tuesday Noon I had taken ten grains of Blue Pill—And
the disquieting Sensations ceased.—But on the next day a com-
mencing Salivation took place—& I will answer for it, that out of
the foul Ward of a Hospital even you have never seen a Head so
swoln, or a physiognomy so frightfully deformed as that of your
poor friend at this moment. I have very nearly lost the voluntary
power of ejecting the mucus from my Throat—& as to eating, it is
impracticable.—The result is—that I shall distress you, when you
see me—& you can do me no good.—I do not feel the slightest
wish or craving for the Laudanum; nor do I believe, that it would
even alleviate my sufferin[g]s. But yet I grieve for the too apparent
failure of the experiment—

                                              S. T. Coleridge.

1745. *To J. H. Green*

Address: J. H. Green, Esqre | &c &c | Lincoln's Inn Fields | 36? or 46? It is
one or the other.
MS. Pierpont Morgan Lib. Hitherto unpublished.
Postmark: Highgate, 19 May 1832.

                                  Friday Night—[18 May 1832]
My dear friend
    It annoys me to teize you; but Mr Hardman has during the last
fortnight made so many applications for the return of Brown's
Alcuin, and Mr Gillman as the conducting pipe communicating to
the fluid, a chalybeate Astringency of it's own, and I have as
regularly forgot, as I had resolved, to remind you of the same—
and as further, all the motives against your coming, representable
by determinate figures (1, 2, 3, 4—&c) annexing thereto the thereby
impregnated 0 0 (= aughts or naughts) as expressing the absence
or removal of all motives for it, have in no respect undergone any
change, save for the worse, since I wrote to you—but still I am in
a state, in which I can neither communicate or receive any pleasure,
in which you could not help being shocked, without the least
chance of doing me any good—and I, too probably, should be
weak enough to be affected by the effects on your feelings—*there-
fore* I must intreat you to put the tiny tract in an envelope, & send
it directed to me or Mr Gillman by the 3d. Post.
    I cannot help a nascent suspicion, that the Incidents of the last
four or five days have shaken Mr Gillman's faith in the infallibility
of the routine Tests, the Pulse, the Tongue, the *face*-complexion,
and the non-production of pain by local pressure, more than he
will as yet allow even to his own mind. The distinction between

Disorder & Disease is no less important than it is just; but like the terms Nervous, Dyspepsia, Asthenia & hypersthenia, &c &c, are excellent stuffing for the Tick Bed of respectable Routine.

If contrary to my present anticipation a favorable change should take place 'in the body of this death'—& with such a change the craving to see you will return, as the craving for a pinch of snuff follows the first glass of Wine in a man, who has abjured the Snuff Box, from Bed Time till the post-prandium of the following day— it shall without fail be announced to you.

Are you personally acquainted with Dr Wilson Phillip ?[1]

My poor—or my rich, Brother Colonel Coleridge, who has placed himself, I understand, under the care of Mr Brodie, called in his Carriage this morning—but I would not expose him to the fatigue of getting out of his Carriage, & climbing 5 flights of Stairs, in order to behold a Mask of Syphilis, as a Venus *sub* Medicis et Mercurio, when he had expected to see the Son of his Father. Poor Harriet, who had been hard at work in scouring the House, & had not attended on me as usual, burst into hysteric weeping as she first fixed her eyes on me—& at last sobbed out— I could not have believed any thing so frightful, in your countenance—Mr G. repeats, over and over, on his now almost daily visit—Odd!—it is very Odd!—from whence I venture to infer that this fierce Salivating, whether it prove kill or cure, must be placed under the Rubric of Accident.

Pray, remember me affectionately to Mrs Green—& with highest respect and love to your Mother, whose kindness at St Lawrence is a Tenant that will defy all process of ejection from the Heart & Brain of, dear Friend,

your obliged

S. T. Coleridge

P.S. I have read and with care Professor Park's Dogmas of the Constitution.[2] He does me the Honor of quoting a part of a sentence from me—but I cannot flatter myself with the notion, that he had done more than barely *look at* the Essay.—I feel and therefore do not hesitate to avow, the persuasion, that a morning's Conversation with me would have made Professor Park's Lectures abundantly more satisfactory to the Man, he is evidently becoming.

---

[1] Alexander Philip Wilson Philip (1770?–1851?), physician and physiologist, was the author of numerous medical works, several of which were translated into various languages.

[2] John James Park, *The Dogmas of the Constitution: Four Lectures delivered at King's College, London*, 1832. For Coleridge's annotations in this work see *Notes, Theological, Political, and Miscellaneous. By Samuel Taylor Coleridge*, ed. Derwent Coleridge, 1853, pp. 223–8.

If *14* lines sufficed to justify the name of a Sonnet, the off-slough of my 'Youth & Age' might appear per se, as such Sonnet.[1]

> Dew-drops are the Gems of Morning,
> But the Tears of mournful Eve.—
> Where no Hope is, Life's a Warning
> That only serves to make us grieve,
> > In our old Age[2]—
> That only serves to make us grieve
> With oft and tedious taking-leave,
> Like a poor, nigh-related Guest,
> Who may not rudely be dismiss'd,
> Yet hath outstayed his welcome While
> And tells the Jest without the smile!
> O! might *Life* cease! and selfless Mind,
> Whose total *Being* is *Act*, alone remain behind![3]

S. T. Coleridge

1746. *To William Worship*

Transcript made by Professor R. C. Bald from a copy in the handwriting of Mrs. Gillman. Hitherto unpublished.

[May 1832]

. . . specially of the Plexus Solaris; but its headquarters in the interspace between the pit of the Stomach and the navel but often extending by sympathy to the rectum with all the disquieting miseries of tenesmal irritation. During the paroxysms which would last for days with a few hours' intermission of stupor rather than Sleep I could neither lie sit nor stand but from morning to night kept pacing my room like a Leopard in his Den to the tune of groans & prayers—praying earnestly for Death but likewise for Grace to add ever 'But thy will not mine be done'. As soon as an interval of ease returned, the affection shifted to the sciatic nerve of one or of both thighs—& I became a compleat cripple—[Laudanum, which I had taken in enormous doses for 32 years lost all its anodyne powers,][4] & at last I proposed to leave it off. But Dr

---

[1] These lines were first published under the title, *An Old Man's Sigh. A Sonnet,* in *Blackwood's Magazine,* June 1832, with the date '18th May, 1832— Grove, Highgate'. The poem is preceded by a prose note, 'What is an English Sonnet?'.

[2] At this point an additional line appears in the version of the poem printed in *Blackwood's Magazine*:
  Whose bruised wings quarrel with the bars of the still narrowing cage.

[3] These last two lines were not included in the version of *Youth and Age* published in *Poetical Works,* 1834.

[4] Passage in brackets partly erased in copy.

Prout[1] and my friends Mr Green and Mr Gillman could not give their consent to a step which they regarded as bordering too near on suicidal. Well! I struggled for another month but finding no improvement I resolved on leaving off the Laudanum at once & what Dr Prout . . .

1747. *To William Blackwood*

Pub. Annals of a Publishing House. William Blackwood and His Sons, *by* M. Oliphant, 2 vols., 1897, i. 419.

May 26, 1832.

I have no means of procuring a frank; and I cannot but fear that the disproportion between the contents of my last, and the postage of an Edinburgh letter from London, may argue a some-what unconscientious self-appreciation on the part of the Writer, and the more so that it omitted what yet was a fact foremost and apparent in my mind; *videlicet*, the sense of your kind attentions to me, my cordial thanks for the 'Odd Book', and my old friend De Quincey's 'Klosterheim'.[2] It is now about the second year of my imprisonment to my Bad [Bed?] Book Attic, and from fever and languor I crawl through a book as cumbrously as a Fly through a Milk-splash, and the more the book interests me the slower is my progress. And I have read nothing since the 'Quentin Durward'[3] which would compare in interest with 'Klosterheim': and in purity of style and idiom, in which the Scholar is ever implied, and the scholarly never obtrudes itself, it reaches an excellence* to which Sir W. Scott, with all the countless unaffected conversa-tional charms and on-carryingness of his Diction, appears never to have aspired, rather than to have fallen short of. The 'Odd

---

[1] William Prout (1785–1850), physician and chemist. In 1831 Prout de-livered a course of Gulstonian lectures, the 'Application of Chemistry to Physio-logy, Pathology, and Practice'. The lectures were reported in the *London Medical Gazette* and led to a controversy in that journal with A. P. W. Philip, whom Coleridge mentions in the preceding letter.

[2] De Quincey's *Klosterheim; or, The Masque* was published by William Black-wood in 1832.

[3] Referring to a passage in ch. xxix of *Quentin Durward*, Coleridge says in a marginal note: 'From *The Ancient Mariner* [lines 414–19] stolen and (as usual) *spoilt* in the attempt to disguise the theft'. See *Coleridge's Miscellaneous Criticism*, ed. T. M. Raysor, 1936, pp. 336–7.

* With a few exceptions, as 'knock up', 'were pulled up', the inevitables of that human iscoria [scoria?] from which no writer in his senses ever hopes to secure an immunity. *N.B.*—In writing this I had read only to page 230. I have since finished and carefully revised the volume, and for all that follows from page 23 I have much to say which De Quincey will suffer me to say to himself should I have strength to put it down. [Note by S. T. C.]

Book' I hope to commence to-morrow. I refer to it now chiefly as
an excuse for expressing the regrets I felt and feel that Mr K. left
London, and that I had no opportunity of shaking [his hand] and
giving him an old Poet's and Fellow-Christian's blessing. But what
shall I say of what I owe to you for the delight and comfort and
instruction of the Ed. Magazine, and especially for the whole
series of the two years, during which Sickness and Sorrow have
made such a visitor and Bedside Comforter a *Friend indeed*, for it
has been a Friend in Need. If I were to express half of what I think
and feel concerning the Magazine I should give the heartless
slanderers of the Catilinarian press a tempting pretext for charging
me with flattery. But, nevertheless, I should accuse myself of
cowardice and ingratitude if I hesitated to avow and assert my
conviction that in the long, never-flagging Height and Sustained-
ness of irony, in the continuity, variety, and strength of wing, and
in the value, the worth, the deep importance of the moral and
political truths which it has streamed forth with eloquent wisdom,
'Blackwood's Magazine' is an unprecedented Phenomenon in the
world of letters, and forms the golden—alas! the only—remaining
link between the Periodical Press and the enduring literature of
Great Britain. If ever I was delighted with what, at the same
moment, I felt as a gross flattery, it was on the Belief entertained
by several of my friends that the 13 articles on Reform, the
French Revolution,[1] &c., had been contributed by me; and if per-
fect identity of sentiment, principle, and faith and feeling could
excuse the mistake, it might stand within the conditions of a
Pardon. But at no period of my life could I have produced such a
union of the Popular and the Profound. Your Magazine is every-
where, and therefore supersedes the necessity of any further pub-
lication. Still I cannot but long to possess these, and its congeners
of the last three years, in a couple of volumes printed like the
'Klosterheim'.

Having now given the relief of an *Outlet* to the 'gathering of the
waters', to the feelings and convictions that have so long been
astir within me, do me the justice to believe that it is from far
other impulses than those of authorial vanity and craving for
Praise that I give vent to my Regret that no notice was taken of
my 'Essay on the Constitution; or, Church and State according
to the Idea', a copy of both the first and the second edition of
which I expressly desired the Publisher to transmit to you. If I

---

[1] The French Revolution of 1830, which caused the abdication of Charles
X on 2 Aug. and led to the establishment of the Liberal Monarchy under
Louis-Philippe, was to exert a strong influence on the movement for reform in
England.

know my own heart, it is the deep sense I have of the truth, urgency, and importance of the Principles set out in that work, which alone made me not ambitious of, but anxious for, its being noticed in your Magazine; and allow me to observe that Mons. Thiers' speech on the question of hereditary Peerage was almost a translation from the first part of my Essay.

I will now try to pay virtually half the postage of this letter by transcribing for you, if worth your acceptance, a pathetic over-flowing Sonnet[1] of your truly obliged

S. T. Coleridge.

1748. *To Henry Nelson Coleridge*

MS. Victoria University Lib. Hitherto unpublished.

My dear Henry   [Endorsed 10 June 1832]

Quamvis vix adhuc desaeviit Virus Hermaphroditicum, with it's intergingival hillocks of sponge, the bigness, the aching, the drivelry and the devilry (i.e. the fetor), yet the Head and Features are re-appearing—and I no longer behold in my glass a Hottentot Venus sub medicis, with the characteristic Feature transplaced. I got up at noon, laved, shaved and shirted myself: & hope that I shall be able to sit up till tea time. It is now ½ past 4. I owe part of my strength, however, to the influence of the Cordial Ether Draught, which Mr Gillman administered to me last night, at 11 o'clock.

For the last 3 weeks it has been [my] intention to speak to you when you came, on a subject which when you *did* come, I as regularly forgot. It is this. Three applications have been made, two per letter in my own hand, within the last 8 months to Messrs. Baldwin & Cradock, Pater-noster Row, requesting a statement & settlement of the Friends & Lay Sermons, of which for the last 16 or 17 years they have been the Cellarers & Sellers.[2]—Promises have been returned—and broken. Likewise, Mr Pickleherring, *the* Aldus,[3] or Elzevir[4] of Chancery Lane, has been as fruitlessly

---

[1] Coleridge included a somewhat different version of the lines which he had previously sent to Green in his letter of 11 Jan. 1832. In forwarding them to Blackwood he entitled them *An Elegiac plusquam sesqui Sonnet to my Tin Shaving-pot.* Mrs. Oliphant printed the lines with the present letter. Op. cit. i. 421.

[2] Coleridge's publisher, Rest Fenner, failed in Mar. 1819. Baldwin was named one of the assignees in bankruptcy. See Letters 1202, 1204–5, 1725, and 1749.

[3] Aldus Manutius (1450–1515), Italian classical scholar, celebrated printer, and founder of the Aldine Press. In 1829 William Pickering adopted the trade-mark of the Aldine Press, an anchor entwined with a dolphin.

[4] Elzevir, the name of a famous family of Dutch printers in the 17th century.

importuned for something like an account of the two high-priced
Editions of my Poetic Works.—Now I know, that a long time ago
being in much distress of mind for want of 25 or 30£, owing, two
thirds of it, to an engagement for a distressed pair of female
former Intimates[1]—the more unfortunate as I had if not made yet
implied a promise to the Gillmans, that I should refuse it on the
score of absolute inability. But my fortitude turned tail—I had
expectations of obtaining 30£ from an Annual for two Poems, one
finished, the other wanting only a few concluding Stanzas—which
I should receive before the Bill came due &c—. But lo!—the
Annualist jockeyed me, & I was at the same time taken ill—.[2]
Basil Montagu coming to see me, I confided to him the weight
upon my mind, and he with his wonted promissory Munificence
and characteristic prosiliency of Undertaking relieved me of the
burthen, con prestezza—Unluckily he had accomodated his friend
& publisher, Pickleherring, with a large sum of ready money last
week & left himself bare—but that made no difference—'Draw
on Pick. for the 30£ at 6 weeks date, & he shall accept it'—I did
so—but lo! toward the close of the time dear Basil found, it would
be inconvenient to take the Bill on his own account—& made
Pickleherring put down the Sum, as advanced to me on account
of the Poems, sold or hereafter to be sold.[3]—Nothing but the knock
me down disqualification of my long long illness could have pre-
vented me from composing a couple of Sheets for Blackwood's
Magazine—[MS. breaks off thus.]

1749. *To Baldwin and Cradock*

Address: Messrs. Baldwin and Cradock | Publishers | Pater Noster Row
MS. Cornell University Lib. Pub. Nineteenth-Century Studies (*Cornell*), 54.
Postmark: Highgate, 30 June 1832.

Friday, 29 June 1832
Grove, Highgate

Dear Sirs

In very truth I owe an apology (I wish, I could offer an *excuse*)
to you for my delay in acknowleging the receipt of your friendly

[1] In his letter to Hall of 4 Dec. 1828 Coleridge mentions his efforts to col-
lect £20 for Mrs. Morgan and her sister. The £30 loan of 1829 was all the money
Coleridge received from Pickering. See Letter 1653.

[2] Coleridge obviously refers to Frederic M. Reynolds, who 'jockeyed' him
concerning payment for contributions to the 1830 *Keepsake*. See Letters 1667
and 1669.

[3] In Aug. 1829 Coleridge sent Pickering a bill due on 7 Nov. (See Letter
1668.) On 17 Nov. he renewed the loan, which he promised to pay by 10 Feb.
1830. See Letter 1679. There was 'no *profit*' from the 1828 *Poet. Works*. See
Letter 1639, p. 760.

note with the inclosed check of a 102£.[1] But tell the truth and shame the Devil—tho' at the price of going halves in the shame with His cerco-ceronychous (*i.e.   tail-horn-hoofed*) Majesty![2]—An almost two years' confinement to my bed-room (and for the greater part of the latter half of the time to my Bed) pain alternating with far more intolerable bodily inquietude, and the Languors with the torpor of the Organs of motion, which still *dog* and retard my convalescence, have tended to aggravate an old bad habit of mine —viz. a sort of cowardly awe and superstitious reverence for the *Seals* (whether wax or wafer) of my Correspondents' Letters, with the consequent suspension *sine die* of all knowlege of their contents—which might perhaps by a very partial Judge be referred to a taste for the MAGNIFICENT, on the strength of the old Adage— *Omne ignotum pro magnifico*[3]—but to confess the honest truth, was and is a very idle and mischievous Trick: and for which I had not the excuse of Debt, or the anticipation of a dunning Bill. This morning, however, my Conscience got me into a corner, and vowed that there she would keep watch and ward, till I had discharged my debt to her—& accordingly I opened my Nephew's Letter and to my 'confusion of face' found your Note & check as the inclosure—[4] But be assured, my dear Sirs! that I feel grateful to you for your kind attentions to my interests, & remain with great respect

Your obliged

S. T. Coleridge

1750. *To Eliza Nixon*

Transcript Coleridge family. Pub. E. L. G. ii. 446.

23rd July 1832—

Dear Eliza

I return you Mrs Rundle's Cook-away Book,[5] with many thanks —but how could such a meagre transcript from some Sausage wife's Receipt Scrawl have obtained so extensive a sale! I positively could not live out of it half a week. I have lost a full pound of flesh by the mere hasty skimming thro' it—In the whole 449 pages, I have found but 4 possible Dinners—1st Tripe & Onions— 2 Cowheel—3 Pigs' feet & Petitoes—4 Black puddings! And the

---

[1] This was money due to Coleridge from the assignees of the bankrupt estate of Rest Fenner. See Letter 1725.

[2] Cf. *Omniana, or Horae Otiosiores*, 2 vols., 1812, i. 197, and *Literary Remains*, i. 287.

[3] Tacitus, *Agricola*, 30.   [4] See preceding letter.

[5] The publication in 1808 of Mrs. Maria Eliza Rundell's *A New System of Domestic Cookery. By a Lady* was one of John Murray's most lucrative undertakings. By 1841 sixty-five English editions had appeared.

first & last of these Mr Gillman would not let me have—Even
Irish Stew is not mentioned!! and as to Vegetables why 'the
Lady' must have been all her life tethered in a Battersea Cabbage
Garden, with a simple prospect of a Potatoe Field in the distance,
& an occasional Glimpse of a Turnip Waggon from over the Hedge
—Covent Garden must have been a Terra Incognita, not even
named in her Map—O by the Soul of Dr Kitchener, and the Esprit
of Monsieur Ude,[1] the 'New System of Domestic Cookery' is as
surely a pickpocket humbug of Mister Murray, as I am

dear Eliza | Your aff. Friend

S. T. Coleridge—

1751. *To J. H. Green*

Address: J. H. Green, Esqre | &c | Lincoln's Inn Fields
MS. Pierpont Morgan Lib. Hitherto unpublished.
Postmark: Highgate, 26 July 1832.

Thursday, 26 July 1832

Grove, Highgate—

My dear Friend

What think you of the following 'Premonitory'? I cannot
afford, myself, to have a few score Copies struck off, pasted upon
a parallelogram Board, & set in motion, like genuine Ligna Vitae,
as Placards ambulant! (We have plenty of ligneous Doctors: why
not a few additional Dr Lignums?—) Should I send it to the Board
of Health? or to Lord Melborne?[2] There ought to be a Premium,
an £ ‖ S ‖ D Honorarium, offered for such Contributions; but *I*
would make a present of it to a Government, of whom and of whose
measures I am, you know, so glowing an admirer that it may be
fairly questioned whether the Devil himself can in this respect
outrival me. Besides, I am jealous of the Glory of this new-
imported Nabob, from the Indian Jungles,[3] his Serene Blueness,
Prince of the Air—lest he should have the presumption—for there
is no bounds to the arrogance of these Oriental Imports—to set
himself up in Hell against Lords Grey, Durham, & the Reform-Bill.
Fool! as if filling the Church-yard could be reckoned an equal
service with stripping and emptying the Church!—

---

[1] Dr. William Kitchiner published his *Apicius Redivivus, or the Cook's
Oracle*, in 1817; Louis E. Ude was not only a cook but a writer on the art of
cookery.

[2] William Lamb, second Viscount Melbourne (1779–1848), was appointed
home secretary in the Grey ministry in Nov. 1830.

[3] A violent epidemic of Asiatic cholera occurred at Jessore in Bengal in
1817 and was followed by the gradual spread of the disease to Europe. It first
appeared in England in Oct. 1831 and in London in Jan. of the following year.

(916)

The communication of, and counsel-craving about, this elegant Iatro-poesy was not, however, the principal end & object of this letter—but to beg you to bring with you on Sunday next your two concluding Lectures of the Zoological Course, on the Characteristics of Man.—I wish to look over again the passage on the *Federative* Character of the N. W. Branch of the Japetic Race—in reference to our Sunday Business. God bless you,

& your's &

S. T. Coleridge

Address premonitory to the Sovereign People: or the Cholera cured beforehand, promulgated *gratis* for the use of the Useful Classes, specially of those resident in St Giles's, Bethnal Green, Saffron Hill, &c—by their Majesties', i.e. the People's, loyal Subject,

DEMOPHILUS MUDLARKIADES.[1]

To escape Belly-ache
Eat no plums nor plum-cake!
Cry, Avaunt, New Potato!
And don't get drunk, like old Cato!
Ah beware of Dys Pipsy,
And there*före* don't get tipsy!
For tho' Gin and Whisky
May make you feel frisky,
They're but Crimps for Dys Pipsy.
And nose to tail of Dys Pipsy
Comes, black as a Porpus,
The Diabolus ipse
Call'd, Cholery Morpus!

And oh! och! my dear Honeys!
There is no Cure for *You*
For Loves nor for Moneys:
And you'll find it too true.
Och! the Halloballoo!
Och! och! how you'll wail
When the horn-and-hoof'd Vagrant
Shall turn you as blue
As the Gas-light unfragrant
That gushes in jets from beneath his own Tail!
Then swift as the Mail
He at length brings the Cramps on,
That will twist you, like Sampson.

---

[1] For another version of these lines see Letter 1757.

So without further blethring,
Dear Mud-larks, my Brethren!
Of all Scents and Degrees,
(Yourselves with your SHES)
Forswear all Cabàl, Lads!
Wakes, Unions, and Rows,
Hot Drams and cold Sallads:
And don't live in Styes that would suffocate Sows!
Quit Cobbett's, O'Connel's, and Belzebub's Banners,
And white-wash at once your Guts, Rooms, and Manners!
                    VIVAT Rex Popellus!
                    VIVAT Regina Plebs!
                        Hurra! 3 times 3 thrice
                    repeated.—Hurra!—

1752. *To J. H. Green*

Address: J. H. Green, Esqre | &c &c | Lincoln's Inn Fields
MS. The Carl H. Pforzheimer Library. Hitherto unpublished.
Postmark: 1832.

                                        Monday [6 August 1832]
My dearest Friend
  H. N. C. and Sara being very desirous that I should be present
at the christening of my Grand-daughter, Edith to be—& I myself
wishing to stand beside Mrs Coleridge at this second birth of our
common Off-spring[1]—in proof that the lack of Oil or Anti-friction
Powder in our Conjugal Carriage-wheels did not extend to our
parental relations—(and in fact, bating living in the same house with
her there are few women, that I have a greater respect & *ratherish*
liking for, than Mrs C——) & this being fixed for Thursday—I
write now to say, that Wednesday & Friday are *open* days—for
I mean to postpone Tuesday's and ante-date Friday's Air-Bath—
& take it on Thursday, as a *Cosmetic* as well as Circulator of the
Capillary Fluids—so as to return viâ Hamstead by 3 o'clock, P.M.—
            God bless you, | &
                                        S. T. Coleridge

  [1] Edith Coleridge, who was born on 2 July 1832, was baptized by the Rev.
James Gillman on Thursday, 9 Aug. Coleridge was able to attend the christen-
ing. His daughter reported that the family snatched 'a golden opportunity of
a most sunny season of my dear Father's health'. According to Mrs. Coleridge,
her husband 'talked incessantly for full 5 hours'. See E. L. Griggs, *Coleridge
Fille*, 1940, p. 74, and *Minnow among Tritons*, ed. Stephen Potter, 1934, p. 165.

1753. *To James Gillman*

Address: James Gillman, Esqre
MS. Victoria University Lib. Hitherto unpublished.

[6 August 1832]

My dear Gillman

Have you made, or can you make up your mind decisively whether or no you can join me at Henry's christening Dinner, on Thursday, 5 o'clock? If there be even a decent chance of your coming, I need not say how much your presence would be preferred to that of any possible Substitute who might be asked, were your Coming impracticable.—A verbal answer[1] by Beal or little Sara will be enough for

S. T. Coleridge

1754. *To Henry Nelson Coleridge*

Address: H. N. Coleridge, Esqre | New Court | Lincoln's Inn.   *Favored by Mr Kinderley.*
MS. Victoria University Lib. Hitherto unpublished.

Tuesday Night. [7 August 1832]

My dear Henry

I shall have both pleasure and interest in reading your Essay on Hesiod[2] & in comparing it with it's second or plagiary Rain-bow in the Ebony.[3] Gillman cannot come—I inclose his answer to my note. My own scheme is—that I have ordered the Fly (not the Reading Fly) for Thursday at $\frac{1}{2}$ 11, A.M., wherewith I shall proceed to Jonathan's, Great Marlborough St,[4] & after my Air-bath

---

[1] Gillman's reply is written on the verso of Coleridge's letter:

From what has occurred nearly every Evening these last few nights & the chances are that the same may continue, makes the necessity almost imperious that I should remain more within call than at Hampstead—I had thought of driving over in the Evening to pay my respects & look at the festive folks for a short time, but *certainly* not of *dining* with *them*. Thus it stands with me my dear Friend to my utter regret & disappointment for many reasons.

Hubble! Bubble! toil! and trouble!

J. G.—

[2] Coleridge refers to an article, 'Life and Writings of Hesiod', which appeared in the Mar. 1832 issue of the *Quarterly Review*, 1–39. Southey points out that H. N. Coleridge also contributed another article, 'Greek Elegy', to the same periodical for Oct. 1832, pp. 69–100. See *Southey Letters*, iv. 307.

[3] The second article to which Coleridge refers is entitled 'Hesiod', and appeared in *Blackwood's Magazine* for Aug. 1832, pp. 165–76.

[4] Jonathan Green, M.D. (1788?–1864) conducted an establishment for fumigating and other baths at 40 Great Marlborough Street.

return viâ Downshire Hill, so as to be delivered at your door by
½ 2—post-dating my Tuesday's & antedating my Friday's Bath,
partly as a *Cosmetic* to do credit to little *Mottle* & the Gossips, and
partly as an accelerative Circulator of the Capillary Fluids on my
own & the Dinner's Account.

I am happy to say that the mala fides, which had been supposed
of James Harding, proves to be an unjust charge—at all events,
if meditated, it was res infecta. . . . [MS. cut off.]

1755. To Mrs. Gillman

Pub. Coleridge at Highgate, *by Lucy E. Watson, 1925, p. 146.*

[13 August 1832][1]

My dear Friend,—A letter from Mr. Kennard has announced to
me a loss too great, too awful for common grief, or for any of its
ordinary forms.

A state of deepest mental silence, neither prayer nor thanks-
giving, but with my whole mind soul and spirit fixed on God is
what I now feel.

Steinmetz was translated to a yet more intimate communion
with his God and Saviour yesterday morning, perfectly tranquil,
and without having had any return of delirium since Friday last.
From the hour I began to love him—and this was at a very early
period of our acquaintance[2]—I have ever anticipated this event,
and you well know have often, after his taking leave of me, said,
'Alas! there is death in that hand!'[3]

But whether he has passed at once into a state of self-conscious
being, or whether his life is hidden in God—there is [in ?] a blessed
and divine sleep to grow and evolve into the angel—in God and
with God he is!

S. T. Coleridge.

[1] This letter was written immediately after Coleridge learned of the death
of his young friend and disciple, Adam Steinmetz. See next letter.

[2] Mrs. Coleridge wrote to Poole that Steinmetz 'left my poor S. T. C. a
Legacy of £300. I believe he had felt much for his friend at the loss of his
Pension. . . . I believe Mr Stutfield had introduced him at Highgate. C. sent to
the father of the youth to know if his son was of *sound mind* when he made the
Will; his answer was, "perfectly".' *Minnow among Tritons*, ed. Stephen Potter,
1934, p. 172.

[3] Coleridge had made the same comment about Keats's hand after Green
had introduced the two poets at a chance meeting in Apr. 1819. See *Table
Talk*, 1852, p. 195 and n. For Keats's extraordinary account of Coleridge's con-
versation on this occasion, see *The Letters of John Keats*, ed. H. E. Rollins,
2 vols., 1958, ii. 88–89.

1756. *To J. P. Kennard*[1]

Address: M. Kinnaird, Esqre | Grove Place | Hackney
MS. Fitz Park Museum, Keswick. Pub. Letters, *ii. 762*.
Postmark: Highgate, 13 August 1832.

Grove, Highgate.
13 August, 1832.

My dear Sir

Your Letter has announced to me a Loss too great, too aweful, for common Grief or any of it's ordinary forms and outlets. For more than an hour after, I remained in a state which I can only describe as a state of deepest mental silence, neither Prayer nor Thanksgiving, but a prostration of absolute Faith, as if the Omnipresent were present to me by a more especial Intuition, passing all Sense and all Understanding. Whether Death be but the cloudy Bridge to the Life beyond, and Adam Steinmetz has been wafted over it without suspension, or with an immediate resumption, of self-conscious Existence; or whether his Life be hidden in God, in the eternal Only-begotten, the Pleroma of all Beings and *'the Habitation'* both of the Retained and the Retrieved, therein in a blessed and most divine Slumber to grow and evolve into the perfected Spirit—for Sleep is the appointed Season of all Growth here below, and God's Ordinances in the Earthly may shadow out his ways in the Heavenly—in either case, our Friend is *in* God, and *with* God. Were it possible for me even to *think* otherwise, the very Grass in the fields would turn black before my eyes, and Nature appear as a Skeleton fantastically mossed over beneath the weeping vault of a charnel House![2] Deeply am I persuaded, that for every man born on earth there is an appointed task, some remedial process in the Soul known only to the Omniscient: and this thro' divine grace fulfilled, the sole Question is whether it be needful or expedient for the Church that he should still remain— for the Individual himself 'to depart and be with Christ' must needs be GREAT Gain.—And of my dear, my filial Friend we may with a strong and most consoling Assurance affirm, that he was eminently One

> Who being innocent did even for *that* cause
> Bestir him in good deeds!
>
> Wise Virgin He and wakeful kept his Lamp
> Aye trimm'd and full: and thus thro' grace he liv'd

---

[1] This letter was intended for John Peirse Kennard (1798–1877), who later named his second son Adam Steinmetz. See *Letters*, ii. 762 n., and Letters 1755, 1789, and 1818.

[2] Cf. *Table Talk*, 14 Aug. 1832.

In this bad World as in a place of Tombs
And touch'd not the Pollutions of the Dead[1]—

and yet in Christ only did he build a hope—yea, he blessed the
emptiness, that made him capable of his Lord's Fullness, gloried
in the Blindness that was receptive of his Master's Light, and in
the Nakedness that asked to be cloathed with the wedding-garment
of his Redeemer's Righteousness.—'Therefore say I unto you, my
young Friend, Rejoice! and again I say, Rejoice!'—

The effect of the event communicated in your Letter has been
that of awe and sadness on our whole Household. Mrs Gillman
mourns as for a Son, but with that grief which is felt for a departed
Saint. Even the Servants felt as if an especially loved and honored
Member of the Family had been suddenly taken away. When I
announced the sad tidings to Harriet, an almost *unalphabeted* but
very sensible Woman, the Tears swelled in her eyes, and she ex-
claimed—'Ah, Sir! how many a Thursday Night, after Mr Stein-
metz was gone & I had opened the Door for him, I have said to
them below—That dear young Man is too amiable to live: God will
soon have him back.' These were her very words—Nor were my
own anticipations of his Recall less distinct or less frequent. Not
once, or twice only, after he had shaken hands with me on leaving
us, I have turned round with the tear on my cheek, and whispered
to Mrs Gillman—Alas! there is *Death* in that dear Hand!—

My dear Sir! if our society can afford any comfort to *you*, as
that of so dear a friend of Adam Steinmetz cannot but be to *us*, I
beseech you in my own name, and am intreated by Mr and Mrs
Gillman to invite you to be his representative for us, and to take
his place in our Circle. And I must further request, that you do not
confine yourself to any particular evening of the week (for which
there is now no reason) but that you consult your own convenience
& opportunities of Leisure.—At *whatever* time he comes, the frater-
nal Friend of Adam Steinmetz will ever be dear & most welcome to

                                                              S. T. Coleridge

1757. *To Henry Nelson Coleridge*

Address H. N. Coleridge, Esqre | 1 New Court | Lincoln's Inn
MS. Victoria University Lib. Hitherto unpublished.
Postmark: Highgate, 29 August 1832.

                                                    Tuesday [28 August 1832]
My dear Henry
    You expressed a wish for a conservative MSS of my Cholera
cured beforehand—

---

[1] The last two lines are taken from *The Destiny of Nations*, 177–8.

I hope and trust that nothing less desirable than Business has prevented my seeing you—

I am setting about the corrections of the Poems in good earnest[1]—

God bless you, and yours, or rather our's—

S. T. Coleridge

If I had had money enough (the negation of which hypothesis might be proved as a Corollary to the thetical fact, that I had no money at all—ergo—Q.E.D.) I would have the following iatro-gnomonic prophylactic Anthro[po]philous Doggrel so printed as to secure a facile legibility to a current eye—(mem. if Eyes run with water, for which we have a prophet's authority, Jeremiah passim, then eyes may run, as the eating of a Dumplin proves that the man can eat: and tho' it is more commonly held, that men run with their legs, yet that the Leg may run is well exemplified in the justly celebrated Hic jacet of 'my Wife, Peg Who had no issue but one in her leg; and she was so clever & so cunning, That while one leg stood still, the other kept running.'—N.B. My passion for a piece of neat Logic has seduced me into the Parenthetical.) Da Capo, therefore—I would have, I say, a number of Copies struck off, pasted to parallelograms of Deal, and sent abroad as Placards Ambulant. With so many ligneous Doctors a few additional Doctor Lignums cannot fairly be complained [of]—and by way of attract-ing notice and giving authority to the thing, I would have each superscribed in red Capitals, THE BOARD OF HEALTH. I must confess, however, that the Sweet-wort of my Philanthropy was barmed and hopped by feelings of a less gentle order—the jealousy, to wit, and impatiency, with which I resented the presumption of that herd of Cholerophilists, who would set up this travelling Nabob from the swamps & jungles of Hindostan against the Lords Gray, Durham and the Reform Bill. Fools!—as if filling the Churchyard could be deemed an equal service in Hell with emptying and stripping the Church!—

---

[1] Coleridge refers to the preparation of the three-volume edition of his *Poetical Works*, 1834. On 24 July 1832 H. N. Coleridge had written to Miss Trevenen, a friend of the family: 'We are meditating another & cheaper edi-tion of his [Coleridge's] poems; the former editions were much too dear. Some new pieces will appear, & as I hope, a short autobiography, in which the dates shall be correct at least.' [MS. Mr. A. H. B. Coleridge.] On 16 Aug. 1832 Mrs. Coleridge wrote to Poole: 'Henry is preparing his Uncle's poems for the press, in a cheaper edition and is collecting everything he can to add to the Vols—could you have the goodness to spare us what you have by you?' In Oct. 1832 she thanked Poole for his 'goodness in transcribing the Poems' and added: 'S. T. C. had no previous copy—the republishing the Poems is his own concern only he is so dilatory he will never do it without help.' See *Minnow among Tritons*, ed. Stephen Potter, 1934, pp. 168 and 174.

CHOLERA CURED BEFORE HAND: Premonitory promulgated
gratis for the use of the useful Classes, specially those resident in
St Giles's, Saffron Hill, Bethnal Green, &c—and likewise, inasmuch
as the good man is merciful even to the Beasts, for the benefits of
the Bulls and Bears of the Stock Exchange.[1]—

> Pains ventral, subventral,
> In stomach or entrail
> Think no longer mere prefaces
> For Damns, Grins and Wry Faces;
> But off to the Doctor, fast as ye can crawl:
> Yet far better 'twould be not to have them at all.

> Now to 'scape inward aches
> Eat no plums nor plum-cakes;
> Cry, Avaunt, New Potato!
> And don't drink, like old Cato.
> Ah beware of Dis* Pipsy,
> And therefòre don't get tipsy!
> For tho' Gin and Whisky
> May make you feel frisky,
> They're but Crimps to DIS PIPSY:
> And nose to tail with this Gypsy
> Comes, black as a Porpus,
> The DIABOLUS ipse
> Call'd, Cholery Morpus:
> Who with Horns, Hoofs and Tail croaks for Carrion to feed him,
> Tho' being a Devil, nobody never has see'd him.

> Ah! then, my dear Honeys!
> There's no Cure for you
> For Loves, nor for Moneys—
> You'll find it too true!
> Och! the hallabaloo!
> Och! och! how ye'll wail!
> When the offal-fed Vagrant
> Shall turn you as blue
> As the gas-light unfragrant

[1] These lines were first published in *Poetical Works*, 1834, ii. 142. See also
Poems, ii. 985.

* Sometimes erroneously written Dyspepsia; but there can be little doubt,
that Dis is the Diminutive of Dyonesia, or some such Christian Name. The
Sir-name, Pipsy, is probably but a fondling name for an infant Daughter of the
Pip Family. [Note by S. T. C.]

From a portrait of Samuel Taylor Coleridge painted by Moses Haughton in 1832 and now in the possession of Christ's Hospital

That gushes in jets from beneath his own Tail:
    Till, swift as the Mail,
    He at last brings the Cramps on,
    That will twist you, like Sampson.

    So without further Blethring,
    Dear Mudlarks! my Brethren!
    Of all scents and degrees
    (Yourselves with your Shes)
    Forswear all Cabal, Lads!
    Wakes, Unions and Rows;
    Hot Drams and cold Sallads;
And don't pig in Styes that would suffocate Sows!
Quit Cobbet's, O'Connel's and Belzebub's banners,
And white-wash at once your Guts, Rooms, and Manners.

    Philodemus Coprophilus,
    Physician prophylactic to their
    Majesties, the He and She People.

    Vivat Rex Popellus!
    Vivat Regina Plebs!

1758. *To Moses Haughton*[1]

Address: M. Haughton, Esqre | *51*. Great Marlborough Street
MS. Public Library of New South Wales, Sydney, Australia. Hitherto unpublished.
Postmark: 13 ⟨September⟩ 1832.

                Grove, Highgate
                Wednesday Night.
                12 Septr 1832.

Dear Sir

    I propose, not hearing from you to the contrary, to leave High-
gate on Saturday Morning by the 11 o'clock Stage to Tottenham
Court Road, so as by aid of a Hackney Coach to be with you at 12—
and then to return by the Stage from Holborn, which starts at
4 o'clock—allowing 20 minutes for a Hackney Coach or Cab from
Marlborough St to Middle Row, Holborn, I shall have three hours
& 40 minutes at your Service—which will be as long, perhaps, as I
can in the present state of my health continue to sit.[2] And on the

---

   [1] Moses Haughton, the younger (1772?–1848?), to whom this letter is
addressed, was a miniature painter and engraver.
   [2] Haughton's portrait of Coleridge is at Christ's Hospital. It was presented
in 1864 by Mary Green, the daughter of Jonathan Green. It was Green who

Tuesday following I hope to be with you from 2 till 4. For Mr & Mrs Gillman will not hear of my not returning to dinner, or risking the chill dusk of the now commencing Autumn. Give my blessing & a kiss to little Moses Cartwright Haughton, &

believe me, dear Sir, | with every kind wish, | Your's truly,

S. T. Coleridge

1759. *To J. H. B. Williams*

MS. Cornell University Lib. Pub. Some Letters of the Wordsworth Family, ed. L. N. Broughton, 1942, p. 107.

Grove Highgate.

Octr. 12, 1832

My dear Williams

This Work[1] has risen in public estimation, since the time that it fell apparently dead-born from the Press, and for a series of years continued in a state of suspended Animation—the greater part of this Edition having been sold off by the Desponding Publishers for *waste paper*. Such has not been the case, my dear Friend! with *your* character in *my* respect and regard. The best compliment, I can pay you—and it is a high compliment—is, that what you *were* when you first received these Tragedies, you *continue* to be. And so likewise do the Regard and Respect of your old Friend

S. T. Coleridge.

1760. *To James Gillman*

Address: James Gillman, Esqre. | Hotel Royal | Calais
[Readdressed in another hand] Highgate—Middlesex.
MS. Mr. Robert H. Taylor. Hitherto unpublished.
Postmark: 13 October 1832.

13 October, 1832.

My dear Gillman

Mrs Gillman will cheerfully pay the ultra-marine postage of this Letter, on the mere chance of it's influencing you to stay away another week or so—

And free from Sick-rooms, free from midnight Calls
To sojourn yet awhile among the Gauls.

COLERIDGE.

What an affectionate Wife! what a complimentary Request! We

kept the establishment in Marlborough Street where Coleridge was taking his bi-weekly 'Air-bath'. See Letters 1752 and 1754.

[1] According to Broughton (op. cit., 107 n.) the sheet containing this letter bears evidence that it was once a flyleaf in the volume containing *Piccolomini* and *Wallenstein*, 1800'.

are all quite happy without you—and every thing (with exception of my Right Thigh which is at this very moment playing the Devil with me, and the Devil playing his Grandam in it) is going on right cannily: 'and Mr Williams gives great satisfaction'—to me especially, for whom he brings up alternately Tripe and Sausages, medicines of my own prescription but which he leaves Cookie to compound.—

But verily and in sober earnest, my dear Friend! I am anxiously desirous that you should consent to convalesce in quiet, and to take in an Elijah Meal[1] of Strength and Spirits that may last you thro' the Winter.[2] And this is Mrs Gillman's intreaty, & earnest wish— which has strengthened, since she received a budget of good News from Susan Steele. Our Love to James: and kind remembrances to Mr and Miss Robarts.—I believe, I have nothing more to say even if this sciatic paroxysm would allow me to say it—

> For with grunts I indite,
> And grin while I write
>   COLERIDGE.

By the bye, in proof of commencing Desquamation I wrote the following Lines, and regret that I cannot at present peel off a strip large enough to make a real Fac Simile for you.—

> Why, sure, such a wonder was never yet seen!
> An Autograph on an Auto-pergamene!
> A Poet's own Name, and own Hand-writing both,
> And the Ink and the Parchment all of his own growth—
> The Ink his own Blood and the Parchment his Skin—
> This from 's Leg, and the other from 's razor-snipt chin—
>   S. T. Coleridge—

God bless you, my dear Gillman! Get well, keep well, and integrate your Sternum in mirth and quiet.—   S. T. C.

1761. *To James Gillman, Jr.*

Address: The Reverend | James Gillman | Highgate
MS. Boston Public Lib. Pub. with omis. More Books: a Bulletin, *1939, p. 412.*

Friday, 9 November 1832.

My dear James

I scarcely think that a Father can feel a livelier interest for a Son's Well-being and Well-doing (= $\epsilon \dot{v}\pi\rho\alpha\xi\acute{\iota}\alpha$) than I feel in

---

[1] Cf. 1 Kings xvii. 6.

[2] Writing to Poole in Oct. 1832, Mrs. Coleridge reports that Gillman 'is now at Paris for his Health, after a surgical operation, a tumour being cut from the neck'. *Minnow among Tritons*, ed. Stephen Potter, 1934, p. 173.

your's: and I do you but justice when I add, for your own sake, and
from my faith in the foundation, the abiding Substratum of your
character, tho' this is, doubtless, greatly enhanced by the accessory
circumstance, that your Father is the Friend of a most important
portion of my life, and your Mother a most dear and holy Name to
me—a Blessing which plays, like an auspicious Flame, on my
nightly Sacrifice of praise and thanksgiving.

My dear James! I am little *dis*contented with you—and not at
all *mal*content. All I want and wish, but this I do want, I do most
earnestly wish, is to see you rise one round higher on the Ladder of
Thought and Feeling. Believe me, that He who takes his footing on
the notion of the *Gentlemanlike*, will hardly attain, much less realize,
the *idea* of a Gentleman: while the Christian—supposing the same
social *Manège*, the same advantages of outward training—the
Christian, respectful or forbearing to other men thro' the conscious-
ness of his own actual defects and deficiencies, yet standing in awe
of Himself from the knowlege of what he is *called* to be, is capable
of becoming and aspires to become, who not overlooking the hues
and qualities that difference man from man still looks thro' them;
and in every exercise of prayer is compelled to lose them in the
contemplation of the Reason, one and the same in all men, and the
responsible Will and mysterious permanent Identity common to all
men, and constituting while they contra-distinguish our Humanity
—the Christian, for whom in this very habit of feeling respect for
every man, even because he is a Man, there arises that *manner* of
shewing respect to others which implies & with the ease and un-
consciousness of all *continual* feelings claims & anticipates respect
for himself—the Christian *comprehends, includes* the *Gentleman*. Or
shall I not rather say, he is the *Apotheosis* of a Gentleman? I was
once asked for a definition of Good Prose and replied—'Proper words
in their proper places.' And what then is good Verse, rejoined the
Querist: and my answer was—'The *most* proper words in the *most*
proper places.'[1] So to the ? what should a well-born Layman be?
I would say—'A Gentleman'—and what then a Clergyman? 'A
Gentleman in his Court-dress, as always in attendance on the King
from whom all Gentry is derived.' For the Clergyman is a Christian,
whose specific *business*, whose recognized *profession* it is, at all times
to *remember* that he is a Christian, and were it but by his Dress, and
by a somewhat more heedful composure in his habitual demeanour,
to remind *others* that he is so.—

But both as Clergyman & Christian—or rather, as a Christian,
and therefore a fortiori as a Clergyman, you have a threefold
Ground of Respect, each ground acquiring and indeed producing

[1] Cf. *Table Talk*, 3 July 1833.

it's own appropriate *manner*. First: *negative*—i.e. the respect you owe to a man, as a man. Composure, mildness, and the absence of all passion, *overliness* and contempt or contumely you would owe to your *self* even tho' they were not owing to the individual in your presence. But God, who permits him to retain *his* Image, makes him your Creditor for this negative Respect, at least. Secondly: *positive*—namely, the respect, you feel for intrinsic worth, or in a less degree for the eminent gifts and talents with which the Person has been endowed. Thirdly, and as the intermediate of the first and second—Respect for the Relations, both social & natural, as so many ordinances of the Divine Providence. I respect a Senior, a Superior in rank or station, a Matron, with the same feeling and on the same principle as I take off my Hat when I enter the Aisle of a Church. The Apis might be a clumsy Ox; but I would shew respect to him in reverence of the higher power of which he was the appointed Symbol: and in my obeisance to William the fourth I should feel myself discharging the debt of reverence, which as an Englishman I owe to the King that can do no wrong, that never dies.

Further, my dear James! as a Christian and a Moralist you will know and will hold it a duty of Self-reverence to avail yourself of the knowlege, that to be wronged confers on you in the same moment a superiority over the person who has wronged you, which you forfeit in proportion as you retaliate. In the very act of *retaliating* you change your position and lose your moral Vantage-ground. Worst of all, should the Impulse make you forget the permanent, the inalienable, indefeasible Relation, in which the Person has stood to you, and in which you stand to that Person. The more he forgets himself, the more do you remember *him*. I do not mean, I do not wish, that you should not shew that you felt the wrong, and with an emotion proportioned to your love and respect for the Author of it but let it be the impulse of the next moment to sacrifice the feeling on the altar of Memory and Gratitude: and let the scum, which has boiled up on the surface, remind you of the precious metal that glows beneath—the affections, the solicitudes, the love-travail of half a Life. I would have you connect a tender, a pleasurable feeling even with such a one's Foibles, whenever they were instrumental to or commingled with his well-purchased enjoyments, the alleviations of Cares and toils undertaken in no small part for your sake, and of which you have reapt and are reaping, the fruits. Life itself, this mortal Life, is but a trifle in a wise man's contemplation, and if you are a wise man, you will not let the trifles of Life upset you. Lastly, one of the securities for respecting and being respected is as seldom as possible to make your muscles the substitu[te] for your Tongue. What can be conveyed by *words*, express as seldom and as little as you can, in any other way.

God bless you &

S. T. Coleridge

1762. *To Thomas H. Dunn*

Facsimile Advertiser, *Adelaide, South Australia, 28 July 1934.*

Thursday, Dec. 6.

1832

Mr Coleridge's kind respects to Mr Dunn: and if Mr Dunn should have on sale the Opii Liquor Sedatives of Battley, which (Mr C. believes) is Half a Crown an Ounce; Mr Coleridge would be much obliged to Mr Dunn to spare him the accompanying Phial of it—but if he has it not, then to fill the Phial with Laudanum—.

Mr. C. will not suffer the New Year to arrive without having settled his arrears with Mr. Dunn, of which he has kept account, perhaps less to his creditor's disadvantage than Mr. D. himself has lately done.[1]

1763. *To Henry Nelson Coleridge*

Address: Henry Nelson Coleridge, Esqre | 1. New Court | Lincoln's Inn
MS. Victoria University Lib. Hitherto unpublished.
Postmark: 5 January 1833.

[5 January 1833]

My dear Henry

It struck me, that you answered rather doubtfully, as if, I mean, your *Feeling* could not return a full Accord—when I spoke to you of Mrs Hathaway's Legacy. If, as I indeed told you, it had been a 100£, or any Sum above it, I should have had no second thought, or rather, the Thought would have existed only in the act or determination of transferring it to the Mother of my Children. But whatever the Sum had been, tho' but a 5 or 10£, yet if she wished or wanted it for Hartley,[2] there could not have been a moment's

---

[1] This concluding paragraph, which does not appear in the facsimile, is taken from the text printed in the Adelaide *Advertiser*.

[2] Although he continued to be a source of anxiety to both his parents, Hartley Coleridge published in 1833 a volume of *Poems*, with a 'Dedicatory Sonnet' to his father; and a prose work, *Biographia Borealis; or, Lives of Distinguished Northerns*. Coleridge annotated the latter work. The annotations are included in Derwent Coleridge's republication of the work in 3 vols. under the title, *Lives of Northern Worthies*, 1852.

Much of Hartley's *l*iterary work appeared in magazines and annuals. For

hesitation. I will not add, if she wanted it for herself—for that would be self-slander, even to imagine, that I could have made it a question at all.

But *supposing*, that nothing of this is the case—knowing, that in relation to so small a Sum, Sarah and I at this present moment stand much on the same footing, as to occasional remunerations to Servants, and the et cetera of small duties and small wishes, I had a pleasure in treating the matter as a rule & confession of *Parity*, and therefore thought of adding 19 to 10 = 29, and then dividing into $14\frac{1}{2} + 14\frac{1}{2}$. But if you have the least ground for suspecting, that Mrs C. has the least wish for aught attainable by the whole, & not attainable by the Half—if in short she have any thing in her thought of more importance than mine—namely, than the discharging of the minor gratitudes, & acknowlegements—(and I should consider, in *her*, Dress & handsome *Appearance* as *much* more; as duties to you and becoming [to] hers[elf]) then, *for* Heaven's sake, let it never [be] remembered that I had ever made [it] a question; or had ever any other feeling, than the wish, that it had been 2900£ instead of 29£—for her sake; and that *she* might enjoy what I could not—what, alas! would be to *me* but as a Burst of Sunshine into the Room of a bed-stricken Cripple.—God bless you! Fervently, and swelling up thro' my prayers for myself, do I pray that the Cloud may have, if not passed over, yet have risen higher, and with more eyelets of blue sky, for my dear innocent Sara—by the time, we next meet.

S. T. Coleridge

P.S. Perhaps, you will find occasion to learn what Mr Lonsdale's impressions were & are respecting the Revd. James Gillman—You know, that both his Father & I are adverse to it, even if [it] were in his power.

collections of his poems see *Poems by Hartley Coleridge*, ed. Derwent Coleridge, 2 vols., 1851, and *New Poems of Hartley Coleridge*, ed. E. L. Griggs, 1942; for a collection of his miscellaneous prose writings see *Essays and Marginalia. By Hartley Coleridge*, ed. Derwent Coleridge, 2 vols., 1851. Hartley's 'Shakspeare a Tory and a Gentleman' and 'On the Character of Hamlet' reveal genuine critical insight; and 'Brief Observations upon Brevity', 'Books and Bantlings', and 'Ignoramus on the Fine Arts' show a mastery of the familiar essay in the tradition of Charles Lamb.

1764. To John Sterling[1]

Address: John Stirling Esqre | Knightsbridge
MS. Indiana University Lib. Pub. Memories of Old Friends, being Extracts
from the Journals and Letters of Caroline Fox, *ed. H. N. Pym, 2 vols., 1882
(2nd edn.), i. 161.*
Postmark: Highgate, 18 March 1833.

Monday afternoon [18 March 1833]

My dear Stirling

With grief I tell you, that I have been & now am, worse, far
worse than when you left me—God have mercy on me, & not with-
draw the influence of his Spirit from me! I can now only thank you
for your very kind attentions to your most sincere,

afflicted Friend
S. T. Coleridge

P.S. Mr Green is persuaded that it is Gout which I have not
strength enough to throw from the nerves of the Trunk to the
extremities.—

[1] John Sterling (1806–44), one of Coleridge's disciples. He first met Coleridge
in 1827. His report of Coleridge's conversation on that occasion reveals an
admiration amounting almost to reverence. The last sentence pays special
tribute to Coleridge: 'When he dies, another, and one of the greatest of their
race, will rejoin the few Immortals, the ill understood and ill requited, who have
walked this earth.' In Oct. 1834 Sterling wrote to Gillman that he had travelled
the road to Highgate 'with keen and buoyant expectation, and returned with
high and animating remembrances oftener than any other in England'. This
'tone of rapture and panegyric' did not last, however, and in a letter written in
July 1844, only two months before his own death, Sterling charged Coleridge
with plagiarism and indolence. See *Essays and Tales, by John Sterling*, ed. with
a memoir of his life, J. C. Hare, 2 vols., 1848, i, p. xxv; *Letters*, ii. 772 n.; and
Anne K. Tuell, *John Sterling*, 1941, pp. 260–3. See also Letter 1795 n.

That the change in Sterling's estimate of Coleridge was in great measure due
to the influence of Carlyle seems certain. When Sterling met Carlyle in Feb.
1835, he was still an avowed Coleridgean. Carlyle, however, regarded Coleridge
as 'a man of great and useless genius'—an opinion which he had formed during
a brief personal association in 1824–5 and one which time had only served to
strengthen. It was inevitable that his biased judgement should have swayed
a man of Sterling's light, volatile, and unstable temperament.

When in 1851 he came to write his *Life of John Sterling*, a work to which
Sterling owes his reputation, Carlyle gave full expression to his antipathy to
Coleridge. He devoted an entire chapter to him and pointed to the harmful
influence of Coleridge's teaching on the 'ingenuous young English head, of those
days'. Did not Coleridge, he exclaimed, 'procreate strange Centaurs, spectral
Puseyisms, monstrous illusory Hybrids, and ecclesiastical Chimeras,—which
now roam the earth in a very lamentable manner'? Carlyle declared that
Sterling had for a time been 'dazzled and bewildered' by Coleridge's 'transient
fantasies and theosophic moonshine', and to his account of Sterling's brief
experience as a curate in 1834–5, he added the following comment: 'This
clerical aberration,—for such it undoubtedly was in Sterling,—we have ascribed

1765. *To J. H. Green*

Address: J. H. Green, Esqre | &c &c | Lincoln's Inn Fields
MS. Pierpont Morgan Lib. Pub. Letters, *ii. 767.*
Postmark: Highgate, 8 April 1833.

Sunday Night. [7 April 1833]

It is seldom, my dearest Friend! that I find myself differing from you in judgements of any sort. It is more than seldom, that I am left in doubt and query on any judgement of your's of a *practical* nature—for on the good ground of some 16 or more years' experience I feel a take-for-granted faith in the dips and pointings of the needle, in every decision of your *total* mind.—But in the instance, you spoke of this afternoon, viz. your persistent rebuttal of the Temperance-Society Man's Request, tho' I do not feel *sure* that you are not in the Right, yet I do feel as if I should have been more delighted, and more satisfied, if you had intimated your compliance with it. I feel, that in this case I should have had *no* doubt; but that my mind would have leapt forwards with content, like a key to a loadstone.

Assuredly, you might—at least, you would have a very promising chance of effecting considerable *Good*—and you might have commenced your address with your own remark of the superfluity of any Light of Information afforded to an habitual Dram Drinker respecting the unutterable evil and misery of his thraldom. As wisely give a physiological Lecture to convince a man of the pain of Burns, while he is lying with his head on the bars of the Firegrate, instead of snatching him off. But in stating this you might most effectingly & preventively for others describe the misery of that condition in which the impulse waxes as the motive wanes. Mem. There is a striking passage in my FRIEND on this subject[1]—

to Coleridge; and do clearly think that had there been no Coleridge, neither had this been,—nor had English Puseyism or some other strange enough universal portents been.' Carlyle insisted that it was years before Sterling 'got the inky tints of that Coleridgean adventure completely bleached from his mind', but that the process had already begun in 1836, 'in the solitude of Floirac', near Bordeaux. See R. W. Armour and R. F. Howes, *Coleridge the Talker*, 1940, pp. 109–12 and 446; Thomas Carlyle, *The Life of John Sterling*, New York, 1900, pp. 52–62, 104–5, 134, and 140; and C. R. Sanders, *Coleridge and the Broad Church Movement*, 1942, pp. 147–76.

[1] The passage to which Coleridge refers reads:

It is an undoubted fact of human nature, that the sense of impossibility quenches all will. Sense of utter inaptitude does the same. The man shuns the beautiful flame, which is eagerly grasped at by the infant. The sense of a disproportion of certain after-harm to present gratification—produces effects almost equally uniform: though almost perishing with thirst, we should dash to the earth a goblet of wine in which we had seen a poison infused, though the poison were without taste or odour, or even added to the pleasures of both. Are not all our vices equally inapt to the universal end of

& a no less striking one in a School boy theme of mine, now in Gill-
man's Possession, & in my own hand, written when I was fourteen,
with the simile of the treacherous Current & the Maelstrom[1]—But
this might give occasion for the suggestion of one new charitable
Institution, under Authority of a Legislative Act—namely, a
Maison de Santé (what do the French call it?) for Lunacy & Ideocy
of the *Will*—in which with the full consent of, or at the direct
instance of the Patient himself, and with the concurrence of his
Friends, such a person under the certificate of a Physician might be
placed under medical & moral coercion. I am convinced, that
London would furnish a hundred Volunteers in as many days from
the Gin-shops—who would swallow their glass of poison in order to
get courage to present themselves to the Hospital in question—
And a similar Institution might exist for a higher class of Will-
Maniacs or Impotents.—Had such a House of Health been in
existence, I know who would have entered himself as a Patient
some five & 20 years ago.—

  2 Class—To the persons still capable of self-cure—and lastly, to

human actions, the satisfaction of the agent? Are not their pleasures equally
disproportionate to the after harm? . . . The sot would reject the poisoned
cup, yet the trembling hand with which he raises his daily or hourly draught to
his lips, has not left him ignorant that this too is altogether a poison. I know,
it will be objected, that the consequences foreseen are less immediate; that
they are diffused over a larger space of time; and that the slave of vice hopes
where no hope is. This, however, only removes the question one step further:
for why should the distance or diffusion of known consequence produce so
great a difference? Why are men the dupe of the present moment? Evidently
because the conceptions are indistinct in the one case, and vivid in the other;
because all confused conceptions render us restless; and because restlessness
can drive us to vices that promise no enjoyment, no not even the cessation
of that restlessness. This is indeed the dread punishment attached by nature
to habitual vice, that its impulses wax as its motives wane. No object, not
even the light of a solitary taper in the far distance, tempts the benighted
mind from before; but its own restlessness dogs it from behind, as with the
iron goad of Destiny. (*The Friend*, 1818, i. 175–7.)

[1] This theme was first published in the *Illustrated London News*, 1 Apr.
1893, where it is dated 19 Jan. 1791. Coleridge refers to the following passage:
'Alas! at the moment we contract a habit we forego our free agency. The re-
mainder of our life will be spent in making resolutions in the hour of dejection
and breaking them in the hour of passion. As if we were in some great sea-
vortex, every moment we perceive our ruin more clearly, every moment we are
impelled towards it with greater force.'

Two autograph copies of this theme have survived. The manuscript to which
Coleridge refers in the present letter eventually came into the possession of
E. H. Coleridge. (See *Letters*, ii. 768 n.) Another copy appears in *Liber Aureus*,
a three-volume manuscript album into which James Boyer of Christ's Hospital
caused certain students to copy their best compositions in prose and verse.
For a description of the *Liber Aureus*, which is now in the British Museum,
see T. J. Wise, *Two Lake Poets . . .*, 1927, pp. 51–53.

the young who have only begun—& not yet begun—and the urgency
of connecting the Temperance Society with the *Christian* Churches,
of all denominations—the *classes* known to each other—& deriving
strength from *religion*. This is a beautiful part or might have been
made so of the Wesleian Church—

These are but raw Hints. But unless the Mercy of God should
remove me from my sufferings earlier than I dare hope or pray for,
we will talk the subject over, again: as well as of the reasons *why*
Spirits in any form, as such, are so much more dangerous morally &
in relation to the forming [of a] Habit than Beer or Wine—Item—
If a Government were truly paternal, a healthsome and sound Beer
would be made universal—aye, and for the lower Half of the
middle classes Wine might be imported, good and generous, from
6d to 8d per quart—

God bless you & your | ever affectionate
S. T. Coleridge.

1766. *To John Sterling*

Address: John Stirling, Esqre | Knightsbridge
MS. Indiana University Lib. Hitherto unpublished.
Postmark: Highgate, 12 April 1833.

Thursday [11 April 1833]

My dear Sir

I am more than grieved by the contents of your Note, and
earnestly adjure you—now especially when

> The March Wolf romping with the April Kid
> Mangles his quiv'ring play-mate—

to submit to a week or fortnight's strict confinement to the House,
or rather to any rooms the temperature of which can be preserved
uniform—yet not such as to render you afterwards susceptible of
injury from the average weather of May & June—and surely you
should not delay an hour to consult some medical friend, not likely
to confound excitement of Irritation with Inflammation, and who—
in case, anti-phlogistic measures should be necessary, knows enough
of your past & present state to judge what you require and what
you can bear. For the ensuing six weeks you cannot be over careful
—The Breeze, the Shade, the Sunshine, the Hot, the Cold, are all
treacherous.

The Author of the Prose Faust[1] has been so good as to send me
a Copy—I will therefore return your's—but let me know, at what

---

[1] Abraham Hayward (1801–84), essayist, published his prose translation of
Goethe's *Faust* in 1833.

place your Knightsbridge Carrier sets up in Town—that I may direct our Highgate Carrier—I am myself a little better, my breathing easier; but clearly under the influence of the mercury, affecting my gums & salivary glands.—A Grain and a Half of Calomel divided into three doses, taken at the interval of 24 hours each—and yet this has sufficed to effect a salivation—in what a state my veno-glandular system must be!

Pray, do not run the slightest risk.—I should be vexed to *see* you, tho' glad to hear from you—

God bless you | & | Your obliged Friend
S. T. Coleridge

1767. *To J. H. Green*

Address: J. H. Green, Esqre | &c &c | Lincoln's Inn Fields
MS. Pierpont Morgan Lib. Hitherto unpublished.
Postmark: Highgate, 15 April 1833.

Sunday Night: 14 April 1833
Grove, Highgate.

My dear Friend

From Mr Porter I learn, that this Influenza or Weather-blast is so truly epidemic, that there is scarcely a House in our Vicinity in which some—& many Houses in which all—are affected—Similar accounts we hear thro' Mr Williams, himself a Sufferer, of London. Hence the accident of missing a visit from you to day, which I should have thought nothing of under ordinary circumstances, has suggested the fear that yourself or Mrs Green may have been on the sick list. Be so good as to let me have a single line from you by return of Post—just to say, how you are. Our own has been a House of Sickness—but all, I trust, all convalescent. Mr & Mrs Gillman were both violently attacked—Mr G. quite delirious for about 12 Hours.

I am myself in the average of my endurable state. I awake about 5 o'clock, & with occasional interpositions of 5 or 10 minutes' forgetfulness remain so & tolerably quiet till 8 or ½ 8 when I take my Opiate Draught & my Gruel. Then comes on the Expectoration which after the first unlading of the glands continues more or less thro' the day.—I get up about 2 or 3—take my bit of cold fowl, with difficulty chewed & swallowed, about 5—then try to eke out, sip by sip, my pint of Wine, of which Gillman, . . . [seems to *me* unreasonably jealous]¹ for I take the opiate draught, containing two *very* small tea spoonfuls of Laudanum only once in the 24 Hours—not a third of what I used to take twice a day.—

¹ 2¾ lines heavily inked out in MS.; only the words in brackets are decipherable.

After dinner I am chilly, & not able to read—the Cup of Tea a
little enlivens me, probably by quickening the digestion of the
food, scanty as the meal is—& at about 10, my Bed is made, & in
about half an hour commences the *Delirium* in both my Legs &
Feet, of Heat, intense Itching, & the Sensation of a Blow-up—
This remits into an itchiness of my Arms, Back &c—under which I
fall asleep—& with one or two inter-wakes sleep till day-light—
And thus you have the History of my 24 Hours. I have not gone
backward—I make no progress.—May God grant me removal, or
the power of using the time assigned to me—

God bless you | &
S. T. Coleridge

1768. *To J. H. Green*

Address: J. H. Green Esqre | &c &c | 46. Lincoln's Inn Fields
MS. Pierpont Morgan Lib. Hitherto unpublished.
Postmark: Highgate, 25 April 1833.

Thursday 25 April 1833.

My dear Friend

Tho' your letter very imperfectly relieved the apprehensions, it
confirmed, it was in some measure a Comfort to me, were it only
that it gave a definite object to my Prayers, and blended some
warmth and light of Love with the mist and fog of self-concerning
fear and heaviness, out of which even my Thanksgiving could not
ascend. For this is one of the worst afflictions of long continued
Sickness, that all our reproachful Recollections and gloomy
Fancies eddy round and round the Thought, and under the name
and form of SELF (because we dare not derive them from God)
acquire a phantom unity, a pseudo-hypostasis.

Is the East Wind of itself sufficient to account for this super-
lative Epidemic, by it's meagre & rasp-like texture, it's thirstiness
of Heat and Moisture, it's antagonism with the hot Sunshine, it's
rapid motion, and it's persistency? Or may we suppose, that in it's
long Journey over the vast Steppes, the enormous Depressions,
Moon-holes, and Dead Seas of Scytho-tartar Asia it has been
freighted with contraband waves of more specific quality? Ex. gr.
with nitrous Salts in infinitesimal subdivision? I remember at
Malta a drying wind that made the wooden Window-shutters, the
Tables, the very Tea-caddies split and go off as Pistols. But it
produced no effects on the Health. On the other hand, the occa-
sional wind from the Barbary Coast, loaded with Sand so subtle
that the Maltese believe that it passes thro' Glass, produced com-
plaints on the head, eyes, chest and mucous membrane that bore

no distant analogy to the symptoms of the present Fever.—I expect
Mr Stirling here this afternoon, who is going with his Wife & child
to Bonn, on the Rhine. If he come, I shall request him to call at
your House, to learn from the Servant how you are, & to let me
know by return of Post. Need I say, in what anxiety I must remain
till I hear of your assured Convalescence? Would not 3 or 4 of your
Namesake's[1] Caloric Baths be a probable Clearer off, & Preventive
of Relapse?

At Enfield there is a Lectureship vacant, for which James
Gillman is a Candidate[2]—& Mr Gillman, uninformed of your
Illness, has requested me thro' Mrs G. (it is 5 months since I have
seen *him*) to ask you if you did not know the Holts of Enfield, or a
Mr Holt, a medical Man there—and if you did, whether you could
interest him in favor of James, who by favor of the Vicar is to read
& preach there, as probationary. You might call him a theological
Protégé of mine— But do not trouble yourself about this, till you
are (which God grant speedily!) out and stirring.

I am myself as usual—only that my Teeth are worse & worse, &
distemper my left eye.—My Love & Sympathy to Mrs Green.—
You seal your two last Notes with *black* wax—God bless you!

S. T. Coleridge

1769. *To John Sterling*

Address: John Stirling, Esqre. | Knightsbridge
MS. Indiana University Lib. Hitherto unpublished.
Postmark: Highgate, 8 May 1833.

Grove, Highgate
Tuesday Night
7 May 1833

My dear young Friend

—for so permit yourself to be called by an old man, more than
half as old again as his years—

Under ordinary circumstances I should not have permitted my-
self to be made uneasy by the simple fact of not having seen you or
heard from you, for a week or so. But with this Influenza in my
thoughts—within the Tail of which we are still immersed, tho' the
Nucleus of the Malign Star has passed onward—and with what I
have learnt from you of your constitutional predispositions to
pulmonary excitement—I should be ashamed of myself, if I were

[1] Jonathan Green. See note to Letter 1754.

[2] James Gillman, Jr., failed to obtain the lectureship at Enfield. For a short
time he acted as undermaster in the Highgate Grammar School. See A. W.
Gillman, *The Gillmans of Highgate*, 1895, p. 29.

not uneasy. I am myself a hair's breadth better, & on Sunday went in Mr Gillman's Carriage to Enfield to hear James Gillman read & preach—& very proud I was of my young Protégé—and yesterday in a Fly I took a two hours' Airing with Mrs Gillman—who with Henry Gillman & my favorite Hand-maid, Harriet, left our house semi-desolate this Morning on a visit to her Sister near Deal. Bless her! she wanted a sea-change, & I pray to God, that it may exert it's usual restorative influence on her.

If you can, I know you will inform or let me [be] informed, how you are—& that you will receive this Scrawl as a mark that you are not absent from the thoughts & affection

of your sincere Friend
S. T. Coleridge

1770. *To Thomas Pringle*[1]

MS. British Museum. Pub. with omis. 'Samuel Taylor Coleridge and Thomas Pringle', *by E. L. Griggs*, Quarterly Bulletin of the South African Library, *1951, p. 7.*

[June 1833 ?][2]

My dear Sir

You have done much honor to an incondite suggestion, which I attempted to convey in words during a relaxation of bodily pain

---

[1] This fragment, of which only a rough draft has come to light, was probably addressed to Thomas Pringle, who became secretary of the Anti-Slavery Society in 1827.

[2] The present letter must have been written in June, during the parliamentary discussion of the 'Act for the Abolition of Slavery throughout the *British* Colonies, for promoting the Industry of the manumitted Slaves, and for compensating the Persons hitherto entitled to the Services of such Slaves'. The bill was passed by the House of Commons on 7 Aug. 1833, by the House of Lords on the 20th, and received the royal assent on 28 Aug. To take effect on 1 Aug. 1834, the parliamentary act provided 20 millions sterling as compensation to the planters. Provision was also made for apprenticeships as a transitional preparation for liberty. The Negroes were bound to work for their masters three-fourths of the day during this period, and were subject to punishment if they failed to give the due amount of labour. In return the masters were to provide them with food and clothing. Children under six years of age were to be at once free, and provision was to be made for their religious and moral instruction. A resolution later passed by the House of Commons against the continuance of the transitional system led the colonial legislatures to reduce the length of the indentured apprenticeships. Thus on 1 Aug. 1838, rather than 1840, the Negroes gained their freedom. See T. C. Hansard, *Parliamentary Debates*, 1833, xx, p. xxviii; *Encyclopaedia Britannica*, 1910–11, xxv. 225; and E. L. Griggs, *Thomas Clarkson*, 1936, pp. 165–6.

For Coleridge's comments on slavery see *Table Talk*, 8 and 17 June 1833; *Notes, Theological, Political, and Miscellaneous. By Samuel Taylor Coleridge*, ed. Derwent Coleridge, 1853, pp. 221–3 and 309; and Letter 1782.

and while my attention was render[ed] discontinuous by it's teizing remnants. And now I write from my bed, the distemper having assumed the form [of] a biliary overflow—and deprest tho' calmed by the effects of Calomel and a Black Dose. But I write from my anxious wish, not to convince *you* who already both think and feel all, I can say, but to help you with that penny-weight of authority that an ardent & almost life-long Denouncer of Slavery may have in impressing on the influential Combatants for Emancipation the great Truth, that for men in the state of the W. India Negros motives grounded on even the most obvious calculations of future Instance, tho' that Future should be but for a few years (qy. *months* ?), will be powerless against the dictates of his [their] present animal impulses—The World has not been [their] Friend, nor the World's Law—& the inevitable result has been, that the motives of this World have proportionally little force for them. No! It is a body of Death into which Religion alone can awake the spirit of life—it must be the great Truths of the Gospel, which like the Solar Light to the eye, at once correspond to and evoke the essential constituents of our Humanity, the ideas which subsist *potentially* in every man, however bedimmed by unblest circumstances & the absence of education (i.e. their never being *educa*[*te*]*d*)—for they form the Image of God, in which God *created* men, and by which he contra-distinguished from all the creatures, whom by the life, his spirit had given, & the Law which his Word had imposed, he had enforced the Chaos to *become*.—

Now next to the knowlege—for in this case Faith *is* Knowlege—of an Almighty God, the Father of Spirits, and best conveyed—for even to little children it is adequately conveyed—as a Father and Universal Governor, the most momentous truth is the Fact of a FALL, and that all the miseries of the World are the consequences of this Fall—and thence to deduce the true notion of human Freedom—viz. that Control from without must ever be *inversely* as the Self-government or Control from within,[1] unless men are to fall abroad into the state of wild beasts, or more truly of wild Fiends. Now as in the very lowest state a man cannot be forced into action by mere physical force, like the parts of a machine, but must act by the determining of his Will, the moral forces nearest to physical must be substituted—bodily pain, and Fear from the experience & anticipation of Pain. Man is made a Beast—& alas! by Man in defiance of and most impious contradiction to the

---

[1] Cf. *Table Talk*, 15 June 1833: 'The necessity for external government to man is in an inverse ratio to the vigour of his self-government. Where the last is most complete, the first is least wanted. Hence, the more virtue the more liberty.'

common Creator's Fiat. But this is not all that this great truth involves. It can be to awake in the mind of the *Slave* by human Law, that even in Slavery he may be free with a freedom, compared with which his oppressor is a pitiable Slave—[MS. breaks off thus.]

1771. *To Mrs. Gillman*

Address: Mrs Gillman | Grove | Highgate
MS. Victoria University Lib. Hitherto unpublished.
Postmark: Ramsgate, 3 July 1833.

[3 July 1833]

My dearest Friend

After a very pleasant passage I arrived safe & found Mr Gillman with Henry on the Pier, but Mr G. not expecting any one this evening; but fully relying on you, me, and Harriet arriving to-morrow evening. He has provided the very best Lodgings, to my Taste, that I have ever seen in Ramsgate—& only a guinea & a half a week.—Now the *sooner*, you and Harriet can come, the better on all accounts—as James to my surprize is gone—Surely, he must have misinterpreted your letter—as either he must have forgotten his Post-script informing you, that Mr G. had taken No. 4, Bell vue—or you overlooked it.—

Mr Gillman was rather uncomfortable this morning, but feels himself now much better, having been relieved by his Physic. I observed, that he walked very much more like his former self—. . . [MS. cut off.]

1772. *To Mr. Ely*

MS. Editor. Hitherto unpublished.

4. Belle Vue Place
[July 1833]

Half a Pound of Mr Ely's plain Rappee—the same of which he had a quarter of a Pound some days back—Mr Coleridge will call on Mr Ely, as he goes to the Bath.

1773. *To J. G. Lockhart*

Address: G. Lockhart, Esqre | 4. Spenser Place
MS. National Library of Scotland. Pub. Review of English Studies, *October
1934, p. 454.*

> 4, Belle Vue Place.
> Friday
> [12] July 1833[1]

My dear Sir

I gathered from something you said, that the Standard is for-
warded to you. If I have not made a false inference, be so kind as to
let me have the two or three last, if you have retained them—and
I will return them in the course of to-day or tomorrow.

It would be doing poor Justice to myself to say, that I thank
you for the *pleasure*, which the introduction to your Wife & Children
has given me: for I feel, that it has done my heart good, and that in
my remembrance of Mrs Lockhart, I shall have one more affection
to be glad of. God bless her, and you, and your's!

> I am with sincere regard, | my dear Sir, | Your obliged
> S. T. Coleridge

1774. *To Mrs. J. G. Lockhart*

Address: Mrs Lockhart | 4. Spenser Place
MS. Fitzwilliam Museum, Cambridge. Hitherto unpublished.

> 4. Belle Vue Ramsgate
> 14 July 1833.

Dear Madam

I have persuaded Mr and Mrs Gillman to let their joint *wishes*
overcome *her* fears, i.e. to gratify themselves by accepting your &
Mr Lockhart's kind invitation to us for tomorrow. All that Mr
Gillman dare venture on, in the way of eating, is a Lamb Chop—&
you know, that my powers in the same line are not much more
extensive. Mrs Gillman, who has accepted me as her Amanuensis,
intreats me to say for her whatever, she knows, I should say for
myself—which I comprize in assuring you, my dear Mrs Lockhart,
that I am with affectionate regard for you & your's

> your obliged—permit me to say—Friend
> S. T. Coleridge

[1] In a letter to her brother of 10 July 1833 Mrs. Lockhart wrote that 'yester-
day' the family had taken a house at 4 Spencer Place, Ramsgate, for a month
or two. She also mentioned having seen Coleridge 'who is grown very old and
frail and lives at the opposite side of the town'. The present letter was written,
therefore, on Friday, 12 July. Mrs. Lockhart's letter was published in the
East Kent Times, Ramsgate, on 11 July 1934.

1775. *To Mrs. J. G. Lockhart*

Address: Mrs Lockhart | 4. Spenser Place
MS. National Library of Scotland. Pub. East Kent Times, *Ramsgate, 11 July* 1934.

4, Belle Vue Place
Ramsgate.
Tuesday Evening
22 [23] July, 1833.

My dear Madam

As Mr Gillman, who spite of wind and weather loitered about the Pier till the Steam-pacquet arrived, could not descry Mr Lockhart, I fear, you may not see him till tomorrow—. Under the expectation of his arrival as this evening, we had proposed to call on you tomorrow afternoon, about a ¼ before three, & to have proposed your going with us (by *your*, I mean all—*You*, Walter, Charlotte, Miss Scott,[1] &c) to the Jewish SYNAGOGUE, which not Jewish but christian Ignorance has named the TEMPLE—where Mr Mayer, the Minister, has offered to shew us all that is to be shewn—And then, if you would further like to see the place lighted up, & their ceremonial Service, on Friday Evening, of course I should be happy to accompany you. I happen to be a favorite among the Descendants of Abraham: and Mr Montefiere,[2] the Munificent Founder of this Synagogue, has expressed a strong Wish to be introduced to the Author of THE FRIEND. His Father, lately deceased, was without exception the most beautiful old Man, I ever saw—Beauty in the form of Nobleness & Venerableness.—I therefore intend to be at the Synagogue on Friday.—On this plan (tomorrow, I mean) you might return to Spenser Place by half past 4—before your dinner hour at the latest.

With an old man's Love & Blessing to Walter and his Sister, and including as I can safely do, Mr & Mrs Gillman's Feelings in my own, I am, my dear Madam,

with many dear recollections & with | affectionate Esteem |
Your obliged | Friend
S. T. Coleridge

[1] Coleridge refers to Scott's niece, Anne Scott, daughter of Thomas Scott.

[2] Moses Haim Montefiore (1784–1885), philanthropist. Having amassed a fortune, he retired from business in 1824 and devoted himself to the amelioration of the lot of the Jewish race at home and abroad. A baronetcy was conferred on him in 1846.

1776. *To Mrs. J. G. Lockhart*

Address: Mrs Lockhart | 4. Spenser Place
MS. National Library of Scotland. Pub. Review of English Studies, *October 1934, p. 455.*

[23 July 1833][1]

Dear Mrs Lockhart

We shall gladly expect you a little before 3 tomorrow: & we shall have returned at least some 20 minutes before there can be any chance of Mr Lockhart's arrival.

As I perfectly co-incide with his judgement on the late debates, so (had I been in town & in competent health) should I have sympathized with his desire to *see it out.*—Alas! alas! the want of *Principle!* May God bless you | &

S. T. Coleridge

1777. *To Mrs. J. G. Lockhart*

Address: Mrs Lockhart | 4. Spenser Place | Ramsgate
MS. State University of Iowa. Hitherto unpublished.

26 July, 1833—. Ramsgate.

May God bless you, Mrs Lockhart, and your Husband, and Walter & Charlotte—this is the fervent uplifting of the Heart and Spirit of an old Man, who is glad to have seen and known you—

S. T. Coleridge.[2]

To a Cataract
from near the summit of the precipice of a Mountain—

A fragmentary recollection of an Ode, in which the Writer attempted an accomodation of the regular Pindaric Scheme of metrical correspondence, by Strophe, Antistrophe, and Epode to a Language in which, as in the English, *Accent*, or the comparative *Stroke* of the voice on the Syllables, is substituted for the *Quantity*, or comparative *prolongation* of the Sounds.—In English Feet, therefore, the ◡, or *short* of the Greek & Latin, and the – or *long*, must be interpreted as *unaccentuated* or *accentuated* Syllables.—Thus—

Cretic [pyrrhic ?] or Dibrach   Bŏdy̆, Mŏney̆, Spĭrĭt.

Tribrach   Nŏbŏdy̆

Dactyl   (What?)   Nō bŏdy̆ ?

---

[1] Mrs. Lockhart accepted Coleridge's invitation to visit the 'Jewish SYNAGOGUE' on Wednesday, 24 July. See preceding letter.

[2] Coleridge's letter is written at the end of the MS.

Amphibrach   No Body—but a Soul

Anapest At the close / of the Day / when the Ham / let is still.

Spondee God came.—Egypt.—Turmoil. Our Language has very
few *verbal* Spondees. We must form them by Monosyllables. Thus
in the Psalms (– – means a *Spondee*; – ᴗ ᴗ a Dactyl) God came¹ /
up with a² / Shout, our³ / Lord with the⁴ / Sound of a⁵ / Trumpet⁶–/*
Such a Line is called an Hexameter—i.e. a Line of 6 feet, all of
which are either Dactyls or Spondees, the 5th being always a
Dactyl and the 6th a Spondee.

Trochee Lightly, merry.—N.b. at the end of an Hexameter a
trochee counts for a Spondee—from the natural *throw up* of the
Voice, as in '*Trumpet*' in the Hexameter from the Psalms.**

Amphimacer   Britons swear—We are free.

Bacchius   The Lord came.

Anti-bacchius   Plinlymmon: Helvellin.†

These are the *simple* feet—many might be added, as *composite*
feet, under the names of Ionics, Paeans, Epitrites, &c—which are all
requisite in order to *scan* the metre of the Paradise Lost—but the
above will suffice for such Dwarf Poets, as the Writer of the fol-
lowing Fragment.—

                                        S. T. Coleridge.
                    To a Cataract‡
                        &c
                    Strophe
    Unperishing Youth!   – – ᴗ ᴗ –
    Thou leapest from forth   – – ᴗ ᴗ –
    The Cell of thy ceaseless Nativity! ᴗ – ᴗ / ᴗ – ᴗ / ᴗ – ᴗ ᴗ

* Psalm xlvii. 5.
** Similar comments appear in *Friendship's Offering* for 1834, p. 164, in the
note which Coleridge prefixed to a group of poems included under the general
heading, *Fragments from the Wreck of Memory: or, Portions of Poems composed in
early Manhood.* In 1798–9 Coleridge was experimenting with hexameters, both
in translations from the German and in original composition. See *Poems*, i.
327, and Letters 261, 266, and 292–3.
    † In the MS. Coleridge interchanged the examples of the bacchius and anti-
bacchius.
    ‡ First published *Quarterly Review*, Mar. 1834, p. 26, and included in *Poetical
Works*, 1834, under the title, *On a Cataract from a Cavern near the Summit of a
Mountain Precipice.* The words *Improved from Stolberg* were prefixed to this
title in *The Poems of S. T. Coleridge*, 1844, p. 336. On p. 371 Sara Coleridge

Never Mortal saw $- \cup - \cup -$
The Cradle of the Strong One: $\cup - \cup / \cup \cup / --$
Never Mortal heard $- \cup / - \cup / -$
The Gathering of his Voices— $\cup - \cup / \cup \cup / --$
The deep-mutter'd Charm of the Son of the Rock,
Which he lisps evermore in his slumberless fountain!
There's a Cloud at the Portal, a Veil at the Shrine—
         **** (a line wanting)[1]
It embosoms the Roses of Dawn,
It entangles the shafts of the Noon;
And into the Bed of it's Stillness
The Moonshine sinks down as in Slumber—
That the Son of the Rock, that the Nursling of Heaven
May be born in a holy twilight.

Antistrophe.

The Wild Goat in awe
Looks up, and beholds
Above him the Cliff inaccessible!
Thou, at once full-born,
Madden'st in thy Joyance;
Plungest, shatter'st, whirl'st,
Life invulnerable!
         &c &c

Meant to have been finished, but *somebody* came *in*, or some*thing fell* out—& tomorrow—alas! tomorrow!

                                        S. T. C.

1778. *To J. H. Green*

Address: J. H. Green, Esqre | &c &c | 46. Lincoln's Inn Fields
MS. Pierpont Morgan Lib. Pub. E. L. G. ii. 447.

                                        [26 July 1833]

My dearest Friend
    If you did not know me, I should be afraid of your thinking me thankless and loveless from my neglect of writing to you. I went to Ramsgate, in the intention of reviewing our Logic, your transcripts of which I had taken with me, and in the hope of rendering

pointed out that her father's lines were 'an expansion' of a poem by Count Stolberg (F. L. Stolberg), and printed the German original, *Unsterblicher Jüngling*. See also *Poems*, i. 308, and ii. 1126.
    [1] The missing line reads:
         At the shrine of his ceaseless renewing.

the Chapters already written a fit preparation for, & foundation of, the more important third Part—on the IDEAS, or the resolution of the Sense, the Understanding into the Reason, in the evolution of which I joyfully know that you have had at least an equal co-productiveness with myself—if indeed this be not (as on reflection I find it to be) a false and misplaced introduction of the Distinct into the One—For it would puzzle either of us to determine conscientiously the priority or relative Origination of what with ever-intenser faith I dare call the Truths.—But partly from the precarious state of our Friend, Gillman's Health, which however has been, I think, progressive, my anxiety to have, if possible and as soon as possible, some arrangement made, of partnership finally & immediately, for Mrs Gillman's sake, some anxieties in addition respecting James Gillman's prospects & state of mind; & lastly, my own daily Bathings, receivings & returnings of Visits, specially from the Lockharts (Mrs L., Sir Walter Scott's favorite Daughter, is truly an interesting and love-compelling Woman) & from a member or two of the House of Commons, Beaumont of Northumberland[1] &c, of whom when we meet—& lastly, from my own progression in health & countenance, tho' not much in diminished decrepitude—day has followed day, without any work, but that I have read thro' the four folios of Bingham's Antiquities of the Christian Church,[2] found a *continued* series of historical evidences of the truth of my Convictions; have had a great treat in a thorough enjoyment & examination of Canterbury Theatre [Cathedral ?]; Visiting & (I have reason to believe) com-forting Southey's Brother, Captn. Thomas Southey, with his very large family—& the feelings I have left behind with them may perhaps be a means with God's influence, of making the SOUTHEY feel his unkind neglect of me—& God knows! it is wholly & ex-clusively from my persistent regard for *him* & *his* better Being, that I desire it—&c &c—that in short, all I have done is to have attained a younger & healthier *face*, and a less uncomfortable state of bodily sensations, than I had when I left you. I have certainly been much benefited, in praesenti, by the warm salt Shower Baths—standing with my legs in a Tub at the temperature of near a 100, & receiving from 30 to 40 gallons of salt water of from 90 to 100—.

As I was crawling up the Hill towards Belle Vue, where we lodge, a stately old Lady, certainly not less than 80, was coming down—I was making way to give her the Wall—when with an unexpected

---

[1] Thomas Wentworth Beaumont (1792–1848), M.P. for Northumberland 1818–26 and 1830–7.

[2] Joseph Bingham (1668–1723), *Origines Ecclesiasticae, or the Antiquities of the Christian Church*, 10 vols., 1708–22.

alacrity of motion she made the outward Curve, & with grave solemnity said—No, Sir! You are the far Elder. It is my *Duty* to make way for the *Aged*.—

However, Mr G's anxieties begin to counteract the beneficent effects of the Sea-air & Baths—& we are to return tomorrow (Saturday, 27 July) by the Steamer—It is possible, therefore, that I may see you on Sunday. With my affectionate Love to Mrs Green, I am, my *dearest* Friend,

Your's most *entirely*
S. T. Coleridge.

1779. *To Henry Nelson Coleridge*

MS. Victoria University Lib. Hitherto unpublished.

[August 1833][1]

My dear Henry

I am returned, & have brought back Mr Gillman with me, better beyond the fullest extent of my *Hopes*, and only short of those Wishes, which the Fancy hides from the Understanding.—Mrs Gillman too looks so well as really to acquit Mr Lockhart of all intentional flattery, when on my asking him whether he did not see a striking likeness to the present Marchioness of Lansdown he replied—Nay! that is a compliment to the Marchioness which could scarcely be tolerated from one of her Lovers in her May of Life—. Lastly, I too am said to have not been retrograde: and the effects of Dyasson's Warm Salt Shower-Baths were such, as to make me long and yearn day after day for our dearest Sara, & prompted many & many a calculation as to the total difference in your expenditure—if for six or eight weeks a comfortable & well-situated House could be procured for the whole *Kit* (as it might be) for 4£ a week!—Pray, let me see or hear from you. I am always thinking & dreaming about Sara.—While repeating *metres* to Mrs L.—the following fragment of an attempt at an English Pindaric rushed on my Memory.[2] Tell me *truly*, that is, tell me—how it falls on your

[1] With this letter Coleridge included the poem, *To a Cataract*, along with the following dated note:

Caetera desunt. Some*thing* fell *out*, or some*body* came *in*—& so Tomorrow—alas! the Sunset gorgeous Horizon—the inarrivable Horizon of that Hope-Lie, Tomorrow!

S. T. Coleridge
August, 1833—

i.e. of every Man's *Year*—Novr. 30th, of *his* Life!

[2] A reference to the lines *To a Cataract*, which Coleridge had sent to Mrs. Lockhart on 26 July 1833. Since the text of this poem in *Poetical Works*, 1834, differs but slightly from the version in the present letter, the lines are omitted here. H. N. Coleridge published the poem in the *Quarterly Review*, Mar. 1834, in an article entitled 'Translations of Pindar'.

ear. I have read the article on the Greek Lyric Poetry with delight[1]
—& only wish it had been fuller—& double the Length—
My faithful love to Mrs Coleridge—& a double father's Blessings
on our Grand-children—

S. T. Coleridge.

1780. *To Mrs. Dowling*

Address: Mrs Dowling
MS. New York Public Lib. Hitherto unpublished.

Saturday Noon. [3 August 1833][3]

Dear Madam—
or rather as my hand was on the move to write, My dear Mrs
Dowling! I have done my best—but pre-engagements not the less
binding because I regret that they should be an obstacle to my
indulging my wish on the present opportunity, put it out of my
power to avail myself of your & Mr D's *very kind* Invitation—
Independent of it's *friendliness*, which indeed has never been
wanting on your part toward me, it would have been exceedingly
gratifying to me to have had the pleasure and without flattery I
might say the honor of spending a social evening with such a party
as will ornament your table—. I feel an especial disappointment
with regard to the American Philosopher, were it but as the Country-
man of my dear & honored Washington Allston—But what can
not be had, must be forgone—and believe me, dear Mrs Dowling,
with sincere regard

your obliged
S. T. Coleridge

1781. *To Thomas Pringle*

Address: T. Pringle, Esqre. | Holly Terrace | Highgate
MS. Yale University Lib. Hitherto unpublished.

In the present letter Coleridge is writing to Thomas Pringle, the editor of
Friendship's Offering, concerning his contributions to that annual. (See also
Letters 1782, 1784–5, 1787, and 1792.) The following poems were published in
the 1834 issue:

---

[1] See *Quarterly Review*, July 1833, pp. 349–81, for this article by H. N.
Coleridge.
[2] Mrs. Dowling was the sister-in-law of James Kenney, the dramatist. See
Appendix B, Letter 1013A.
[3] This letter was written on the Saturday preceding Emerson's visit to
Highgate on Monday, 5 Aug. 1833. For Emerson's account of this meeting see
R. W. Armour and R. F. Howes, *Coleridge the Talker*, 1940, pp. 208–10.

My Baptismal Birth-day. Lines composed on a sick bed, under severe bodily Suffering, on My Spiritual Birthday, October 28th.

Fragments from the Wreck of Memory: or, Portions of Poems composed in early Manhood:

    I.—*Hymn to the Earth.*
    II.—*English Hexameters, written during a temporary Blindness, in the year 1799.*
    III.—*The Homeric Hexameter described and exemplified.*
    IV.—*The Ovidian Elegiac Metre described and exemplified.*
    V.—*A Versified Reflection.*

Love's Apparition and Evanishment. An Allegoric Romance.

Lightheartednesses in Rhyme.

    I.—*The Reproof and Reply.*
    II.—*In Answer to a Friend's Question.*
    III.—*Lines to a Comic Author, on an Abusive Review.*
    IV.—*An Expectoration, or Splenetic Extempore, on my joyful departure from the City of Cologne.*
    Expectoration the Second.

Aug. 6—1833

My dear Sir

From successive interruptions I have not had time or spirits to turn over my wilderness of Papers—but I think, I can promise you a fragment of a Hymn to the Earth in English Hexameters, of some 50 lines or so[1]—if you should think likely to be acceptable, as a curiosity in English Verse—This I hope to find tomorrow—but send the above trifles,[2] in proof that I have not forgotten you—

S. T. Coleridge—

On my spiritual Birth-day, October 28—Lines composed on a Sick-bed under severe bodily Suffering, by

S. T. Coleridge

My Baptismal Birth-day.[3]

Born unto God in CHRIST—in Christ, my ALL!
What, that Earth boasts, were not lost cheaply, rather
Than forfeit that blest Name, by which we call
The HOLY ONE, the Almighty God, OUR FATHER?
FATHER! in Christ we live: and Christ in Thee.
Eternal Thou, and everlasting We!

[1] First published in *Friendship's Offering* for 1834. The poem has thirty-three lines. It is a free translation of F. L. Stolberg's *Hymne an die Erde*. See *Poems*, i. 327.

Sara Coleridge points out that *The Homeric Hexameter* and *The Ovidian Elegiac Metre*, which were also first published in *Friendship's Offering* for 1834, were translated from Schiller, and prints the German originals in *The Poems of S. T. Coleridge*, 1844, pp. 371–2. See *Poems*, i. 307–8, and ii. 1125.

[2] In the MS. the two poems which follow precede Coleridge's letter.

[3] First published in *Friendship's Offering* for 1834. See *Poems*, i. 490.

The Heir of Heaven, henceforth I dread not Death.
In Christ I live, in Christ I draw the Breath
Of the true Life. Let Sea, and Earth, and Sky
Wage war against me: on my front I shew
Their mighty Master's Seal! In vain *they* try
To end my Life, who can but end it's Woe.

Is that a Death-bed, where the CHRISTIAN lies?
Yes!—But not *his*: 'tis DEATH itself, *there* dies.

S. T. C.

A FORCE is the provincial term in Cumberland for any narrow
Fall of Water from the summit of a Mountain Precipice.

The following stanza (it may not arrogate the name of Poem) or
versified Reflection was composed while the Writer was gazing on
three parallel FORCES on a Moonlight Night at the foot of a part of
the Saddleback Fell.[1]

On stern BLENCARTHUR'S perilous Height[2]
The Wind is tyrannous and strong:[3]
And flashing forth unsteady light
From stern Blencarthur's skiey Height
As loud the torrents throng!
Beneath the Moon in gentle Weather
They bind the Earth and Sky together:
But O! the Sky, and all *it's* Forms, how quiet!
The Things, that seek the Earth, how full of noise & riot!

S. T. Coleridge

[1] In *Friendship's Offering* for 1834 this and the preceding paragraph are
printed as a prefatory note to *A Versified Reflection*.

[2] These lines, to which E. H. Coleridge and J. L. Lowes assign a date of
1800, are entitled *A Versified Reflection* in *Friendship's Offering* for 1834. The
lines were first published without Coleridge's knowledge as one of 'Three Scraps'
in *The Amulet* for 1833, with the title, *A Thought suggested by a View of Saddle-
back in Cumberland.* (See Letter 1596 n.) Lowes follows E. H. Coleridge in
pointing out that the first two lines of Coleridge's poem were adapted from a
poem by Isaac Ritson. See *Poems*, i. 347, and J. L. Lowes, *The Road to Xanadu*,
1930, pp. 604 *j* and *k*.

[3] The phrase 'tyrannous and strong' occurs in Wordsworth's *The Waterfall
and the Eglantine*, which Coleridge in Aug. 1800 copied and sent to the Bristol
printers for the second edition of *Lyrical Ballads*. (See headnote to Letter 346.)
The phrase also occurs in line 42 of *The Ancient Mariner* in a passage first pub-
lished in *Sibylline Leaves*, 1817. See Lowes, op. cit. 604 *j* and *k*.

1782. *To Thomas Pringle*

Address: T. Pringle, Esqre | Holly Terrace | Highgate
MS. Cornell University Lib. Pub. with omis. 'Samuel Taylor Coleridge and
Thomas Pringle', by E. L. Griggs, Quarterly Bulletin of the South African
Library, *1951, p. 7.*

[Endorsed Aug. 13, 1833]

My dear Sir

My only motive for wishing to learn, whether your Volume will
have room enough for the insertion of the *Madrigal*[1] is—that if
there should be room, I would send you a greatly improved Copy of
the same, especially in respect of the irregularity in the distances of
the corresponding Rhymes in that, I gave you—as well as in the
greater *perspicuity* in the Allegory. But I presume, that when the
Proof Sheet is sent me, I may, if I find the Madrigal inserted, sub-
stitute the improvements, as corrections, only that it will make 4
or 6 lines more than the Copy in your possession.

But, if inserted, it will not altogether appropriately fall under the
head of *Levities*:[2] & would have better followed the Poem of one
Stanza—

On stern Blencarthur's perilous height—[3]

But n'importe. This is a trifle. It is *light* enough, God wot!

I read with much interest the Earl of Belmore's Speech[4]—&
could have wished that the Lord Chancellor had more fairly met the
one argument, which is sufficiently plausible to depress the hopes, if
not perplex the moral resolves, of a thinking honest man—that,
namely, grounded on the improbability that any wages that can be
offered by the Planters should stimulate any *body* of men forming
the great majority of the Population, to labor throughout the year
in such a climate, & with such extent of fertile Soils, when the
Labor of some twenty days would enable the man to roam about
with his Gun & Fishing Rod, & yet feed & cloath his family accord-
ing to all *their* wants & wishes. It is very easy to say as Lord B.
in fact does say—Well! then—let the West India Islands or the

---

[1] A reference to *Love's Apparition and Evanishment. An Allegoric Romance*,
first published without *L'Envoy* in *Friendship's Offering* for 1834, where the
poem is signed and dated 'S. T. Coleridge, *August*, 1833'. See Letter 1394 and
note. See also Letter 1784.

[2] As Coleridge suggested, this poem was not printed under the general head-
ing *Levities*, later changed to *Lightheartednesses in Rhyme*. See Letter 1785.

[3] See preceding letter for the text of this poem.

[4] Somerset Lowry-Corry, second Earl Belmore (1774–1841), formerly
governor-in-chief of Jamaica. On 12 Aug. 1833 he spoke in the House of Lords
against certain provisions in the Act for the Abolition of Slavery. T. C. Hansard,
Parliamentary Debates, 1833, xx. 507–14.

Planters therein go to the Devil, who has long had a lawful *Lien* upon them—& we will drink East India Sugar, & the Ch. of the Exch. raise the same amount of Taxes.—It is easy to say this for a Man who pleases to throw the whole guilt of the Slave Trade & Tenure on the W. I. Proprietors—but I and others who regard *them* as only the Executive Ministers & Functionaries of a *National Act*, find all this very unsatisfactory. We want a more human[e] & hope-giving ans[wer.] . . . [Conclusion and signature cut off.]

1783. *To Thomas H. Dunn*

Pub. Advertiser, *Adelaide, South Australia, 28 July 1934.*

Wednesday, 14th August, 1833.

My Dear Sir—

It is high time that I should settle my account with you. There was neither cause nor reason why you should have remained un-paid for so unconscionable a time, but that I, before my sudden start to Cambridge,[1] had been too ill and listless to think of anything, and you too delicate to remind one of a debt to yourself. However, better late than never. Any time after the 22nd of this month it will be QUITE CONVENIENT to me to discharge it, and therefore be so kind as before that time to let me have—not the Bills, but the total amount. My money is not so bad, nor my calculating however so weak, as to suffer you to CHEAT YOURSELF—the only person in the world you are at all disposed to cheat.

[1] In late June 1833 Coleridge went to Cambridge with Gillman and Green to attend the meeting of the British Association, where he met William Rowan Hamilton on the 27th. On his return to Highgate he reported to H. N. Coleridge: 'My emotions at revisiting the university were at first overwhelming. I could not speak for an hour; yet my feelings were upon the whole very pleasurable, and I have not passed, of late years at least, three days of such great enjoyment and healthful excitement of mind and body. The bed on which I slept—and slept soundly too—was, as near as I can describe it, a couple of sacks full of potatoes tied together. I understand the young men think it hardens them. Truly I lay down at night a man, and arose in the morning a bruise.' See R. P. Graves, *Life of Sir William Rowan Hamilton*, 3 vols., 1882–9, ii. 49, and *Table Talk*, 29 June 1833. See also *Minnow among Tritons*, ed. Stephen Potter, 1934, p. 176.

1784. *To Thomas Pringle*

MS. The Carl H. Pforzheimer Library. Hitherto unpublished.

[August 1833]

My dear Sir

   If you like the Poem better as it stands in the Proof, pray, retain it—I will trust your taste & judgement rather than my own.

                                                     S. T. C.[1]

instead of 'a Madrigal'—put 'an Allegoric Romance'—

> Like a lone ARAB, old and blind,
> Some Caravan had left behind;
> Who sits beside a ruin'd Well,
> Where the shy Dipsads bask and swell!
> And now he cowers with low-hung Head aslant,
> And listens for some human sound, in vain:
> And now the Aid, which Heaven alone can grant,
> Upturns his eyeless face from Heaven to gain!
> Even thus, in languid mood and vacant hour,
> Resting my eye upon a drooping plant,
> With brow low-bent, within my garden-bower,
> I sate upon it's Couch of Camomile:
> And lo!—or was it a brief Sleep, the[2] while
> I watch'd the sickly Calm and aimless Scope[3]
> Of my own Heart?—I saw[4] the Inmate, HOPE,
>   That once had made that Heart so warm,
>   Lie[5] lifeless at my feet!—
>   And LOVE stole in, in maiden form[6]
>   Toward my[7] arbor Seat!
> She bent and kiss'd her Sister's lips,[8]
>   As she was wont to do:
>   Alas! 'twas but a chilling Breath,
>   That woke enough of life in death
>   To make HOPE die anew.[9]

---

   [1] In the MS. the poem, *Love's Apparition and Evanishment*, precedes the letter. Someone, presumably Pringle, has crossed out Coleridge's letter.

   [2] When, like some Birth of shadowy twilight, [Cancelled version of line above.]   [3] without aim or Scope, [Cancelled words in line above.]

   [4] as tho' [Cancelled words in line above.]

   [5] Lay [Cancelled word in line above.]

   [6] The Spirit of Love in female form, [Cancelled version of line above.]

   [7] Hard by that [Cancelled words in line above.]

   [8] Coleridge first wrote and then cancelled the following words:
            She bent, methought, &c &c as in the Proof.

   [9] In *Friendship's Offering* for 1834 and in *Poetical Works*, 1834, *Love's*

1785. *To Thomas Pringle*

Address: T. Pringle, Esqre.
Facsimile South African Bookman, *December 1912, p. 12.*

[August 1833]

My dear Sir

Your messenger disappeared right quickly, & was out of Call and Recall, before our little Cook, Sarah, returned to the Door to give him the Note that accompanies this—& which had been written before your paquet arrived.—

I prefer 'Light-heartednesses' to Levities,[1] and the more so for the out-of-the-wayness of the new minted former—as better suiting both the verses, and their perpetrator.

I sadly quarrel with our modern Printers for their levelling spirit of antipathy to all initial Capitals, thus ruin'd well for ruin'd Well.[2] I greatly approve of the German Rule of distinguishing all Noun-Substantives by a Capital: & at least, all *Personifications* shall be in small Capitals: see—hope[3]—[4]

Good night. I hope you are asleep, for it is on the stroke of Midnight.

S. T. Coleridge.

P.S.—The Asps of the sand-desarts ancient[ly] named *Dipsads*.[5]

1786. *To Charles Aders*

Transcript Cornell University Lib. Pub. Some Letters of the Wordsworth Family, *ed. L. N. Broughton, 1942, p. 108.*

18 Aug. 1833
Grove, Highgate.

My dear Sir,

Forgive me for wasting any portion of your valuable time by drawing your attention to any want or perhaps whim of my own—

Apparition and Evanishment runs to twenty-eight lines, and the published texts vary considerably from that of the present letter.

[1] For a list of the poems printed in *Friendship's Offering* for 1834 under the general heading, *Lightheartednesses in Rhyme*, see headnote to Letter 1781.

[2] *Love's Apparition and Evanishment* line 3. See *Poems*, i. 489.

[3] See lines 17 and 28 of *Love's Apparition*.

[4] The remainder of this letter is not in the facsimile; the text is taken from *Modern Language Review*, July 1917, p. 353, where the letter is reprinted.

[5] In *Friendship's Offering* this sentence is printed as a footnote to the word 'Dipsads' in line 4 of *Love's Apparition and Evanishment*—'Where basking Dipsads hiss and swell'. In *Poetical Works*, 1834, this line was altered to read: 'Where the shy sand-asps bask and swell.'

not perhaps, tho' God knows! I am not conscious of . . .[1] or vanity. But I have several letters to write on the subject of individual interest, either to the writer or the Receiver in proportion to the universal interest of the contents—and likewise have not seldom to send off at the spur of the moment when [what ?] I had too little time or too much indolence to transcribe,—and which yet afterwards I regret, not to have retained. Now what I wish to learn from your practical experience is, whether there is either any copying machine, within a moderate price, which I, the very awkwardest, and most *hand* or rather *paw*-impotent of Earth's featherless Bipeds, could easily manage—or any means that would make the original legible while it preserves one or more copies, as I have heard of a thin paper written upon with a sort of *Style* instead of a *Pen*—which perhaps might be still better in some respects—tho' I confess, the letters, which I received from Mr. Chance, which were thus written, betrayed the mode in which they were written, and the *purpose* for which that mode had been adopted—viz. that of retaining a *copy*, which seems somewhat alien from the spirit of free offhand communication, somewhat too *prospective*, and savoring too much of a man's looking forward mainly to himself, while he is acting a selbst-entäusserung to his correspondent. But the subjects, and the nature of the subjects, in the letters which I have in view, will, I trust help to exempt me from this charge.—In few words, do you know of any Copy-*taking* or Copy-*making* simple machine or mode, which will cost only a few pounds?

In order in some slight measure to repay you for the postage of this scrawl, if Henry Gillman does not take it, I will put down on the now blank third side or page of this sheet, in hopes that you may read it to dear Mrs. Aders, a little poem I composed from a rude conception which I accidentally found in one of my many old 'Fly-catchers' (Fliegen-fänger) or Mss Day Books for *impounding* (Einsperrung) Stray Thoughts, as I was lying in my bed, some three or four mornings ago, after my Gruel.[2]

I heard with unspeakable anguish and indignation of a scene

---

[1] Word illegible, as noted by the transcriber. At the top of the transcript Mrs. Aders wrote: 'The original of this letter was given by Mr Aders to his young friend Frd. Pfeffel—this copy is by him—Dec. 3rd 1835.' At the end of the letter she added: 'The mistakes and omissions corrected from the original letter by me—Eliza Aders.' There is a second but less accurate transcript of this letter in the Central Library, Auckland, New Zealand.

[2] The transcript of this letter contains a copy of *Love's Apparition and Evanishment*. The poem is signed, 'S. T. Coleridge aetatis suae *63 Fie! old gentleman*'. The text differs somewhat from those published in *Friendship's Offering* for 1834 and in *Poetical Works*, 1834, and the word 'Dispads' is misspelled in the transcript.

that had lately taken place, by an incursion of the *little* Doctor's wife—and almost involuntarily, tho' to myself only, expectorated my spleen in three or four stanzas, which I have not yet made outward in Ink or Pencil, but which I will sometime or other put you in possession of.

With my kindest love to Mrs. Aders, whom I both love and esteem with my whole self, Head, Heart and senses, I am, my dear Mr. Aders,

your Sincere Friend
S. T. Coleridge.

1787. *To Thomas Pringle*

MS. Goodspeed's Book Shop. Hitherto unpublished.

Thursday ½ past 11. [22 August 1833]

My dear Sir

This your Note with it's inclosure was delivered to me some ten minutes ago, as I was undressing for Bed. I however have stayed to make the only requisite correction—and re-inclose it—in order that it may be returned to you before I get up tomorrow morning—

Good Night & God | bless you | &
S. T. Coleridge—

1788. *To Anne R. Scott*

Address: Miss Anne R. Scott | Precincts | Canterbury
MS. Jesus College Lib., Cambridge. Pub. E. L. G. ii. 449.
Postmark: Highgate, 26 August 1833.

Grove, Highgate
Monday, 26 August, 1833

My dear Miss Scott

If our acquaintance had been of longer standing, I should not have needed to assure you, that at no one moment did I ever believe, suppose, or even think of, *your* having contributed either Ground or Material to Lockhart's GOOD JOKE, in any other than some such way, as that which your obliging Letter has now recalled to my mind. The circumstance had escaped me; but I now distinctly remember it—and I venture to conjecture, that the cause of my having forgot it may have been, that my Discussion, tho' *occasioned* by the remark of our Fellow-passenger, was—in my own feeling at least—chiefly addressed to *you*.[1]

---

[1] While he was at Ramsgate in July 1833, Coleridge saw much of the Lockharts. He also became acquainted with Anne R. Scott, Sir Walter's niece, and on a journey from Ramsgate to Canterbury, where he visited Southey's

Permit me, dear Miss Scott, to repeat, that *your* having any other concern in the Representation, excepting as having unconsciously suggested the Date, Scene, and Dramatis Personae to our good Friend's Comic Muse, or at the utmost some slight Hint for the Opening of the Plot—a Hook, as it were, for the story to hang from—never occurred to me even among the possibilities of this world. It would have stood in too violent a contrast with the impression, I had retained, of your character and whole frame of mind. But independently of this, Women are too veracious creatures, and set too little value on a good Joke—a certain degree of Obtuseness in this respect I have ever considered among the characteristic traits, nay, *charms*, of Womanhood: and have a

brother Thomas and his family, he unexpectedly found that she was travelling in the same carriage. A woman who apparently kept lodgings was the only other passenger. On her arrival in Canterbury Miss Scott sent Mrs. Lockhart an enthusiastic account of Coleridge's conversation during the journey. Lockhart seized on her glowing description and turned it into a jest at Coleridge's expense. Mrs. Thomas Southey reported Lockhart's remarks to Coleridge. He replied with a 'playful' letter in which, nevertheless, he revealed his annoyance at Lockhart's ridicule. Subsequently, Mrs. Southey informed Miss Scott of the contents of Coleridge's letter. Quite naturally Miss Scott was disconcerted, and on 24 Aug. 1833 she sent Coleridge a letter of apology and explanation reading in part:

Were the Subject any other than the one I am about to address you upon, I can hardly say how much I should feel gratified by addressing a letter to you, but, at the present moment I feel nothing almost but very keen sensations of pain, under the sense of being much injured in any passing opinion you might have formed of me. . . . In writing a hurried Note to her [Mrs. Lockhart] the evening I arrived here, I told her how much delighted I had been with my good fortune in meeting with you, with perhaps more enthusiasm than people usually express themselves; and alluding to . . . your talent of raising people for the time above themselves, and making them capable for the moment of feeling and comprehending Subjects, at other times out of their reach, I said you had conversed on various subjects, . . . [and] that a good Woman, who I imagine kept lodgings, only was in the carriage. On her observing that a gipsy life after all was the pleasantest—you observed that it was a common opinion but it might easily be proved to be a fallacy, and entered into a most delightful conversation—naming the heads of it—which remains imprinted on my mind, while at the same time—my own note to Mrs. Lockhart . . . was almost forgotten. My Note however *was written* in an abrupt manner and in that familiar and half playful way that intimate friends may use, certain of being understood by those they address, but which certainly is liable to misapprehension by another. Yet if Mr. Lockhart used my expression I *know* it must have been to illustrate a gift which you possess so remarkably. . . . I feel ashamed to have written so much at length; but I should have been still more cruelly pained to have lain a day longer under the imputation of repeating or designedly uttering conversations. . . . I must beg your indulgence for all I have been obliged to confess in order to clear the matter, and I shall feel much relieved by hearing from yourself or through Mrs. Southey that my explanation has been satisfactory to you. [MS. Mr. A. H. B. Coleridge.]

hundred times noticed it, not only in amiable Females, but in the most intelligent, and of the finest talents: and often, when I have laughed heartily at the simplicity, with which the whole *Joke* of a Tale, told only *as* a Joke, has been over-looked on the sudden moral feeling excited by the supposition of it's actual occurrence, I have been conscious of an inward Love-thrill the meanwhile, and an enlivened *respect*: for it was truly *feminine*. Dorothy Words-worth, the Sister of our great Poet, is a Woman of Genius, as well as manifold acquirements; and but for the absorption of her whole Soul in her Brother's fame and writings would, perhaps, in a different style have been as great a Poet as Himself. Once, she being present, I told one of these good stories, the main drollery of which rests on their utter *unbelievability* as actual fact—viz—of a Surgeon, who having restored to life two or three persons who had attempted to hang or drown themselves; and having been afterwards impor-tuned by them for Help and Maintenance on the plea, that having forced life upon them against their own will and wish, he was bound to support it; had resolved, that he would never interfere in any such accidents without having first ascertained whether the individual wished it or no. On a summer day, while on a water-party, one of the Rowers in some unaccountable way fell over-board and dis-appeared. But on his re-emersion the Surgeon caught hold of his Hair & lifting his head & chest above the water said—Now, my good Fellow! did you really mean to drown yourself! What is your own wish?—0—0. 0—(sobbed out the man)—a sickly *Wife*—and seven small children!—'Ha! POOR Fellow! No Wonder then!'—exclaimed the Surgeon, and instantly popped him under again.—The party were all on the brink of a loud Laugh, when Dorothy Wordsworth, with tears sparkling in her eyes, cried out—Bless me! but was not that very *inhuman*!—This stroke of exquisite simplicity & true singleness of heart, made us almost roll off our chairs; but was there one of the Party, that did not love Dorothy the more for it?—I trust, not one.—

Now I have but one request to make, my dear Miss Scott! that you will not infer from my playful Letter to Mrs Southey, that I entertain, or even on the first Hearing felt, the slightest resent-ment, or the least *touch* of unkindness, towards Mr Lockhart. I laughed as unfeignedly as well as as heartily as any one of his jovial Hearers; nor should I have noticed it but that I thought my gallantry as a Man, or in words that better become both me and my Age, my courtesy as a gentleman called in question; and even for the example's sake did not choose, that the supposed excess of my intellectual powers should be made an excuse for a palpable defect of good sense and good manners.

I can readily understand and enter into the mood, in which Lockhart related the anecdote; and am not, believe me, one of those profound sages, who delve deep for motives and feelings, that lie on the surface: and who most often dig *aslant*, and the deeper they delve, the farther they are from the object of their search. Mr Lockhart, I have no doubt, had been previously expressing in strong terms his high opinion of my powers as a Poet: and nothing *sets off* a thing better, than a sharp contrast—the same principle which makes us all enjoy Butler's

> And like a Lobster boil'd, the Morn
> From Black to Red began to turn.[1]

Remember me with affectionate respect to your Mother, and Sister, and be assured that I remain

with esteem, regard, and general | recollections, sincerely your's,

S. T. Coleridge

1789. *To J. H. Green*

Address: J. H. Green, Esqre | 46. Lincoln's Inn Fields.
MS. Pierpont Morgan Lib. Hitherto unpublished.
Postmark: Highgate, 3 September 1833.

Monday Night, 2 Septr. 1833—

My dear Friend

Mr Kinnaird has been with me this afternoon, to ask the fulfillment of my promise to stand God-father for his child[2]—and I have engaged, God permitting, to take a Fly and be with him at Hack[n]ey by or before 12 o'clock on Thursday Next. If, therefore I do not see you on Wednesday, I shall not *expect* to see [you] before Thursday—tho' on no account of my own.

Henry Coleridge goes off Devon-ward for his part Vacation and part Registering Barristership to morrow. I wonder, the Whigs employ such an inveterate Tory! But I forgot—Lord Brougham by way of a (not very veracious) Self-denying Egoism, & a popularity-sop, has consigned the selection to the Judges. But the recent

---

[1] *Hudibras*, Part II, Canto ii, lines 31–32. Coleridge again quoted the lines in making a distinction between fancy and imagination: 'The Fancy brings together images which have no connection natural or moral, but are yoked together by the poet by means of some accidental coincidence; as in the well-known passage in Hudibras.' *Table Talk*, 23 June 1834.

[2] A reference to John Peirse Kennard's son, born in June 1833 and named Adam Steinmetz for Coleridge's late friend and disciple. Coleridge attended the christening on 5 Sept. 1833. It was young Kennard to whom Coleridge addressed his celebrated letter of 13 July 1834.

Equinoctials have frightened him out of the *Steamers*: indeed, his Father has written to interdict the Hazard.

When we meet, I shall, I hope, be prepared to explain to you my present apprehensions, that it will be well to preface a part at least of what you have read to me, as a means of reconciling with right reason the belief, or believed Antecedents & Accompaniments of the essential Belief of the Christian Church, rather than as an attempt to give an historical or narrative Character to Beings, whose practical moral interest for us is superseded by the divine Omnipresence. As far [as] these Hierarchies tend to make the idea of the Tetractys, of the co-immanence of the Unity in the Distinctity, and of the co-existence of hypostasized Distinctities with the hypostatic Tri-unity, more clear—(klarer & auch mehr *deutlich*) I receive them with Joy—but under the dread of climbing up to stand on my own shoulders, I feel more confident satisfaction in particularizing the great general ideas (of which I consider it the height of my present state to see that they *are* and *must be*) by their application, first to the primal Fall, and then to the Creatures, as a gradual re-elevation. Besides, I dread even the appearance of an approximation to the Neo-platonic Proclo-plotinian Scheme & Process.—

Don't forget the Pen-knife. This vile tool in it's product may remind you, as the difficulty of being legible does,

> my very dear Friend, | Your obliged & affectionate
> S. T. Coleridge

1790. *To J. P. Kennard*

Address: J. P. Kinnaird, Esqre | Hackney
MS. Mr. W. Hugh Peal. Hitherto unpublished.

> Monday Noon
> [Endorsed 9 September 1833]

My dear Sir

Please God, I will be with you by Two o'clock, or (if I call at Mr Stutfield's) by ½ past, at the latest. I shall quit Highgate a quarter before One. The Dinner Hour is therefore of no importance—Nay, I should prefer 5. I thank you for the Pens—tho' I am sure, that you receive the most acceptable remuneration in the knowlege, that I had had health, and grace to employ them to the full extent of the powers, that have been entrusted to me.

Of Ramsgate when we meet. I am uncertain whether I shall be successful in persuading Mrs Gillman to accompany me tomorrow.

> Your's, my dear Sir, | Most truly
> S. T. Coleridge

1791. *To F. Nixon*

Address: Mr F. Nixon
MS. Yale University Lib. Hitherto unpublished.

Tuesday Evening—[22 October 1833 ?]

If Mr F. Nixon should happen to have the Volumes of the Black Dwarf and Old Mortality, Mr Coleridge would be much obliged to him for the Loan of them till tomorrow night.

1792. *To Thomas Pringle*

Pub. The Poetical Works of Thomas Pringle. With a Sketch of His Life, *ed.* Leitch Ritchie, 1839 (2nd edn.), p. cx.

Thursday, October 24, 1833.
My dear Pringle,

I am indeed very unwell—perhaps worse in spirits than in body— so oppressive is the gloom of the fear of a relapse. I have barely looked at your kind letter. As I never had the slightest thought of any remuneration of this kind, if I supposed that in any way, *direct* or *indirect*, it came from *your* pocket,[1] I should not hesitate to re-enclose it. But I still pray, and heartily trust, I may yet see you to question you on this. Till then God bless you.

Your afflicted but very sincere friend and thorough *esteemer*, with friendly affection,

S. T. Coleridge.

1793. *To J. H. Green*

Address: J. H. Green, Esqre | 46. Lincoln's Inn Fields.
MS. Pierpont Morgan Lib. Hitherto unpublished.
Postmark: Highgate, 29 October 1833.

Monday Night [28 October 1833]
My dear Friend

Will you, if it be not *much* inconvenient, have my Mss note in one of the blank leaves or pages at the beginning of the *Waterland* transcribed for me ? That I mean on Pantheism as the only possible *speculative* Atheism: & that it *is* Atheism: & that Socinianism stops short of it, only because it is lazy, and lily-livered[2]—shrinks

---

[1] Coleridge had obviously received payment for his contributions to *Friendship's Offering* for 1834.

[2] Coleridge refers to his note in the fly-leaves of a copy of Daniel Waterland's *A Vindication of Christ's Divinity*, 1719. This volume is in the British Museum. For Coleridge's comments see *Literary Remains*, iv. 223–4.

from the ugliness of it's own thought and Ergo—halts, and turns
out of the strait road, & *cowering* down to ease itself from the
drastic effects of it's own *cowardice* looks to the eyes of my *refined*
imagination like a *poached* Egg with a *crack* in it.—

Perhaps, your Amanuensis may find time to copy the other Mss
at the beginning & at the end on the IDEA of the Trinity, & the evil
of the absence of the same in Waterland & Bull—and that on the
importance of the Identity of the Jehovah of the Old with the
Word, or υἱὸς μονογενής of the New Testament.[1]—I should like to
have these transferred into my Fly-Catcher. But now I think of it,
you might as well bring the Volume itself with you; and I can
transcribe them myself or get James to do it.—

I wish that if you can find at the German Bookseller's 'Joannis
Henrici Heinrichs Apocalypsis Graece, perpetuâ annotatione illus-
trata'—in 2 vol.—Gottingae apud Dietrich, MDCCCXXI—you
would buy it for me—or even order it.[2]—

In part to compensate for the 3d. of the 2d. post—& by way of
a consoling prospect of an end to such intrusions on your purse &
patience, I send you the Epitaph, I rewrote last night, or rather
re-*thought* (for I am now first to re-*write* it) on an Author not
wholly unknown; but better known by the initials of his Name than
by the Name itself—which he fondly Graecized—ἔστησε. ἔστησε:
κεῖται· ἀναστήσει[3]—. Hic Jacet, qui stetit, restat, resurget.—

God bless you, my dearest | Friend and your

ESTEESE.

On a Tombstone.[4]

Stop, Christian Passer-by! Stop, Child of God!
And read with gentle heart. Beneath this sod
A Poet lies: or that which once was he.
O lift one thought in prayer for S. T. C.
That he, who many a year, with toil of breath
Found Death in Life, may here find Life in Death.
Mercy for Praise, *to be forgiven* for Fame
He ask'd, and hop'd thro' Christ. Do Thou the Same!

[1] See *Literary Remains*, iv. 221–2, 226–7, and 233–4.
[2] For Coleridge's annotations in this work see *Literary Remains*, iii. 167–70.
[3] See Letter 459 (ii. 867 n.).
[4] First published under the title *Epitaph* in *Poetical Works*, 1834, ii. 152,
where the poem is dated '9th November, 1833'. See *Poems*, i. 491.

1794. *To Gioacchino de' Prati*[1]

Address: J. De Prati, LL.D. | 32 Upper Norton Street | Portland Place
MS. New York Public Lib. Pub. E. L. G. ii. 451.
Postmark: Highgate, 30 October 1833.

Tuesday Night—29 Octr 1833
Grove, Highgate

My dear De Prati

I learn by the Times of to day that you are in Town, & your address. I was much interested at the sight of your name in your first appeal in favor of your *name*-honored Friend—I recognized the warmth & kindliness of your nature in thus coming forward, and did full credit to your chivalry. But in the distinct remembrance of the Quarterly Review, and the consequent association of the name, Buonaroti, with the atrocity of Robespierre and the bedlamism of Baboeuf, and himself made prominent in my recollection by the singular circumstance of, first, the unmixed character, and secondly, by the longaevity, of his *Monomania*, I could not, from my knowlege of the present state of the public mind, but exceedingly doubt the *prudence* of the attempt, relatively to yourself, and it's *expediency* relatively to poor Buonaroti.[2] For believe me, De

[1] In 1829, during his residence in England, Prati was imprisoned for debt, and after his release visited his old friend, Filippo Buonarroti, in Brussels. Following the July 1830 Revolution in France, he spent some time there and joined the Society of Friends of the People. He returned to England in 1831. See M. H. Fisch, 'The Coleridges, Dr. Prati, and Vico', *Modern Philology*, Nov. 1943, p. 111.

[2] *The Times* of 29 Oct. 1833 contained a letter from Prati written on the 26th in defence of Filippo Buonarroti (1761–1837), an Italian political agitator. In 1796 Buonarroti took part in the conspiracy of François N. Babeuf against the Directory. Babeuf was executed on 28 May 1797. Buonarroti was exiled. In 1828 Buonarroti published at Brussels his *Conspiration pour l'Égalité, dite de Babeuf*. The work was reviewed by Southey in the *Quarterly Review*, Apr. 1831, pp. 167–209.

Prati's letter in *The Times* reads in part:

Yesterday, when I reached town, on my way to Paris, for the purpose of offering my assistance to F. Buonarroti, I was happy . . . to learn . . . that Buonarroti was released.

The object for which I appealed to the sympathy of the British public having been thus accomplished, I beg all those who have sent any contributions to claim them back. . . . I return my thanks both to the press and the public for the readiness with which they answered my call. The bitterness, however, it met with in some quarters, and the ungenerous misrepresentations of Buonarroti's whole course of life, prove at once the necessity of my acting as a thoroughly devoted friend. . . .

Now that I have fulfilled the duty of a friend, allow me to perform that of an historian. Permit me to ask who is that 'Z.' who assumes the character of accuser and judge of Buonarroti? Of what country is he, and where is the evidence to substantiate his accusation? In what point would Buonarroti

Prati! even those men who out of pure shame must profess to a readiness to forgive him for having *once* entertained such opinions, will be the first to make a merit of withholding all mercy from him, for having *retained* them. *I* think & feel more charitably, because from the very outset I hoped in no advancement of humanity but from individual mind & morals working onward from Individual to Individual—in short, from the *Gospel*—. This in my first work, the Conciones ad Populum, I declared, in my 23rd year: and to this I adhere in my present 63rd. Liberty without Law can exist *no where*: and in nations in a certain state of general information & morality, Law without Liberty is as little possible. But in the state, which France *is*, and which England is becoming, there seems to me an equal incapability of either Law or Liberty.—Therefore, that which some of my Contemporaries denounce in Buonaroti as crazy or criminal Obstinacy in Error, in the face of a guilt-reapt, horror-harvested Experience, I am more disposed, *in this individual Case*, to wonder at & almost admire, as a persistency in Hope, spite of Disappointment, in *Humanity* in despite of *Men*.—You should, I think, have made yourself better acquainted with the detail of the Facts, before you hazarded the assertions respecting Louis Philippe, and his actuation by the Austrian Court—tho' with your remembrances I can scarcely condemn you for any thing worse than impolicy. If I am not deceived in my conjecture respecting the Times 'Correspondent Z', this Mr Izzard, tho' no great Wisard, is a worthy Man & a Lover of the Freedom which alone *You* would call such—but who at Florence believed himself to have learnt facts of Buonaroti's character & habits, which could not, if believed, but have prejudiced him.—But this is a mere conjecture of mine.—

I have (or rather, ought to have) two volumes of your's—Vico's Nuova scienza[1]—but unfortunately I had yielded to the request of a friend & relation, to lend them to him[2]—& he is now in Devonshire

outrun Robespierre? . . . With what view . . . does 'Z.' state that Buonarroti's work was published in France, when it was printed and published at Brussels two years before the revolution of July, 1830? . . .

In bearing my frank testimony to Buonarroti's sincere devotion to the cause of human advancement, I did not intend to eulogize his political system; I have rejected it, as I reject all political systems by which modern publicists have intended to promote the happiness of nations. I have rejected them all, because I consider any form of government vicious and ephemeral which is not the result of a high moral conception, and which requires military power and capital punishment for its support.

[1] Coleridge had received Prati's copy of Vico's work in 1825. See Letter 1457.

[2] In the first edition (1830) of his *Introductions to the Study of the Greek Classic Poets*, a volume mainly devoted to Homer and the only one of a projected series, H. N. Coleridge included a brief notice of the controversy concerning the authorship of Homer. To his second edition (1834) he expanded his

& will not return till the end of November—but I should be most happy to order another Copy for you, if one can be found in London—or any other work, as a quid pro quo—or if you will let me have your address, to remit the former, as soon as I can recover them—

I have, till of late, been a prisoner for nearly 3 years to my Bedroom, and for the far larger portion to my *bed*—hourly praying against the Desire of Death, which thro' constant Pain & *Miserableness* I was unable to suppress—. In this state incapable of attending to any thing extrinsic, I will rely on your forgiving me if I ask—whether or no you returned the Volumes of Lessing's Work which you once took home with you?[1]—If you have, I must account for them as for any other broken set, by my own forgetfulness & confusion.—Mr Gillman has had, but thank God! is greatly recovered from, a severe seizure—a dyspeptic attack almost counterfeiting apoplexy—and dear Mrs Gillman is at this moment confined to her Bed from the shock & bruise of a sudden Fall, her foot catching in a *Ruck* of the Carpet.—

I shall, however, be glad to see you, should Choice or Chance direct your steps Highgate-ward—& to learn what your prospects are—for poor and prospectless myself, except as a Christian, I have not lost the interest of sympathy with my juniors.—Give me a line by return of Post—for I remain with unabated kind wishes your's truly,

S. T. Coleridge

1795. *To John Sterling*

Address: John Stirling, Esqre | Knights Bridge
Readdressed in another hand] Trinity Hall | Cambridge
MS. Professor F. W. Hilles. Pub. wth omis. Letters, ii. 771.
Postmark: 30 October 1833.

Tuesday Night [29 October 1833]
Grove, Highgate

My dear Sir

I very much regret, that I am not to see you again for so many months.[2] Many a fond dream have I amused myself with, of your

account of the Homeric question and added a translation of the third book of Vico's *Scienza Nuova*, 'On the Discovery of the true Homer'.

Coleridge believed in the multiple authorship of the *Iliad*. See *Literary Remains*, i. 262–3; *Robinson on Books and Their Writers*, i. 320–1; *Coleridge the Talker*, ed. R. W. Armour and R. F. Howes, 1940, pp. 181–2 and 336–7; and *Table Talk*, 12 May 1830 and 9 July 1832.

[1] Coleridge's annotated copy of Lessing's *Sämmtliche Schriften*, 30 vols., 1796, is in the British Museum.

[2] In Apr. 1833, as Coleridge wrote to Green on the 25th, Sterling was leaving for Bonn on the Rhine. When the present letter was written, Sterling had

residing near me or in the same house, and of preparing with your & Mr Green's assistance, my whole system for the Press, as far as it exists in writing, in any *systematic* form—that is beginning with the Propyleum, On the Power and Use of Words—comprizing Logic, as the Canons of *Conclusion*; as the criterion of Premises; and lastly, as the Discipline, and Evolution of Ideas—and then the Methodus et Epochae, or the Disqui[si]tion on God, Nature, and Man—the two first great Divisions of which, from the Ens super Ens to the FALL, or from God to Hades; and then from Chaos to the commencement of living Organization—containing the whole scheme of the Dynamic Philosophy, and the Deduction of the Powers & Forces—are complete—as is likewise a third, *composed* for the greater part by Mr Green, on the application of the Ideas, as the *Transcendents* of the Truths, Duties, Affections &c in the Human Mind.—If I could once publish these (but alas! even these could not be compressed in less than three Octavo Volumes), I should then have no objection to print my MSS Papers on positive Theology—from Adam to Abraham—to Moses—the Prophets— Christ—and Christendom.—But this is a Dream! I am, however, very seriously disposed to employ the next two months in preparing for the Press a metrical translation (if I find it practicable) of the Apocalypse,[1] with an introduction on the Use & interpretation of Scriptures—a Prophecy &c—and a *perpetual* illustration, as the Germans say—. I am encouraged to this by finding how much of *Original* remains in my Views, after I have subtracted all that I

not only returned from his visit to the Continent, but as the address shows, he was already at Cambridge, where he had gone to prepare himself to take orders. He was ordained deacon on Trinity Sunday 1834 and served as curate at Hurstmonceaux for eight months.

According to J. C. Hare, Sterling had read Coleridge's *Confessions of an Inquiring Spirit* 'in manuscript with delight and sympathy, had been permitted to transcribe them, and had adopted the views concerning Inspiration expressed in them'. In Oct. 1834 Sara Coleridge wrote to a friend: 'Mr Green has the sole power over my father's literary remains, and the philosophical part he will himself prepare for publication; some theological treatises he has placed in the hands of Mr Julius Hare . . . and his curate, Mr Sterling, (both men of great ability).' In 1840, however, H. N. Coleridge published the *Confessions* 'from the Author's MS.' Sterling had lost his enthusiasm. He thought the book 'very slight & obvious to those familiar with German writers as Coleridge himself was, & the tone of discovery is therefore rather inappropriate'. In the following year he complained that the book was 'full of timidity and equivocation'. See *Essays and Tales, by John Sterling,* ed. with a memoir of his life, J. C. Hare, 2 vols., 1848, i, p. cxxix; *Memoir and Letters of Sara Coleridge,* ed. Edith Coleridge, 2 vols., 1873, i. 111; and Anne K. Tuell, *John Sterling,* 1941, pp. 249–53 and 264–5.

[1] Coleridge had earlier spoken of making such a translation. See his second *Lay Sermon,* 1817, p. 14 n.

have in common with Eichhorn & Heinrichs—I write now to re-
mind you, or to beg you to recall to my Memory, the name of the
more recent work (Lobeck?)[1] which you mentioned to me—&
whether you can procure it for me or rather the Loan of it.—Like-
wise, whether you know of any German Translation & Commentary
on Daniel, that is thought highly of?—I find Gesenius's[2] Version
exceedingly interesting, & look forward to his Commentaries with
delight.—You mentioned some works on the numerical Cabbala,
the Gematria (I think) they call it—But I must not scribble away
your patience—and after I have heard from you, from Cambridge,
I will try to write to you more to the purpose—for I did not begin
this Scrawl, till the hour had past, that ought to have found me in
bed—With sincere regard

Your obliged Friend
S. T. Coleridge

1796. *To Mrs. Charles Aders*

Address: Mrs. Aders, favoured by H. Gillman[3]
Transcript Cornell University Lib. Pub. Letters, ii. 769.

[November 1833 ?]

My dear Mrs Aders

By my idleness or oversight I have occasioned a very sweet
vignette to have been made in vain—except for its own beauty.
Had I sent you the Lines that were to be written on the upright
Tomb, you and our excellent Miss Denman[4] would have first seen
the dimensions requisite for letters of a distinctly visible and
legible size, and secondly, that the homely, plain, *church yard
Christian* Verses would not be in keeping with a Muse (tho' a lovelier
I never wooed), nor with a Lyre, or Harp, or Laurel, or aught else
Parnassian or allegorical. A rude old Yew Tree or a mountain Ash
with a grave or two or any other characteristic of a Village rude
Church-yard—such a hint of a Landscape was all, I meant, but if
any figure rather that of an elderly man

---

[1] C. A. Lobeck (1781–1860), German classical scholar and author of *Aglao-
phamus; sive, de theologiae mysticae Graecorum causis libri tres*, 2 vols., 1829.

[2] H. F. W. Gesenius (1786–1842), German orientalist and biblical critic.
The first volume of his well-known commentary on Isaiah (*Der Prophet
Jesaja*) was published in 1821, but the work was not completed until 1829.

[3] The address is taken from a note by E. H. Coleridge. See *Letters*, ii. 769 n.

[4] At the top of the transcript Mrs. Aders wrote: 'The original of the fol-
lowing letter I have given to Miss Maria Denman—Eliza Aders.' Later the
MS. came into the possession of Arthur Coleridge. See *Arthur Coleridge. Remi-
niscences*, ed. J. A. Fuller-Maitland, 1921, p. 42. The MS. letter has not come
to light.

Thoughtful, with quiet tears upon his cheek.
    (*Tombless Epitaph*—see Sibylline Leaves)

But I send the lines, and you and Miss Denman will form your own opinion.

Is one of Wyville's Proofs[1] of my face worth Mr Aders' acceptance? I wrote under the one I sent to Henry Coleridge this line from Ovid, with the translation thus

    S. T. Coleridge Ætat. suae 63.
    Not / handsome / was / but was / eloquent
    Non formosus erat, sed erat facundus Ulysses.[2]

Translation

    'In truth, he's no beauty!' cry'd Moll, Poll, and Tab,
    But they all of them own'd He'd the gift of the Gab.

My best love to Mr Aders and believe that as I have been, so I ever remain your affectionate and trusting Friend
                                        S. T. Coleridge—

P.S.—*I* like this Tomb stone very much.[3]

The lines when printed would probably have on the preceding page this advertisement

    Epitaph on a Poet little known, yet better known by his [the]
        Initials of his Name than by the Name itself.

                    S. T. C.

    Stop, Christian Passer by! stop, Child of God!
    And read with gentle heart. Beneath this sod

---

[1] Coleridge refers to a half-length drawing by Abraham Wivell (1786–1849). An engraving of this drawing made by T. B. Welch appears as the frontispiece in *The Works of Samuel Taylor Coleridge, Prose and Verse*, Philadelphia, 1840; a second engraving by J. F. E. Prudhomme forms the frontispiece of vol. i of *The Complete Works of Samuel Taylor Coleridge*, ed. W. G. T. Shedd, 7 vols., 1853.   [2] Ovid, *Ars Amatoria*, ii. 123.

[3] According to E. H. Coleridge, the present letter 'refers to the new edition of his poetical works which Coleridge had begun to see through the press. Apparently he had intended that the "Epitaph" should be inscribed on the outline of a headstone, and that this should illustrate, by way of vignette, the last page of the volume'. (*Letters*, ii. 769 n.) In the *Poetical Works*, 1834, however, the poem appears without any illustration. See also *Poems*, i. 491 n,

A Poet lies: or that, which once seemed He.
O lift one thought in Prayer for S. T. C.
That He, who many a year with toilsome breath
Found Death in Life, may here find Life in Death.
Mercy for praise—*to be forgiven* for Fame
He ask'd, and hoped thro' Christ. Do Thou the same.

1797. *To J. H. Green*

Address: J. H. Green, Esqre | &c &c | 46. Lincoln's Inn Fields
MS. Pierpont Morgan Lib. Hitherto unpublished.
Postmark: 4 November 1833.

Sunday Night. [3 November 1833]

My dear Friend

Would it, think you, justify the expence, to purchase from the Bible Society (the *Church* Bible Society) a *Quarto* Bible with the Apocrypha between the Old and New Testament—in sheets: and to have them half-bound in three or four Volumes interleaved?— I am almost heartless, when I cast on me [my eye ?] on my wilderness of Scraps, and Booklets little better, or less volatile & fugitive. If I had such a Book, I certainly would begin the New Year (God prolonging my life & vouchsafing competent Health) with the first of Genesis, and make a point of reading one or more chapters every night—so that I might hope at the end of the year to have left behind some 3 or 400 Chapters, corrected according to my best judgement, aided by the best recent German Versions—and on important points availing myself of Hurwitz's Aid as to Original Text—while longer Notes I could write in a separate Book, carefully paged—and thus referred to in the interleaves of the Bible.—

If the thing strikes you, as desirable in itself, & plausible in the chance of it's execution—would you make some enquiry, as to what the expence would be, Copy, interleaving and binding?—

I was sorry not to have intercepted you before you left the House—so as to have learnt what you thought of Mrs Gillman. I am very low & disquieted about her—& Mr Gillman seems to apprehend some injury beyond the Bruise on the Cap & ball of the Knee—& Mr Tottill[1] a wrench of the Pelvis.—I pray fervently that God in his Mercy will suffer this cloud to pass from over us.—

My kind Love & Respects to Mrs Green and your honored

Mother.—

S. T. Coleridge

[1] A reference to G. L. Tuthill. See Letter 927.

1798. *To John Sterling*

Address: John Stirling, Esqre | Trinity Hall | Cambridge
MS. Indiana University Lib. Hitherto unpublished.
Postmark: 4 November 1833.

Monday, 4 Novr. 1833.

My dear Sir

I had sate down to write a letter to you—but a Visitor with certain claims upon me has arrived, and as I am not certain whether he will leave me in time for the Post, I must amerce you in a shilling extra—for I cannot leave even for a single post the arrival of the Valuable Books from Cambridge, or my sense of your and Mr Thirlwall's[1] kindness unacknowleged—But for my letter you must wait till Wednesday—

May God bless you | and
S. T. Coleridge

1799. *To J. G. Lockhart*

Address: J. S. Lockhart, Esqre | 24 Sussex Place | Regent's Park.
MS. British Museum. Hitherto unpublished.
Postmark: Highgate, 6 November 1833.

[5 November 1833]

My dear Sir

To shame the Devil is so good a thing, that one ought not to think it dear tho' at the cost of a Blush or two on one's own face— a sort of tender suffusion by reflection from the crimsoning Soot of the old Enemy's Visage—such as the youthful St Dunstan's from the glow of the red-hot Pincers, in a picture by Schalken, or Elsheimer.—[2]

I had promised a reverend Friend, who answers to the unlucky twy-bestial name of Cattermole, the not unlaurreled [*sic*] Secretary of that Royal Society of Literature, of which I, alas! *was* a Royal Associate, every year fastened anew to that great Pillar of British Mecaenatism by an aurea catena of a hundred Links, weighing collectively 105£ (n.b. pounds *sterling*) till the Fitz-clarences stole it with nine others in order to emblazon *d'or* the black cross Bar on their paternal Coat of Arms—tho' methinks, the sinister Unicorn,

---

[1] Connop Thirlwall (1797–1875), historian, became bishop of St. David's in 1840. On his return from Cambridge in June 1833, Coleridge spoke 'with the greatest interest' of Faraday and Thirlwall. See *Table Talk*, 29 June 1833. See also *Conversations at Cambridge* [by R. A. Willmott], 1836, pp. 1–36, for an account of Coleridge's conversation 'under the clock at Trinity . . . [in] Mr. Thirlwall's Rooms'.

[2] St. Lawrence not St. Dunstan was burned alive. Adam Elsheimer (1574– 1620) painted the *Martyrdom of St. Lawrence*.

copper-gilt, might have sufficed to emblem the monstrum hybridum, Bastardy—excuse this digressive 'sfogarsi', quamdam eructatiun-culam irae—well, I had promised Felis Mustyphlu[s] to look over a Mss of his, and to return it by a certain day—which thro' indis-position of two kinds, I had suffered to elapse, and a week of days besides, re infectâ.—At length, came a Letter which partly from the confusion of an upbraiding Conscience, and in part from the actual great resemblance of the hand-writing and the formation of the folding, I took for granted to be from Mr Cattermole. It might have lain on the table before me for some half-hour, while I was screwing up my nerves to the opening it, when, lo! Mr C. himself was announced. I hastily put the letter in my pocket—and with an—O my dear Cattermole! how sorry I am, that my procrastina-tion should have given you this trouble &c &c—an hour or two passed, while I looked thro' the Mss with him—and he left with my mind quite disburthened of the concern, letter included. But this morning, Nov. 5, which looks as grim and gloomy as Guy Fawx himself could have done, my Camerina, Harriet, took down my clothes to brush; and when I rose to my Noon Breakfast, which is likewise my Dinner, the Letter, which with other ignoble papers she had dispocketed, lay again on my table—& heaven knows! without the slightest intention of reading it, but only because so many old Letters with unbroken seals have an *idle* Look, and in fact have brought disrepute on me, I broke open the seal, and meaning to throw it into the fire just unfolded the Note contained—which I have made a point of doing, since my misfortune of throwing one with a 5£ note in it—and so caught '24, Sussex Place, Regent's Park'.—

And now, my dear Sir! I can only say that I regret this: but that if Mr Millman be still in town, & it be not too late, I shall be happy to meet him on any day, you & Mrs L. may appoint—and should choice or chance direct him Highgate-ward, on any day from 12 to 10 at night, shall think myself honored by a Call from him—

Dear Mrs Gillman has met a most unhappy Fall; and tho' there is neither dislocation or fracture of Hip, or Thigh, yet such was the Bruise & I *fear* the Wrench, especially in the Cap and Ball of the Knee, as to ensure a long confinement to Bed or Sopha. May God of his mercy grant, that this heavy Cloud may pass from over us! For need I tell you, that She is the Life, Love, and sanctifying Spirit of this House-hold—yea, I might say & with truth, of this Neighbor-hood.—

Henry N. Coleridge thought so highly of the grace and metrical movement of a little poem, which will with 4 or 5 other scraps appear in the *Friendship's Offering* (an Annual edited by my friend,

Pringle), that I am encouraged to inclose a corrected Copy of it, for Mrs Lockhart—if she finds it legible[1]—& to leave as little blank space as possible, I add an Epitaph on a Writer better known by the Initials of his Name, than by the name itself.—Suppose an upright Tombstone—

S. T. C.

Stop, Christian Passer-by! stop, Child of God!
And read with gentle heart. Beneath this sod
A Poet lies: or that which once seem'd He.
O lift one thought in prayer for S. T. C.
That he who many a year with toil of Breath
Found Death in Life, may here find Life in Death.
Mercy for[2] Praise, to be forgiven for Fame,
He ask'd, and hoped thro' Christ. Do Thou the Same.

ἔστη. κεῖται. ἀναστήσει.
Stetit: restat:resurget.
ΕΣΤΗΣΕ

With affectionate respect to Mrs Lockhart, and my blessing on Walter & his Sister believe me, my dear Sir,

Your's sincerely
S. T. Coleridge.

1800. *To E. F. Finden*[3]

Address: W. T. E. Finden, Esqr | 11. Southampton Place | Euston Square
MS. Mr. W. Hugh Peal. Pub. E. L. G. ii. 454.
Postmark: Highgate, 7 November 1833.

6 Novr 1833.

Mr S. T. Coleridge presents his respects to Mr Finden.
There are two pen or pencil Drawings of him at Highgate, the one (& in point of something like expression, the best) taken off hand, some 15 years ago, by Mr Lesly[4]—another, done very recently,

---

[1] The MS. letter in the British Museum originally included an additional page now in the Cornell University Library. The recto of this page contains lines 4 and 7–17 of *Love's Apparition and Evanishment*, the verso the address and postmark.

[2] N.b.–'for' in the sense of 'instead of'.—[Note by S. T. C.]

[3] This letter was intended for Edward Francis Finden (1791–1857). Lamb had recently written to Coleridge: 'Mr. Finden, an artist of some celebrity, is desirous of publishing an Engraving of you . . . can you lend him your head?' *Lamb Letters*, iii. 389. Finden's engraving of Thomas Phillips's portrait of Coleridge forms the frontispiece of the second edition of *Table Talk*, 1836.

[4] A reference to C. R. Leslie's drawing of Coleridge made in 1818 and now in the possession of Mr. A. H. B. Coleridge. See Letters 1147 and 1184. Leslie's drawing is reproduced as a frontispiece to vol. v of the present edition.

by a young German Artist[1]—a Likeness, certainly; but with such unhappy Density of the Nose & ideotic Drooping of the Lip, with a certain pervading *Wooden[n]ess* of the whole Countenance, that it has not been thought guilty of any great Flattery by Mr Coleridge's Friends.—Such, as they are, however, either is at Mr Finden's Service—or perhaps, the Artist may be induced to see them—& to select one or the other—& judge, whether the defects of the later portrait may not be removed.

Mr S. T. C. will be found at home, 'the Grove, Highgate' any day, *after 1* o'clock. His ill health does not permit him to mention an earlier hour.—A Friend of S. T. Coleridge's wrote under a portrait of him—'A glow-worm with a pin stuck thro' it, as seen in broad day-light.'—

1801. *To Sara Coleridge*

MS. Mr. A. H. B. Coleridge. Pub. Coleridge Fille, *by E. L. Griggs, 1940, p. 68.*

[November 1833]

My dearest Sara—Night after night has my last and most fervent prayer been that of humble Intercession for you & for my other suffering Friend, Mrs Gillman.[2]—I thank God who has thus far given ear to my Prayers, and trust in his Mercy—Your affectionate Father

S. T. Coleridge

1802. *To Henry Nelson Coleridge*

Address: H. N. Coleridge, Esqre
MS. Victoria University Lib. Hitherto unpublished.

[Early December 1833][3]

My dear Henry

Yesterday I awoke virtuously resolved to devote the few hours, that constitute my day, to the tossing over *of papers*—when lo! just after 12 came the Revd Mr——distressed on some points of

---

[1] The pencil sketch of Coleridge by J. Kayser is dated 1833. See Coleridge's poem, *To the Young Artist, Kayser of Kaserwerth* [Kaiserswerth], *Poems*, i. 490.

[2] Not only had Sara Coleridge been seriously ill, but Mrs. Gillman had suffered a severe fall in Oct. 1833. See *Minnow among Tritons*, ed. Stephen Potter, 1934, pp. 174–8, and Letters 1763, 1779, 1794, 1797, and 1799.

Early in 1834 Sara Coleridge gave birth to twins, both of whom died on 16 Jan. 1834. H. N. Coleridge's lines, *On Berkeley and Florence Coleridge*, were included in Coleridge's *Poetical Works*, 1834, ii. 149.

[3] This letter was probably written shortly after H. N. Coleridge returned from Devonshire at 'the end of November' 1833. See Letters 1789 and 1794.

*From a pencil sketch of Samuel Taylor Coleridge drawn by J. Kayser in 1833
and now in the possession of Mr. A. H. B. Coleridge*

Faith—& detained me in bed till 3—On the point of going, he was supplied by the Reverends Cattermole and Stebbing[1]—& in short, I was quite exhausted—This morning again, just as I was preparing for work, came Mr D. Stuart, & his Daughter.—In short, I will do what I can—but do not let my doings or no doings interfere with the Progress of Pickering—The *first* Poem, you inclose, was *Southey's*—the second certainly not mine.—Neither has the least resemblance to my mind—tho' the first I always liked—

S. T. Coleridge

I promise myself, that I shall write to you in a day or two—

1803. *To Dinah Knowe*[2]

Address: Mrs | Dinah Noe
MS. Mr. W. Hugh Peal. Pub. The Gillmans of Highgate, *by A. W. Gillman, 1895, p. 20C.* This MS. is badly torn.

January the first, 1834.

I have it not in my power, nor [i]s it within my Means, t[o] offer any thing fit to be called [a] New Year's Gift; but [I hope], that Dinah Noe will accept the inclosed trifle,[3] as an [ac]knowlegement of her late dutiful and affectionate Attentions to Mr Gillman during his Illness; and no less to her dear Mistress, the best of Good Women, Mrs Gillman—from Mr & Mrs Gillman's Friend & House-mate

S. T. Coleridge

1804. *To Henry Nelson Coleridge*

MS. Mr. Robert H. Taylor. Hitherto unpublished.

Saturday Night [4 January 1834][4]

My dear Henry

I forgot to do what I had intended to do, in case you called on me,—viz. to beg you to give my thanks and gratulations to my

---

[1] Henry Stebbing (1799–1883), poet, preacher, and historian. In collaboration with Richard Cattermole, Stebbing edited the *Sacred Classics, or Select Library of Divinity*, 30 vols., 1834–6.

[2] Dinah Knowe, for many years a faithful 'Maid and Janitress' in the Gillman household and the wife of Gillman's coachman. See Letter 1323 and A. W. Gillman, op. cit., p. 20 c.

[3] 'Three guineas', according to Mrs. Lucy E. Watson. *Coleridge at Highgate*, 1925, p. 8 n.

[4] The present letter refers to a New Series of the *Gentleman's Magazine*, the first number of which was issued on 1 Jan. 1834. William Pickering and John Bowyer Nichols were the co-proprietors.

poetic Publisher, Mr Pickle-herring,[1] on the resuscitation of
SYLVANUS URBAN.[2] Tell him from me, that the improved Form &
Look of the Work do him *credit*—that the first three Articles are
cheering pledges of a new life in a venerable Body—that if he or the
Editor[3] will rigorously maintain the great merit of the Gentleman's
Magazine—viz—freedom from all *faction, love* even to *dotage* of the
Past, delight in all, that is capable of *becoming* an abiding past;
& the *judicia* even with the amiable *Pre*judices of an English
GENTLEMAN, Scholar, and of whoever *intelligently* drinks, 'CHURCH
& KING'; the Magazine will assuredly reassume it's old *Primatecy*.—
But had PICKLE-HERRING any influence on the literary manage-
ment of the Work, I would suggest the seeking out of a *learned*, a
truly *Old-book Elizabethian & James the first* Scholar, or Scholars,
for the Reviewer—I would strongly recommend the keeping up of
the love of Antiquity in all points, *in men & Volumes*, as well as in
seats & Buildings—and a recurrence (as in the *old* Volumes of the
G. M. when your Grandfather, the Revd John Coleridge, wrote in
it)[4] to learned Criticism, and to the Biography of the middle age &
the Restoration of Literature—Hugo de St Victore,[5] Ambrosius,
Petrarch &c &c &c. Keep *clear* from every vulgarism of the Day—
& I dare answer for the culmination of Pickle-herring's Gent.
Mag. . . . [Remainder of manuscript missing.]

---

[1] Throughout the MS. Coleridge's 'Pickle-herring' has been altered to
'Pickering'.

[2] In 1731 Edward Cave (1691–1754) founded the *Gentleman's Magazine*,
which he edited under the pseudonym 'Silvanus Urban, Gent.'

[3] John Mitford (1781–1859), editor of the *Gentleman's Magazine*, 1834–50.

[4] The Rev. John Coleridge (1719–81) 'occasionally sent letters on scholas-
tic points connected with Biblical lore to the *Gentleman's Magazine*, whose
editor described him as "our ingenious contributor" '. See Lord Coleridge, *The
Story of a Devonshire House*, 1905, p. 14.

[5] 'Hugo de Saint Victor, Luther's favourite divine, was a wonderful man,
who, in the 12th century, the jubilant age of papal dominion, nursed the
lamp of Platonic mysticism in the spirit of the most refined Christianity.'
Table Talk, 25 May 1832. According to J. L. Haney, a copy of Hugh of St.
Victor's *De Sacramentis Christianae Fidei*, 1485, bears this inscription: 'This
rare and intrinsically valuable volume was presented to me, S. T. Coleridge,
by my friend, the Revd. Edward Irving, 3 July, 1829. Grove, Highgate.'
See *Coleridge*, ed. E. Blunden and E. L. Griggs, 1934, pp. 118–19.

1805. *To J. H. Green*

Address: Professor (J. H.) Green | &c &c | 46. Lincoln's Inn Fields.
MS. Pierpont Morgan Lib. Pub. E. L. G. ii. 454.
Postmark: Highgate, 18 March 1834.

Grove, Highgate
[17] March 1834

My dearest Friend

This night, Monday, 9 o'clock Harriet noticed a peculiar red streak or splash, running from my left eye, which had been for many days at morn and night *weepy* and *weak*, down the cheek along by that old tumor of my left cheek, which I date from the Top of the Brocken, Hartz, Midsummer Midnight, 1800—or 1799, I forget which.—I have been this whole day unwell—& with my old duodenal umbilical uneasiness while I lay in bed, & when I got up, sick & wind-strangled.—As soon as Harriet noticed the red streak, I immediately felt by the application of my finger a sensible difference of Heat between that [and] the corresponding part near the other Ear—& sent for Mr Taylor[1]— who deems it a slight Erysipylas, or ERISYPALOTÖID ERYTHEMA—the very thing that carried off my Acquaintance-friend, Sir George Beaumont, who had likewise the same tumour, in nape of the neck & below the chin, in 5 days from it's first very unalarming appearance—Now as I should like to see you before I went, if to go I am—& leave with you, the sole Depositarium of my Mind & Aspirations, what God may suggest to me—therefore, if you can, come to me during the week.

S. T. Coleridge

1806. *To Henry Nelson Coleridge*

MS. Victoria University Lib. Pub. with omis. Table Talk, *1835, ii. 224 n. and 306 n.* This letter is written in the fly-leaves of a copy of Francis Bond Head's *Bubbles from the Brunnens of Nassau, by an Old Man,* 1834. The volume, which was published by John Murray, is inscribed, 'Mrs H. N. Coleridge From the Publisher'.

18 March, 1834.
Grove, Highgate

My dear Henry

I, the most incurious of all sensitive animals, do feel very curious to know, who is the Writer of this Book.[2]—The strange discrepancy

---

[1] Gillman's assistant. See *Coleridge,* ed. E. Blunden and E. L. Griggs, 1934, p. 227.

[2] The following sentence from a paragraph included under the date, 16 Apr. 1834, in the first edition of *Table Talk* (1835) shows that Coleridge soon had his curiosity satisfied concerning the authorship of *Bubbles*:

of his account of the *Maltese* with my own recollections startled me.
Had he been speaking of the *Messinese*, I should have recognized
the truth to the Hair of a Cheek-Mole!—But this variation of mine
& the other 'Old Man's' recollections is a trifle. But how can I
account for the Anglo-gentlemanly, the sensible & kindly mind
breaking forth every where in the first half of the Volume, as con-
trasted with the strange, *one-sided* representation of our public
Schools—which, with full admission on *my* part of their Defects, or
rather *Deficiencies*, or still better, their *Paucities*, amounts to a
double Lie, a Lie by exaggeration, and a Lie by *Omission*—And [of]
the Universities—even relatively to Oxford 30 years ago it would
have been Slander—to Cambridge, as it now is, blasphemy!—And
then his absurd attribution of the National Debt of 800 millions, to
the predominance of *Classical* Taste, and Academic Talent! And
his strange ignorance that without the rapidly increasing National
Debt Great Britain could never have become that mo[n]strous
Mammon-bloated *Dives*, or Woden-Idol of stuffed Pursemen, *part*
of whose unrighteous Wealth this Debt constitutes!!

But what can Sir Francis Head, in the 'Bubbles', mean by talking of the
musical turn of the Maltese?

To Coleridge's mention of Head's 'Bubbles', H. N. Coleridge appended a foot-
note beginning, 'I have the following note by Mr. C. on this work'. He then
printed (with changes) the first two paragraphs of the present letter, beginning
with the words, 'How can I account for the Anglo-gentlemanly', etc. He also
added a caustic comment of his own:

Perhaps if the author of the 'Bubbles' had not *finished his classical studies at
fourteen*, he might have seen reason to modify his heavy censure on Greek
and Latin. As it is, it must be borne with patience.—Ed.

After reading the critical comments in *Table Talk*, F. B. Head on 29 Aug.
1835 sent H. N. Coleridge an angry letter calling his attention to the statements
in the footnote 'signed by yourself'. The letter concludes:

I will not occupy your time by expressing to you astonishment that your
Uncle should have discovered Slander and blasphemy in my bubbles, that
he should have affixed the same to me by name, altho' *my* work was pub-
lished anonymously, and that having done this in a private note, you should
deliberately have thought it adviseable to print and publish it.
    However early I may have left my school I was there long enough to learn
that no person should allow an inoffensive statement to be termed '*a double
lie*', a lie by exaggeration and a lie by omission, and I have therefore requested
my friend Major Wells to deliver to you this letter with a request that you
will be so good as to render me that written apology, which I am sure you
will be sensible is only my due.

H. N. Coleridge immediately sent an elaborate apology for publishing the
passage from Coleridge's letter and promised to withdraw it 'at the earliest
opportunity in my power'. When the second edition of *Table Talk* appeared in
1836, the paragraph containing the reference to Head and his *Bubbles* and the
appended footnote were omitted from the entry for 16 Apr. 1834.

In short, at one moment I imagine that Mr Frere, or you, or any other Etonian, or Alumnus of Westminster or Winchester, might be the Author—at another, fall back to Joseph Hume, Dr Birkbeck,[1] Edingburgh or Aberdeen.

S. T. C.—

Do ask Lockhart, if it may be dared.

One constant blunder of these New-broomers (or Broughamers)— these Penny Magazine Sages and Philanthropists,* in reference to our Public Schools, is to confine their view to what the School-Masters teach the Boys, with entire oversight of all, that the Boys are excited to learn from each other, and of themselves—with more geniality, even *because* it is *not* a part of their compelled school Knowlege.—An Etonian of 15's knowlege of the St Lawrence, Mississippi, Missouri, Orellana &c &c will be, generally, found in exact proportion to his knowlege of Issus, Ilissus, Hebrus, &c— as modern Travels & Voyages are more entertaining & fascinating than Cellarius[2]—or Robinson Crusoe, Dampier, & Captn Cook than the Periegesis.[3] Compare the *Lads* themselves from Eton &c with the alumni of the New-broom Institutions, & not the lists of School-lessons: & be that the Criterion![4]—*S. T. C.*

---

[1] George Birkbeck, M.D. (1776–1841), founder of the Glasgow and the London Mechanics' Institutions in 1823 and 1824.

* That variety who prescribe solitary imprisonment for Burglary, Highway-robbery &c might be distinguished as Felon-trappists: & these again distinguished from the humane Philleantists, who plant man-gins, spring-guns &c in their grounds, by naming the latter *Villain trap*ists—the 'Villain' interpreted midway between the original *Villan*us, = peasant, & the modern *product* or hominifact of our peasantry—ex. gr. Poachers, or Cottage Boys a nutting or Orchard-robbing—which latter, any where within 10 miles of the Metropolis, & 5 of any large Town, is to be excepted from the 8th Commandment for all males & females not 14 years *old. S. T. C.*

[2] Christoph Cellarius (1638–1707), author of numerous works on ancient history and geography.

[3] A description of the habitable world written in Greek hexameters by Dionysius Periegetes.

[4] This paragraph was included in the first edition of *Table Talk* as a footnote to an entry dated 8 July 1833. H. N. Coleridge retained the quotation in the second edition of *Table Talk*, 1836, but his statement that it was 'pencilled by Mr. C. on a blank page of my copy of the "Bubbles from the Brunnens"' was amended to read, 'pencilled by Mr. C. on a margin'.

1807. *To Henry Nelson Coleridge*

Address: H. N. Coleridge, Esqre
MS. Victoria University Lib. Hitherto unpublished.

My dear Henry   [March 1834][1]
It was no illness, but an accident of *Forget* divided between me
and Ramsgatina—i.e. our Mary from Ramsgate.

I have only the MSS German Wallenstein[2]—and am doubtful
whether I have or have not Schiller's Poems; and if I have, in how
many days I might be lucky enough to turn up the Needles in the
Hay-loft. But I doubt not, that from Mr Green you can have both.
I send back the Lewis[3]—I have been exceedingly amused likewise
with Peter Simple.[4]—

How *could* the latter third of the 'Bubbles' have been of the
same Author with the first two thirds?

Your last sentence has fallen like Lead or cold water on my heart.

I am not up—so excuse this ragged Bob-tag of a Note—

                                                Bless you &
                                                    S. T. C.

Did I give you the accompanying Lines—are they worth publishing?

Item—would there be any objection to those vigorous Lines on
Milner & Butler with the motto 'Facit indignatio versus'[5] those I
mean, on occasion of Butler's assent to the Calumnious Abuse of
Blanco White?[6]

[1] The reference to *Bubbles* suggests that this and the preceding letter were
written about the same time.

[2] For a discussion of these MSS. see Walter Grossmann, 'The Gillman-
Harvard Manuscript of Schiller's *Wallensteins Tod*', *Harvard Library Bulletin*,
Autumn 1957, pp. 319–45, and *Poems*, ii. 598 n.

[3] Coleridge refers to M. G. Lewis's *Journal of a West Indian Proprietor*,
1834. See *Table Talk*, 20 Mar. 1834.

[4] F. Marryat, *Peter Simple*, 3 vols., 1834. See *Table Talk*, 5 Mar. 1834.

[5] Cf. Juvenal, i. 79.

[6] In Coleridge's *Poetical Works*, 1834, ii. 80, the names of Milner (John
Milner, 1752–1826, bishop of Castabala and vicar-apostolic of the western
district of England) and Butler (Charles Butler, 1750–1832, Roman Catholic
lawyer) are left blank, and the poem is entitled *Sancti Dominici Pallium; a
Dialogue between Poet and Friend, found written on the blank leaf at the beginning
of Butler's Book of the Church*. (A reference to Charles Butler's *Vindication of
'The Book of the Roman Catholic Church'*, 1826.) The 'Calumnious Abuse' of
White to which Coleridge refers took place at a meeting of the British Catholic
Association and is commented on at length in Blanco White's *Letter to Charles
Butler, Esq. on his Notice of the 'Practical and Internal Evidence against Catho-
licism'*, 1826. Indeed, it was his reading of this *Letter* which led Coleridge to
compose his poem in June 1826. See Letters 1569 and 1607.

Milner's death occurred on 19 Apr. 1826, and in publishing the poem in
the *Standard* and the *St. James Chronicle* in May 1827, Coleridge added the

1808. *To William Pickering*

Address: Mr Pickering | Publisher | Chancery Lane
MS. Cornell University Lib. Hitherto unpublished.

8 April 1834
Grove, Highgate

Dear Sir

Be so good as to let Master Edward Parry, the Bearer, a young Brother Blue-coat of mine, have the second and third Volumes of my Poems as soon as they come out:[1] and place them to the account of your

obliged

S. T. Coleridge

To Mr W. Pickering.—

following note to Milner's name, possibly because he wished to avoid giving the appearance of a personal attack on a man who had recently died: 'These lines were written before this Prelate's decease.' A note added in a manuscript copy of the poem is more explicit:

Tho' unnecessary, I trust, for those who know the Author, it may be hereafter proved expedient, to state that these Lines were written before Dr Milner's Death. Dr M. survives in his Publications: and it was these, as personified under the Name of their Author, that the Poet had alone in his contemplation.

[1] The three volumes of Coleridge's *Poetical Works* of 1834 were published separately, but all were issued before 25 July, the date of the poet's death. According to the *Literary Gazette* (p. 231), the first volume was published on 29 Mar. Volumes i and ii were reviewed in the same periodical on 17 May. The publication of the third volume was delayed until July. It was listed among the 'New Books' in the *Literary Gazette* on 19 July. H. N. Coleridge reviewed all three volumes in the *Quarterly Review* for Aug. 1834, pp. 1–38. A note inserted at the end of the issue of the *Quarterly* (p. 291) shows that the review was printed prior to Coleridge's death: 'It is with deep regret that we announce the death of Mr. COLERIDGE. When the foregoing article on his poetry was printed, he was weak in body, but exhibited no obvious symptoms of so near a dissolution.'

The *Poetical Works* of 1834 contained all of the poems published in 1829 and numerous additional poems, the larger number of which had not previously been published. Two poems by J. H. Green and one by H. N. Coleridge were also included. This edition had been under way since 1832, and, as Coleridge's letters suggest, was carried forward mainly through the efforts of H. N. Coleridge. Coleridge, however, took an active hand in its preparation, and, as was his custom, made corrections and alterations in the text of many of the poems. Turnbull, for example, lists twenty-three poems of which the text differs in the editions of 1829 and 1834. Likewise, E. H. Coleridge points out that Coleridge 'altered and emended the text of 1829, with a view to the forthcoming edition of 1834', and draws attention to the changes appearing in the 1834 text of *The Destiny of Nations, Songs of the Pixies*, and *Christabel*. However much, therefore, H. N. Coleridge may have contributed by collecting materials, by prodding his uncle, and by seeing the volumes through the press, the fact remains that Coleridge himself was responsible for the text of his *Poetical Works* of 1834. See Letters 1757, 1796, 1802, and 1807; Campbell, *Poetical Works*, 555; *Biographia Epistolaris*, ed. A. Turnbull, 2 vols., 1911, ii. 297 and 324; and *Poems*, i. pp. iii–iv and viii, and vol. ii, pp. 1161–6.

1809. *To Thomas Hurst*

Pub. Letters Hitherto Uncollected, *58.*

Tuesday, April 9th [8th], 1834.

My dear Sir,—Mr. Gillman tells me that he delivered to me, I know not how long ago, a letter from you respecting the *Aids to Reflection,* and, therefore, though I have no recollection of it, I doubt not it was so; for my memory, never of the strongest, has through long illness and accumulated indisposition, become pitiably intenacious; the memory indeed being a plant that has its root and trunk in the body, especially the stomach and bowels, though its branches and blossoms are in the head. However, better late than never.

I hereby authorise you to dispose of my share of the edition of the *Aids to Reflection,* and of the Essay on *The Constitution of the Church and the State, According to the Idea,* as your own judgment may direct.[1] For I can truly say, that though not worth a shilling of my own in the world since King William the Fourth took my poor gold chain of a hundred links—one hundred pounds—with those of nine other literary veterans, to emblazon d'or the black bar across the Royal arms of the Fitzclarences,[2] I would yet rather lose ten times a hundred pounds than ever suspect you of an unkind act towards

Your very sincere friend,
S. T. Coleridge

---

[1] After going into bankruptcy in 1826, Thomas Hurst 'made two or three efforts to regain credit and business', among them the partnership with Chance, which was dissolved in 1831. Ultimately he 'was reduced to the mortifying state of seeking an asylum for old age, as an inmate, and dependant on the charity of the Charter House, in which he died in the year 1850'. See Letters 1540 and 1720, and *Auto-Biography of John Britton,* 2 vols., 1850, i. 210 n.

[2] In a letter to her brother Hartley written on 5 Aug. 1834, not long after her father's death, Sara Coleridge says: 'A week before his [Coleridge's] illness Mr. Cattermole had announced to him that his pension was to be continued from last April.' (*Coleridge,* ed. E. Blunden and E. L. Griggs, 1934, p. 228.) The files of the Royal Society of Literature do not, however, contain any record of such a proposal. Cattermole may have referred to a civil list pension such as those received by Sharon Turner (1835) and James Millingen, both former Royal Associates. Coleridge, however, received no such pension. See headnote to Letter 1707.

1810. *To the Court of Assistants of the Worshipful Company*
of Haberdashers

MS. New York Public Lib. Pub. E. L. G. ii. 455.

Grove, Highgate
27 May, 1834

Gentlemen

The Living of Leiston in your presentation is vacant: and one of
the Candidates is the Reverend James Gillman, Fellow of St John's
College, Oxford.[1] Among the weightier Testimonials and from
higher Authority, which he will, doubtless, lay before you, con-
descend to accept that of the humble Individual, whose Name is
subscribed, and who at an advanced age writes from a Bed of Sick-
ness under convictions, that subordinate every worldly motive and
predilection to more aweful Interests.

I have known the Revd James Gillman from his Childhood, as
having been from that time to this a trusted Inmate of the House-
hold of his dear and exemplary Parents. I have followed his pro-
gress at weekly Intervals from his entrance into the Merchants'
Taylors' School, and traced his continued improvements under the
excellent Mr Bellamy to his Removal, as Head Scholar, to St John's
College: and during his academic Career his Vacations were in the
main passed under my eye. I was myself educated for the Church at
Christ's Hospital, and sent from that honored and unique Institu-
tion to Jesus College, Cambridge, under the tutorage and discipline
of the Revd James Bowyer who has left an honored name in the
Church for the zeal and ability with which he formed and trained
his Orphan Pupils to the Sacred Ministry, as Scholars, as Readers,
as Preachers, and as sound Interpreters of the Word. May I add,
that I was the Junior School-fellow in the next place, the Protégé,
and the Friend of the late venerated Dr Middleton, the first Bishop
of Calcutta. And assuredly whatever under such Training and such
Influence *I* learnt, or thro' a long life mainly devoted to Scriptural,
Theological and Ecclesiastical Studies, I have been permitted to
attain, I have been anxious to communicate to the Son of my
dearest Friends, with little less than paternal solicitude. And at all
events I dare attest, that the Revd James Gillman is pure and
blameless in morals, and unexceptionable in manners—equally
impressed with the importance of the Pastoral Duties as of the

---

[1] James Gillman failed to obtain the living at Leiston. In 1836, however, he
was presented by St. John's College, Oxford, with the living at Barfreston,
Kent. See A. W. Gillman, *The Gillmans of Highgate*, 1895, p. 29.

Labors in the Desk and the Pulpit: and that his mind is made up to preach the *whole* truth in Christ.

Accept, Gentlemen! the unfeigned Respects of your aged humble Servant,   S. T. Coleridge

1811. *To Eliza Nixon*

Transcript Coleridge family. Hitherto unpublished.

June 7th 1834—
From my Bed of Pain—

My dear Eliza

I was about to send you my kindest love & Regard by Mr Elliot—but recollected that the Words might not come with as much propriety *through* his juvenile mouth, as *from* that of the grey-haired Poet, your poor infirm Cripple of a Friend—but whose affection for you is the exact reverse of his Body, for the *older* it is— the stronger it becomes—The two last Vols. of Love & Pride[1] have lingered on the table by my sick-bed side, read by me 4 or 5 pages at a time, as my weakness permitted, which did not permit me to read any thing of more serious interest—& yet I wanted something to call off my attention from my own uneasy Sensations—From my Youth upward the most unpleasant if not the most worthless Object of direct Thought has ever been my individual Self—and to be forced in upon my*self*, to be compelled to think about myself, I regard among the saddest aggravations of Sickness—I write now to re- quest you to take on yourselves the Time that the two Vols. have been detained, beyond what was assigned to this Household—And yet the Work is worth your ordering it for a second reading—if I have not left you time for its first sojourn with you—

Believe me, my dear Eliza, | Most sincerely your Friend
S. T. Coleridge—

1812. *To Eliza Nixon*

Transcript Coleridge family. Pub. E. L. G. ii. 457.

June 14th—1834

Thanks, dear Eliza, for your sweet flowers so Van Huysum-like arranged—But warmer thanks and from deeper down in the Heart for your far sweeter letter—That my Sense is from illness become obtuse to the *fragrance* of Flowers, I but little regret, but O! let my eyes be closed when their *Beauty* is no longer revealed to me—& finds no counterpart in my mind[2]—

---

[1] Theodore E. Hook, *Love and Pride*, 3 vols., 1833.

[2] For Coleridge's poetic tributes to Eliza Nixon see *Poems*, ii. 1009–10.

1813. *To Eliza Nixon*[1]

Pub. Catalogue of Sotheby and Co.

[June 1834 ?]

Once on a time, I beheld a flower of late Summer, the fairest Daughter that ever Late Summer brought forth: and I saw a large Dewdrop fall on her; on this fair Flower I mean. How gladly she seemed to welcome the glittering stranger—She drank in lustre from his sight and renewed her fragrancy in his freshness. Surely she loved him—yea in the pit and central cell of her Petals she found a place for him wherein to rest. But ah! fair is too often fickle. And whether it were, that joy in full dress is wont to have Satiety for his train-bearer, or that even on the purest Brilliants custom will breathe a tarnish, I know not. But so it was, that after a while the Flower began to feel her inmate as a Weight or (to say the least) as little better than some superfluous chance-mate from the sweeping Water-pot, as the menial Gardener strode onward. . . .

1814. *To Mrs. Gillman*

Pub. Coleridge at Highgate, *by Lucy E. Watson, 1925, p. 154.*

4 July, 1834.

Do not forget to look over the first three or four chapters of 'Bishop Sandford's Life'.[2]

God bless you now and for ever, and

Your most affectionate and most grateful
S. T. Coleridge.

1815. *To Mrs. Dashwood*

Address: Mrs Dashwood | Bodvyddan [Bodrhyddan ?] | St Asaph
MS. Yale University Lib. Hitherto unpublished.
Postmark: 7 July 1834.

Grove, Highgate. July 5, 1834

My dear Madam

After the long, long time of confinement to my Bed-room, and for the latter two thirds of the Trial to my *Bed*, a time passed in low involuntary moaning and inward almost continuous prayer—but likewise, God be praised! with inward peace and unclouded clearness and serenity of mind—it is no slight addition to the satisfaction,

[1] According to the Sotheby catalogue this note was 'written for Eliza Nixon'.
[2] *Remains of Daniel Sandford*, ed. with a Memoir by his son, John Sandford, 2 vols., 1830. See *Table Talk*, 17 Aug. 1833 (note) and 5 July 1834.

I derive, from the (*within the last eight days*) sensible and progressive improvements of my bodily feelings and animal spirits, and the slower and less marked but still very perceptible diminution of the sinking and *faintiness* at and just below the pit of the stomach, of the wearisome expectorating Cough, the difficulty of Breathing, and the asthmatic panting on any the least exertion, and from the softening and increasing mobility of my lower Limbs, the ligaments of which had become contracted and the muscles hardened, more particularly of my left knee and leg, so that I required the support of both the Maids in the few steps from my Bed to the Chair, while the Bed was made—I have this morning walked across the room to the window to look once more at the pretty Gardens and the glorious landscape, with the assistance of one and of my walking stick—it is, I repeat, no light addition to, no untasted ingredient in, my joy and thankfulness at this apparent Dawn of Convalescence, that I find myself able to answer your *most* kind letter to Mr Gillman, in my own name and with my own *hand*. To the several successive proofs, I have received, of your friendly recollections of me, and of the affectionately deep interest, you have taken in my Weal and Woe, my labors, my aspirations and my hopes, O how many many Letters, and long ones too, have I not composed and mentally directed to you, with my eyes closed and my Back supported by the piled up sloping Pillows! But, alas! the bodily power was deficient, and still more that animal Volition, wholly distinct, nay, different *in kind*, from the moral Will (as different as any other faculty or function of the animal Life and the Organic Structure) but which—call it Volition, or spontaneous Impulse—is the indispensable antecedent and *conditio sine quâ non* of every exertion of the voluntary Muscles.

My dear Madam! it would be the self-complacent Hypocrisy of morbid self-reviling Saintship, if I pretended that my Conscience accused me of any intentional deliberate wrongs to my fellow-creatures, of commission or omission, of word, wish or deed. 'Against thee, O my God! have I sinned',[1] against thee only and against my own spirit—in opportunities lost from procrastination and from bodily indolence, both only too compatible with energetic activity of mind and unremitting effort! But in sinning against myself, I have sinned indirectly against my fellow-men! And this my Conscience made me *know* during the months when I had lost all hope of recovery, yet saw as little probability of a speedy removal—and dared not *pray* for the latter: for I knew myself an undischarged Debtor, a hitherto unfaithful Trustee with the intrusted Talents still on my person; and in earnest *resolve* indeed, on

---

[1] Psalm li. 4.

the road towards the due dispensing of the same to their rightful claimant, Christ's Church militant on earth! How then could I dare lift up my heart to God with the desire to lie down by the way-side, and sleep the sleep of Death?—But, God be praised! his grace and fatherly chastisements had long humbled me to trust wholly and *exclusively* in the perfected righteousness of the Redeemer and Saviour, abjuring all plea and claim in myself to the all-merciful Father, save only my own exceeding need of mercy.

Therefore, my dear Madam! I was under no danger of finding a temptation to self-glorying in your too favorable expressions, your too exalted estimate of my moral and intellectual Being in your kind letter to Mrs Gillman. I was assured, that they proceeded from your love and inward honoring of a Light not mine, but of which you believed yourself to see the translucence thro' the earthly Vessel, the fragile and clouded Lamp vase, thro' which the Light gleamed.

But as little did any depressive sense of Obligation disturb or bedim my grateful affection for [the] draft inclosed,[1] large in amount as it is. For I knew that the kindness had it's reward in your own Heart: and I knew, that I had neither right nor cause to be ashamed of a Poverty, which had not been in any degree the result or consequence of Idleness, or Dissipation, or vicious Sensuality, or the want of continuous labors to honorable Objects with pure aims, and which a cruel & dishonest breach of Contract on the part of my Superiors had alone brought to Dependence—just in the very month when it pleased the Almighty to prostrate me on a sick bed. But on both these two last subjects I will speak more at full in my next letter, if I am favored with a continuance of my present convalescence. Only I must not omit to say, that had I been a Duke or a Millionaire, I could not have had more skilful, more constant medical tendance, from Mr Gillman & my dear Friend, Professor Green. But there being no organic disease discoverable, all that could be done was to watch from day to day, and to alleviate the Symptoms, as they successively rose.—But I have sat up and written as long as my medical Inmate thinks right—& besides I may lose the Highgate Post.

May God bless you, my dear Madam! and your obliged & affectionate Friend S. T. Coleridge.

[1] 'A Mrs. Dashwood wrote to Mrs. Gillman at the time of illness in terms of fervent admiration & love respecting my father. Just before, she had expressed a hope that he would accept of a small annuity from her.' Sara Coleridge to her brother Hartley in a letter dated 5 Aug. 1834. See *Coleridge*, ed. E. Blunden and E. L. Griggs, 1934, p. 228.

1816. *To Eliza Nixon*

Transcript Coleridge family. Pub. with omis. Letters, ii. 773.

July 9—1834

My dear Eliza

The 3 Vols. of Miss Edgeworth's Helen ought to have been sent in to you last night—and are marked as having been *so sent*.—And indeed knowing how much noise this Work was making & the great interest it had excited I should not have been so selfish as to have retained them on my own account. But Mrs Gillman is very anxious that I should read it & has made me promise to write my remarks on it & such reflections as the contents may suggest— which in awe of the Precisians of the Book society I shall put down on separate paper—The young people (Mr E & J) were so eager to read it that with my slow & interrupted style of reading, it would have been cruel not to give them the priority—Mrs Gillman flatters me that you & your sisters will think a copy of my remarks some compensation for the delay—

God bless you, my dear young friend—You I know will be gratified to learn & in my own writing the still timid but still strengthening & brightening Dawn of Convalescence within the last 8 days—

S. T. Coleridge—

The two Vols.[1] that I send you are making a rumour and are highly & I believe justly extolled—They are written by a friend of mine, a remarkably handsome young man—whom you may have seen on one of our latest Thursday evening Conversaziones—I have not yet read them but keep them till I send in Helen & longer if you should not then have finished them—

1817. *To William C. Saunders*

Address: William C. Saunders | to the care of | Harrison Latham | Liverpool
MS. Mr. Foster W. Bond. Hitherto unpublished.
Postmark: 10 July 1834.

Grove, Highgate
10 July, 1834

'Rich Men, who keep accounts at various Banks,
Should not give Autographs: to *Strangers*, ne'er!'
So said a shrewd Attorney, one who ranks
High 'mongst the Jews, and in th' Old Bailey Sphere.

---

[1] Henry Taylor's *Philip Van Artevelde*, 2 vols., 1834.

But I keep none: and therefore have no fear
In letting loose my hand-writing and name,
To gain such fair Extension to my FAME!

S. T. Coleridge

To Mr William C. Saunders

1818. *To Adam Steinmetz Kennard*

Transcript in Editor's possession. First pub. Literary Gazette, *9 August 1834,*
p. 547. Coleridge wrote this letter 'in the Album of young Kennard—his god-
son'.

To Adam Steinmetz Kennard[1]

13th July 1834. Grove, Highgate.

My dear Godchild

I offer up the same fervent prayer for you now as I did kneeling
before the altar when you were baptized into Christ, & solemnly
received as a living member of His spiritual body, the Church. Years
must pass before you will be able to read with an understanding
heart, what I now write. But I trust that the all-gracious God, the
Father of our Lord Jesus Christ, the Father of Mercies, who by His
only begotten Son (all mercies in one sovereign mercy!) has re-
deemed you from the evil ground, & willed you to be born out of
darkness, but into light; out of death but into life; out of sin but
into righteousness, even into 'the Lord our Righteousness';[2] I trust
that He will graciously hear the prayers of your dear parents, &
be with you as the spirit of health & growth in body, & in mind. My
dear Godchild! you received from Christ's minister, at the baptismal
font, as your Christian name, the name of a most dear friend of
your father's, & who was to me even as a son, the late Adam
Steinmetz;[3] whose fervent aspirations and ever paramount aim,
even from early youth, was to be a Christian in thought, word, &
deed, in will, mind & affections.

I too your Godfather, have known what the enjoyments &
advantages of this life are, & what the more refined pleasures which
learning and intellectual power can bestow, & with all the ex-
perience that more than threescore years can give, I now on the
eve of my departure declare to you (and earnestly pray that you
may hereafter live & act on the conviction) that health is a great
blessing; competency obtained by honourable industry, a great

[1] Adam Steinmetz Kennard was born in June 1833 and was christened on
5 Sept. See Letter 1789.
[2] Jeremiah xxiii. 6 and xxxiii. 16.
[3] Adam Steinmetz died on 12 Aug. 1832. See Letters 1755-6.

blessing; & a great blessing it is to have kind, faithful & loving friends & relatives, but that the greatest of all blessings, as it is the most ennobling of all privileges, is to be indeed a Christian. But I have been likewise, thro' a large portion of my later life, a sufferer, sorely afflicted with bodily pains, languor, & manifold infirmities; & for the last 3 or 4 years have with few & brief intervals, been confined to a sick room, & at this moment, in great weakness & heaviness, write from a sick bed, hopeless of recovery, yet without prospect of a speedy removal. And I thus, on the brink of the grave, solemnly bear witness to you, that the Almighty Redeemer, most gracious in his promises to them that truly seek Him, is faithful to perform what He has promised, & has preserved under all my pains & infirmities, the inward peace that passeth all understanding, with the supporting assurance of a reconciled God, who will not withdraw his spirit from me in the conflict, & in his own time will *deliver* me from the Evil One. O my dear Godchild! eminently blessed are they who begin *early* to seek, fear, & love their God, trusting wholly in the righteousness & mediation of their Lord, Redeemer, Saviour, & everlasting High Priest, Jesus Christ. O! preserve this as a legacy & bequest from your unseen Godfather & friend,

S. T. Coleridge

1819. *To J. H. Green and Mrs. Gillman*

Pub. Coleridge at Highgate, *by Lucy E. Watson, 1925, p. 159.*

July 24, 1834.

Most dear Mr. Green, most dear Mrs. Gillman, my especial Friends,—

Do impress it on my nephew and son-in-law, Henry Nelson Coleridge, and through him on all who bear my name, that I beg, expect, and would fain hope of them according to their means, such a contribution as may suffice collectively for a handsome Legacy for that most faithful, affectionate, and disinterested servant, Harriet Macklin. Henry can explain. I have never asked for myself.[1]

S. T. Coleridge.

[1] According to Gillman, Coleridge wrote this affecting note 'at about ½ 7 o'clock in the evening of the 24th July 1834—1½ hours before he became comatose & eleven only before his death, which took place at ½ 6 A.M. on the 25th'. For an account of the death, burial, and grave of Coleridge see Appendix A.

APPENDIX A

THE DEATH AND BURIAL OF COLERIDGE

The last days of Coleridge's life, his death, the post-mortem examination, and his burial are described in a letter of 5 August 1834 from Sara Coleridge to her brother Hartley:

On the evening of the 19th he [Coleridge] appeared very ill & on Sunday the 20th of July came a note—which I opened—Henry being at Church. We sent to him there & he went to Highgate immediately. My dear father had often seemed near death before so that it was not impossible that he might rally. Still from the tone of the note I mourned him as one about to be taken from us. Henry returned in a few hours. My father since he first felt his end approaching had expressed a desire that he might be as little disturbed as possible. He took leave of Mrs Gillman & did not wish even to see his beloved friend Mr Green. The agitation of nerves at the sight of those dear to him disturbed his meditations on his Redeemer to whose bosom he was hastening & he then said that he wished to evince in the manner of his death the depth & sincerity of his faith in Christ. Henry, however, was resolved to enter his room & see him for the last time. He was just able to send his blessing to my mother & me, though he articulated with difficulty & speaking seemed to increase his pain. Henry kissed him & withdrew—never to see him living again. He continued to suffer much pain in the chest or bowels & had an impression that there was water in the chest. Mr Green brought a physician who examined him with a stethoscope & thought there was not much water. Henry continued to visit the Grove but made no attempt to see my father again, & we all agreed that it would be useless for my mother & myself to go to Highgate or for Derwent or you to come up. Mr Taylor, Mr Gillman's Assistant, . . . constantly attended on my father, which was better than his seeing Mr Gillman—such interviews would have been too agitating to both. . . . My father had a most faithful & affectionate Nurse in Harriet, an old servant of the G's, & a few hours before his death he raised himself a little in bed & wrote six or seven lines recommending *her* for a legacy. . . . The writing, though feeble, is readable. On Thursday Henry brought word that by injections of laudanum the medical attendants had succeeded in easing my father's sufferings. This was a great relief indeed to our minds. He was able to swallow very little—but had taken some arrow-root & brandy & a dose of Laudanum. He had told Harriet that he had no feelings of dissolution upon him & feared his end would be long & painful. Thank God this was not so. On Wednesday—no Tuesday [Thursday?] he saw Mrs Gillman for the last time & took leave of James Gillman. James then saw him raise his head in the air—looking upwards as in prayer—he then fell asleep—from sleep into a state of coma, Torpor, as I understood it, and ceased to breathe at half past six in the morning of Friday [25 July]. Mr Green was with him that night till he died. In the middle of the day on Thursday he had repeated to Mr Green his formula of the Trinity. His utterance was difficult—but his mind in perfect vigour & clearness— he remarked that his intellect was quite unclouded & he said 'I could even be witty'. . . . He had made a solemn injunction on Mr Gillman that his body should be opened—which was accordingly done by Mr Taylor & another able young Surgeon—his friends, of course, declining such a trial themselves. Henry has their accurate report.[1] There was more than a pint of water in the chest, & the heart & liver were enlarged. But nothing was observed which could be ascribed to laudanum, & the internal pain & uneasiness which he has suffered from all his life, & which my mother remembers his complaining of before he ever had recourse to opium, is supposed to have been some sympathetic nervous affection.[2] . . .

[1] The following copy of a 'Report of Examination of the body of S. T. Coleridge' was probably made from the 'accurate report' mentioned in Sara Coleridge's letter:

External Appearances

Abdomen tympanitic and very tense—Body loaded with fat—
Internal—Thorax

Adhesions between the surfaces of the left pleura to a small extent—left lung crepitating—healthy—left bronchial tubes contained a small quantity of fluid but not overcharged. Right pleura strongly adherent in many places —between it and the cartilages of the 5th, 6th, & 7th ribs was a cyst containing about half a pint of bloody serum of a very deep colour. The cavity on the right side contained at least three quarts of bloody serum. Right lung gorged with serous fluid—bronchial tubes dilated. The air tubes throughout exhibited marks of former inflammation, by the thickened and congested state of the lining membrane. Heart loaded with fat—half as large again as natural. Dilatation of both ventricles and hypertrophy of the left. Valves healthy. A Deposit of caseous matter not quite amounting in hardness to cartilage was found beneath the lining membrane of the aorta, the sinus of which was dilated more than usual.

Abdomen.

Liver pale—of exceeding softness, so as to break down on the slightest pressure. Gall bladder enormously distended with pale-coloured bile. Stomach empty—lining membrane inflamed throughout, with patches of ulceration towards the cardiac extremity. Intestines natural—some congestion of the coats of the caput coli—but hardly amounting to inflammation. Other Viscera healthy. [Transcript Coleridge family.]

[2] On 2 Nov. 1835 Gillman sent Joseph Cottle a general report of the postmortem examination:

After Mr Coleridge's decease, his body was inspected by two able anatomists, appointed by Mr Green: a task too painful for either him or me to perform. The left side of the chest was nearly occupied by the heart, which was immensely enlarged, and the sides of which were so thin as not to be able to sustain it's weight when raised. The right side of the chest was filled with

Appendix A

The funeral took place on Saturday the 2nd of August. It was attended by Mr Green, James Gillman, Mr Kinnaird [Kennard], Mr Steinmetz (father of the youth who left my father a legacy), Mr. Stutfield, Mr. Sterling (a young Clergyman—a disciple of my father's who begged to be allowed to follow him to the grave & came from Cambridge on purpose)—Henry, & Edward, who came from Eton sending his own family without him to Ottery. Mr Gillman was ill in bed—Mr Mense [Mence] read the service. Our dear father's remains were placed in a vault in Highgate churchyard beside those of Miss Harding—they had been in the coffin for some days. . . . The funeral was handsome—a hearse & four—abundance of plumes—two mourning carriages &c.

THE GRAVE OF COLERIDGE

On 2 August 1834, as Sara Coleridge wrote to her brother, Coleridge's 'remains were placed in a vault in Highgate churchyard beside those of Miss Harding'. The vault was located on the site of the old chapel of the Free Grammar School at Highgate, the chapel having been torn down in 1833 and the area thrown into the burial ground

a fluid enclosed in a membrane having the appearance of a cyst, amounting in quantity to upwards of three quarts, so that the lungs on each side were completely compressed—This will account sufficiently for his bodily sufferings, which were almost without intermission during the progress of the disease, and will explain to you the necessity of subduing these sufferings by narcotics, and of driving on a most feeble circulation by stimulants—which his case had imperatively demanded—This disease, which is generally of slow progress, had it's commencement in Coleridge more than 30 years before his death. [MS. The Wellcome Historical Medical Museum.]

Gillman's report was printed in *The Times* on 8 June 1895, and reprinted in the *Lancet* on 15 June, with the following comment:

The account here given of the *post-mortem* examination was probably not intended for professional perusal, and is therefore not so precise and definite as to be quite clearly interpreted. Thus it is somewhat puzzling to define the condition described in the right pleura. The large 'cyst' mentioned could hardly have been a hydatid. It is more likely, we think, that it was really a pleural effusion, which seemed to be encysted from the presence of adhesions of the lung to the chest wall. If this be so then this effusion may be regarded as dropsical in character, occurring towards the close of life in a subject of chronic cardiac dilatation. The account which describes the enormous size of the heart and the extreme tenuity of its walls is silent as to the pericardium, but such a degree of enlargement may well have been due to universal adhesion of the heart to the pericardial sac, from the inflammation of the latter in early life. The record, however, suffices to prove that this intellectual giant must have suffered more than the world was aware of, and it can be understood that his 'indolence' as well as his opium habit had a physical basis. (A. W. Gillman, *The Gillmans of Highgate*, 1895, pp. 35–37.)

adjoining the school. In January 1843 Henry Nelson Coleridge died and his body was interred in a tomb close by the vault where Coleridge had been buried more than eight years earlier. Not long afterwards, Sara Coleridge arranged to have her husband's tomb enlarged, and in July 1843 her father's remains were placed in a new outer coffin and reinterred in what was now the family vault. Mrs. Coleridge was buried in this vault in 1845, Sara herself in 1852, and her son Herbert in 1861. There, among other tombs, the Coleridge vault stood uncovered 'in the old church-yard, by the road side' until 1866.

In that year the present chapel of Highgate School (until 1832 the Cholmeley Free Grammar School) was erected on the site where the old school chapel had stood. The Crawley family gave the chapel in memory of G. A. Crawley, a governor of the school from 1847 to 1862. The foundation-stone was laid on 24 March 1866, and Bishop Tait, bishop of London, consecrated the new school chapel on 29 May 1867. Built on pillars four feet or more above the level of the ground, the chapel extended over that part of the graveyard containing the Coleridge family vault. The only vault disturbed by the erection of the chapel was that of Mary and John Schoppens, who had died in 1718 and 1720. One of the foundation piers of the new chapel divided this vault, thus making the removal of the coffins necessary. The area beneath the chapel now took on the appearance of a crypt, but the side facing the burial ground was left open. Thus in 1873 Edith Coleridge says of the grave of her mother, Sara Coleridge: 'In the old churchyard of Highgate (now enclosed in a crypt under the school chapel) her remains lie, beside those of her parents, her husband, and her son.'

A chapel and grounds lying adjacent to the school had been granted by Bishop Grindal to Sir Roger Cholmeley in 1565, for the benefit of the newly founded Free Grammar School at Highgate. Over the years the chapel belonging to the school became a place of worship for the inhabitants of Highgate, and early in the seventeenth century the land adjoining the chapel was consecrated as a burial ground for the hamlet. In 1830 a parliamentary Act authorized the governors of the school to tear down their old chapel and to transfer its site and the remaining burial ground to the Commissioners for Building Churches, to serve as a place of interment belonging to a new church to be built on another location in Highgate. The master, scholars, and governors of the school were to have seats in the new church '*rent free for ever*'. As a result, St. Michael's Church was erected across from The Grove, Highgate, some little distance from the school, and the Consolidated Chapelry District of St. Michael was established. The Church was consecrated on 8 November 1832.[1] The old school chapel was torn down in 1833, and until its closing in 1857 the graveyard, including the site of the former chapel, served St. Michael's Church as a burying ground. Indeed, an Order of the Queen in Council, dated 25 June 1857, which closed the graveyard on 4 July 1857, 'with the exception of now existing family vaults', specifically mentions 'the Old Burial-ground of the consolidated chapelry of Saint Michael, Highgate'. Likewise, the governors of Highgate School possess a 'Faculty' dated 21 June 1865 'for erecting a Chapel on the Burial ground belonging to the Consolidated Chapelry District of St. Michael, Highgate, Middlesex'. It would seem, however, that the burial ground was not transferred to the Commissioners for Building Churches or to St. Michael's Church, but remained the property of Highgate School until 1867, for among the papers of the governors there is 'a Conveyance dated 7 May 1867, whereby the Governors of the School conveyed the old Burial ground to the Bishop of London'.

On visiting the Coleridge vault several years ago, the distinguished novelist, Ernest Raymond, found it in a 'pitiable state—neglected, gaping, and partly surrounded by rubbish in a crypt that appears to be a dump for discarded iron, a receptacle for blown litter and leaves and a convenient place for tramps to sleep in'. Nobody, as far as he could discover, knew who owned the part of the grave-yard covered over by the school chapel or who was responsible for the care of the Coleridge vault;[2] and since the school authorities could

---

[1] Coleridge himself attended the consecration. Afterwards, the bishop of London, C. J. Blomfield, complimented him, saying, 'You must have perceived, Mr Coleridge, that the substance of my Sermon was taken from your Work on Church & State'. (Sara Coleridge to Mrs. Derwent Coleridge, 30 Nov. 1832. MS. in the possession of Mr. A. H. B. Coleridge.)

[2] Inquiries made by several newspaper representatives also failed to fix the responsibility for the maintenance of the Coleridge vault. A writer in the *Evening Standard* of 27 Jan. 1960, for example, reported that Highgate School was 'clearly free from blame, since it does not own the land'. The same writer also quoted Mr. David Witty, the senior assistant solicitor of the Hornsey Borough Council: 'We have the care of the graveyard, but not of the crypt, in which Coleridge lies.' A year later, the *Hornsey Journal* of 24 Feb. 1961 reported: 'With the closing of the burial ground, its upkeep became the responsibility of Hornsey Borough Council, but the council have always maintained that the part of the burial-ground which was incorporated in the crypt is no longer a part and therefore not their responsibility. The school, on the other hand, maintain that they never took over the tomb.' A recent inquiry addressed by the present editor to the Hornsey Borough Council in 1963 brought a more definitive answer from the town clerk:

'With reference to your letter of the 21st January 1963, I think that the following extract from a letter written on the 1st June, 1949, by a church-warden of St. Michael's Church, Highgate, gives you all the information you require:—

give no guarantee that the area would thenceforth be maintained in a more satisfactory condition, the late Walter H. P. Coleridge, the poet's great-grandson, the late Anthony Derwent Coleridge, a great-great-grandson, Mr. Raymond, and the Revd. Harry Edwards, the Vicar of St. Michael's, met to discuss the possibility of Coleridge's remains and those of his family being removed to the churchyard or to the interior of St. Michael's Church. Subject to the granting of a faculty, which was later obtained, the Churchwardens and the Council readily agreed to a reburial in St. Michael's Church. Accordingly, with the co-operation of the Society of Authors, Mr. Raymond launched a public appeal for funds to carry out the project. Sponsored by John Masefield, John Betjeman, Richard Church, Cecil Day-Lewis, Christopher Fry, J. E. Morpurgo (Director, National Book League), Sir Harold Nicolson, Kathleen Raine, Mrs. Louise A. Arabin (Mayor of St. Pancras), Sir Bernard Waley-Cohen (Lord Mayor of London), and Sylva Norman, this appeal met with an enthusiastic response from Coleridge admirers all over the world. In fact, the fund was over-subscribed, and it was planned to use the balance remaining 'for the maintenance of the new tomb and the memorial stone, for the endowment of an annual lecture on Coleridge, and for the decoration of the memorial on the

"With reference to the burial ground at Highgate, I write to say that this was closed by an Order of the Queen in Council dated the 25th June, 1857. The Order was passed under the Burial Act, 1855. . . .

"By a further Act, the Burial Act, 1855 (18 and 19 Vict. cap. 128), it was provided that where an Order in Council had been issued for the discontinuance of burials in any churchyard or burial ground, the churchwardens were required to maintain the burial ground in decent order and also do the necessary repair of the walls and other fences, and the costs and expenses were to be repaid by the Overseers upon the certificate of the churchwardens out of the rate made for the relief of the poor. . . . By section 269 (2) of the Local Government Act, 1933 it was provided that where a certificate was given after the commencement of that Act (that is, after the 1st June, 1934) in order to obtain repayment from the general rate fund, the functions and liabilities of the Parochial Church Council of the parish (to which the churchwardens' liabilities had passed by virtue of the Parochial Church Council (Powers) Measure, 1921) should be transferred to the Council of the Borough etc.

"In fact the Parochial Church Council of Highgate has never made a certificate with a view to recover the expenses of maintaining or repairing the closed churchyard, but were they to do so, as they are properly entitled to do, the result would be that the liabilities of the Parochial Church Council relating to the maintenance and repair of the closed churchyard would pass to the Borough."

'You will see from this that following the closure of the churchyard on the 4th July, 1857, the churchwardens—and subsequently the Parochial Church Council—were responsible for its maintenance and the Hornsey Borough Council have not at any time been so responsible.'

anniversary of the poet's death'. A trust has now been established by St. Michael's Church.[1]

On 28 March 1961 the remains of Coleridge and the other members of his family were removed from the dilapidated vault under the Highgate School chapel, placed in new coffins, and reinterred in a new brick tomb beneath the nave of St. Michael's Church. A memorial stone of Westmorland slate inscribed by Mr. Reynolds Stone with Coleridge's own *Epitaph*—'Stop, Christian passer-by'— was placed above the vault halfway down the middle aisle of the church. In an impressive ceremony held in St. Michael's Church on 6 June 1961 the memorial was dedicated by the Rt. Revd. H. Montgomery Campbell, lord bishop of London. The Revd. Anthony Derwent Coleridge and John Daniel, a Senior Grecian from Christ's Hospital, read the Lessons, and John Masefield, the Poet Laureate, delivered an address. A great-great-grandson of the poet, Mr. A. H. B. Coleridge, was represented by his daughter, Priscilla. Also among those attending the service were Mr. Walter H. P. Coleridge, two of the poet's great-great-grandchildren, Mrs. Phyllis Coleridge Hooper and the Revd. Nicholas Coleridge, and other members of the Coleridge family; a colonel of the 15th–19th, the King's Royal Hussars (formerly the King's Light Dragoons, Coleridge's old regiment), T. S. Eliot, I. A. Richards, Agatha Christie, Sir B. Ifor Evans, Sir Mark and Lady Turner, Canon Adam Fox of Westminster Abbey, representatives of Highgate School, the Society of Authors, the Charles Lamb Society, the Keats–Shelley Memorial Association, the Royal Society of Literature, the Dove Cottage Trust, and of many universities and libraries, English and foreign. Fittingly, Coleridge is now buried directly across from No. 3, The Grove, where he spent the last years of his life.

---

[1] The following statement appeared in the summer 1962 issue of *The Author*:

COLERIDGE'S TOMB

Dear Sir,

We would like to convey to the Society of Authors our warm appreciation of the magnificent help and co-operation given in raising the Samuel Taylor Coleridge fund for re-entombment; of Ernest Raymond's work in accepting the burden and expense of the treasuryship; and of the generosity of members of the Society who personally contributed to the Appeal.

The income from the balance of the fund, which amounts to £539 8s., will be used in accordance with the Declaration of Trust, drawn up for the due commemoration of Samuel Coleridge and his family buried with him, and for the benefit of the fabric of St. Michael's Church, Highgate, where they are now interred.

> Harry Edwards, *Vicar*
> Richard Lyttelton
> James R. Hudson, *Churchwardens.*

Appendix A

THE WILL OF COLERIDGE

The copy of Coleridge's will deposited in Somerset House, London, is not in the poet's handwriting but bears the following autograph notation at the top of the first page: 'My Will, revised by myself, and corrected with my own hand, previously to the Signing: S. T. Coleridge.' The codicil, which is dated 2 July 1830, is, however, entirely in Coleridge's handwriting.

Highgate, September 17th 1829

This is the last Will of me, Samuel Taylor Coleridge.—I hereby give and bequeath to Joseph Henry Green, of Lincoln's Inn Fields, Surgeon, all my Books, manuscripts, and personal Estates and Effects whatsoever— except the Pictures and Engravings herein after bequeathed—upon Trust, to sell & dispose of all such part thereof, as shall not consist of money, according to his discretion, and to invest the Produce thereof and also all money which I may leave at my Death, and that shall be due to me from the Equitable Assurance Office, or elsewhere, in the Public Funds, in the name of the said Joseph Henry Green; and he shall pay the Dividends of the Stock to be purchased therewith, to my Wife, Sarah Coleridge, during her Life; and after her death, pay the same Dividends to my Daughter, Sara Coleridge, she being un- married, and as long as she shall remain single. But if my daughter, Sara Coleridge, shall before or at the time of my death have married (unless indeed she (which may the Almighty in his Mercy forefend!) should be left a Widow, wholly unprovided for by her husband's Will & Property or otherwise, in which case the former disposition of this Testament is to revive and take place) I then give the Dividends of the Stock purchased to be equally divided between my three Children, Hartley Coleridge, the Revnd Derwent Coleridge, & the aforesaid Sara Coleridge; or if one of these, my three Children, should die, then to be equally divided between the two Survivors, and the whole Dividend of the Stock to be paid to the last Survivor.—Still, however, it is my Will, that each of the three, namely, Hartley, and Derwent, and my Daughter Sara, should retain the Right and Power, each, of bequeathing the third part of the Principal after the death of the last Survivor, according to his or her pleasure. And my Will is, that notwithstanding any thing herein and before contained, & it is my desire, that my Friend, Mr Joseph Henry Green, shall in lieu of selling my Books have the option of purchasing the same at such price as he shall himself determine, in as much as their chief value will be dependent on his possession of them. Nevertheless, it is my Will, that in case the said Joseph Henry Green should think it expedient to publish any of the Notes or Writing made by me in the same Books, or any of them; or to publish any other manuscripts or writings of mine, or any letters of mine, which should any be hereafter collected from, or supplied by, my Friends & Correspondents, then my Will is, that the Proceeds & all benefit accruing therefrom, shall be subject to the same Trusts, and to be paid to or amongst such Persons as shall be entitled to my said personal Estate, herein before bequeathed—The Pictures and Engravings belonging to me, in the House of my dear Friends, James & Anne Gillman, my more than Friends, the Guardians of my Health, Happiness, and Interests, during the fourteen years of my Life that I have enjoyed the proofs of their constant, zealous, and disinterested affection, as an Inmate and Member of their family, I give & bequeath to Anne Gillman, the Wife of my dear friend, my love for whom, and my sense of her unremitted goodness, tenderness, and never wearied kindness to me, I hope & humbly trust, will follow me, as a part of my abiding Being, into that state into which I hope to rise, through the merits and mediation, and by the efficacious Power of the Son of God, incarnate in the Blessed Jesus, whom I believe in my Heart, and confess with my mouth, to have been from Everlasting the Way & the Truth, and to have become Man that for fallen and sinful Men he might be the Resurrection, & the Life. And further I hereby tell my Children, Hartley, Derwent, & Sara, that I have but little to leave them; but I hope and indeed confidently believe, that they will regard it as a part of their inheritance, when I thus bequeath to them my affection & gratitude to Mr & Mrs Gillman, and to the dear friend, the companion, partner, and help-mate of my worthiest studies, Mr Joseph Henry Green.

Further to Mr Gillman, as the most expressive way in which I can mark my relation to him, and in remembrance of a great and good man, revered by us both, I leave the Manuscript volume lettered, Arist: Manuscript—Birds, Acharnians, Knights, presented to me by my dear Friend & Patron, the Honorable John Hookham Frere, who of all the Men that I have had the means of knowing during my Life, appears to me eminently to deserve to be characterized as ὁ καλοκἀγαθὸς ὁ φιλόκαλος.

To Mr Frere himself I can only bequeath my assurance, grounded on a Faith, equally precious to him, as to me, of a continuance of those Prayers, which I have for many years offered for his temporal and spiritual well Being.—And further in remembrance that it was under this, Mr Gillman's, Roof, I enjoyed so many hours of delightful and profitable communion with Mr J. H. Frere, it is my wish that this volume should after the demise of James Gillman Senr. belong, and I do hereby bequeath the same, to James Gillman Junior, in the hope that it will remain as an Heir-loom in the Gillman Family.

On revising this my Will, there seemed at first some reason to apprehend that in the disposition of my Books, as above determined, I might have imposed on my Executor a too delicate Office. But, on the other hand, the motive from the peculiar character of the Books is so evident, and the reverential sense, which all my Children entertain of Mr Green's character both as the personal friend of their Father, and as the Man most intimate with their Father's intellectual labors, purposes, and aspirations, I believe to be such, as will I trust be sufficient to preclude any delicacy that might result from the said disposition. To my Daughter, Sara Coleridge, exemplary in all the relations of life in which she hath been placed, a blessing to both her Parents and to her Mother the rich reward, which the anxious fulfilment of her maternal Duties had, humanly speaking, merited, I bequeath the Presentation copy of the Georgica Heptaglotta [*sic*], given me by my highly respected Friend, William Sotheby Esqre—And it is my Wish, that Sara should never part with this volume: but that if she marry & should have a daughter, it may descend to her, or if daughters to her eldest daughter as a memento, that her Mother's accomplishments & her unusual attainments in ancient & modern Languages were not so much nor so justly the object of admiration, as their co-existence with Piety, Simplicity, and a characteristic meekness, in short with mind, manners, and character so perfectly feminine. And for this purpose I have recorded this my Wish in the same or equivalent words, on the first Title Page of this splendid Work—

To my Daughter in law, Mary Coleridge, the Wife of the Revnd Derwent Coleridge, whom I bless God that I have been permitted to see, & to have so seen as to esteem & love on my own judgement & to be grateful for her on my own account, as well as in behalf of my dear Son I give the interleaved Copy of the FRIEND, corrected by myself & with sundry Notes & additions in my own Hand-writing, in Trust for my Grand-Son Derwent Coleridge; that if it should please God to preserve his life, he may possess some memento of the Paternal Grandfather who blesses him unseen and fervently commends him to the Great Father in Heaven, whose Face his Angels ever more beholdeth (XVIII Matth: 10).—And further as a relief to my own feelings by the opportunity of mentioning their names that I request of my Executor that a small, plain gold mourning Ring with my Hair may be presented to the following Persons: namely to my oldest Friend, & ever-beloved Schoolfellow, Charles Lamb, and in the deep and almost life-long affection, of which this is the slender record, his equally beloved Sister Mary Lamb, will know herself to be included. 2—To my old and very kind Friend, Basil Montagu Esquire. 3—To Thomas Poole Esqre of Nether Stowey The dedicatory Poem to my Juvenile Poems, & my Fears in Solitude render it unnecessary to say more than that what I then, in my early manhood thought and felt, I now, a grey-haired Man, still think & feel. 4 To Mr Josiah Wade, whose zealous friendship and important services during my residences at Bristol I never have forgotten, or while Reason & Memory remain, can forget. 5 To my filial friend, dear to me by a double Bond, in his Father's right & in his own Launcelot Wade. 6—To Miss Sarah Hutchinson.—

To Robert Southey, & to William Wordsworth, my Children have a debt of Gratitude & reverential affection on their own account: and the sentiments, I have left on record in my Literary Life & in my Poems, and which are the convictions of the present moment, supersede the necessity of any other memorial of my Regard and Respect.

There is one thing yet on my Heart to say, as far as it may consist with entire submission to the Divine Will, namely, that I have perhaps too little proposed to myself any temporal Interests either of fortune or literary reputation, and that the sole regret I now feel at the scantiness of my means arises out of my inability to make such present provision for my dear Hartley, my first-born, as might set his feelings at ease, and his mind at liberty from the depressing anxieties of the To Day, and exempt him from the necessity of diverting the Talents, with which it has pleased God to entrust him, to subjects of temporary interests: knowing, that it is with him, as it ever has been with myself, that his Powers and the ability and disposition to exert them are greatest, when the motives from without are least or of least urgency. But with earnest Prayer, & through Faith in Jesus the Mediator, I commit him, with his dear Brother and Sister, to the care and Providence of the Father in Heaven, and affectionately leave this my last injunction—My dear Children *love* one another.

Lastly, with awe & thankfulness I acknowledge, that from God who has graciously endowed me, a creature of the Dust and the Indistinction with the glorious capability of knowing Him, the Eternal, as the Author of my Being and of desiring and seeking Him as it's ultimate End, I have received all Good, and Good alone. Yea the evils from my own corrupt yet responsible Will, He hath converted into Mercies, sanctifying them as instruments of fatherly chastisement for instruction, prevention, and restraint. Praise in the Highest, and Thanksgiving and adoring Love to the I AM with the co-eternal Word and the Spirit proceeding, One God from everlasting to everlasting! His Staff and his Rod alike comfort me!

Samuel Taylor Coleridge

Witnesses.
Anne Gillman
Henry Langley Porter

Grove, Highgate: 2 July, 1830
This is a Codicil to my last Will and Testament.

S. T. Coleridge.

Most desirous to secure, as far as in me lies, for my dear Son Hartley Coleridge the tranquillity indispensable to any continued and successful exertion of his literary talents, and which from the like character of our minds in this respect I know to be especially requisite for his happiness; and persuaded that he will recognize in this provision that anxious Affection by which it is dictated—I affix this Codicil to my last Will and Testament:

And I hereby give and bequeath to Joseph Henry Green, Esquire, to Henry Nelson Coleridge, Esquire, and to James Gillman, Esquire and the Surviver of them and the Executor and Assigns of such Surviver the Sum, whatever it may be, which in the Will aforesaid I bequeathed to my Son, Hartley Coleridge, after the decease of his Mother, Sarah Coleridge, upon trust. And I hereby request them, the said Joseph Henry Green, Henry Nelson Coleridge and James Gillman, Esquires, to hold the Sum accruing to Hartley Coleridge from the equal division of my total bequest between Him, his Brother Derwent and his Sister Sara Coleridge after their Mother's decease—to dispose of the

Interest or Proceeds of the same portion to or for the use of my dear Son, Hartley Coleridge, at such time or times, in such manner and under such conditions, as they, the Trustees above named, know to be my Wish, and shall deem conducive to the attainment of my Object in adding this Codicil, namely, the anxious wish to ensure for my Son the continued means of a Home, in which I comprize Board, Lodging and Raiment—providing, that nothing in this Codicil shall be so interpreted as to interfere with my Son, Hartley Coleridge's freedom of choice respecting his place of residence or with his power of disposing of his Portion by Will, after his decease, according as his own Judgement and affections may decide.

S. T. Coleridge
2 July 1830.[1]

Witnesses
Anne Gillman
James Gillman Jun:

---

[1] On 11 Aug. 1834 Joseph Henry Green, the executor, testified under oath that 'the whole of the deceased's Goods Chattels and Credits do not amount in Value to the Sum of *Three thousand* Pounds'.

Filed with the will in Somerset House there is an affidavit dated 11 Aug. 1834 and signed by Joseph Hardman and Henry Taylor, who 'made Oath . . . that they knew and were well acquainted with Samuel Taylor Coleridge . . . for some years before and to the time of his death and also well acquainted with his manner and character of handwriting and subscription'. After examining the will and codicil they declared that 'they do verily and in their consciences believe the sentence at the top of the said Will and also the several interlineations therein . . ., the whole body series and Contents of the said Codicil, [and] the subscription to the said Will and Codicil . . . to be all of the proper handwriting . . . of the said deceased'.

APPENDIX B

ADDITIONAL LETTERS, 1795–1831,
RECEIVED TOO LATE FOR INCLUSION IN THE
CHRONOLOGICAL SERIES (IDENTIFIED BY A OR B
FOLLOWING THE LETTER NUMBER)
AND CERTAIN LETTERS
PRINTED IN VOLUMES I–VI FROM PUBLISHED SOURCES
OR FROM TRANSCRIPTS AND NOW REPRINTED
FROM MSS.

93 A. *To Joseph Cottle*

Address: Mr Cottle | Bookseller
MS. Pierpont Morgan Library. Hitherto unpublished.

[November 1795][1]

My dear Friend

Let the Rose's Men be working off the last sheet till twelve o'clock, if you can—as I particularly wish to get the Lectures printed compleat to day—and am writing copy as hard as I can— you shall have your's by one o'clock. And can you for one day permit the Hot presses to suspend your work—and work this last half sheet of my lectures?

Your's affectionately
S. T. Coleridge

97 A. *To Josiah Wade*

Address: Mr Wade | No 5 | Wine Street | Bristol
MS. Mr. James M. Osborn. Hitherto unpublished.
Stamped: Worcester.

Sunday Afternoon [10 January 1796]

My dear Mr Wade

I had written and put the letter in the post before I received your's—and of two evils I prefer putting you to the expence of two

[1] This letter, which Cottle erroneously endorsed '1796', was written in Nov. 1795 while Coleridge was preparing his three political lectures for publication. Delivered in Bristol in Feb. 1795, these lectures were: *A Moral and Political Lecture*, first published in Feb. 1795; *On the Present War*; and *The Plot Discovered*. The first two lectures were published together as *Conciones ad Populum*, the preface being dated, '*Clevedon, November 16th*, 1795'. The third lecture bore the following alternate title and the date on the front wrapper: '*A Protest against Certain Bills. Bristol; Printed for the Author, November 28*, 1795.' See T. J. Wise, *Bibliography*, 8–13, and *Two Lake Poets . . .*, 1927, pp. 57–59; Campbell, *Life*, 44 n.; and Letters 81, 83, and 93. The three lectures are reprinted in *Essays on His Own Times*, i. 1–98.

Letters rather than leave you in any suspense concerning the receipt of your's—The five pound is perfectly adequate to all my expences, both here and at Birmingham—I entirely approve of the plan on which you have persuaded Mrs Coleridge to act—Altho' the new paper at Manchester is rather against the success of my work—inasmuch as it renders it less necessary—But 'hang it! (as James Jennings said of his "Times, a Satire") it has merit and must succeed!!'—

I am rejoiced to hear your intelligence concerning the printing— We equally in time as well as opinion must have coincided in our *thinkings* about Charles Danvers—God bless him! Little Charles Barr particularly begs his Love to you—What an exquisite little fellow Samuel Barr is—

I am going to meeting—Mr & Mrs Barr desire their remembrances—

Excuse my putting you to the expence of postage for such a naked nonentity of a Letter & believe me gratefully & affectionately
Your's
S. T. Coleridge

105 A. *To Joseph Cottle*

Address: Mr Cottle | Bookseller | High-Street | Bristol
MS. Rugby School. Hitherto unpublished.

[February 1796][1]

—I shall be in Bristol by eleven o'clock to morrow with the remaining Copy—this I have sent as the man will be with you before 9.—What a dreadful night!

God bless you, my dear Sir! and believe sincerely
Your FRIEND[2]
S. T. Coleridge.

Mrs Coleridge desires her Love to you as to a Brother.

The parcel is to be saved for Mr Gilbert[3]—

[1] This letter was written not long before the publication of Coleridge's *Poems on Various Subjects*, Apr. 1796. Along with his letter Coleridge sent Cottle the first 36 lines of *Epistle iv. To the Author of Poems* [Joseph Cottle] *published anonymously at Bristol in September 1795*. In Letter 106 Coleridge included the remaining lines of the poem.

[2] In the MS. of the poem addressed to Cottle, Coleridge began with the words 'High honor'd FRIEND' and then wrote above them 'Unboastful Bard'. In Letter 106 he wrote: 'The poem to begin thus—Unboastful Bard!'

[3] William Gilbert (1760?–1825?), author of *The Hurricane: a Theosophical and Western Eclogue*, 1796. As J. L. Lowes points out, Coleridge printed in *The Watchman*, p. 302, 'a cento of extracts' from this poem before it was published. See *The Road to Xanadu*, 1930, pp. 162–3, 202–3, 504, and 521; and *Early Rec.* i. 62–69, and ii. 325–46 (pages misnumbered).

Appendix B

111. *To Joseph Cottle*

Address: Mr Cottle
MS. Brown University Library. Pub. with omis. Collected Letters of Samuel
Taylor Coleridge, *i. 190.* The earlier text of this letter was drawn from the
Collection of Alfred Morrison, 1895, ii. 249.

[*Circa* 19 March 1796][1]

My dear Cottle

I have finished all the Copy for the Watchman which I need
supply till Monday—of course I have to night & tomorrow for you.
Mrs Southey is with her Sister—and I have the Evening alone & in
peace—my spirits calm. I shall consult my poetic honor and of
course your interest more by staying at home than by drinking Tea
with you.—I should be happy to see my Poems out by the con-
clusion of next week—and shall continue in stirrups—that is—
shall not dismount my Pegasus till Monday Morning—at which
time you will be able to thank God for having done with

your affectionate | Friend always, | but author evanescent,

S. T. Coleridge

145. *To Joseph Cottle*

MS. Cornell University Lib. Pub. with omis. Collected Letters of Samuel
Taylor Coleridge, *i. 241.* The earlier text of this letter was drawn from *Rem.* 115.

[Octr 18–1796][2]

Dear Cottle

I have no mercenary feelings, I verily believe; but I hate *bartering*
at any time and with any person—with you it is absolutely intoler-
able. I clearly perceive that by allowing me half the profits of the
present Edition & 20 guineas on the sale of a second Edition, you
will get little or nothing by the *additional* poems, unless they should

[1] Cottle erroneously endorsed the MS. of this undated letter 'April 95
Coleridge'. In publishing the letter in *Early Rec.* i. 140, and in *Rem.* 67, he did
not date it.

[2] Coleridge did not date this letter, the date of 'Octr 18—1796' appearing
in the MS. being in Cottle's handwriting. In publishing the letter in *Early Rec.*
i. 209, and more fully but with omissions in *Rem.* 115, Cottle added 'Stowey'
to the date. The letter, however, was written from Bristol in Oct. after Cole-
ridge and Lloyd had spent a week at Stowey early in that month. See Letters
142, 144, and 163; and Mrs. Henry Sandford, *Thomas Poole and His Friends,*
2 vols., 1888, i. 160–1.

In the present letter Coleridge tells Cottle he wishes to publish 'the *best*
pieces together, & those of secondary Splendor at the end of the Volume'; in
his letter of 1 Nov. 1796 he reported to Poole that his poems had come to a
second edition and explained that those of 'inferior merit' were to be charac-
terized as 'Juvenilia' and printed last.

be sufficiently popular to reach a third Edition which soars above
our wildest expectations. The only advantage, you can derive
therefore, from the purchase of them on such terms, is simply—that
my poetry is more likely to sell, when the whole may be had in *one*
volume, price 5S—than when it is scattered in two Volumes—the
one 4s—the other possibly 3S.—In short, you will get nothing
directly; but only indirectly from the probable circumstance, that
these *additional* poems added to the former, will give a more rapid
sale to the second Edition than it could otherwise expect—& cause
it, possibly, to be re-reviewed at large—add to this, that by
omitting every thing political I widen the sphere of my Readers.
So much *for you*— now for *myself.*—You must see, Cottle! that
whatever money I should receive from you, would result from the
circumstance that would give me the same or more, if I published
them on my own account—I mean, the *Sale* of the Poems.—I can
therefore have no motive to make such conditions with you, except
the wish to omit poems unworthy of me, & the circumstance that
our *separate properties* would aid each other by their union—and
whatever advantage this may be to me, it is, of course, equally so *to
you.*—*The only difference* between my publishing the poems on my
own account, and yielding them up to you, the only difference, I
say, independent of the above-stated differences, is that in the one
case I retain the property for ever,[1] in the other case I lose it after
two Editions.—

However, I am not solicitous to have any thing omitted except
the ludicrous poem[2] which is immoral & the Sonnet to Lord
Stanhope[3]—only I should like to publish the *best* pieces together,

[1] Coleridge retained the copyright of the '*additional* poems' published in
the second edition of 1797. In 1815 he told Byron that the compositions
'inserted' in the second edition of his *Poems* were his own property. See Letter
963 (Appendix B, p. 1034).

[2] *Written after a Walk before Supper, Poems,* i. 37. These lines, which
Coleridge quoted in Letter 19, refer to the Rev. Fulwood Smerdon, Vicar of
Ottery St. Mary, and 'Spouse'. Coleridge did not republish the poem. Smerdon,
who died in Aug. 1794, is the subject of Coleridge's *Lines on a Friend who
Died of a Frenzy Fever induced by Calumnious Reports.* See *Poems,* i. 76, and
Letters 68 and 69.

[3] The sonnet, *To Earl Stanhope,* was omitted from Coleridge's *Poems* of
1797 but was reinserted in the third edition of 1803. For Coleridge's complaint
in 1807 against Cottle for publishing the sonnet in 1796 and for sending Stan-
hope 'the book [*Poems on Various Subjects,* 1796], and a letter', see Letter
655. Among the Coleridge MSS. in Rugby School, however, the following can-
celled dedication appears on the verso of the Preface of 1796: 'To Earl Stan-
hope A man beloved of Science and of Freedom, these Poems are respectfully
inscribed by The Author.' See *Poems,* ii. 1137. See also Letters 83 and 436;
The Watchman, 1 Mar. 1796; *The Cornell Wordsworth Collection,* 1957, item
1722; *The Friend,* No. 2, 8 June 1809; and *Letters, Conversations and Rec.* 116.

& those of secondary Splendor at the end of the Volume; and this, I think, the best Quietus of the whole Affair.

Your's affectionately
S. T. Coleridge

148. *To Joseph Cottle*

MS. Cornell University Lib. Pub. with omis. Collected Letters of Samuel Taylor Coleridge, *i. 248.* The earlier text of this letter was drawn from *Early Rec.* i. 54.

November 5th
1796

Dear Cottle

A Devil has got possession of my left temple, eye, cheek, jaw, throat, & shoulder—a Devil—a very Devil—& his Name is Legion! I cannot see you this evening—I write in agonies—Pray, contrive that the apologetic note to the younger Mr Eden may be conveyed to him as soon as possible.[1]—

Do not forget Bowles's Hope[2]—as you write to the Robinsons[3] to day, you may as well write to him on the Sheet of Paper, which I have sent you—on one side of which I have written two or three Lines—

The PORTER is not come—but the *source* of the Castalian Fount lies deep—it is *Lethe.*

Your affectionate | friend & Brother,
S. T. Coleridge

184. *To Joseph Cottle*

Address: Mr Cottle | Bookseller | High Street | Bristol *Single*
MS. Birmingham University Lib. Pub. with omis. Collected Letters of Samuel Taylor Coleridge, *i. 319.* The earlier text of this letter was drawn from a bookseller's catalogue. The upper half of the first page of this MS. is cut off. In the MS. Cottle endorsed Coleridge's letter 'Stowey 1796', and it appears under that erroneous date in both *Early Rec.* i. 190, and *Rem.* 102.

[Early April 1797][4]

. . . any *sense*, puzzles [me]—: after the four first lines these should have succeeded[5]—

---

[1] In *Early Rec.* i. 189, this sentence is printed as a postscript to Coleridge's letter to Cottle of 6 Jan. 1797.

[2] W. L. Bowles, *Hope, an Allegorical Sketch,* 1796. Coleridge quotes two stanzas from this poem in Letter 156.

[3] G. G. and J. Robinson, London booksellers. Their names appear on the title-pages of both the first and second editions of Coleridge's *Poems,* 1796 and 1797.

[4] See Letter 184 of the present edition, vol. i, p. 319, notes 3 and 5.

[5] With the proof-sheet obviously in hand, Coleridge here expresses his irritation over the misprinting of the *Lines: Written at the King's Arms, Ross, for-*

Friend to the friendless, to the sick man Health,
With generous joy he view'd his modest wealth;
He heard the Widow's heaven-breath'd prayer of praise;
He mark'd the shelter's Orphan's tearful gaze;
And o'er the portion'd Maiden's snowy cheek
Bade bridal Love suffuse it's blushes meek.

Then a new paragraph &

If near this roof thy wine-cheer'd moments pass
Fill to the Good man's name one grateful[1] glass:
To higher zest shall Memory wake thy soul,
And Virtue mingle in th' ennobled bowl!
But if, like mine, thro' Life's &c.—

But never mind it—the poem may, perhaps, be reprinted in the *Errata.*—In the Sigh without any reason, certainly without any bidding, you have huddled together the four Stanzas into *one*.

In the Religious Musings I would wish you to make the following alterations. Let the second paragraph begin

Yet thou more glorious, than the Angel Host, &c

and instead of When heedless of himself the scourgéd Saint &c—let it be What time his Spirit with a brother's love &c[2]— ...

My dearest Cottle

I love & respect you, as a Brother. And my memory deceives me woefully, if I have not evidenced by the animated turn of my conversation, when we have been tête à tête, how much your company interested me.—But when last in Bristol the day I meant to have devoted to you, was such a day of sadness, that I could *do nothing*—On the Saturday, the Sunday, & the ten days after my arrival at Stowey I felt a depression too dreadful to be described—

So much I felt my genial spirits droop!
My Hopes all flat, Nature within me seem'd
In all her functions weary of herself.

Wordsworth's conversation &c rous'd me somewhat; but even now

merly the House of the 'Man of Ross', and goes on to suggest that the poem might be reprinted in the Errata of his *Poems*, 1797. This was not done. See also Letter 195, in which Coleridge writes to Cottle: 'The Man of Ross is altogether misprinted; and cannot be made intelligible in these Errata.'

It may be added that Letter 194, at least the part referring to the *Man of Ross*, may have been fabricated by Cottle from the present mutilated manuscript. See Letter 51 for the earliest draft of this poem.

[1] cheerful [Cancelled word in line above.]

[2] Neither of these changes was made in *Religious Musings* in 1797.

I am not the man, I have been—& I think, never shall.—A sort of calm hopelessness diffuses itself over my heart.—Indeed every mode of life, which has promised me bread & cheese, has been, one after another, torn away from me—but God remains! I have no immediate pecuniary distress, having received ten pound from Lloyd's Father at Birmingham.—I employ myself now on a book of morals in answer to Godwin, & on my Tragedy . . .

David Hartley is well & grows—Sara is well, and desires a Sister's Love to you—

Tom Poole desires to be kindly remembered to you—I see they have reviewed Southey's Poems, & my Ode in the Monthly Review —Notwithstanding the Reviews, I, who in the sincerity of my heart am *jealous for* Robert Southey's fame, regret the publication of that Volume. Wordsworth complains with justice, that Southey writes *too much at his ease*—that he too seldom 'feels his burthen'd breast

Heaving beneath th' incumbent Deity.'

He certainly will make literature more *profitable to him* from the fluency with which he writes, & the facility, with which he pleases himself. But I fear, that to Posterity his Wreath will look unseemly—here an ever living Amaranth, & close by it's side some Weed of an hour, sere, yellow, & shapeless—his exquisite Beauties will lose half their effect from the bad company, they keep.— Besides, I am fearful that he will begin to rely too much on *story & event* in his poems to the neglect of those *lofty imaginings,* that are peculiar to, & definitive of, *the* POET. The *story* of Milton might be told in *two pages*—it is this [whic]h distinguishes *an* EPIC *Poem* from a *Romance in metre.* Observe the march of Milton—his severe application, his laborious polish, his deep metaphysical researches, his *prayers to God* before he began his great poem—all, that could lift & swell his intellect, became his daily food.—I should not think of devoting less than 20 years to an Epic Poem. Ten to collect materials, & warm my mind with universal Science—I would be a tolerable mathematician, I would thoroughly know mechanics, hydrostatics, optics, & Astronomy—Botany, Metallurgy, fossillism, chemistry, geology, Anatomy, Medicine—then *the mind of man*— then the *minds of men*—in *all* Travels, Voyages, & Histories. So I would spend ten years—the next five in the composition of the poem—& the five last in the correction of it—So I would write, haply not unhearing of that divine and nightly-whispering Voice, which speaks to mighty Minds of predestinated Garlands starry & unwithering!—[1]

God love you & S. T. Coleridge

[1] Cf. *Poems,* i. 174, lines 35–39.

284. *To Charles Parry*

MS. Cornell University Lib. Pub. Collected Letters of Samuel Taylor Coleridge *i. 520*. The earlier text of this letter was drawn from a transcript.

June 25th 1799

My dear Fellow! my dear Parry! we are safe at Clausthal—.[1] The Coach horse near Clausthal fell down; but old Kutscher took a walk up & down, mumbling a charm, then fell to, & up rose the horse—Greenough & I lost our way and after much hallooing in which we were mocked by some fine echoes we recovered our Party—We were however amply repayed by the sight of a wild Boar with an immense Cluster of Glowworms round his Tail & Rump.—Vale, φιλτάτη μοι Κεφαλή!—God bless you again & again, my dear Fellow—& my kind Love to Frederic—& when I have the Night Mair, I shall probably dream of him a top of me under that charming Tree where we slept so warm & comfortable, some two miles from a Village called Mentfelde [Mollenfelde].[2]

God bless you
S. T. Coleridge

285. *To George Bellas Greenough*

Address: Den Herrn Greenough | Göttingen
MS. Pierpont Morgan Lib. Pub. with omis. Collected Letters of Samuel Taylor Coleridge, *i. 520*. The earlier text of this letter was drawn from a transcript made by Professor Edith J. Morley.

[Brunswick, 6 July 1799]

My dear Greenough—God bless you! And eke Carlyon, and Charles Parry, & little Fred.—Health & Happiness be with you all.—The date of this Letter, at present in it's infancy, or rather in the very act of Delivery, (for Letters come into Existence with their Heads forward, in which respect, as in some others, they agree with young

---

[1] On 24 June Coleridge and Chester set off from Göttingen on the first stage of their return journey to England. They were accompanied as far as Braunschweig by Carlyon and Greenough. See *Wordsworth and Coleridge*, ed. E. L. Griggs, 1939, pp. 231–3, and note to Letter 284 in vol. i, p. 520 of the present edition.

[2] In Charles Parry's unpublished letters the name of this place is spelled Mollefeld. The Parry brothers, Coleridge, and several others left Göttingen at half past four on Saturday, 22 June 1799, to visit a castle some four or five hours distant. On their way they attempted to secure lodgings at Mollenfelde, became involved in an altercation, and were forced to spend the night under a tree. This 'amusing adventure' is also described by Clement Carlyon (*Early Years and Late Reflections*, 4 vols., 1836–58, i. 35–38) and Gillman (*Life*, 138–9). See also *The Notebooks of Samuel Taylor Coleridge*, ed. Kathleen Coburn, vol. i, 1957, item 447 3.28 *f31* and note.

Children) the date, I say, is July 6th, 1799, Saturday Morning ½ past 8.—On Wednesday Morning after quitting you we took a melancholy Stroll on the Ramparts, then called on the Kaufmann & begged him to take our Places in the Post auf Hamburg for Saturday, & then walked forth for Helmstadt [Helmstedt].—With coat on my arm, & hat in hand, I walked before & Chester behind, & never stopped till we reached Helmstadt, which is 23 miles from Brunswick—they called it 5 G. M. but it certainly is not—for we walked it exactly in 7 Hours.—Well—when we arrived there, we were *overdone*—behind my ears, all down the side of [my] neck, a longitudinal Bladder, the colours shifting prettily betwixt blue & Red—& such another on my Forehead—. Chester had acquired a whitloe on his nose, with one dot of black—& the Bile had occupied his Face—Red, white, black, & Yellow—poor Chester!—God bless him!—He fell down on his bed at Helmstadt, and in the literal sense, *fell* asleep.—I drest myself (i.e. undrest myself & put on the same cloaths again) and delivered my letter to Hofrath Bruns—I saw his wife, a pretty affable Woman; but the Hofrath was at the Library. I left my letter & Card; but had scarcely arrived at my Inn, when Bruns came after me—welcomed me with great kindness, took me in his arms to the Library, where we rummaged old Manuscripts, & looked at some Libri Rarissimi for about an Hour—(N.B.—The Library resembles strikingly the Libraries of some of the little Colleges at Oxford and Cambridge.) After this he took me to his House, spoke to me of a little Translation which Lowth[1] had made in his Presence of an Ode of Ramler's[2]—talked of England, & Oxford, where he had resided some years & I found, that he had been intimate with many of my Father's Friends—eat Butterbrod in his arbor with him & his Wife—a sweet Woman!—another Professor & Wife came—smoked a Pipe—all comfortable—all even affectionate to me—went away at past eleven—Bruns having promised to send the next morning to Beireis &c—

So passed Wednesday—i.e. Arsenic. Now for Verdegris.—On Thursday morning received a note from Bruns that Beireis would see me & Chester at 10 o'clock—at ten Bruns came, introduced us to Beireis, & left us there.—Beireis!—A short man, drest in black, with a very expressive Forehead—& small eyes—He went strait to work—asked no questions—offered no Civilities—but full of himself

---

[1] Robert Lowth (1710–87), professor of poetry at Oxford, 1741–50, became bishop of London in 1777.

[2] K. W. Ramler (1725–98), German poet and for many years professor of logic and literature at the cadet school in Berlin. For Coleridge's reading of Ramler's translations of Horace see *The Notebooks of Samuel Taylor Coleridge*, ed. Kathleen Coburn, vol. i, 1957, item 373 3.15 *f16* and *17*.

even to Retching began instantly—'You wish to see my Things
—what do you wish to see—To see all, or half, or quarter is impos-
sible, in one or in two Days—name the collection—Pictures, or
Coins, or Minerals, or Anatomical Preparations, or, or, or, or, or, &
&c &c.'—Now I had heard that his Coins & Minerals were really
admirable—so I would *not* see them—I was afraid of too much
Truth, that Poisoner of Imagination!—besides, for Coins I don't
care a dam!—& Minerals—have I not seen Professor Wiedemann's,
& the Duke of Brunswick's, & Greenough's Collection? So I chose
his Pictures—O Lord! it was a Treat!—His Eloquence, which is
natural & unaffected, really surprized me—in the space of half an
hour I counted on my fingers at least half a million Sterling, that he
had given as purchase money—The earliest attempts of all the
great Masters, & their last Performances—Cranach, & Holbein,
Michael Angelo, Raphael, Correggio, &c &c &c—& behind each a
Distich, of Beireis's own Composition—I wondered at all with broad
eyes, hands uplifted!! like two Notes of Admiration & such a stupid
Face of Praise, that Beireis fell in raptures—Extacied as I was
with each & all, yet I never forgot to turn to the Back of each
Picture, & read aloud with admiring Emphasis the Latin Distich—
still trying the Experiment, whether I could not rise above Beireis's
Self-Praises—in vain! My most extravagant Compliments were as
German Mustard to Cayenne Pepper!—Some originals of Correggio
he certainly has—but of Rafael assuredly none—after all, his
German Pictures are, in my opinion, the most valuable.—But hang
his Pictures—it was the *Man* that interested.—I asked him once
with great earnestness whether he had not drawn on himself the
Envy of all the European Sovereigns! O Ja! entsetzlich! was his
answer. But (rejoined I) it is lucky for you that the French Revolu-
tion has happened—or beyond a Doubt you would have to fear an
Invasion!—On my Honour, even this was not too Extravagant.—
At last, after three hours' Picture-seeing, during which he spoke
constantly & always eloquently, I begged him, with trembling
voice & downcast eyes, to favor our thirsty Ears with only the
'Geschichte seines weltberühmten Demants'—to *see* it would be
too great a request—Immediately he gave us a narration, quite
as entertaining tho' not so probable as the story of the Wonderful
Lamp—then took me to see his Eating Duck of Brass, which quacked
like rusty Hinges—tho' Beireis asked me seriously, if I could dis-
tinguish it from a real Duck's Quack!—I shut my eyes—lifted up
both my hands—listened—& cried—Herr Jesus!!!! On our return
from these Machineries into his Parlour then—yes—then he shook
my hand friendlily—& out of his Pocket he pulled the Diamond—
apparently, a semi transparent Pebble almost as large as my Fist!—

I will write again from Celle—for now I must interrupt my Narration, to talk of piteous Care—No Chest, no Portmanteau!—the Kaufman has heard this Morning, that it ought to have been here on the first of July—My Stars! what shall I do!—Last night I sprinkled my shirt with [water], hung it up at the window, & slept naked—for my *one* clean Shirt I *must* keep till I get to Hamburg.— Heaven! I stink like an old Poultice!—I should mislead any Pack of Foxhounds in Great Britain—Put a Trail of Rusty Bacon at a Furlong Distance, & me at a mile, and they would follow *me*—I should hear a cry of Stop Thief close at my ears with a safe Conscience—but if I caught only the Echo of a Tally Ho! I should climb up into a Tree—! You know me too well, to suspect Hyperbole— I stink damnably—& that's the Truth! Lord a mercy on those poor Imps that are condemned to live between the Toes of the Devil's Dam who wears black Worsted Socks, & uses Turney Sarat for Corn Plaster—O those that lived under the Devil's Tail have a Heaven in Comparison—Mercy—& my Books—I shall be ruined—on the Debtors' Side in Newgate—just 5 Yards distant from Sodomy, Murder, & House-breaking—Soul of Lessing!—hover over my Boxes!—Ye Minnesänger! fly after them!—Dear Greenough!— Dear Parry! Carlyon—Fred—I go—the Kaufman had forgotten to take place—so we go with the Package—Chester has got St Antony's Fire in his Legs—& his Arse is sore—

Your affectionate
S. T. Coleridge

368. *To Thomas N. Longman*

Address: Messrs Longman & Rees | Paternoster Row | London.
MS. Longmans, Green & Co. Ltd. *Pub.* Collected Letters of Samuel Taylor Coleridge, *i. 654.* The earlier text of this letter was drawn from a transcript. *Stamped*: Keswick.

Monday Dec. 15
1800

Dear Sir

It gives me great pleasure that I am able to inform you, that the last sheet of the Lyrical Ballads is sent off—I have already commenced Negotiations for securing them a fair & honest Review.—I should advise, that 3 or 4 Copies should be sent to different people of eminence: one to Mrs Jordan, (who intended to sing stanzas of the Mad Mother in Pizarro if she acted Cora again—) one to Mrs Barbauld—and one to Mr Wilberforce—if you agree with me,

Appendix B

Mr Wordsworth will write appropriate complimentary Letters with each—With neither of these has Mr W. any acquaintance— I propose it only as likely to push the sale.—Of their ultimate & permanent success, I have no doubt—I am especially pleased that I have contributed nothing to the second Volume, as I can now exert myself loudly & every where in their favor without suspicion of vanity or self-interest. I have written Letters to all my acquaintance whose voices I think likely to have any Influence. In all this I am guided, if I know my own heart, wholly & exclusively by my almost unbounded admiration of the poems—. The second Volume is indeed greatly superior to the first.—

Now for myself. In Christmas week I shall be in London, & will explain to you the delay in my Manuscript—tho' indeed the explanation is short enough. After I had finished the work & written you, I was convinced by a friend that a long account which I had given of the Illuminati would raise a violent clamour against me & my publisher—yet I had said nothing but what I am assured was the truth—at the same time Mr Wordsworth who had been in a different part of Germany offered me the use of his Journal tho' not of his name—I immediately resolved to throw my work into Chapters instead of Letters, & substitute my friend's account of Germany farther south, than I had been, instead of the obnoxious Letters. This however would have taken so little time that you would have had the copy, within a week or ten days at most later than the day appointed—but at that time a complaint seized my head & eyes, which made it impracticable for me even to read, & after a six weeks' continuance, during which time I had in vain used Leaches, Blisters, & God knows what, it was carried off by six large Boils which appeared behind my ear down to my Shoulder & which are not yet quite healed.— I leave this place the day after Christmas Day, & you may depend on it that from the first of January to the printing of the last page your Printer shall not have to complain of an hour's delay.

Mrs Coleridge & my two Children are well. You will present my best respects to Mrs Longman & believe me, dear Sir,

with a great sense of your constant Civility

Your obliged humble / Servant,
S. T. Coleridge

Appendix B

463 A. *To the Editor of the 'Morning Post'*

Pub. Morning Post, *7 October 1802.*

[Early October 1802]

Mr. EDITOR,

The following Verses were composed before daylight, on the morning appointed for the departure of a very worthy, but not very pleasant, visitor; whom, it was feared, the rain might detain. If you give it a place in your paper, it must be under the title of

AN ODE TO THE RAIN.[1]

463 B. *To William Calvert*[2]

MS. Mr. Jonathan Wordsworth. Hitherto unpublished.

[13 October 1802][3]

Dear Calvert

I thank you for your kind present—the gift is good, & the givers better—Mrs Calvert has been exceedingly kind in troubling herself with Derwent—for a very troublesome little Fellow I fear she must have found him—. Wordsworth, with his Wife & Sister, walked on with me, drawn forward mile after mile by the interest of much to hear & much to tell after so very unusual & important an absence,[4] till they found themselves considerably more than half way on the road to Keswick—& Mary & Dorothy were so impatiently eager to see Derwent, that they determined to go on, & unless too fatigued to return early tomorrow morning—a sort of rapid *Incog.* business. If they stay longer than tomorrow they will call—if not, you will be good enough to consider this as a mere accident—as their *apparitions* only—for in truth they hoped to have concealed their rapid *in and out* even from themselves, by way of a poetic Hyperbole which often borders very near on an Irish Bull, you know.—They send their kindest & best remembrances—

Your's with unfeigned esteem

S. T. Coleridge

---

[1] See *Poems*, i. 382, and David V. Erdman, 'Unrecorded Coleridge Variants', *Studies in Bibliography*, ed. F. T. Bowers, vol. xi, 1958, p. 158. For Coleridge's estimate of this poem see Letter 464.

[2] William Calvert, the brother of Wordsworth's benefactor, Raisley Calvert, lived at Windy Brow, 'scarce half a mile' from Greta Hall. See Letter 378.

[3] Dorothy Wordsworth's *Journal* establishes the date of the present letter. '[*October*] *13th* [*1802*], *Wednesday*. Set forwards with him [Coleridge] towards Keswick, and he prevailed us to go on. We consented, Mrs. C. not being at home.' On the evening of 14 Oct. the Wordsworths called on the Calverts. *Journals of Dorothy Wordsworth*, ed. E. de Selincourt, 2 vols., 1952, i. 183.

[4] Coleridge refers, of course, to the journey which Wordsworth and Dorothy made to France previous to the former's marriage on 4 Oct. 1802.

Appendix B

470 A. *To Davies Giddy*[1]

Address: Davies Giddy Esqre | Tredrea | near Redruth | Cornwall
[Readdressed in another hand] *Marazion*
MS. Royal Institution of Cornwall. Hitherto unpublished.

Crescelly, near Pembroke, Nov. 27. 1802.

Dear Sir

I write to you at the request of our friend, T. Wedgewood, who is on a shooting scheme here, to make the following Inquiries of you—whether you could learn from any of your shooting Friends, in what part of Cornwall the best Cock-shooting is ?—How far such part, or parts, may be from a tolerable Inn ? At what time of the year ? Whether the woodcocks make a long or short sojourn with you ? Whether the Covers are Woods, or only Furze & Fern ? Whether there be other Game, as Snipes, near the same places ?—

T. Wedgewood is sorry, that he has not been able hitherto to procure the portable Barometer for you; but as Mr Leslie is now on his way home from the Continent, T. W. hopes that he shall soon have it in his power to send you one.—He desires his kind remembrances to Mr, Mrs, and Miss Giddy.

He has employed me, as his Amanuensis, as writing disagrees with both his head & Stomach—& bids me add, that he makes a hundred apologies for giving you this Trouble.—

I am, dear Sir, | both for Mr Wedgewood & for myself | your's with sincere esteem,

S. T. Co'eridge

Direct to Mr T. W. at Cote-house near Bristol

581 B. *To Unknown Correspondent*

MS. University College Library, London. Hitherto unpublished.

Grosvenor Square—Monday Morning [26 March 1804]

Dear Sir

Sudden Indisposition, the ordinary effect of such Changes of weather, stopped me at a Friend's House in Argyll Street on my

---

[1] Davies Giddy, later Gilbert (1767–1839), friend of Humphry Davy, became president of the Royal Society in 1827. Coleridge first met Giddy in Aug. 1799. See R. S. Woof, 'Coleridge and Thomasina Dennis', *University of Toronto Quarterly*, Oct. 1962, pp. 37–54.

way to you & to Mr Horner.[1] When I say, that tho' about to leave
the Kingdom in a day or two I am *sorry* for it, believe me, I express
in homely phrase no every-day Feeling & am, dear Sir, respectfully

your sincere Well-wisher

S. T. Coleridge

626 A. *To Lady Holland*[2]

Address: The Right Honorable | Lady Holland | Holland House
MS. Private possession. Hitherto unpublished.
Postmark: 27 September 1806.

Saturday Morning,
26 [27] Septr. 1806.
348, Strand.

Madam

I was at Parndon at the time, your Ladyship's very flattering
Invitation arrived; and did not receive it till late last night. I fear,
that I must leave Town for the North so soon, that I shall not be
able to express my acknowlegements for the honor designed me, in
person. I can only say, that it would have been a pleasure, which I
had long wished for, tho' never anticipated: and am at present only
too conscious, that I owe the honor wholly to that kindness of
nature, which makes Mr W. Smith think and speak too highly of
those, who can be thought well of at all. Having been so long absent
from my country, and therefore—I am grieved yet forced to add—
absent too from all, that pursue noble purposes by honorable means,
I should be ashamed not to feel myself more than ordinarily pleased
by any commands from Holland House—for with most unfeigned
respect,

I am, | Madam,

Your Ladyship's | obliged and | obedient humble Servant,

S. T. Coleridge

---

[1] Evidently Francis Horner (1778–1817), English politician, who settled in
London in Mar. 1803. See *Memoirs and Correspondence of Francis Horner,
M.P.*, ed. Leonard Horner, 2 vols., 1843, i. 215. Coleridge refers to Francis
Horner in Letter 1604. [2] See Letter 626 and note.

Appendix B

649 A. *To Sara Hutchinson*

Address: Miss S. Hutchinson | T. Clarkson's, Esqre | Bury St Edmonds
MS. Dove Cottage. Hitherto unpublished fragment. This manuscript appears to be the second half of a foolscap sheet, of which the first leaf is torn off. The recto of the MS. contains a copy in Coleridge's handwriting of most of Andrew Marvell's poem, *On a Drop of Dew*. The verso contains the last four lines of the poem, the address, and this fragment to Sara Hutchinson. (From information kindly supplied by Miss Nesta Clutterbuck, Librarian.)

[May 1807][1]

... I pray you, write immediately 2 or 3 lines to me, at Mr Wade's, Bridge-Street, Bristol—just to let me know how you were, and how you are.—

683 A. *To J. J. Morgan*

Address: Mr. J. J. Morgan | St. James's Square | Bristol
MS. British Museum. Hitherto unpublished.
Postmark: 1 March 1808.

Tuesday Morning [1 March 1808]

My dear Morgan

Wordsworth arrived here on Saturday.[2] The Evening before a strange Eruption took place in my right Leg, and Foot (n.b. the intolerable *restlessness* in my right knee & thigh had been one of my sorest grievances during the whole of my confinement) and on the night following a similar Eruption took place in my left leg. I felt myself greatly and suddenly relieved in my visceral and vital parts, & in all my upper Half; but what is to be the result, whether it be the Harbinger of Recovery or of Dropsy, will be known by the result. If the former, I will endeavor to deserve it; if the latter, I am prepared for it. The Eruption is a mixture of Boils, or rather exquisitely sore Bumps, with a multitude of interspersed red Spots, the size of a Shilling, but oblong rather than round.—O dear Friend! it is mortifying to me to disclose these woeful Infirmities—but so is so!—I wrote to Mrs Coleridge entreating her to send Derwent by

---

[1] This fragment, which appears on paper watermarked 1806, was written at Bristol, where Coleridge arrived in early May 1807 and where he remained until early June. He and Mrs. Coleridge reached Nether Stowey on 6 June. Sara Hutchinson, as Letter 647 shows, left London for Bury St. Edmunds on 4 May. There she remained until June, when she set off for Halifax to join the Wordsworths. They found her at Halifax when they arrived there on 12 June. See Mrs. Henry Sandford, *Thomas Poole and His Friends*, 2 vols., 1888, ii. 182, and *Middle Years*, vol. i, Letters 302–5.

[2] Wordsworth had come to London, in part to see Coleridge, in part to make arrangements for the publication of *The White Doe of Rylstone*. See Letter 709.

Mr Estlin; and have received an answer, a second indeed, in which she conjures, & prays to me, not to *command* it, with no other argument, than the time of year, the possibility that he may have one of his feverish fits in the road, and the unfitness, & probable reluctance, of young Estlin to take care of him. I shall & can say nothing, till my own plans are determined—greatly as I have been excited & perhaps (for the time, like any other strong Stimulus) bettered by my friend's arrival & conversation, yet still my Judgement tells me, that I am TRIFLING—that the enemy is undermining the Citadel—& that a little better or a little worse is as nothing, till by having continued for some weeks under the immediate eye of Dr Beddoes I can be at rest, as to the *?* 'in what state am I really?' 'What *may* I hope? what *must* I expect?'—

As to Mrs C. I am weary at heart of writing to her. Whatever anxiety she may have for her Children she exhausts in momentary Scoldings and Fretfulnesses; but as to looking a *week* forward, it is out of her nature. And Mr Wordsworth, who has just left her, tells me, it is in vain to expect it. He says, 'her unimpressibility is almost a moral miracle'.—Now all her doleful Terrors concerning the state of Derwent's Eyes are gone—vanished!—all a trifle—&c—Merciful Heaven! if *I* have sinned, what have my sweet Babes done, that their Fate should be controlled and regulated by so unthinking, unfeeling a Being?—And yet according to her Letter to part with Derwent—O! she could not get over it—! She, that three years ago permitted him to remain with Sara Hutchinson 10 or 11 months [weeks?][1]—& at last he was sent back by Sara, without a *hint* from the mother, sent back by her with tears, and after a long struggle from her great love for the child, & pleasure she had in him, because she found the Boy's affections growing daily stronger toward her, & thought it *wrong* to rob the Mother of them—and after this, merely for the pleasure of an *idle visit*, by the Lord! she left the Brood for [two?][2] Months TO A SERVANT. And now, forsooth! [she wo]uld be broken-hearted, that he should be *with his Father*, under the care

[1] Derwent Coleridge was with Sara Hutchinson at Park House near Ullswater in Oct.–Nov. 1805—'to his great improvement', according to Dorothy Wordsworth. See *The Early Letters of William and Dorothy Wordsworth* (1787–1805), ed. E. de Selincourt, 1935, p. 534.

[2] MS. torn by seal. On 10 Feb. 1805 Dorothy Wordsworth reported to Mrs. Clarkson: 'Mrs Coleridge is coming on Tuesday to spend a few days with us on her Road to Liverpool. We had a note from her on Thursday saying that two days before Mary Stamper had gone to Church to be married without saying a word to her and the next day had come for her wages. This when Mrs Coleridge was preparing for a journey and had intended leaving the Children to her care! Luckily she has got a young Woman to take the charge who has worked for her and is remarkably fond of them.' Ibid. 444 and 481.

of two Women, of whose exceeding kindness & fondness for him & Sara she herself had spoken so warmly, that (I *thank* her for that!) it was *my* motive for first visiting at your House.

I shall say nothing, till my Plans are settled—then I *must* say, aye, and *have it done*! God knows! to *command* any one is opposite to my nature—to command a woman, the mother of my Children, an anguish—but 'to *command*' is the sad result of the want of being beloved—and what *can* I do, but my Duty?—Surely, they are my Children, as well as her's—and her's as well as mine. My own gratifications therefore I will never consult—; but neither must I *blindly* follow her's; that conduct must I pursue, which the Interest, the Virtue, the general Well-being of the Children themselves imperiously dictate to me. If after this I am called a Tyrant, I must appeal to God, and my own poor bleeding Heart.

I have been obliged during the last week or more to write at least a Quire of letter paper in letters & replies to great & little men in order to procure the Discharge of Mrs Wordsworth's Brother, impressed from a merchant Ship—& have succeeded, as far as the Admiralty have any power. As I never *exerted* and stretched my Interest so much before, it has given me no sma[ll] additional knowlege of the World. With every blessing that can be breathed for[th from] a grateful & loving Spirit, I love & bless your Wife & her Sister [and am *tr*]uly your Friend,

S. T. C.

701. *To Thomas N. Longman*

Address: Mr Longman | Paternoster Row
MS. Longmans, Green & Co. Ltd. Pub. Collected Letters of Samuel Taylor Coleridge, *iii. 99.* The earlier text of this letter was drawn from a transcript.

[Early May 1808]

My dear Sir

I will take upon me the correction of the Sheets of 'the White Doe'.—I seriously hope, that nothing in my last, which was wholly intended to amuse you, has given you offence—Upon my honor, you were not even in my Thoughts—I reasoned with A, X. Y, & Z., exactly as a Mathematician—

be assured, my dear Sir! I highly respect you—

S. T. Coleridge

709. *To Thomas N. Longman*

Address: Messrs. Longman, Hurst, Rees, & Orme | Booksellers | Paternoster Row
MS. Longmans, Green & Co. Ltd. Pub. Collected Letters of Samuel Taylor Coleridge, *iii. 115.* The earlier text of this letter was drawn from a transcript.
Postmark: 23 May 1808.

[Endorsed Courier office]
[23 May 1808]

Dear Sir

I am painfully surprized by the extract from Mr Wordsworth's Letter.

Mr W. came to town, among other motives, to publish his Poem. He offered Terms—did not choose to submit his work to your previous inspection—& of course felt them, as declined. I did not see the matter in exactly the same light, as he did. I thought, that in the purchase, not of a total Copyright, but of a mere first Edition —& that at a very handsome price—and that too from an Author, whose last publication had not been so favorably received, as his admirers anticipated—a Publisher had an undoubted *Right* (in the *equity* between man & man, as well as in the vulgar Sense of the word) to have the means of some distinct Information concerning it's nature, and the probability of it's immediate Sale, from some *indifferent* Judge. As to it's intrinsic merits He might perhaps be disposed to rely on the Author's own opinion & that of his particular friends; but what is this to the persons, who are to purchase a first Edition at a risk, which can be made to answer only by a quick return?—I advised him to leave the Poem with me, & to appoint me his plenipotentiary—He did so—Mr T. Rees was so good as to pass an hour or two with me—we read part of the Poem & discussed the whole—he made his report to you—& the result was, that tho' still in favor of the prudence of your first proposal you however acceded to Mr Wordsworth's Proposal. I informed him of this—received his full confirmation—found by an after letter that his opinions differed from mine with regard to one essential in the Tale of the Poem—therefore confined myself to the correction of mere verbal inaccuracies—which I found very few & very trifling—when I received a letter from Miss Wordsworth, who always, except where she expresses the contrary, writes in her Brother's name & authority, from which the following is the Extract—'We are all *very anxious* that the White Doe should be sent to the Press AS SOON AS POSSIBLE. The corrections cannot be of a very difficult or troublesome kind—We think it of the UTMOST IMPORTANCE, that it should come out before the buz of your Lectures is settled.'

My Lectures will finish in about a fortnight—I appeal to you, &
to common Sense, whether my transmission of the Poem can be
deemed a 'misinterpretation' of the above? or whether after
having been authorized to negociate, after the result had been
confirmed (not to say, received with thanks) and after I had been
thus spurred on, it is exactly agreeable with common English to
speak of 'Mr Coleridge's having sent A Mss poem of MINE to you'—
A!—

God bless you, my dear Sir!

& S. T. Coleridge

P.S. I had sent it before; but retracted it, in order to write out the
parts which spite of the Author's present opinion, I yet wished to
alter, in hopes that his opinion might alter.—'Tis a strange World,
Mr Longman!—especially with those, who have to do with
Authors!—

721 A. *To J. J. Morgan*

MS. Bodleian Library. Hitherto unpublished fragment.

4 Dec. 1808
Grasmere, Kendal.

. . . circumstances which they would mourn over rather than con-
demn, while I am subscribing myself, dear Morgan,

their and your | obliged and affectionate
S. T. Coleridge

762. *To Thomas N. Longman*

Address: Messrs. Longman, Rees & Co | Paternoster Row | London
MS. Longmans, Green & Co. Ltd. Pub. with omis. Collected Letters of Samuel
Taylor Coleridge, *iii. 202.* The earlier text of this letter was drawn from a
transcript.

Greta Hall, Keswick.—
Thursday Night. [27 April 1809]

Dear Sir

It gave me much concern, first that contrary to my direction
some books belonging to you were sent hither from London among
my own; and secondly, that after having been properly packed up
for my friend, Mr De Quincey, to take with him to town, they were,
as I find, forgotten and left behind. Immediately on my return to
Grasmere (for I must remain here and at Penrith, till the first
Number of 'The Friend' has been sent off) they shall be additionally
secured, and forwarded to you by the Waggon, Carriage paid.

Appendix B

You will have seen by my Prospectus the general nature of my weekly paper, which will be circulated to those, that order it, by the general Post, it having been registered &c as a Newspaper. It has been often asked, whether 'The Friend' is to exclude *Politics* altogether? My answer is: If by Politics be meant the Events of the Day, Public Papers, or Discussions thereon, or attacks on or defences of particular measures, or particular men in or out of power, in short, personal & party politics, Yes! all these the Friend will exclude. But if the word 'Political' be taken in it's wider sense, so as to include whatever relates to the public conduct of men and nations, I must answer, No! for the Object of my Work is, as far as in me lies and in those who assist me, to draw the attention of the country to Principle and Principles instead of mere Expedience & *prudential* maxims, in *every thing*—in Literature, in the fine Arts, in Morals, in Religion, in Legislation, and in international Law. The first number will be sent from Penrith by Thursday's Post, May 12 [11], so as to be in London & all places equi-distant on Saturday Morning, 14 [13] May. Any service, you might find it in your power to render it, I need not say, will be acknowleged & remembered gratefully by me.

Ill-health, and still more the consequent morbid Low-spirits amounting almost to despondency, joined to the unworthy Reception of Southey's Madoc & Wordsworth's Poems, hung such a weight on every attempt I made to finish two Poems, four fifths of which had been written years ago, that I at last gave up the Thought altogether. I once remarked, that there were Beauties & Excellences enough in the very *worst* of Shakespere's Plays to ensure it's damnation had it appeared in the present age. Now it is most certain, that my Poems do not contain either in kind or degree the qualities which make Wordsworth's poems so dear to me & many much greater men, and so repulsive to others—But it was enough that I am known to be the particular Friend both of Southey & Wordsworth to draw upon me the whole clamor of those who have waged war against them. I told Jeffray that it was rather hard upon me, that for the poems, which I have published, I received the not-undeserved censure that my style was too highly ornamented, and deviating from simplicity by a too constant employment of the strongest words & boldest figures of Poetry. Even the ancient Mariner, the only poem of any size that has appeared since—& that anonymously—was yet every where criticized in the Reviews, as '*Laboriously* beautiful'—and 'over-polished in the diction with *Dutch* Industry'—And now for *no*-poems at all, but only for my acquaintanceships, I am abused in every Review & Magazine, in time & out of time, for the *simple* &

puerile: tho' it is a fact, that I was the very first person who commenced the attack on mock-simplicity in the Sonnets (in one of the early Monthly Magazines) signed Nehemiah Higgenbotham —. I have however some reason to believe that Jeffray is well inclined to make me the amende honorable—at least, if I may believe his own letters.—These objections however are perhaps the offspring of Low-spirits in great measure—But the alteration, I have made in the plan, I made from sober reflection.—The poems in my possession are of two sorts—1. Poems of such length that either of them with the necessary notes would make a small volume, when completed.—Of these not a line has ever appeared in any form—. 2. Poems, all of which are completed, & corrected for the Press, the longest of which is a thousand lines—a second 700—the others from 300 to 10 lines—which altogether amount to four thousand lines, and printed as the last Edition of my Poems would with the notes make near 400 pages. But of these[1] tho' all are my own property, yet several have already appeared, tho' very different from their present form, in the Morning Post—these however are of small consequence from their minor size &c and the A. Mariner (which in any future Edition Wordsworth will withdraw from the L. Ballads, now sold out) in the L. B—My Wish therefore is to publish these, as a second, or 2nd & 3rd Volu[mes] of *my Poems*— the first being 'Poems written chiefly from the age of 17 to 25'— the second—'Poems from 25 to 33'—and hereafter to publish whatever I may publish by the name of the particular Poem—as 'The three Graves, a Sexton's Tale, by S. T. C.'—&c—

Now as the first Volume is your *property*, I have no objection to dispose of the absolute Copyright of the second, or second & third (as with notes & critical preface it will make, as I find by accurate measurements, two Volumes of the same size with the last Edition of the first) both for that reason, and in order that any defect of immediate Novelty from the Ancient Mariner having past thro' several Editions in the L. B. (for the same objection scarcely applies to those that have appeared occasionally & often without my knowlege, in different channels & at very distant dates) may be fully counterbalanced by the certainty of the whole advantage (whatever that may chance to be) derived from any present or future reputation, that I may chance to obtain.—It shall be at your own command on what day the Poems shall be put to the Press, and within what time completed—only it is my particular

---

[1] At this point in the MS. Coleridge wrote and then cancelled the following passage: (tho' excepting two or three small verses in the second Volume of the annual Anthology).

Wish, that they should be printed under my own Eye by Brown, of
Penrith, & the difference in the *Price* will nearly pay the carriage to
London if not wholly. He prints excellently, & his Type is quite
new from Wilson, of Glasgow.

For the copy-right I ask 120£.—Brown could begin any day
after May 21st.—

When you write, be so good as to send my account for Books &c—

Mr Southey's little Boy the night before last had an attack of the
Croup; but thank Heaven! by instant Bleeding at the Jugular, and
a blister on the Throat, the Danger seems past.—

Respectfully, dear Sir,

S. T. Coleridge

828 A. *To Dr. Edward Jenner*

Pub. The Life of Edward Jenner, M.D., *by John Baron, 2 vols., 1827, 1838, ii.
175.*

7, Portland-place, Hammersmith,
near London, 27th Sept. 1811.

Dear Sir,

I take the liberty of intruding on your time, first, to ask you
where and in what publication I shall find the best and fullest
history of the vaccine matter as preventive of the small-pox. I
mean the year in which the thought first suggested itself to you,
(and surely no honest heart would suspect me of the baseness of
flattery if I had said, inspired into you by the All-preserver, as
a counterpoise to the crushing weight of this unexampled war) and
the progress of its realization to the present day. My motives are
twofold: first and principally, the time is now come when the
Courier (the paper of the widest circulation, and, as an evening
paper, both more read in the country, and read at more leisure
than the morning papers,) is open and prepared for a series of
essays on this subject; and the only painful thought that will
mingle with the pleasure with which I shall write them, is, that it
should at this day, and in this the native country of the discoverer
and the discovery, be even *expedient* to write at all on the subject.
My second motive is more selfish. I have planned a poem on this
theme, which after long deliberation, I have convinced myself is
capable in the highest degree of being poetically treated, according
to our divine bard's own definition of poetry, as '*simple, sensuous,*
(i.e. appealing to the senses, by imagery, sweetness of sound, &c.)

and impassioned.'—O, dear sir! how must every good and warm-hearted man detest the habit of mouth panegyric and the fashion of smooth falsehood, were it only for this,—that it throws a damp on the honestest feelings of our nature when we speak or write to or of those whom we do indeed revere and love, and know that it is our *duty* to do so; those concerning whom we feel as if they had lived centuries before our time in the certainty that centuries after us all good and wise men will so feel. This, this, dear sir, is true FAME as contradistinguished from the trifle, reputation; the latter explains itself, quod iste *putabat*, hic *putat*, one man's echo of another man's fancy or supposition. The former is in truth φήμη, *i.e.* ὃ φάσιν οἱ καλοκἀγαθοί, through all ages, the united suffrage of the Church of Philosophy, the fatum or verdict unappealable. So only can we live and act exempt from the tyranny of time: and thus live still, and still act upon us, Hippocrates, Plato, Milton. And hence, too, while reputation in any other sense than as moral character is a bubble, fame is a *worthy* object for the best men, and an awful duty to those, whom Providence has gifted with the power to acquire it. For it is, in truth, no other than benevolence extended beyond the grave, active virtue no longer cooped in between the cradle and the coffin. Excuse this overflow, and let me only add, that most grateful am I, and a consolation it is to me for my own almost uselessness, that what I could most have wished to have done,—yea, had in lazy indefinite reveries early dreamt about doing,—has been effected in my own lifetime, and by men whom I have seen, and many of whom I have called my friends; in short, that I have known and personally loved Clarkson, Davy, Dr. Andrew Bell, and Jenner.

But while I gratify my own feelings I am pressing painfully on yours. I will, therefore, avail myself of an accident to change the subject. A very amiable lady, a particular friend of mine, and dear to me as a sister, has been subject generally once or twice in a year to a severe tooth-ache. She has many decayed back teeth; so many, as to put extraction almost out of the question; and besides, from the circumstances of the case, and the manner in which her face, eyes, and head are affected, I am convinced that the locality of the pain is in a great measure accidental; that it is what I have heard called a nervous rheumatic affection, and possibly dependent on some affection of the stomach or other parts of her inside. She is single, about six and twenty, has excellent health and spirits in all other respects, and bears this affliction with more than even feminine patience. Hot topical applications, such as tinctures of the pyrethrum, with ether, oil of cloves, &c. &c. give only momentary relief, or rather palliation. Her last attack was in November last, when she was confined to her bed more than a month by it, and reduced to a skeleton. Yesterday she had a return, and I am sadly afraid of another fit of it. Should you remember any case in point in the course of your practice, and be able to suggest any mode of treatment, I will not say that I should be most thankful, but only that you will make a truly estimable family both grateful and happy. My friend, Mr. Morgan, has under Mr. Andrews, to whom you were so kind as to give him a letter of introduction, got rid entirely of his complaint. Though I still suspect it to have been symptomatic of some *tendency*, at least, to schirrus in some of the viscera, the liver probably. I have somewhere read or heard, that ipecacuanha in very large doses, so as not to act as an emetic, but as a sudorific, has effected great cures in rheumatic affections of uncertain, and, as they say, *nervous* kind. I have not yet read the answers, &c. &c. of Davy and Murray on the oxymuriatic, whether a chemical element or a compound; but I own, that in Davy's first communication to the R. S. I appeared to myself to see a laxer logic than is common with him. I judge merely as a logician, taking the facts for granted, and applying the rules of logic as an algebraist, his rules to X. Y. Z.—With every wish for your life and health, believe me, dear sir,

Most sincerely your respectful friend and servant,

S. T. Coleridge.

Be pleased to remember me to Mr. Pruen should you see him.

837 A. *To Joseph Hardcastle*

Address: Joseph Hardcastle, Esqre | Old Swan Stairs | London Bridge
MS. Mr. W. Hugh Peal. Hitherto unpublished.
Postmark: 12 November ⟨1811⟩.

7, Portland Place Hammersmith.
12 Novemb[e]r 1811.

Mr Coleridge takes the liberty of addressing a Prospectus[1] of his Lectures to Mr Hardcastle, and conscious to himself that his best efforts have been and will be directed to the impressing on the minds and hearts of his Readers or Auditors, that true Taste is indissolubly connected with the moral sense and that inward Harmony with Man and Nature which Religion alone can give, he feels encouraged to hope that his present Undertaking will not be without such

[1] This letter is written in the blank pages of a Prospectus of Coleridge's lectures at the London Philosophical Society in 1811–12. See Letters 835 and 841.

favorable recommendation as it may fall in the way of Mr Hardcastle to give it, among his Friends and Acquaintance. Mr Coleridge begs leave to add his respectful remembrances to Mrs Hardcastle and Daughters.

881 A. *To Miss Smith*[1]

MS. Mr. W. Hugh Peal. Hitherto unpublished.

[*Circa* 7 December 1812][2]

Mr Coleridge presents his respectful Compliments to Miss Smith, and hopes, that in soliciting her permission to wait on her at any hour not pre-occupied, he is not taking an undue liberty.

Mr and Mrs Kenny[3] had given Mr Coleridge the prospect of being introduced to Miss Smith at their House; but the unfeigned admiration inspired by the Isabella of Saturday Evening (the first time, Mr C. had the opportunity of seeing Miss Smith, as far at least as continued Tears permitted him to see her) has rendered him impatient under the Hope delayed—he being too anxious to make any alterations, whether in addition or omission, which Miss Smith may wish or suggest.—

886 A. *To Mrs. James Kenney*[4]

MS. Boston Public Lib. Hitherto unpublished fragment.

71, Berners' Street.—
[February 1813 ?]

... (I suppose they mean complying, & indifferent as to omissions, always assenting to them gladly, & often pleading for them against

---

[1] Miss Smith played the role of Donna Teresa in Coleridge's *Remorse*, which opened at Drury Lane on Saturday, 23 Jan. 1813, and ran for twenty nights. See Wise, *Bibliography*, 83.

[2] In the present letter Coleridge mentions having seen Miss Smith in the part of Isabella on 'Saturday Evening'. Miss Smith first appeared at Drury Lane as Isabella in Southerne's *Fatal Marriage* on Tuesday, 1 Dec. 1812. The performance which Coleridge attended was that of Saturday, 5 Dec. As the contents suggest, this letter was written before the rehearsals of *Remorse* began. Writing to Wordsworth on Monday noon, 7 Dec. 1812, Coleridge remarks: 'The Rehearsal of my Play commences this week.'

[3] See next letter.

[4] See Letter 891 to James Kenney, the dramatist. Kenney married Holcroft's widow in 1812. See *Robinson on Books and Their Writers*, i. 68.

the wishes of the actor & Manager)[1] but at the same time, the most indolent in doing any thing, either by private Influence or by the public Press, in my own or their favour.[2] I wish you had been so good as to send to me . . .[3]

. . . I shall therefore say no more—than to conjure you & Mr Kenny not to attribute any Voluntary Neglect to your obliged

& affectionate Friend,
S. T. Coleridge

945 A. *To J. J. Morgan*

Address: J. J. Morgan, Esqre, Mrs Smith's, | Ashley, Box | Bath
MS. British Museum. Hitherto unpublished.

16 August, 1814

My dear Friend

I have informed both Mr Daniel, and my excellent friend, Wade, that as soon as Allston has done with me, I shall migrate to Ashley for a month or so.—I did not call at Porter's for one *cause* & for one *reason*—the first necessitating, & the latter obligatory, each independent of the other. First, I was taken so unwell, after dinner, that I was obliged to sit all the afternoon & evening in the Kitchen by the Kitchen Fire, feverish & shivery. It would have been madness to have gone out. Secondly, I recollected Porter's behaviour to Wade—& tho' I have no resentment for myself, I have no right to waive that which I have on the part of a friend. Hood heard from Kiddle, that you sate expecting me—& said—'I *am sure*, Coleridge never would dine or wine at Porter's, till P. had made a satisfying Apology or Confession to Wade. I am *sure*, that he would not do it.'

Of my own portrait[4] I am no judge—Allston is highly gratified with it, & promises himself that it will be even better than Mr King's—which in it's present state is the most looking-glassish, ipsissimous, living flesh & blood thing, I ever beheld. I cannot

---

[1] In writing to John Rickman on 25 Jan. 1813 Coleridge made the same point and added that Arnold (Samuel James Arnold, the manager of Drury Lane) and Raymond (J. G. Raymond, the stage manager) had given him the name of '*the Amenable Author*'. See also Letter 887, in which Coleridge says he has been nicknamed 'the anomalous Author'.

[2] Arnold had urged Coleridge to exert himself to reply to the attacks on *Remorse* in the daily press. See Letter 886.

[3] The MS. of this fragmentary paragraph is now covered over by a piece of tissue. For the reading I am indebted to Mr. R. S. Woof and Mr. John Alden, Keeper of Rare Books, Boston Public Library.

[4] For a reproduction of Washington Allston's portrait of Coleridge see *Collected Letters*, iii. 509.

believe, that mine will be equal; because King's is so very far finer a face. I am not *mortified*, tho' I own I should better like it to be otherwise, that my face is not a manly or representable Face— Whatever is impressive, is part fugitive, part *existent* only in the imaginations of persons impressed strongly by my conversation— The face *itself* is a FEEBLE, unmanly face. I never perceived this so intuitively, as in comparing my portrait with King's, both nearly in the same state of forwardness.—The exceeding *Weakness*, Strengthlessness, in my face, was ever painful to me—not as my own face—but as *a* face.—

I am hesitating whether I should send a letter of C. Lamb's to you—but hang it! I will—& will pay the Postage—it recalled old times—but I don't understand the *Gos-lettuces*[1]—

On Wednesday Allston is to finish my face—& he will require two Sittings after that—I trust, Thursday and Saturday—If so, I will be with you on Monday—

I have had another angry letter from the Irish Fellow, about his India subject for a Tragedy—challenging the papers, he sent me.— Papers! were they not sent to the man, he desired them to be sent to?—Pray, ask my dear Sisters—(no! Megrim shan't be my *Sister*.) As far as I recollect, they furnished no temptation from the softness of the Paper to make *any* use of them—Damn the Paddy! he almost threatens to cut my Throat, & make a Tragedy of me, without Remorse—

I shall write again by this Post both to Street & to Stuart.

In reading Charles Lamb's Letter, I had an odd perplexity of Feeling—a Wish, that *you* had had the place[2]—& yet an incapability either for you or for myself to wish any thing that should confine us in London—God grant that with a quiet Conscience I could never be out of the sight of green Fields, or out of company with you, Mary & Charlotte—tho' the two latter quarrel with me in a very inexplicable way—for they don't hate me—& I never hear any thing like praise, or sugar comfits, from them—tho' I endeavor to get 'em by saying all the sweet things, I can. Perhaps it is from mere ignorance & not from disinclination. I will therefore write down a few sheets full of the soothing, handsome speeches,

---

[1] Coleridge refers to a letter from Charles Lamb of 13 Aug. 1814: 'What is gone of that frank-hearted circle, Morgan and his cos-lettuces?' *Lamb Letters*, ii. 131–2. Cos lettuce is a variety of lettuce from the island of Cos. For Lamb's explanation of his use of the term see his letter to Coleridge of 26 Aug. 1814.

[2] On 13 Aug. 1814 Lamb informed Coleridge that Rickman had become 'Clerk to the House of Commons' and that Edward Phillips had 'strangely stept into Rickman's Secretaryship'. *Lamb Letters*, ii. 132. Rickman had been secretary to Charles Abbot (later Lord Colchester), Speaker of the House of Commons since 1802.

that they *may* make me—with exact rules & directions for the time & place of administering them—

Your Cousin,[1] Long Ashton, is the greatest Fool, I ever encountered. But I must say nothing about Relations by Gore, or I shall have Mary at me—& *therefore* & *of course*, in the 'black is white' Line, Miss Charlotte! and vice versâ—in short, they are no better than sworn Conspiratresses against me—and I pay no regard to their conjoint testimony. If I could contrive to make them quarrel with each other, I should have some chance—otherwise, tho' not only innocent, but even virtuous, I am left in the Lurch—for *you* never say a word, instead of joining with me as they join with each other.—

S. T. Coleridge.—

I shall send off a Box of Books & Cloathes, by the Canal—directed to Long Ashton's Brother, Ben:[2] who seems to have had a Benjamin's mass of common sense given him. But how to get them from Bath to Ashley—aye! there's the Rub.—Perhaps, if there is a Wag[g]on from Bristol thro' Chippenham, that might be the better way. My respects to Sally, of the brown Eyes 'an excellent gift in woman'—& to Mr Bill, Truant and Stick-attractor.—

955 A. *To John Chubb*

Address: John Chubb, Esqre. | Bridgewater | Somerset Post paid
MS. Fitzwilliam Museum, Cambridge. Hitherto unpublished.

My dear Sir 24 Jan. 1814. [1815][3]

An old friend of mine, a man of whom I know no other fault, nor after ten years' intimacy have ever discovered any, but that of having in too many instances acted on the notion that others were as honest as himself, has so far entangled himself in the Toils of an unprincipled Scoundrel by an act of indiscreet confidence & misplaced Kindness, that tho' there is little Debt [doubt ?] that the Law would determine in my friend's Favor yet the other Party might from mere malignity put him to Trouble, which he dreads not on his own account but for his Wife's—an amiable & excellent woman, in a very ticklish state of Health, and on whom any Fright might have even fatal Consequences. For in palliation of my friend's

---

[1] Ben Morgan's brother lived in Long Ashton, near Bristol. See postscript.

[2] Ben Morgan, the Bath chemist. See Letters 942–3, 950, and 952.

[3] In the present letter Coleridge mentions his 'Letters to Judge Fletcher', which appeared in the *Courier*, Sept.–Dec. 1814. In Nov. 1814 Coleridge told both Kenyon and Stuart that he was removing to Calne, Wiltshire. (See Letters 954–5.) Coleridge's letter, therefore, was written in 1815.

(1031)

Confidence I ought to say, that the ungrateful Wretches are two of her own nearest Relations—and I have certain knowlege, that the main motive of one of them is Revenge, in consequence of my friend's having refused to admit his Visits on account of Reports, which he had not taken the proper means to repel, tho' often prest to do so—As we do not wish him to know where my friend is, & he has lately offered to settle this matter and instead of claiming a pretended Debt to pay part at least of a true Debt owing to my friend, I have taken the Liberty of begging you to put the inclosed Letter into the Bridgewater Post Office, on the 26th, and to take up any Letter which may come in answer directed—J. J. Morgan, to be left at the Post office, Bridgewater—and inclose it in a letter for *me*, Calne, Wiltshire.[1]

I was delighted to hear from Mr and Mrs Kenyon so very pleasing an account of Morley.—I have not for years met with persons that seem so worthy of Love & Esteem as the Kenyons. They will be a great acquisition to your neighbourhood.—

I am myself engaged in finishing a Drama, and a large theological Work on Revelation considered only as antedating the discoveries of Philosophy—so that the Mysteries of Religion are as the *Facit* of a Sum in Books of Arithmetic, to prevent wanderings out to supersede science—in short, that what are now Truths of Revelation, is [are ?] to be & if true must & will become Truths of Reason—and this I have endeavored to shew in the Doctrines of the Logos, and of original Sin—i.e. not ab Adamâ, but de *origine* de fonte—or *originating* Sin in opposition to *derived* or *acquired*—But my wretched Health makes it a slow & often interrupted Task—Did you see my Letter[s] to Judge Fletcher in the Courier, signed an Irish Protestant?—

Be assure[d], that absence has in no wise weakened the impression with which I was since I best knew you[2]

with unfeigned and affectionate | Esteem, my dear Sir,

your obliged & grateful

S. T. Coleridge

---

[1] In 1813 Morgan fled to Ireland to escape his creditors. By May 1814 he was back in England. See Letters 893 and 927-8. A notation probably made by Chubb in the MS. indicates the addressee of the 'inclosed Letter' mentioned above: 'Mr. W. M. Brent No. 12 Kirby St. Hatton Garden London.'

[2] Coleridge's friendship with John Chubb dates back to 1797. See Letter 203.

963. *To Lord Byron*

Address: For the Rt Honble Lord Byron | To Mr Murray's *care* | Mr Murray,
Bookseller, | Albermale Street | London.
MS. Lovelace Papers. Pub. Collected Letters of Samuel Taylor Coleridge, *iv.*
559. The earlier text of this letter was drawn from a transcript.
Postmark: 30 March 1815. *Stamped*: Calne.

> Calne, Wilts.
> Wednesday [29 March], Easter Week—1815.

My Lord

I feel that I am taking a liberty for which I shall have but small
excuse and no justification to offer, if I am not fortunate enough to
find one in your Lordship's approbation of my design: & unless
You should condescend to regard the writer as addressing himself
to Your Genius rather than your Rank, and graciously permit me
to forget my total inacquaintance with your Lordship personally in
my familiarity with your other more permanent Self, to which
your Works have introduced me. If indeed I had not in *them* dis-
covered that Balance of Thought and Feeling, of Submission and
Mastery; that one sole unfleeting Music, which is never of Yester-
day, but still remaining still reproduces *itself*, and powers *akin* to
itself, in the minds of other men;—believe me, my Lord! I not only
could not have hazarded this Boldness, but my own sense of pro-
priety would have precluded the very Wish. A sort of pre-established
good-will, not unlike that with which the Swan, instinctively, takes
up the weakling Cygnet into the Hollow between it's wings, I knew
I might confidently look for from one who is indeed a Poet; were I
but assured, that your Lordship had ever thought of me as a fellow-
laborer in the same Vineyard, and as not otherwise unworthy your
notice. And surely a fellow-laborer I *have* been, & a co-inheritor of
the same Bequest, tho' of a smaller portion; and tho' your Lord-
ship's ampler Lot is on the sunny side, while mine has lain open to
the North, my *growing* Vines gnawed down by Asses and my richest
and raciest Clusters carried off and spoilt by the plundering Fox.
Excuse, my Lord! the length and 'petitionary' solemnity of this
Preface, as attributable to the unquiet state of spirits, under which
I write this Letter, and my fears as to it's final reception. Anxiety
makes us all ceremonious.

Long since from many and respectable Quarters I have been
urged—and my Circumstances now compel me—to publish in two
Volumes all the poems composed by me from the year 1795 to the
present Date, that are sanctioned by my maturer Judgement, all*

---

* with the exception of one or at most two poems in that juvenile collection,
the copy-right of which belongs to Messrs Longman & Co—so disposed of by

that I would consent to have called mine if it depended on my own will. Of these the better Half—comprizing the Poems of greatest comparative importance, from their Length and from the Interest of the Subjects, and (*me* saltem judice) from their superior worth— exist only in manuscript—The remainder consist, I. of a selection from Poems, which have at very different periods appeared in different Newspapers, London & Provincial, and in other yet more obscure and equally perishable Vehicles, most of them without my consent or previous knowlege, many imperfectly, all of them in- correctly. 2. of the Poems published in the Lyrical Ballads and omitted in Mr Wordsworth's Collection of all his minor Poems, as was agreed on mutually by us—& which, tho' much called for, have been out of Print for some years, in consequence of Mr Wordsworth's determination not to re-edit the Lyrical Ballads separately. To these I have added a few of the better compositions inserted in the second Edition of my juvenile Poems, & which are my own property.[1]—The whole have been corrected throughout, with very considerable alterations and additions, some indeed almost

one who knew that it was never considered by me or by himself, as a copy- right, & having received for the three Editions but 20£, my whole *poetic* profits, (the 'Remorse' not included, as a theatrical accident) and against which I have to put near 100£ lost by 'the Watchman', and nearly three times that sum by 'the FRIEND'—chiefly in consequence of not half the Subscriptions having been received, & those, that were, at such distant periods as to make the money of no service to me.—It was this unfortunate Volume which subjected me to the Lash of your Lordship's Satire—not unjustly, as far as respects the Poems themselves—but permit me to say, not quite so fairly as to the Author, who published them, God knows! 'his poverty, and not his will consenting', and never thought of them as other or better than the not unpromising attempts of a young man. A Laugh at their obscurity, false splendor and buckram Diction neither did or could offend me, who had myself ridiculed these faults in them in the third of 'the Sonnets by Nehemiah Higgenbotham' pub- lished in the second Number (I think) of the monthly magazine.—But it was unjust and has been injurious to me, that having run the gauntlet for one set of faults and published nothing *reviewable* in the interim, I should be attacked in almost every other number of the Edinburgh Review & of half a dozen other publications for the very opposite, merely because I happened to be an Acquain- tance of Mr Wordsworth & Mr Southey. But so it was! The cataracts of anony- mous criticism never fell on them, but I was wet thro' with the Spray; & without any participation in the Praise, which their merits extorted even from Calumny itself. [Note by S. T. C.]

[1] This comment shows that Coleridge did not relinquish to Cottle the copy- right of the new poems in the 1797 edition. See Letter 145 (Appendix B). The copyright of the first edition, *Poems on Various Subjects*, 1796, originally be- longed to Cottle. For the receipt see Letter 114, p. 195, note 1. As Coleridge's note to the present letter shows, Cottle subsequently sold the copyright of the 1796 edition to Longman. In the Preface to *Sibylline Leaves*, 1817, Coleridge mentions 'the first edition of his juvenile poems, over which he has no controul'.

re-written. 3. The Remorse, enlarged, the Plot altered, the character of Teresa re-written, and those of Albert and of the Inquisitor nearly so.—A general Preface will be pre-fixed, on the Principles of philosophic and genial criticism relatively to the Fine Arts in general; but especially to Poetry: and a particular Preface to the Ancient Mariner and the Ballads, on the employment of the Supernatural in Poetry, and the Laws which regulate it—in answer to a note of Mr W. Scott's in the Lady of the Lake.—Both Volumes will be ready for the Press, by the first Week of June.—

Now, my Lord! if I offer these myself to the Booksellers, and unprotected, I know too certainly, that they will take advantage of my Distresses; but if your Lordship would have the goodness to allow me to send the MSS Volumes to you, as soon as they are fit for your perusal, and if you should be led to think well of them, which my Hopes flatter me that you will, so that you could with inward satisfaction recommend them to some respectable Publisher (I should rather, it were *not* Longman) your weight in society and the splendor of your name would, I am convinced (& so is Mr Bowles who in truth suggested this application so far as to lead me to flatter myself, that if you rejected, you would at least not be offended by, it) treble the amount of their offer, and [they would] be ashamed to propose such terms to your Lordship, as without remorse they would attempt to extort a concession to from my poverty. Some years ago a Publisher of the first Note offered me a 100£ for a first Edition = 1000 Copies of a Volume of Poems. I did not then wish to publish at all—but a year & a half after I went to him, and foolishly enough let him know, that I was exceedingly distressed, having from forgetfulness delayed the payment to the Assurance Office (which I have done for the last 17 or 18 years in order to secure something for my Widow) to the very last Day—and the only friends, I could apply to, able to advance the money, were out of town.—He instantly offered me 100£ for the *Copy-right* in perpetuum![1]—In like manner I have earnestly wished to employ myself at such times, as my spirits were not quite equal to original Composition, in a translation of the Persiles, Galatea, Novels, Voyage to Parnassus, and Numantium, of Cervantes: with an Essay on the Don Quixote—as likewise a translation of all Boccaccio's works, the Decameron excepted.—I wrote to Mr Murray—and wished, not any sum in advance, but merely to know whether he would purchase them when compleated—& I described at large the merits & the kind of merit, of those exquisite performances, which

[1] In 1807, 1809, and 1811 Coleridge wrote of negotiations with Longman for an edition of his poems. See Letters 647, 762, and 824.

if translated in the spirit of the original, in the same genuine rhythm of unaffected yet harmonious Prose, could not but be a great acquisition to our English Literature, and a classical Work.— He did not even condescend to return me an answer—whether because I had the open-heartedness to dissuade him from hazarding any money on the translation of the Faust of Goethe, much as I myself admired the work on the whole, & tho' ready to undertake the translation—from the conviction that the fantastic character of it's Witcheries, and the general Tone of it's morals & religious opinions would be highly obnoxious to the Taste & Principles of the present righteous English Public, I know not—. But the consequence was, that some other Gentleman is employed in translating one of the works of Cervantes, which I had proposed.—I cannot conclude a letter already, I fear, unduly long without intreating your Lordship's mildest construction of a Liberty, which, great as it is, most certainly did not spring from any want of unfeigned respect to your Lordship from, my Lord! your Lordship's obedient Servant,

S. T. Coleridge.

969 A. *To R. H. Brabant*

MS. Harvard College Lib. Hitherto unpublished fragment.

Calne.—
[June 1815 ?]

. . . But till Logic is studied in good earnest, and the whole system of Lockian Pseudo-psychology subverted, there is little chance of the philosophic Truth being listened to. Locke's whole Book (as far as it is different from Des Cartes)[1] is one $\Sigma \acute{o}\phi\iota\sigma\mu\alpha$ $\acute{\epsilon}\tau\epsilon\rho o\zeta\eta\tau\acute{\eta}\sigma\epsilon\omega\varsigma$[2]— = the fallacy, that the Soil, Rain, Air, and Sunshine, *make* the Wheat-stalk & it's Ear of Corn, because they are the conditions under which alone the seed can develope itself.[3]

My kindest respects to Mrs Brabant, & her Sisters—& affectionate Endearments to your Little ones—

S. T. Coleridge

---

[1] For Coleridge's discussion of Locke and Descartes in 1801 see *Letters* 381–4.

[2] Cf. *Biog. Lit.* i. 94.

[3] Cf. *Notes, Theological, Political, and Miscellaneous. By Samuel Taylor Coleridge*, ed. Derwent Coleridge, 1853, p. 263, and *The Philosophical Lectures of Samuel Taylor Coleridge*, ed. Kathleen Coburn, 1949, Lecture XIII, p. 379.

980. *To Lord Byron*

Address: Lord Byron | Piccadilly | London
MS. Lovelace Papers. Pub. Collected Letters of Samuel Taylor Coleridge, *iv.*
597. The earlier text of this letter was drawn from a transcript.
Postmark: 17 October 1815. *Stamped*: Calne.

17 [15] Octr 1815
Calne

My Lord

I have no better way of expressing the grateful sense, I have, of
your Lordship's very kind letter, than by informing you of what
I have done in consequence. A few Friends at Bristol undertook the
risk of printing two volumes for me, which are now entire in the
Printer's possession: a copy of which I shall take the liberty of for-
warding to your Lordship, previously to the Publication. Should
your opinion be favorable, I shall then offer the Edition and the
Copy-right for sale to the London Booksellers. I am so little known
to your Lordship that I scarcely dare venture to say what yet I
know to be true—that your Censure, however extensive it should
be, would be welcomed by me with unfeigned pleasure, as a mark of
your kindness. The first Volume is entitled, Biographical Sketches
of my own literary Life and Opinions, on Politics, Religion, Philo-
sophy and the Theory of Poetry, my object to reduce Criticism to
a system, by the deduction of Canons from Principles involved in
our faculties. The Chapters on the Γένεσις and Functions of the
Imagination, it's *contra*-distinction from the Fancy (as to which I
unexpectedly find my convictions widely different from those of
Mr Wordsworth, as explained in the new Preface to his Collection
of his poems) and the conditional Necessity of the Fine Arts.—The
second Volume I entitle, Sybilline Leaves: as a collection of all
the Poems, that are my own property, which I wish to have pre-
served.—

All my leisure Hours I have devoted to the Drama, encouraged
by your Lordship's advice and favorable opinions of my compara-
tive powers among the tragic Dwarfs, which exhausted Nature
seems to have been under the necessity of producing since Shake-
spear.—Before the third week in December I shall, I trust, be able
to transmit to your Lordship a Tragedy, in which I have endeavored
to avoid the faults and deficiencies of the Remorse, by a better
subordination of the Characters, by avoiding a duplicity of Interest,
by a greater clearness of the Plot, and by a deeper pathos. Above
all, I have labored to render the Poem at once tragic and dramatic.
May I be permitted to inquire whether it will be too late for repre-
sentation after Christmas, if it be presented by the 12th of Decem-
ber—on the supposition, that the Piece is approved?—

During my stay in London I mentioned to Mr Arnold or Mr Rae my intention of presenting three old plays adapted to the present stage. The first was Richard the second—perhaps the most admirable of Shakespear's historical plays, but from the length of the Speeches, the entire absence of female Interest, and (with one splendid Exception) it's want of visual effect, the least *representable*, in the present state & postulates of the Stage. I had conceived a new Plot: and a new female Character. But this was brought out, with what success I know not.—The second Play, which I mentioned to Mr Arnold, & I believe, to Mr Rae, was B. & F's Pilgrim—this I had determined to re-write almost entirely, preserving the outline of the Plot, and the main Characters—; to have laid the scene in Ireland; and to have entitled it, LOVE'S METAMORPHOSES.—This too has, I understand, been brought out.—But the third was that, on which I not only laid the greatest stress, and built most hope, but which I have more than half written, and could compleat in less than a month, was the BEGGAR'S BUSH—The first act is entirely my own—in the others three fifths at least of the language & thought are original—in short, a few of the characters, and the Story, comprise all, I have borrowed. I was struck with the application of the fable to the present Times.—And this too (*the third of the only three Dramas, I ever thought of as rifacciamenti*) the Newspapers have announced as about to be brought out at Drury Lane for Mr Kean.—Will your Lordship condescend to inform me, whether, I. the Newspaper account has any foundation—& 2. if so, whether the Piece is already prepared so as to preclude my services, I should say my presentation of my Rifacciamento as a candidate? —Having mentioned my intention to Mr Arnold, and having from him received the assurance, that the pre-existence of the Story and some of the Characters in Beaumont & Fletcher would be no objection to it's acceptance, I seem to myself to have some slight claim on the Theatre.

We had a company of Players at Calne, some little time ago— and very far superior to my expectations. There was a female Actress, Miss Hudson, who pronounced the blank Verse of Shakespear, & indeed Verse in general, better than I ever heard it pronounced, with the solitary exception of some passages by Mrs Jordan. She hit the exact medium between the obtrusive Iambic March of Recitation, and that far better yet still faulty style which substituting *Copy* for *Imitation* & assuming that the Actor cannot speak too like natural Talking, destroys all sense of Metre—& consequently, if it be metre, converts the language into a sort of Prose intolerable to a good ear. It was a real Luxury to hear her give the speech of Portia (on Mercy). I could not have believed, that it had been possible to have rendered the part of Teresa in the Remorse so interesting & pathetic as she made it. The whole Audience were in Tears—& in Jane Shore she was almost faultless.—In private Life she was much respected. Where she is now, I know not. The Calne Company, I know, she has left.—

Of the Actors the best incomparably was a Mr Glendore, who acted the Ghost in Hamlet, and Banquo in Macbeth better than I ever saw them acted on the London Stage—& I say this with more confidence, because Mr Bowles (& I might add several of his Friends who were with him) was equally struck and of the same opinion, declaring both the most perfect display of action, *for the parts*, that he had ever witnessed. He is a gentlemanly *Comedian*— and if his Voice be powerful enough (which I have no reason to *doubt*, but of which from the smallness of the Calne Theatre I cannot judge) I should think him a great acquisition to a London Theatre for all the respectable second characters in Tragedy and Comedy— For instance, he shewed great powers in the character of Isidore— Cassio, in Othello—Orlando, in As you like it—&c. In the Heir at Law he acted Dick Dowlas in a manner that led me to think highly of his Talents in genteel Comedy, for the only fault was that he appeared too much a gentleman by Habit. I owe it to him to ac- knowlege, that I derived assistance in one of the characters in my Tragedy by imagining him as acting it, while I was composing. I promised that if I had an opportunity, I would mention his name to your Lordship: and as he is now in London, I shall take the liberty of giving him an introduction to Mr Dibden or Mr Rae.—

I hope, your Lordship will pardon my having applied to you for an answer to questions, which I might more properly have addressed to the official managers.—Among my poems there is one respect- ing yourself—which, I assure you, was written all but the last stanza and half of another before the publication of your Childe Harold and indeed before I had ever seen a line of your composi- tions except in the Review which occasioned the poem. You will see that the stanza & a half written since are mere completions of the Thought—you were to me an *abstract* Being at that time, and that the Possible has become real, is an accident. As I have no claim to Prophecy (for not having seen any composition of your Lordship's I had no ground even for conjecture) so I would avoid the suspicion of antedating a poem in order to give the appearance of it—.

Your Lordship's obliged Servant,

S. T. Coleridge

1013 A. *To J. J. Morgan*

Address: J. J. Morgan, Esqre | Calne | Wilts
MS. British Museum. Hitherto unpublished.
Postmark: Highgate, 24 June 1816.

24 June 1816
Monday—

My dear Morgan

It was not till Thursday that I could talk with Mr Stuart, after four days of as fretting and feverous expectation as I ever passed— On Friday I was or thought myself obliged to yield to Mrs Dowling's (Mrs Kenny's Sister) request to be examining Master in Classics and Belle[s] Lettres on the examination day of her Husband's School—besides it's being a sort of respect to Gillman who attends on the Family and Scholars. This detained me till past Post-time— on that night at $\frac{1}{4}$ before Eleven poor Jeremiah Joyce[1] (the best of the Unicorn Parsons & who had just emerged out of all his difficulties) died suddenly. He had dined out at the bottom of the Hill with Abernethie & a few others—walked home by 10—on entering the house complained of a pain in his Chest, drank some warm water and having discharged the contents of the Stomach declared himself relieved and lying down on the Sofa expired without a pang or struggle. Mrs Joyce thought him in a fainting-fit, and sent for Gillman who came without a moment's delay but only to find the pulseless remains of his poor friend and neighbor—All the trouble fell on G—who was indeed so agitated that he could not hold a pen—so that I was obliged in common humanity to write all the letters to Joyce's different Friends, Executors &c on Saturday—So much for the causes of (which in this instance are adequate reasons for) my silence.—

Well—on Thursday Stuart came and I had a two hours' Talk or more with him in Lord Mansfield's Grounds—and read him the first half of your Critique—His answer was plain and direct.— First, that with regard to the fine Arts,[2] and to public places of all kinds the Courier never interested itself; & never inserted any

---

[1] Jeremiah Joyce (1763–1816), miscellaneous writer. In 1794, while serving as tutor to the sons of Earl Stanhope, Joyce was arrested, the charge being high treason. 'Pitt is said to have directed the arrest in order to irritate Stanhope, his brother-in-law.' After twenty-three weeks' imprisonment Joyce was found not guilty and acquitted. He was minister of the Unitarian chapel at Hampstead at the time of his death.

[2] As the present letter shows, Coleridge was prepared to render Morgan 'all the assistance' in his power, and this reference may be to the proposed continuance of his essays, 'On the Principles of Genial Criticism concerning the Fine Arts', which he had described to Stuart in Sept. 1814. (See Letters 944 and 951.)

thing but to oblige some individual[1]—unless for instance a single Essay or series of Essays on the *political* tendencies &c—as Essays not as Accounts or Criticisms. From the very nature of the Thing, he says, all this belongs to the great *Morning*-papers. 2. That for a man who *morally* and in his *habits* could be relied on as *regularly* attached to the Courier, and who could and would undertake the literary-political part, he scarcely knew of any limitation of Salary— If it was not done well, he should think 2£ too much; and if done impressively, 12£ a week too little.—Such was his reply.—But since Street's return, and having now the Courier every evening, I am really so shocked at the damnable immorality of the principles supported in that paper, which is now little less than a systematic advocate of the Slave-trade and all it's West-India Abominations, besides every other mode of Despotism & Ministerial Folly, that I have resolved myself never to let an article of mine contribute to the *sale* of that paper—Besides, they are playing false, as well as their Masters, with the Catholic Question—& Street will never let my Essays be published, even if I did not (as I shall do) retract them.[2] He has had his Cue from Castlerag and Carlton House, I doubt not. Therefore without waiting for your answer I have written to day to Perry, stating all I think and know of you with exception of your name—and defining all the assistance that I could give—

Partly from the state of the weather, but in a much greater degree from suspense and bustle I have not been so well for the last 10 days; but only in one instance did there recur any alarming symptom as to the main disease—On Wednesday night about an hour before bed time I was taken as by surprize, with a sensation of indefinite *Fear* over my whole Frame; but it was not accompanied with any craving for Laudanum, and I fought up against it and went to bed. I had a wretched night—and next morning the few drops, I now take, only increasing my irritability, about noon I

---

[1] In 1816 Coleridge dictated his essays on *Bertram* to Morgan. These essays, which appeared in the *Courier* in Aug. and Sept. 1816, were certainly composed after 8 July, since on that date Coleridge was still looking forward to the production of *Zapolya* as a melodrama at Drury Lane 'at or before Christmas'. His abortive attempts to deal with the management concerning the performance of *Zapolya* even as a melodrama and the 'insolent and unfeeling caprice' with which Kinnaird treated him undoubtedly account, in part at least, for his attack not only on *Bertram* but also on the 'Supreme Committee of Management' of Drury Lane. See Letters 1001, 1011, 1016, 1023, 1025, 1030, 1043, 1053, and 1213, and *Biog. Lit.*, chs. xxiii–xxiv.

[2] For references to Coleridge's 1816 essays on the Catholic Question see Letters 1008, 1010, 1025, and 1030. Coleridge was still trying to recover his MS. in Jan. 1819. See Letters 1170 and 1173 (the latter as printed from MS. in Appendix B).

called on G. for the performance of *his* part of our mutual Engagement, & took enough and *barely* enough (for more, I am certain, would have been better) to break the commencing Cycle before the actual Craving came on.—To day I am much better.—If I do not write to Mary or Charlotte tomorrow the reason will be that I have not an answer from Perry; and you may rely on a letter by Thursday.

I have written a *very long* and elaborate Letter this morning to Mr Frere, with my printed Sheets[1]—so that I must hurry this Letter to the Post.—Mr Gutch most imprudently has been *lending* the Sheets to the ferocious Blue Stockings of Bristol, Mrs Carrick &c—who declare the work unreadable—*No body* could understand great part of it—THEY never read any thing so *dull* as the philosophical Chapters &c.—Now is not this abominable? For it will really mischief the sale of the work[2]—My Love to Mary and Charlotte—& to Charles & M. Lamb if with you.—

Your's most faithfully
S. T. Coleridge—

1041 A. *To Samuel Curtis*

Address: Mr S. Curtis | Printer | Southampton Place | Camberwell
MS. Cornell University Lib. Hitherto unpublished.
Postmark: Highgate, 18 January 1817.

Highgate
Saturday afternoon—[18 January 1817]

Dear Sir

This is the first day on which I could sit up long enough to correct the Sheets of the Friend[3]—but on opening them I can make neither head or tail of the Sheets. I sent you a division of them into Essays, with a motto to each, and a translation of the same, which translation together with all other Translations that might occur in the body of the Essay I directed to be printed at the end of the Essay, divided from it by a Line, and headed—TRANSLATIONS.— Till this is explained, I do not know how to correct the Sheets or to what purpose it would be—for assuredly no one can expect me to put my name to a work, which is not properly my own—for the

---

[1] On 2 July 1816 Coleridge delivered to Frere the printed sheets, as far as they were ready, of the *Biographia Literaria* and *Sibylline Leaves*. See Letters 1014 and 1018.

[2] In Letter 1022 Coleridge rebuked Gutch for lending the printed sheets of the *Biographia* to 'my Enemies at Clifton'.

[3] The new edition of *The Friend*, 3 vols., appeared in Nov. 1818. See Letter 1148.

arrangement of a work is a vital part of the work.—I see that you have received the mottos—for one of them is printed as a Note.[1]— You remember, Sir! my letter—& your answer in which you acknowleged that my desires were just and reasonable, and that you would take care to comply with them.—Be so good as to let me know how this is—& believe me

with respect | Your's faithfully
S. T. Coleridge

P.S. Be so good as to send back the Mottos & Directions. I have no objection, Sir! henceforward to send off the MSS Copy in such a state, that it may be corrected at Camberwell—and as soon as the second Sermon can be closed up,[2] I will send you week after week portions of the Friend before I do any thing else—till you have six weeks' work before hand.—But I can engage to do this on no other condition, than that every iota of my MSS, and every form of arrangement, are to be printed exactly as sent by me—tho' I have no objection to, nay rather shall consider myself obliged by, any advice, or suggestion of whatever kind; but the ultimate decision must be with me.

1100 A. *To William Ayrton*

Address: W. Ayrton, Esqre
MS. Knox College Lib. Hitherto unpublished.
The manuscript of this letter was discovered and brought to my attention by Professor Paul A. Lacey while the present volumes were being printed. I take this opportunity, therefore, gratefully to acknowledge his courtesy and that of the Librarian of Knox College.

Saturday Morning, 24 Jany. 1818.

Dear Sir

I have this moment received your polite invitation, for I cannot be ignorant that it is to *your* favorable opinion that I owe so flattering a distinction from the Phil[h]armonic Society:[3] to which my best claim must be my sense of their merits, and a passionate Love

---

[1] The printer did not follow Coleridge's directions. In vol. i. the translations of the mottoes for the first two essays appear in footnotes. Thereafter the translation is printed immediately after the motto at the beginning of each essay.

[2] *A Lay Sermon, addressed to the Higher and Middle Classes, on the existing Distresses and Discontents*, 1817.

[3] Coleridge had been asked to dine with members of the Philharmonic Society, an invitation illness forced him to decline two days later. See his letter to Ayrton of 26 Jan. 1818 (Letter 1103).

of the divine Art, the taste for which the Society has adopted the noblest and most effective means of forming and reforming, in the higher ranks. I thank you sincerely: and could I invoke the Manes of Mozart, and embody the spirit of his strains in verse, I would attempt to express what the Lovers of Harmony owe to your generous enthusiasm. I scarcely know whether I ought to congratulate you on the scanty justice awarded you in the late Trial.[1] If to have essentially served a man, and to have been rewarded by roguery and ingratitude can render me your fellow-sufferer, I may presume to call myself such.—

As the answer is required 'on or before Thursday' now past, I do not know exactly whether I should or should not write to Mr Watts,[2] to make known my sense and acceptance of the Honor. I will even venture it—Unfortunately, your address is neither in Charles's[3] Note to me, nor in your note to him: so that I must trouble him with the conveyance of this and of the accompanyment, of which I solicit your favorable acceptance. The Ticket admits a Lady and Gentleman: and tho' there could be no substitute in my feelings for the pleasure of seeing you among my Auditors, yet I must inform you that it is transferable ad libitum.[4]—I am, dear Sir! with unfeigned respect

Your obliged Friend and Servant

J. Gillman's, Esqre   S. T. Coleridge
Highgate

where, if chance or choice should lead you this way, I should be much gratified by a friendly call.

---

[1] After visiting Italy in 1816 to engage singers for the Italian opera at the King's Theatre in London, William Ayrton (1777–1858) produced for the first time in England Mozart's *Don Giovanni* in 1817. Despite a successful season, disputes of the company forced Ayrton to resign as musical director.

[2] Probably Alaric A. Watts, sub-editor of the *New Monthly Magazine* at this time.

[3] Coleridge may refer to Charles Lamb, with whom Ayrton was on terms of intimacy.

[4] Coleridge's course of lectures in the Great Room of the Philosophical Society of London began on 27 Jan. 1818.

1122. *To Thomas Boosey, Jr.*[1]

MS. Boston Public Lib. Pub. with omis. Collected Letters of Samuel Taylor Coleridge, *iv. 844.* The earlier text of this letter was drawn from a bookseller's catalogue.

Wednesday, 25 Feby. 1818
Highgate

Dear Sir

I return the Sterne and two Vol. of Swift with sincere acknow-legement.—Do you happen to know where I could find Turner on Witch Craft—it is an old folio[2]—

Brerewood's tract begins where I have put in the Slip of Paper.—The first treatise I have never been able to light on; but this is a Whole in itself.—Byfield's Work is interesting only as it leads to the history and origin of the Controversy—and as a specimen of the Bigotry and mob-adulation of the Puritans, of that age—at least of too many of them.[3]—The first great Reformers, nay, Calvin himself in his best works, breathe a far other spirit—and in a marked degree the Founders and Martyrs of the Church *in* England, till Errors on both sides brought it to be the Church of England as by Law &c.—

Believe me | with unfeigned respect, | dear Sir, | Your obliged
S. T. Coleridge

1173. *To William Mudford*

Address: Mr Mudford | Courier office
MS. Mr. W. Hugh Peal. Pub. with omis. Collected Letters of Samuel Taylor Coleridge, *iv. 896 and 912* (Letters 1162 and 1173). The earlier text of this letter was drawn from the *Canterbury Magazine* (Sept. 1834 and Jan. 1835) where it is printed as two letters.

[19 January 1819]

Dear Sir

I thank you for your kind and in all points judicious Letter. In my last night's Lecture I had pre-resolved to avail myself of it—

[1] This letter was undoubtedly addressed to Boosey, from whom Coleridge was obtaining books for his course of lectures at the London Philosophical Society in 1818. See Letter 1120.

[2] Coleridge may refer to John Webster's *The Displaying of Supposed Witch-craft*, 1677. A copy of this work containing annotations by Coleridge is in the British Museum.

[3] Coleridge was evidently sending Boosey 'an old Book of James Ist reign' presented to him by a 'Mr West, Surgeon, at Calne, Wiltshire'. The volume contains two works, Richard Byfield's *The Doctrine of the Sabbath Vindicated, in a confutation of a treatise of the Sabbath, written by M. Edward Breerwood against M. Nic. Byfield*, 1631, and Edward Brerewood's *A Second Treatise of the Sabbath, or an Explication of the Fourth Commandment*, 1632. See Letter 978 and note.

yet still exceeded. I will try hard, that my next Monday's shall be within the limit—which, I fully agree with you, is the utmost that a Lecturer ought to inflict on a subject demanding any *catenation* of Thought.[1] Mrs Gillman, who was prevented from coming with us by sudden indisposition, had promised to explain my apparent neglect with regard to the Queen's Character—in short, the missing sheets,[2] which she had herself seen, were sought for in all possible and impossible Holes and Corners—in vain! And all, we could discover, was that Henry had been seen burning some paper, or rather with the Tinder which on the Servant's entering he had dropt & run off—and which the Maid had not told his Mother of, because she knew that it was one of the very few *whipping* matters in the penal or rather *natal* law of this family. If it would be of the *least service*, & you will send me the fragments,[3] I will compleat them: for I have a distinct remembrance of all, I wrote at that time, tho' I do not know what the parts are that are missing.—My Catholic Letters were sent long ago—years ago—. I must apply to Mr Street.[4] I see that Dr Stoddart espouses the Catholic Cause—so I suppose, that the Courier will remain neutral.—I try and try—keep my mind religiously open to every argument from the partizans of the (so miscalled) Cath. Emancipation—but still my convictions remain the same. I believe in my Conscience, that the separation of Ireland from this Country would be a less ultimate Evil—I hope, I need not tell you, that no theological point enters into my grounds of reasoning. Tho' they had adored Spiders instead of Wafers, and prayed to Beetles and Onions, I should not regard it as an objection. No! I use no Argument which our Houses of Parliament would not have acted upon before Luther was born.—I have conversed with the best and wisest Advocates of the measure—with more than one *Minister of State*—but never could get a fair answer to my objections, or an adequate counterbalance.—With all this, I can readily

---

[1] In the *Canterbury Magazine*, Sept. 1834, Mudford printed these first three sentences as a separate letter with the following prefatory comment: 'I ventured to suggest to him [Coleridge], that he made his lectures too long for a mixed auditory, more especially as their matter was not of that flimsy, superficial character, that would admit of the attention being withdrawn and brought back at pleasure, without sustaining any intermediate loss. . . .' The present letter, which may have been written after the fifth philosophical lecture of 18 Jan. 1819, was Coleridge's reply.

The remainder of Coleridge's letter appears, with omissions, as a separate communication in the *Canterbury Magazine*, Jan. 1835.   [2] See Letter 1157.

[3] Mudford says he did not return the fragments; in Jan. 1835 he printed them in the *Canterbury Magazine*, pp. 32–33.

[4] On 8 Jan. 1819 Coleridge had written to Mudford for the return of his 'two or three Letters on the Catholic Question'. See also Letter 1013 A (Appendix B).

believe that were I the conductor of the Courier, I might see justi-
fying reason for remaining neutral.

I hope, that some Saturday or Sunday Choice or Chance may
lead you Highgate-ward to,

dear Sir, | Your obliged
S. T. Coleridge

P.S. Would it be possible (i.e. for *you*) to put my advertisement
in rather a more advanced station ?—

1180 A. *To James Gillman, Jr.*

MS. Pierpont Morgan Lib. Hitherto unpublished.

24 Feby. 1819: Highgate.

Dear James

By little and little, stone upon stone, the Temple of Solomon was
finished: for Solomon was a wise Youth. The Masons who bustled,
by thousands, about the foundations of the Tower of Babel, after a
quarrelsome Jostle, with Hubble Bubble, Toil and Trouble, left it
at last unfinished: for these Babel Brick layers were very self-con-
ceited; of course, very silly Youths. Like our wholesale Reformers,
and Westminster Jacobins or frenchified Jackanapes, they would
do all at once. And in this way you may make a handome Soap
Bubble, but not a Temple. Now the purpose of Education, the
Object of being sent to school, is no other than to build up your
mind into a Temple for the good spirit to dwell in: and Goodness
and Learning are to stand, like Moses and Aaron, on each side
of the Altar.[1]—

For this reason I now give you two Rules, and two only for the
present, in order that you may not have more to learn than you can
remember and practice. For without Practice there is no memory
that can be relied on. And these are but short Rules: the first for
CONSTRUING, the 2nd for your Ellis's Exercises.[2]

Rule 1. Before you begin to construe a Greek or Latin sentence,
read the whole aloud, distinctly. If you catch yourself stammering
at any word, spell it, and then begin again. Having read it off
'*trippingly over the tongue*',[3] then examine word by word what you
already know the English of, and *parse* it to yourself however well

---

[1] There are in the British Museum (Egerton MS. 2800) several fragments
written for James Gillman, Jr.: 'Historical Mementos' (ff. 92–98), 'Conver-
sation between a Tutor and his Pupil' (f. 175), rules for scanning and making
hexameter and pentameter verses in Latin (ff. 183–4), and others.

[2] William Ellis, *A Collection of School Exercises*, 1782.

[3] *Hamlet*, III. ii.

you may remember it—and every word, you are not *quite* certain of, look out in your Lexicon or Dictionary, and then be *sure* to compare it with the correspondent Declension, or conjugation in your Grammar.—Having done all this, then begin with the first words and do not change the order in which they stand in the Greek or Latin, as long as it makes sense in *our* language.—I would wish you to try what you can do by your own cleverness for a little while: and then I will both write out and explain to you the *exceptions*, that is, the instances in which a position of words is quite plain in the Greek or Latin but would be nonsense in English. Such as Fartum comedit Jacobus uvis refertum—a Pudding eats James plum, while the Latin says plain as a pike staff that it is James who eats a Plum-pudding.

Rule 2.—from Ellis's Exercises—

First, read the English so as to understand the *sense*—and it would not be amiss, if you were to try whether you could not say the same thing in other words, even in English. Having done this, do not look at the English side any more; but first put the Latin into the grammatical Numbers, cases, tenses &c, then construe your own Latin, and ask yourself whether it expresses the same *sense* as the English Words.—Thus, suppose the English to be—Shew dutiful affection to your Father and Mother—and the Latin to be— Sum pius erga paren[te]s. Sis pius erga parentes, expresses the exact same *sense* as the English: and if you had first fixed the *sense* in your mind, instead of thinking of the particular English words, you would not get puzzled, confused, and fluttered at your challenges.—

Bear these two rules in mind, dear James, for your own sake, for your Father's & Mother's sakes and at the earnest request of your loving Friend,

S. T. Coleridge.

1217 A. *To Joseph Hughes*[1]

Pub. Memoir of the late Rev. Joseph Hughes, A.M., *by John Leifchild, 1835, p. 464.*

24th November, 1819.

Dear Sir,—Having no one in the circle of my common acquaintance who is at once competent and interested in religion *theologically*, I had additional pleasure in the opportunity of conversing with you.

---

[1] Joseph Hughes (1769–1833) became in 1793 the assistant minister of the Baptist Church, Broadmead, Bristol, where he was associated with the Revd. John Ryland. He met Coleridge at Cottle's house, probably in 1795. Hughes moved to the Baptist Church in Battersea in 1796 and remained there until

In part, from constitutional temperament not duly disciplined; but in part likewise from the very circumstance above mentioned, my thoughts, all born and shaped inwardly in consequence, and in solitary meditation, communicate their own continuity, and (to use a phrase of Jeremy Taylor's) *agglomeration*[1] to my conversation. Whenever the so rare occasion presents itself of conversing concerning these subjects, I am most conscious that I hurry forwards, *run over*, and tread upon my own arguments, and leave at last on my auditor an impression of dazzle and crowd, where so much has been said that little or nothing can be distinctly remembered. When indeed I am on my guard:—as for instance, when I am ostensibly, and, as it were, officially engaged in *teaching*, and my companion is with me as my acknowledged pupil,—then I err, if at all, in the opposite extreme; by anxiety in arrangement, and in the effort to secure for my pupil a firm footing at each step, and to obtain proofs from himself that he has full possession of the ground before I advance. And even in conversation, I can affirm most sincerely that any interruption, or admonition that I have lost the bit and curb, and am reducing the conversation to a mono-drama, or dialogue (in which one of the two *dramatis personae* is forced to act the mute) of tongue *versus* ear, is received by me not only thankfully, but with unfeigned pleasure. I wish from my very heart that every one of my acquaintance, not to say my friends, made a point of doing this. '*Lente! ferruminandus est!*'

Of no mean importance therefore, as a *service*, would it be, and a solid gratification, if you should have at any time half an hour's leisure that you could employ in drawing my attention to any passages in my 'Friend,' or 'Lay Sermons,' which shall have struck you during the perusal of them as *objectionable*, whether as unscriptural in the doctrine or rash and uncandid in the application or language.

My philosophy (as metaphysics) is built on the distinction between the Reason and the Understanding. He who, after fairly attending to my exposition of this point in the 'Friend,' (vol. I. p. 254–277,) and in the Appendix to the *first* Lay-Sermon, can still

---

the year of his death. Soon after the founding of the British and Foreign Bible Society in 1804, he became one of the secretaries. Coleridge presented a copy of *The Friend*, 1818 edition, to Hughes with the following inscription: 'The Rev. Mr. Hughes, from the author. In testimony of esteem and regard, and in the humble hope that the bread cast on the fluctuating waters of the author's mind by Mr. Hughes in early manhood, and years long gone by, will be here found neither innutritious nor unmultiplied. Highgate, Nov. 1819.' J. Leifchild, op. cit., 465 n. The annotated copy of *The Friend* presented to Hughes is now in the library of Manchester College, Oxford. See *Notes and Queries*, 29 June 1940, p. 455. See also Letter 1211, which is addressed to Hughes.

[1] Cf. *Sibylline Leaves*, 1817, p. 106.

find no meaning in this distinction,—if it still appear to him the same as if I had attempted to contra-distinguish a black from a *negro*,—for him the perusal of my *philosophical* writings, at least, will be a mere waste of time. I can only suggest to him, in prevention of any contemptuous feelings and judgments on his part, that from the first philosopher, Pythagoras, even to the present age, there has not been a single century in which this distinction has not been made and impressed by some one or more philosopher or divine of acknowledged eminence; that in the works of others it is clearly *implied*, though not *expressed*; and that, in some, sundry errors and obscurities are attributable to the confusion of terms, from the absence of a previous distinction. But, should the reader admit that the distinction conveys a *meaning*, he admits in fact that it is a *truth*; and I should dare hope, that for him the Essays on Method in the third volume would be intelligible throughout, and serve as the first elements, or alphabet, of my whole system— should it be the will of the Most High that I should live and have power to publish it. As among the secondary and merely confirmative arguments, I would challenge any learned Unitarian to give such an interpretation of the φρόνημα σαρκός, σύνεσις τῶν συνετῶν, ἐκ κόσμου, &c. as would not impeach the philosophic apostle of the puerile and tautological truism that folly is folly, and wicked opinions displeasing to God.

I am most solicitous on this point, from the deep conviction, grounded in constant experience, that it is to the mistaken identification of reason and the understanding that the undervaluing of,—nay, the suspicious aversion to,—all intellectual ἄσκησις among so many truly pious Christians is owing; and on the other hand, the over-rating of the intellects of sundry impious men and writers, who in fact are eminent (if eminent at all) in those faculties which differ from animals in degree only, except as far as that the reason irradiates these even in despite of their possessors, who, in this life of probation, and while even the shadow of the image of God is yet vouchsafed to them, *cannot* be as base as they themselves try to become; but who (comparatively) are idiots in all that is properly and peculiarly *human*.

I fear, that if my thoughts are intelligible, my writing will scarcely be legible,—but be so kind as to divide the fault between the pen and your obliged friend.

S. T. C.

Appendix B

1320 A. *To Unknown Correspondent*

Pub. Memoir of the late Rev. Joseph Hughes, A.M., *by John Leifchild, 1835, p. 274.* The following extract is taken from a letter which Coleridge addressed to a 'Mr. M—.', a cousin of Joseph Hughes.

[Highgate, November 1822][1]

I took it for granted that I should not return a discourse of Mr. Hughes without having to acknowledge more than *your* kindness in the *loan* of it. But high as my respect for your cousin's both intellect and character ever has been, I did not on *such* a subject anticipate the *great* and unusual gratification I have received from the repeated perusal of the present discourse. It is throughout as happily expressed as it is judiciously conceived. Nay, it possesses a union of excellence that is rare indeed: it is perspicuous and intelligible for all readers who are capable of reading with more than their *eyes*, and yet possesses the liveliest marks of originality, i.e. of origination in the writer's own mind and heart, and not merely in his memory or his bookshelf. To say much in little, the sermon is nowhere *below* the gospel point, nor *above* the point of human nature under gospel aids. I have found but one objectionable, *not* sentence, but—word, and that only in the biographical appendix. I allude to—'*the* Owen, *the* Siddons, *the* sublime, tremendous, super-tragical Kean, &c.' It is indeed a mere trifle, which I should not have probably even observed but for its extreme unlikeness and incongruity with the simplicity and sober dignity of Mr. Hughes's style and temper.[2]

1381 A. *To Mr. Bald*

Address: Mr Bald | 36 | Lincoln's Inn Fields
MS. Private possession. Hitherto unpublished.
Postmark: ⟨13 March⟩ 1824.

Grove, Highgate
Saturday
13 March 1824.

Dear Sir

An Islamite would have sighed & resigned himself to the Decree of Fate, & were I infected with practical predestination I might myself have been tempted to suppose it predetermined that we

---

[1] John Owen (1766–1822), the principal secretary of the British and Foreign Bible Society, died on 26 Sept. 1822. On 27 Oct. Joseph Hughes delivered a funeral sermon. It was published in 1822. The present letter, in which Coleridge comments on this sermon, was probably written in Nov. 1822.

[2] John Leifchild, op. cit., p. 274, says that in a second edition of Hughes's sermon 'the passages to which Mr. C. refers were struck out'.

should not meet. But this not being the case, I only complain of
Mrs Gillman's Emissary as either a very heedless or very faithless
Messenger: inasmuch as from the time I quitted the house to the
moment, that I stood in no very mannerly sort staring at the
Carriage, the Coachman and Yourself on my return to it, I had
never left the Square or rather Trapezium, of which our Row of
Houses forms one side, & which is my ordinary περιπατεῖον; and
only once the Grove or Walk of Trees immediately adjacent. I was
in fact expecting you, & about the time of your arrival had walked
to the end of the Trees toward the Church to see what o Clock it was,
where I met indeed, & remained some time in chat with, one of our
neighbours, but still within sight.—I was more than once summon-
ing up resolution to ask the Coachman whether it was Mr Gillman
that was wanted, but the impression on my mind was, that it was
Mr Robarts, M.P., whose medical Attendant Mr G. is—& that it
might be deemed an impertinence. Under these circumstances I
cannot without trifling with words offer any *apology*, unless the
statement of the fact may be so called, joined with a very sincere
expression of Regret, and the Assurance that every opportunity
of enjoying an hour's conversation with you, or in any way of
indemnifying myself for the loss of it this morning, will be eagerly
embraced by,   dear Sir, | Your's very respectfully
                                               S. T. Coleridge

1389. *To William Wordsworth*

Address: W. Wordsworth, Esqre.
MS. Mr. Jonathan Wordsworth. *Pub. with omis.* Collected Letters of Samuel
Taylor Coleridge, *v*. 353. The earlier text of this letter was drawn from *Letters*,
ii. 733.

                                    Monday Night, [12 April 1824]
Dear Wordsworth
    I did not venture to trust your MSS by our common Carrier; and
partly the continued Rain, and partly a flush of pharmacopœétic
business, prevented either of Mr Gillman's two Pupils going to
town with the pacquet on Saturday, and this Morning. Dear
Dorothy was neither aware of the *Crush* of unperformed & ac-
cumulated Business that ill-health & a multitude of time-wasters
& requests, I wanted courage to say No to had layed on me—nor
of the slowness with which I proceed especially where there is any
Collating, or turning from one book to another—Three whole days
the going thro' the first book cost me—tho' only to find fault. But

I can not find fault, in pen and ink, without thinking over & over again, & without some sort of an attempt to suggest the alteration —& in so doing how soon an hour is gone—so many half seconds up to half minutes are lost in leaning back in one's chair & looking up in the bodily act of contracting the muscles of the brows & forehead & unconsciously attending to the sensation.—Had I the MSS with me for 5 or 6 months, so as to amuse myself off and on, without any solicitude as to a given day; and could I be persuaded, that if as well done as the nature of the thing (viz. a *translation*, *Virgil* in English) renders possible, it would—not raise; but simply —sustain your well-merited fame, for pure diction, where what is not idiom is never other than logically correct; I doubt not, that the inequalities could be removed.—But I am haunted by the apprehension, that I am not feeling or thinking in the same spirit with you, at one time; and at another, too *much* in the spirit of your writings. Since Milton I know of no Poet, with so many *felicities* & unforgettable Lines & Stanzas as you—And to read therefore page after page without a single *brilliant* note, depresses me—& I grow peevish with you for having wasted your time on a work *so* much below you, that you can not *stoop & take*. Finally, my conviction is: that you undertook an IMPOSSIBILITY: and that there is no medium between a prose Version, and one on the avowed principle of *Compensation* in the widest sense—i.e. manner, genius, total effect—. I confine myself to *Virgil* when I say this.—

I must now set to work with *all* my powers & thoughts to my Leighton, & then to my Logic; and then to my Opus Maximum— if indeed it shall please God to spare me so long—which I have had too many warnings of late (more than my nearest Friends know of) not to doubt.—

N.B. One great Joy, I have in John Coleridge's reversionary Wind-fall is that it will clap the extinguisher on the *Quarterly* Scheme, which gave me more pain than I thought fit to express— For to John & his Sister Fanny & to them alone, I have feelings that tell me what the ties of Blood may be—. My kind love to Dorothy.

S. T. Coleridge

1453 A. *To Joseph Hughes*

Pub. Memoir of the late Rev. Joseph Hughes, A.M., *by John Leifchild, 1835, p. 466.*

Grove, Highgate, May 12th, 1825.

My Dear Sir,—I have for some time past been reading and reflecting earnestly and actively on the subject of a Metropolitan

University, now in agitation, and I could conveniently comprise the results of my meditation and researches in three discourses, the chief contents of which would be:—

A. The history and origin of European universities generally.

B. The more interesting facts and features in the histories of the more celebrated universities at home and abroad; especially the university of Paris.

C. Construction and constitution of British and Continental universities; and reduction of the same to three *kinds* or classes.

D. The origin and proper sense of the term university; and the right and only adequate frame of a university stated—*i.e.* an ideal university, developed from the germenal [*sic*] idea to the full-grown tree of knowledge, with all its branches.

E. The advantages, individual and national, moral, intellectual, and political, of a true university; deduced from reason, and established by proofs of fact, and historical evidences.

F. Cambridge and Oxford national blessings; but not true universities. On the *collegiate* form, with the arguments *pro et contra*. Is a great city a proper place for a university? Is it equally proper? Has it any peculiar advantages? What are the disadvantages and objections? Which over-balance?

G. A full *exposé* of the plan and means of the greatest practicable approximation to the ideal of a university at the present time, given in detail, with proof that the plan would comprehend all the several advantages on which all the different parties have grounded their particular schemes, is exposed to fewer obstacles, and removes or precludes the most formidable.

Conclusion. Display of the probable consequences on the wealth, worth, and character of the country at large, and of the metropolis in particular.

That I could render these subjects highly interesting, and even entertaining, I dare confidently promise myself. But, would the announcement of the same excite an interest of *curiosity*? Would the anticipation of what I might have to offer attract a sufficient number of respectable auditors to liquidate the expenses of room, advertisements, &c., with a surplus equal to what, with the same exertion of head and hand, I should earn in my own attic by a quieter industry? I say, *hand*; because I should compose and write out each of the three discourses, as I should do were they then going to the press; though probably I should make no use of the MSS. in speaking, and consider the writing as but one method of carefully *premeditating* my address. (And I put the query, because, in my present circumstances, I cannot *HONESTLY give* the time.) The fatigue and painful sensations with which public speaking and the great city always oppress me I would willingly undergo, and willingly give or give up the pleasurable quiet of domestic study, if I were led to believe the affirmative to this my last question,—viz., should I be likely to promote a useful and desirable object? Should I do more good by the *vivâ voce* promulgation of my sentiments, and the grounds of the same? These are the questions which, being unable to decide for myself, I anxiously entreat you to answer, to the best of your judgment, and from what you know and have observed of the *public mind*, and the prevalent tone of feeling.

A single line of yours,—'I think you would have a sufficient audience,' or,—'I fear, not,' would be enough, and would seriously *serve*, I need not add, oblige;

S. T. C.

1530 A. *To Mrs. T. Farrer*

MS. Cornell University Lib. Hitherto unpublished.

25 May 1826.

Dear Madam

I shall be most happy to avail myself of your & Mr T. Farrer's kind invitation; and only regret, that in the present very uncertain state of my health I can only do so *conditionally*—viz. that I am well enough to leave home without danger. I trust, that this will be the case, & I assure you, that nothing, but positive inability, will prevent me—for I am with sincere respect

Your obliged
S. T. Coleridge

1705 A. *To Joseph Hughes*

Pub. Memoir of the late Rev. Joseph Hughes, A.M., *by John Leifchild, 1835, p. 468.*

Grove, Highgate, 14th Jan. 1831.

My Dear Sir,—I will offer no apology for thus obtruding on your time: for the subject, *i.e.* the character of England, Protestantism, and Christianity are so dear to you, that the removal of the least stain from either, or the chance of doing so, would be regarded as an ample compensation for a heavier loss. I have been this day reading, 'Otto von Kotzebue's New Voyage Round the World.'

Colburn, 1830. Some two years ago, I read his first voyage.[1] Have you seen them? He is evidently prejudiced against our missionaries, and there is a sort of Russo-gallican sentimentality in his tone of thinking, with a low wish to flatter Russia and the Greek Church at the expence of both Protestantism and Romanism, so that I take his statements with great caution, and am quite prepared to hear that he has both exaggerated and distorted the facts. But the same or similar statements, very plausibly set forth in both voyages, and which, if believed, must place your British Missionary Society on a par with the Franciscan and Dominican Friars of New California, and in truth disclose a woful scene of folly and fanaticism, spiritual pride, and lust of temporal power, masked under spiritual purposes; with the names of the missionaries, &c. &c., both at Tahiti and in the Sandwich Islands, ought not to remain uncontradicted, if false; and if in any measure true, God forbid that they should remain ineffectual to the removal of such an opprobrium on the Protestant Church! I have long regretted the too general unfitness of the men chosen as missionaries, with some splendid exceptions in the East Indies; have long regretted that the instructors of the missionaries had not previously convinced them that civilization and Christian faith ought to move *pari passu*, mutually aiding each other. But I was not prepared for errors of so malignant a nature as Kotzebue lays to the charge of Bingham and others. My health scarcely allows me to prove such a wish, otherwise I should express, what I cannot help feeling, a strong desire some time or other to converse with you, and with some sincere Christians interested in and acquainted with the Missionary proceedings, on the subject generally.[2]

---

[1] Otto von Kotzebue's two narratives were published in English translations: *A Voyage of Discovery into the South Sea and Beering's Straits for the Purpose of exploring a North-East Passage, undertaken in the Years 1815–1818*, 3 vols., 1821, and *A New Voyage round the World in the Years 1823–1826*, 1830.

[2] The falsifications of Kotzebue were admirably exposed, in a reply, by the Rev. W. Ellis; and Mr. Coleridge, through the medium of Mr. Hughes, had his mind perfectly disabused on the subject. [Note by John Leifchild.]

Appendix B

1720. *To David Scott*

Address: David Scott, Esqre | Lauriston St. | Edinburgh
MS. in the Trevelyan Papers deposited in the Library of The University of
Newcastle upon Tyne. (G.O.T. 34.) Pub. Collected Letters of Samuel Taylor
Coleridge, vi. 875. The earlier text of this letter was drawn from the Memoir
of David Scott, by William Bell Scott, 1850, p. 48.
Postmark: Highgate, 19 November 1831.

Grove, Highgate.
19 Novr 1831

Dear Sir

For twelve years or more, weak and interrupted Health, and the
nature and object of the Studies, to which the hours, that Ill-
health left in my power, have been devoted—studies, the Honor of
which, if any, will be posthumous, and the advantage that of others
—have rendered my visits to London rare and at long intervals.
But during the last eighteen months my life has been but one
chain of severe sicknesses, brief and imperfect convalescence, and
capricious Relapses. It is comparative health and comfort for me
when the morbid action, whether gout or nervous rheumatism,
passes down and settles for a time in the great sciatic Nerve of one
or the other thigh—but then I am a cripple, and my boldest
excursion, a crawl up and down the Grove Walk before our front-
door. At present, I am confined to my bed-room.—At no time of
my life had I much intercourse with Booksellers or Publishers—
the Trade, as they call themselves—and my little experience has
all been of the most unfortunate kind. Were I to sum up the whole
cash receipts from my published works, I should find the sum total
something like this:

£. S. D   £ S D
0: 0: 0   −300. 0. 0.

The little, I ought to have had, was lost in a fraudulent Bankruptcy,
—and the House, by which my latest publications, the Aids to
Reflection, and the Essay on the Constitution in Church and State
according to the *Idea*, were printed & published, have dissolved
their partnership, I understand—I have found no reason for with-
drawing my confidence in the honor and integrity of the Partners,
Messrs. Hurst, Chance, & Co—but whether the business is, or is
[*not*] *to be*, continued, I am wholly uninformed.—

With this exception, I know of no one Individual in the Trade,
with whom I have any acquaintance—nor do I believe that there is
one, of London Publishers, at least, with whom *my* Name and
authority would act otherwise, than as a counter-weight. For the
Quarterly Review never notices any work under my Name—the

Appendix B

Edingburgh has reviewed only such, as seemed to furnish an occasion for vilifying the writer—and the minor Reviews sometimes, I hear, mention my name but never in any reference to my Works. I question, whether there ever existed a man of letters, so utterly friendless, or so unconnected, as I am, with the Dispensers of contemporary reputation, or the Publishers, in whose service they labor.—

Such is the answer, I must return to your friendly Letter, adding only the assurance, that I acknowlege and duly appreciate the compliment, payed to me, in having selected a poem of mine for ornamental illustration and an alliance of the Sister Arts, Metrical and Graphic Poesy—and that I would most readily have complied with your request, had it been in my power. Believe me, dear Sir, with every friendly wish,

your's respectfully
S. T. Coleridge.

INDEX

Aaron, 1047.

Abbot, Charles, later Lord Colchester, 1030 n.

Abenezra, 689 and n.

Abercromby, James, 341 and n.

Abernethy, John, 49 n., 50, 53 n., 191, 375, 576, 1040.

Abraham, 1–3, 20, 689 n., 738, 967.

Abraham Ibn Daud, 8 and n.

Abud, Wm. and Mrs., 385–6.

Achmetes, 326 and n.

Ackermann, Rudolph, 752 and n., 753, 757, 762, 883.

Acts, 622 and n., 784.

Adam, 377, 689 and n., 723, 967.

Adelaide, Queen, 867 n.

Aders, Charles, Letters to, 129, 261, 266, 287, 355, 406, 696, 751, 756, 764, 882, 955; 129 n., 261 n., 263, 271, 272 n., 319, 366–9, 370 n., 409, 513, 531–2, 543–4, 554, 568, 582 and n., 588, 652–3, 662 n., 663, 747 n., 748, 828, 956 n., 969.

Aders, Mrs. Charles, Letters to, 262, 271, 317, 365, 366, 368, 531, 543, 544, 545, 553, 567, 581, 651, 662, 671, 968; 129 n., 130, 261 and n., 262, 266, 288, 355, 370 n., 407, 409, 513, 582 n., 662 nn., 665, 670, 679, 696–7, 718 and n., 747 n., 751–3, 757–8 and n., 762 and n., 840, 882–4, 956 and n., 957, 968 n.

Advertiser, Adelaide, 930 n.

Æschylus, 192, 570; Prometheus, 142–3 and nn., 209, 463, 712 and n., 729 and n.

Æsculapius, 348.

Agrippa, Cornelius Heinrich, 579.

Alcuin, 900 and n., 908.

Alexeyev, M. P., 161 n.

Allen, Robert, 218.

Allgemeine Encyclopädie, 191 and n.

Allsop, Thomas, Letters to, 15, 22, 32, 38, 52, 78, 93, 100, 102, 115, 118, 119, 139, 144, 150, 164, 176, 179, 181, 187, 188, 201, 202, 209, 211, 213, 216, 221, 224, 233, 238, 247, 248, 249, 263, 272, 274, 279, 313, 315, 354, 358, 409, 411, 417, 418,

429, 445, 667, 673, 788, 789; 15 n., 16 n., 22 n., 33 n., 50, 72 n., 74 n., 79 n., 107 n., 117 n., 118–19, 127 n., 142 n., 144 n., 149 n., 151 n., 152 n., 178 n., 182 n., 189 n., 201 n., 202 n., 203 n., 204 n., 229 nn., 234 n., 272 n., 315 and n., 316, 346 n., 347, 360 n., 379, 410–11, 563 and n., 667 n., 672, 790 n., 850 n.

Allsop, Mrs. Thomas, Letter to, 315; 202, 210–11, 213, 215, 216 n., 217–18, 221, 224–6, 233, 235, 238, 240, 248, 252, 264–6, 314–15 and n., 346 n., 347, 355, 358–9, 431, 447, 674, 790.

Allsop, Thomas and Mrs., Letter to, 346.

Allsop family, 181, 238–40, 248, 252, 316, 347, 354–5, 358–9, 447.

Allsop, Miss (sister), 144 n., 145, 152 n., 158–9, 187–8, 224.

Allston, Washington, 159 n., 208, 422, 949, 1029 and n., 1030.

Althorp, John Charles Spencer, Viscount, later third Earl Spencer, 883 and n., 903.

Ambrosius, 976.

Amici, G. B., 523 and n.

Amulet, The, see under Coleridge, S. T., Special Topics, Literary Annuals.

Anaxagoras, 326 n.

Anderson, 503.

Anderson, John (servant), 350, 498, 860.

Andrea del Sarto, 588.

Andrews, Mr., 1027.

Anne, Queen, 901, 905.

Annual Anthology (1800), 1024 n.

Anster, John, Letters to, 332, 793; 138 n., 187 and n., 211, 234, 332 n., 334 n., 338, 360, 733 n., 792, 793 n., 794 n., 898.

Antrobus, Mr. and Mrs., 395, 397–8.

Apocalypse, 2, 51, 280 n., 520 n., 550, 557–8, 569–71, 683–4, 784, 967 and n.

Apocrypha, 683, 900, 970.

Apollo, 635, 804.

Index

Old Testament, 2, 4, 5, 27, 51, 87, 92, 94, 433, 440, 444, 558, 611, 894–5, 963, 970.
Pentateuch, 900.
Septuagint, 683, 900.
Vulgate, 900.
Bichat, M. F. X., 597 and n.
Bijou, The, see under Coleridge, S. T., *Special Topics, Literary Annuals.*
Bingham, Hiram, 1056.
Bingham, Joseph, 947 and n.
Biographia Britannica, 905 and n.
Biographia Scoticana, 300 and n., 301.
Bird, Miss, 769.
Birkbeck, George, 979 and n.
Blackwood's Magazine, 30, 123 n., 124 n., 125–6 and n., 128 n., 164, 165 n., 166 n., 167, 169–70 and n., 186, 187 n., 190, 210 n., 219, 265, 498, 578, 730 n., 771, 783, 801, 809 n., 820–1 and nn., 837 n., 838–9, 872, 884, 910 n., 912–14, 919 and n.
Blackwood, William, *Letters to*, 165, 167, 820, 836, 911; 124 n., 165 n., 166 n., 167 n., 603 n., 820 n., 821 n. 884, 911 n., 913 n.
Blake, William, 130 n.
Blizard, William, 738 and n.
Blomfield, C. J., Bishop of London, 846 and nn., 902 and n., 905, 995 n.
Blomfield, E. V., 490 n.
Bloomfield, Benjamin, 41 and n.
Bloxam, Mr., 647–8.
Blundell, James, 739 and n.
Boccaccio, 756 n., 1035.
Boehme, Jakob, 125 and n., 136 n., 370, 897, 898 n.
Bohte, J. H., *Letter to*, 304; 162, 251.
Bond, C. R., 900 and n.
Boosey, Thomas and Sons, *Letter to*, 42; 43 n., 44 n.
Boosey, Thomas, Jr., *Letter to*, 1045; 1045 n.
Bowles, W. L., 1007 and n., 1035, 1039.
Boyer, James, 618 n., 843, 934 n., 983.
Boyle, Captain R., The Voyages of, 354. (*See also* i. 653.)
Brabant, R. H., *Letter to*, 1036.
Brabant, Mrs. R. H., 1036.
Bradley, Miss, 378, 390, 392, 394, 404–6, 656.
Brandrams, the, 393.

Brent, Charlotte, *Letter to*, 280; 42 n., 281 n., 437, 619, 775 and n., 914 and n., 1020, 1026–7, 1030–1, 1042.
Brent, W. M., 1032 n.
Brerewood, Edward, 1045 and n.
British Critic, 328.
Brodie, Benjamin C., 851 and n., 909.
Brougham, Henry Peter, Lord, *Letter to*, 668; 115, 116 n., 173 n., 175 and n., 445 n., 681, 710 and n., 854–7 nn., 858–69 and nn., 883, 952, 960, 979.
Brown, John (printer), 1025.
Brown, Mr., 298.
Browne, Mary Ann, 735 and n.
Browne, Sir Thomas, 125 n.
Brownrigg, Elizabeth, 489 and n.
Bruce, James, 650 n., 651 and nn.
Bruno, Giordano, 136 n., 228 and n., 326, 332 n., 579.
Bruns, Herr, 1011.
Brunswick, Duke of, 1012.
Brutus, the elder, 117.
Bull, George, 510, 963.
Buller, Sir Francis, Judge, 258.
Bullock, Betsy, 42 and n., 131, 186, 209.
Bunyan, John, 712.
Buonarroti, F., 964–5 and nn.
Burgess, Mr. (Ramsgate), 305, 419, 514.
Burnet, Gilbert, 198 and n., 199, 300 and n.
Burns, Robert, 855 n.
Burton, Henry, 294–5 and nn.
Burton, Robert, 45 and n., 68 n., 81 n., 82, 142, 374.
Butler, Charles, 481 and n., 660, 713 and n., 980 and n.
Butler, Samuel, author of *Hudibras*, 960 and n.
Butler, Samuel, later Bishop of Lichfield, 647 and n., 650, 658.
Byfield, Richard, 1045 and n.
Byron, Lord, *Letters to*, 1033, 1037; 24 n., 161 n., 206 and n., 287 and n., 312, 379 n., 380 n., 421 and n., 436–7 and n., 449 n., 564, 755, 1006 n., 1034 n., 1039.

Cabbala, 17, 968.
Cadell, R., 603 n.
Cadell, T., 613, 836.
Calamy, Edmund, 477.

Index

Index

Index

Index

Cottle, Joseph, *Letters to*, 1003, 1004, 1005, 1007; 80 n., 198 n., 992 n., 1003–8 nn., 1034 n., 1048 n.
Courier, The, 30, 131, 203 n., 206 n., 219 and n., 235, 397, 650, 761, 1025, 1031 n., 1032, 1040–1 and n., 1046–7.
Coutts, Thomas, 101 n., 758 n.
Coutts, Mrs. Thomas, later Duchess of St. Albans, 101 and n., 211, 468, 758 n.
Cox, F. A., *Letter to*, 786; 786 n.
Cradock, Charles, 125 n., 913.
Cranach, L., 1012.
Cranmer, Mr., 227.
Cranmer, Thomas, Archbishop of Canterbury, 905 and n.
Crawley, G. A. and family, 994.
Critical Review, 733 and n.
Critici Sacri, 480 and n.
Croker, John Wilson, 903, 905–6.
Croly, George, 683 and n.
Crompton, Mrs. and family, 84, 890 and n.
Cromwell, Oliver, 515.
Cromwell, Oliver (biographer), 189 and n.
Cromwell, Thomas, *Letter to*, 178; 178 n., 179 n., 189 and n.
Cruikshank, George, 564.
Cruikshank, R., 829 n.
Cumberland, Richard, 625 and n.
Currie & Co., 346.
Curtis and Fenner, *see under* Fenner, Rest.
Curtis, Samuel, *Letter to*, 1042.
Curtis, Thomas, 163, 437–8.
Curtis, Sir William, 257 and n., 707–8.
Cuvier, G. L., 372.
Cyrus, 685, 688.

Dampier, W., 979.
Dana, Richard Henry, 207 and n., 208.
Daniel, Book of, 280 n., 520 and n., 550, 557, 561, 568–9, 571, 683, 968.
Daniel, Henry (Bristol physician), 1029.
Daniell, John Frederic, 289 n., 372 and n., 850–1 and n., 852.
Dante, 15, 26, 36, 166, 302, 403 and n., 489, 541, 714 and n.
Danvers, Charles, 1004.
Dashwood, Mrs., *Letter to*, 985; 987 n.

David, 404, 683, 685, 688.
Davies, Edward, 343 n., 857 n.
Davison, John, 510 and n., 549.
Davy, Sir Humphry, *Letter to*, 410; 130, 301, 309, 349 n., 389 n., 409 n., 410, 630, 1016 n., 1026–7.
Davy, John, 349 and n.
Davy, Martin, 249 and n.
Dawes, John, *Letter to*, 228; 228 n., 229 nn., 230 n., 234, 243, 245, 248, 255 n.
Defoe, Daniel, 979.
Delafosses, 386.
Democritus, 683.
Demosthenes, 280.
Denman, Maria, 408 and n., 968 and n., 969.
De Quincey, Thomas, *Letter to*, 161; 161 n., 255 n., 528 n., 911 and n., 912, 1022.
Descartes, 1036 and n.
De Soires, Miss, 41.
Des Voeux, Sir Charles and Lady, 377 and n., 388, 395–8.
Deuteronomy, 20 n.
De Vains, Mr., 118.
De Vere, Aubrey, 893 n.
De Wette, W. M. L., 407.
Dibdin, T. F., 526 and n.
Dibdin, Thomas J., 1039.
Dinah, *see under* Knowe, Dinah.
Diogenes Laërtius, 14 n.
Dionysius Periegetes, 979 and n.
Divett, Mr., 499–500, 706.
Dobrizhoffer, Martin, 96 and n., 268 n.
Doddridge, Philip, 197 and n. *See also under* Leighton, Robert, *Editions of*.
Domville, Mr. and Mrs., 825 and n.
Donatus, 454 n.
Donne, 26.
Douglas, Mr., 350.
Dowling, Mr., 222 and n., 949, 1040.
Dowling, Mrs., *Letter to*, 949; 222 n., 949 n., 1040.
Dryden, John, 15, 729 and n., 905.
Dubois, Edward, 12 and n.
Dudley and Ward, John William Ward, Viscount, later Earl of Dudley, 670 and n., 671–4, 679–81, 710, 717–18.
Duncombe, Thomas S., 903 and n.
Dundas, Capt. and Mrs., 377.

Index

Iliff, Frederick, 647, 650, 655, 658, 665.

Ilive, Jacob, 900 n.

Illuminati, 1014.

Illustrated London News, 934 n.

Ingram, Mr., 504, 709.

Irenaeus, 552, 558.

Irving, Edward, 280 and n., 284, 286–7 and n., 301, 362, 365, 368–9, 370 n., 372, 447, 453 n., 461, 470 n., 473–4 and n., 475–6, 520–2, 549–50, 557, 570, 661–2, 676–7 and n., 719, 746, 785, 840 and n., 976 n.

Irving, Washington, 208 and n.

Isaac, 1.

Isaiah, 20 and n., 688–9, 968 n.

Isherwood, Robert, 173 n.

Jackson, Wm., 66 n.

Jacob, 1, 296, 415, 561, 879.

Jacobi, F. H., 454 n.

James I, 295, 478 and n., 976.

James, Epistle of, 252 and n., 784.

James, Miss, 532.

James, William, 58 n., 63 n., 68 n., 69 n., 109 n.

Jameson, Robert, *Letter to*, 363; 149 n., 225 and n., 245, 254 n., 268, 347, 412, 429, 447, 672, 674.

Jamieson, John, 343 n.

Jane (servant), 260.

Jane Shore (Nicholas Rowe), 1039.

Jasher, Book of, 900 and n.

Jebb, John, 545 n.

Jeffrey, Francis, 421, 475, 734 and n., 1023–4.

Jenner, Dr. Edward, *Letter to*, 1025.

Jennings, James, 1004.

Jerdan, William, 329 and n., 754 n.

Jeremiah, 923, 989 and n.

Jerment, George, *see under* Leighton, Robert, *Editions of*.

Jezirah, Book of, 8 and n.

Job, 122, 296 and n., 556, 895 and n.

John, 2, 46, 48, 51, 87, 90, 480 and n., 537 and n., 550, 552, 556, 562, 569, 583, 595, 600, 611, 615 n., 622 and n., 683, 725, 784, 850, 890 and n., 893, 903.

John Bull, 286, 397, 472 n.

John XXII, Pope, 326 n.

Johnson, 172 n.

Johnson, Miss, 372.

Johnson, Dr. Samuel, 637.

Johnston, Sir Alexander and Lady, 388 and n., 389, 393, 395, 397 and n., 459 and n.

Johnston, Frederick and William, 329–30 and n., 340, 345, 358, 550, 553.

Jonah, 186, 250 and n., 289, 523.

Jones, Mr. and Mrs., 374, 386, 392, 397, 402, 497, 515, 757, 768.

Jones, T., *Letter to*, 186.

Jonson, Ben, 26, 173.

Jordan, Mrs., Dorothea, 1013, 1038.

Joseph (servant), 366.

Josephus, 3, 569–70.

Joshua, 900 and n.

Joy, Wm., 125 n.

Joyce, Jeremiah and Mrs., 1040 and n.

Jude, Epistle of, 622 and n., 784.

Judges, 900.

Juvenal, 511, 639, 980 and n.

Kant, Immanuel, 14 and n., 264 n., 332 n., 421, 896 and nn.

Kaye, Mr. and Mrs., 514–15.

Kayser, J., 974 and n.

Kean, Edmund, 33, 179, 269 and n., 1038, 1051.

Keate, John, 450, 487, 505, 508, 520, 535, 543, 585, 647 and n., 650.

Keate, Mary, *see under* Coleridge, Mrs. Edward.

Keats, John, 920 n.

Keble, John, 58 n., 60–63 nn., 65–67 nn., 69 n., 72 n., 74 n., 84 n., 103 n., 112 n., 195 n.

Keepsake, The, see under Coleridge, S. T., SPECIAL TOPICS, *Literary Annuals*.

Keith, Lord, 398.

Kelly, Ellen, 262–3, 271, 288, 318–19, 366 and n., 367–8, 372–3, 407, 554, 758, 810.

Kelly, Frances Maria, *Letters to*, 22, 745; 22 n.

Kelly, Michael, 161 n.

Kennard, Adam Steinmetz, *Letter to*, 989; 921 n., 960 and n., 989 nn.

Kennard, J. P., *Letters to*, 921, 961; 920, 921 n., 960 and n., 989, 993.

Kenney, James, 949 n., 1028 and n., 1029.

Kenney, Mrs. James, *Letter to*, 1028; 222 n., 1028 n., 1040.

Kent, Duke of, 129 n.

Kent, Elizabeth, 293 and n.

Index

Penrose, Lewellin, 646.
Perry, James, 886 and n., 888.
Perry, James (ed. *Morning Chronicle*), 1041–2.
Persius, 639.
Pestalozzi, J. H., 452 n.
Peter, 198 n., 200, 290, 689 n.
Petrarch, 976.
Petronius Arbiter, 402 and n., 732.
Pettigrew, Thomas J., *Letter to*, 128 ; 129 n.
Petvin, John, 117 n.
Philip, A. P. Wilson, 909 and n., 911 n.
Phillips, Edward, 1030 n.
Phillips, Thomas, *Letter to*, 158 ; 159 n., 463 and n., 588–9, 973 n.
Phillips, Mrs. Thomas, 158–9.
Philo Judaeus, 542 n.
Philpott (Ramsgate), 185, 401.
Pickering, William, *Letters to*, 782, 803, 822, 981 ; 276 n., 493 and n., 559 n., 672 and n., 674 n., 699–700, 710 n., 760, 766, 782 n., 803 and n., 830, 913–14 and nn., 975–6 and nn.
Pindar, 467 n.,'496, 675, 944, 948 and n.
Pitt, William, 269, 734 and n., 1040 n.
Plato, 13–15 and n., 331 n., 538, 542 and n., 598, 676, 844, 903, 976 n., 1026.
Plotinus, 421.
Pocock, George, 670–1 and n., 679, 718 and n.
Poole (or Pole), Matthew, 480 and n.
Poole, Thomas, *Letters to*, 160, 661, 841 ; 31 n., 54, 77 n., 110, 113, 119 n., 160 n., 250 n., 409 n., 525 n., 551 n., 659 n., 661, 680 n., 800 n., 842 n., 871 n., 874 n., 920 n., 923 n., 927 n., 1000, 1005 n., 1009.
Pope, Alexander, 577 and n.
Pople, W., 287.
Porson, Richard, 829 n., 830 and n.
Porter, Henry Langley, 666, 936, 1001.
Porter, Joseph (Bristol), 1029.
Porter, S. T., 207 n., 342 n., 373 n., 763 n.
Porteus, Beilby, 198 and n.
Potter, John, 843 and n.
Poulton, Mr., 524–5.
Powell, 186, 259–61.
Pownal, Mr. and Mrs., 350.
Prati, Gioacchino de', *Letters to*, 452, 488, 578, 767, 964 ; 424 and n., 426–

7 and n., 450, 452 n., 453 n., 454 n., 470 n., 488 n., 964 n., 965 n.
Preda (servant), 317.
Predl, Catharine de, 588, 652–4.
Prickett family, 101, 687–8.
Prideaux, Humphrey, 843 and n.
Pridham, Mary, *see under* Coleridge, Mrs. Derwent.
Pridham, Mrs., 588.
Priestley, Joseph, 893–4.
Pringle, Thomas, *Letters to*, 732, 867, 939, 949, 952, 954, 955, 957, 962 ; 732 n., 856 n., 858 n., 867 n., 939 n., 949 n., 954 n., 973.
Prout, William, 376 and n., 911 and n.
Proverbs, 879 and n.
Pruen, Mr., 1027.
Prynne, William, 294 n., 300 and n.
Psalms, 327 and n., 556, 607, 611, 681–2 and nn., 685, 688, 724–5, 866, 890 and n., 945 and n., 986 and n.
Pythagoras, 14, 26, 598, 1050.

Quarles, Francis, 573.
Quarterly Magazine, 528 n.
Quarterly Review, *Letter to* Editor of, 733 ; 29 and n., 43, 51, 92–93, 126, 163, 281, 305 n., 361 n., 422, 425, 437, 441–2, 454, 470 and n., 471, 475, 477 n., 509, 520–1, 525 and n., 566 n., 603 n., 668, 670, 733 and n., 735 and n., 754 n., 787 and n., 854 and n., 875 n., 876, 919 n., 945 n., 948 n., 949 n., 964 and n., 981 n., 1053, 1057.
Quillinan, Edward, *Letter to*, 307 ; 247 n., 255 n., 305 and n., 588 n.

Rabelais, 26, 821, 831, 901.
Rae, Alexander, 1038–9.
Ramler, K. W., 1011 and n.
Raphael, 15, 653, 1012.
Rapin, Paul de, 627.
Raymond de Sabunde, 326, 332 n.
Raymond, J. G., 1029 n.
Reade, John Edmund, *Letter to*, 849 ; 849 nn.
Reece, Mr., 271 and n.
Rees, T., 1021.
Reform Bill, *see under* Coleridge, S. T.
Reich, Dr., 421–2, 425.
Reil, J. C., 191 and n.
Retzsch, Moritz, 43 n.
Revelation, *see under* Apocalypse.

Index

Tertullian, 552, 714 n.
Theodosius, 590 n.
Thiers, Louis A., 913.
Thirlwall, Connop, 543 n., 971 and n.
Thomas à Becket, 35.
Thomas à Kempis, 205.
Thompson, George, 732 and n.
Thomson, Thomas, 851 and n.
Thucydides, 192.
Ticknor, George, 269 n.
Tieck, Ludwig, 35 and n., 190, 269.
Times, The, Letter to Editor of, 606 ;
  133, 173, 189 n., 219, 242 n., 413,
  430 n., 606 and n., 840–1, 855 n.,
  856 n., 862 n., 866 and n., 871–2,
  964 and n., 965, 993 n.
Timothy, 683 and n., 784.
Titian, 289.
Titus, 683 and n., 784.
Titus (Roman emperor), 28 and n.
Tobin, Mrs. James, 810, 816.
Todd, H. J., 343 n.
Todd, Mrs. Mary Evans, *Letter to*,
  101 ; 101 n., 218.
Tomalin, J., 265 n.
Tooke, Andrew, 348 and n., 492.
Tooke, J. Horne, 491 and n.
Torah, 5 and n., 481.
Trevenen, Miss E., 923 n.
Treviranus, G. R. and L. C., 349 and
  n., 351.
Trollope, A. W., 618 and n.
Trotter, Mrs. Coutts and daughter,
  395, 397.
Tulk, C. A., *Letters to*, 9, 17, 40, 86,
  136, 171, 238, 240, 281, 291, 303,
  324, 327, 338, 352, 419, 604, 606,
  608, 610, 612, 614, 616, 620 ; 9 n.,
  10 n., 18 and n., 40 n., 68 n., 86 n.,
  88 n., 89 n., 90 n., 175 n., 279 n.,
  283 n., 292 n., 295 and n., 324 n.,
  332 n., 409 and n., 435 n., 438, 583–
  4, 609–10, 612, 620, 682.
Tulk, Mrs. and children, 10, 19, 41,
  91, 138, 175–6, 238, 242, 281, 284,
  293, 295, 303, 327, 338, 352, 383
  and n., 409 and n., 419–20, 605,
  609.
Turner, 1045.
Turner, Edward, 851 and n., 852.
Turner, Miss, 159.
Turner, Sharon, 343 n., 857 n., 982 n.
Tuthill, G. L., 970 and n.
Twiss, Horace, *Letter to*, 242 ; 242 n.

Tyler, James, 58 n., 61 n., 63 n., 75 n.
Tyrrell, Frederick, 53 and n.

Ude, Louis E., 916 and n.
Underwood, Mr., 499.
University College, *see under* London,
  University of.
Unknown Correspondent, *Letters to*,
  42, 152, 235, 237, 295, 303, 341,
  379, 402, 414, 449, 531, 666, 690,
  731, 772, 822, 885, 1016, 1051.
Ure, Andrew, 851 and n.
Urfé, H. D'., 35.

Vesalius, A., 740.
Vespasian, 677.
Vico, G. B., 445 n., 454 and n., 465,
  470 and n., 498, 579, 965 and n.
Villiers, Charles P. and Thomas H.,
  783 and n.
Virgil, 302 and n., 347 and n., 353–4
  and nn., 489, 541 and n., 569, 584,
  605, 691 n., 692, 771, 1052–3.
Voltaire, 638.
Voss, J. H., 43 n., 691 n., 771 and n.

Wade, Josiah, *Letter to*, 1003 ; 1000,
  1018, 1029.
Wade, Launcelot, 182 and n., 1000.
Wakley, Thomas, 740 and n.
Walden, Baron Howard de, 257 and n.
Walker, Anthony, 477 and n.
Walker, Curzon, 655, 665–6.
Walker, Mrs. John, *Letter to*, 665 ;
  654–5.
Walker, John (lexicographer), 135 n.
Walker, Sidney, *Letter to*, 654 ; 528 n.,
  567 and n., 568, 570–1, 666.
Wall, William, 432 and n.
Warburton, William, 199 and n.
Ward, George, 250 n.
Warton, Thomas, 627.
Waterland, Daniel, 510 and n., 962
  and n., 963.
Watson, Dr., 785.
Watson, John, *Letter to*, 693 ; 181 and
  n., 186, 204 and n., 211–12, 221,
  226–7, 245 and n., 247, 256, 264–5,
  286–8, 303–4, 335, 375, 423, 550,
  552–3, 693 n.
Watson, Richard, Bishop of Llandaff,
  16, 538.
Watson, Seth B., 49 n.
Watt, James, 707 and n.

PRINTED IN GREAT BRITAIN
AT THE UNIVERSITY PRESS, OXFORD
BY VIVIAN RIDLER
PRINTER TO THE UNIVERSITY